D1466303

McDougal, Littell
Economics

George G. Watson, Jr.

McDougal, Littell & Company

Evanston, Illinois
New York   Dallas   Sacramento

The Author

George G. Watson, Jr. is Director of the Center for Economic Education at the Lincoln Filene Center for Citizenship and Public Affairs, Tufts University, and a high school economics teacher at Winchester High School in Winchester, Massachusetts. He is a past president of the National Council for the Social Studies and of the National Association of Economic Education Directors.

Consultants

Robert Beisch, *Social Studies Teacher, Ottumwa High School, Ottumwa, Iowa*

Edgar Bravo, *Social Studies Teacher, Miami Edison Senior High School, Miami, Florida*

Judith H. Bristol, *Assistant Director, Social Studies Department, Houston Independent School District, Houston, Texas*

Pat Collage, *Social Studies Teacher, Fairview High School, Fairview, Pennsylvania*

Ena Gordo, *Social Studies Teacher, Miami Senior High School, Miami, Florida*

Chester Harrison, *Social Studies Teacher, Modoc High School, Alturas, California*

Contributors

James I. Clark, *Teacher and Writer, Evanston, Illinois*

Donald G. Fell, *Executive Director, Florida Council on Economic Education, Tampa, Florida*

Dean Folkes, *Social Studies Teacher, Wheeling High School, Wheeling, Illinois*

Denny L. Schillings, *Social Studies Teacher, Homewood-Flossmoor High School, Flossmoor, Illinois*

ISBN 0-86609-096-7

Acknowledgments and Credits: See page 561

No part of this book may be reproduced or transmitted in any form or by any means, electronic or mechanical, including photocopying, recording, or by any information storage and retrieval system without permission in writing from the Publisher.

Copyright © 1986 by McDougal, Littell & Company
Box 1667, Evanston, Illinois 60204
All rights reserved. Printed in the United States of America.

86 87 88 89 90 / 15 14 13 12 11 10 9 8 7 6 5 4 3 2

Table of Contents

UNIT 2 *American Capitalism* 102

List of Charts and Graphs

CHAPTER 10   The Role of Government

CHAPTER 11   Monetary Policy

CHAPTER 12   The Federal Budget

CHAPTER 13   Challenges to the Market Economy

CHAPTER 14   Current Economic Issues

CHAPTER 15   International Trade

CHAPTER 16   Less Developed Countries

READING

Readings

Special Features of *McDougal, Littell Economics*

McDougal, Littell Economics combines strong organization and clear writing to form a powerful approach to teaching economics. The combination of clear definitions, practical examples, selected readings, and special features will appeal to both students and teachers. These distinctive characteristics include the following:

1. **Readable Sections.** Each section combines three parts to give students a clear and deep understanding of economic concepts and issues.

   ■ **Development** of the central concepts basic to understanding economics. Each section begins with an Overview and a list of Economic Vocabulary. In the text, key terms are highlighted and clearly defined.

   ■ **The Case Study** in each section demonstrates how the concepts discussed in the section affect the life of an actual person or group. The case study shows students how economic concepts operate in daily life.

   ■ **The Reading** is an article by an influential writer about the concepts developed in the section. Several readings are excerpts from classic works in economics.

   ■ **The Section Review** includes questions on vocabulary and basic economic facts.

2. **Teachable Chapters.** Each chapter follows a clear pattern.

   ■ **The Opening Page** states the basic learning objective for each of the three sections in the chapter.

   ■ **The three Sections** consist of Development, Case Study, Reading, and Review.

■ **The Americans at Work** feature in each chapter highlights an individual and his or her career.

■ **The Economic Skills** feature in each chapter focuses on practical knowledge that will help students perform basic economic tasks in their daily lives.

■ **The Chapter Summary and Review** consists of a review of each section and questions designed to promote critical thinking and analyses of graphs.

3. **Well-organized Units.** Each unit includes three to five chapters and the following special features.

   ■ **The Unit Opening Pages** feature a large illustration introducing the theme of the unit, and a list of the chapters in the unit.

   ■ **The Unit Review** ends each unit with questions about using Economic Concepts, Applying Economic Skills, Current Economic Issues, and Economic Reasoning.

4. **Helpful Teaching Aids.** These materials support the text:

   ■ **Special Treatment of Charts and Graphs.** Each chart or graph includes an Explanation and Skills Questions to help students analyze graphic information in the chart or graph.

   ■ **The Glossary** in the back of the text defines important terms in economics.

5. **Ancillary Materials.** A Teacher's Manual, Test Program, Transparencies, and Activities accompany the textbook.

Introduction to Economics

CHAPTER 1

Basic Economic Issues

1 Economic Questions

Objective: to become familiar with the terms used in economics and the questions economists try to answer

2 Scarcity

Objective: to understand and analyze the economic problem of scarcity faced by individuals and societies

3 Opportunity Costs

Objective: to understand opportunity costs and evaluate tradeoffs involved in economic decisions

1 Economic Questions

SECTION OVERVIEW

Your grandparents probably never attended a class called Economics. Yet, they had to think about how to meet their needs for goods and services. Today's world is more complex. A knowledge of economics, the study of how people and countries use their resources to produce, distribute, and consume goods and services, is important to everyone now. Your understanding of economics will influence how you earn a living and help you make better economic decisions. This first section will explain the basic questions studied in Economics.

ECONOMIC VOCABULARY

economics	consumer goods	producer	scarcity
consumer	services	resources	capital goods

Economic Goods and Services

People begin to learn about economics when they are still very young. Even before they start school, they make two very important economic discoveries. They find that there are lots of things in the world they want. They also find that they cannot have them all. There is a big gap between what they want and what they can have.

Later, young people learn another lesson. When they watch television commercials, they discover that there are thousands of things they or their parents could buy. Gradually, they settle into the two major economic roles: consumer and producer.

In the role of consumer, a person buys goods and services for personal use, not for resale. Consumer goods are products, such as food, clothing, and cars, that satisfy people's economic needs or wants. Some consumer goods, such as food, do not last a long time. Other goods, such as cars or VCRS, last longer. Sooner or later, though, consumer goods are used up. Services are actions, such as haircutting, cleaning, or teaching. Services are used up at the time they are provided.

A producer makes the goods or provides the services that consumers use. A person who makes lemonade and then sells it is producing a good. A person who shovels snow during the winter or clerks in a store is providing a service. Students working after school or during the summer earn money to buy some of the things they want—records, books, or a car. They are learning about the role of the producer.

Types of Resources

In order to produce something, however, a person must first have the right resources. Resources are the materials from which goods and services are made. There are three kinds of resources.

Consumers make choices among a variety of products every day. These market choices influence how resources are used.

1. **Human resources** are people. A person's knowledge, skills, attitudes, and ability to work determine that individual's value as a human resource.
2. **Natural resources** are raw materials, such as land, water, oil, timber, iron ore, and coal, from which goods are made.
3. **Capital resources** are the money or property, such as tools, machines, and buildings, that are used to produce consumer goods or services.

A person's role as producer depends on available resources. People or businesses without enough of the right kinds of resources cannot produce the desired goods or services. For example, shoveling snow is a service that requires two types of resources. To shovel snow, both a human resource—a person willing and able to work—and a capital resource—a shovel— are needed. If either of these resources is missing, production will stop. If a person catches a cold and is unable to work, his or her level of production will go down. If the snow shovel breaks, production will probably stop completely.

The Importance of Scarcity

The economy as a whole, like an individual, can produce only products for which it has the right kinds of resources. No economy can produce the things people want if it does not have enough of the right kinds of resources. And no economy has an unlimited supply of resources. In other words, there is a scarcity of resources. Scarcity is the situation that exists when demand for a good, service, or resource is greater than supply. In Economics, you will study how people use their resources to make the goods and provide the services they want. Economics is also the study of how people decide who will get the goods and services produced. Human wants tend to be unlimited, but human, natural, and capital resources are, unfortunately, limited.

Economic Questions Nations Ask

Individuals and countries face the basic problem of scarcity. Economists are interested in how people deal with this problem. The following are economic questions that every country must answer:

1. What goods and services will be produced?
2. How will goods and services be produced?
3. Who will get them?
4. How much will be produced for now and how much for later?

Different countries form different answers to the question "What goods and services will be produced?" Each answer depends heavily on the resources available to each country. Countries whose natural resource is oil can produce oil if they also have adequate human and capital resources. A country's answer to the first economic question also depends on the country's policies and priorities. Any change in a country's situation or leadership may cause it to produce different amounts of certain goods and services. A country at war, for instance, usually chooses to produce more military and fewer civilian goods and services.

Many possible mixtures of goods and services can be produced with a country's human, natural, and capital resources. Thus, the first question raises many others. For instance, are more goods and services for consumers wanted? If so, is it better to produce more shoes or more electric dishwashers? Does the country want more capital resources? If so, then what tools and machines must be produced? Which public policies are favored? Do people want more national defense or better health care, more roads or better schools? Economists are very interested in nations' answers to these questions. They also study the ways a country makes its economic choices.

The answer to the question "How will goods and services be produced?" is related to each country's basic economic system and the knowledge and skills of its work force. For instance, agricultural products in the United States are produced in a different way from those in China. Only 4 percent of American workers are engaged in agriculture, while 76 percent of the work force in China is involved in agricultural production. Agricultural goods are produced in different ways in China and the United States because of differences in workers' training, available technology, soil, and climate.

The first two questions deal with the production of goods and services. The "Who will get them?" question concerns the way goods and services are distributed to consumers. Does the country want to help certain groups, or does it want all to share equally in goods and services? Should a person's share of the goods and services be based on his or her contribution to production? Or should it be based on some other factor, such as need? Each society will form different answers to these questions based on its own customs and values.

Capital or Consumer Goods?

The question "How much will be produced for now and how much for later?" involves two decisions. First, the country must decide whether its natural resources should be used now or conserved for later use. Second, it must decide what mix of consumer goods and capital goods it wants. Capital goods are goods that are used to produce other items. Tools, machines on an assembly line, and buildings are examples of capital goods. Some items can be either capital or consumer goods.

The decision on the relative amounts of consumer and capital goods to produce is extremely important, for it will shape a country's economy for years to come. On the one hand, by creating more capital goods (machines, tools, factories) the country is adding to its capital resources. With more capital resources, the country will be able to produce more consumer goods and services in the future. On the other hand, by deciding to produce more consumer goods the country will be able to satisfy some of the immediate needs and wants of its population.

Important Choices

All countries must answer the basic economic questions. Each wants answers that will best satisfy its people and protect its self-interests. The answers to economic questions involve important choices both for countries and for individuals. These choices reflect values and priorities, and both limit and create opportunities. Your study of economics will help you to understand the basic economic issues facing you and the country. Understanding economics will help you to make more effective economic choices now and in the future.

REVIEWING THE CONCEPT

Developing Vocabulary

1. Write a definition for each of the following terms and indicate where you found the definition.

economics
consumer
consumer goods
services
producer
resources
scarcity
capital goods

2. Explain the difference between consumer goods and capital goods.

Mastering Facts

1. Explain how the production and consumption of goods are related to economic scarcity.
2. What are the three kinds of resources that are necessary to produce goods and services?

How to Read Economic Graphs

In order to make wise economic choices, you need to understand information about the economy. Businesspeople, economists, news reporters, and others use graphs to illustrate economic activity. A graph is a diagram that shows the relationship between two changing items. Graphs are very useful in showing trends and changes in economic activity.

The grid, or framework, of a graph is made with two basic lines, each called an axis. The vertical axis measures one item; it is also called the y-axis. The horizontal axis, or x-axis, measures a second item. The point at which the vertical and horizontal axes meet is called the zero point. It is also called the origin. The scale of measurement for each axis starts at the zero point. From the zero point, each axis is marked off in equal units. Since the items measured on each axis can change in quantity, each item is called a variable. Price and quantity are two variables often shown on economic graphs.

When the grid has been made and labeled, specific points are marked on the graph. Each point represents a certain amount of each of the two variables. After several points are marked on the graph, the pattern in the relationship between the two variables can be seen.

The graph shows the relationship be-

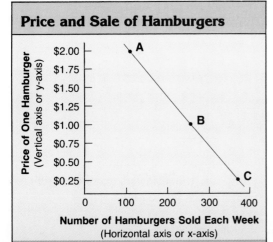

Price and Sale of Hamburgers

Price of One Hamburger (Vertical axis or y-axis)

$2.00 · A
$1.75
$1.50
$1.25
$1.00 · B
$0.75
$0.50
$0.25 · C

0   100   200   300   400

Number of Hamburgers Sold Each Week
(Horizontal axis or x-axis)

Explanation

To secure the basic information a graph offers, note the title of the graph and the labels of the vertical and horizontal axes. Remember that a graph always shows a relationship between two changing items. Before you can interpret and apply the economic information, you must first comprehend, or understand, what the graph says.

Graph Skills

1. What does the horizontal axis measure? The vertical axis?
2. What unit of measure is used on the x-axis? On the y-axis?
3. Which part of the graph shows the relationship between variables on the horizontal axis and on the vertical axis?

tween price and the sale of hamburgers at a fast food restaurant. The following explanation will help you to analyze and interpret economic graphs.

To interpret a graph accurately, you must be able to show your understanding of its meaning. In this case, the meaning of the graph is in the relationship between price and the number of hamburgers sold. In other words, a correct interpretation of this graph will lead you to understand what higher or lower hamburger prices will do to

sales. Answer the following questions to interpret the graph correctly.

1. If hamburgers are priced at $2.00, how many will be sold in one week?
2. If hamburgers cost 25 cents, how many will be sold in one week?
3. How many hamburgers will be sold in a week if each costs $1.00? If each costs 50 cents?
4. At what price could the owner expect to sell 150 hamburgers each week?
5. What generalization can you make about lower prices and the volume of sales?
6. What generalization can you make about the influence of higher prices on sales?
7. Explain why this graph alone cannot tell you at which price the owner will make the most money. What information do you need to be able to determine the best price for the owner to charge?

ANALYZING THE CASE STUDY

An economic question every family deals with is how much the family spends on food, a basic consumer good. A graph can clarify the relationship between the family's total income and the percentage spent on foods. Use the following steps in economic reasoning to make a graph and better understand this basic economic question.

STEP 1   Define the Question

1. Suggest a title for a graph that would show various incomes and the percentages of income spent on food.
2. What label would you apply to the x-axis that measures family income?
3. What label would you apply to the y-axis that measures the percentage of income spent on food?
4. What economic question will your graph help to answer?

STEP 2   Graph Economic Relationships

1. Make a graph with horizontal and vertical axes, using the labels you chose in Step 1. Remember to write the title of your graph above the grid.
2. Develop a grid, using $5,000 as your unit of measurement for the x-axis. Use 10 percent units for the y-axis.
3. Mark and label each of the following three points on the graph:
   Point A represents families with income of $12,000. These families spend 38 percent of their income on food. To locate this point, find $12,000 on the y-axis. Move straight up until you are directly across from 38 percent on the x-axis. Mark and label this point A.
   Point B represents families with income of $18,000. They spend 31 percent of their income on food. Mark the point directly above $18,000 on the x-axis and directly across from 31 percent on the y-axis. Label it B.
   Point C represents families with income of $24,000. They spend 29 percent of their income on food. Mark and label this point C.
4. Sketch a line running through points A, B, and C. The line will not be straight; rather, it will curve slightly. The line you draw will help you see the relationship between the two variables. Using the line, you can estimate the percentage of income families at different income levels will spend on food.

STEP 3   Interpret Graphs

Using your graph, answer these questions.

1. Which point represents the families that spend the highest percentage of their income on food?
2. What is the income level of the families that spend the highest percentage of their income on food?

Family Income and Food

Point	x-axis Total Family Income	y-axis Percentage of Family Income Spent on Food
A	$12,000	38 percent
B	$18,000	31 percent
C	$24,000	29 percent

Explanation
Information for a graph often is presented in a chart. The chart above provides statistics that show the relationship between three families incomes and the proportion of their income spent on food.

Chart Skills
1. What group of families is represented by point B?
2. What does the x-axis represent?

3. What is the income level of the families that spend the lowest percentage of their income on food?
4. As family income increases, what happens to the percentage of income spent on food?
5. Use the line you sketched to predict the percentage of a $21,000 family income spent on food.

STEP 4   Apply Your Knowledge

1. Draw and interpret a graph using the information in the chart. Based on the graph, what conclusion can you reach about the percentage of income spent on housing as family income increases?
2. Estimate how many hours you studied each day for the past two weeks. Use this information to draw a graph. What con-

clusions can you reach about your study patterns from the graph?

Enrichment Activities

1. Find a graph in a newspaper or magazine. Identify what the x-axis and the y-axis each measure. What units are used on each axis? Is each axis marked off in equal units? What idea does the graph demonstrate?
2. Graphs are extensively used in mathematics, particularly algebra. Use a high school mathematics book or an encyclopedia to help you define what each of the following terms mean in algebra: coordinate, ordered pair, and function. Explain how each of these terms could be used in economics. How are mathematics and economics similar?

Family Income and Housing

Point	x-axis Total Family Income	y-axis Percentage of Family Income Spent on Housing
A	$12,000	23 percent
B	$18,000	30 percent
C	$24,000	33 percent

Explanation

The chart shows the relationship between family income and the proportion of that income spent on housing.

Chart Skills

1. What group of families is represented by point A?
2. What does the y-axis represent?

READING

The Gift of the Magi

by O. Henry   (1862-1910)

The information in the first part of each section is extended through a reading. Each reading is taken from an article or book in order to show how the economic issues discussed affect you. This reading is a short story by William S. Porter, better known as O. Henry. The story was first published in 1906. In it, O. Henry describes the difficult choices facing two New Yorkers, Della and Jim, in the early 1900s. Because of limited capital resources, Della and Jim had to make some difficult choices. As you read, consider what economic questions Della and Jim had to answer. How are their questions and answers similar to your own?

❝One dollar and eighty-seven cents. That was all. And 60 cents of it was in pennies. Tomorrow would be Christmas Day. She had been saving every penny she could for months, with this result. Twenty dollars a week does not go far. Expenses had been greater than she had calculated. They always are. Only $1.87 to buy a present for Jim. Her Jim.

Many a happy hour she had spent planning for something nice for him. Something fine and rare and sterling—something worthy of the honor of being owned by Jim.

Now, there were two possessions of the James Dillingham Youngs in which they both took a mighty pride. One was Jim's gold watch that had been his father's and his grandfather's. The other was Della's hair. Had the Queen of Sheba lived in the flat across the airshaft, Della would have let her hair hang out the window some day to dry just to depreciate Her Majesty's jewels and gifts. Had King Solomon been the janitor, with all his treasures piled up in the basement, Jim would have pulled out his watch every time he passed, just to see him pluck at his beard from envy.

So now Della's beautiful hair fell about her, rippling and shining like a cascade of brown waters. It reached below her knee and made itself almost a garment for her. And then she did it up again nervously and quickly. Once she faltered for a minute and stood still while a tear or two splashed on the worn red carpet.

On went her old brown jacket; on went her old brown hat. With a whirl of skirts and with the brilliant sparkle still in her eyes, she fluttered out the door and down the stairs to the street.

Where she stopped the sign read: "Mme. Sofronie. Hair Goods of All Kinds." One flight up Della ran, and collected herself, panting. Madame, large, too white, chilly, hardly looked the "Sofronie."

"Will you buy my hair?" asked Della.

"I buy hair," said Madame. "Take yer hat off and let's have a sight at the looks of it."

Down rippled the brown cascade.

"Twenty dollars," said Madame, lifting the mass with a practiced hand.

"Give it to me quick," said Della.

Oh, and the next two hours tripped by on rosy wings. Forget the hashed metaphor. She was ransacking the stores for Jim's present.

She found it at last. It surely had been made for Jim and no one else. It was a platinum fob chain simple and chaste in design. As soon as she saw it she knew that it must be Jim's. It was like him. Quietness and value—the description applied to both. Twenty-one dollars they took from her for it, and she hurried home with the 87 cents. With that chain on his watch Jim might be properly anxious about the time in any company. Grand as the watch was, he sometimes looked at it on the sly on account of the old leather strap that he used in place of a chain.

When Della reached home, she looked at her reflection in the mirror long, carefully, and critically.

"If Jim doesn't kill me," she said to herself, "before he takes a second look at me, he'll say I look like a Coney Island chorus girl. But what else could I do—oh! what could I do with $1.87?"

The door opened and Jim stepped in and closed it. He looked thin and

very serious. Poor fellow, he was only 22—and to be burdened with a family! He needed a new overcoat and he was without gloves.

Jim stopped inside the door, as immovable as a setter at the scent of quail. His eyes were fixed upon Della, and there was an expression in them that she could not read, and it terrified her. It was not anger, nor surprise, not disapproval, nor horror, nor any of the sentiments that she had been prepared for. He simply stared at her fixedly with that peculiar expression on his face.

Della wriggled off the table and went for him.

"Jim, darling," she cried, "don't look at me that way. I had my hair cut off and sold it because I couldn't have lived through Christmas without giving you a present. It'll grow out again—you won't mind, will you? I just had to do it. My hair grows awfully fast."

"You've cut off your hair?" asked Jim.

"Don't you like me just as well, anyhow? I'm me without my hair, ain't I?"

Out of his trance Jim seemed quickly to wake. He enfolded his Della.

Jim drew a package from his overcoat pocket and threw it upon the table.

"Don't make any mistake, Dell," he said, "about me. I don't think there's anything in the way of a haircut or a shave or a shampoo that could make me like my girl any less. But if you'll unwrap that package you may see why you had me going a while at first."

White fingers and nimble tore at the string and paper. There lay The Combs—the set of combs, side and back, that Della had worshipped for long in a Broadway window. Beautiful combs just the shade to wear in the beautiful vanished hair. Her heart had simply craved and yearned over them without the least hope of possession. And now, they were hers, but the hair that should have adorned the coveted adornments was gone.

But she hugged them to her bosom, and at length she was able to look up with dim eyes and a smile and say: "My hair grows so fast, Jim!"

And then Della leaped up like a little singed cat and cried, "Oh, oh!"

Jim had not yet seen his beautiful present. She held it out to him eagerly upon her open palm. Jim tumbled down on the couch and put his hands under the back of his head and smiled.

"Dell," said he, "let's put our Christmas presents away and keep 'em a while. They're too nice to use just at present. I sold the watch to get the money to buy your combs. And now suppose you put the chops on."

The magi, as you know, were wise men—wonderfully wise men—who brought gifts to the Babe in the manger. They invented the art of giving Christmas presents. Being wise, their gifts were no doubt wise ones, possibly bearing the privilege of exchange in case of duplication. And here I have lamely related to you the uneventful story of two foolish children in a flat who most unwisely sacrificed for each other the greatest treasures of their house. But in a last word to the wise of these days let it be said that of all who give gifts these two were the wisest. Of all who give and receive gifts, such as they are wisest. Everywhere they are wisest. They are the magi. **99**

From "The Gift of the Magi," by O. Henry.

UNDERSTANDING THE READING

1. What economic questions did Della and Jim each want to answer?
2. What resources did Della and Jim each have?
3. How did Della solve her economic problem? How did Jim solve his economic problem? Would you have done what each of them did?

Section 1 Review

Understanding Economic Questions

1. What evidence suggests that human wants are unlimited?
2. What are the four basic economic questions countries must answer?
3. What is the function of a graph?

Economic Questions Today

1. List three products you think most Americans want more of today. What resources are needed to produce each?
2. For what economic questions must the United States find answers today?

3. Is there a difference between how the government and how consumers answer basic economic questions? Explain.
4. **Challenge:** Choose one of the following current economic concerns. Write a paragraph explaining how the basic questions economists ask apply to this issue.
   a. Should the United States increase funding for the space program?
   b. Should energy companies be allowed to build nuclear power plants?
   c. What types of warnings should be put on foods that may cause cancer?

2 Scarcity

SECTION OVERVIEW

You experience scarcity every day. You want more time for this, more money for that. The economic problem of scarcity, the imbalance between limited resources and unlimited wants, concerns everyone in a variety of ways. Each individual and each community must balance limited resources and increasing demands. In this section you will learn the causes of scarcity and how to think about scarcity as an economic issue of personal and national importance.

ECONOMIC VOCABULARY   recycling   poverty level

Causes of Scarcity

Since resources are limited and economic wants are unlimited, scarcity is a basic concern for everybody. Can resources ever meet all demands? Probably not. People will always have needs and wants. People always need some things, such as food and clothing. These items are consumed quickly and must be replaced. People also want other items, such as television sets, cars, and stereo equipment, even though they are not necessary. Even the very rich, who seem to have everything, manage to find new things to buy.

Countries, as well as individuals, face scarcity. No country has all the resources it could use. The United States has vast resources of all types. Still, the United States imports large amounts of oil and minerals to make up for scarcities of these natural resources. Many of the minerals come from southeast and central Africa. These areas, in turn, face scarcities of other resources. During the 1980s, for example, they have faced a severe food scarcity because of lack of rain.

Human and capital resources also are scarce in many countries. As a nation, the United States faces a shortage of qualified high school science teachers. A capital resource that is scarce in the United States is modern steel-making machinery. Many of the nation's steel mills today are older and less efficient than mills in other countries, such as Japan and West Germany.

Scarcity can result from several conditions. First, scarcity frequently results from poor distribution of a resource. Water covers 75 percent of the earth's surface. In a desert, however, water is a scarce resource. It is not easy to distribute the abundant water of one area to relieve the severe shortage of another.

Second, the notion of scarcity may depend on personal perspective. You may feel hungry in the middle of the afternoon. Your hunger results from a scarcity of food. Yet, your experience of food scarcity is quite different from that of someone suffering from malnutrition or famine. Someone near death from starvation would consider your afternoon hunger from an entirely different perspective.

Third, scarcity sometimes results from a rapid increase in demand. In these cases, scarcity lasts only a short time. In 1983, a particular brand of doll became a very popular Christmas gift. The desire for the doll far exceeded the available supply. Newspapers carried stories of people who fought to get these dolls. People ran want ads offering hundreds of dollars for one of the dolls. After the Christmas season, demand for the dolls decreased. The scarcity of dolls became less severe.

Dealing with Scarcity

A society can deal with the problem of unlimited wants and limited resources in four ways.

1. People can simply do without some of the things they want. Selecting the most important goods and services and doing without the others is by far the most widespread way of dealing with scarcity.
2. People can create more resources. At times, new natural resource locations, such as oil fields, can be found. Workers can be taught new skills. Better tools can be invented. All these things make it possible to produce more goods and services so that people can have more of what they want.
3. People can produce more by making better use of the resources they already have. The sun has always been a resource available to people. In the past 20 years, people have begun to make better use of the sun for heating homes and generating power.
4. People can redistribute goods and services so that everyone has enough—that is, no one has too much and no one has too little. Taxing adults to provide schools for children is a simple form of redistribution.

Each of these four ways of dealing with scarcity is limited and not totally satisfactory. The first method, simply doing without certain things, is often unpleasant and sometimes dangerous. Doing without a stereo or a new bicycle may be unpleasant. For people living in poverty, though, the choice may be between adequate food and adequate health care. The problem then is that doing without food or health care can be dangerous.

Creating more resources is often desirable but not always possible. One of the most basic resources is land—a very difficult resource to create. Some cities, such as Amsterdam in the Netherlands, Boston, and Chicago, have built up land that was once covered with water. This method, though, is costly and difficult. At times, new resources may create additional problems. In the 1950s, the new resource of nuclear energy was viewed as an unlimited source of low-cost energy. However, in the 1980s safety problems related to nuclear energy have appeared. Some of these problems may never be solved. Until inexpensive solutions are found, nuclear energy will not end the problem of scarce energy.

More often now people are making better use of existing resources. Many people, for example, recycle products. Recycling is the process of using materials more than once. Since the 1960s, growing numbers of people have been taking their old newspapers, aluminum cans, scrap metal, and glass bottles to local recycling centers. These materials then are used to make new products. Even recycling, though, has limits. For example, no one has yet found a method for recycling plastics.

The fourth method, redistributing goods and services, is often difficult. People who have more goods and services than others usually are reluctant to give up what they have. For example, in the United

These workers are tapping one of the most important of all limited resources—oil.

States 1 doctor serves every 612 persons. In wealthy urban areas, the ratio is 1 doctor for every 350 to 400 persons. In poor and rural areas, 1 doctor provides for 900 to 1,000. Americans in wealthier communities with more doctors might be reluctant to lose their doctors to poorer areas. Further, the doctors themselves probably would oppose efforts to even out their distribution in the country.

Continuing Scarcity

The problem of scarcity is directly related to boundless human wants. Increasing the amount of goods and services available does not necessarily end scarcity. Consider what has happened in America since the English founded a colony at Jamestown, Virginia, in 1607. The leader of the colony, Captain John Smith, was a strong leader who believed colonists should work hard. Smith told the colonists, "he that will not work, shall not eat." To Smith, a day's work was done in four hours. Today, almost 400 years later, Americans often work at least eight hours a day to produce what they consider necessary goods and services. Though people now work longer and more efficiently than did the Jamestown colonists, scarcity remains a problem.

Individuals, like societies, must deal with the problem of scarcity. You probably want many things—clothes, entertainment, money for traveling. You may also have several resources—time, energy, money, talent, knowledge and skills, charm, intelligence, imagination. Yet, your resources are limited. Scarcity forces you to decide what you want most. Societies also must make such choices. Each economy has a certain amount of human, natural, and capital resources, but even more wants. People want food, clothing, housing, transportation, and many other things. The study of economics will help to clarify how people and countries can best use resources to meet these wants.

REVIEWING THE CONCEPT

Developing Vocabulary

1. What is the difference between personal needs and personal wants? Give an example of an item that one person might need and another person might want.
2. What is recycling?

Mastering Facts

1. Give examples of three different conditions that may cause scarcity.
2. In what four ways can a society deal with shortages? What problems might develop with each?

3. List four examples of materials that can be recycled.
4. Explain how war makes the problem of scarcity more severe.

5. Contrast the amount and type of work people did in colonial Virginia with the work of people today. What do these differences suggest about scarcity?

Who Goes Hungry?

How a country decides to use its resources determines the kind and amount of scarcity its people experience. Edward Rodi of Houston stands in line for coffee and doughnuts at an emergency shelter. He has lost his job, exhausted his savings, and knows the stomach cramps of real hunger. Once he had been a cook in a Chicago restaurant. Now food is scarce for Rodi.

Rodi is not alone. Despite storage bins crammed with corn, wheat, and dairy products, some Americans experience food

This family probably experiences poverty. What evidence from the picture suggests this observation?

scarcity. Accurate numbers are difficult to determine. In 1983, over 46 million Americans lived at or below the official poverty level. The poverty level, according to the government, is the minimum amount of money an individual or a family requires to meet basic needs. For a nonfarm family of four in 1983, the poverty level was defined as an annual family income of $10,180. However, less than half of those with income below the poverty line received food stamps from the federal government to help them buy food.

In New York, researchers from the Albert Einstein College of Medicine surveyed people seeking emergency food. One-third of the parents surveyed reported going without food so their children could eat. In 1983, the Massachusetts Department of Public Health studied 1,500 poor children. The study results indicated that 10 percent of the children examined were chronically malnourished.

Growing concern about hunger in the United States prompted President Reagan to study the problem. His Task Force on Food Assistance reviewed federal and private food programs. Some Americans regard the evidence of hunger in the United States as anecdotal—stories about specific individuals, rather than accurate figures. The government's search for statistics on hunger continues. Meanwhile, food scarcity remains a problem in a country that produces 30 percent more food than it consumes.

ANALYZING THE CASE STUDY

STEP 1 Clarify the Issue

1. Which two of the following questions are most useful in defining the problem of hunger, the scarcity of food:
   a. How many Americans are going hungry daily? Monthly? Yearly?
   b. Do you think that most Americans believe a hunger problem exists the United States? Explain.
   c. What may be the causes of chronic hunger in the United States?
   d. If hunger is a problem, who should be responsible for doing something about it?
   e. What other questions need to be asked to provide an understanding of the issue of hunger in the United States today?
2. Use your answers to the questions you chose to write a paragraph about the problem of hunger as it currently exists in the United States. Use the concept of scarcity in your paragraph.

STEP 2 Gather Evidence

1. Using this case study, give an example of statistical evidence of hunger in the United States. Identify an example of anecdotal evidence of hunger.
2. Label each of the following as either statistical or anecdotal evidence of hunger in the United States.
   a. Demand for emergency food increased in 19 cities by an average of 71 percent in 1983.
   b. Dorothy Human lost her $17,500 secretarial job and her husband John's trucking business went bankrupt.

After running out of unemployment compensation from the government, Mrs. Human reported, "I'm at the point where I don't have the food and I don't feel like eating."
   c. The 1983 Food Stamp Program cost $19.2 billion.
3. Explain how statistics and anecdotes each are useful in describing the problem of hunger.

STEP 3 Consider Alternatives

1. Identify three consequences for each of the following solutions to the problem of hunger:
   a. Grow more food.
   b. Start open door kitchens in every community.
   c. Give food surpluses to the poor.
   d. Expand the food stamp program.
   e. Create jobs for the unemployed.
2. What do you need to know in order to decide how to solve Edward Rodi's problem of hunger? What information do Americans need to know to deal with the issue of hunger?

STEP 4 Make a Decision

1. Why is food considered scarce even in a country like the United States that grows more food than it consumes?
2. What should be done to help prevent people from going hungry in the United States today?

Enrichment Activity

1. Write a paragraph explaining what you consider to be the most important problem of scarcity in the United States? In the world?
2. Make a list of five examples of scarcity facing the United States today. For each example, suggest a method of lessening the degree of scarcity. Then, describe the costs of each method you suggest.

Wartime Scarcity

by Paul Samuelson   (1915-   )

Major disasters frequently cause scarcity. If you have lived through a severe earthquake, tornado, or flood, you may recall shortages of food, medical care, or shelter. One of the worst economic problems occurs when a society has to answer the basic economic questions and deal with scarcity during time of war. Immense resources are needed to equip an army. In addition, thousands or even millions of workers become soldiers, thereby creating a labor scarcity. This reading analyzes why the scarcity caused by World War II differed in the United States, Germany, and the Soviet Union. The reading is taken from *Economics: An Introductory Analysis*, a classic economics textbook by Paul Samuelson. Since 1940, Samuelson has taught economics at the Massachusetts Institute of Technology. During the 1960s he was an adviser to President Kennedy and President Johnson. In 1970, he won the Nobel Prize in Economics. As you read, consider how wartime scarcities differed in each country.

66 In the decade before World War II, the 1930s, the United States and Germany each faced high unemployment. Millions of workers in each country were without work.

After 1940, the United States was able to provide most of the military supplies for the Allied Forces, and still enjoy civilian living standards higher than ever before. This was made possible largely by taking up the slack of unemployment. On the other hand, Hitler's war effort began in 1933, long before any formal declaration of war. His war effort stemmed from a period of unemployment severe enough to win him the votes to get

Women entered factories because of scarcity of male labor in the 1940s.

into power peacefully. He used previously unemployed workers and plants to produce German war goods instead of increasing civilian consumption. Still a third case is that of the Soviet Union in World War II. Unlike the United States and Germany, the Russians had little unemployment before the war. They were already producing as much as they possibly could. They had no choice but to substitute war for civilian goods—with subsequent hardships on civilians. **"**

From *Economics: An Introductory Analysis*, by Paul Samuelson.

UNDERSTANDING THE READING

1. How did the economies of the United States, Germany, and the Soviet Union differ at the beginning of World War II?
2. Which nation's economy benefited most from that nation's efforts to fight the war?
3. Which nation had to cut back most on production of consumer goods in order to produce military goods? Which nation suffered the most severe scarcity problems?

Section 2 Review

Understanding Scarcity

1. Compare the scarcity problems that the United States, Germany, and the Soviet Union faced because of World War II and the ways in which each country responded to the problem.
2. What evidence suggests that hunger is a problem in the United States?
3. Compare the amount of food the United States produces with the amount it consumes. How does this information help you to understand scarcity?
4. How was the poverty level defined in 1983? Who determined the poverty level in that year?

Scarcity Today

1. Name three resources that are scarcer today than they were 10 years ago. Identify a resource that you expect to be scarcer when you are an adult.
2. Do you expect the problem of food scarcity in the United States to be re-duced by the year 2000? Explain why or why not.
3. Scarcity of time is often a big problem for high school students. How do you decide on allocating your time among the different things you have to do? What do you do if you cannot find enough time to do everything? What are the consequences of such a decision? Can you think of any other solutions to the problem of scarcity of time?
4. Explain how recycling can help people today deal with scarcity. Do you recycle any products? If so, list them. If not, describe how you could begin to recycle three different products.
5. **Challenge:** If your average monthly income were cut in half, what changes would you make in how you spent your money? If your monthly income doubled, how would you use the extra money? How is scarcity related to the amount of money you have?

3 Opportunity Costs

SECTION OVERVIEW

Opportunities are chances to improve your situation. Opportunities, however, may cost you something. If you spend time watching television, you cannot spend the same time at the library. If you buy a car, you cannot spend the same money for a stereo. This section will help you understand that every economic choice involves opportunity cost. You will learn to evaluate tradeoffs involved in your economic decisions.

ECONOMIC VOCABULARY

real costs
opportunity cost

tradeoff
economic model

production possibilities
model

Choices Involve Tradeoffs

All production involves a cost. This cost is not counted simply in terms of money but also in terms of the resources used. The various resources used in producing a good or a service are the real costs of that product. In building a bridge, for example, the real costs of the bridge are the human, capital, and natural resources it consumes. To build a bridge requires the labor of many people, including engineers and construction workers. The capital resources these people use include a variety of tools and machines. Building a bridge also requires natural resources, such as iron ore and coal. These natural resources are used to make the steel that is used in constructing the bridge.

Since resources are limited and human wants are unlimited, people and societies must make choices about what they want most. Each choice involves costs. The value of time, money, goods, and services given up in making a choice is called opportunity cost. For example, a person might have a choice between spending an evening at the movies or staying at home to study. The opportunity cost of going to the movies is the studying that could have been done in the same time. If a person has more than two choices, then more than one opportunity cost also exists. That person could earn money baby-sitting or could watch television. If one of these things is done, the opportunity costs of doing it are the other things that could have been done instead.

Likewise, when steel is used to make a bridge instead of a hospital, the loss in hospitals is the opportunity cost of making the bridge. In fact, any resources used for the bridge are then no longer available for something else.

When people make a choice between two possible uses of their resources, they are making a tradeoff between them. A person who goes to the movies instead of studying is making a tradeoff between two

Almost every activity involves tradeoffs between possible uses of available resources. What resources are being used by the student in this picture? What tradeoffs has the student made?

uses of time. However, tradeoffs seldom involve only two choices. For instance, steel can be used for products other than bridges and hospitals. Steel also can be used for sports arenas, coat hangers, screwdrivers, skyscrapers, and a thousand other things. So the tradeoff between using steel for bridges or for hospitals could just as easily have been stated as a tradeoff between coat hangers and skyscrapers, or sports arenas and screwdrivers.

To make choices that best satisfy human wants, people must be aware of all the tradeoffs. Then, society will understand the true costs of making one decision rather than another, and can make the decision that best fits its values and goals.

Using Economic Models

How can the concepts of opportunity costs and tradeoffs be used to help explain how the economy works? One way is to construct a simple plan of the economy called an economic model. This simple plan helps economists to analyze economic problems, seek solutions, and make comparisons between the economic model and the real world. An economic model is a little bit like a model airplane. It helps to explain how the real thing works, even if it does not fly. When models are used to help solve economic problems, their usefulness depends on the assumptions made about the world.

An economic model useful in understanding opportunity costs is a production possibilities model. A production possibilities model is a simple graph that shows the production choices open to a country. Such an economic model demonstrates the tradeoffs a country must make to increase production of a particular item. What are the assumptions of the production model? First, only two kinds of goods can be produced. Second, the country's resources can be used to produce either good.

For example, assume that a make-believe country called Alpha can produce only two kinds of goods: missiles and televisions. The same productive resources, such as skilled electronics workers, iron ore, and factories, can produce either missiles or televisions. If Alpha uses all of its resources to produce missiles, it can make 100,000. If it uses all of its resources to produce televisions, it can make 10,000,000. If Alpha uses

23

half of its resources to produce missiles and half to produce televisions, it can make 50,000 missiles and 5,000,000 televisions. The chart and graph show possibilities.

Consequences of Choices

The model shows what choices Alpha faces. By analyzing the opportunity costs and tradeoffs shown in the graph, the people of Alpha can see the effects of whatever production choices they make. Suppose for the moment that Alpha is producing 5,000,000 televisions and 50,000 missiles (possibility C in the chart). Alpha's leaders decide that they need a stronger armed forces. They will need more missiles. So they change their production plans. They now will produce 2,500,000 televisions and 75,000 missiles (possibility B in the table).

Looking at their situation carefully, Alpha's leaders see that the opportunity cost of those 25,000 extra missiles will be 2,500,000 televisions. In other words, Alpha will have traded off 2,500,000 televisions for 25,000 missiles.

Applying the Model

What is true for make-believe Alpha is true for countries in the real world. A million dollars spent on a missile cannot be spent on televisions. Conversely, a million dollars spent on televisions cannot be spent on a guided missile. The economic model allows such tradeoffs to be measured so that a country can make sound choices on how it will use its resources. First, however, a country must decide whether it needs more televisions or more missiles.

Economic Choices in Alpha

Production Possibilities in Alpha: Graph

Production Possibilities in Alpha: Chart

Possibilities	Televisions (millions)	Missiles (thousands)
A	0	100
B	2.5	75
C	5	50
D	7.5	25
E	10	0

[ ] Alpha can produce any combination of missiles and televisions in this area.

[ ] Alpha cannot produce any combination of missiles and televisions in this area.

The line is called the production possibilities curve. Alpha also can produce any combination below the line but no combination above the line.

Explanation

The graph and chart show the same information. On the graph, television production is measured on the horizontal axis and missile production on the vertical axis. The possibilities in the chart appear as points on the graph. The line joining the points includes all the other ways in which Alpha could produce using all of its resources.

Graph Skills

1. Should the production possibility curve containing points A, B, C, D, and E be considered part of the [ ] or the [ ] area? Explain.

2. Compare the scales used on the two axes. How does one unit on the y-axis differ from one unit on the x-axis?

Choosing Today or the Future

One of the most important choices a society makes is between producing capital goods and producing consumer goods. If a nation increases its production of consumer goods, its people will live better lives today. However, if a nation increases its production of capital goods, its people may live better in the future.

Production possibility curves show the choices open to a society at one point in time. In the future, changes in technology, resources, or the skills of the work force may shift the production possibility curve. By increasing production of capital goods, societies can increase their ability to produce goods. As a result, the production possibility curve moves upward and to the right. The society then can produce more of each good than it previously could have produced. Analyzing graphs showing different uses of resources will help make clear this idea.

The two graphs show the production possibility curves for microchips, miniaturized electronic circuits. Microchips can be used for such desired consumer goods as home computers, or for such capital goods as industrial robots that could increase production in the future. The nation can choose to produce any mixture of home computers and industrial robots that is on or below today's production possibility curve, the solid curve on each graph.

Choosing between home computers and industrial robots is an example of a choice a society must make. Society must decide what it wants and what it is willing to give up to get it. The same applies to you individually. Since every economic decision requires a choice, economics is a study of tradeoffs. When you analyze each side of a tradeoff, you can make better decisions.

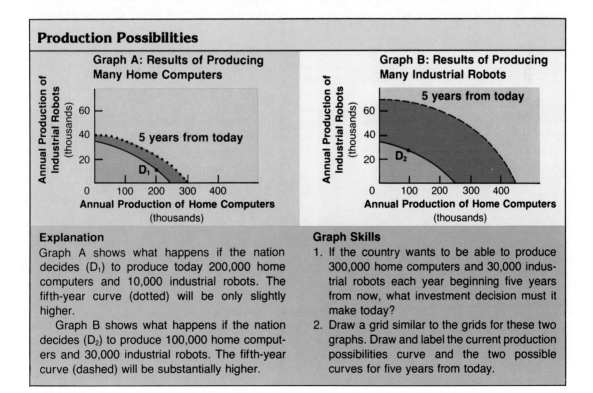

Production Possibilities

Graph A: Results of Producing Many Home Computers

Graph B: Results of Producing Many Industrial Robots

Explanation

Graph A shows what happens if the nation decides (D_1) to produce today 200,000 home computers and 10,000 industrial robots. The fifth-year curve (dotted) will be only slightly higher.

Graph B shows what happens if the nation decides (D_2) to produce 100,000 home computers and 30,000 industrial robots. The fifth-year curve (dashed) will be substantially higher.

Graph Skills

1. If the country wants to be able to produce 300,000 home computers and 30,000 industrial robots each year beginning five years from now, what investment decision must it make today?
2. Draw a grid similar to the grids for these two graphs. Draw and label the current production possibilities curve and the two possible curves for five years from today.

REVIEWING THE CONCEPT

Developing Vocabulary

1. Explain the difference between real costs and opportunity costs.
2. Give an example of a tradeoff in your daily life.
3. Explain the relationship between an economic model and economic choices.
4. What is a production possibilities model? Explain the purpose of this type of economic model.

Mastering Facts

1. Why are economic choices necessary?
2. Identify two types of costs involved in every economic choice.
3. Why is it important for a society to be aware of tradeoffs when making economic choices?
4. What determines the usefulness of an economic model?
5. What are the consequences of a society's choices in producing either capital goods or consumer goods?

CASE STUDY

The Value of a College Education

An understanding of opportunity costs and tradeoffs is important personally to high school students, as well as everyone else. Sooner or later, high school students must

College graduates expect to make up for lost time and work experience.

make choices about what to do after graduation. This year, about 2.5 million students will graduate from high school. The decisions they make will effect the rest of their lives. Some will choose to go to college; some will want to get full-time jobs; others will decide to obtain technical job training. In every case, economic reasoning will help students make better choices.

Consider the costs and tradeoffs connected with a decision to go to college. Is a college education worth the expense in terms of immediate and future personal growth and economic well-being?

The chart shows lifetime earnings estimates for Americans based on their levels of education. What is the general relationship between a person's education and that individual's earning power? How much is your high school diploma worth in terms of earning power? What is a college degree worth? How valuable is post-college schooling?

The opportunity costs of going to college involve a loss of income and a loss of practical job experience while attending college. The tradeoffs involved in going to college include using time and money now to gain greater advantages in the future. But what would happen if the actual tuition and other costs of a college education were invested now? Could you invest $30,000 now, for instance, forego a college education, and with your investment returns still have the same lifetime earning power as a college-educated person? What are some other considerations in making this choice?

Education and Earning Power

Education Level	Projected Lifetime Earnings	
	Males	Females
Less than 12 years	$ 845,000	$500,000
High school	$1,041,000	$634,000
1–3 years college	$1,155,000	$716,000
4 years college (degree)	$1,392,000	$846,000
5 or more years college	$1,503,000	$955,000

Source: Census Bureau.

Explanation

This chart demonstrates one value of education. It shows how much money males and females with various amounts of education are each likely to earn in their lifetimes.

Chart Skills

1. Compare and contrast the effect of education on projected lifetime earnings for males and females.
2. How much more can a male high school graduate expect to earn than a male who does not graduate? How much more can a female high school graduate expect to earn than a female who does not graduate?

ANALYZING THE CASE STUDY

Copy and complete the chart that follows on a separate sheet of paper to analyze the opportunity costs of a college education.

Opportunity Cost of College

Costs	Tradeoffs	Criteria
1. Spend four years at school	Better standard of living for lifetime	+
2.		
3.		
4.		

Explanation

The chart contains three columns to help you evaluate the opportunity costs and tradeoffs of a college education. After considering each entry, decide whether it encourages (+) or discourages (−) you from going to college.

Chart Skills

1. Using your economic knowledge, explain the meaning of opportunity cost.
2. Explain the meaning of tradeoff.

STEP 1 Clarify the Issue

1. List three more opportunity costs of a college education.
2. For each opportunity cost, identify its tradeoff.

STEP 2 Consider Alternatives

1. Evaluate the combined impact of each opportunity cost and tradeoff. If the combined impact encourages you to choose college, enter a plus (+) under Criteria. If the combined impact discourages you from attending college, enter a minus (−).
2. Costs for a single year at Massachusetts Institute of Technology are over $15,000. Costs at the University of Texas at Austin are over $4,500. Figure out the real cost of a college education in both of these schools. Compare opportunity costs and tradeoffs.

Make a Decision

Is a college education worth the time and money involved? Give at least two reasons to support your decision.

Enrichment Activities

1. Assume you could obtain a $30,000 loan to cover the cost of your college education. Think about the economic reasons you could use to convince a banker or relative to lend you $30,000 now for investment instead of college.

To help in preparing your presentation to the lender, make a list of five reasons for investing in a college education. Make another list of five reasons for using the money intended for a college education to invest in your own small business. Which reasons seem most convincing to you? To a parent? To a banker?

2. Think of another economic decision you might make this year (to buy a car, for example). Apply the steps in economic reasoning about costs and tradeoffs to that possible decision.

READING

Land for Food and Energy

by Lester R. Brown   (1934-   )

When you buy a pizza or get a tank of gas, the prices you pay are linked to the costs of food and energy. Food and energy costs influence the price of almost everything. This reading is taken from *Building a Sustainable Society,* by Lester R. Brown. It analyzes how these costs will be determined in the future. The author is president of Worldwatch Institute, a private research institution that studies global issues. As you read Brown's comments, consider how changing costs for food and energy will affect you.

"As efforts to create a sustainable society based on renewable resources gain momentum, agriculture seems destined to play a larger part. Agriculture can produce energy as well as food. The sharp rise in oil prices is certain to bring higher food prices over the long term. Since grains can be changed into liquid fuel, the market value of agricultural goods will be based on their value as energy. The distinction between agriculture and energy will fade as the price of oil begins to set the price of food.

Land once valued solely for its food production will acquire additional value because of its energy-production potential. Energy crops may displace food crops; farmers will produce trees for fuel. With proper management, efforts can increase food and energy production without intensifying the competition between the two.

Farmers grow crops that can be used for food or to produce fuel.

New techniques for managing land for both food and energy are beginning to emerge, mostly in Asia. The dual use of land to produce both food and energy may become commonplace in the post-petroleum world. In the United States Western Plains, for example, land could be used both for livestock grazing and for erecting windmills to generate electricity. Similarly, land flooded in the production of hydroelectric power could also be used for intensive fish farming.

As the transition to a sustainable society gains momentum, entirely new professions and jobs will emerge as new industries form. For governments, making the transition to a sustainable society may become an all-absorbing activity. **"**

From *Building a Sustainable Society,* by Lester R. Brown.

UNDERSTANDING THE READING

1. In what two ways can land be used?
2. What is meant by a sustainable society? For what reasons is a sustainable society desirable? Is our present situation a sustainable society? Explain.
3. What choices need to be made to create a sustainable society?

Section 3 Review

Understanding Opportunity Costs

1. Describe two economic choices you made today. What opportunity costs and tradeoffs were involved in each?
2. What economic choices will you have to make to plan for your life after graduation from high school?
3. Why are the economic choices of government more complicated than personal economic choices?
4. For each of the following economic choices, give examples of opportunity costs in terms of time or goods:
   a. studying for a final exam on the night before the exam
   b. buying a VCR
   c. sleeping until noon on a Saturday
   d. taking a part-time job
   e. going to graduate school
   f. riding a bus to school
   g. playing on the school basketball team
5. What does the cartoon on this page suggest about the cost of a college education to the parents of many students?

Opportunity Costs Today

1. If all high school graduates decided to go to college, what economic choices would colleges face? State governments? The federal government?
2. Why do individuals facing similar economic choices often make different decisions about what to do?
3. List four activities you may choose to do tonight. Explain the opportunity costs and tradeoffs involved in each choice.
4. Your friend wants to start a rock group. Identify three economic choices related to that activity. What costs and tradeoffs are involved? What is your advice to your friend?
5. **Challenge:** What production choices must nations make regarding the use of their natural resources? Which of these choices are made by the government? What are the most important goals for the government to achieve? Which of these goals are related to economics? Which are not?

Drawing by H. Martin; © 1980 The New Yorker Magazine, Inc.

President Gorman, distinguished faculty, honored guests, members of the Class of 1980, and impoverished parents. . .

Americans
at Work

Meet Joseph F. Littell
Educational Publisher

"In this business you look for opportunities," said Joseph F. Littell, editor-in-chief of McDougal, Littell & Company, a textbook publishing company in Evanston, Illinois. The search for publishing opportunities led Joseph Littell and Fred McDougal to start their own company.

While working together for another publisher, McDougal and Littell found that the larger textbook companies were not responding to specific needs of some classroom teachers. The two decided to combine their publishing experience and start their own company. "That was in 1969," Mr. Littell recalled. "We had talked with a lot of teachers about the kinds of materials they wanted to use in their classrooms. Large companies with large sales forces needed large national markets for their textbooks. We thought that by starting a small publishing company without a national sales force, we could develop texts to meet the particular needs of a smaller number of teachers throughout the country. Our first publishing effort was a high school modern literature series. Supply met demands—the series was successful."

McDougal, Littell & Company grew rapidly by responding to new opportunities. Basic economic questions need publishing decisions. What will be published? How will the company's human and capital resources be used? What kind of textbooks do teachers and students want?

The decision to publish *McDougal, Littell Economics* demonstrates the role of an editor-in-chief. Through regular meetings and surveys, Mr. Littell maintains contacts with teachers to become aware of classroom needs. Mr. Littell found that economics teachers wanted a text that emphasized concepts and had specific examples. Teachers liked the use of case studies and readings to reinforce basic concepts.

Mr. Littell directed a team of writers, consultants, and editors to develop such a text. During preparation of the book, several chapters were used and evaluated in various schools. Because the book's material was used in classrooms before publication, Mr. Littell could tell the sales representatives, "We've tried this out with students, and it works."

What other opportunities will the company pursue? Mr. Littell commented, "We're still growing, getting into new fields. But we haven't changed our basic publishing philosophy. We still keep a close eye on costs and resources—as well as publishing opportunities."

ECONOMIC

Making a Personal Budget

High school students, like everyone else, have unlimited wants and limited resources. Therefore, students will want to use their income as effectively as possible.

Choices must be made concerning spending and saving. Can you afford another video cassette? Can you afford not to save? You can find the answers to these questions. With a budget, your choices and alternatives become clearer, and you can learn to use money more effectively.

Copy and complete the chart to help you develop a useful personal budget.

STEP 1   Know Your Real Income

List all sources of money you can rely on. Money resources may include allowance, part-time jobs, babysitting, errands, interest on savings. If you have a job, note all deductions from your paycheck. Record only your take-home pay as income.

STEP 2   List Fixed Expenses

Fixed expenses are set in advance and must be paid regularly. Examples of fixed expenses are car or rent payments, auto insurance premiums, and tuition. Many people

Your Monthly Budget

Monthly Sources of Income		Monthly Fixed Expenses		Monthly Flexible Expenses		Monthly Optional Expenses	
Type	Amount	Type	Amount	Type	Amount	Type	Amount
1.		1.		1.		1.	
2.		2.		2.		2.	
3.		3.		3.		3.	
4.		4.		4.		4.	
5.		5.		5.		5.	
6.		6.		6.		6.	
Total		Total		Total		Total	

Explanation

The chart contains four columns that you can use to keep a monthly budget.

Chart Skills

1. What is your total monthly income?
2. What are your total monthly expenses?

include savings as a fixed expense because they regularly save a part of their income.

STEP 3   List Flexible Expenses

Flexible expenses are necessary but change with circumstances. Food, clothing, and gasoline are examples of flexible expenses.

STEP 4   List Optional Expenses

Optional expenses vary and are not always necessary. They may include entertainment, personal care, or school supplies.

STEP 5   Total Income and Expenses

Compare income and expenses. Obviously, expenses should not exceed income. Most people cannot follow their budget exactly. One expense may turn out to be higher than planned, while another may be lower. A consistent pattern of overspending suggests that the budget should be readjusted or followed more closely.

ECONOMIC SKILLS TODAY

1. Explain the differences between fixed, flexible, and optional expenses. Give examples from your own expenses.
2. Why must budgets be flexible?

Enrichment Activities

1. Keep track of your actual income and expenses for a month. Record how much you spend for food, entertainment, clothing, school supplies, personal care, transportation, and miscellaneous items. In which category do you spend the most? The least? If you wanted to reduce your expenses, what changes would you make in your budget?
2. Compare your monthly expenses with

Average Expenses of Students

Item	Percentage of Total Expenses
Entertainment	35
Food	29
Clothing	11
School supplies	10
Savings	5
Personal care	4
Transportation	3
Other	3

Explanation

The chart shows the average expenses of a group of high school students.

Chart Skills

1. What two items account for 64 percent of the students' total expenses?
2. What percentage of income does an average student save?

the average expenses in the expense chart. Figure out what percentage of your income is allocated for each item listed in the chart. List the categories in which your percentages clearly match the average percentages. Identify the categories that show the greatest difference. Are your personal expenses basically similar to the average expenses for high school students? How can a personal budget help you to deal realistically with scarcity and promote effective economic decisions?
3. Imagine that you are the head of a household of four, and your annual income is $15,000. Use your local newspaper to determine rent, food, clothing, and transportation costs. Make a family budget identifying its monthly income and expenses.

CHAPTER SUMMARY

Economic Questions

The basic economic questions individuals and nations face are: (1) What goods and services will be produced? (2) How will they be produced? (3) Who will get them? (4) How much will be produced for now and how much for the future? The answers to these questions depend on a country's human, natural, and capital resources, and also on its customs and values. Each country will answer these questions in a different way.

Scarcity

The basic issue in economics is how people can use a limited supply of productive resources to meet their unlimited and competing wants. A society can deal with this problem of scarcity in four ways: (1) by selecting the most important goods and services and doing without the others; (2) by creating more resources; (3) by making better use of the resources already available; (4) by redistributing existing goods and services so that everyone has enough and no one has too much or too little.

Opportunity Costs

Each economic choice to use productive resources involves sacrificing opportunities to use those resources in other ways. A nation can make the choices that best satisfy its people only if it understands what the tradeoffs are. Economic models help explain the production choices available to a nation. Generally, nations and individuals make economic choices that best fit their values and goals.

CRITICAL THINKING QUESTIONS

Economic Questions

1. Use three current newspaper articles that deal with economic choices. For each article, identify the conflict between limited resources and unlimited wants.
2. Give three examples of economic choices you must make this week. How can your study of economics help you make better choices?
3. What is the basic service your school provides you and your community? How does your school answer each of the four basic economic questions?

Scarcity

1. Identify five photographs from this text that show examples of natural, capital, and human resources. What are some of the real costs associated with their use?
2. Find five photographs from magazines that show different types of resources. Write a short essay explaining:
   a. how the use of each resource would have been different 100 years ago.
   b. how the use of each resource might change a century from now.
   c. two generalizations about various resources.

Opportunity Costs

1. Why is it necessary for a nation to make careful decisions about how to allocate its resources?
2. Why is it necessary for an individual to make careful decisions about how to allocate personal resources?
3. What are the opportunity costs of taking

Land for Food or Fuel

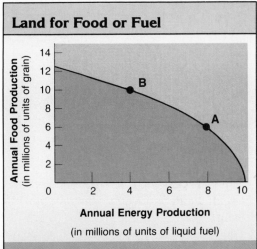

Annual Food Production (in millions of units of grain) vs. **Annual Energy Production** (in millions of units of liquid fuel)

Explanation

The graph shows the tradeoff between using land to produce food and to produce fuel.

Graph Skills

1. What happens to the production of crops for energy as the production of food crops decreases? Increases?
2. If the country were producing 10 million units of grain for food each year, how much energy could it produce?

Charting Land Use Choices

Annual Energy Production (units of liquid fuel)	Annual Food Production (units of grain)
0	
2	
4	
6	
8	
10	

Explanation

The points on a curve in a graph can also be listed in a chart. The left side of this chart corresponds to the horizontal axis on the graph. Both measure annual energy production in units of liquid fuel.

Chart Skills

1. What unit is used to measure annual food production in the graph in the chart?
2. Explain how a chart shows a relationship between two variables more precisely than does a graph.

a two-week vacation in the summer for a working adult? A high school student? An elementary school student?

DEVELOPING ECONOMIC SKILLS

Use the graph to help you answer the questions that follow it.

1. If the nation were at point A on the graph, and farmers were encouraged to increase food production to 9 million bushels of grain, how much would energy production decrease?
2. If the nation were at point B on the graph and wanted to increase food production to 9 million bushels, what would happen to energy production?
3. Copy the chart on a separate sheet of paper. Complete the chart by analyzing the graph to determine the maximum

amount of food that can be produced at each level of energy production.

APPLYING ECONOMICS TODAY

1. Do you think everyone should attend college? Why or why not? What trade-offs are involved in your opinion?
2. What tradeoffs will society have to make as oil and other energy prices increase?
3. **Challenge:** How much does it cost to have your car tuned up at a garage? What would it cost if you were to do the tuneup yourself? List all the factors that must be taken into consideration. Which method of caring for your car is cheaper? Which method is better for your car? Which is better for you?

CHAPTER 2

Economic Systems

1 Traditional Systems

Objective: to understand how economic decisions based on habits and customs are made in a traditional economic system

2 Command Systems

Objective: to understand how economic decisions based on centralized planning are made in a command system

3 Market Systems

Objective: to understand how economic decisions based on the interactions of buyers and sellers are made in a market system

36

1 Traditional Systems

SECTION OVERVIEW

Compare the ways you and a friend spend money. Each of you not only spends your money in different ways but probably also uses different procedures to determine what to buy. For example, you may buy the least expensive gasoline available. Your friend may buy the brand that his or her parents have always purchased. Similarly, countries make different decisions about basic economic questions. They also use different procedures to arrive at economic policies. This section will help you to understand how traditional economic systems make decisions based on long-standing customs.

ECONOMIC VOCABULARY

culture   traditional systems   command systems   market systems

Three Basic Types of Systems

In studying an economic system, you first need to analyze the system's answers to the four basic economic questions: What goods and services will be produced? How will they be produced? Who will get them? How much will be produced for now and how much for later? Second, you need to analyze the ways those answers are reached. The way a society makes economic decisions says a great deal about its culture. Culture is a society's entire way of life. It includes the society's language, housing, food, clothing, religion, family life, and political system. A society's economic system is only one part of its culture. That system influences, and is influenced by, all the other parts.

Economist Robert L. Heilbroner found a simple way to look at the different methods of economic decision making. He said that economic systems can be classed into three main types or a mix of those types. Economies operate: (1) by tradition, (2) by command, and (3) by the market.

Traditional systems base economic decisions on what always has been done in the past. In traditional systems, habits and customs are very important guides to making decisions. Command systems use a group of leaders or central authority to answer the basic economic questions. In these systems, government planning heavily influences decisions. Market systems rely on exchange, barter, or a network of prices. Decisions in a market system usually are made by merchants, consumers, and businesspeople interested in getting the best product for the best price.

No economy makes all of its decisions in only one of these three ways. Every economy is a mixture of all three. The economy of the United States is basically a market system. Some decisions, though, are made by tradition or by command.

Traditional System Characteristics

Until recently, tradition was by far the most widespread system for making economic decisions. It is still common in many parts

37

of the world. Traditional economies are tied to methods that developed long ago by trial and error. People in these economies generally produce the same items their ancestors made, using the same methods their ancestors used. Jobs are handed down from parents to children so that skills can be retained and the economy can survive. In some rural areas of the world, parents teach their children how to plow soil, milk cattle, thatch roofs, and weave baskets. Often in traditional cultures, males and females do different jobs.

Answers to the questions "for whom" and "how much" in traditional cultures are fixed by custom, habit, religion, or law. For example, the Bushmen of the Kalahari Desert in southern Africa follow custom in making economic decisions. In this traditional hunting society, custom sets the rules for sharing the kills among the hunters and their families. The largest share usually goes to the best hunter. In this way, the best hunters are able to survive when game is scarce. But in times of plenty, the fa-vored hunters share their positions so that no one eats more than any other.

In traditional cultures, change comes slowly. When change does come, it is not always welcomed and may even be bitterly opposed. The fight of the Plains Indians against the building of railroads across the United States is an example of such resistance. The Iron Horse and the white settlers who traveled on it were a threat to the Plains Indian economy. These machines and people were rapidly killing off the buffalo, the Indians' most important natural resource. The Plains Indians depended on the buffalo's flesh for food, its skin for clothing and tents, its dung for fuel, and its bones for tools.

The Eskimos' Traditional System

Before Europeans settled in North and South America, most of the cultures in these areas had traditional economic systems. One of the best known is that of the North American Eskimo. The Eskimos

Contact with Europeans caused the Eskimos to modify their traditional economic system. For example, the Eskimos shown here will sell these dried fish. In former times, they would have eaten the fish or traded them for other goods.

today are changing and losing many of the old ways as they mix more with other people in the United States and Canada. The following account, written by an explorer in 1913, shows the role that tradition played then in the Eskimo economy.

66 It was the vanishing of the caribou from the inland coastal plain that drove the Eskimo down to the coast. Now it seems that the caribou are having a slight chance. In large districts where formerly they had to face the hunter, their only enemy is now the wolf. . . . [T]he Eskimo expects to find everything next year as he found it last year; and so the belief dies hard that the foothills had an endless supply of caribou. But when starvation had year after year taken off families by groups, the Eskimo finally realized that the caribou in large numbers were a thing of the past. They were so firmly impressed with the fact that now they are sure that no caribou are in the interior. They had once thought they would be there forever. 99

Factors for Change

The disappearance of the Caribou from their traditional area changed the Eskimo economy. Wars, climate, and other outside forces can cause traditional economic systems to change. In the 1860s, Japan depended almost wholly on farming. Then, contact with Western nations led to the rapid growth of Japanese industry and trade in the 20th century. Finally came World War II and, after the war, military occupation by the United States. All of these factors helped to transform Japan's economic system into one based more on the market than on tradition.

Many countries in Asia, Africa, and Latin America are now subject to outside influences. Some changes—improved seed and plows, for example—are easily ac-cepted. Others, such as the idea of women working outside the home, are fought because they conflict with deeply held values of the culture.

In a traditional culture, then, economic choices are limited. People do things "the way they are supposed to be done" because in the past the society survived by choosing what it considered to be the best method of performing a task. The people may not know any other way.

A person in a traditional economy is like a member of a family. The family member may disagree with other members but must go along just the same. Similarly, people in traditional economies believe that their way of doing things and their elders' choices are right. They find it hard, if not impossible, to believe that any other or better methods may exist.

REVIEWING THE CONCEPT

Developing Vocabulary

1. What aspects of life are included in a group's culture?
2. Write a brief definition of the following:
   a. traditional system
   b. command system
   c. market system

Mastering Facts

1. Until recently, which type of economic system was most common?
2. In what parts of the world today are you most likely to find a traditional economic system?
3. List four outside forces that can cause change in a society using a traditional economic system.
4. What is the major disadvantage of a traditional economic system?
5. What is the major advantage of a traditional system?

Navajo Choices Today

Individuals who grow up in a traditional system usually live just as their parents did. However, when members of traditional systems leave, they temporarily face a difficult decision. Marlene Sandoval grew up on the Navajo Indian Reservation in New Mexico. Two of her high school teachers arranged for her to attend college in Atlanta, Georgia. Now, she must decide whether or not to return to the reservation. If she returns, her opportunities for a career will be limited, but she will stay in close touch with her family and the traditions of the Navajo Indians. If she seeks opportunities elsewhere, she may find a better job. However, she will risk losing touch with the traditions of her ancestors and family.

Traditions are still very important to the Navajo. One of the traditional economic activities still widely practiced is weaving. Navajo weavers have been famous for their distinctive designs, uses of color, and weaving patterns for over 200 years. According to Navajo custom, women have always been the weavers. Neither their equipment nor their methods have changed much over the years. Strangers have tried to introduce the spinning wheel, but Navajo women have rejected it. They still favor their traditional method of hand spinning. Centuries ago, Spanish settlers showed the Navajo a new type of loom. Still, Navajo weavers continue to use their own kind of loom.

Navajo weavers create a wide variety of weaves in numerous patterns and colors. Many of their designs are rare. Some are unique to Navajo weavers. Excepting some intricate patterns that are sketched in the sand, the weaver creates patterns from memory. Those familiar with Navajo culture easily recognize the traditional Navajo patterns.

Although the Navajo Indians have tried to maintain their traditions, they have been greatly affected by outside influences. Changing conditions led the Navajo Tribal Council to establish a Department of Resources. This department manages the use of resources on Navajo lands in the Southwest. Hundreds of Navajos now cut timber, mine coal and uranium ore, recover natural gas and oil, and work in other industries located on the reservation. These resources have brought the Navajo tribe some prosperity. The Navajos have invested much of their wealth in a variety of enterprises and programs designed to benefit all Navajos.

Nevertheless, modern opportunities, such as mining and industrial work, seriously threaten the traditional Navajo lifestyle. Today, many Navajos, like Marlene Sandoval, are better educated than their parents. These children face difficult

With traditional dress and modern ideas, this Navajo woman faces the future.

choices between modern careers and traditional activities. All of the choices have both costs and benefits. The challenge for Marlene and other young Navajos is to maintain the best of the modern opportunities and traditional customs.

ANALYZING THE CASE STUDY

STEP 1   Clarify the Issue

1. In the past, how did the Navajo people answer basic economic questions?
2. What elements of a traditional economic system are evident in the Navajo Indian culture?
3. What modern opportunities exist for the Navajo today?

STEP 2   Consider Costs and Benefits

1. What factors enter into a college-educated Navajo's decision about career and lifestyle? Compare the benefits of traditional and modern living. What tradeoffs must be made, and what are the opportunity costs?
2. How do modern opportunities threaten the traditional system?

STEP 3   Make a Decision

1. How do particular skills and interests influence a young Navajo's decisions about a career?
2. Why is the past likely to influence the economic decisions of a young Navajo more than those of teenagers in other cultures today?

READING

Life in a Turkish Village

by Joe E. Pierce   (1924-   )

Two of the most important decisions you will make in your life concern your career and marriage. The way you approach these decisions will depend heavily on the culture in which you live. If you lived in a traditional rather than a market economic system, your approach to work and marriage would be quite different. This reading, taken from *Life in a Turkish Village* by Joe E. Pierce, describes work and marriage in a traditional economy. It shows how tradition influences some basic life choices. Pierce is an **anthropologist**, a person who studies the culture of various groups of people. As you read, compare decision-making in this traditional economy with the way you make decisions.

66 The cold, hard winter passed, and most of the people had enough to eat and lived to see the spring. Some died, of course, but the villagers rarely knew why. So far as the people could see, there were no solutions to these problems, for it had always been so, and when anyone asked why, they were always given the answer that it was the will of Allah.

One morning, after the snows had gone, but the bitter cold winds were still blowing across the hills, his father was fastening the heavy

41

wooden yoke onto the oxen when Mahmud came into the room that was reserved for the animals.

"Let's go together and plow this morning, my son," the older man said.

"What can I do, my father?" the boy responded with enthusiasm.

"You can best watch today, my son, but soon you must help, for you will some day have to plow the fields alone."

As they walked along, Mahmud examined the plow very carefully, because he knew that one day he would probably have to make one like it. This was the only piece of equipment that they would need that day, as it would take about a month, working from sunup till sundown, to plow the four acres that his father had decided he would cultivate this year. Whenever he finished turning the soil, he would replace the plow with a heavy log and ride this, behind the same pair of oxen, over the field several times to break up the heavy clods and shake stones loose from the dirt. However, the first and most difficult job was to break the hard-packed, rocky ground so that the seeds could take root and grow.

It took the two of them well over an hour to reach the spot to be planted, and the sun was well up in the sky when they arrived. They did not begin to plow immediately, because the ground had to be cleared of the larger rocks first. This made it much easier for the oxen to pull the dull wooden plowshare through the very hard earth. Picking up the stones, which ranged in size from that of an acorn to a small melon and which lay scattered thickly over the surface of the ground, they made neat piles of rock outside the area to be plowed. These stacks began to look like small buildings, and Mahmud liked to pretend that these structures were the houses of a village of little people, and he made up all kinds of stories about what happened to these people.

By shortly after the noon hours they had cleared nearly half an acre, which was twice as much as a man could plow up in one day, so Mahmud sat down to rest, and his father took up the plow and began the long hard job of following the oxen back and forth across what would soon be his wheat field.

Days passed, each very much like the first, and all of the rocks were cleared from the surface. The ground was broken, and Mahmud followed his father and picked up many more stones that had been turned up during the plowing. Finally, after all this had been done, and his father had decided that they had broken all the land that he and his family could properly tend that year, Mahmud was allowed to ride on the clod-breaking log (harrow). His body added weight to the implement, which made it more efficient, and also gave father and son a chance to work more closely together so that Mahmud could learn how to be a man.

As the weeks and months went by, Mahmud grew older and entered school, just as his parents had said that he would. Each morning he walked to 2 kilometers [about 1.2 miles] to the city in company with the

42

A Turkish woman prepares a meal using traditional methods.

other school-age children, taking half a loaf of bread and some fruit for lunch, and returned in the evening. School life was very different from that in the village, but when he was at home things went on pretty much as they always had.

Even in the village, however, things new to Mahmud happened occasionally, and one evening he heard his father and mother talking softly in the hallway between the two living rooms. They were whispering so that no one could understand what they were saying, but this only made him want more than ever to hear, and so he edged nearer to where they were standing and listened intently, in the shadows near the doorway. The conversation concerned his older sister who was nearly 16 and old enough to be married.

"What will you tell them?" his mother asked.

"I don't know just yet," his father answered.

"But they will come tomorrow, and you know that they have been here twice already. They will want to know tomorrow, and you cannot wait until then to decide," the wife insisted.

This reminded Mahmud of the two special visits in recent weeks by the mother and father of one of his friends who lived just down the street. He had not understood their purpose then, but the family had come to look over his sister as a prospective wife for their son who would soon be old enough to go into the army and should be married before he left. Thinking back on the visits, Mahmud remembered how his sister had each time been told well in advance that they were coming and that she had spent hours getting dressed, preparing fruits and nuts for the visitors, and asking her mother if she should do this or that when they arrived.

At the very first knock she ran to the door. As they came in, she kissed first the back of the hand of the man and lifted it to her forehead, then did the same to the woman. Mahmud's mother and father had also welcomed the guests. Then the men had gone into the men's room and the women into the women's. As they sat talking, the visitors would call in and ask for this or that, and Mahmud's sister would run to bring what they asked for as quickly as she could. On the second visit the mother had asked her to make some coffee, and she had very carefully and skillfully demonstrated her ability to handle cooking utensils. They had seemed pleased, and his sister appeared to be happy, but he did not quite understand it all.

Now it became clear, as he listened to the talk of his mother and father. The visitors had thought his sister would make a good wife for their son or they would not have come back again. Now that they were coming a third time, it meant that they might very well ask for a final decision about the arrangements. If they were not completely satisfied, they might come once more, but Mahmud's mother felt that they should have an answer ready before tomorrow, just in case the boy's parents did want to settle it all then.

The prospective husband was of good family. He was quite nice looking, a hard worker, and the daughter liked him, from a distance of course, as she was not allowed to talk with boys his age. There seemed to be no obvious reason for not accepting, but Mahmud's father was worried about how much money the family would give. He realized that his daughter was an unusually pretty girl and that this was only the first family to ask. He wondered if they should accept if the man offered them 5,000 lira, bargain for more, or just wait for a better offer, but Mahmud's mother said that almost any girl in the village was worth that much, and Fatma should be worth much more.

This was not a sale of their daughter, because all the money would be used to buy furniture for the couple after they were married and to pay for the wedding feast. Still, the more they could get, the better their daughter would be able to outfit her household. After much discussion it was decided that they would not accept less than 6,000 lira, but that would be a fair amount considering that Fatma would go into a fine family and, after all, she was getting an exceptional husband out of the deal too.

Mahmud wondered why no one in the village ever married people from the city, or other villages, but he knew that for some reason this was forbidden. Someone said that there was a village somewhere, where the people were also their relatives, to which young people could go to marry, but he had never known of anyone who had done it. He wondered also if there really were such a place, and if so where it was, but these things he did not know.

Late in the day a knock was heard on the door sounding their arrival. Again he watched as his sister went to the door, kissed the hands of the visitors respectfully, and jumped to serve their every wish. Finally, after a rather long visit, the man asked Mahmud's father what he thought of arranging a marriage between the two young people. He had been cautious, approving with some hesitancy, until the man offered 7,000 lira in payment to cover the wedding costs. With the amount offered it would have been almost impossible for anyone not to enter wholeheartedly into the agreement, and it was settled that within a few weeks the couple would be married. **99**

From *Life in a Turkish Village*, by Joe E. Pierce.

UNDERSTANDING THE READING

1. What is an anthropologist? What types of activities would both an anthropologist and an economist study?
2. What choices were made for Mahmud because of his Turkish culture? What choices were made for Fatma?
3. Explain how marriage decisions were made in this traditional economic system in Turkey.
4. Would Mahmud or Fatma expect their lives to be very different from their parents' lives?
5. In what way do you consider your choices to be most different from those of Mahmud or Fatma?

Section 1 Review

Understanding Traditional Systems

1. Which of the following statements are true and which are false? Reword the false ones to make them true.

   a. The way a society makes economic decisions reflects its natural resources.
   b. Decisions in a traditional system are based on shared social values.
   c. In a traditional economic system, most people go to school in order to learn an occupation.
   d. Traditional economic systems tend to be highly industrialized.
   e. Children in a traditional economic system usually follow in their parents' footsteps.

2. What kinds of changes are rather easily accepted by a traditional culture? Not easily accepted? Give two examples of each kind of change.

Traditional Systems Today

1. How do people, culture, and resources affect the way decisions are made in a traditional economy?
2. Do you expect to follow the same occupation as one of your parents? Why or why not?
3. What difficulties might an inventor face in a traditional economy?
4. What economic considerations might have an affect on your choice of marriage partner?
5. **Challenge:** What kinds of conflicts might arise when women in a traditional economy begin working outside the home?
6. **Challenge:** What opportunities do Navajo Indians have today that they did not have in the past? How do these opportunities affect the economic choices each Navajo must make today?

2 Command Systems

SECTION OVERVIEW

Your parents decide where you live and go to school. Your teachers influence what and how much you study. You have experienced what someone experiences when authority plans and controls important decisions. In some countries, the government is the authority that plans and controls important economic decisions. This section will help you to understand how command economic systems make economic decisions based on centralized planning.

ECONOMIC VOCABULARY   planned economy

Command System Characteristics

In a command economic system, a group of central planners answers the basic economic questions. These planners have the power to make economic decisions for society as a whole. Many of the great cultures of the past, such as Egypt and Rome, were command economies. Today, the Soviet Union, Cuba, and China almost always use the command system. Other countries, such as Sweden and the United States, use the command system in part.

A command economy, also known as a planned economy, answers the "what to produce" question in several ways. Leaders of a country may decide to produce what they want for themselves—such things as palaces or works of art. The rulers of ancient Egypt, for example, built huge pyramids in honor of dead kings and queens. In contrast, the leaders may decide to produce what they believe is good for the people—such as modern weapons or schools. Finally, they may decide to produce what they think the people want—such as low-cost housing or cheap food. Whatever the choices, the leaders of a command system decide what to produce.

In command economies, the leaders also answer the "how to produce" question. They decide how many people will work, which workers will get jobs, and where they will work. The Soviet Union, for example, has a central planning agency called Gosplan. It assigns to each factory or farm its production goals, its machinery and supplies, and its work force.

By setting wages, the leaders of a command economy also answer the "for whom" question. That is, they decide how much of the country's goods and services each worker will be able to buy. Leaders can decide to provide some goods and services (such as housing or medical care) to everyone. They can deny other goods (such as cars) to all but a favored few. Also, by the way they set prices and fix production goals they can control who is able to buy goods and services.

Command Systems in Action

A hard problem that most command economies face is determining how much of each good or service will be wanted at the prices that are set. If the planners do not predict buyers' wants, or if factories do not meet production goals, either shortages or surpluses of goods will result. People may have to wait a long time for some goods to be delivered. Other goods may have to be stored because the demand for them is smaller than the supply.

Often, punishments and rewards are used in command economies to back up the planner's decisions. Leaders encourage people to work harder by reminding them that their society values their work. The results of their hard work will benefit all of society, not just the owners of their company. Sometimes, individual workers receive real rewards—more pay or a promotion—for hard work. Punishments for poor production range from wage cuts to imprisonment. Workers sometimes refuse to speak to or associate with other workers who are not doing their jobs well.

Command economies are able to act quickly. Central planners can meet war, famine, natural disasters, and other emergency situations with prompt action. Economic change can be brought about much faster than in traditional economies. Leaders in a command economy often can overcome the opposition of those who do not want to change their traditional ways. For this reason, individuals in traditional societies who want to change their economies often try to establish a command system.

In the command economy of China, the government decides what and how much to produce. Workers such as these try to meet quotas set by government planners. Most wages and prices are also determined by the government.

Democratic Government Planning

It is important to understand that some elements of a command economy can exist in either a democracy or a dictatorship. Many democratic countries use a command system to make some of their major economic decisions. In the democratic countries of Britain, France, Sweden, and Japan, the government owns some important industries. Government planners in these countries make many of the decisions on how to invest in capital goods and how many consumer goods to produce. The important difference between a democracy and a dictatorship is not an economic one. It is a political one. The difference is that in a democracy, average citizens have some influence on economic planning. Through their votes, they can remove the planners if

47

the planning decisions turn out to be foolish or unfair. In a dictatorship, average citizens have little or no influence on the decisions the planners make.

Even in market economies, some decisions are made by command. In the United States, for example, the federal government has controlled prices and wages in wartime, and occasionally in peacetime as well. State, city, and town governments restrict the use of private property by means of zoning laws. Federal, state, and local antipollution laws regulate the dumping of wastes into the air and water. All these laws represent government commands. Businesses and people are told that they must do some things and may not do other things.

People in every economy allow others to make some of their decisions for them. In a traditional culture, the right to make decisions that will affect others is based on strong, shared social values and beliefs. In a command economy, the right to make decisions is based on political power. People may think their only choice is to obey the commands of those in power. They also may believe that their leaders are better able than they are to choose for the common good. Consequently, these citizens support their country's command system.

REVIEWING THE CONCEPT

Developing Vocabulary

1. How are the basic economic questions answered in a command economy?
2. Explain why a command economy also can be called a planned economy.

Mastering Facts

1. List three factors that determine what is produced in a command economy.
2. How does a command economy decide for whom it will produce?
3. What are the advantages and disadvantages of a command economy?
4. How does shopping for consumer goods in the Soviet Union differ from shopping in the United States?

Making Decisions in the Soviet Union

One citizen of the Soviet Union who agrees with that country's command system is Klara Nijasbayeva. She manages a carpet factory in Alma-Ata, in the south-central region of the Soviet Union. Her factory produces about 1 million square yards of high quality carpet each year. All of it is sold, because carpets are in great demand in the Soviet Union.

If Nijasbayeva managed a factory in the United States or some other market economy, she probably would raise her prices until sales began to fall. With the increased income, her factory could produce more carpet. Alternatively, she might lower the quality of the carpet so that the factory could produce more, sell more, and increase her company's profits.

Since the economy of the Soviet Union is basically a planned economy, however, Nijasbayeva does not have these options. Basic decisions about prices and production levels are made centrally, not by individual factory managers. Nijasbayeva cannot make decisions based on what is best for her or her factory. Rather, she must do what the planners believe is in the best interests of the entire society. Raising prices is not allowed. Nijasbayeva explains this policy by saying, "That would be unfair to workers in other factories. One worker would be exploiting another."

Her factory cannot increase production until it receives increased amounts of raw materials. Nijasbayeva cannot simply order and receive greater supplies. In the Soviet Union, factories cannot compete for resources. Each factory is allocated certain amounts of raw materials. Nijasbayeva likes the Soviet system better than a competitive price system. "In a market system," she says, "other bidders might offer higher prices, and I might not get the raw materials I need."

What is Nijasbayeva's chance of getting more resources from the planners? Planners in the Soviet Union follow a pattern similar to the system that is common to most large American corporations. Lower level managers make projections of how much their section can produce. Then, middle and upper level managers use these estimates to make other forecasts. Central planners make the final projections. The central planners try to analyze all the variables in obtaining resources and carrying out production. Then, they issue a plan to guide the corporation or country through the coming year.

Nijasbayeva may request more resources, but the planners will decide whether her factory gets them. The planners may conclude that the additional wool she requests for carpets would be better allocated for sweaters. If that situation occurs, then despite demand Nijasbayeva will not be able to produce more carpets.

The workers in this Soviet carpet factory are protected from competition and from the ups and downs of the market. However, they depend on the decisions of government planners for supplies of raw materials.

ANALYZING THE CASE STUDY

STEP 1 Clarify the Issue

1. What characteristics of the Soviet Union's command economy affect the Soviet consumer?
2. How is planning in an American corporation today similar to planning in a Soviet factory?

STEP 2 Consider Costs and Benefits

1. According to Nijasbayeva, what advantages does a command system offer her factory?
2. Which aspects of a command system help the government to pursue its goals? Which make life easier for Russians?
3. Which aspects of a command system keep the government from realizing its goals? Which aspects make life more difficult for Russians?

49

1. How would a factory employee's work in a command economy be similar to such an employee's work in a market economy like that of the United States? How would it be different?
2. Would you prefer to manage a factory in a market system or in a command system? Explain your answer.

Enrichment Activities

1. During World War II, the United States economy took on many aspects of a command economy. List five examples of a command system at work in the United States during World War II. What problems did American consumers face? What problems did the government have then? Talk with at least three people who lived during World War II. Ask each of them about the problems consumers and the government faced. Do their memories match what you have read in books about the period?
2. The United States government is currently deregulating, or lessening its control of, several industries. This deregulation includes decontrol of the fares and routes of the airline and trucking industries. Talk with your parents and friends' parents to find out what they know about government regulations. Are they in favor of government regulation of some parts of their lives?

READING

The Art of Queuing

by Hedrick Smith   (1933-   )

When you go shopping, you may sometimes be bothered by long lines. No economic system has been able to eliminate lines. People are willing to wait, if the good or service they want is valuable enough. In many countries where consumer goods are in short supply, long lines are common. In the command system of the Soviet Union, consumers often must wait to purchase items. This reading is taken from *The Russians,* by the *New York Times* writer Hedrick Smith. As you read, consider how a command system could respond to the problem of long lines.

66 The urge for a touch of class, for something better than others have, has put new pressure on that classic Russian institution—the queue. Customers the world-over wait in lines, but Soviet queues have a dimension all their own, like the Egyptian pyramids. They reveal a lot about the Russian predicament and the Russian psyche. And their operation is far more intricate than first meets the eye. To the passerby they look like nearly motionless files of mortals doomed to some commercial purgatory for their humble purchases. But what the outsider misses is the hidden magnetism of lines for Russians, their inner dynamics, their special etiquette.

The only real taste of stoical shopping vigils in recent American history were the predawn lines at service stations during the gasoline crisis in the winter of 1973–74. That produced a wave of national self-pity in America. But it was temporary and only for one item. Imagine it across the board, all the time, and you realize that Soviet shopping is like a year-round Christmas rush. The accepted norm is that the Soviet woman daily spends two hours in line, seven days a week, daily going through double the gauntlet that the American housewife undergoes at her supermarket once, maybe twice a week. . . .

Personally, I have known of people who stood in line 90 minutes to buy four pineapples, three hours for a two-minute roller coaster ride, 3 and a half hours to buy three large heads of cabbage only to find the cabbages were gone as they approached the front of the line, 18 hours to sign up to purchase a rug at some later date, all through a freezing December night to register on a list for buying a car, and then waiting 18 more months for actual delivery, and terribly lucky at that. Lines can run from a few yards long to half a block to nearly a mile, and usually they move at an excruciating creep. Some friends of ours, living in the southwest part of Moscow, watched and photographed a line that lasted two solid days and nights, four abreast and running all through an apartment development. They guessed there were 10,000–15,000 people, signing up to buy rugs, an opportunity that came only once a year in that entire section of Moscow. Some burned bonfires to keep warm out in the snow, and the crackling wood and din of constant conversation kept our friends awake at night.

Consumers in a command economy may have to wait in long lines to purchase goods if planners predict demand inaccurately.

Yet despite such ordeals, the instinctive reaction of a Russian woman when she sees a queue forming is to get in line immediately—even before she knows what is being sold. Queue-psychology has a magnetism of its own. Again and again, I have been told by Russians that anyone's normal assumption on seeing people up front hurrying to get in line is that there must be something up there worth lining up for. Never mind what it is. Get in line first and ask questions later. You'll find out when you get to the front of the line, or perhaps they'll pass back word before then. A lawyer told me she once came upon an enormous line stretching all through the Moskva Department Store, and when she asked those at the end of the line what was on sale, "they said they didn't know or else snarled at me and told me not to interefere. I walked up 20 or 30 yards asking people and no one knew. Finally I gave up asking."

Nina Voronel, a translator of children's literature, said she happened to be at an appliance counter one day buying an ordinary hand mixer for 30 rubles when a clerk carried in a box of East German wall-lamps. . . . "I told the salesgirl 'I'll take one. Put me down for one and I'll go pay the cashier.' And while I went to the cashier, a line of about 50 people formed. How they found out about it, I don't know, word spreads—that is the way we always learn here. Practically everyone in the store was there. It didn't matter whether they needed the lamps or not. People here don't just buy what they need, but whatever they see that is worth having. Some may sell those lamps. Some may give them to friends. But mostly they keep them on the shelf. A lamp is always needed. Good fabrics are always needed, fur coats, fur hats, good winter boots, bright summer dresses, floor rugs, dishes, enamel pots and pans, kettles, good woolen cardigan sweaters, umbrellas, a decent purse, a nice writing table, and a typewriter . . . That is why people are so quick to join a line. It might be any of those things. . . .'

Once formed, moreover, Soviet lines are more fluid than they appear. . . .Undercurrents work within them. In most stores, for example, the shopper's ordeal is prolonged by the requirement to stand in not one, but three lines for any purchase: the first to select her purchase, find out its price and order it; the second to pay a cashier somewhere else in the store and get a receipt; and the third, to go pick up her purchase and turn in her receipt.

But in a dairy store one Saturday morning, I found out that the game is both simpler and more complex than that. I went in to buy some cheese, butter and bologna sausage which were, unfortunately, in three separate departments, each with its own line. *Nine lines!* I groaned inwardly. But rather quickly, I noticed that veteran shoppers were skipping the first stage. They knew what most items cost, so they went directly to the cashier for their receipts. After a bit of studying prices, that was what I did, too. Then, receipts in hand, I went to the cheese line, the longest—probably 20 people—to get the worst over with first. But I was in line less than a minute when the lady in front of me turned around and asked me to hold her place. She darted off to the butter-and-milk line. The cheese line was moving so slowly that she got her butter and milk and returned before we had moved forward three feet. I decided to take the risk, too, and got back with my butter while the cheese line was still inching along. Then it dawned on me that the entire store was churning with people getting into line, holding places, leaving, returning. Everyone was using the cheese line as home base. That was why it was barely moving: it kept expanding in the middle. So once again, I got the elderly gentleman behind me to hold my place and went off to buy my bologna. Once again, it worked. In the end it took me 22 minutes to buy butter, sausage and cheese, and instead of being furious, I felt oddly as if I had somehow beaten the system with all those shortcuts. **99**

From *The Russians*, by Hedrick Smith.

UNDERSTANDING THE READING

1. Why did Nina Voronel buy a wall lamp? How did she explain why people are quick to join a line?
2. What did the author do to master the art of queuing?
3. How would you explain the Russian reaction on seeing a queue form? If goods were abundant, would queues disappear? Why or why not?
4. Explain why shortages and queues might occur in a command economy. Can you make any assumptions about what types of products Soviet leaders prefer to manufacture? Explain.

Section 2 Review

Understanding Command Systems

1. Identify two past cultures that were command economies. Identify two present countries with command economies.
2. Who makes production decisions in a command economy? How are such decisions enforced?
3. Give three examples of decisions made by command in the economy of the United States today.
4. Explain in a paragraph the following statement: "A command economy can exist in a country with a democratic government or a dictatorship."

Command Systems Today

1. How do the problems facing a factory manager in the Soviet Union differ from those facing an American factory manager? Which manager is in the more difficult position? Explain your answer.
2. Why are some consumer goods scarce in the Soviet Union? How do planners contribute to the problem?
3. What are the most difficult decisions facing economic planners in a command economy?
4. Businesses in the United States often take surveys to determine consumer

needs and wants. Would consumer surveys be valuable in a command economy? Explain your answer.

5. Why might worker motivation be a problem in a command economy? Why might workers in a command economy be more motivated than workers in a market economy?

6. Chernenko was a Soviet leader who died in 1985. In the cartoon on this page, what surprises the individual speaking?

7. What is the longest time you have ever waited in line to purchase an item? What did you purchase? Would you be willing to wait in a long line on a weekly basis for this item? Explain your answer.

8. **Challenge:** The Soviet Union is second only to the United States in total value of manufactured products. However, the standard of living of consumers in the Soviet Union is far below the United States standard of living. What does this situation suggest about the way planners in the Soviet Union have decided to use the manufacturing capabilities of the Soviet Union?

"WHAT!? THIS LINE IS FOR CHERNENKO? I THOUGHT IT WAS FOR SHOES!"

3 Market Systems

SECTION OVERVIEW

Think of three economic decisions you made in the past week. Did you buy an item because you thought the price was low? Did you agree to work for a neighbor because you needed some extra money? Did you make any decision on the basis of price, quality, or personal preferences? If so, then the forces of the market system were influencing you. This section will help you to understand how market systems make economic decisions based on interactions between buyers and sellers.

ECONOMIC VOCABULARY

supply	capitalism	profit	private property
demand	invisible hand	profit motive	freedom of exchange

Market Economy Organization

In a market economy, the basic economic questions are answered by the exchanges of buyers and sellers. The quantity of a good or service that a producer will provide at each of its possible prices is called supply. The quantity of a product consumers want at each of its possible prices is called demand. The interaction of supply and demand determines what, how, for whom, and how much of a product will be produced. In a market system, no overall planning occurs as it does in command systems.

The guiding principle of market systems is self-interest. Individuals do what they believe will help them most. Sellers want to sell at the highest possible prices. Buyers want to buy at the lowest possible prices. The agreements that buyers and sellers reach answer the four basic economic questions.

The economy of the United States is an example of a market system called capitalism. Capitalism is a type of market system in which private individuals and businesses own most of the resources.

In a large market economy such as that of the United States, millions of people make individual economic decisions about supply and demand. When so many people make decisions, what prevents chaos? What ensures that enough coffee, milk, and meat will be available for consumers to buy? How can enough trucks be ready for merchants to ship their goods? Can enough workers be found to produce what customers want? How can any order exist when people make these decisions without the help of leaders or traditions?

Adam Smith's Invisible Hand

One of the first people to try to explain how a market system operates was the Scottish economist Adam Smith. His best-known book, *The Wealth of Nations,* was published in 1776. Market systems were just developing then in Europe and America. Smith believed that a market economy could serve society well without relying on traditions or a ruler's commands to coordinate economic decisions.

In order to explain how a market system makes decisions, Smith first had to explain how individuals make decisions. Smith believed that each producer and consumer would make economic decisions based on self-interest. For example, given a choice between two similar products, a consumer would choose the less expensive item. Producers would prefer to supply items that consumers will buy rather than those they will not buy.

Individuals acting in self-interest, said Smith, would compete, or try to outdo one another. Just as runners compete to win a race, producers would compete with one another to win consumers' money. Each producer would try to provide goods and services that are better and less expensive than those of the others. Consumers would compete with one another to purchase the best goods for the lowest prices. The result of competition, said Smith, would be that everybody would get wanted goods and services. Then, the best interests of the entire society would be met.

A market system, therefore, works in a way quite different from a traditional or command system. In a traditional system, custom determines the best interests of society. In a command system, a ruler or a group of central planners decides what economic policies will help society most. In a market system, no single person or group determines what is best for society.

Smith said that the market economy seemed to be controlled by an invisible hand. He meant that each individual who "intends only his own gain" is "led by an invisible hand to promote an end which was no part of his intention. . . . By pursuing his own interest he frequently promotes that of society . . ." The concept of the invisible hand, then, is the belief that the best interests of a society usually are met when people compete to achieve individual self-interests. According to Smith, there is little need for government involvement in the economy. Smith trusted the invisible hand to coordinate the market system.

Market System Characteristics

How does the market system answer the basic economic questions? Producers and consumers together answer the question of "what to produce." Producers compete for the business of consumers in order to make a profit. Profit is the difference between what it costs to make something and the price at which it sells. If producers think that they will earn higher profits by switching to different goods and services, then they will switch.

The profit motive, or desire to make money, determines the behavior of producers. Consumers' purchases express their beliefs about what should be produced. Every consumer purchase is an order to producers to provide a greater supply of that good or service.

The producers and owners of resources answer the "how to produce" question. Owners of human resources sell their labor for the highest wages they can obtain. Owners of natural and capital resources also seek the highest prices they can get. Producers are seeking profits; so they want to produce goods and services at the lowest cost. Those who find a way to sell their goods at lower prices than others will increase their sales and profits. Then, other producers who want to stay in business will have to copy their methods. Consequently, successful ways of making and selling products very quickly spread throughout an entire industry.

The question "for whom to produce" is answered at the same time as the "what" and "how" questions. The income that people get as profits, wages, rent, or interest determines their ability to buy the goods and services that have been produced. High-income people are better able to buy products than are low-income people.

The decisions of consumers and producers answer the questions of "how much now" and "how much in the future." Consumers want to purchase goods and services for immediate use. Producers want to purchase capital goods so that more items can be produced in the future. Items useful to both consumers and producers will be sold to whomever is willing to pay the most for them. Steel, for example, can be used to make such consumer goods as cars or such capital goods as cranes. Makers of steel will sell their product to the manufacturer offering the best price.

Market System Requirements

Most countries make at least some economic decisions through a market system. Some countries, including the United States, use the market system to make most economic decisions. Since the government often modifies the workings of the market, these economies are sometimes called modified market systems. Like command systems, a market system can exist in a wide variety of political situations. For example, the market system flourishes in the United States and Japan, which are politically free countries. In other countries, such as Chile, South Africa, and the Philippines, the market system works despite a lack of political freedom or equality. Regardless of political systems, to operate efficiently a market system must have four components: (1) private property, (2) freedom of exchange, (3) competition, and (4) profit motive.

The first component of a market system is private property, or resources owned by individuals and companies. These resources do not belong to society as a whole,

In the market economy of the United States, most economic decisions are made by private individuals and businesses.

as they might in a traditional or a command economy. In the United States, most human, natural, and capital resources are privately owned. Individuals and companies make decisions on how to use these three kinds of resources.

Second, a market system requires freedom of exchange. This freedom allows buyers and sellers to trade or sell goods or services at whatever terms they can agree on. In a traditional or a command system, custom or planners may establish the price of an item. In the united States, businesses can sell most products at any price they can convince consumers to pay.

The third and fourth components are competition and the profit motive. Both are necessary parts of Adam Smith's invisible hand. Competition allows consumers to

57

choose among goods and services and human, natural, and capital resources. The profit motive leads producers to seek the best price agreements with consumers. It also leads businesses to seek the lowest prices from their suppliers. Competition allows the most efficient producers to get the most business. Further, competition gives consumers the chance to get the products for which they are willing to pay.

REVIEWING THE CONCEPT

Developing Vocabulary

Find an article in a newspaper that illustrates or uses each of the following:
supply
demand
capitalism
invisible hand
profit
profit motive
private property
freedom of exchange
Prepare to report to the class on the way each concept is illustrated.

Mastering Facts

1. What economic activities take place in all markets?
2. What are the four requirements for the efficient working of a market system?
3. When did Adam Smith publish *The Wealth of Nations?* In what nation was he born?
4. Describe Adam Smith's concept of the invisible hand and the role it plays in the operation of a market system.
5. What are the benefits of competition in a market economy?

CASE STUDY

Day Care Centers: A Market Response

As consumers change the ways they live, they become more willing to pay for different goods and services. One of the greatest changes in the United States in the past 40 years has been the increase in the number of women working outside the home. This change has caused important changes in the types of services for which families are willing to pay.

Cecilia Rasko, for example, is about to take a job outside her home. Since her husband already is working, they need to provide care for their 5-year-old daughter, Linda, and their 6-year-old son, Brian.

Neither Cecilia nor her husband has relatives nearby. Neither of their employers provides child-care facilities. Virtually all of their neighbors work away from home

during the day. When the Raskos turned to their telephone book, though, they found several ways to satisfy their need for child care. They were amazed to see several dozen entries in the book listed under the category, "Day Nurseries, Nursery Schools, and Kindergartens."

Day care centers are an example of the American market system responding to changing needs. In 1947, only 19 percent of women with children under the age of 18 worked outside the home. By 1983, over 60 percent of women in this category were employed. As more women like Cecilia entered the labor force, more families needed help in caring for their children. The demand for day care centers increased. To meet this demand, churches, community

Day care centers reflect market demands.

organizations, and profit-seeking individuals became suppliers. By the mid-1980s, 120,000 day care centers were licensed by cities or states. These centers provided care for over 1.2 million children. Most were small, handling only a few children. Today, about half of all day care centers are run for profit. Almost 10 percent of the owners direct more than one center in a national or local chain.

Experts predict that the need for day care will continue to grow. By 1990, over 11 million children under 6 years of age will need care during the day. Relatives or friends will care for many of these children in informal arrangements. Many, though, will go to day care centers. During the rest of the century, child care outside the home should continue to be a growing industry.

ANALYZING THE CASE STUDY

STEP 1 Clarify the Issue

1. What change in the economy increased the need for day care centers?
2. What problems did the Raskos face

when Cecilia decided to take a job outside the home?

STEP 2 Gather Evidence

1. What three groups began day care centers? What were the motives of each group? Were these three groups responding to the market system?
2. List three consequences of the increase in the numbers of women working outside the home.
3. Describe the natural, capital, and human resources required to start a day care center. How would the market system provide these resources?

STEP 3 Consider Costs and Benefits

1. Identify the opportunity costs and trade-offs facing the Rasko family as Cecilia takes a job.
2. Identify the opportunity costs and trade-offs to society when millions of household workers enter the job market.

Enrichment Activities

1. Find out how many day care centers are in your community. Contact three or more to learn when they were started, why they were started, and how they have changed in recent years. Explain in a report how a particular day care center exemplifies the market system at work.
2. Listed below are four goods and services that developed rapidly during a certain era. Each grew in response to a change in consumer demands. In a one-page report on one of these items, explain why consumer demand for the item changed during that time.
   a. subcompact cars in the 1970s
   b. professional baseball teams in the early 1900s
   c. high schools and colleges in the 1960s
   d. suburban housing developments in the 1950s

Choosing a System

by Robert Heilbroner   (1919-   )

Markets for food and clothing have existed throughout recorded history. For thousands of years, farmers and craft workers have sold their products in small markets that exist in traditional or command economies. However, in the past few centuries market-dominated economies have developed. This reading, taken from *The Making of Economic Society,* by Robert Heilbroner, explains how market systems differ from the other systems. Heilbroner teaches economics at the New School for Social Research in New York. He is one of the most respected writers on economics today. As you read the excerpt, consider what is distinctive about market economies.

"**B**ecause we in the United States live in a market-run society, we are apt to take for granted the puzzling nature of how a market economy works. But assume for a moment that we could act as economic advisers to a society that had not yet decided on its type of economic organization.

We could imagine the leaders of such a nation saying, "We have always experienced a highly tradition-bound way of life. Our men hunt and cultivate the fields and perform their tasks as they are brought up to do by the force of example and the instruction of their elders. Likewise, women are brought up with the knowledge of how to weave, cook, and care for children. We know, too, something of what can be done by economic command. We are prepared, if necessary, to require by law that many of our people work on community projects for our national development. Tell us, is there any other way we can organize our society so that it will function successfully—or better yet, *more* successfully?"

Suppose we answered, "Yes, there is another way. Organize your society along the lines of a market economy."

"Very well," say the leaders. "What do we then tell people to do? How do we assign them to their various tasks?"

"That's the very point," we would answer. "In a market economy, no one is assigned to any task. In fact, the main idea of a market society is that each person is allowed to decide for himself or herself what to do."

There is confusion among the leaders. "You mean there is no assignment of some people to mining and others to cattle raising? No manner of designating some for transportation and others for weaving? You leave this to people to decide for themselves? But what happens if they do not decide correctly? What happens if no one volunteers to go into the mines, or if no one offers to become a railway engineer?"

"You may rest assured," we tell the leaders, "none of that will happen. In a market society, all the jobs will be filled because it will be to people's advantage to fill them."

Our respondents accept this with uncertain expressions. "Now, look," one of them finally says, "let us suppose that we take your advice and allow our people to do as they please. Let's talk about something specific, like cloth production. Just how do we fix the right level of cloth output in this 'market society' of yours?"

"But you don't," we reply.

"We don't! Then how do we know there will be enough cloth produced?"

"There will be," we tell him. "The market will see to that."

"Then how do we know there won't be too much cloth produced?" he asks triumphantly.

"Ah, but the market will see to that too!"

"But what is this market that will do these wonderful things? Who runs it?"

"Oh, nobody runs the market," we answer. "It runs itself. In fact there really isn't any such thing as *'the market.'* It's just a word we use to describe the way people behave."

This shopping mall holds a variety of shops. In a market economy individuals choose what they do for a living.

"But I thought people behaved the way they wanted to!"

"And so they do," we say. "But never fear. They will want to behave the way you want them to behave."

"I am afraid," says the leader of the delegation, "that we are wasting our time. We thought you had in mind a serious proposal. What you suggest is inconceivable. Good day. **"**

From *The Making of Economic Society,* by Robert Heilbroner.

UNDERSTANDING THE READING

1. According to Heilbroner, what is the main point of a market system?
2. How does the way jobs are filled in a market system differ from the way they are filled in a traditional or command system?
3. Why did the leaders think a market system was inconceivable?

Section 3 Review

Understanding Market Systems

1. Explain the role of self-interest in a market system.
2. Complete the statements below by matching them with the correct terms.
   competition
   freedom of exchange
   each person
   profits
   self-interest
   a. In a pure market economy, _____ makes basic economic decisions.
   b. Market systems depend on the _____ of buyers and sellers.
   c. In a market economy, _____ allows only the most efficient producers to succeed.
   d. Producers in a market economy seek

   _____.

   e. In a market economy, people buying and selling material goods and one another's skills have _____.

3. According to Robert Heilbroner, what are two ways in which a market economy differs from a traditional or a command economy?

Market Systems Today

1. Give examples to show that market economies can work in a variety of political systems.
2. Should businesses be concerned only with profits? Explain.
3. What do you think the role of government should be in a market economy? Explain your answer.
4. In a market economy, who decides how to use basic resources? How do these decisions affect the system's answers to the basic economic questions?
5. **Challenge:** Give three examples of economic activities today that are not based on self-interest. Would these activities take place in a pure market economy? Explain your answer.

Americans at Work

Meet Randy Sher
Career Counselor

Like many Americans, Randy Sher had to find out about the realities of the modern job market the hard way. In 1977 Randy Sher was divorced and unemployed, and had two children to support. At one time she had been a school teacher, but teaching jobs were hard to find. She began retraining as a paralegal. Sher learned, however, that this field also was overcrowded.

Sher realized that she lacked the skills employers demanded. Frustrated, she began to study the ways businesses operated and the employment needs they had. She analyzed the economy and the ways it was changing. In 1979, she put her knowledge of the economy to work when she started counseling women on job retraining and employment trends. She now heads her own career counseling firm, A Better Way. Randy Sher emphasizes constant learning. "Women have to stop and focus on where this country is going," she said. Workers "are all going to be trained and retrained two or three times in [their] lives."

Career counseling is a rather new profession. A century ago the economy offered only a few different opportunities for most people. As the nation's economy changed, however, people had more career opportunities. By World War II, millions of people were working in many different commercial and industrial jobs. The number and variety of job opportunities meant that young people could no longer rely solely on their parents for information on careers.

Since World War II, the economy has changed at an ever-increasing rate. For students graduating from school and ready to choose their first full-time job, the opportunities are endless. Further, people are increasingly likely to change careers. More than ever before, individuals are changing careers after 10 years of work. Career counseling, then, has become important to workers of all ages. As the economy continues to change rapidly, career counseling probably will become even more important.

Career counseling is a growing profession.

Finding a Job

Today, 9 out of every 10 Americans who want to work are employed. If you do not already have a job, the chances are great that you will soon begin to search actively for one. The marketplace, though, does not hire just anyone. In fact, teenage unemployment is traditionally about twice as high as the overall unemployment rate. In the mid-1980s, nearly 24 percent of all teenagers who wanted to work were unable to find a job. Where you look for work and the techniques you use in applying can be the difference between getting the job and remaining unemployed.

If you were to begin looking for a job today, for what would you be qualifed? Where would you look for job opportunities? What kinds of jobs are open to teenagers? Why? Could you develop or would you need a résumé? Knowing how to find a job is a valuable skill in a market economy.

STEP 1 Look for a Job

Several sources may be used when job hunting. One of the simplest but often overlooked is word-of-mouth. Let friends and relatives know you are looking and ask them whether they know of any job openings. Another way that is often successful is to go to the supermarkets, fast-food restau-rants, stores, and shopping centers near your home. Ask the manager whether any jobs are available now or in the near future. Fill out applications for jobs. Leave your name, address, and telephone number so that they can contact you if any jobs become available.

Newspaper ads are a good source of job openings, as are school counselors and teen job services. Often schools have bulletin boards where job openings are posted. Also, public bulletin boards in stores list job openings. Private job agencies may be used, but be very cautious. Unlike public job agencies, the private firms charge a fee, sometimes a percentage of your salary. Whichever source you use, do not be shy about seeking a job. If you want to work, you must be willing to look for a job.

STEP 2 Fill Out an Application

After you find a job that is available, you must show your potential employer why your are the right person for the job. In a sense, you are now selling a product—yourself. You want the employer to purchase your abilities rather than those of someone else.

Usually the employer will ask you to fill out an application. This step can be critical.

Your potential employer must select candidates to interview, often using only the application as a guide. Read the application through before beginning to write. Make sure you understand what information is being requested. If you are unsure, ask questions. Write neatly, and provide complete information.

Often an employment application requires that you give names of friends or acquaintances as references. Your prospective employer may contact these people to find out about your work habits and skills. Be sure to get permission to use names.

STEP 3   Write a Résumé

Employers looking for permanent, full-time workers often require a résumé—an outline of your educational and employment background—in addition to an application. Some employers may want a résumé for part-time employment. In any case, a prospective employer will be impressed if you have prepared a résumé. Writing a résumé while you are still in school provides practice at a skill you will need again in the future. Be sure your résumé is typed neatly and includes your name, address, telephone number, educational background, work history, special skills, and references of individuals who can attest to your work abilities. If possible, have someone else read your résumé.

STEP 4   Prepare for an Interview

Assuming that all has gone well, the final step in the process of finding a job probably will be an interview. Your potential employer, having read your application, now wants to meet the real person. Know some-

"IT HAS COME TO THE COMPANY'S ATTENTION, CREEDMORE, THAT YOU ARE DRESSED FOR SOMETHING OTHER THAN SUCCESS."

thing about the company before going to the interview. First impressions are most important: be on time, dress neatly, comb your hair. Appearance is not everything, but a good appearance will help you. Be polite, answer questions thoughtfully, speak clearly, and, when you leave, thank the interviewer for talking with you.

If you do not get the job, do not be discouraged. Most people have missed a job at some time. Keep on trying; this is one case where persistence usually pays.

ECONOMIC SKILLS TODAY

1. List and explain three sources to use when job hunting.
2. What does the above cartoon suggest about how to impress an employer?

Enrichment Activities

1. Go to several businesses near you and obtain copies of applications. How are the applications similar? How are they different?
2. Prepare a résumé that you might use when applying for a job.

CHAPTER SUMMARY

Traditional Systems

The traditional system answers basic economic questions by means of custom, habit, religion, or law. Generally, such methods limit economic choices. Until recently, the traditional system was the most common in the world, and it is still found in many areas of Africa, Asia, and Latin America. However, outside forces—especially wars and the influence of Western nations—are introducing changes. Frequently, changes are resisted. A traditional culture accepts change more easily when the new ideas do not conflict with the culture's values.

Command Systems

Command systems use a group of planners to answer basic economic questions. The planners are able to act quickly, overcome opposition, and organize a society's resources. However, they have difficulty in matching supply with demand. Two major countries that use the command system today are the Soviet Union and China. Democratic nations, such as Britain, France, Sweden, and Japan, use the command system in part.

Market Systems

A market system answers basic economic questions by means of the invisible hand of exchange between buyers and sellers, who operate out of self-interest. Market systems require four things in order to operate: private property, freedom of exchange, the profit motive, and competition. The economic system of the United States is mostly a market system.

CRITICAL THINKING QUESTIONS

Traditional Systems

1. What are the advantages of a traditional economic system?
2. What are the economic disadvantages of a traditional system?
3. Who makes the economic decisions in a traditional system?

Command Systems

1. What kinds of nations might find that a command economy is most suited to their needs? Why?
2. What factors might persuade nations with a command economy to move toward a market economy?
3. Explain how a command economy in a democratic country is different from one in a dictatorship. Give an example of a democratic country that uses a command economic system.

Market Systems

1. What impressions of the American economy might a first-time visitor from the Soviet Union have?
2. What items are bought and sold in a market economy that are not exchanged in a command economy?
3. Explain the role of competition in a market economy.
4. What role does the government play in the regulation of competition in a market economy?

DEVELOPING ECONOMIC SKILLS

Copy the chart, "Answering Basic Economic Questions." Fill in each category to show how the different economic systems answer the basic economic questions.

APPLYING ECONOMICS TODAY

1. In your library, research one of the traditional cultures mentioned in this chapter. Describe the ways that people in the culture make decisions about jobs and marriage.
2. Consult recent periodicals for articles on changes in the economies of China and the Soviet Union. How are their economies changing today? Provide specific examples to support your answer.
3. **Challenge:** Research the market economy of Japan and then describe it in several paragraphs. What attitude do the Japanese have toward competition? What role does the Japanese government play in that nation's economy?
4. **Challenge:** Use the information in a United States history book to describe the economy of two American colonies in the 1600s. Identify the traits of each colony as traditional, command, or market. Which colony is more like the economy of the United States today?

Answering Basic Economic Questions

	Traditional Economy	Command Economy	Market Economy
What should be produced?			
How should it be produced?			
Who gets what is produced, now and later?			
How much should be produced?			

Explanation

The chart will help you compare how basic economic questions are answered in three different kinds of economies.

Chart Skills

1. What are the three different kinds of economies compared?
2. With what subject do all four basic economic questions deal?

CHAPTER 3

Economic Growth

1 Specialization

Objective: *to understand how specialization promotes growth and interdependence among nations*

2 Decisions on Growth

Objective: *to understand how economic growth is stimulated in command and market systems*

3 Evaluating Growth

Objective: *to understand and analyze the costs and benefits of economic growth*

1 Specialization

SECTION OVERVIEW

American pioneers learned to be self-sufficient. Frontier families grew their own food, made their own clothes, and built their own homes. Your world is vastly different from the world of the pioneers. During your life, you probably will never develop the variety of skills common among pioneers. Instead, your economic skills probably will be more specialized. This section will help you to learn how specialization promotes growth and interdependence among people.

ECONOMIC VOCABULARY

geographic specialization

occupational specialization

resource specialization

division of labor

mechanization

social interdependence

Specializing with Resources

The most successful way of dealing with scarcity is wiser use of existing resources. A common way of using such resources is to specialize. For example, New England farms produce such crops as apples and potatoes. With the help of greenhouses, however, oranges could be grown as well. It is much cheaper, though, to import oranges from warmer regions, such as Florida or California. The warmer climate gives these regions a geographic advantage in growing some foods. Geographic specialization describes a region's production of goods and services that make use of that region's particular resources.

Occupational specialization means that each person concentrates on developing one skill rather than several. It is easier for one person to be a doctor, a plumber, or a farmer than to try to be all of these things at once. By specializing, people can pro-duce more goods and services than they could if each tried to do all the jobs that others do.

In resource specialization, natural, capital, or human resources are used in a particular way. A doctor who likes children may choose to specialize and become a pediatrician. A steel company that invented a process for making rolled steel might specialize in making that kind of steel. A city of mostly skilled workers may try to attract industries that need skilled workers.

When each worker on a job does the one task for which he or she is trained, the total job will be completed faster than it would be if each worker did many jobs. This process of dividing jobs into several tasks is called division of labor. An auto assembly line is a good example of the division of labor. Each worker performs a very specific task, such as attaching a mirror, in the job of assembling an automobile. Dividing jobs into smaller tasks, how-

69

ever, has allowed the use of machines to do the work. The use of machines to increase production is called mechanization. Division of labor makes it possible to take advantage of the special skills of some workers but also may create new problems. The auto worker who does the same task again and again often loses all interest in the work.

Specialization, division of labor, and mechanization increase total production. Consumers then have not only a wider range of goods and services from which to choose but also more than they could produce for themselves. Think of all the things people use during the course of a single day—clothes, cars, books, dishes, food, houses. Then imagine how much time people would need to produce all of these things themselves.

Changes in the economy have forced people to rely on one another more and more. This increasing social interdependence carries costs as well as benefits. A drought in the wheat belt can cause bread prices to rise elsewhere. A coal miners' strike may increase consumers' electric bills. Most economic problems are related to one another. One small change in the economy can affect people everywhere.

World economic growth has increased social interdependence among countries as well as within countries. As countries specialize in order to grow, each becomes more dependent on other countries for goods. By 1980, world trade in terms of dollars had reached almost $2 trillion.

Skills and Specialization

Specialization occurs because each of us is different. You have distinct talents, strengths, weaknesses, and personality traits. When you choose freely, you base your choice on your own traits and desires. At the same time, others also are choosing freely. All people try to satisfy their wants by doing jobs they like and are able to do.

Sooner or later, these choices are bound to conflict. Too many people want the same things. Some jobs must be done, but nobody wants to do them. Those who like to be different may find that others are cramping their style. If others do not want what you can give, you may not be able to do what you most want to do. Often you must adjust your choices because of the choices others make. Economic growth will result if you choose to use your economic resources wisely.

REVIEWING THE CONCEPT

Developing Vocabulary

1. How does geographic specialization differ from occupational specialization?
2. What is resource specialization?

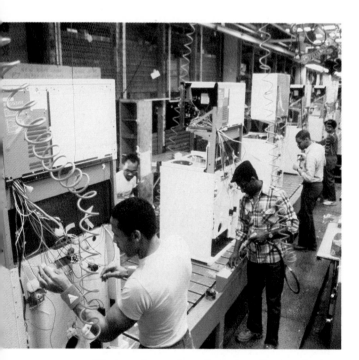

Workers in modern factories often specialize in performing specific tasks.

3. Define specialization, division of labor, and mechanization. How do they work together?
4. What is social interdependence? How has it developed?

Mastering Facts

1. What are the four ways in which people deal with the problem of scarcity? What are the advantages and the disadvantages of each?
2. List the advantages of geographic specialization. What effect does geographic specialization have on trade? On the consumer? On the nation's economy?
3. What are two advantages and two disadvantages of occupational specialization. Explain your choices.
4. Explain why a doctor who chooses to become a pediatrician is an example of resource specialization.
5. What advantage does your family, as consumers, gain when the use of specialization, mechanization, and division of labor increases production?

Can a Robot Do Your Job?

Economic growth resulting from specialization has made life easier. Specialization is likely to continue, but no guarantee exists that it will continue to make life better. One example of specialization that will affect work in the future is the robot.

The use of robots for specialized work is increasing slowly in industries throughout the world. Japan currently leads the world in the robot industry, having in use five times as many robots as the United States. Over 200 Japanese companies produce robots. Robots are partially responsible for Japan's rapid economic growth over the past 20 years.

The United States is expected to become a leader in the production and use of robots. From 12 in 1979, the number of robot companies in the United States had increased five times by 1984.

Robots represent a further step in specialization. Specially designed robots can weld automobile frames, but others are more versatile. One American-made robot can handle 70 percent of all jobs currently done by other types of robots. This robot can do tasks as diverse as welding and assembling electronic parts. As robots are improved, they can be used in various ways to promote economic growth.

Undoubtedly, robots will replace many workers. Economic growth through changes in technology often results in some loss of jobs. At this time, estimating how many workers robots will replace is difficult. Robots also will create jobs, though fewer than they will eliminate. Workers will be needed to maintain and monitor robots and computers. These people will be vitally important to the smooth operation of any company using robots.

Experts disagree on precisely how many jobs robots will eliminate and how many they will create. Since the jobs lost and those created will be quite different, though, few of the displaced workers are

71

The word robot comes from a Czech word meaning drudgery. Robots such as this welder are often used to perform jobs that are difficult, dangerous, or unpleasant.

create jobs. Robots will change how people work. Some experts predict that the effects of changes resulting from the use of robots and computers will be positive. Many people will become more productive and so will be able to work less time. American workers may work only 30 hours a week and have six or more weeks of vacation each year. With more leisure time, people will have more opportunity to travel. Then industries based on travel and vacations may grow. Airlines, restaurants, hotels, and resorts may benefit indirectly from the increasing use of robots.

Further, robots could be used in dangerous and unpleasant jobs, freeing people to work in safe, enjoyable jobs. Robots might allow companies to update their methods of production more easily. In that case, individuals able to learn new tasks quickly would become increasingly valuable to their employers.

Another result of the use of robots is a greater emphasis on person-to-person contact. Consumers still prefer to deal with humans rather than machines. Consequently, in a world of robots and computers, customer service representatives are even more important.

Not all of the effects of robots on economic growth may be desirable. Increases in productivity do not necessarily result in shorter workdays. Further, because of robots some jobs, including those of unskilled workers, may become more specialized. For many people, work then may be less enjoyable. Robot-promoted growth will not be without costs.

Preparation for your future should include preparation for living in a world with robots. You may want to be one of the skilled professionals who design or service robots. If not, though, you will still need to develop solid learning skills so that you can adapt to a changing world.

likely to be retrained for the new jobs. As often occurs in economic changes, the people who pay the costs and those who receive the benefits will not be the same. Growth that benefits one group of people, or the general public, may cause serious hardships for others.

Robots will do more than eliminate and

72

Robots in the United States

Year	Sold by U.S. Manufacturers	In Use in U.S.
1979	1,367	5,000
1982	6,300	11,300
1984	15,950	37,250
1987	34,950	115,200
1990	125,400	359,200
1992	274,000	810,000

Source: International Resource Development, Inc.

Explanation

The chart contains statistical information on the actual and projected sale and use of robots in the United States.

Chart Skills

1. How many robots will be in use in the United States in 1992?
2. How many more robots will United States manufacturers sell in 1992 than were sold in 1982?
3. Is there a relationship between the number of robots sold and the number used in the United States? Explain.

ANALYZING THE CASE STUDY

STEP 1   Examine Change

1. How do robots demonstrate increasing specialization?
2. What types of skills will increase in importance in the future? What is the meaning of these changes in relation to your career training?
3. Will robots create or eliminate jobs? Explain.

STEP 2   Consider Costs and Benefits

1. List the economic costs and benefits of increased specialization.
2. Do the economic benefits outweigh the costs? Explain.
3. How does the cartoon on this page suggest one of the advantages of robots over human workers?

STEP 3   Make a Decision

1. Do you think specialized job training or a more general business background will be of greater economic benefit to you? Why?
2. What decisions do you need to make in the next two years to prepare yourself for the job market of the future? What information do you need to make these decisions?

Enrichment Activity

During the past century, specialization has affected many parts of the culture of the United States. Research one of the topics below and write a report on the ways it shows the influence of specialization.

1. Subjects taught by individual teachers in a high school
2. The kickers and the return team in the game of football
3. The designated hitter on a baseball team
4. Magazines dealing exclusively with specific topics
5. Diet-oriented foods

"Of course, if you're not feeling well take the rest of the day off!"

The Wealth of Nations

by Adam Smith   (1723-1790)

In 1776, Adam Smith's best-known book, *The Wealth of Nations,* was published. His ideas continue to influence economists today. Smith, a teacher of logic and philosophy, believed that the economy of the British empire would be more productive if trade and other economic activities were less regulated. He believed that without interference, trade would occur naturally in a way that would benefit everyone. Smith believed that the value of a product was equal to the labor that went into making it. By increasing the productivity of each worker, then, a nation would increase its total wealth. In this reading, taken from *The Wealth of Nations,* Smith describes how specialization increased production in a pin factory. As you read, consider how applicable Smith's ideas are today.

66 The greatest improvement in the productive powers of labor comes from effects of the division of labor. Consider for example the pin-maker: a worker not educated to this business, nor acquainted with the use of the machinery employed in it, could barely make one pin in a day and certainly could not make 20. But in the way in which this business is now carried on, no person does all jobs. One worker draws out the wire, another straightens it, a third cuts it, a fourth points it, a fifth grinds it at the top for receiving the head; to make the head requires two or three distinct operations. It is even a trade by itself to put the pins into the paper. The important business of making a pin is, in this manner, divided into about 18 distinct operations.

I have seen a small factory of this kind where 10 men only were employed, and where some of them consequently performed two or three distinct operations. But though they had little machinery, they could, when they exerted themselves, make among them about 12 pounds of pins in a day. There are in a pound upwards of 4,000 pins of an average size. Those 10 persons, therefore, could make among them upwards of 48,000 pins in a day. Each person, therefore, making a tenth part of 48,000 pins, might be considered as making 4,800 pins in a day. But if they had all worked separately and independently, and without any of them having been educated in this business, none of them could have made as many as 10 pins in a day.

In every other art and manufacture, the effects of the division of labor are similar to what they are in this one. In many of them, though, the labor can neither be so much subdivided, nor reduced to so great a simplicity of operation. The division of labor, however, promotes a proportionable increase of the productive powers of labor. The separation of different trades and employments seems to have taken place in

Smith—prophet of the free market.

consequence of this advantage. This separation, too, is generally carried furthest in those countries which enjoy the highest degree of industry and improvement. In every improved society, the farmer is generally nothing but a farmer; the manufacturer, nothing but a manufacturer. The labor, too, which is necessary to produce any one complete product is almost always divided among a great number of hands.

This great increase of the quantity of work accomplished through the division of labor results from three different circumstances: first, the increase of each worker's skill; second, the saving of the time which is commonly lost in passing from one type of work to another: and last, the invention of a great number of machines which make work easier, and enable one person to do the work of many.

This division of labor, from which so many advantages are derived, is not originally the effect of any human wisdom. It developed through very slow and gradual consequence of a certain tendency in human nature to trade, barter, and exchange one thing for another. **"**

From *The Wealth of Nations*, by Adam Smith.

UNDERSTANDING THE READING

1. Summarize Adam Smith's argument that specialization increases the productivity of workers.
2. What are the three circumstances that cause productivity to increase through specialization?
3. According to Smith, what characterizes the most productive countries?
4. What does Smith claim to be the reason for the division of labor, or specialization? Do you agree with Smith's reasoning? Why or why not?
5. Give three examples of how the division of labor and the use of machines have increased production.

Section 1 Review

Understanding Specialization

1. In our present-day society, what has caused social interdependence?
2. Compare the advantages and disadvantages of social interdependence for you as an individual, for all Americans, and for the global community.
3. Give one example of how specialization has affected your life today.
4. Name one item you used today that resulted from geographic specialization.

Specialization Today

1. Volvo and Saab, automobile manufacturing firms in Sweden, have reorganized their assembly lines so that each car is built from start to finish by a team of eight workers. What do you think the

advantages of such an arrangement might be? What do you think its disadvantages might be? Would you prefer to work in one of these factories or in a conventional factory?

2. How do you suppose pins are made today? Would it be more or less difficult to find workers for Smith's pin factory?

3. As jobs become more specialized, they also tend to change more quickly. How can you prepare to work in a world where jobs are specialized and change rapidly?

4. In what products does the United States specialize? Are they a result of geographic specialization? Are they a result of resource specialization?

5. Think about the career choice you must make in the near future. How are your talents, strengths, and personality traits related to the career choices you are considering?

6. **Challenge:** Analyze five tasks you perform regularly. Are any of these tasks specialized aspects of larger jobs? Could you perform any of these tasks more efficiently if you divided the task into smaller actions?

This team of auto workers assembles a car from start to finish.

2 Decisions on Growth

SECTION OVERVIEW

Your growth determines what you will be like in the future. You can influence your physical growth by the food you choose to eat and the amount of exercise you get. You also can influence your academic growth. You can choose to study hard or to study just enough to pass. Similarly, countries can choose their rate of growth. In this section, you will learn how economic growth is encouraged in a market system, exemplified by American capitalism, and in a type of command system called socialism.

ECONOMIC VOCABULARY

socialism   communism   consumer cooperative

Using Capital Resources

If you spent all the money you have now, you might be able to buy many of the things you want. However, you probably would choose not to spend all of your money right now. You realize that by saving some now, you will have more for the future. Societies also must save some of what they produce today in order to have more for tomorrow. If a society used all its resources to produce consumer goods, its people would have only a brief period of prosperity. Every society must produce capital goods as well as consumer goods in order to meet future economic needs. Long-range economic growth depends on the continued production of capital goods.

Everyone who works contributes to the growth of capital resources. Suppose you earn $72 a week, working evenings in an auto repair shop. How do you contribute to the growth of capital resources? If your manager paid you exactly what the customer paid the company for your repair work, what would happen to the company? What would happen to the business if no money were saved to replace old tools and equipment? Your labor must be valuable enough to earn more than just the money to cover your wages.

When your manager bills customers for the work you did, the amount will be large enough not only to cover the company's costs but also to invest in capital resources. Your labor may earn your company $100 a week. Since you are paid $72, you are helping the company to collect $28 a week. Some, or all, of this money can be used for capital resources. When your company uses this money to buy new equipment, it expects future returns from the equipment to justify the purchases.

The example of a part-time auto repair worker demonstrates how the economy operates. For instance, if a person works 40 hours a week, costs to cover wages might be produced in 30 hours. Then, the other 10 hours of work could cover operating costs of the business. One of these operating costs is investment in capital resources in order to produce more in the future.

Ownership of Capital Resources

The use of capital resources determines how a society will grow. In a capitalist system, such as the United States, the owners of businesses control capital resources. In the auto repair shop, the owner decides how the business will grow. The manager may decide to replace the old tools, hire more help, or expand the shop, for example. The manager makes decisions based on how the company will earn the most profits.

Many countries with market systems are basically capitalist. No country is purely capitalist, though. In a pure capitalist system, all capital resources would be privately owned. The government would have no control over the ways those resources were used to promote growth. In all countries today, governments place some limits on the ways individuals and businesses can use their resources. Government regulations often prohibit certain investments because they are harmful to the overall community.

Countries with command systems usually are directed by some kind of socialism, an economic system in which the public owns and controls most of the capital goods. Among the many socialist countries in the world today, none practices pure socialism. In all, private individuals own and control some resources. In the People's Republic of China, a socialist system, the government makes most of the basic economic decisions. Individuals, though, farm small plots of land. They decide how to use this resource.

History of Socialism

The idea of socialism has existed for thousands of years. Some of the ancient Greeks and early Christians practiced forms of socialism. In the United States during the 1800s, several groups started socialist communities. In these communities, all property was jointly owned and all work shared. One of the most famous examples of these communities was Brook Farm in Massachusetts. This experimental community lasted from 1841 to 1847.

Modern socialism bears the strong influence of Karl Marx, a German philosopher and economist who lived between 1818 and 1883. Marx was a brilliant, fiery man who made his living writing articles and essays for newspapers and journals.

Like all economists, Marx was greatly influenced by the era in which he lived. During the mid-1800s, capitalism was developing. Working conditions in factories then were much worse than working conditions today. Laborers worked long hours in dangerous conditions for low pay. They had little protection from ruthless managers. Marx was struck by the misery many workers faced. To him, the conflict between workers and owners was sharp and brutal. In addition, like many leading thinkers of his day Marx believed that the world was constantly changing. Ways of making goods and relationships among people were always evolving. The writings of earlier economists, such as Adam Smith, also strongly affected Marx's writings on economics.

The various influences on Marx came together to shape his ideas about history and economics. He believed that history revealed a constant struggle between different economic groups. The groups in conflict would change as the economy changed. In earlier times, the conflict was between slaves and slaveowners, or peasants and landowners. In the industrial society, said Marx, the conflict would be between owners and laborers.

Marx believed that changes in the economy would cause changes throughout a society. The most basic changes were often technological, as in the ways people

People today often work in large factories where many people do the same tasks or jobs.

made goods. A series of changes in Europe led to the development of capitalism.

Marx viewed capitalism as an advancement over earlier economic systems. By breaking down old economic restrictions, capitalism allowed production to expand rapidly. This increase in production, said Marx, was tied to specialization, division of labor, and mechanization. As companies grew in size and efficiency, they would slowly push smaller, less efficient companies out of business. Group production would replace individual producers: the giant shoe factory would replace the village cobbler. People in society would increasingly realize they were dependent on one another. As a result, they would realize that their self-interest would be served by policies that helped everyone. According to Marx, replacing individual production with group production would be the first step from capitalism to socialism.

Marx also believed that group ownership would replace individual ownership.

As capitalism gave way to socialism, workers would gain control and ownership of capital resources. Wealth would become more evenly divided in society. Socialism would evolve out of capitalism.

Marx thought that some countries, including the United States, might evolve peacefully from capitalism to socialism. He said, however, that history shows that people in power rarely give it up without struggle. Consequently, the workers would have to be ready to fight to change the system. Marx believed that a violent revolution to overthrow capitalism would be necessary in most countries.

Marx thought society would continue to change after socialism had replaced capitalism. Socialism would give away to another economic system, communism, a more extreme form of socialism. Marx viewed socialism as a halfway step between capitalism and communism. The trends toward worker ownership of capital resources and equal distribution of wealth would continue under communism. Eventually, all people would be both workers and owners, and everyone would have an equal share of wealth. Without the conflict between owners and workers, government would have little to do. Marx predicted that government would slowly whither away.

Marx was considered a radical in his time. Nevertheless, many of the ideas he supported as socialist—free public education, for example—are now accepted. Many radical movements claimed to be carrying out his goals. Though Marx believed violent revolution was justifiable, he did not support all of those who claimed to be his followers. Near the end of his life, he became so upset with the actions of those who used his name that he declared, "I am not a Marxist," Today, many socialists do not consider themselves Marxists.

Growth in Two Systems

Both capitalists and socialists claim that their economic system will promote economic growth. The two systems promote growth in different ways, however.

Under capitalism, capital resources are privately owned. Consequently, private individuals and businesses decide how the economy should grow. Thousands, or millions, of people make individual decisions about how to use capital resources. These people feel most directly the benefits of growth or the problems related to lack of growth. In a socialist economy, capital resources are publicly owned. The public, usually through the government, determines how to use these resources to promote growth. The benefits of growth or problems related to lack of growth affect the entire public.

Capitalists and socialists each claim that their system provides a fairer way to promote growth. Both systems are widespread in the world today, and all nations have elements of each. Economic growth is a vital issue that affects all people, regardless of what they call themselves.

REVIEWING THE CONCEPT

Developing Vocabulary

How are communism and socialism similar? How are they different?

Mastering Facts

1. Why must societies invest in capital goods as well as consumer goods?
2. In a capitalist system, who decides how much of the country's resources will be invested in capital goods? What is the opportunity cost of this decision? What circumstances would bring about government involvement in this decision?
3. In a socialist system, who decides how much of a country's resources will be invested in capital goods?
4. How did Marx believe that capitalism and socialism were related?
5. According to Marx, why would communism evolve?

CASE STUDY

Cooperative Growth

In each economic system, decisions on economic growth greatly affect the jobs of workers. At the Puget Consumer's Cooperative, or PCC, a food store in Seattle, Washington, the decisions made are popular with the employees. "I have never been happier working in a place," says Carol Bergin of her job at the PCC. Another employee agrees that the PCC is an excellent place to work. "It would be a hard place to leave," says Tom Schooley.

The popularity of the PCC may be explained by two of its unusual features that combine capitalist and socialist traits. First, like other capitalist businesses, the PCC succeeds or fails based on how well it competes in the market. Its managers must develop policies that allow the store to compete successfully. Like socialist businesses, however, workers control management of the store. Bergin, Schooley, and the rest of the 100 employees of PCC share in managing the store. The result, says Tom Schooley, is "a sense that you do have control over your life and your job."

The second unusual feature of the PCC is that its customers are also its owners. PCC is an example of a consumer cooperative, a form of business in which the consumers who purchase from the business share in the ownership of the business. As in other capitalist businesses, the owners are private citizens. As in socialist businesses, however, the decisions the PCC makes must serve the interests of the consumers. In the PCC, the consumers are also the owners.

Cooperatives, or coops, are used in a great variety of ways in the United States. Examples of coops include credit unions, mutual insurance companies, group health plans, rural electric cooperatives, rural telephone cooperatives, housing cooperatives, and college stores. Cooperatives have a long history in the American economy. You or your family may have firsthand experience with them.

Many of the food coops that exist today started less than 30 years ago. Most began as food-buying clubs in which members took turns shopping or packing or delivering orders. As these food coops grew, they

In a consumer cooperative, people who purchase from a business are also the owners of the business. Some gas stations are run as cooperatives.

expanded their variety of goods, acquired storefront space, and even hired staff. Some sold to nonmembers at slightly higher prices. The Puget Consumer Cooperative has 15,000 members and 3 stores.

What would it be like to work for a cooperative like the PCC? The growth of the business would depend on you in several ways. Your decisions, as well as your working ability, would be part of the cooperative's success or failure. You would have to become more involved with your company in buying and selling decisions and practices. Workers manage the stores using a system of elected staff committees. Several advisory committees make recommendations to a steering committee that consists of elected representatives from each department. The steering committee makes all staff and store operation decisions, but workers can appeal any decision, bringing it to a full staff vote.

Members and the staff share responsibility for coop planning of policy to promote growth. Members own the coop, having provided most of the PCC's capital. An elected board of trustees makes decisions about finance. It also determines such policies as senior citizens' and handicapped persons' discounts and price subsidies for certain essential foods. Members may serve on boards and committees or influence policy by voting on important issues. It is possible, of course, for members to use the services of the coop without such extensive participation.

The success of the PCC and other coops has attracted attention. Two of the reasons for the PCC's success are prices and incentives. Food prices at the PCC are 11 to 28 percent lower than supermarket prices. Since employees are also managers, they have a stronger incentive to work harder than supermarket employees. Members share in the successful growth of the enterprise. As companies everywhere look for ways to lower prices and encourage their employees to work harder, coops are taking on added importance.

ANALYZING THE CASE STUDY

STEP 1 Clarify the Issue

1. What is a cooperative?
2. What are some types of coops in the United States?

STEP 2 Consider Costs and Benefits

1. List the costs and benefits of being part of the Puget Consumer Cooperative.
2. Do cooperatives define costs and benefits in the same way as other businesses? Explain.

STEP 3 Make a Decision

1. Would you like to join the PCC? Explain why or why not.
2. If you managed a local supermarket, what would your economic concerns about the PCC include?

Enrichment Activity

Find out about coops in your community. Contact them to learn about their prices, organization, and membership. Make a table or chart to summarize your findings.

READING

A.D. 2033

from U.S. News and World Report

Economic decisions made today will determine how the economy of the nation grows in the future. Investments in new technology will influence what new products and businesses develop and how people work. This reading from *U.S. News and World Report* predicts how the economy will change in the next 50 years. As you read, decide which of these predictions you think are probable.

"IF the United States economy can manage a steady takeoff in the next couple of years, it may well climb for at least the balance of this century.

Predictions for the Future

Category	1980- 1989	1990- 1999	2000- 2009
Overall Economic Growth (percent per year)	2.6%	2.7%	2.4%
Increase in Prices (percent per year)	5.8%	4.2%	3.4%
Increase in Personal Income (percent per year)	1.6%	1.8%	1.7%
Unemployment Rate (average)	8.5%	6.2%	5.3%

From: *U.S. News and World Report* and **Wharton Econometric Forecasting Associates**.

Explanation

This chart shows predictions of four basic economic trends over three decades.

Chart Skills

1. According to the predictions, during which decade will the economy grow fastest?
2. During which period shown on the chart will jobs be easiest to find? How old will you be then?

Only after the year 2000 will that rise, powered by the thrust of new technology, show signs of fatigue and settle back to a slower pace.

Even so, the surge will be strong enough to produce 50 years from now a "new country"—one resplendent [shining brightly] with new products, new jobs, new opportunities—says Joseph Wahed, chief economist for Wells Fargo Bank in San Francisco.

American industry will be rebuilt and redesigned. Automated factories will replace the aging, inefficient plants of today. Only 1 out of 10 workers will toil in the auto, steel, textile, and other smokestack industries that symbolize this country's first Industrial Revolution.

Most of the others will earn livings by producing new generations of electronic marvels and by providing a proliferating array [growing variety] of information, advice, and services to society.

Big corporations will grow even bigger, but there still will be room for aggressive entrepreneurs, particularly in services and fast-moving high-technology fields.

The government's role will expand, too, and voters will insist on continued protection of public health and safety, the environment and other quality-of-life factors, as well as federal aid for society's less able.

Result: The American standard of living, both in terms of incomes and amenities [convenience items] will "improve significantly this century and will continue to improve as far as the eye can see into the next century," predicts economist Irving Leveson of the Hudson Institute in Croton-on-Hudson, New York.

Barring unforseen calamities [problems], most experts agree that the most perilous period in the next half-century may well be the present. Will the budding economy flower? Or will domestic-policy mistakes or debt defaults abroad knock the economy on its back?

Nobody knows for sure, but the odds favor growth. Forecasters at Wharton Econometric Associates in Philadelphia predict a 3.1 percent average annual growth rate—after inflation [a general rise in prices]—in the nation's total output of goods and services over the 10 years to 1992.

That's a sharp turnabout from the 1.2 percent decline in 1982 and the no-net growth of the past four years. It also is a shade higher than the average for the 1970s.

83

Because the recovery from the recent recession is expected to last longer than average, the momentum should enable the economy to attain new heights over the next 20 years.

However, the pace of business will begin to cool at the turn of the century. By that time, the impetus from new job-creating investment in high technology will have ebbed. What's more, population growth will slacken, reducing the demand for products. As a result, Wharton forecasters see an average annual growth rate of about 2 percent for the first 20 years of the next century.

Such a script means that there is very little chance of another Great Depression. Unemployment will fall from more than 10 percent this year to perhaps half that rate by the beginning of the next century.

The gap between the haves [wealthy] and have-nots [poor] may widen for a while as social-welfare spending is restrained. But Sandra Shaber of Chase Econometrics in Bala-Cynwyd, Pennsylvania, believes this trend could be mitigated [modified], or even reversed, as long-term growth broadcasts its benefits. "A rising tide does tend to lift all ships," she notes.

However, the lesson of recent times will not be lost. "People will remember that it took a costly recession to bring down inflation," says Kurt Karl, a Wharton economist. For that reason, the public will be more tolerant of higher unemployment if it is seen as needed to tame inflation.

The business cycle will not end, especially if the government, as most experts predict, allows market forces to work more freely. Only if the market's effects on society become too harsh will there be a "swing back to more control" by Washington, says economist Gary Stacey of the Battelle Memorial Institute in Columbus, Ohio.

Economists see virtually no chance of the government's engaging in aggressive national economic planning, but they do see it acting as a referee and a protector of the public good. "As society becomes more complex," says A. George Gols, chief economist for the Arthur D. Little consulting firm in Cambridge, Massachusetts, "government will be asked to make more rules."

There will be no substantial repeal of social programs and protections, such as unemployment pay, which have sprung up since Roosevelt's New Deal. Nor will there be any major add-ons, except for perhaps an insurance plan to cover castastrophic illnesses. Increasingly, Washington will perform the role of fiscal middleman—collecting taxes but financing functions through state and local governments and private agencies.

Nonetheless, urgent public problems will need to be addressed in the years ahead. Crumbling roads, bridges, and other public facilities will require substantial outlays. Also, no matter what party is in office, pressures will build for programs to retrain displaced workers, aid for depressed regions, tax incentives to stimulate research, and changes in antitrust laws to allow American firms to compete more effectively overseas.

But the most dramatic economic change in the next 50 years will be the renewal of the private sector as it departs its old manufacturing base and advances further into what some call the "Information Age."

American industry will give up its grubby, sometimes menial [low-level], assembly-line jobs to the lower-wage regions of Asia, India, Africa, and South America.

That's not to say that industries such as autos and steel will disappear. Fifty years from now, there almost certainly will be fewer United States auto makers. They will be producing worldwide and will be engaged in more cooperative ventures with foreign manufacturers, here and abroad.

Similarly, a much smaller United States steel industry will concentrate on specialty products rather than on mass production of steel. "Steel no longer will be an important industry," says Lillian Deitch, vice president of the Futures Group in Glastonbury, Connecticut.

Instead, tomorrow's growth will be fueled by the developing high-technology industries: Home computers, industrial robots, genetic engineering, electronic medical devices—and scores of exotic applications not yet known.

About 8 out of every 10 workers will be employed in making computers and providing services and information to society. "The biggest growth will be in jobs that require people to operate electronic equipment," predicts Hudson's Leveson.

Development of vast computer networks will allow companies to desert crowded urban centers for the more pleasant surroundings of suburbia [areas near cities] and smaller communities.

Corporations also will change the way they operate. The big will become bigger to compete against their foreign counterparts all over the globe. But new giants will emerge, many of them organized as joint ventures and other cooperative arrangements rather than the traditional manufacturer-wholesaler-retailer relationships.

"The big companies in 2033 are not going to be General Motors-type vertically integrated companies," says Geoffrey Greene of Wharton, "but trading companies to compete in world markets and financial supermarkets to serve a more sophisticated public."

As new industries are spawned and old industries are automated, the nation's productivity—or output per worker—will stage a comeback, allowing companies to keep closer control of costs.

Industry will become even more decentralized not only across the United States but throughout the world, as telecommunications links decision makers in distant locations and transforms the production process.

Interchangeable parts and portable assembly kits—the auto industry's "world car" concept—will emancipate [free] manufacturing of the future from the bondage of the large-plant assembly lines of the past. "General Motors may still be in Detroit," says Wharton's Greene, "but few, if any, cars will be made in Detroit."

Robots also will speed the trend toward smaller, more flexible factories. "It will be less expensive to reprogram a computer in the smaller factory of tomorrow than it is to retool today's outmoded, large industrial plants," says Roy Amara, president of the Institute for the Future in Menlo Park, California.

Market information will become more detailed. This, in combination with more flexible production, will enable business managers to "target production more tightly to particular markets," adds John White, senior vice president at Arthur D. Little.

Indeed, many experts see within the next two decades the spread of "production on demand," in which an order placed by a consumer from his or her home computer will automatically trigger factory production.

At the same time, as menial production tasks are ceded [given] to other countries, American management will use the exploding information technology to take on the role of "global managers" for all sorts of worldwide ventures.

That leadership role—and the very survival of United States firms in a tougher international market—will depend, says Halder Fisher of Battelle, on the greater willingness of American companies to take long-term investment risks, even at the expense of short-term profits. **"**

From *U.S. New & World Report.*

UNDERSTANDING THE READING

1. Write a one-sentence summary of the main point of this article.
2. According to economists mentioned in the article, how will the role of government change?
3. How will the relationships between the economy of the United States and the economies of other nations change in the future?
4. List three changes discussed in this reading that will affect you.

Section 2 Review

Understanding Decisions on Growth

1. What is a consumer cooperative?
2. What advantages might socialism have over capitalism?
3. What advantages might capitalism have over socialism?
4. As a consumer, would you prefer to live in a country with a capitalist or a socialist system? Why?
5. As a producer, would you prefer to live in a country with a capitalist or a socialist system? Why? How does your answer to this question compare with your answer to question 4?

Decisions on Growth Today

1. Explain the advantages of government ownership of passenger railroads, such recreational areas as national parks, and the post office. List and explain any disadvantages of such ownership.
2. **Challenge:** Should the government operate a program to provide health insurance for all Americans? Explain.

3 Evaluating Growth

SECTION OVERVIEW

When you were 8 years old, you probably could barely wait to grow up. Adults could stay up late, they had money, and no one told them what to do. By now you realize that growth is not without problems. Similarly, economic growth has both advantages and disadvantages. Economic growth will make finding a job and a comfortable place to live easier for you. However, economic growth may cause such problems as air and water pollution. In this section, you will learn about the costs that accompany the benefits of economic growth.

ECONOMIC VOCABULARY

nonrenewable resources   hidden costs

Advantages of Economic Growth

In recent years, many people have argued that economic growth is a mixed blessing. The advantages of growth are fairly clear. As people produce more goods and services, the average standard of living goes up. Growth also keeps people employed and earning income. It provides people with more leisure time, since they can decrease their working hours without decreasing their income. Growth provides the government with additional tax revenues, which enable it to spend more on programs for education, water and air purification, medical care, highway construction, and national defense.

Disadvantages of Growth

What are the disadvantages, then? Some economists point out several. Four of them are: (1) use of natural resources that cannot be replaced, (2) generation of waste products, (3) destruction of natural environ-

ments, (4) uneven growth among different groups in society.

By growing constantly, the economy uses up more and more natural resources each year. Many of them, such as oil and natural gas, are nonrenewable resources: they cannot be replaced. It is expensive to look for new resources, and as the easily accessible supplies are used up, the prices of resources go up. As these prices go up, so do the costs of products made with them. Soon a time will come, critics of growth say, when the nonrenewable sources of energy—oil, gas, coal—will be too expensive to be useful.

Critics point out that economic growth carries hidden costs. These costs are not reflected in the market price of goods and services. They are also known as third-party or social costs. One hidden cost is the waste generated in producing many goods. This waste often causes air or water pollution. Cleaning up pollution is becoming more important and more expensive each year. Also, the damage that pollution can

Sometimes, economic growth results in the ravaging of natural resources, such as by this strip mine.

cause to health is alarming. Further, as the population and the economy grow, the ordinary waste products of life grow as well. Garbage disposal, for example, has become a serious problem for most major cities. Finding places to dump waste is getting both harder and more costly.

Economic growth causes more than just air and water pollution. Growth also leads to the destruction of forests, wetlands, beaches, mountains, oceanbeds. Controlling destruction costs money. Thus, the economy may not grow as fast as it would if we did not have to worry about the destruction. For example, strip mining, a popular and cheap way of getting coal out of the ground, involves stripping away the surface of the land. But this method destroys the original landscape, leaving ugly, barren hills. As strip mine owners are required to restore the land, the cost of doing so turns up in the price of coal. When coal is more expensive, industries that use it may cut

back production or raise their prices to make up the difference. Either action can slow down economic growth.

Economic growth is a measure of the economy as a whole. But such a measure says little about those parts of the United States whose economies are growing more slowly than others. The economies of some parts of the country, in fact, may not be growing at all. Many older cities, for example, stopped growing years ago. Others are shrinking. Between 1970 and 1980, St. Louis lost nearly 27 percent of its residents. During the same period, Cleveland's population dropped by 23 percent, Buffalo's by 22 percent, Detroit's by 21 percent, Pittsburgh's by 18 percent, and Chicago's by 11 percent. People are moving away from these cities to find work. Jobs are easier to find in the suburbs and the newer cities of the South and West.

Further, not everyone shares equally in growth. One group of people may benefit from growth but another may not. The period of economic growth in 1983 and 1984, for example, helped middle and upper income families more than poor families. Some economists stress that the goal of society should be balanced growth rather than growth any way it might occur. Then all parts of the country and all groups of people could benefit equally.

Counting Benefits and Costs

Decisions about economic growth are not easy to make. In the past, growth has allowed poor people to improve their economic condition. During periods of growth, people have felt optimistic about their future. Nevertheless, continuing economic growth at the pace of today may permanently damage our world, polluting air, land, and waters, and using up natural resources.

In considering the benefits and problems of growth, it is necessary to recall that to survive, every economy needs three kinds of resources that depend on one another. If these resources are overused to promote economic growth now, future growth may be much slower. Growth, however, sometimes provides solutions to problems.

REVIEWING THE CONCEPT

Developing Vocabulary

1. List four renewable resources that could replace nonrenewable resources.

2. What is a hidden cost? Use an example in your answer.

Mastering Facts

1. What are the advantages of economic growth for you as a consumer? As a producer?
2. List four disadvantages that can result from economic growth. Explain each.
3. List and explain three social costs of economic growth. Which of them are hidden costs?
4. Why is uneven growth a result of economic growth?

CASE STUDY

Costs of Growth

One of the advantages of economic growth is the creation of new jobs. Bruce Gilchrist and Ariaana Shenkin have jobs that did not exist 20 years ago. Gilchrist is the director of the Center for Computing Activities at Columbia University. Shenkin is his research assistant. They are just two of the thousands of workers who make their living operating a computer. Millions of other Americans have jobs that computers have made easier.

Gilchrist and Shenkin realize that the progress responsible for their jobs has its costs as well. The introduction of computer typesetting, for example, spelled unemployment for many Linotype and other machine operators. Gilchrist and Shenkin studied what happened to a few families when, over the four-year period 1974–1978, three major New York City newspapers reduced their employment of typesetters by almost half.

Among those who lost their jobs was a 58-year-old man who had spent 30 years as a typesetter. He had a wife and son to support and a sizable mortgage to pay. For a year after being laid off, he tried unsuccessfully to obtain another printing job. Because his wife became sick during this period, he and his family received no income for six months after his unemployment insurance expired. His doctor suggested that he see a psychiatrist to help him through his depression. The typesetter replied that he did not need a psychiatrist, he needed a job. Today, he works as a telephone operator, earning less than half his former salary.

Another of the workers studied was a Linotype operator whose family had to seek counseling after he was laid off. His 17-year-old son recently enlisted in the navy because he felt that the pressure at home had become too heavy. He explained that his father, who had been mild mannered, now easily lost his temper. This typesetter's wife had never held a job before her husband lost his job. She went out to work, and the family lived on her paycheck for almost a year. Her husband now has three jobs. His wife commented: "The three jobs he now has to work at to make ends meet will be the death of him."

In all, the Gilchrist and Shenkin study traced 44 of the people who had lost their jobs during the conversion to computer typesetting. The workers ranged in age from 34 to 55. Their average wage had been $27,000. Three of the 44 found full-time jobs in printing. The remaining workers continued to seek employment. Many tried retraining programs, but found that employers were reluctant to hire older, experienced persons as beginners.

Properly trained workers can take advantage of new jobs created by economic growth.

As might be expected, younger people were more likely to find other employment. Excepting one, however, none of the operators under 40 years of age obtained a high-paying job. More than a year after losing their jobs, many of the workers had taken jobs delivering flowers, polishing glass, stock-clerking, or driving taxis. Others did such odd jobs as painting and home repairs to earn income.

Technological advance, and along with it the loss of some jobs, greatly accelerated after the Industrial Revolution. Although groups have tried, none has successfully resisted technological change. This change has brought about improvements in production that, in turn, have led to lower costs and prices, greater demand, and more material abundance. Where advances have reduced the number of jobs on the one hand, they have created jobs on the other. Widespread acceptance of farm machinery, for example, reduced the need for farmers. However, it greatly increased demand for workers to manufacture machines and perform numerous other jobs related to them. The growing computer industry has created thousands of jobs in manufacturing, sales, and service. As the study of the typesetters shows, though, displacement can be devastating for individuals.

Retraining in new skills is only one solution to the problem, and that is not a simple one. Retraining probably is more useful to the young than to the old. The questions of what skills will be in demand in the future and what job guarantees may be offered are difficult to answer. Regardless of demand, most retrained workers must begin again at entry levels. Also, how to pay for retraining remains a controversial question. Currently, the federal government, businesses, and unions all do some retraining. Primarily, though, work education is still an individual responsibility.

ANALYZING THE CASE STUDY

STEP 1   Clarify the Issue

1. List five jobs that you believe will need fewer workers because of computers.
2. List five jobs that you believe will need more workers because of computers.
3. Overall, have computers contributed to the growth of our economy? If so, how? Give examples. If not, why?

STEP 2   Examine Costs and Benefits

1. How would the costs differ in retraining a 30-year-old and a 60-year-old worker?
2. Ultimately, who pays for retraining programs? Explain.
3. What are the economic costs of not retraining workers? The social costs? Who pays these costs?
4. What are the benefits to the economy of retraining workers?

5. Do the economic advantages of technological growth outweigh the social costs?

STEP 3   Consider Alternatives

1. What alternatives are available to the worker who has been displaced by technology? Is age a factor? Explain.
2. What alternatives can the government use to deal with displaced workers?
3. What responsibilities does an employer have to the stockholders or owners of a business? To its employees, both those being displaced and those remaining?
4. What role, if any, do unions have in regard to displaced workers?

STEP 4   Summarize the Benefits

Explain your views on the economic costs and benefits of computers.

READING

Technology and Growth

by Paul Ehrlich   (1932-   )
and John Holdren   (1944-   )

Advances in technology will bring economic growth that will change your life. Technological advances may give you a shorter work week, cheaper food, and higher quality products than your parents had. These same advances may bring with them damage to the environment, resulting in health problems and more expensive products for you. In this reading, Paul Ehrlich and John P. Holdren examine the impact of technology on our lives. Ehrlich, a biologist, is well known for his studies of the effects of population growth. Holdren is an energy expert at the University of California at Berkeley. As you read, consider how changes in technology affect different economic groups.

    "Those who have called attention to the misuses of technology, and to the fact that technology cannot solve all problems, have been unfairly labeled antitechnology, and extremists.

If technology is indeed neither good nor bad, as we believe, then one should be able to discuss its potential and limitations openly, without being called names. To our knowledge, no responsible observer has seriously suggested that technology be abandoned or that everyone return to hunting and gathering. Those who have rushed to technology's defense should deal with the real issues: how to focus technology on genuine human needs, how to minimize bad side-effects, and how to recognize that some problems do not have purely technological solutions.

A particularly unfair attack on those who have questioned the present course of technology has been that they are condemning the poor both at home and abroad to continued poverty. It is beyond dispute that technology is an essential ingredient if the bulk of humanity is to be provided a decent existence. But this does not mean that the answer is simply more of the same kinds of technology that have helped to create today's problems, and it does not mean that a particular technological scheme is wise simply because it is well intentioned. We need more transportation, but fewer automobiles. We need more housing, but less suburban sprawl. The world may need more aluminum and steel for communications networks, bridges, and railroads, but the United States certainly does not need more beverage cans.

It appears to us that certain representatives for technology are attempting to use the legitimate needs of the poor to justify trying outlandish technological circuses that have no real relevance to those needs. These representatives seem to be suggesting that the only route to

Developments in technology have helped create great wealth, but they have not ended poverty. Cities often include both wealthy and poor areas.

prosperity for all is the raising of today's wasteful technologies to ever higher levels of waste. In other words, we will not be able to give the poor many crumbs until our own loaf, already more than ample, gets even bigger. Implicit in this philosophy is the assumption—perhaps even the desire—that the present unfair distribution of the fruits of technology will endure.

We do not believe this is the only possible future. Further, it is certainly not the most desirable one. Under the current system, the standard of living for the poor rises agonizingly slowly while the increasing demands by the already comfortable damage the earth.

We suggest an alternative. It is based on the proposition that what Western society has been calling development is really overdevelopment. In other words, we are consuming more resources than the environment can long endure. The solution would seem to be de-development for the United States—and, to a lesser extent, for Europe, the USSR, and Japan. At the same time, semi-development should be pursued in what today are poor countries. In this process, the diversion of resources and energy from frivolous uses in the overdeveloped countries to necessity-oriented uses in the underdeveloped countries would hasten an adequate standard of living in the underdeveloped countries and ecologically rational standard in the developed countries.

To any but the most defensive technologist, it should be obvious that this is not a proposal to destroy technology. De-development and semi-development would involve the abandonment of some technologies, the modification of others, and the invention of some new ones. Few would deny, we suspect, that the sooner we abandon the technologies of war the better. Similarly, the existing technologies of power generation and agriculture must be modified to reduce their environmental impact, and we need altogether new technologies for recycling, for farming in tropical rain forest areas, and for solar energy. The list could be greatly expanded, but the message is clear; on balance, these enterprises will require more science and technology, not less. At the same time, they will surely fail if we are unsuccessful in grappling with the nontechnological issues that accompany them. We must eliminate discrimination, inequity, and exploitation, and we must stabilize both population and consumption. **99**

From "Technology and De-Development," by Paul Ehrlich and John Holdren.

UNDERSTANDING THE READING

1. Why did Paul Ehrlich and John Holdren write this article? What is their view of technology?
2. What do the authors mean by the terms semi-development and

de-development? Why are these terms important to understanding the viewpoint of the article?

3. Summarize the authors' conclusion. Do you agree or disagree? Explain your position.

4. Is the present distribution of the benefits of technology fair? Why or why not? Explain.

Section 3 Review

Understanding Evaluating Growth

1. Choose a social cost and explain how it has affected you.

2. What effects does economic growth have on our environment?

3. Compare the advantages and disadvantages of economic growth. Write a paragraph that states your conclusions on whether or not economic growth is worth the costs.

Evaluating Growth Today

1. Most Americans, when comparing themselves with their parents, expect to maintain a higher standard of living, and have more material possessions and sooner. How are these expectations related to economic growth?

2. What are the hidden health costs of air pollution? Who pays them?

3. If it were possible to limit economic growth, would our slower growth affect poor, backward countries? How?

4. Does psychological damage carry an economic cost? Explain your answer.

5. Would it be economically justifiable for government to pay a subsidy to displaced workers who cannot maintain their former income in new jobs? Explain why or why not.

6. **Challenge:** Certain kinds of air pollution cause acid rain, which destroys vegetation, wildlife, and buildings, and may damage humans. What might be the economic costs and benefits of eliminating acid rain?

Pollution hurts plants, animals, and people.

Americans *at Work*

A house is a family purchase.

Meet Margaret Richards
Real Estate Broker

Margaret Richards went into real estate after her children were grown and her husband had died. To become a real estate broker, she went to school to pass a state exam. Richards had to learn a great deal about technical subjects, such as property surveys, mortgages, title changes, closing costs, and zoning. To succeed in the business, however, Richards believes that a broker must also like and understand people. Margaret Richards was interviewed by Studs Terkel for his book, *Working*. In the following excerpt, Margaret Richards talks about her work as a realtor, its rewards and challenges.

"Being a realtor is something I enjoy very much . . . The niftiest part is to be in on the ground floor of the decision making. A house is the largest investment a family can make . . . It becomes pretty vital in the lives of people . . . they always ask your advice . . . About neighborhoods, schools, parks. The most rewarding thing for me personally is to work with young people buying their first house. . . .

One of the nicest parts is the continual influx of people from all over the country, all ages. . . . I find it stimulating to be exposed to someone that isn't cut out of the same piece of cloth as I am. . . .

I started as a secretary and then went into the sales end of it. It's infinitely more lucrative. The commission is six percent of the first fifty thousand dollars and five percent on anything above that . . . This is a very competitive area. There are many seasoned, highly professional realtors in this area. So you do step on each other's toes . . . About twenty years ago there were many part time ladies in this field. This is frowned upon and no longer condoned . . . I think that's good. [But] a woman realtor makes very good sense . . . By and large, it's the woman who buys the house. Most men . . . let the wife decide, as long as the price is right . . . Naturally a woman can better understand a woman's needs and find what she's looking for.

Of course, you get tensions. I just had a three-thousand-dollar deal fall apart . . . Another broker brought in an offer on it . . . This last year, from the first of April until the middle of August, I had [only] one Sunday at home . . . It can be very tiring.

[Yet] to me, the most exciting thing in the world is picking up the phone and having someone say, 'Some friends are coming to town. Can you help them?' . . . I'm excited about seeing them and getting to know them."

Filing Income Tax Returns

Anyone earning $3,300 or more must complete income tax forms every year. The completed tax forms must be mailed to a regional office of the Internal Revenue Service (IRS) before April 16. Employers withhold part of employees' salaries to pay taxes directly to the government. Completing a tax return involves the following steps.

STEP 1   Collect Tax Return Information

Income sources may vary, including wages, tips, and interest from savings and investments. An employer must send all workers a statement of wages and taxes at the end of every year. This statement, a W-2 form, indicates gross salary—the amount earned before taxes and social security were deducted. The W-2 also shows the amount the employer withheld and sent directly to the state and federal governments for state and federal income taxes and the Federal Insurance Contributions Act (FICA), usually referred to as social security.

Paycheck stubs also show total amounts withheld for the year to date in each category. The last paycheck stub of the year should show the same figures as the W-2.

Banks and savings-and-loan institutions also are legally required to send their customers form 1099. That form shows the amount of interest paid on each account during the year.

STEP 2   Obtain Tax Forms

Copies of government tax tables and tax return forms usually are mailed to the taxpayer. They are also available at banks and savings and loans as well as post offices and federal government offices. The IRS, a part of the Treasury Department, offers assistance to taxpayers at no charge. It is listed under U.S. Government Agencies in the telephone book.

STEP 3   Understand Tax Tables

The amounts of tax people pay is affected by the number of exemptions, filing status, and income size. Tax calculations are based on these three factors.

First, every taxpayer may take one exemption for himself or herself, so $1,000 of income is exempt, or free from taxation. An individual over 65 years of age is allowed an additional exemption, as is a person who is blind.

Second, filing status depends on whether the taxpayer files a return as a single person or as a married partner filing either jointly or separately. Another category,

head of household, generally refers to an unmarried person with dependents.

Third, the amount of income received is an important factor in determining the amount of tax owed. The larger the income, the higher the percentage of that income a person pays for federal personal income tax. The lowest tax rate for single taxpayers is 11 percent on income over $3,300. As income increases, the rate for additional income also rises, to a maximum of 50 percent.

STEP 4 Calculate Tax

Completing tax returns has become easier over the last several years. Most students file the 1040EZ tax form. This form can be used if the taxpayer meets the following conditions: (1) the filing status is single; (2) no more than one exemption is claimed; (3) all income is from wages, salaries, tips, and interest; (4) interest income is $400 or less; and (5) taxable income is less than $50,000.

The sample form illustrates this kind of return. John Mill had a part-time job washing windows in an office building. At the end of 1983, his employer gave him a statement of wages and taxes (Form W-2). John found that he had earned $1,844 (line 1). His savings-and-loan institution sent him a form (1099) saying that he had earned $15 in interest on his savings account (line 2). He then added all his income together and found that he had a total adjusted income of $1,859 (line 3). After he subtracted $1,000 for his personal exemption (line 6), his taxable income was $859 (line 7). According to the tax table, he owed no tax because that amount was less than $3,300. Looking at his W-2 again,

John saw that his employer had deducted $59 for income tax (line 8); so he filed his return and received a refund (line 10). If he had not filed his return, he would have lost the $59.

ECONOMIC SKILLS TODAY

1. Using the Form 1040EZ, determine the amount of tax on wages of $2,625 and $70 of interest income.
2. If you contribute $25 to a charitable organization, how will your taxes be affected?

Income Tax Return

Department of the Treasury · Internal Revenue Service

Form 1040EZ Income Tax Return for Single filers with no dependents

OMB No. 1545-0675

1984

Name & address Use the IRS mailing label. If you don't have one, please print:

Please print your numbers like this.

1234567890

Print your name above (first, initial, last)

Social security number

Present home address (number and street)

City, town, or post office, State, and ZIP code

Presidential Election Campaign Fund
Check box if you want $1 of your tax to go to this fund. ▶

Figure your tax

1 Total wages, salaries, and tips. This should be shown in Box 10 of your W-2 form(s). (Attach your W-2 form(s).)   **1**

2 Interest income of $400 or less. If the total is more than $400, you cannot use Form 1040EZ.   **2**

Attach Copy B of Form(s) W-2 here

3 Add line 1 and line 2. This is your **adjusted gross income**.   **3**

4 Allowable part of your charitable contributions. Complete the worksheet on page 21 of the instruction booklet. Do not enter more than $75.   **4**

5 Subtract line 4 from line 3.   **5**

6 Amount of your personal exemption.   **6**   1 000 00

7 Subtract line 6 from line 5. This is your **taxable income**.   **7**

8 Enter your Federal income tax withheld. This should be shown in Box 9 of your W-2 form(s).   **8**

9 Use the **single** column in the tax table on pages 31-36 of the instruction booklet to find the **tax** on your taxable income on line 7. Enter the amount of tax.   **9**

Refund or amount you owe

10 If line 8 is larger than line 9, subtract line 9 from line 8. Enter the amount of **your refund**.   **10**

11 If line 9 is larger than line 8, subtract line 8 from line 9. Enter the **amount you owe**. Attach check or money order for the full amount, payable to "Internal Revenue Service."   **11**

Sign your return I have read this return. Under penalties of perjury, I declare that to the best of my knowledge and belief, the return is true, correct, and complete.

Your signature   Date

For Privacy Act and Paperwork Reduction Act Notice, see page 41.

CHAPTER SUMMARY

Specialization

To grow, a country must use its available resources efficiently. Specialization helps to achieve the most efficient use of resources. Specialization occurs in several ways: (1) geographic specialization, (2) occupational specialization, and (3) resource specialization, which includes mechanization and division of labor. The result of the trend toward more specialization is increasing social interdependence.

Decisions on Growth

To grow, an economy needs capital goods because they are used to produce other goods and services. Each company must reserve money to replace and update its tools, machines, and factories, as well as to expand to meet demand. In capitalist countries, individuals and businesses own and control most of the capital resources. In socialist countries, the public owns the resources. There, the leaders or planners make decisions about the country's production of capital goods and consumer goods. According to Karl Marx, these two economic systems, capitalism and socialism, are but steps to a final system, communism.

Evaluating Growth

One benefit of economic growth is an increasingly higher standard of living. The costs are numerous. Among them are: (1) depletion of natural resources that cannot be replaced, (2) problems in disposal of a growing amount of waste products, (3) pollution of the natural environment, and (4) uneven growth among different groups.

Everyone in some way pays the hidden social costs of economic growth, such as air and water pollution.

CRITICAL THINKING QUESTIONS

Specialization

1. Divide the United States into four general geographic areas—north, south, east, and west. List any geographic and resource advantages for each area and explain whether and how they are specialized to use these resources.

2. Using your favorite candy bar, make a list of the candy ingredients, such as chocolate, peanuts, and sugar, and the wrapper elements, such as paper and aluminum. Where are the natural resources for these ingredients found and where are they processed? Explain how geographic specialization is necessary to produce your candy bar.

3. List the countries the United States depends on for any products, foods, or resources. List any countries that depend on the United States. Explain how this interdependence came about. Explain how interdependence may affect decisions of industrial planners.

Decisions on Growth

1. In the United States, consumer rather than capital goods are emphasized. Is such emphasis characteristic of market systems? How do market systems grow? Who makes economic decisions in a market system?

2. Explain the major differences among capitalism, socialism, and communism.

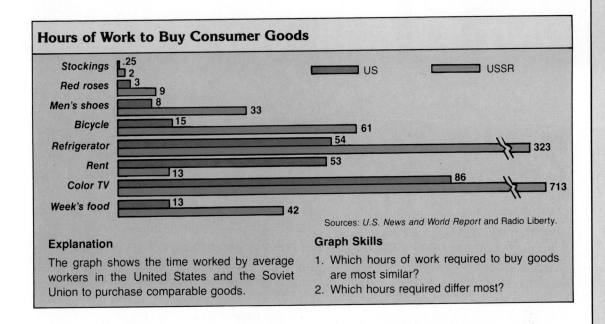

Hours of Work to Buy Consumer Goods

	US	USSR
Stockings	.25	2
Red roses	3	9
Men's shoes	8	33
Bicycle	15	61
Refrigerator	54	323
Rent	53	13
Color TV	86	713
Week's food	13	42

Sources: *U.S. News and World Report* and Radio Liberty.

Explanation

The graph shows the time worked by average workers in the United States and the Soviet Union to purchase comparable goods.

Graph Skills

1. Which hours of work required to buy goods are most similar?
2. Which hours required differ most?

Evaluating Growth

1. Compare the benefits and costs of our level of economic growth. Evaluate the importance of each. Can growth be accomplished without negative consequences? Explain.
2. Using your list of benefits and costs, determine the effects on society of each.
3. Using your list of costs, explain how, in a capitalist, socialist, and communist system, changes would be made to eliminate or at least lessen them.

DEVELOPING ECONOMIC SKILLS

Use the graph to help you answer the following questions.

1. How many hours must the average American work to buy a bicycle? How many hours must the average Russian work for the same product?
2. For what item does the Russian work fewer hours than the American?
3. What assumptions about planning for the growth of consumer goods production can you make about the Soviet Union and the United States?
4. Can you determine from the graph anything about the mix of capital and consumer goods in either of the countries represented? Why or why not?
5. If you could add any other two items to the graph, what would they be? Explain why you chose these items.

APPLYING ECONOMICS TODAY

1. Think about the way you expect to live 10 years from now. What major consumer goods—a car, color television, stereo—do you expect to own? What growth is necessary to produce these goods? Are you willing to pay the costs of this growth? Why or why not?
2. **Challenge:** The southern and western areas of the United States—the Sunbelt region—are growing while the older cities of the Northeast and Midwest are declining. What has influenced this growth? What are the consequences for the residents of each area?

USING ECONOMIC CONCEPTS

Basic Economic Issues

1. What are the four basic economic questions every society must answer?
2. What are four ways to deal with scarcity? What influences a society's choice of a solution to the problem?
3. Why does every choice involve opportunity costs and tradeoffs?
4. For what purposes are economic models used? Why are models helpful?
5. **Challenge:** What are the opportunity costs of attending college for four years? What are the real costs?

Economic Systems

1. What are the three main types of systems for making economic decisions? How does each system answer the basic economic questions?
2. What four components do market systems require in order to function?
3. **Challenge:** Would supermarkets exist in all three economic systems? Explain.

Economic Growth

1. What are the benefits and costs of economic specialization?
2. How would you measure the economic effects of antipollution efforts? How would a factory owner measure them?
3. **Challenge:** Compare the ways that decisions on growth are made in capitalist, socialist, and communist systems. List two advantages and two disadvantages of each system.

APPLYING ECONOMIC SKILLS

Use the graph and your economic skills to answer the questions.

1. At point A, how many sweaters are produced? How many carpet rolls?
2. What does a point inside the curve, such as point B, represent?
3. What does a point outside the curve, such as point C, represent?
4. What is the cost to society of moving from point A to point D?

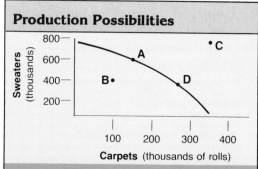

Production Possibilities

Explanation

The graph shows the tradeoff between using wool to produce sweaters and to produce carpets. Each axis is marked off in thousands of units of sweaters or carpets. The curve on the graph shows the relationship between the production of these two products.

Graph Skills

1. What happens to the production of wool for sweaters as the production of wool for carpets decreases?
2. How many sweaters could be produced in place of approximately 200,000 carpets?

ECONOMIC REASONING

Jim is a high school senior who has worked since junior high school. Next September Jim would like to attend college but must pay his tuition himself. Since the college is in a distant suburb, he would like to buy a car with part of his savings to make commuting faster and more convenient than would the bus.

The purchase price of the car, however, is only a small portion of the money necessary to possess it. Gas and insurance, as well as any repairs the car may need, enter into its cost. Jim needs money for tuition, too, and he does not know how often he will be able to work while attending college full-time.

STEP 1   Clarify the Issue

1. Which question below best clarifies the problem Jim faces?
   a. Will other costs make a car purchase more expensive than Jim realizes?
   b. Does Jim have enough money to pay for a car and his tuition?
   c. Does Jim need a car, or does the bus provide adequate transporation?
   d. Should Jim attend college or get a full-time job?
2. Explain why you agree or disagree with each statement below.
   a. Everyone needs a car for transportation in the suburbs.
   b. It is important to get to and from school as quickly and comfortably as possible.
   c. Jim's parents should pay his tuition.
   d. A college education is more important than a car.

STEP 2   Analyze Costs and Benefits

List the economic costs and benefits of each of these alternatives.
1. Jim could buy the car, start classes, and continue to attend college as long as his money lasts.
2. Jim could take the bus and save all his money for tuition.
3. Jim could delay entering college until he has saved enough money to buy a car and pay the college tuition.

STEP 3   Make a Decision

What is the best solution to Jim's problem? Explain your answer.

CURRENT ECONOMIC ISSUES

1. You may have heard the saying, "There is no such thing as a free lunch."
   a. If your employer runs a cafeteria that serves lunch to you at no charge, is your lunch free?
   b. What is your opportunity cost of the cafeteria lunch?
   c. What is your employer's opportunity cost of the lunch?
   d. What tradeoff do you make when you choose to eat in the cafeteria?
2. How has specialization in the past changed the ways people work? What changes are occurring today because of increased specialization?
3. What would be the economic effect on you of producing fewer cars but more buses and railroad and subway systems? On the environment? On the economy of the country?
4. Select from any source, other than this textbook, three photographs that demonstrate the advantages of economic growth and three that demonstrate the disadvantages. What similarities and differences appear in each picture? What do the people look like in each photograph? What changes would you make to overcome the disadvantages portrayed in the photographs?

UNIT 2

American Capitalism

CHAPTER 4

Our Market System

1 Consumers and Demand

Objective: *to understand the significance of demand in the United States market economy*

2 Producers and Supply

Objective: *to understand the significance of supply in the United States market economy*

3 Equilibrium Price

Objective: *to understand the relationship between demand and supply in setting prices in a market system*

1 Consumers and Demand

SECTION OVERVIEW

What are the goods and services you desire in life? To many people, a nice place to live, an education, and a car are important. What determines what you want? How do you decide what to buy? The products you and other consumers demand help determine how the economy works. This section will help you understand demand and how consumers fulfill their demands based on need, prices, and available alternatives.

ECONOMIC VOCABULARY

demand schedule	demand curve	substitution effect
law of demand	elasticity of demand	complementary products

Demand and Prices

In a market economy, buyers and sellers answer the basic economic questions. The actions of buyers and sellers set the prices of goods and services. The prices, in turn, determine what is produced, how it is produced, who will buy it, and what will be the mix of consumer and capital goods. Supply, the quantity of a product that suppliers will provide, is the seller's side of a market transaction. Suppliers usually want the price that allows them to make the most money. Demand, the quantity of a product consumers want, is the buyer's side of a market transaction. Buyers will want the price that gives them the most value for the least cost.

One place to see how demand works is an auction. An auction is a market where goods are sold to the highest bidders. Because the items are sold one at a time, buyers must quickly decide what prices they are willing to pay. If not, they risk seeing the item go to someone else who is willing to pay more. Imagine now that you are at an auction with about 100 other people. The auctioneer brings out a used electric popcorn maker, and you decide you would like to own it. In order to get it you will have to outbid all the others who want it. How do you decide how high to bid?

Since you know you will have to pay for the popcorn maker right away, you look into your wallet. Only a $5 bill is there. You know that you have another $15 in your desk at home, and that your companion will lend you that amount if you return it tomorrow. You know that a brand-new popcorn maker sells for $14. A used one is not worth quite that much to you. You decide you are willing to go as high as $10 but no higher. Besides, if you spend all your money, you will not have anything left to buy popcorn, oil, salt, and butter.

What factors so far have influenced you? Your decision is the result of your tastes (for popcorn), your available cash income (the $5 you carry), your wealth (the $15 at home), and your credit (the loan your friend will make). You have also had to think of the price of a substitute (a new popcorn maker) and the price of related items (such things as popcorn and salt).

The bidding starts at $1, and five people take part in the bidding. When the price goes up to $6, one person drops out. That person wants to spend $5 for the item. A second person drops out at $8, and two more drop out when the bids reach $9. That leaves only one—you. The popcorn maker is yours for $9.

Changes in Quantity Demanded

Economists use a tool called a demand schedule to study demand. A demand schedule is a chart that shows how much of a product consumers demand at several different possible prices. The chart here shows a demand schedule for popcorn makers at the auction.

The popcorn maker demand schedule illustrates the law of demand, which indicates that as the price of an item increases,

Popcorn Maker Demand Schedule

Price	Quantity Demanded
$11	0
10	1
9	1
8	3
7	4
6	4
5	5
4	5
3	5
2	5
1	5

Explanation

The demand schedule shows how many popcorn makers could have been sold at each of the possible prices (if more than one had been for sale). Since all five bidders stayed in the auction through $5, five machines could have been sold at that price or anything less than $5. When the price went up to $6, though, only four could have been sold. At $9, only one buyer remained—you. And you would have dropped out if the price had gone higher than $10. At $11, there would have been no demand at all for a used popcorn maker.

Chart Skills

1. As price increases from $5 to $6, what happens to the quantity demanded?
2. In general, what happens to the quantity demanded as the price increases?

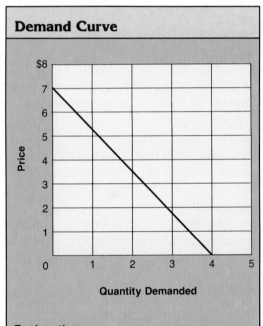

Demand Curve

Explanation

Quantity demanded usually increases as price declines, so demand curves usually slope down to the right.

Graph Skills

1. What quantity is demanded at $5? $2?
2. At what price is the quantity demanded two? Three? Four?

a smaller quantity will be bought. Likewise, as the price of an item falls, a larger quantity will be bought.

A demand schedule can be graphed. A demand curve is a line on a graph showing how much of a product consumers demand at different possible prices.

Effects of Price Changes

Consumers are more sensitive to some price changes than to others. You may not want to buy a car if its price goes up 10 percent. But if the price of salt goes up 10 percent, chances are you will pay the extra amount rather than go without salt. The degree to which changes in price cause changes in quantity demanded is called elasticity of demand. The number of cars demanded changes greatly as car prices change; so the demand for cars is highly elastic. The demand for salt is more inelastic: people buy nearly the same amount even though the price of salt changes.

There are two basic reasons for elasticity of demand. The first concerns the relationship between income and the cost of the product. A car, for example, may easily cost 50 percent of your annual income. Salt probably costs less than 0.0001 percent of your annual income. The smaller the proportion of your income that a product costs, the more inelastic is its demand.

The second reason why demand is elastic or inelastic concerns whether or not a substitute product is available. If you are close to public transportation, for example, your demand for a car is more elastic than it would be if you had no alternative means of transportation. The demand for butter tends to be elastic because margarine is available as a substitute. The demand for gasoline tends to be inelastic—and will remain so at least until vehicles using a different, low-cost fuel become available.

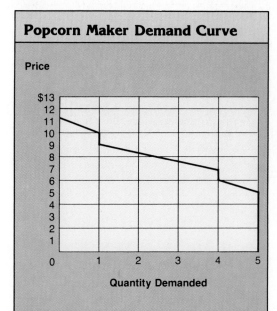

Popcorn Maker Demand Curve

Price

Quantity Demanded

Explanation

The quantity demanded for popcorn makers, even at a very low price, is five. As price increases, quantity demanded slowly decreases. At $11, the quantity demanded is zero.

Graph Skills

1. How many popcorn makers are demanded when the price is $7?
2. Use the graph to determine how many people want to buy popcorn makers if the price is $6.50.
3. How does the graph for popcorn makers illustrate the law of demand?

Demand decreases as prices increase.

107

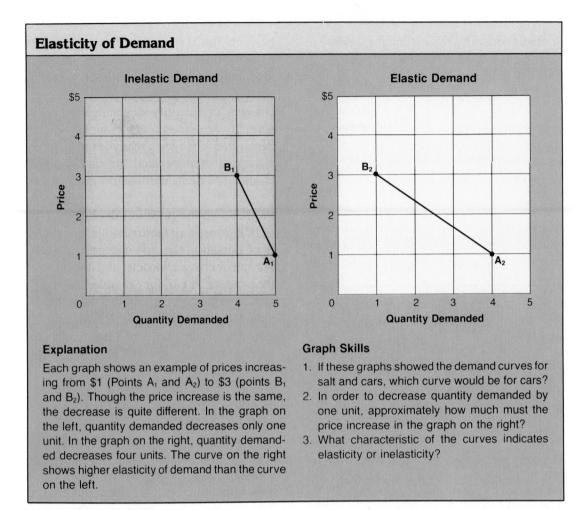

Elasticity of Demand

Inelastic Demand

Elastic Demand

Explanation

Each graph shows an example of prices increasing from $1 (Points A₁ and A₂) to $3 (points B₁ and B₂). Though the price increase is the same, the decrease is quite different. In the graph on the left, quantity demanded decreases only one unit. In the graph on the right, quantity demanded decreases four units. The curve on the right shows higher elasticity of demand than the curve on the left.

Graph Skills

1. If these graphs showed the demand curves for salt and cars, which curve would be for cars?
2. In order to decrease quantity demanded by one unit, approximately how much must the price increase in the graph on the right?
3. What characteristic of the curves indicates elasticity or inelasticity?

Shifts in Demand

A demand curve is like a snapshot. It shows the relationship between quantity demanded and price at one instant in time. If the price of a product changes and everything else remains the same, quantity demanded changes and will move to a new point on the demand curve. However, several factors influence demand, and each may create an entirely new demand curve.

First, as consumers earn more money they are able to spend more. Consequently, the price of an item, though unchanged, seems lower. If your weekly income increased $50, you might go to more movies. The same idea applies to groups of consumers. If total consumer income increases, demand increases. If consumers' income decreases, products become relatively more expensive; so demand decreases.

Second, more than one product often satisfies a consumer's demand. If the price of pork doubled, many consumers would buy substitutes, such as beef or chicken. Demand for those products would increase while the demand for pork would decline. Changes in demand for a product caused by changes in the price of substitute products is called the substitution effect.

Third, demand for a product is influenced by the price of goods or services used with that product. For example, hot dog

Variations in Demand

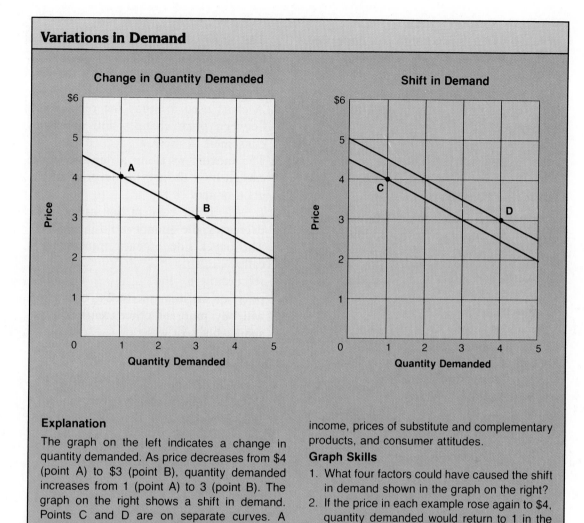

Change in Quantity Demanded

Shift in Demand

Explanation

The graph on the left indicates a change in quantity demanded. As price decreases from $4 (point A) to $3 (point B), quantity demanded increases from 1 (point A) to 3 (point B). The graph on the right shows a shift in demand. Points C and D are on separate curves. A change in a factor other than price caused the shift. Among these factors are changes in income, prices of substitute and complementary products, and consumer attitudes.

Graph Skills

1. What four factors could have caused the shift in demand shown in the graph on the right?
2. If the price in each example rose again to $4, quantity demanded would return to 1 in the graph on the left, and 2 in the graph on the right. Explain.

buns are generally used with hot dogs. If the demand for hot dogs suddenly decreases, the demand for hot dog buns probably will decrease also. Products used in combination with each other are called complementary products. A shift in the demand for a product will cause a similar shift in the demand for its complements.

Fourth, possibly the most common shift in demand results from changes in consumers' attitudes. Attitudes toward popular music shift quickly. A group or singer in great demand today may be virtually forgotten in a month.

If change occurs in any of these four factors, the old demand schedule and demand curve are no longer accurate. A new schedule and curve are needed.

The new demand schedule and curve represent a shift in demand for a reason other than price. If a change in price had caused the change in demand, no new curve would have been needed. A change in price causes a change along the same curve. However, since a shift in a nonprice factor caused the change in demand, the old demand schedule and curve are no longer accurate. Demand shifted, so a new schedule and curve were needed to show the change.

REVIEWING THE CONCEPT

Developing Vocabulary

Complete each statement below with the correct term from the list that follows.

> supply
> demand
> law of demand
> demand curve
> demand schedule
> elasticity of demand
> substitution effect
> change in quantity demanded
> complementary products

1. A graph that shows the amounts consumers are willing to buy is a _____.

2. The seller side of each transaction is called _____.

3. The _____ is usually greater for very expensive products.

4. A chart used to study the relationship between price changes and quantities consumers desire is a _____.

5. The movement along a demand curve caused by a change in the price of the good or service is a _____.

6. _____ is the concept that as the price decreases, the quantity sold increases.

7. The buyer side of each transaction is called _____.

8. According to the _____, when the price of an item increases, consumers will buy more of other items that are similar but cost less.

Mastering Facts

1. What do sellers want most to achieve?
2. What do buyers want most to achieve?
3. Why is elasticity of demand greater for some items than for others.

CASE STUDY

The Bicycle Boom

When attitudes change, demand for products shifts. Until the 1970s, for instance, many Americans thought that bicycles were only for children. Ann Syndergaard was one of millions of American children who grew up in the 1950s and 1960s. Like other children, Ann rode her sturdy one-speed bicycle everywhere. After Ann turned 16 and got her driver's license, she rarely rode her bicycle. However, by 1972 Ann's attitude toward bicycles had shifted. At age 23, she bought a new, lightweight 10-speed bicycle. Thousands of other American

adults did the same. Between 1970 and 1973, bicycle sales increased dramatically. Analyzing the factors that influence demand can explain the sudden boom in bicycle sales.

An increase in the quantity demanded is sometimes caused by a decrease in price. Prices of bicycles, however, did not decrease between 1970 and 1973. Instead, bike prices increased about 25 percent more than did prices for other goods. Consequently, the increase in demand for bicycles came from a factor other than a decline in price. The increased demand could have been caused by one of four nonprice factors: (1) an increase in consumers' income, (2) an increase in the price of substitute products, (3) a decrease in the price of complementary products, or (4) a change in consumers' attitudes.

The first three of these factors probably had little effect on the demand for bicycles. Between 1970 and 1973, the average consumer's income changed little. The prices of substitute products for bicycles, such as other forms of transportation, did not increase very much. The prices of complementary products, such as bicycle accessories and tires, did not decline significantly.

The remaining explanation for the increase in demand is that consumers' attitudes changed during the early 1970s. During this period, sales of several types of sports equipment rose. The estimated number of tennis players in the United States, for example, almost tripled between 1970 and 1975. This change suggests that the attitude of consumers toward recreation and exercise changed. Adults became more concerned about health and physical fitness. Bicycling became a popular form of exercise. The changing demands of consumers caused an increase in demand for bicycles. By 1975 the bicycle boom had ended, since bicycle production was half the 1973 level. By then, however, Americans no longer viewed bicycles as toys only for children. Even after 1975, bicycle production was above the 1970 level. Such increased production pointed to a long-term shift in the demand curve. Ann, like millions of other adult Americans, valued bicycles for recreation and exercise.

Trends in Bicycle Production

Year	Number Supplied by Producers in the United States (in millions)	Number Supplied by Producers outside the United States (in millions)	Total Supplied (in millions)
1965	4.6	1.0	5.6
1970	5.0	1.9	6.9
1971	6.6	2.3	8.9
1972	8.8	5.1	13.9
1973	10.1	5.1	15.2
1974	10.1	4.0	14.1
1975	5.6	1.7	7.3
1983	6.3	2.7	9.0

Source: Bicycle Manufacturers Association of America.

Explanation

The chart shows the number of bicycles supplied to the United States market for 1965, 1970 to 1975, and 1983. The middle two columns show how many bicycles were made domestically and how many were imported for sale in the United States. The last column is the sum of the middle two columns.

Graph Skills

1. In 1965, how many bicycles were supplied by producers in the United States? By producers outside the United States?
2. During what years did the number of bicycles supplied to the United States market go over 13 million?

ANALYZING THE CASE STUDY

STEP 1 Clarify the Issue

1. What are the reasons for differences in elasticity of demand?
2. What caused the demand curve for bicycles to shift after 1970?
3. Why did the demand curve shift to the right rather than the left?

STEP 2 Examine Change

1. In which years did production decline from the prior year? During which year did production decline the most?
2. What percentage of bicycles produced for the United States market were imported in 1970? In 1973? In 1983?

STEP 3 Draw Conclusions

1. Summarize how demand for bicycles changed between 1965 and 1983.

2. How were bicycle imports affected by changes in demand between 1965 and 1983? From the import figures, what conclusions can you draw about American bicycle manufacturers' ability to produce during this period?
3. Based on the changes in bicycle prices between 1970 and 1973, how elastic was the demand for bicycles?
4. What was the trend in bicycle sales between 1975 and 1983?

Enrichment Activity

Take a survey of 10 adults. Find out how many rode bicycles as children and how many ride now. Ask those who ride now why they ride. Make a table or chart indicating your results. Share your information with the class.

READING

Clothes, Price, and Beauty

by Thorstein Veblen   (1857-1929)

Look around your school and notice the similarities in how students dress. Demand is often influenced by psychological needs. One of the most famous books on American culture is *The Theory of the Leisure Class,* by Thorstein Veblen. Veblen wrote the book from the perspective of an outsider analyzing a culture. In many ways, Veblen himself was an outsider. He was born to Norwegian immigrant parents and, like many children of immigrants, learned English as a second language. His book, published in 1899, caused a sensation with its sharp satire and unusual insights. As you read this excerpt taken from *The Theory of the Leisure Class,* consider why you want certain clothes.

❝Except for the instinct of self-preservation, the tendency to imitate others is probably the strongest and most persistent of all economic motives. In an industrial community this imitation expresses itself in some form of conspicuous waste. That is, individuals demonstrate their wealth by openly wasting their money on items with no practical use. Thus, after the most basic physical wants have been provided for, the need of

112

conscious waste uses up any increase in the output of goods.

Consider how we judge clothes. The approval with which we look upon fashionable attire is by no means pure make-believe. We readily, and usually sincerely, find those things pleasing that are in style. Shaggy dress-stuffs and bright colors, for instance, offend us at times when the fashion is goods of a high, glossy finish and neutral colors. The high-gloss of a patent-leather shoe has no more intrinsic beauty than a similar high gloss on a threadbare sleeve; and yet there is no question but that well-bred people in Western cultures instinctively cling to the one as great beauty, and avoid the other as offensive.

A beautiful article which is not expensive is considered not beautiful. In this way it has happened, for instance, that some beautiful flowers are viewed as offensive weeds. These varieties are rejected as vulgar by those people who are better able to pay for expensive flowers. Still other flowers, of no greater natural beauty than these, are grown at great cost and call out much admiration from flower-lovers whose tastes have been developed in a polite environment. **99**

From *The Theory of the Leisure Class*, by Thorstein Veblen.

UNDERSTANDING THE READING

1. What does Veblen mean by conspicuous waste?
2. According to Veblen, what are the two strongest economic motives?
3. What accounts for differences in taste?
4. What is the relationship between income and consumption?
5. Give examples of conspicuous waste in your buying habits or those of your friends.

Section 1 Review

Understanding Consumers and Demand

1. What two kinds of needs are satisfied by the things a person buys?
2. Explain how Thorstein Veblen viewed the demand for clothes and flowers. What type of influences did Veblen think affected demand?

Consumers and Demand Today

1. Is conspicuous consumption common today? What evidence can you offer to support your answer?

2. List 10 purchases you would make if your weekly income were to double that you are now unable to make. How much money per week would you need to be completely satisfied?
3. **Challenge:** Give two examples of goods or services for which your demand is highly elastic. Give two examples of goods or services for which your demand is highly inelastic. Why is your demand for some products more elastic than for other products?

2 Producers and Supply

SECTION OVERVIEW

The goods and services you want can be obtained by providing for the needs or wants of others. For example, during the gold rush of 1849, Levi Strauss, a California peddler, struck it rich by providing heavy, durable pants for miners and cowboys. The manufacturing of Levi's is now a multibillion-dollar industry. What will be produced, how much will be produced, and who will produce it are important questions that directly affect you as a consumer. This section will help you understand the relationship between supply and price in a market economy.

ECONOMIC VOCABULARY

profit	law of supply	elasticity of supply
supply schedule	supply curve	

Producing for Profit

The job of sellers is to supply what buyers demand. Like those of the buyer, the seller's actions are influenced by a number of things. A major influence on sellers is the profit motive. Profit is the difference between what it costs to make a good or provide a service and the price for which

Supply Schedule for Tennis Rackets

Price	Quantity Supplied
$50	115,000
45	100,000
40	85,000
35	70,000
30	50,000
25	40,000
20	30,000
15	20,000
10	10,000
5	0

Explanation

According to the chart, no seller is willing to supply any tennis rackets for only $5. When the price is $10 a racket, sellers are willing to supply 10,000 rackets. At $50 a racket, however, the sellers are willing to supply 115,000 tennis rackets.

Chart Skills

1. What happens to quantity supplied as price increases?

2. Approximately how many tennis rackets would be supplied if the price were $13?

3. What is likely to happen to consumption when the price of a racket is $50.

the good or service sells. The larger the difference, the greater the profit. Profits, therefore, are determined by two things: what it costs to make a product and the price people are willing to pay for it. For each price consumers offer, sellers are willing to offer a different amount of a good or a service.

The seller wants to make the highest profit possible on goods or services sold. Profit is not the only motive that affects sellers, but it is one of the most important. Some sellers, for example, are willing to keep their profits lower than they could be in order to avoid taking risks. Others would rather work less and take a smaller profit. Also, laws and rules limit the pursuit of profits. They include laws against hiring children, laws that set maximum hours and minimum wages for workers, and workplace safety rules.

It is possible to show a supply schedule similar to the one for demand. A supply schedule shows how much of a product sellers will supply at different possible prices. The supply schedule for tennis rackets, for example, shows how many rackets sellers are willing to supply at each of several possible prices. In general, as prices increase, the supply of rackets also increases. Conversely, as prices decline, the supply of rackets also declines.

Changes in Supply

The supply schedule illustrates the law of supply: the higher the price offered, the more of a product sellers are willing to supply. The supply schedule can also be placed on a graph, which shows the law of supply as a supply curve.

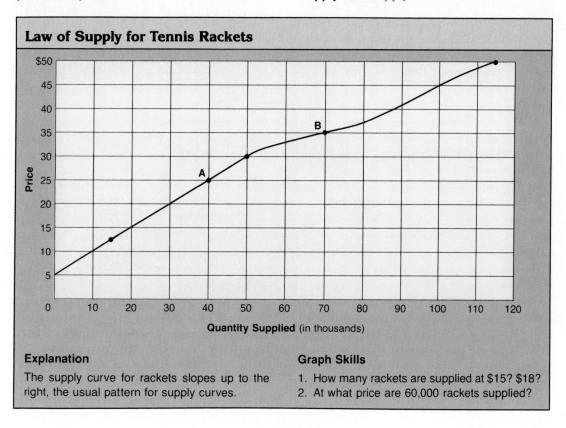

Law of Supply for Tennis Rackets

Price / Quantity Supplied (in thousands)

Explanation

The supply curve for rackets slopes up to the right, the usual pattern for supply curves.

Graph Skills

1. How many rackets are supplied at $15? $18?
2. At what price are 60,000 rackets supplied?

Elasticity of Supply

Suppliers are more sensitive to some price changes than to others. The degree that quantity supplied changes as the price changes is called elasticity of supply. Just as elasticity of demand varies among products for consumers, elasticity of supply varies among products for suppliers. The major reason that elasticity of supply varies is the variation in the costs of increasing production of different products. It is relatively easy to increase or decrease supply of a product that requires common resources and is simple to produce. Record albums are an example. The supply of record albums is, therefore, elastic. Automobiles require complex factories and are difficult to make. The supply of automobiles is relatively inelastic. The graphs show the curves for elastic and inelastic supply.

Factors Influencing Supply

A supply curve shows the relationship between price and quantity supplied. Any change in price will cause a change in the

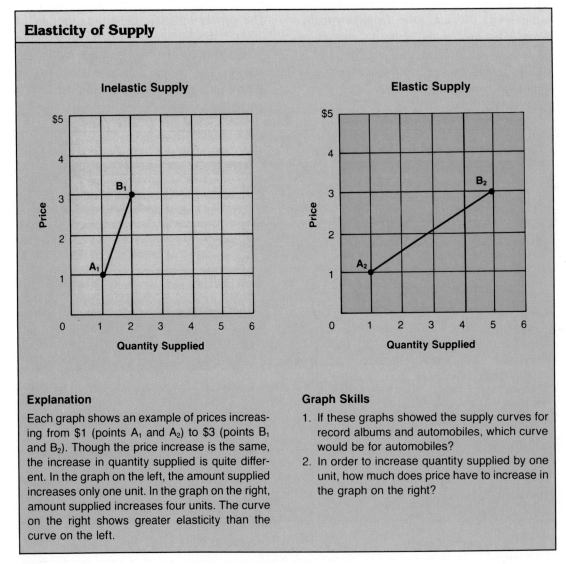

Elasticity of Supply

Inelastic Supply

Elastic Supply

Explanation

Each graph shows an example of prices increasing from $1 (points A_1 and A_2) to $3 (points B_1 and B_2). Though the price increase is the same, the increase in quantity supplied is quite different. In the graph on the left, the amount supplied increases only one unit. In the graph on the right, amount supplied increases four units. The curve on the right shows greater elasticity than the curve on the left.

Graph Skills

1. If these graphs showed the supply curves for record albums and automobiles, which curve would be for automobiles?
2. In order to increase quantity supplied by one unit, how much does price have to increase in the graph on the right?

quantity supplied. Like demand, supply is influenced by factors other than price. If any of these factors change, the entire supply curve will shift. Three factors besides price influence supply.

First, producers can cut the cost of production by developing less expensive means of production. By decreasing the cost of production, they can produce more at any given price. At times, producers must shift to a more expensive method of production. If machinery is destroyed by war or fire, producers may have to use older, more expensive methods. This change decreases the amount produced at any given price.

Second, prices of human, natural, and capital resources often change. These changes affect a producer's ability to supply goods at a certain price. Increasing costs decrease the ability of producers to supply products at a given price. Decreases in costs allow a producer to increase production but keep the same price.

Third, suppliers will change their production in order to increase profits. Consider a company that produces both television sets and radios. If the price of radios increases and the price of television sets stays the same, the company will increase its production of radios. To do so, it may have to reduce its production of television sets.

Relationship of Price and Supply of Tennis Rackets

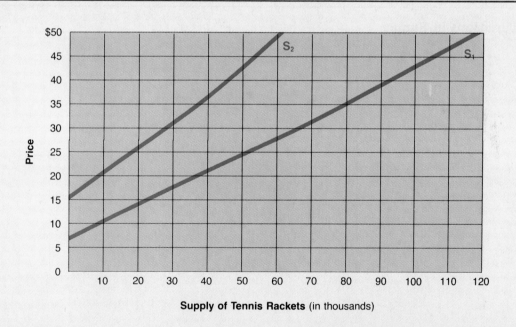

Supply of Tennis Rackets (in thousands)

Explanation
Both supply curves slope upward to the right. Supply curve S_2 is to the left of S_1. The increase in factory rents raised the cost of producing tennis rackets. As a result, companies will produce fewer rackets at any given price.

Graph Skills
1. How many tennis rackets will be produced at $25 on S_1? On S_2?
2. What price would be necessary to encourage suppliers to produce 40,000 tennis rackets on S_1? On S_2?

If the price of radios decreases, the company may increase television set production.

A change in any one of these factors affects the entire supply schedule and curve. Old supply schedules and curves then are no longer accurate. A new schedule and curve are needed. For example, the supply curve S_1 shows the relationship between price and quantity of tennis rackets supplied at a given time. Supply curve S_2 shows what would happen if factory rents increased. It would cost suppliers more to produce each tennis racket.

Changes in price cause a change in quantity supplied. On a graph, this change is shown by movement from one point to another on a supply curve. Changes in factors other than price, however, cause a

shift in the entire supply curve. Consequently, a new supply curve is needed. The graphs here show the difference between a change in quantity supplied and a shift in a supply curve.

REVIEWING THE CONCEPT

Developing Vocabulary

1. Define profit. Explain how a company determines whether it has made a profit.
2. Construct a supply schedule that shows your willingness to work at a part-time job of your choice.
3. Plot the supply curve for the supply schedule developed for question 2.
4. Explain how your willingness to work illustrates the law of supply.

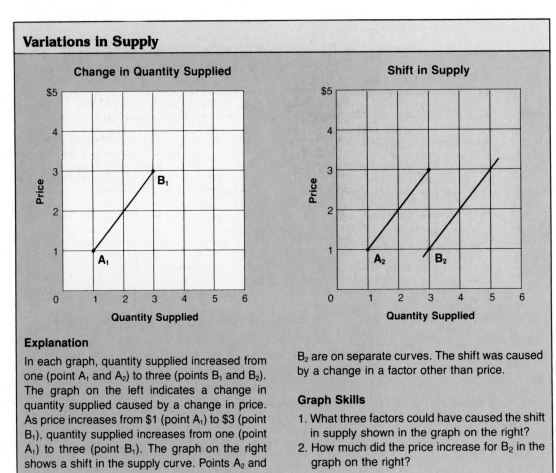

Variations in Supply

Change in Quantity Supplied

Shift in Supply

Explanation

In each graph, quantity supplied increased from one (point A_1 and A_2) to three (points B_1 and B_2). The graph on the left indicates a change in quantity supplied caused by a change in price. As price increases from $1 (point A_1) to $3 (point B_1), quantity supplied increases from one (point A_1) to three (point B_1). The graph on the right shows a shift in the supply curve. Points A_2 and

B_2 are on separate curves. The shift was caused by a change in a factor other than price.

Graph Skills

1. What three factors could have caused the shift in supply shown in the graph on the right?
2. How much did the price increase for B_2 in the graph on the right?

118

Mastering Facts

1. What is probably the major influence on sellers? What are two other influences?
2. List three kinds of laws and rules that limit the pursuit of profits.
3. What happens to profits as the difference between production costs and selling prices increases? Decreases?
4. What circumstances would influence new suppliers to enter the market?
5. Explain the basic differences between a shift in supply and a change in the quantity supplied.
6. What is the principal reason why elasticity of supply varies among products for suppliers?

Processed Food

One basic need of all people is food. Changes in the supply of food affect everyone. Arthur Stupay, a packaging industry analyst, says that changes in food packaging alone will change how people live in the future. A new type of container "is as great as anything developed in personal computers and two-way cable [communication], . . . and is the most far-reaching and technologically advanced product that has come from [human] imagination."

This new packaging method is only one change in the continuing change in the supply of food. For thousands of years, people focused their lives around gathering, growing, hunting, and preparing food. They slowly developed better ways to process food so that it would last longer and taste better.

In modern times, the processing of food has increased dramatically. Consider some typical breakfast foods—orange juice, eggs, bacon, coffee. Each of these foods can be made, or significantly changed, in a laboratory in order to supply what consumers want. As a consumer, you can have orange juice without oranges, eggs without yolks, bacon without meat, and coffee without caffeine. In addition,

you can use artificial salt, nonfattening sugar, and nondairy cream to make your breakfast more convenient.

The increase in the supply of processed food could have resulted from any of four changes. They include: (1) a decrease in the cost of resources used to make processed foods; (2) a decrease in the prices of other products made by suppliers of processed foods; (3) an increase in the prices consumers were willing to pay for processed foods; and (4) an improvement in the methods of processing food.

The first two changes have not greatly affected the supply of processed foods. The cost of resources to make foods has not decreased enough to explain the increase in supply. The costs of other goods that food-processing companies could make have not increased enough to explain why the companies would shift production to making processed food.

The last two changes did influence the supply of processed foods. Over the past 40 years, families and individuals have been increasingly willing to buy foods that would save them time in preparation. As consumers felt their time to be more valuable, they became more willing to pay more for con-

These boys are taking advantage of the convenience of processed foods.

venience. Suppliers, reacting to the change in price, were willing to increase supply.

Improvements in the methods of processing food have repeatedly allowed suppliers to increase the supply at a given cost. In 1795, a French candymaker, Nicolas Appert, developed the first canning method. By the 1820s, canning was a growing industry in the United States. During World War I (1914–1918), food drying became increasingly common. New methods were developed to dry food in large volumes. During the 1920s, Clarence Birdseye developed a process to freeze foods quickly and still preserve their quality.

The food-processing industry received a boost from World War II. Researchers developed better methods for preserving and packaging foods sent to soldiers fighting overseas. This research provided soldiers with instant foods, mixes, and heat-and-serve meals. After the war, the methods of production were used by companies supplying goods for the consumer market.

After World War II, suppliers continued to develop new processed foods. They used a wider variety of chemicals to produce foods that were tastier and easier to make. Now, the list of ingredients on a package of food may include dozens of additives to preserve the food, improve its nutritional value, and make it more attractive to consumers.

Some consumers think food processing has gone too far. James Tilotson, head of technical research and development at a major fruit juice company, is aware of these feelings. "You do not want people clubbed over the head with technology. What we try to do is present food that is more convenient and better tasting."

ANALYZING THE CASE STUDY

STEP 1   Clarify the Issue

1. How does the development of the processed food industry illustrate the workings of the law of supply?
2. Give three examples of processed food not mentioned in the case study.
3. Is the supply of processed foods elastic or inelastic? Why?

STEP 2   Consider Costs and Benefits

1. List the economic costs of processed food. Which economic groups are hurt by processed food?
2. List the economic benefits of processed food. Which economic groups are helped by processed food?

STEP 3   Predict Futher Change

1. Using the information from Step 2, predict whether the groups helped by processed food and the benefits obtained will increase the demand for processed food. Will producers increase the supply of these products?
2. Describe the lunch diet of a typical high school student today. Are your lunches different from those your parents had when in high school? What do you think your children will have for lunch when they reach high school? Write a paragraph describing the production and supply trends you think will continue.

The Popcorn Industry

from Everybody's Business: An Almanac

Popcorn is one of the most popular foods in the United States. Annual popcorn consumption is over 42 quarts per capita. The growth of the popcorn industry illustrates the response of sellers to a perceived demand, the use of marketing techniques, and the impact of changing market conditions on sellers. This reading, taken from the book, *Everybody's Business: An Almanac,* describes these changes. As you read, consider how the development of the popcorn industry demonstrates the relationship between supply and demand.

"Popcorn is symbolic of and indispensable to the nation's mainstream amusements. It is linked to baseball, circuses, and the movies. Americans eat some 400 million pounds of popcorn annually. The industry supports a Popcorn Institute that tests poppers and offers tips on popcorn safety. Popcorn is most popular in the Midwest, least popular in Manhattan. The American Dental Association endorsed it as a snack in preference to sugared treats.

Yet at the beginning of the 20th century, popcorn was a rarity in American grocery stores. Popping machines were invented in 1885. After that, gaily painted wagons sold popcorn on town and city street corners. The 1897 Sears, Roebuck catalog advertised a 25-pound sack of popcorn, still on the cob, for $1.00.

American Indians had used popcorn for thousands of years. Archaeologists have used radiocarbon dating to prove that ears of popcorn found in a New Mexico cave were 5,600 years old. Later, farmers in the Midwest grew and popped small quantities for their families. Only in the 1900s could an Iowa farmer's son named Cloid H. Smith make it a national institution.

In 1914 Smith formed the American Pop Corn Company and packaged his first 1-pound packages of popcorn. He shelled, graded, and cleaned it by hand with the help of his mother. The family coined the name Jolly Time to evoke associations of festivity.

This brand-name popcorn was an instant success. By the end of the first year Smith's company had sold more than 75,000 pounds of popcorn. Smith moved his operations into bigger quarters, and in 1926 the American Pop Corn Company incorporated in Iowa.

Jolly Time popcorn promised its customers reliable popping, but the cardboard packages posed problems. Smith's high-quality corn lost its pop because it dried out when left too long in the cardboard boxes.

American Can Company bailed Jolly Time out of its trouble in 1925, designing an airtight metal can. The cheerful red, white, and blue can carried the motto, "Guaranteed to Pop."

121

The producers of popcorn increased demand for their product by associating it with movies. Later, producers associated popcorn with soft drinks and television.

When movies became popular, theater managers at first barred popcorn from their lobbies after moviegoers complained that the scent and noise of popcorn broke the spell of on-screen drama. During the Depression the moviehouse managers changed their minds, largely because they needed cash. The popcorn sold in theater lobbies turned out to be, in some cases, almost as profitable as admission tickets. By 1947, 85 percent of the nation's theaters sold popcorn. Sales boomed. In 1948, 300,000 acres of midwestern farmland were planted in popcorn—an increase from 20,000 acres in 1900.

Then came television. Starting in 1949, moviegoing dwindled, and with it, popcorn consumption. The Popcorn Institute met in gloom. The Institute recognized that the American public had come to associate popcorn exclusively with movies.

The popcorn planners noticed Americans drank a lot of Coca-Cola. The Institute approached the Coca-Cola Company with the proposal that Coke could be promoted even more effectively in tandem with a dry, salted snack that led to thirst. Coke-popcorn ads strove to persuade American TV watchers that Coke was best when accompanied by popcorn.

A survey of Chicago TV owners in 1951 proved the success of the Coke-popcorn promotions. Fully 63 percent of TV watchers munched popcorn from one to four nights a week, and another 10 percent ate popcorn five or six nights each week. Sales of electric home poppers began to boom.

Today two-thirds of all the popcorn produced in the world is consumed in American homes, much of it in front of the TV. **99**

From *Everybody's Business: An Almanac*, edited by Milton Moskowitz, Michael Katz, and Robert Levering.

UNDERSTANDING THE READING

1. Who was responsible for making popcorn a national institution?
2. What evidence points to the increased supply of popcorn in the 1900s?
3. How can suppliers increase consumer demand for their products?
4. Do new products satisfy needs that already exist, or must sellers create the needs as part of marketing the product? Explain your view.

Section 2 Review

Understanding Producers and Supply

1. Give an example of a product with an inelastic supply schedule. Explain why it is inelastic.
2. Does a supply curve guarantee actual sale of the quantities shown? Explain.
3. Jolly Time popcorn sales declined in 1949. Was this decline a result of a change in demand or a change in quantity demanded? During this period might the substitution effect have been important? Why or why not?
4. How elastic is the demand for popcorn?
5. How elastic is the supply of popcorn?

Producers and Supply Today

1. What were the advantages and disadvantages of associating popcorn consumption with the movies?
2. The reading about popcorn offers an example of an individual creating a supply for an unmet demand. If you were given an opportunity to open a small store in your school, what products would you supply to satisfy the demands of student consumers?
3. Do you think a person like Cloid H. Smith could succeed in the United States today? Give reasons for your opinion.
4. **Challenge:** Predict what will happen in each of these situations according to the law of supply.
   a. Foreign nations cut off all oil shipments to the United States, causing oil prices to increase. What should happen to the production of oil from oil wells in the United States?
   b. The use of artificial materials decreases the use of cotton to make clothes. Cotton prices drop. What should happen to the production of cotton?
   c. Increased investment in railroads creates a better train system. Since people have less need for cars, prices of cars drop. What should happen to the number of cars produced?

3 Equilibrium Price

SECTION OVERVIEW

You probably try to balance time among going out with friends, doing homework, and earning money. In economics there must be a balance between the consumer and the producer. Prices reflect this balance. In this section you will learn how prices are set in a market economy.

ECONOMIC VOCABULARY   equilibrium price

Reaching the Right Price

In a market economy, prices are the result of the needs of both buyers and sellers. Sellers will supply more goods at higher prices than at lower ones. Buyers will buy more goods at lower prices than at higher ones. Some price is satisfactory to both buyers and sellers. At that price the supply —quantity offered for sale—equals the demand—quantity people are willing to buy. Since no surplus or shortage exists, there is no pressure on price to change. This point is called the equilibrium price. At the equilibrium price, the amount producers will supply and the amount consumers will buy are the same.

The demand schedule for T-shirts shows that at $1 per T-shirt, consumers see a great bargain and will buy 100,000 T-shirts. But suppliers do not see it that way. At $1, T-shirts are no bargain for them. At that price, they will not supply any T-shirts. At $2 a T-shirt, they will supply 2,000 T-shirts, but consumers will buy only 80,000 T-shirts. The demand for T-shirts is great enough to support a higher output and a higher price. As the price increases, the quantity producers will supply also in-creases, but the quantity consumers will buy decreases. The quantity producers will supply and the quantity consumers will buy is the same—15,000 T-shirts—at $5. This amount is the equilibrium price.

The equilibrium point is point A— 15,000 T-shirts at $5 apiece. If T-shirt makers tried to earn more profits by raising the price to $7, they would want to supply 35,000 T-shirts (point B). The consumers, though, want to buy only 9,000 T-shirts at that price (point C). So the suppliers are stuck with 26,000 unsold T-shirts.

Supply and Demand for T-Shirts

The 26,000 T-shirts are a surplus. On the graph, a surplus occurs at any price where the supply curve is to the right of the demand curve. With such a large surplus, suppliers have no choice but to roll the price back toward its equilibrium point. If, however, consumers were to offer only $2 a T-shirt, the suppliers would want to supply only 2,000 T-shirts (point D). But at that price (point E), they would be swamped by a demand for 80,000 T-shirts. This excess demand would drive the price back up toward its equilibrium point. Hence, supply

Supply and Demand Schedule for T-shirts

Price	Quantity Supplied	Quantity Demanded
$10	100,000	1,000
9	70,000	3,000
8	50,000	6,000
7	35,000	9,000
6	25,000	12,000
5	15,000	15,000
4	9,000	25,000
3	5,000	50,000
2	2,000	80,000
1	0	100,000

Explanation

The chart combines a supply schedule and a demand schedule. Included are the quantity of T-shirts producers will supply and the quantity consumers will demand at each price from $1 to $10.

Chart Skills

1. At what price will producers supply only 2,000 T-shirts?
2. At what price will consumers demand only 3,000 T-shirts?

Supply and Demand Curves for T-Shirts

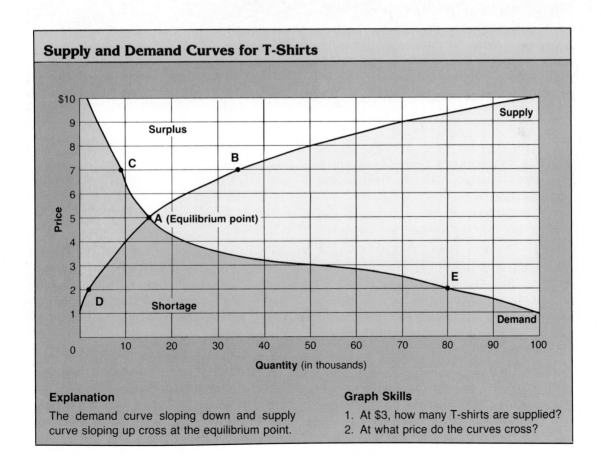

Explanation

The demand curve sloping down and supply curve sloping up cross at the equilibrium point.

Graph Skills

1. At $3, how many T-shirts are supplied?
2. At what price do the curves cross?

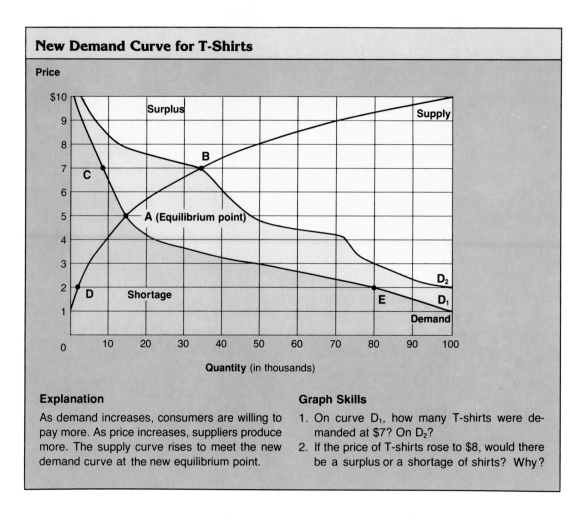

New Demand Curve for T-Shirts

Price

(graph showing Price on vertical axis from $1 to $10, Quantity in thousands on horizontal axis from 0 to 100. Labels include: Surplus, Supply, B, C, A (Equilibrium point), D, Shortage, E, D₂, D₁, Demand.)

Quantity (in thousands)

Explanation

As demand increases, consumers are willing to pay more. As price increases, suppliers produce more. The supply curve rises to meet the new demand curve at the new equilibrium point.

Graph Skills

1. On curve D_1, how many T-shirts were demanded at $7? On D_2?
2. If the price of T-shirts rose to $8, would there be a surplus or a shortage of shirts? Why?

---

would be short by 78,000 T-shirts. On the graph, a shortage occurs at any price where the demand curve is to the right of the supply curve.

The market price also determines who will get the 15,000 T-shirts. They will go to those consumers who can and want to spend $5 on a T-shirt. The market price, then, serves to ration goods and services.

As long as the demand and supply curves remain unchanged, the equilibrium point will stay at the same price. If the demand or supply shifts, however, a new equilibrium point will be reached. For example, if T-shirts become fashionable, consumer demand for them will increase.

Similarly, if supply shifts, then a new equilibrium point is reached. Suppose suppliers developed a new sewing machine that

could produce T-shirts more cheaply. Then suppliers could produce more T-shirts at any given price.

Alternatives to the Market Price

Sometimes a society decides that the free market is not the best provider of goods and services. To choose who will have vital items, such as food, shelter, and medical care, societies may try some other method. One method is to let people stand in line or put their names on a waiting list. Price controls are often used during times of severe shortages to make sure that the prices of important items, such as food and gasoline, do not go too high. The price of rental housing is controlled by law in some American cities today. During World War

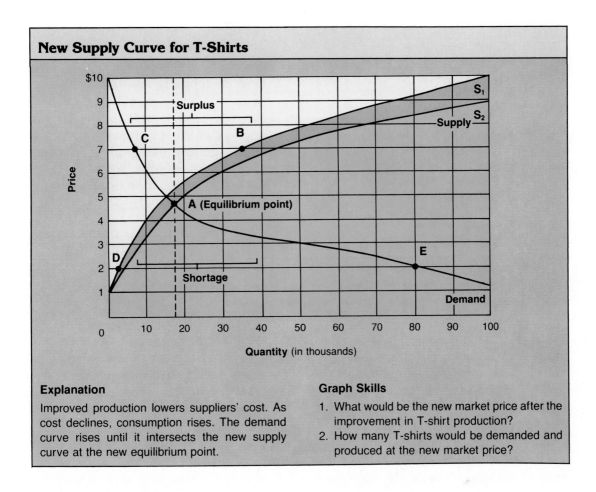

New Supply Curve for T-Shirts

Explanation

Improved production lowers suppliers' cost. As cost declines, consumption rises. The demand curve rises until it intersects the new supply curve at the new equilibrium point.

Graph Skills

1. What would be the new market price after the improvement in T-shirt production?
2. How many T-shirts would be demanded and produced at the new market price?

II, people were issued ration stamps for meat, butter, sugar, canned goods, shoes, and gasoline. Each person was thus able to get the minimum amount of these goods needed to survive. Price controls and ration stamps were also discussed in recent years as a way of dealing with temporary shortages of gasoline and heating oil.

In some cases, the price of an item is not allowed to fall below a certain price. In order to encourage farmers to produce large supplies of corn, wheat, milk, and other products, the government agrees to prevent the prices of these goods from going too low. This system of keeping prices at or above market level takes some of the risk out of operating a farm. It ensures that the supply of food will not decline drastically because of a fall in prices.

These alternatives to market prices all

have side effects. When prices are not allowed to rise to their market level, suppliers may not supply as much of a good or service as consumers want. In other words, shortages develop. These shortages can sometimes become quite serious. Nevertheless, if prices are kept lower than their market level, more people may be able to buy the product. When prices are not allowed to drop to their market level, suppliers may be supplying more of a good or service than consumers want.

The market, then, coordinates the needs of producers and consumers. In some ways, groups of people are like market economies. We need things from others and others need things from us. Somehow, we all find our own equilibrium point. Everyone gets what he or she most needs and can afford.

REVIEWING THE CONCEPT

Developing Vocabulary

1. Define equilibrium price.
2. What happens to the equilibrium price when a surplus exists? A shortage?

Mastering Facts

1. How do supply and demand interact to produce an equilibrium price?
2. How do suppliers react to increases in prices of products supplied?
3. How do buyers react to increases in prices of products consumed?
4. Draw a graph showing supply, demand, and equilibrium price. What portion of the graph represents a shortage? What portion indicates a surplus?

The Home Computer Industry

In a market system, people make decisions about what to buy. Thus, the equilibrium price may change over short periods of time. The rapid fall in home computer prices resulted from actions of individuals and firms as they responded to changes in technology and demand and supply.

In 1985, computer owners numbered 50 million throughout the world. You have

Two children learn to use a home computer.

probably heard or seen commercials promoting various computers. Perhaps you and your family have resisted buying one because you believe you do not know enough to make an intelligent choice. You may have been put off by the technical jargon, or maybe you are waiting for prices to drop.

Economics can help explain what has been happening in the market for home computers. As recently as 1977, personal computers were made by a handful of manufacturers at the rate of a few thousand a year. Limited production and rising demand kept prices high until technological advances along with supply and demand changes lowered everyone's cost.

A personal computer can be adapted to a variety of uses. As more users realized the computer's power to boost their productivity, demand steadily increased.

If only demand for computers had increased, buyers would have expected a steady increase in prices. As often happens, however, demand stimulated research, enabling manufacturers to improve their product and production efficiency. This development lowered prices and increased sales and profitability. Strong demand brought new producers into the market, increasing competition; so prices dropped even lower. The pioneer firms had to improve their product and reduce prices to compete. For example, the equilibrium price of a top personal computer in 1979 was $1,150. By 1983, the equilibrium price of an improved version of that model was only $375.

No one can predict with certainty where computer technology will lead. Consumers can hope that competition in the computer industry will continue to improve the home computer and reduce its price.

ANALYZING THE CASE STUDY

STEP 1   Clarify the Issue

1. Explain what caused the change in the price, quality, and number of suppliers of home computers in the past decade.
2. List changes in supply and changes in demand that could bring prices down.

Which of these changes in supply and demand actually occurred in the computer industry? How did they affect price?

STEP 2   Consider Costs and Benefits

1. What economic and technical problems could limit the demand for home computers? The supply?
2. What could limit the supply of home computers?
3. For what reasons are many consumers reluctant to buy home computers?

STEP 3   Examine Alternatives

1. What will happen to supply and demand when the equilibrium price of home computers comes down?
2. Suggest a solution to each problem you identified in Step 2.
3. Compare the advantages and disadvantages of learning through a textbook and learning through a computer. Which do you prefer?

READING

Competition and Behavior

by Robert Heilbroner   (1919-   )

How does your desire to earn and save money shape your behavior? Throughout the American economy, the desire for money produces competition. Competition helps set the market equilibrium price. This reading describes how this process of setting equilibrium price shapes behavior. Like the reading for Chapter 2, Section 3, this reading is taken from *The Making of Economic Society,* by Robert Heilbroner. As you read, consider how your attitude toward money affects your behavior.

66 The transition to a market society between 900 and 1500 led to a new form of social control to guide the economy.

What was this new form of control? It was a pattern of social behavior, of normal, everyday action that the new market imposed on society. And what was this pattern of behavior? In the language of the economist, it was the drive to maximize one's income by the best possible bargains in the marketplace. In ordinary language, it was the profit motive.

The market society had not, of course, invented this motive. During the Middle Ages, people bought and sold goods at town markets. However, these markets were a means of supplementing a livelihood. They were not necessary for most people.

With the rise of the market economy, however, the profit motive became widespread and important. Now everything was for sale. An individual sold his or her labor in a market. Society assumed no responsibility for taking care of the individual. Therefore, the price at which a laborer made the bargain for wages was all-important. So it was with the capitalist. A good bargain could spell riches—and a bad one, ruin. Thus, the profit motive was spread throughout society. It was a powerful force for shaping human behavior.

The new market society did more than merely allow people to follow their economic self-interest. It created a social environment in which people could be controlled in their economic activities. With the drive for profits, it now became possible to direct people's energies by raising or

Grocery shoppers compete with one another to purchase items they want. Stores, in turn, compete with one another to sell goods and services to consumers.

lowering the rewards offered for different tasks. If more shoes were needed, the market could attract that effort by raising the rewards for the land, labor, and capital employed in shoe manufacture. Or if society wished to reduce the supply of hats, the market could reduce economic rewards—wages, rents, profits—of hat manufacturers. Thus, the drive toward income maximization was a powerful tool for allocating society's resources.

Note, however, that this regulatory device required more than just the profit motive. Equally necessary was a mobility of the factors of production.

The market society also brought about the mobilization of life—that is, the breakdown of ties of place and position in society. Any job or activity was now open to all comers. Competition appeared. Now any worker and any employer could be displaced from a task by a competitor who would do the job more cheaply or better.

For individuals displaced, competition must have seemed harsh and unjust; but for society as a whole, it was an advantage. What competition did was to contain the economic drive. By pitting seller against seller, it made it difficult for any single person to gain a personal advantage.

Competition not only prevented the seller from using his or her economic power to general social disadvantage, but it also restrained the buyer. No single buyer could force prices below the cost of production, for other eager buyers would quickly outbid him or her. And this competition worked in the market for resources, as well. Clearly, no laborer could ask for more than the normal wage if he or she wanted employment. But neither would the laborer have to take less than the normal wage. If a single employer cut wages, workers could find better wages elsewhere.

Now we begin to see the complex nature of the price control mechanism provided by competition. In the marketplace, buyer and seller faced one another in a contest. Every buyer sought to pay as little as possible and every seller sought to gain as much as possible. By itself this would be merely a tug of war about the outcome of which one could say very little. But because sellers on one side of the tug of war were themselves engaged in a contest with one another, and because buyers at the other end of the rope were engaged in a similar contest, the outcome of the contest was quite predictable. While prices of goods might sway back and forth in the short run, the interaction of supply and demand always brought them back towards the costs of production in the long run.

Only one final point remains to be noted. We have seen how a competitive market economy operated to fulfill the wants of society. But who was to say what its wants were?

In pre-market economies, such a question did not pose problems. The wants of such societies were established by ageless tradition or by rulers. But in a market society, wants suddenly take on a new dimension. The wants of society are expressed by millions of daily orders placed by an entire community. As these orders enter the marketplace they affect the prices at which goods sell. Thus shifts in prices become, in effect, signals to producers: rising prices signal an increase in demand; falling prices signal the opposite.

In this way the market society puts the consumer into a position of extraordinary importance. Producers depend on the consumer's ability and willingness to buy. If consumers do not want a good or service, or if they do not wish to buy it at its offered price, that good or service will go unsold. In a market society, the consumer determines the ultimate [final] pattern of economic activity. **99**

From *The Making of Economic Society,* by Robert Heilbroner.

UNDERSTANDING THE READING

1. How does Heilbroner define the profit motive?
2. How did the development of a market society differ from the economic activities of earlier societies?
3. According to Heilbroner, what are two results of competition?
4. Who determines the wants of society?
5. What will happen to a product that costs more to produce than consumers are willing to pay for it?

Section 3 Review

Understanding Equilibrium Price

1. List three ways, other than the market, by which a society may share its goods and services. What effect do these actions have on the supply?
2. What happens to the supply of goods and services when prices are not allowed to rise to their market level?
3. The clothes store where you shop is having a sale. Explain why the store holds a sale and what is its effect on equilibrium price.

Equilibrium Price Today

1. What effect do you think higher salaries for professional athletes might have on the supply of athletes in the short run? In the long run?

2. How might a serious recession affect your college or career plans? How will your actions, multiplied by those of many individuals your age, affect the labor market and colleges? If the recession continued over several years, what actions might colleges take to deal with the problems it caused?

3. **Challenge:** During 1973, a group of Middle East oil-exporting countries cut off oil shipments to the United States. Consequently, not enough gasoline was available at 55 cents per gallon. Some people believed that the solution to the shortage was rationing. Others felt the solution was to raise prices until they reached equilibrium. Give your opinion of which solution is best from an economic point of view? Why?

Americans *at Work*

Meet Don Lusk
Insurance Salesperson

"A successful insurance salesperson takes no for an answer," said Don Lusk, who sells for the Prudential Life Insurance Company in Chicago. "Look at it this way: You make 100 phone calls, asking for appointments. You get three. Out of that three, you make one sale—1 percent. But remember, too, there are hundreds and hundreds of people out there you have not called yet."

On graduating from Roosevelt University in Chicago with a degree in political science, Lusk became a social worker. Five years later, at age 28, he switched careers. Although in changing jobs he left the public sector, Lusk did not stop helping people. He now provides a service most people need. He became one of the 2 million people employed in the insurance industry.

"During the 20 or more years I have been selling," Lusk said, "I have seen the economy go up and down several times. And a downturn soon affects my business. When times are good, businesspeople are good prospects. But when there are layoffs, shrinking profits, and general belt-tightening, you know it—and quickly. Then you look for groups that have lower incomes, perhaps, but relatively more stable jobs—government workers, for example. So I have to pay attention to the economy and be prepared for change."

Economic change has affected Lusk in another way. New federal laws have made many people investment-conscious. One, for example, permits individuals to lay aside up to $2,000 a year for Individual Retirement Accounts (IRAs) and shelter the money from taxation for a time. That money, however, can be set aside in a number of different ways, and the choices can be confusing. Most people appreciate the advice that investment experts can offer to them.

"We will sell life insurance," Lusk said, "but we also deal in IRAs, and in stocks, bonds, money market funds, and other avenues of investment for our clients. So we are not just agents any more. We are also financial advisers. That means we have to know financial markets, where the best interest-earning opportunities lie, and we have to make guesses about the economic future. We read a lot these days. And as an insurance company's services expand, so does that list of people you can call," Lusk concluded, "That makes one out of a hundred not so bad after all."

Comparing Prices

Being a wise consumer is never easy. A wide variety of brands, sizes, prices, and advertising gimmicks influence you when you enter a store. How can shopping in the supermarket result in the best deal for you as a consumer? Learning to make informed decisions about buying food will result in economic skills that last a lifetime. Consider the options available when buying a loaf of bread.

STEP 1 What Kind?

The variety of bread available in the supermarket is confusing—French, white, rye (with or without seeds), fancy or plain, sliced or unsliced. Brands A, B, C, X, Y, Z! First you have to decide what kind of bread you need. After all, bread for sandwiches might not be the same kind you want for garlic bread. Generic bread might be fine for making bread crumbs or turkey stuffing, but it may not do for a formal luncheon. The occasion or purpose can determine the kind of bread you will buy. People can influence your purchase as well. For instance, if you know your grandmother is coming to visit and loves rye bread, you might want to get some for her.

Another factor influencing your decision is advertising. Brands A, B, and C have been around for a long time, and you trust their names. Brand X, however, just sponsored a sports event on local television, so you may be more aware of that product. Brand Z is a newcomer; maybe you want to try it. Advertising influences what you think about various products. Eventually it influences what you buy.

STEP 2 How Much?

After deciding what kind of bread to buy, consumers generally consider price. Brand A costs $1.19 for a 16-ounce loaf; Brand B costs 35 cents for a 12-ounce loaf; Brand C costs 93 cents for a 20-ounce loaf. Some stores indicate the unit price for the items on the shelves. It tells the price per unit—ounce, pound, quart, or liter, for example—for a product. In the case of unit pricing for bread, the store would show the cost per ounce for each loaf of bread.

If the store does not give unit price information, a consumer can easily figure it out simply by dividing the price of the product by the quantity in the package. For example, consider the unit price of the three brands of bread mentioned above. For Brand A, divide $1.19 by 16 ounces. The cost is 7.4 cents per ounce. The cost of brand B is 35 cents divided by 12 ounces, or

2.9 cents per ounce. Brand C is 93 cents for 20 ounces, or 4.7 cents per ounce. The price of an ounce of bread, then, ranges from 2.9 cents to 7.4 cents.

Determining the unit price may also help you decide how much to buy. Although quality or kind of bread contributes to the price, generally the larger the quantity, the less the per-unit cost. Buying in quantity can often help you spend less.

STEP 3　How Good?

Another consideration that figures into what we buy is the quality of the product. Sometimes, evaluating the quality of a product can be difficult for the consumer. For instance, most food products list natural as well artificial ingredients. Some provide nutritional information as well.

Most meat products are graded for quality by the United States Department of Agriculture (USDA). Its quality stamps appear on meats in virtually all food markets. The most common beef grades are Prime, Choice, Good, Standard, and Commercial, in that order of quality. The consumer's decision is a matter of personal taste. However, the higher the quality, the higher the price.

There is yet another gauge of a product's quality. Packaged products are required by law to have a list of ingredients clearly displayed on the label. The ingredients must be listed in order of their greatest content in the product.

STEP 4　Make a Decision

In the end, the decision of what to buy and at what price and quality level is a personal one. Many factors influence buying decisions, and choices are not simple for consumers. Smart buyers must obtain product information and then compare and evaluate that information. Good judgment is a necessary commodity in the marketplace.

ECONOMIC SKILLS TODAY

1. List and explain two factors that influence the buying decisions of consumers.
2. How is the unit price of a product determined?

Enrichment Activity

Make a shopping list of 10 basic food items. Go to a grocery store and find out the range of unit costs for each item. Make a chart showing the most and least expensive ways to purchase each item. Total the figures in each category. How much is the difference between the expensive column and the inexpensive column?

A wise consumer compares prices.

CHAPTER SUMMARY

Consumers and Demand

Demand is the buyer's side of market trans-actions. The quantity demanded for a good or service usually increases as its price declines, and vice versa, because consumers try to obtain the most value for the least cost. Demand is influenced by your income, the prices of substitutes, the price of related items, and your attitudes. The demand for some items is more responsive to price changes, or more elastic, than for others. A demand curve illustrates the law of demand and shows the relationship between quantity demanded and price at one instant in time.

Producers and Supply

Supply is the seller's side of market transactions. The amount of a good or service supplied usually goes up as the price increases because producers want to make the highest profit possible. Supply can be elastic or inelastic. A shift in the entire supply curve may result from changes in the price of materials, the methods of production, or the cost of other products. A supply curve illustrates the law of supply and shows the relation between quantity supplied and price at one instant in time.

Equilibrium Price

In a market economy, the interaction between buyers and sellers determines the price of goods and services. If the price is too low, a shortage will develop, thereby driving up the price. If the price is too high, a surplus will develop and move the item's price down. A society may interfere with market prices by means of price controls and ration stamps.

CRITICAL THINKING QUESTIONS

Consumers and Demand

1. How are demand and the four basic economic questions related?
2. What circumstances affect elasticity of consumer demand?
3. Use examples to show how a change in the quantity demanded differs from a shift in demand.

Producers and Supply

1. What is the relationship between supply and the four basic economic questions?
2. What affects elasticity of supply?
3. Use examples to show how a change in quantity supplied differs from a shift in the supply.

Equilibrium Price

Select from any source, other than this book, 10 pictures of goods and services. Arrange the images in order according to the amount that you would be willing to pay for them. Then ask a classmate to help you arrange them in order according to what you both think they might really cost. Is the order the same? Explain why the order might be different.

DEVELOPING ECONOMIC SKILLS

Use the chart and your economic knowledge to answer the questions.
1. What was the quantity of jeans demanded in May at $18? In September?

2. Is the difference between demand in September and demand in May a change in quantity demanded or a shift in demand? Why?

3. Rank the following seven jobs in order according to how much you would enjoy doing the job:
   babysitting
   lifeguarding at a beach club
   washing and waxing cars
   clearing and cleaning tables
   playing records on radio
   exercising horses
   decorating clothing store windows

4. **Challenge:** Suppose that you have 20 hours a week of free time. Make a supply schedule for the job at the top and the job at the bottom of the list you made in question 3. Show how many of the 20 hours you would work at each job if you were offered $1 an hour, $2 an hour, and so on.
   a. For which job were you willing to work longer at the lower wages? Why?
   b. Were your decisions based on your needs? On others' needs? On market factors? How important to your decision was each factor?

APPLYING ECONOMICS TODAY

Research the work of the Office of Price Administration (OPA) during World War II and write a report on its effect on the American economy. Be sure to describe what happened to prices when the OPA was ended.

Demand Schedule for Blue Jeans

Demand for Blue Jeans in September		Demand for Blue Jeans in May	
Price	Quantity	Price	Quantity
$21	21,000	$21	6,000
18	29,000	18	13,000
15	38,000	15	21,000
12	49,000	12	32,000
9	60,000	9	49,000
6	81,000	6	60,000
3	98,000	3	69,000

Explanation

The chart provides data on the demand for blue jeans during the months of September and May. The amounts under quantity represent the number of blue jeans demanded at each price level. From these two demand schedules it is possible to plot on a graph the demand curve for each month. Showing such information graphically often helps planners in making decisions on future production. With such knowledge a manufacturer could avoid surpluses but still produce enough to fill consumer demand.

Chart Skills

1. What is the basic relationship between the price of blue jeans and the quantity of blue jeans demanded?
2. In which month was the demand greater?
3. If the price of blue jeans declines from $21 to $15 in September, how much does the quantity demanded increase? How much does quantity demanded increase if the same price decrease occurs in May?
4. Suggest two reasons to explain why demand for blue jeans changes during the year.

CHAPTER 5

Competition in the Market

1 Models of Competition

Objective: to understand the different types of competition and the role of each in the United States

2 Economic Markets

Objective: to understand the role of factor markets and product markets in American capitalism

3 Market Interaction

Objective: to understand how competition affects the circular flow between factor and product markets

1 Models of Competition

SECTION OVERVIEW

Competition is part of everyday life. You may compete in schoolwork, sports, or other aspects of life. Competition with others encourages you to try harder to achieve personal and team success. In economics, competition is also important. Business competition results in profits or losses. In this section, you will learn about different types of competition and the role of each in the United States economy.

ECONOMIC VOCABULARY

perfect competition	monopolistic competition	natural monopoly
imperfect competition	oligopoly	patent
differentiated competition	monopoly	copyright

Perfect Competition

One model economists use to help them understand the economy of the United States is the model of perfect competition. Perfect competition is the situation that exists when a market is completely competitive. In such a model, all economic decisions are made solely on price. An economy must have four traits in order to be an example of perfect competition.

First, every good or service (such as shoes, cars, or medical care) would have many buyers and sellers. No one of them would be large enough to control prices. None of them would be able to influence the actions of the others, and none of them would cooperate in setting prices.

Second, all suppliers in the market would make identical products. There would be no differences in quality. Buyers would make their decisions about what to buy based only on market prices. Buyers would ignore such things as advertising and special packaging.

Third, all buyers and sellers would have full knowledge of all market conditions. Producers would know where the cheapest resources could be found. Consumers would know what stores charged the lowest prices. If a woman wanted to buy a new pair of shoes, for instance, she would know what every store was charging for the kind of shoes she liked.

Fourth, there would be perfect mobility of buyers and sellers. Everyone would be free to move in search of the highest profits or the best deal. A lumberjack in Maine, for instance, might find that higher wages were paid to lumberjacks in Oregon. He would be able to move to Oregon.

Competition in the Real World

In a real market economy, perfect competition rarely, if ever, exists. Each of the four conditions is very difficult to meet. First, suppliers of goods and services are not all the same size. Luck, skill, and other factors permit some firms to grow larger than

139

others. Second, not all the producers in an industry make the same product. Third, perfect knowledge of market conditions is hard to achieve in any economy. It would be very hard to know all prices everywhere. Fourth, perfect mobility does not exist. People cannot move every time they hear of a chance to make more money. Nor can producers simply switch from one product to another. Changing production methods is costly and takes time.

Perfect competition also has numerous disadvantages. Perfect competition, it is true, would drive production costs down. But it would mean less money for employees and for profits. In the past, therefore, when competition got too stiff, those who suffered from it organized trade unions or business groups. They forced the prices of resources back up to higher levels. The tactics vary, but the goal is always the same. People try to reduce competition so that they can make more money.

Imperfect Competition

The system of capitalism that exists in the United States today is not an example of perfect competition. Like other market economies, the economy of the United States demonstrates imperfect competition. **Imperfect competition** is the situation that

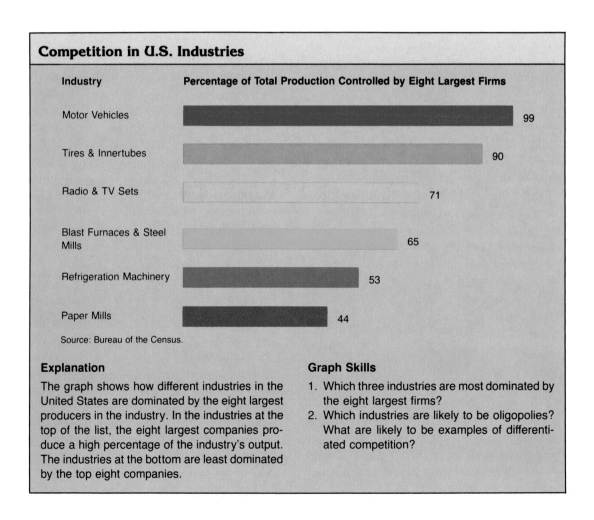

Competition in U.S. Industries

Industry	Percentage of Total Production Controlled by Eight Largest Firms
Motor Vehicles	99
Tires & Innertubes	90
Radio & TV Sets	71
Blast Furnaces & Steel Mills	65
Refrigeration Machinery	53
Paper Mills	44

Source: Bureau of the Census.

Explanation

The graph shows how different industries in the United States are dominated by the eight largest producers in the industry. In the industries at the top of the list, the eight largest companies produce a high percentage of the industry's output. The industries at the bottom are least dominated by the top eight companies.

Graph Skills

1. Which three industries are most dominated by the eight largest firms?
2. Which industries are likely to be oligopolies? What are likely to be examples of differentiated competition?

exists when a market is partially but not completely competitive.

Some imperfect markets show traits of the perfect competition model. For example, the clothing industry has many buyers and sellers, and knowledge of prices and styles is easy to obtain. However, since suppliers do not make identical products, the clothing industry is not an example of perfect competition. Producers make clothes in a wide variety of styles and fabrics. Clothes come in all price ranges. This kind of imperfect competition, in which producers are numerous and prices vary greatly, is called differentiated competition. Some economists call this kind of market situation monopolistic competition.

Another example of imperfect competition is the gasoline industry. Products are nearly identical, and knowledge of prices is easy to obtain. However, since a few large producers dominate the market, the industry is not an example of perfect competition. Further, the prices the major companies charge are usually similar. Therefore, competition is rarely based on price. Through advertising, each company tries to win consumer loyalty to its product. Imperfect competition involving few producers and little price variation is called oligopoly.

The amount of competition in the market varies for each good. In some industries, a handful of companies dominate the market. In other industries, dozens of companies compete with one another.

Monopoly

For any competition to exist, more than one firm must be in a market. A firm that controlled a market would have no competition. The situation in which one seller supplies all the demand for a particular product is a monopoly. A company with a monop-

oly is less pressed to lower prices, improve products, or change production methods.

Monopolies and imperfect competition often result when a company or the government tries to limit competition in an industry. The economy of the United States is based on the profit motive. Each company tries to earn as much profit as it can. A firm that can limit the competition it faces can often increase its prices and profits.

Government also limits competition at times. In a capitalist country that is also democratic, such as the United States, the role of the government is often debated. Some people believe that the economy of the country would run better if the government allowed competition to work freely. Government tries to limit competition in three different situations.

First, the government limits competition when the needs of a group of people can be met most cheaply by a single supplier. These situations are called natural monopolies. Public utilities, such as electric and water companies, are natural monopolies. Two or more companies competing to provide a community with electricity, for example, would be wasteful. Each company would have to duplicate the expenses of the others in producing and distributing electricity. To prevent wasteful duplication, the government has granted a monopoly on selling electricity in each area of the country. To keep electrical power companies from taking advantage of their monopolies, the government regulates the companies' prices and policies.

Second, the government limits competition through licensing. For example, the government has set strict requirements for people who want to become doctors. The purpose of the requirements is to prevent unqualified people from practicing medicine. Without these requirements, more people probably would become doctors,

141

increasing competition in providing health care. Society, through government, has decided to limit competition in order to protect itself from unqualified doctors.

Third, government limits competition by granting patents and copyrights. A patent is an official document that gives an inventor the exclusive right to make, use, or sell an invention for a specified number of years. A copyright is the exclusive right to publish or perform literary, artistic, or musical works for a certain number of years. Patents and copyrights protect the works of inventors and artists from use by competitors for a limited time period. Consequently, inventors and artists can benefit more from their products than they could in perfect competition. In effect, patents and copyrights are temporary monopolies. They are designed to encourage and reward inventors and artists.

Evaluating Competition

Competition in the private enterprise system of the United States is usually imperfect competition. In most instances, more than one supplier can meet the needs of consumers, but perfect competition rarely, if ever, exists.

In other aspects of life, such as school, competition also plays an important role. Like business owners, students often compete with one another for success. Yet, competition is rarely perfect competition.

Basic Models of Competition

Characteristic	Perfect Competition	Imperfect Competition		Monopoly
		Differentiated Competition	Oligopoly	
Number of Firms	Very many	Many	Few	One
Variety in Products	No variety	High	Low	No variety
Price Competition	Very much	Much	Little	None
Competition on Nonprice Factors	None	Some	Very much	None
Current Examples	None	Clothes and furniture	Gasoline and steel	Electric

Explanation

The chart summarizes the basic characteristics of markets with different amounts of competition. The different models are arranged in order from the most to the least competitive. Most industries in the United States are either differentiated competition or oligopoly. Perfect competition does not exist. Monopolies usually exist only with government support.

Chart Skills

1. In the row Number of Firms, what pattern emerges moving from left to right?
2. How are Perfect Competition and Monopoly similar? How they are different?
3. How are differentiated competition and oligopoly different? How are they similar? Why are they each considered examples of imperfect competition?

142

Rather than competing with everyone, you may find that studying with a friend helps both of you. Often, cooperation is better than competition.

REVIEWING THE CONCEPT

Developing Vocabulary

1. List the four traits of perfect competition. Explain how each contributes to perfect competition.
2. Define imperfect competition.
3. What are the differences between the two forms of imperfect competition—differentiated and oligopolistic?
4. What is a monopoly?

5. List three natural monopolies and explain why they are natural monopolies.
6. Compare a patent and a copyright.

Mastering Facts

1. Why does perfect competition not exist in the real world? List and explain four restrictions on competition in the American system of capitalism.
2. Why do most producers try to reduce competition? Why do most consumers want competition?
3. What are the advantages and disadvantages of imperfect competition for the producer? For the consumer?
4. What is the relationship between government and a natural monopoly?

CASE STUDY

Competition in The Air

The amount of competition in an industry usually changes slowly. Occasionally, however, dramatic shifts occur. Amy Clark, a student at the University of Washington in Seattle, benefited from a rapid increase in competition within the airline industry.

Amy wanted to visit her parents in Chicago and her brother in New York during spring break. However, when she first checked air fares she almost changed her mind. The regular trip fare of $1,238 would put a huge dent in her savings. Another check, though, showed that regular air fare was not her only option. By leaving and returning on certain days and by purchasing her ticket early, she could make the trip for $567, less than half the regular fare.

Before 1978, checking various airlines would probably have done Amy Clark little good. At that time the airline industry was

an oligopoly. A few major airlines carried most passengers. Competition was also restricted by the Civil Aeronautics Board, an agency of the federal government. The CAB set fares, determined which carriers would fly which routes, and decided whether new companies would be permitted to enter the industry.

Critics of airline regulation insisted that greater competition would bring down air fares and improve service. They charged that the CAB virtually guaranteed profits to the airlines. The CAB usually allowed airlines to increase their fares whenever costs increased. In 1978, the critics won. Congress voted to deregulate the airlines.

Deregulation sharply increased competition among airlines. No longer could airlines depend on the CAB to protect them from price cuts by other companies. One airline charged $660 for a nonstop New York to Houston flight. A smaller line, making several stops between those cities, charged $150 for the journey.

Deregulation increased competition on nonprice items as well as on price. In order to attract customers, some airlines established special rewards for frequent flyers. Travelers who have flown a certain number of miles on the planes of an airline then are entitled to free flights based on the number of paid miles flown. Consumers benefit from such special programs.

Deregulation also helped the investors who started new airlines. Within five years after deregulation, 20 new airlines had been started. These new companies created new jobs for airline workers and increased service to some communities. Some specialized in inexpensive travel.

Not everyone, though, was helped by deregulation. The major airlines, for instance, lost money. Competition forced price cuts to the point where airlines were not earning enough to cover their expenses. Two airlines went out of business temporarily. Others almost collapsed. Thousands of employees lost their jobs. Those who kept their jobs often had to take large pay cuts. People who had to fly at a moment's notice could not take advantage of special-rate fares. Several airlines raised regular fares to make up for losses on special fares.

Another problem was that after deregulation, airlines could drop unprofitable routes to small communites, and many did. Before deregulation the CAB had forced the airlines to serve many small communities even though flights to these places were less profitable.

Deregulation also raised some questions about air safety. Would airlines reduce safety measures to curb costs? Some airlines cut the amount of time devoted to training flight attendants. Some decreased the amount of experience they required of pilots who flew larger planes. The periods that crew members flew without rest were made longer.

Concerns about safety have caused some people to call for a return to airline regulation. They say that savings to some consumers are not worth increased dangers to all. Defenders of deregulation reply that no clear pattern of increased danger has been established. They insist that the benefits of deregulation far outweigh any of the costs.

The rapid increase in competition in the airline industry has affected passengers, airline workers and owners, and communities. For some, the tradeoffs created by increased competition have not been good. For others, such as Amy Clark, the tradeoffs have made possible an extra trip home.

ANALYZING THE CASE STUDY

STEP 1 Clarify the Issue

1. Explain the effects of deregulation on the role of the federal government in the airline industry.
2. How was competition in the airline industry affected by deregulation?
3. Explain the role of government in a capitalist system.

STEP 2 Consider Costs and Benefits

1. List groups of people who benefited from deregulation of the airline industry. How did they benefit?
2. List groups that were hurt by deregulation. How were they hurt?
3. Which groups are on both lists?
4. Are there any costs or benefits that did not show up in these lists? Explain.

STEP 3 Make a Decision

1. Do you support deregulation of the airlines? Explain your position.

144

Enrichment Activities

1. Find out how deregulation of the trucking industry affected different groups. Decide whether trucking deregulation helped or hurt you overall.
2. Using the travel section of your newspaper, compare airline rates to a particular place, such as New York, Miami, or Acapulco. Make a chart listing the airline, the ticket price, and the special restrictions that apply to the fare. Which airline seems to offer the best package for the consumer?

READING

Parable of the Parking Lots

by Henry G. Manne   (1928-   )

Usually, parking a car is a simple task. However, parking at a large concert or sporting event can be difficult and expensive. This reading, taken from an article by Henry G. Manne, describes how the parking situation at one stadium changed when competition broke down. Manne is a professor at the University of Miami Law School. As you read, consider why competition existed, why it broke down, and what were the effects of less competition.

"In a city not far away there was a large football stadium. It was used from time to time for various events, but the principal use was for football games played Saturday afternoons by the local college team. The games were tremendously popular, and people drove hundreds of miles to watch them. Parking was done in the usual way. People who arrived early were able to park free on the streets. Latecomers had to pay to park in regular and improvised lots.

In the neighborhood of the stadium there were about 25 parking lots. The lots closer to the stadium received more football business than those farther away. Some of the very close lots actually raised their price on Saturday afternoons. But they did not raise the price much, and most did not change prices at all. The reason was not hard to find.

For something else happened on football afternoons. A lot of people who lived nearby went into the parking lot business. It was not a hard thing to do. Typically, a young boy would put out a crude, homemade sign saying "Parking $3." He would direct a couple of cars into his parents' driveway, tell the driver to take the key, and collect the three dollars. The whole system seemed to work fairly smoothly. Though traffic just after a big game was terrible, there were no significant delays parking cars or retrieving parked cars.

But one day the owner of a chain of parking lots called a meeting of all the commercial parking lot owners. They formed an organization known

145

as the Association of Professional Parking Lot Employers, or APPLE. They were very concerned about the Saturday parking business. One man who owned four parking lots pointed out that honest parking lot owners had heavy capital investments in their business, that they paid taxes, and that they employed individuals who supported families. There was no reason, he alleged, why these lots should not handle all the cars coming into the area for special events like football games. "It is unethical," he said, "to engage in harmful competition with irresponsible fender benders. After all, parking cars is a profession, not a business." This last remark drew loud applause. Ethical car parkers, he said, understand their obligations not to dent fenders, to employ only trustworthy car parkers, and to pay decent wages.

Others at the meeting related various tales of horror about nonprofessional car parkers. One homeowner, it was said, actually allowed his 15 year-old son to move other people's cars around. Another said that he had seen a Cadillac parked on a dirt lawn where it would have become mired in the mud had it rained that day. He felt that a professional group such as APPLE had a duty to protect the public from their folly in using those parking spaces. Still another speaker reminded the audience that these "fly-by-night" parking lot operators generally parked a string of cars in their driveways so that a driver had to wait until all cars behind his had been removed before he could get his out. "Clearly," he said, "driveway parking constitutes unfair competition."

Emotions ran high at this meeting, and every member of APPLE pledged $1 per parking space for something mysteriously called a "slush fund." It was never made clear exactly what would be bought with these funds, but several months later a resolution was adopted by the city council requiring licensing for anyone in the parking lot business.

The introduction to the new ordinance read like the speeches at the earlier meeting. It required that anyone parking cars for a fee must have a minimum capital of $25,000 devoted to the parking lot business. They must have liability insurance in an amount not less than $500,000. Finally a special driving test for these parkers (which would be designed and run by APPLE) would be needed. The law also required that every lot charge a single posted price for parking and that any charge in the posted price be approved in advance by the city council. Incidentally, most members were able to raise their fees by about 20 percent before the first posting.

Then a funny thing happened to drivers on their way to the stadium for the next big game. They saw city police in unusually large numbers, who told them it was illegal to pay a nonlicensed parking lot operator for the right to park a car. These policemen also reminded parents that it was against the law for their children to park cars. There were no driveway parking lots that day.

Back at the commercial parking lots, another funny thing occurred. Proceeding from the entrance of each of these parking lots within 12 blocks of the stadium were long lines of cars waiting to park. The lines got larger [and longer] as the lots were closer to the stadium. Many drivers had to wait so long or walk so far that they missed the entire first quarter of the big game.

At the end of the game it was even worse. The confusion was massive. The lot attendants could not cope with the jam-up. Some cars were not retrieved until the next day.

Naturally there was a lot of grumbling, but there was not agreement on what had caused the problem. At first, everyone said there were merely some "bugs" in the new system that would have to be ironed out. But the only "bug" ironed out was a small Volkswagen which was flattened by a careless lot attendant in a large Cadillac Eldorado.

The situation did not improve at later games. The members of APPLE did not hire more people to park cars. Operators near the stadium were not careful to follow their previous practice of parking cars in such a way as to have them easy to reach. Employees seemed to become more unpleasant [to customers]. And the number of dented fender claims rose rapidly. **99**

From "The Parable of the Parking Lots," by Henry G. Manne.

UNDERSTANDING THE READING

1. How did competition work in the real market to solve the problem of football parking space?
2. How did APPLE solve the problem of football parking space? List three negative results of the APPLE solution to the parking problem.
3. What characteristics of perfect competition are illustrated by the story of APPLE?
4. What lesson does the author suggest is to be learned from this parable?

Section 1 Review

Understanding Models of Competition

1. What is the purpose of comparing a perfect competition model to the actuality of the real world?
2. Who would benefit more from perfect competition, producers or consumers?

Models of Competition Today

1. Compare the perfect competition model with the United States economy today. Which of the four traits are present?
2. What might be the result if the electrical company no longer enjoyed its status as a monopoly?
3. Under government regulations, before 1978 airlines did not compete on price. What other bases of competition were left open to them?

2 Economic Markets

SECTION OVERVIEW

You may never have thought of yourself as a factor of production. However, your skills are a resource. The more your skills are in demand, the higher your salary will be. As a consumer you will be using the income from your labor to purchase goods and services on the product market. How much income you receive will determine what and how much you will be able to buy. In this section you will learn how competition works in American capitalism.

ECONOMIC VOCABULARY

factors of production   factor markets   product markets

Factor Markets

In a market economy like American capitalism, three basic resources—land, labor, and capital—are bought and sold for the best price. These resources are called factors of production because they are the things needed to produce goods and services. The markets or exchanges for these factors of production are called factor markets. Producers compete with one another in the factor markets for the resources they need. The prices of these resources are subject to the same laws of supply and demand that affect goods and services. The graphs illustrate the supply curves of these resources.

Resource Prices and Production

Firms decide what to make based on the prices they must pay for resources. If the prices of resources needed for one product go too high, the manufacturer may switch to making a different product. For example, leather seat covers were once standard equipment in cars. Leather was cheap compared to substitutes such as cloth. But after

A young man checks the market for his skills by reading employment ads.

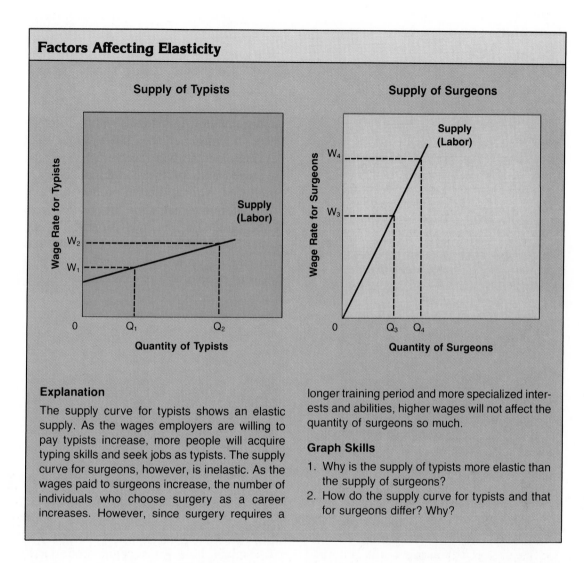

Factors Affecting Elasticity

Supply of Typists

Wage Rate for Typists

Supply (Labor)

W₂
W₁

0   Q₁   Q₂

Quantity of Typists

Supply of Surgeons

Wage Rate for Surgeons

Supply (Labor)

W₄
W₃

0   Q₃   Q₄

Quantity of Surgeons

Explanation

The supply curve for typists shows an elastic supply. As the wages employers are willing to pay typists increase, more people will acquire typing skills and seek jobs as typists. The supply curve for surgeons, however, is inelastic. As the wages paid to surgeons increase, the number of individuals who choose surgery as a career increases. However, since surgery requires a longer training period and more specialized interests and abilities, higher wages will not affect the quantity of surgeons so much.

Graph Skills

1. Why is the supply of typists more elastic than the supply of surgeons?
2. How do the supply curve for typists and that for surgeons differ? Why?

plastic was developed, it gradually became cheaper than either leather or cloth. As a result, automakers began installing plastic seat covers in cars. Leather seat covers then became a luxury. Car manufacturers competing to produce the best product for the lowest cost changed what they were producing because of a change in the factors available for production.

Product Markets for Consumers

In factor markets, individuals trade their land, labor, and capital for income or money. This money or income individuals earn can be the result of rent paid for land, wages paid for labor, or interest paid for the use of capital. Using this income, consumers shop in the product markets. A product market is a market where consumers buy the goods and services they need. When you shop at a supermarket, buy clothes, or see a movie, you are using income in a product market.

Producers compete for the consumers' money in product markets by producing the best products for the lowest prices. Individuals decide what to buy based on these prices and their income. If the price of a product goes too high, consumers adjust

149

Supply of Capital

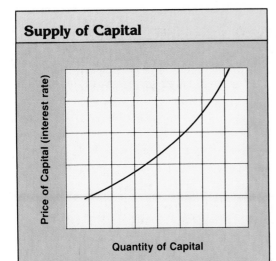

Price of Capital (interest rate) (y-axis)

Quantity of Capital (x-axis)

Explanation

This graph shows the supply curve for capital. Like other items, the supply of capital increases when the price of capital increases. Banks are a major supplier of capital. The amount of capital they will supply for loans is shown on the x-axis. Businesses hoping to expand need to borrow capital from banks. The price of capital is the interest rate a bank charges on a loan. The amount of interest charged on loans is shown on the y-axis. The higher the interest rate businesses are willing to pay, the more capital banks will supply.

Graph Skills

1. Change the graph for capital to show a shift in supply. What circumstances would cause such a shift?
2. Is the supply of capital elastic or inelastic? Explain your answer.

their choices or demands in the product market. A rise in price may influence a consumer to switch to a substitute or do without the product.

Distribution in Product Markets

An important function the product market performs is to answer the question, "Who will get goods and services?" Goods and services that have been produced are distributed in product markets. Money or income will be used in product markets to determine how individuals will share products. A consumer who has a larger than average income will receive a larger than average share of the goods and services produced. Money used in product markets will determine that some households have two, three, or four television sets while other households have one or none. Product markets do not provide goods and services to people who have no money.

REVIEWING THE CONCEPT

Developing Vocabulary

1. List the factors of production and give an example of how businesses use each factor to produce goods or services.
2. With what three basic resources are the factor markets concerned? Who competes for these resources?
3. For whom do product markets operate? Who competes in the product markets?

Mastering Facts

1. Explain how firms compete in factor markets. How do individuals compete in factor markets?
2. How do firms compete with one another in product markets?
3. How do factor markets answer the basic economic question of what to produce? The question of how to produce? The question of for whom to produce?
4. How do product markets answer the question of what to produce? For whom to produce?
5. In the product markets, how do consumers decide where to spend their money?
6. Explain why the elasticity of the supply of labor varies greatly.

Jobs and Growth in the Sunbelt

When demand for a skill decreases, workers who lose their jobs must make economic decisions based on factor markets and individual preferences. Changes in the automobile industry in the 1970s and 1980s caused a decline in the demand for labor in Detroit. Thousands of workers lost their jobs and left Detroit in search of work. Ann and Randy McCoy are two of these people. Their lives were greatly affected by the change in the labor market.

Randy McCoy was a child when he moved with his family from Kentucky to Detroit in 1955. In the 1950s, Detroit was a growing area. Workers could find good jobs in the automobile industry. After graduating from high school, Randy trained as a machinist and found work in a small shop. He and Ann married, bought a house, and had two children. Things went well until economic recession struck the country in 1981. The McCoys realized that the nation's economic problems could cost Randy his job. They heard, through, that jobs were more plentiful in the South. So they moved to the small city of Kerrville, Texas, near San Antonio.

Randy easily found a job in a machine shop in Kerrville. However, wages were lower than in Detroit, and pay raises seemed few and far between. Randy quit and took a job more to his liking in Houston. The McCoys felt uncomfortable in Houston, so they moved again. In Arlington, Texas, Randy found another job, but Ann could not find a job. So, finally, the McCoys went back to Detroit. Ann found a job that paid $150 a week.

"We're having financial problems right now," said Ann McCoy. "Buy if you are going to be broke and unhappy, why not be around your family and friends?"

During the 1970s and 1980s, thousands of families like the McCoys were affected by changes in the labor market. Many workers with good-paying jobs in the northern and northeastern states lost their jobs as the economy changed. This area became known as the Frostbelt. Economic growth was stronger in the Sunbelt—the states in the South and Southwest. Like the McCoys, thousands of people moved from the Frostbelt to the Sunbelt. Not all, though, were disappointed with what they found when they arrived.

Sharon Meyer, for example, moved from Michigan to Houston and took a secretarial job with an energy company. "There's no doubt I made the right decisions," she said. "If you cannot make it here, you probably cannot make it anywhere." The rapid population growth of the Sunbelt suggests that many people agree with Sharon Meyer. America's population increased by 2.2 percent between 1980 and 1982. The South and the West gained 92 percent of that growth. Increases in California, Texas, and Florida alone accounted for more than half of the population growth in the early 1980s.

Two reasons producers moved to the Sunbelt were energy costs and taxes. As energy costs increased during the 1970s, the warm climate of the Sunbelt became more attractive. Businesses and individuals wanted to escape the high cost of heating homes and offices. In additon, Sunbelt states cut taxes in order to attract firms. By moving south, businesses could save substantially on their taxes.

As producers have moved to the South, factor markets have had to readjust. In general, the demand for capital, natural, and human resources has been increasing in the Sunbelt and declining in the Frostbelt. In the capital market, for example, the new and growing businesses in the Sunbelt need to borrow money to start or expand. So demand for capital has been increasing in

the Sunbelt. In the Frostbelt, demand has not been growing rapidly.

The market for natural resources also shows demand increasing faster in the Sunbelt than in the Frostbelt. Construction materials, such as wood, brick, and copper, are in great demand in the Sunbelt. The new industries in the Sunbelt often rely more on skilled labor than on natural resources. Still, demand for the materials they need, such as metals to make airplanes and missiles, is increasing. In the Frostbelt, demand for such raw materials as iron and

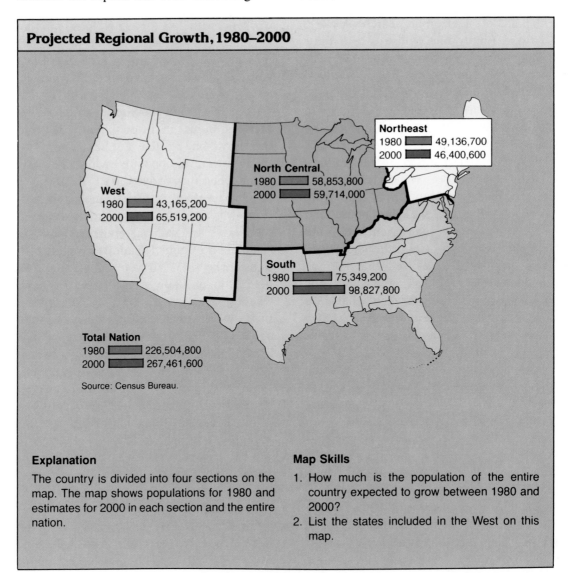

Projected Regional Growth, 1980–2000

Northeast
1980 — 49,136,700
2000 — 46,400,600

North Central
1980 — 58,853,800
2000 — 59,714,000

West
1980 — 43,165,200
2000 — 65,519,200

South
1980 — 75,349,200
2000 — 98,827,800

Total Nation
1980 — 226,504,800
2000 — 267,461,600

Source: Census Bureau.

Explanation

The country is divided into four sections on the map. The map shows populations for 1980 and estimates for 2000 in each section and the entire nation.

Map Skills

1. How much is the population of the entire country expected to grow between 1980 and 2000?
2. List the states included in the West on this map.

Cities in the Sunbelt, such as Dallas, Texas, have grown rapidly because of the tourist, oil, defense, and space industries. Consequently, demand for workers has increased.

coal has not been increasing significantly.

The biggest shift in a factor market, though, has been in the labor market. During the 1970s, 74 percent of all new jobs in the nation were in the Sunbelt. In many areas of the Sunbelt, certain industries have been strong for a long time. Examples of industries that were strong in the Sunbelt long before the 1970s include: the oil industry in Texas and Louisiana; the tourist industry in Florida and Arizona; and the space, airline, and defense industries in California, Texas, and Florida. In general, these industries have been growing since 1970. Consequently, demand for workers in these areas has gone up. Oil rig workers, hotel managers, and engineers have been increasingly in demand. In newer industries, such as computers, demand has jumped even more dramatically.

The growth of all these industries increased demand for workers with special skills in the industries. As these people

moved to the Sunbelt, other people were needed to provide services for them. So the demand for pharmacists, insurance agents, newspaper reporters, and other workers increased. The shift in the factor market affected people in all types of work.

The rapid growth of the Sunbelt population has generally been welcomed by the southern states. However, growth has created problems. Increased population has led to overcrowded schools. Public services, such as sanitation and sewer systems, have been strained. Water shortages are another critical problem, particularly in Texas, Arizona, Florida, and southern California. A shortage of housing, especially in California, has considerably increased the costs of homes for newcomers.

Most people expect Sunbelt growth to continue. The National Planning Association projects that by the year 2000, one out of every five American workers will live in California, Texas, or Florida. The factor markets will have to continue to adjust to shifts in demand for resources.

ANALYZING THE CASE STUDY

STEP 1   Read Maps

1. Which area of the country is expected to lose population between 1980 and 2000?
2. Which area of the country is expected to have the smallest overall change in population between 1980 and 2000?
3. How much is the combined population in the South and the West expected to grow between 1980 and 2000?

STEP 2   Predict Further Change

1. What changes will occur in each of the three factor markets as people move to the Sunbelt?
2. Which factor market will be most affected by the increase in population in the Sunbelt region of the United States?

STEP 3   Make a Decision

List and evaluate three effects the shift to the Sunbelt will have on you and your life. Overall, do you consider these effects good or bad? Explain.

READING

The World Labor Market

by Richard Barnet (1929-   )
and Ronald E. Muller (1939-   )

Factor markets are worldwide today. In this reading, the authors consider the market that affects individuals most directly, the labor market. This excerpt is taken from *Global Reach,* by Richard J. Barnet and Ronald E. Muller. Barnet is a member of the Institute for Policy Studies, a research firm in Washington, D.C. Muller is a professor of economics and international finance at American University in Washington, D.C. As you read, consider how your future may be affected by competition from workers in other nations.

66   **T**he continuing shift of manufacturers to the poorer nations of the world is creating problems for the American worker. Corporate organization on a global scale is a highly effective weapon for undercutting the power of organized labor everywhere. The bases of corporate power, such as capital and technology, are mobile; workers, by and large, are not. The ability of corporations to open and close plants rapidly and to shift their investment from one country to another damages the basis of organized labor's bargaining leverage, the strike. It may be true that when

a plant is closed in the United States and another one is opened in Korea, jobs have not been lost, they have just been traded. However, the trading process does not benefit the worker who has lost his or her job. Unemployed workers in the United States cannot afford to sit home until the uncertain day when their town feels the beneficial effects of industrial expansion overseas.

Management finds that its power to close an entire operation in a community and to transfer everything but the workers out of the country produces a marvelously obliging labor force. The threat of plant closings has caused unions in both Europe and the United States to make fewer demands. In a number of cases unions have pledged not to go on strike. There have been enough cases in which global corporations have used their superior mobility to defeat unions to make the threat credible.

There are also less dramatic alternatives available to management that further weaken labor's bargaining power. Instead of closing a plant completely, a company can cut back on the need for workers. A company making computers in France suddenly fired one-third of its workers on orders from its headquarters in New York. Neither the French government nor the outraged local manager could do a thing about it.

Because it is easier to write a check than to move a worker and his family, the owners and managers of capital, as we have seen, enjoy certain advantages over labor. Further, because lines of authority are kept deliberately unclear in many global enterprises, the local union does not know with whom it should deal. Many union leaders in Europe complain of this in negotiations. They are unable to get a decision out of the local manager and are never sure what issues the local manager has the authority to settle. Labor unions up to this point lack anything like the advanced communications system of the corporations. Thus they [the

American workers and corporations face competition from businesses in other parts of the globe.

unions] have difficulty finding out what the corporation may have paid workers in other countries.

Another problem faced by unions concerns the company's books. The financial records of a large corporation are very complex. This makes it exceedingly difficult for unions to find out how much money the employer is making or, indeed, if the company is really losing money, as its managers frequently claim.

Nonetheless, the exploitation of wage differences in different parts of the world by the global corporations is causing unions to recognize their interests with workers around the world. Union leaders in the United States realize that the army, 34,000 strong, of 30-cents-an-hour child laborers in Hong Kong is a real and growing economic threat to American workers. However, they are confused about what to demand. Should the wages in Hong Kong and Detroit be the same? Not even powerful unions in Europe are making demands for wages equal to those received by workers in the United States. Despite the logic in paying the same wage for the same work for the same company regardless of a race, creed, color, or national origin, the practical union organizer is reluctant to ask for it. Given the risk that the company may decide to pull out altogether, the organizer is happy if the local union can get a few more francs or marks a day. **99**

From *Global Reach*, by Richard Barnet and Ronald E. Muller.

UNDERSTANDING THE READING

1. What advantages do corporations have over labor unions in international markets?
2. Should unions demand that wages be equal internationally? Explain your view.
3. Explain how American consumers benefit from the low wages paid to workers in many foreign countries.

Section 2 Review

Understanding Economic Markets

1. What part do you play in factor markets?
2. What function do you perform in the product markets?
3. Explain the interactions between factor markets and product markets.

Economic Markets Today

1. How does competition help consumers purchase the best products for the lowest prices? Use a consumer product to explain your answer.
2. Give an example of a product that increased in price so much that you, as a consumer, had to use a substitute or do without it.
3. When workers strike in the automobile industry, what happens in factor markets? How do such strikes affect the product markets?

3 Market Interaction

SECTION OVERVIEW

In the American system of capitalism, factor markets where individuals sell resources and product markets where they purchase goods and services are related. There is a circular flow of money between them. Firms would be unable to produce products without paying for labor. They would also be unable to produce goods without individuals to buy goods and services with the income earned on the product market. In the same manner, individuals would not be able to earn income from their labor, land, or capital if firms did not compete for its use. In our private enterprise system, two markets depend on each other just as you and business depend on each other.

ECONOMIC VOCABULARY   circular flow of money

Related Markets

The markets for factors and for products work together. You, as a worker, earn income in a factor market and spend it as a consumer in product markets. Spending in both types of markets is affected by competition between buyers and sellers. This competition in both factor and product markets has two effects. First, factor and product competition provides the consumer with the best product at the lowest price. Second, it encourages business to produce more efficiently.

The automobile industry is an example of how these markets operate in American capitalism. The average American family owns a car. Many high school students hope to buy cars as soon as they can afford them. The automobile industry is an important part of the American economy.

Factor Market Competition

The automobile industry employs 1 out of every 18 Americans. These employees are hired in factor markets where workers compete for the highest paying jobs. Industry also competes here to fill its need for workers. The automobile industry needs thousands of factory workers to assemble cars. Car manufacturers must also compete for employees in many other areas. Research and testing are important, and automakers spend millions of dollars each year trying to find out how to build better cars. Much of this money is used to pay thousands of chemists, engineers, physicists, and technicians.

Automobile manufacturers must compete with other industries in factor markets to obtain the natural resources needed to produce a car. Automakers buy 15 percent of the steel, 27 percent of the zinc, and 11 percent of the aluminum used in the United States. They also buy one out of every three radios produced here and use 25 billion pounds of chemicals every year.

Other manufacturers—of stoves and refrigerators, for example—also require large amounts of raw materials. Each industry competes for the limited supply.

157

When consumers buy products, their wages flow back again to manufacturers.

The auto industry requires the use of large amounts of money to pay employees and purchase raw materials. In addition to employees and raw materials, carmakers must buy capital equipment and pay to advertise their particular product. Information about advantages and technical improvements appears in advertisments. This information influences the consumer's choice of a car. The automobile industry spends over $430 million a year to advertise its cars in the United States alone. This money comes from a number of sources. Some of it comes from the sale of cars; however, buyers do not pay for cars in advance. Until they sell the cars, automakers must borrow money on the factor market for capital. There they compete with other large industries, government agencies, and individuals who also want to borrow money.

Product Market Competition

In product markets, automobile manufacturers compete with one another to sell the most cars. The results of their research and testing are modern and safe vehicles produced as efficiently as is technically possible. In other words, each car manufacturer feels it has produced the best product at the lowest price to meet the needs of a certain group of consumers.

The test of whether an automaker has accomplished this goal will be in the number of cars the automaker can sell. Consumers use their dollars in product markets. Consumer purchases of a new car tell the manufacturer that more of that type of car should be produced.

Since there are many safety, design, performance, and price differences among cars, consumers make economic tradeoffs when they purchase a car. Perhaps getting more miles per gallon of gasoline is more important than sleek styling. Both good gas mileage and sleek styling are available but cost extra. Therefore, an economic choice would be to trade off sleek styling to obtain efficient use of gasoline.

Product and Factor Market Links

Neither factor markets nor product markets operate independently; they are interrelated markets. Each type of market depends on the other, and money from one travels into the other. The circular flow of money is the term used to describe this path that money travels around the economy. The automobile engineer earns income in a factor market. This income is then spent in product markets to satisfy needs and wants.

Circular Flow of Money and Products

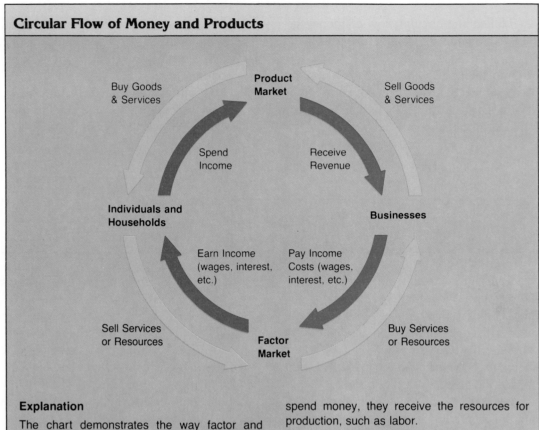

Explanation

The chart demonstrates the way factor and product markets are interrelated. The inside arrows show the flow of money. Money goes from individuals and households to businesses when people buy goods and services. Money flows from businesses to individuals and households when companies buy the resources for production, such as labor. The outside arrows show the flow of the items. When individuals and households spend money, they receive goods and services from businesses. When businesses spend money, they receive the resources for production, such as labor.

Graph Skills

Make a chart showing the flow of economic activity in the automobile industry. Use the chart here as a model, but replace these four terms: (1) Individuals and Households, (2) Product Market, (3) Businesses, and (4) Factor Market. Use these four terms: (1) Workers and Consumers, (2) Automobile Market, (3) Automobile Companies, and (4) Market for Assembly Line Workers.

As it is spent, it flows back to manufacturers, who use it again in factor markets.

In the American capitalist system, this competition influences everyone's behavior. Competition for the factors of production in factor markets and for the consumer's money in product markets results in constantly shifting conditions. Prices and wages constantly change as producers try to increase their profits and consumers try to find better buys. Constant change is a trademark of a modern market system. Consequently, understanding how the economy operates is important to everyone.

REVIEWING THE CONCEPT

Developing Vocabulary

1. How are factor and product markets related to each other?

2. Explain the circular flow of money between factor and product markets.

Mastering Facts

1. What are the two effects of competition in factor and product markets? Explain each of them.

2. Using the automobile industry as an example, explain how factor and product markets work together from a firm's point of view.

3. Using auto assembly workers as an example, explain factor and product markets from a worker's point of view.

Careers in the Future

One part of the American system of capitalism that is constantly changing is the market for labor. Producers are in competition with one another to hire the best workers for the lowest wages. Workers compete with one another to get the best jobs at the highest wages. Producers' needs for workers change constantly. Young people training for a career, then, need to

This young man is preparing for the future by learning to fix electronic equipment.

consider what types of workers will be needed in the future.

Jeff Sosowski is one worker who successfully adjusted to the changing labor market. He had been an assembly line worker in Lordstown, Ohio. The development of robots, though, cost him his job. Robots could do his job at a cost of $2 an hour. Sosowski retrained in robot maintenance. Now he takes care of the machines that took over his job. He likes his new job better than his old one. "I feel a lot better about my job. You have to think." Further, he worries little about future technology taking away his job. As more robots are used, he will be increasingly valuable to his company. More robots, he says, mean "more security for me."

Information to aid individuals in choosing a career is available from a number of sources. The United States Department of Labor, Bureau of Labor Statistics, publishes an *Occupational Outlook Handbook* each year. It lists jobs available in the United States, from academic librarians to writers and editors.

To inform citizens of more current trends in the occupational field, the Bureau of Labor Statistics also publishes an *Occupational Outlook Quarterly*.

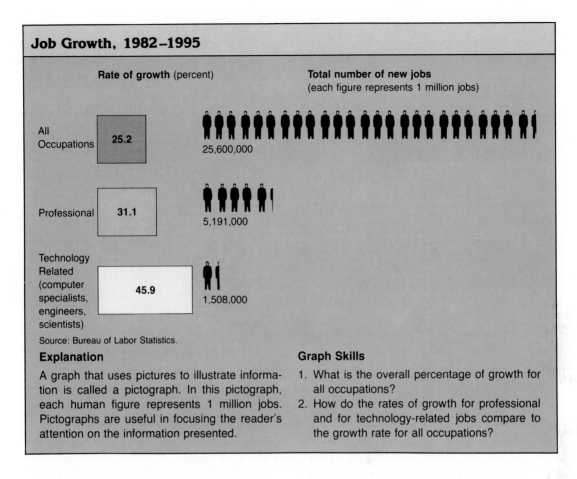

Job Growth, 1982–1995

Rate of growth (percent)

Total number of new jobs
(each figure represents 1 million jobs)

All Occupations	25.2	25,600,000
Professional	31.1	5,191,000
Technology Related (computer specialists, engineers, scientists)	45.9	1,508,000

Source: Bureau of Labor Statistics.

Explanation

A graph that uses pictures to illustrate information is called a pictograph. In this pictograph, each human figure represents 1 million jobs. Pictographs are useful in focusing the reader's attention on the information presented.

Graph Skills

1. What is the overall percentage of growth for all occupations?
2. How do the rates of growth for professional and for technology-related jobs compare to the growth rate for all occupations?

Articles often contain graphics to illustrate a large amount of written material. These graphics—charts, graphs, tables—must be interpreted carefully. For example, the graph in this case study comes from the Spring 1984 issue of *Occupational Outlook Quarterly*. The graph compares the rate of growth in occupations with the total increase in jobs resulting from this growth. The technology-oriented occupations represent an area of employment that began growing rapidly in the 1980s. It is, therefore, small compared to other occupations. While jobs will increase by 45.9 percent, the number of new employees needed will be relatively small.

Planning a career requires careful study of statistics showing which jobs are growing. Further, career planning must include developing the ability to change with the economy. Like Jeff Sosowski, workers need to be able to learn new skills to remain competitive in the market.

ANALYZING THE CASE STUDY

STEP 1 Gather Evidence

1. What occupations are included in technology-related occupations?
2. What time period does the information in the graph cover?

STEP 2 Examine Change

1. Which of the three categories shows the largest percentage of growth?
2. Considering the percentages of growth, why will more jobs be available in professions than in technology-related fields?

161

1. Would it be easier to find a job in a professional area or in a technology-related area?

2. What traditional information is needed before making a choice between a career in a profession and one that is technology-oriented?

READING

The Candlemakers' Petition

by Frederic Bastiat   (1801-1850)

Competition generally brings down prices of consumer goods. Sometimes one supplier in a market makes a product so cheaply and so well that other suppliers cannot compete with it. Then the other suppliers are likely to ask for protection. This reading is taken from an essay by French economist Frederic Bastiat. Though written over a century ago, his argument still applies today. Bastiat was noted for his satire, or use of ridicule. As you read, notice how he makes fun of the candlemakers' petition to eliminate competition. Consider why the French candlemakers were not able to compete with their rival.

66 **P**etition from the manufacturers of candles, lamps, chandeliers, extinguishers; and from the producers of animal fat, oil, and generally of everything used to make lights.

To the Honorable Members of the Congress of France:

We are subjected to the intolerable competition of a foreign rival, who enjoys, it would seem, a superior product for the production of light, at so reduced a price that we have lost business. This rival, who is no other than the sun, carries on so bitter a war against us, that we have every reason to believe that he has been encouraged to compete with us by our country's rival, England.

Our petition is that you pass a law to require the shutting up of windows, skylights, shutters, curtains, and all other openings, holes, and cracks, through which the light of the sun is used to enter our dwellings. Competition from this light harms the profitable manufacturers we have given the country. Our country cannot, therefore, leave us now to struggle unprotected through so unequal a contest.

Here are the reasons for our request. First, by shutting out natural

A monopoly would protect these workers from competition.

light, you thus create the necessity for artificial light, such as candles. Then, industrial pursuits connected with candles will be helped.

If more animal fat must be used to make candles, the need for cattle and sheep will increase. Thus, meat, wool, leather, and above all, manure, this basis of agricultural riches, must become more abundant.

Navigation would also profit. The need for more whale oil would mean thousands of vessels would soon be employed in the whale fisheries. Out of these ships would arise a navy capable of sustaining the honor of [the country of] France.

There is none who would not enjoy an increase of salary and of comforts. The question is, whether you wish for France the benefit of free sunlight or the advantages of expensive artificial light. **99**

From *Petition from the Candlemakers,''* by Frederic Bastiat.

UNDERSTANDING THE READING

1. Is Bastiat for or against monopoly? Explain how you know.
2. According to Bastiat, what groups in France would benefit from a law preventing the sun from lighting people's houses?
3. Do you think the candlemakers faced unfair competition? Explain.

163

Section 3 Review

Understanding Market Interaction

1. Why is the automobile industry so important to the overall economy of the United States?
2. What word or words might replace "crunch" in the cartoon below?

Market Interaction Today

1. Americans had to deal with a scarcity of gas and oil in the 1970s. What methods were used to solve this problem?

2. Choose a product that you expect to purchase in the next year. What economic tradeoffs will you have to make?
3. Specialization is used extensively in the assembly of automobiles: each worker does only a few jobs. How does this specialization affect factor markets? Product markets?
4. **Challenge:** Explain how supply and demand are related to factor markets and to product markets.

Americans *at Work*

Meet Barbara Gardner Proctor
Advertising Executive

In February 1970, Barbara Gardner Proctor was a copywriter for an advertising agency in Chicago. At that time, the agency produced a hairspray advertisement that Proctor thought was tasteless and offensive. When she criticized the ad, she was fired. Proctor decided that, rather than seek another copywriting job, she would start her own agency. Today, her agency, Gardner and Proctor, is a small, but growing and successful company.

Success for Proctor was not easy. She grew up in a poor family in North Carolina and attended a small college in Alabama. After graduation she took a job as a copywriter with an advertising agency. When she was fired, her only resources were her skill and her drive to succeed. Based on these resources, she received an $80,000 loan from the Small Business Administration, a federal agency that assists small businesses. This loan enabled her to start her agency.

One of Proctor's first big accounts was a grocery store chain. She was asked to design an ad campaign for generic foods. These products were unusual and difficult to advertise since generic foods have no brand name with which consumers can identify. Further, although generic foods use wholesome ingredients, they are less than top quality. Proctor designed a campaign emphasizing that generic foods were a healthy, economical alternative to brand-name foods. Her campaign for generic foods was successful, and Proctor's agency was off the ground.

Through her work, Proctor has learned about economics and how advertising affects the answers to the four basic economic questions. She must watch changes in consumers' tastes and suppliers' products. As owner of her own business, she is directly affected by changes in government policies, competition among firms, and trends in advertising.

One change in the economy that Proctor has noticed is the growth of the advertising industry in the United States since World War II. Today, there are over 4,000 advertising agencies in the country. In addition, thousands of businesses, newspapers, radio stations, and TV stations have their own advertising departments. Advertising expenditures amount to over $265 per person each year. This volume suggests that Barbara Gardner Proctor has not been alone in finding success in advertising.

165

Reading Advertising

Business advertising is one of the most widespread traditions in American life. Over 25 percent of all television and radio time and well over 50 percent of most newspapers and magazines are devoted to advertisements. Billboards, handbills, and mail circulars are everywhere. Business advertising is meant to promote specific products and brands. Advertising can provide a positive service by informing the consumer of new or different products. In contrast, advertising can cause unnecessary purchases and confusion over product quality.

A smart consumer uses advertising for its positive results. In order to do that, a consumer must be aware of misleading advertising. By law the advertiser cannot make false claims, but there is nothing illegal about emphasizing only the good qualities of a product, or making undesirable information as inconspicuous as possible. The following steps point out some of the ways you can use advertising to help you rather than mislead you.

STEP 1   Understand Ad Purposes

Advertising is intended to persuade. A good ad makes consumers want to buy a product or use a service. An ad would not be successful if it told all the possible problems with a product, or if it praised its competitors too much. Ads are usually one-sided. Always keep that in mind when evaluating them.

STEP 2   Separate Facts from Opinions

Advertisers make a variety of claims for their products. Some can be demonstrated, other cannot. Facts are usually more helpful to consumers than opinions. However, an opinion or impression may be more significant than a trivial fact.

STEP 3   Evaluate Ad Copy

The following statements are adapted from recent ads. Evaluate each statement as fact or opinion and indicate whether it would influence you.

1. "The finest Swiss quality chronometer money can buy."
2. "Our presses are a world leader in offset newspaper printing."
3. "A system so advanced that it prioritizes mail and messages; specifies the action necessary; even distributes the information to all parties concerned."
4. "Competitors will copy some, possibly even all, of our improvements."
5. "A hotel that is modeled on traditional

lines, yet incorporates every modern convenience."

6. "We introduced the industry's first solid state computer."

STEP 4   Read the Fine Print

Advertisements highlight certain aspects of a product. The aspects that are not highlighted may simply be less important. Or they may be so important that advertisers cannot ignore them, but they do not want consumers to focus on them. The following statements appeared in small print in the advertisements of banks offering high interest rates on a certain type of deposit. Explain how the small print changes the attractiveness of the offer.

1. "This offer may be revised or withdrawn without prior notice."
2. "Rates are subject to change without prior notice."
3. "Interest rates change weekly."

STEP 5   Evaluate Appeals to Emotions

Many ads try to attract consumers by appealing to emotions. Virtually any feeling that many people share can be used by advertisers to sell a product. For each of the items below, explain what emotion the advertiser may be trying to reach.

1. A life insurance ad shows three young children looking sad at a funeral.
2. An automobile ad shows several American factory workers standing in front of an American flag.
3. A diet soft drink ad shows thin people playing at the beach.
4. An ad for a wristwatch that shows wealthy people playing polo.

STEP 6   Contact Advertisers

If you find an ad misleading or offensive, write to the company running the ad. Ads are supposed to convey a positive image of a company. A short letter explaining your dislike of the ad will help the company evaluate the effectiveness of the ad. In addition, if you see an ad you like, compliment the company. A letter praising an ad for effectively conveying accurate information will encourage a company to continue to run high-quality advertisments.

ECONOMIC SKILLS TODAY

1. List and explain two misleading techniques advertisers use.
2. List and explain three other methods advertisers use to sell their products.

Enrichment Activity

Bring in five advertisements. Do they appeal to any emotion in particular? Is the information accurate? Are they misleading in any way? Which appeals most to you?

Advertisements need careful reading.

CHAPTER SUMMARY

Models of Competition

Three economic models describe the workings of economic markets. The first is perfect competition. No real market completely matches this model. The second economic model is imperfect competition. There are two types of imperfect competition. In some, producers are numerous and prices vary greatly. In others, products are nearly identical and knowledge of prices is easy to obtain, but a few large producers dominate the market. The third economic model is a monopoly. Where a monopoly exists, there is no competition. Both imperfect competition and monopolies exist in the American economy.

Economic Markets

Two types of interdependent markets make up a market economy. In the American private enterprise system, competition exists in both types of markets. In factor markets, companies compete for the three factors of production—land, labor, and capital. In product markets, firms compete with one another to sell their products. Here, consumers can choose the best products for their use at prices that fit their income. In product markets, consumers also compete for products that are in short supply. The decisions of consumers and suppliers in product and factor markets determine the answers to the basic questions about production.

Market Interaction

Competition in factor markets and product markets motivates firms to use their resources efficiently. Money flows in a circular pattern between these two types of markets: each depends on the other. Individuals and businesses that own resources obtain money or income by selling their resources. These individuals and businesses then use this money when they shop in product markets as consumers. As they pay for goods and services, the money flows back to firms, which use it to shop again in factor markets.

CRITICAL THINKING QUESTIONS

Models of Competition

1. How does importing foreign cars affect competition in the United States? Does importing cars change the type of imperfect competition that existed before imports became popular?
2. Check the prices of gasoline at two stations that are located very close to each other. Are their prices identical? How do these service stations compete?
3. **Challenge:** What competitive circumstances may contribute to the dominance of a few large firms in some industries? How could other companies be persuaded to enter the market?

Economic Markets

1. How are factor and product markets affected by increases in population? By a labor shift to the Sunbelt? By an international labor market?
2. **Challenge:** What is meant by the best product for the lowest possible price? Is a $10 shirt as good as a $75 shirt? Are the manufacturers of these items competing with each other?

Market Interaction

1. The electric company is a natural monopoly. As a monopoly, does it have any advantages or disadvantages in factor markets? Product markets? Explain.
2. **Challenge:** During World War II (1940s), many parts of the United States economy changed from a market system to a command system. List the effects that this change had on the country's factor markets and product markets.

DEVELOPING ECONOMIC SKILLS

Use the chart to analyze the different costs in making a pair of jeans. Copy the chart and place each production cost listed on the right in the appropriate blank.

1. This chart does not include profit. Explain where profit would be shown.
2. Explain three reasons why the prices of two pairs of jeans may differ.
3. Which of the costs on the chart are for human resources? Explain why the other costs on the chart also include some labor costs.

APPLYING ECONOMICS TODAY

Research a local public utility. Does it pay taxes? Who sets its prices and on what basis? What influence, if any, does the public have on its operations?

Factor Analysis Chart

Costs of Raising Cotton
1.
2.
3.
Total

Costs of Producing Jeans
1. Total Cost of Raising Cotton (from above)
2.
3.
4.
5.
6.
Total

Costs of Selling Jeans
1. Total Cost of Producing Jeans (from above)
2.
3.
4.
5.
Total

Cotton field machinery	$0.49
Sales tax	$0.35
Zippers, buttons, and rivets	$0.42
Land rent	$0.40
Advertising	$0.40
Weavers	$0.62
Retail sales workers	$2.90
Sewing machine workers	$0.43
Cotton field workers	$0.43
Retail store rent	$0.60
Shipping of jeans	$1.95
Factory rent	$0.70

Explanation

The chart provides data for a factor analysis of the costs in making and selling a pair of blue jeans. The specific costs in the column on the right can be grouped under the three types of costs in the column on the left.

Chart Skills

1. What three types of costs does the chart use to group the specific costs?
2. What is the cost of the pair of blue jeans for which this factor analysis was made?

CHAPTER 6

Income and Spending

1 Sources of Income

Objective: to understand the types and sources of income in the United States capitalist system

2 Income Distribution

Objective: to understand how income and wealth are distributed in the United States market system

3 Effects of Spending

Objective: to understand how spending is affected by the multiplier effect and the acceleration principle

1 Sources of Income

SECTION OVERVIEW

You will earn money in several ways throughout your life. Part-time jobs are a major source of income for many high school students. In addition, young people often receive income from their parents or interest on a savings account. Understanding how people earn money will help you consider ways to increase your own income. In this section you will learn about two different ways to analyze the various sources of income of people in the United States.

ECONOMIC VOCABULARY

employee compensation	rent	blue collar worker
proprietor compensation	transfer payment	service worker
corporation profit	white collar worker	farmworker
interest		

Types of Income

People's incomes determine how many of the economy's goods and services they can purchase. In the United States capitalist system there are five basic types of income.

1. Employee compensation is the income earned by working for others. It includes wages and fringe benefits such as health and accident insurance.
2. Proprietor compensation is the income that self-employed people earn.
3. Corporation profit is the income corporations have left after paying all the expenses of the business.
4. Interest is the money received by people and corporations for depositing their money in savings accounts or lending it to others.
5. Rent is income from allowing others to use one's property temporarily. Many people pay rent for an apartment or house. This money is income for the person who owns the property.

This young man earns interest by depositing his money in a savings account.

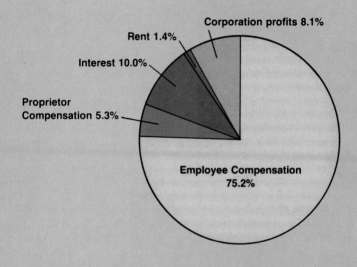

Rent 1.4%

Corporation profits 8.1%

Interest 10.0%

Proprietor Compensation 5.3%

Employee Compensation 75.2%

Source: Bureau of Economic Analysis.

Explanation

A circular graph divided into different slices is called a pie graph. In this pie graph, each slice shows the percentage of total income received from the source indicated for the slice. The size of each slice corresponds to the size of the percentage it represents. Pie graphs are useful in showing, for example, how much of a community's income is spent on each of the services it provides. By studying the pie graph, residents of the community can decide whether or not, in their view, the division of funds is equitable.

Graph Skills

1. What is the largest source of income in the United States economy?
2. What is the smallest percent of income shown in the pie graph?

The total income of the people of the United States is the sum of employee and proprietor compensation, corporation profit, interest, and rent. In each category, people receive this income in return for providing goods or services.

One other type of income is a transfer payment. A transfer payment is money one person or group gives to another, though the receiver has not provided a specific good or service. Gifts, inheritances, and aid to the poor are three examples of transfer payments.

The percentage of income from each of the five sources changes over time. These changes result from changes in the structure of the United States economy. During this century, the percentage of people who work for themselves has generally declined. Increasingly, people are employees and not self-employed.

Income by Type of Work

Another way to examine sources of income is by the type of work people do. Generally, workers fall into one of four broad categories.

1. **White collar workers** are people who do jobs in offices, such as secretaries, teachers, and insurance agents.

2. **Blue collar workers** are people who do jobs in factories or outdoors. Artisans, such as carpenters and plumbers, are blue collar workers.

3. **Service workers** provide services to other individuals or businesses. Janitors, barbers, and police are service workers.

4. **Farmworkers** are people who work on their own farms or those of others.

The income levels of people in each of the four groups have shifted over the years.

Prior to the Civil War, farmworkers earned a high percentage of the nation's

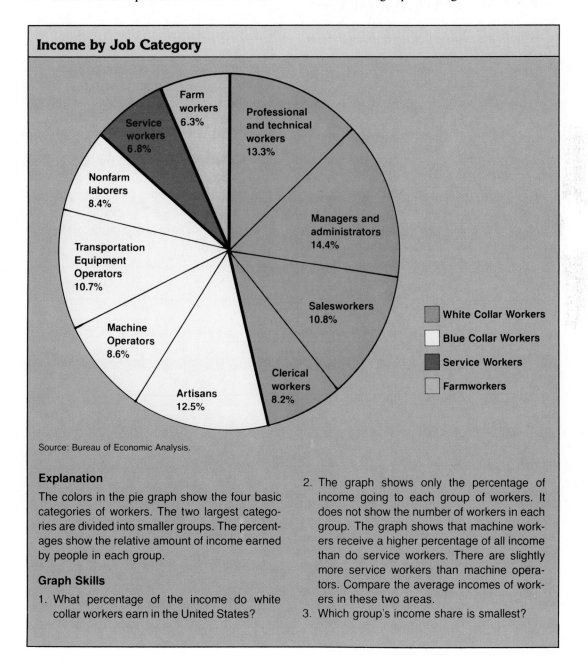

Income by Job Category

Farm workers 6.3%
Service workers 6.8%
Professional and technical workers 13.3%
Nonfarm laborers 8.4%
Managers and administrators 14.4%
Transportation Equipment Operators 10.7%
Salesworkers 10.8%
Machine Operators 8.6%
Clerical workers 8.2%
Artisans 12.5%

White Collar Workers
Blue Collar Workers
Service Workers
Farmworkers

Source: Bureau of Economic Analysis.

Explanation

The colors in the pie graph show the four basic categories of workers. The two largest categories are divided into smaller groups. The percentages show the relative amount of income earned by people in each group.

Graph Skills

1. What percentage of the income do white collar workers earn in the United States?

2. The graph shows only the percentage of income going to each group of workers. It does not show the number of workers in each group. The graph shows that machine workers receive a higher percentage of all income than do service workers. There are slightly more service workers than machine operators. Compare the average incomes of workers in these two areas.

3. Which group's income share is smallest?

income. During and after the Industrial Revolution, farm workers left the farms in great numbers. Many moved to the cities, where they became the blue collar workers in the factories and the construction industries. During the past 20 years, the largest increases in income levels have been in the white collar and service categories. In 1982, over half of all employees in the United States were white collar workers.

Capitalist economies such as the one in the United States are based on the belief that all individuals and groups will try to increase their income. A group's piece of the income pie can increase in two ways. In a growing economy, the incomes of all groups can increase. As the size of the income pie increases, each piece can get larger. The other way a group can increase its income is by increasing its share of the nation's income. By getting a larger percentage of the nation's income, the group increases its piece of the income pie.

REVIEWING THE CONCEPT

Developing Vocabulary

1. What is the difference between employee compensation and proprietor compensation?
2. How does a corporation determine the amount of its profit?
3. Define interest income.
4. Give an example of rental income.
5. Explain how a transfer payment differs from all other sources of income.
6. What is the difference between a blue collar worker and a white collar worker?

Mastering the Facts

1. What are the five basic sources of people's incomes?
2. List and explain the four types of work people do, and give an example of each.
3. Explain the two ways groups can receive larger incomes.

Income for the Lorraines

Most families have more than one source of income. For example, Marc and Claire Lorraine of Waltham, Massachusetts, have four sources of income. Their yearly income, along with that of every family, is figured into the national statistics. Analyzing their income demonstrates how the national statistics are developed.

The Lorraines and their baby son, Henry, live 10 miles outside Boston. Though not wealthy, both enjoy expensive hobbies. Claire likes to ride her horse, Bonne France, and Marc enjoys sailing in their 26-foot sailboat.

Their largest source of income is Marc's business of remodeling homes. In a typical year, he makes $21,000. He owns the business and does most of the work himself. Consequently, he is the proprietor. The type of work he does makes him an artisan.

The second major source of income for the Lorraines is Claire's job as a drafter. She does detailed drawings of floor plans and buildings for a construction company.

Drafters earn wages or salaries for their work. Wages and salaries are types of employee compensation.

Claire's salary as an employee is $14,000 a year. The type of work Claire does makes her a technical worker. The salaries Marc and Claire earn account for most of their income each year.

A third source of income is rent. In 1981 the Lorraines bought a large house that needed extensive repair work. After fixing up the house, they divided it into three apartments. They live in one and rent the other two. Their income from rent is $725 a month, or $8,700 a year.

A fourth source of income for the Lorraines is interest on their savings. Buying and repairing their house took up most of the Lorraines' savings, and much of their income is used to repay the loan on their house. They earn about $700 in interest each year. The total income of the Lorraines is $44,400 per year.

In measuring the national income by job category, all of a family's income is put in the group of the major wage earner. Since Marc has worked the longest and is paid the most, the Lorraines' total family income is counted in the artisan category.

The Lorraines hope their income will increase in the future. They want to buy a farm on the coast of Maine where they could spend more time riding and sailing. As Claire says, "We would not be making a lot of money, but we would be doing what we want."

ANALYZING THE CASE STUDY

STEP 1   Gather Evidence

1. List the four sources of income for the Lorraine family.
2. Determine what percentage of their income comes from each source.

STEP 2   Draw a Graph

Draw a pie graph showing approximately what percentage of the Lorraine income comes from each source.

STEP 3   Read Graphs

If Marc lost his business and Claire became the major wage earner, how would the level of income of the Lorraine family change? How would measurement of the income level change for the graph, Income by Job Category (page 173)?

STEP 4   Consider Costs and Benefits

List the economic costs and benefits to the Lorraines of investing in a farm on the coast of Maine.

The Information Society

by John Naisbitt (1929—)

Your great-grandparents probably earned money working directly with the earth as farmers or miners. Your parents probably earn money working with products or services. They may be manufacturing goods or providing consumer services. What will you work with in the future? According to economic consultant John Naisbitt, you probably will work with information. In this excerpt taken from *Megatrends: Ten New Directions Transforming Our Lives,* Naisbitt says the United States is changing to an information society. More and more jobs will be based on creating, handling, and using information. As you read, consider how you can prepare now to live in an information society.

66 The occupational history of the United States tells a lot about us. For example, in 1979 the most numerous occupation in the United States became clerk, succeeding laborer, succeeding farmer. Farmer, laborer, clerk—that is a brief history of the United States. Farmers, who as recently as the turn of the century constituted more than one-third of the total labor force, now are less than 3 percent of the workforce. In fact, today there are more people employed full-time in our [colleges and] universities than in agriculture.

The second largest classification after clerk is professional, completely in tune with the new information society where knowledge is the critical ingredient. The demand for professional workers has grown substantially since 1960. This demand has grown even more dramatically than the rising need for clerical workers.

Professional workers are almost all information workers—lawyers, teachers, engineers, doctors, architects, accountants, librarians, newspaper reporters, social workers, nurses, and clergy. Of course, everyone needs some kind of knowledge to perform a job. Industrial workers, machinists, welders, and jig makers, for example, are very knowledgeable about the tasks they perform. The difference is that for professional and clerical workers, the creation, processing, and distribution of information *is* the job.

In 1960 professional workers were the fifth largest job category. They numbered about 7.5 million workers, or 11 percent of the workforce. By 1981 that group had more than doubled to 16.4 million workers and made up almost 17 percent of the overall workforce.

In an industrial society the key resource is capital; 100 years ago, a lot of people may have known how to build a steel plant, but not very many could get the money to build one. Consequently, access to the system was limited. But in our new society, the key resource is information. Information is not the only resource, but it is the most important one. We now mass-produce information the way we used to mass-produce cars. In the information society, we have systems to produce knowledge and expand our brainpower. We now mass-produce knowledge, and this knowledge is the driving force of our economy.

The new source of power is not money in the hands of a few, but information in the hands of many.

In an information economy, value is increased not by labor, but by knowledge. By looking at one of our major exports we may realize the value of knowledge. In a day of shrinking United States markets abroad, American companies have little trouble selling their knowledge, their expertise, and their management skills. In 1980 American companies earned $60 billion in overseas sales of services—20 percent of the world market share.

Nevertheless, the notion that knowledge can create economic value is only now beginning to be considered seriously. Edward Denison, an economist with the United States Department of Commerce, did a study to find out which factors contributed most to economic growth from 1948

This advertising agency executive uses information in many forms in his work. In the future, more and more jobs will involve the storage, manipulation, and transmission of information. Fewer and fewer jobs will involve manual labor.

to 1973. Denison concluded that about two-thirds of the economic growth was due to the increased size and education of the workforce and the greater pool of knowledge available to workers.

David Birch, a professor at the Massachusetts Institute of Technology, has demonstrated that of the 19 million new jobs created in the United States during the 1970s—more than ever before in our history—only 5 percent were in manufacturing and only 11 percent were in the goods-producing sector as a whole. Almost 90 percent, then—17 million new jobs—were not in the goods-producing sector. As Birch says, "We are working ourselves out of the manufacturing business and into the thinking business.**"**

From *Megatrends*, by John Naisbitt.

UNDERSTANDING THE READING

1. Give five examples of the kinds of workers whom John Naisbitt views as information workers.
2. According to Naisbitt, how is an information worker different from a worker who simply needs knowledge to do a job?
3. Explain what Naisbitt means when he says, "knowledge can create economic value."

Section 1 Review

Understanding Sources of Income

1. List three examples of a transfer payment. In each example, determine who is transferring what to whom.
2. What is the largest source of income in the United States?

Sources of Income Today

1. What changes might occur in education as a result of the rise of the information society?
2. **Challenge:** In many families now, both husband and wife work. Think of one economic change that has occurred as a result of the two-income family.
3. Why does the office worker in the cartoon feel his job is secure?

"I figure if they fire me, they'll have to pay me a week extra until I clean out my desk."

2 Income Distribution

SECTION OVERVIEW

Few, if any, traits are distributed equally among all people. For example, some people are naturally more intelligent than others. You probably know students who seem to get high grades with little effort and others who work hard to pass. Most often, though, the amount of natural intelligence people have is less important than how they use it. In the economy, distribution of resources is not equal. Some people are rich, others are poor. In this section, you will learn how income and wealth are distributed in the market system of the United States.

ECONOMIC VOCABULARY

income   distribution of income   median   mean   wealth

Income Distribution in the Market

In the market system of the United States, a person's income is determined by how the market values that person's resources and skills. Income is the money a person receives in exchange for work or property. Individuals, such as doctors, whose skills society values, receive high incomes. People who own valuable resources, such as capital to invest or land to develop, also receive high incomes. Those whose skills or resources society values less receive lower incomes. A market system places different values on skills; so incomes of Americans vary. The charts in this section show the distribution of income in the United States. Distribution of income is a term describing the division of income in an economy.

Measuring Distribution

The distribution of income is commonly measured two ways. Each method is useful for measuring income distribution over different periods of time.

One method shows the number of families receiving different amounts of income. This method is useful for showing the gap between the rich and the poor during the course of one year. Over time, however, changes in prices and incomes may distort this measurement.

Another method is more useful for analyzing changes in the distribution of income over a period of several years. To measure income distribution using this method, the population is divided into five equal groups: (1) the richest 20 percent, (2) the next richest 20 percent, (3) the middle 20 percent, (4) the next poorest 20 percent and (5) the poorest 20 percent. Then, each group's percentage of the total national income is measured. This method shows the relative wealth of the poorest 20 percent and the wealthiest 20 percent of the people. Since 1947, the percentage of the national income going to each fifth of the population has remained almost constant.

179

Distribution of Family Income by Income Group

Income	Number of Families	Percent of Families
Under $5,000	3,539,000	5.8
$5,000 to $9,999	7,017,000	11.5
$10,000 to $14,999	8,298,000	13.6
$15,000 to $19,999	7,688,000	12.6
$20,000 to $24,999	7,932,000	13.0
$25,000 to $34,999	12,325,000	20.2
$35,000 to $49,999	9,091,000	14.9
$50,000 and over	5,430,000	8.9
Total	61,320,000	100.0

Explanation

The table shows the distribution of income by families in the United States in 1981. The table shows the number of families in each income category. It also shows the percentage of all families in each category.

Chart Skills

1. What percentage of families received less than $5,000 in 1981?
2. How many families received between $15,000 and $34,999 in 1981?

Distribution of Family Income by Fifths

Percentage of All Income Received

Poorest Fifth of Families	Next Poorest Fifth of Families	Middle Fifth of Families	Next Richest Fifth of Families	Richest Fifth of Families
5%	11%	17%	24%	42%

Explanation

This chart shows how much of the nation's income goes to each fifth of the nation's families. Since the nation has about 60 million families, each fifth represents about 12 million families. The numbers for each group tell the percentage of the nation's income received by that group. In 1981, the poorest fifth of families received 5 percent of the nation's income. Therefore, the 12 million poorest families received a total of 5 percent of all income received by the people of the United States. The richest fifth of families received 42 percent of the nation's income.

Chart Skills

1. How much of the nation's income did the middle fifth of the population receive?
2. How much of the nation's income did the poorest 40 percent of families receive?

Median and Mean Income

Charts on income distribution show the spread of income. To focus on how much a typical family receives, economists look at two different statistics. One is the median income. Median is the middle number in a list of numbers arranged in order. Thus, the median family income is the income of the family in the middle between the richest and the poorest families. In the same year, the median family income in the United States in 1981 was $22,388. In 1981, half of the families earned more than $22,388 and half earned less.

180

Median income families shop carefully for the goods they need. For an average family in the United States, spending for groceries is an important part of their budget each week.

Median income is often used to compare the economic condition of different groups of people. For example, in 1981 the median income for families of white collar workers was $31,101. In the same year, the median income for families of blue collar workers was $23,417.

A second statistic used to indicate how much a typical family receives is the mean. The mean is determined by dividing the total quantity by the number of units. Therefore, the mean family income is the result of dividing the total income of the nation by the number of families. In 1981, the mean family income was $25,838.

Income and Wealth

The money a person receives is income. Income is not the same as wealth. Wealth is any resource that can be used to produce income. An individual's possessions, such as a house, a car, or a stereo, are part of that person's wealth. Each of these could be sold to produce income. Savings accounts and corporation stocks are types of wealth that usually produce income. Labor skills, such as the ability to program a computer, are also a form of wealth. But in determining an individual's wealth, labor skills are not counted because they are difficult to measure. In addition, an individual's debts are subtracted from personal wealth. A person with many valuable possessions but many debts may have no more wealth than a person with few possessions but no debts.

People with similar incomes may have very different amounts of wealth. Consider two women who receive an income of $25,000 a year. One earns all of her income working at a bank. The other receives her $25,000 income from dividends on stock worth $250,000. Aside from the stock the second woman owns, the possessions and debts of the two are similar. The difference in stock ownership, though, is large. The second woman is much wealthier than the first woman.

Though many people own some stock and other forms of wealth, only a small part of the population owns much of the wealth. Only 1 percent of the wealthiest families own about 20 percent of the nation's wealth. The top 8 percent own almost 60 percent. In general, ownership of wealth is distributed far less equally than is income.

REVIEWING THE CONCEPT

Developing Vocabulary

1. Define income distribution.
2. What is the difference between median and mean?
3. How does wealth differ from income?

1. What determines how income is distributed in a market system?
2. What evidence shows that a gap exists between the rich and the poor in the United States?
3. Why is there such a difference between the median and the mean incomes in the United States?
4. How much of the nation's wealth is owned by the wealthiest 1 percent of families in the United States?

CASE STUDY

Poverty in America

The debate on the distribution of income often focuses on the conditions of the poor in the United States. Carla Sanderson is one of America's poor. On November 6, 1982, Carla and her three children dined on frozen waffles and water. Although the children complained, Carla knew that her children would have to eat waffles or nothing. Carla's $718 monthly take-home pay had paid the $365 for the month's rent and utilities, and some other bills. Food stamps were already several days late in arriving. Until they came in the mail, there was no way to purchase food.

Carla had grown up in a middle income family. She found it hard to admit her poverty. She said, "To admit the truth, I am poor. The last week in August we ate oatmeal three times a day because that's what was left in the cupboard; can you believe that?"

In 1982, the Bureau of the Census defined poverty as an income of $9,862 a year for a family of four. This amount was $1,000 more than Carla Sanderson earned as a secretary for a local government agency in a small New England city. According to the Census Bureau study, the number of poor had grown steadily since 1979, when 26.1 million Americans fit the definition. By 1982 the number was 34.4 million, 15 percent of the total population. This number was the highest since 1965, when it stood at 17.3 percent.

Poverty is distributed unevenly in the United States. Of all American households headed by women in the early 1980s, 36 percent lived in poverty. The poor included one out of every three black families and nearly the same proportion of Hispanic families. Of families classified as white, 12 percent were considered poor. Poverty remains largely a big-city problem, but as Carla Sanderson's case suggests, it can be found elsewhere in America too.

About a year before the Sanderson family was forced to eat oatmeal three times a day toward the end of the month, Carla had left her husband in California. He was sick with alcoholism; Carla worried about the safety of their children. Her youngest child was then 2 years old. "I decided it was time to take control of my life again," she said. "I sold my possessions, forwarded 27 cartons to relatives, packed two foam mattresses and three children into my station wagon, and headed home. I was really feeling adventurous—sort of a reverse pioneer—as I headed east in my wagon. I had never camped out and had never done any long-distance driving. Twelve weary days later we arrived." Within two weeks she had found an apartment and a job.

The rent for their new apartment was nearly 50 percent of Carla's income. However, the neighborhood was quiet and near a good elementary school. Carla was determined to stay there no matter how difficult is was to meet expenses.

Carla bought clothing in thrift shops—stores selling used but serviceable clothes. For a time she was eligible for a federally supported bus service to a day-care center for her youngest child. However, she could not afford after-school care for the other two children. They came home each school day to an empty house. Carla received $60 a month from the federal- and state-funded program for parents with children under 18. In 1982, however, government budget cuts eliminated both the bus service and her child aid. Without these government programs, Carla had to rely on income from her job.

Studies indicate that Carla's experience as one of the poor is not unusual. She was poor because her job paid too little to meet her basic expenses. A large portion of Americans living below the poverty level work at least part of the time. Their need for aid is occasional, not constant. A full-time job at a minimum wage provides $6,868 a year; aid payments do not equal that amount.

The pool of working mothers benefits employers who rely on cheap labor. It also benefits the consumers of their products. Among the employers are hospitals; hotels; motels; restaurants; manufacturers of textiles, shoes, and clothing; and employers of such seasonal laborers as fruit and vegetable harvesters.

Unemployment was not one of Carla Sanderson's problems. She had a job, though it did not pay well. Stretching her income to meet daily expenses was her main economic problem. "I don't know

Many people buy generic foods at supermarkets in order to stay within their budgets.

183

what else will happen this winter," she said. "Last year we managed to stay warm, thanks to the federal heating assistance grant. This year there are going to be more cuts—maybe I won't be eligible. Right now, I don't want to know."

ANALYZING THE CASE STUDY

STEP 1   Clarify the Issue

1. What is the definition of poverty used by the government?
2. What is your definition of poverty?
3. Do you expect that a poor person would have a view of poverty that differs from yours or that of the government? Explain your answer.

STEP 2   Gather Evidence

1. How many Americans does the government consider poor?
2. What groups of people are most likely to be poor?

STEP 3   Consider Costs and Benefits

List the economic costs and benefits to society of including a large number of poor people.

The Zero-Sum Game

by Lester Thurow   (1938-   )

For someone to win in basketball, baseball, and football, someone else must lose. Lester Thurow, an economics professor at Massachusetts Institute of Technology and a columnist, calls this a zero-sum situation. Every gain in one place is matched by a loss somewhere else. He considers income distribution a zero-sum game. Every economic decision changes the distribution of income. Whenever someone gains income, someone loses. Thurow argues that people should be aware of these consequences when considering public economic policies. As you read this excerpt taken from Thurow's book, *The Zero-Sum Society,* think about how, in your opinion, income should be distributed.

❝Our economic problems are solvable. For most of our problems there are several solutions. But in each solution someone must suffer large economic losses. No one wants to volunteer this role. Everyone wants someone else to suffer the necessary economic losses, and as a consequence none of the possible solutions can be adopted.

Our political and economic structure simply is not able to cope with an economy that has a substantial zero-sum element. A zero-sum game is any game where the losses exactly equal the winnings. All sporting events are zero-sum games. For every winner there is a loser, and winners can exist only if losers exist. What the winning gambler wins, the losing gambler must lose.

184

When there are large losses to be shared, any economic decision has a large zero-sum element. The economic gains may exceed the economic losses, but the losses are so large as to outweigh many of the gains. What is more important, the gains and losses are not given to the same individuals or groups. On average, society may be better off, but this average hides a large number of people who are much better off and large numbers of people who are much worse off. If you are among those who are worse off, the fact that someone else's income has risen by more than your income has fallen is of little comfort.

Given the problem of loss allocation, it is not surprising that government stands in the middle of winners and losers. Each group wants government to use its power to protect it and to force others to do what is in the general interest. Energy producers want prices to go up, thus the income of energy consumers will go down. Energy consumers want prices to go down and thus the income of producers will be less. Each understands that the government could stop them from having to suffer such losses. Each of us demands what is impossible. But as the demands for protection grow, the basic assumptions of the democratic process are slowly destroyed.

To be workable, a democracy assumes that public decisions are made with a substantial majority of concerned but disinterested citizens who will prevent policies from being shaped by those with direct economic self-interests. Decisions for the good of society are supposed to be produced by those concerned but disinterested citizens. As government grows, however, the number of such citizens shrinks. Almost everyone now has a direct economic stake in what government does in an area such as energy.

Fortunately or unfortunately, we have reached a point where it is no longer possible to solve our economic problems and ignore how the solutions affect the distribution of income. The problems and the options are clear enough that everyone both knows and cares about the effects on everyone's income that will follow. Deregulating the price of energy might be the efficient thing to do, but we have great trouble doing so. Everyone whose income will go down knows it, objects, and stands ready to fight the proposal. Since government must alter the distribution of income if it is to solve our economic problems, we have to have a government that is capable of making decisions about fairness. Whose income ought to go up, and whose income ought to go down? To do this, however, we need to know what is a fair distribution of economic resources. What is a fair procedure for distributing income? Unless we can specify what is fair, we cannot say whose income ought to go down. Unless we can say whose income ought to go down, we cannot solve our economic problems.

This immediately forces a democracy into a difficult situation. Whatever the country decides about the just distribution of resources, there will be a large number (perhaps even a majority) of unhappy voters. Distributional issues are highly controversial and precisely the kind of issues that democracies find most difficult to solve. It is not we versus them, but us versus us in a zero-sum game. **"**

From *The Zero-Sum Society*, by Lester Thurow.

UNDERSTANDING THE READING

1. How does Lester Thurow define zero-sum games? Why does he consider economic decisions similar to a zero-sum games?
2. What is the role of government in zero-sum situations?
3. Why is it difficult for a democracy to deal with zero-sum situations?

Section 2 Review

Understanding Income Distribution

1. The United States economy has grown since 1945. What has happened to the gap between the rich and the poor?
2. Explain whether you would rather have a large income or be wealthy. Why?

Income Distribution Today

1. Explain whether you agree or disagree with the following statement: "The existence of a group of people who receive disproportionately high incomes encourages everyone below them to become more productive."
2. Explain whether you would prefer to work for someone else or start your own small business.
3. **Challenge:** What implications does the rise of the information society have for education?

The performance of students in school influences their income in the future.

3 Effects of Spending

SECTION OVERVIEW

When individuals receive any income, whether as allowance, paycheck, or gift, most of that income is spent. Spending becomes income for someone else. When you spend $5 for a movie, you probably never think of it again. However, the $5 spent for the movie is more than $5 when considered from an economist's point of view. The money each individual spends multiplies throughout the economy as others receive and spend parts of it. In addition, the choice of movie you and others make can lead to investment spending. More movies are made and more theaters built. This section will help you understand how spending results in changes throughout the economy.

ECONOMIC VOCABULARY

multiplier effect   investment spending   acceleration principle

The Multiplier Effect

Nothing in the economy can change without causing changes throughout the entire economy. Think of what happens when workers receive a pay raise. As consumers, these individuals have more money to spend. As they increase their spending, businesses receive greater income. Usually, however, neither consumers nor businesses spend all of their income. Some is saved. The amount each spends differs depending on total income and economic conditions. Each time a dollar is spent, though, the circular flow of money causes a part of it to go into the hands of someone else who spends it again. The $100 that one consumer spends is multiplied by all the other individuals who will receive and then spend parts of the original $100. The process of expanding the number of people and businesses spending money is called the multiplier effect. Each original dollar spent, in effect, multiplies itself by causing more dollars to be spent.

The multiplier effect works this way. Suppose you received $10 for your birthday. Half you save and the other half you spend on a movie. The theater owners then use half, or $2.50 to pay part of the salary of Betty, the cashier. Betty uses $1.25 for a hamburger, and the restaurant owner uses $0.63 to pay the waitress, Cynthia. She, in turn, uses $0.31 to help pay for a new blouse. Each person spent half of his or her income. Some part of the original $10 was received and respent, in effect multiplying the value of the original dollar. The graph and chart show the multiplier effect.

The original amount spent was $10. After this money circulated through the economy another $10 was spent. The total, $20, was twice the original spending. Thus, if people spend half of their income, the multiplier effect is 2. Each original dollar spent causes $2 in extra spending.

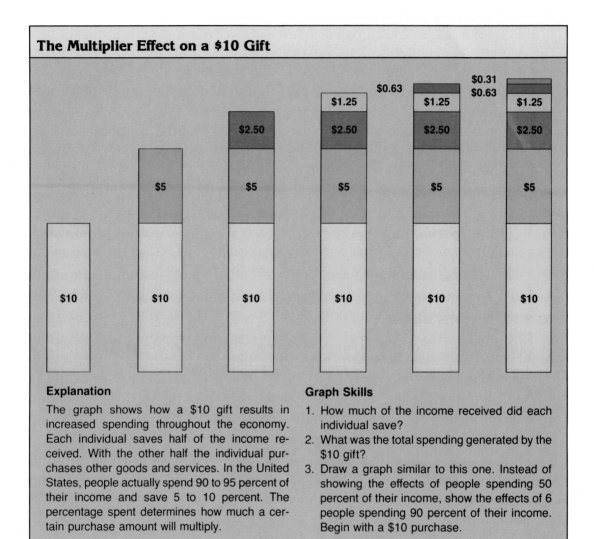

The Multiplier Effect on a $10 Gift

Explanation

The graph shows how a $10 gift results in increased spending throughout the economy. Each individual saves half of the income received. With the other half the individual purchases other goods and services. In the United States, people actually spend 90 to 95 percent of their income and save 5 to 10 percent. The percentage spent determines how much a certain purchase amount will multiply.

Graph Skills

1. How much of the income received did each individual save?
2. What was the total spending generated by the $10 gift?
3. Draw a graph similar to this one. Instead of showing the effects of people spending 50 percent of their income, show the effects of 6 people spending 90 percent of their income. Begin with a $10 purchase.

On a large scale, suppose a manufacturer of motorcycles spends $10 million on a new factory. Various people and firms receive that $10 million. People affected include the workers who build the factory, the contractors who supply the materials for its construction, the architects who design it, the plumbers who put in the pipes, and many more. Part of the money received is spent. Some of it is saved and some goes to the government in the form of taxes.

The multiplier can be any number. For example, if people spent two-thirds of their income, the multiplier would be 3. Each original dollar spent would cause a total of $3 in extra spending.

The Acceleration Principle

A similar principle affects businesses when they spend more on capital goods. Spending on capital goods is called investment spending. For example, a shoe manufacturer has 10 machines. Each one makes 10,000 pairs of shoes yearly, yielding a total output of 100,000 pairs a year. Each ma-

The Acceleration Principle

Year	Sales		Number of Machines	New Machines	New Machines Plus Replacement Machines	
	Amount/% Change				Number/% Change	
1	100,000		10	0	1	
2	110,000	(+10)	11	1	2	(100)
3	120,000	(+9)	12	1	2	(0)
4	120,000	(0)	12	0	1	(−50)

Explanation

The chart shows how an increase in sales can result in an increase in investment spending. Each year, the company is required to set aside the replacement cost of one machine. In years when consumer demand increases, the company is required to pay for an additional new machine as well.

Chart Skills

1. How many more replacement machines must the company pay for in year 2 than in year 1?
2. How much does the change in investment spending vary over the four years shown in the graph?
3. What is the relationship between percent change and amount of sales?

chine lasts 10 years; so the cost of their replacement can be divided over 10 years. The company's total investment spending is, therefore, one machine per year.

Assume that consumers' incomes increase. Consumers now have more money to spend, and so this year they buy 110,000 pairs of shoes—10 percent more than the year before. To meet this new demand, the company will have to pay for an extra machine in addition to the replacement cost of an original machine. The total investment spending is, therefore, two machines. Thus, investment spending has increased 100 percent as the result of a 10 percent increase in consumer spending. This change in investment spending caused by a change in consumer spending is known as the acceleration principle. The chart illustrates this principle.

Notice in the chart what happens if, in the third year, consumers buy 120,000 pairs of shoes. The total investment spending is still two machines, the same as in the second year. In other words, consumer spending has increased another 10 percent, but investment spending has stayed the same. If in the fourth year consumers buy the same number of shoes as in the third year (120,000), the company will have to pay only the replacement cost of an original machine. Total investment spending is now one machine. Consumer spending has remained the same, but investment spending has declined by 50 percent. Although sales are still rising, investment decreases.

Effects of Spending

A decline in investment spending will result in a rise in unemployment. Since the unemployed spend less money, consumer spending declines. Before long, the general economy is in a declining cycle. Investment spending declines because overall spending declines, which causes more declines in investment spending, and so on.

Similarly, when the country's economy is prosperous, unemployment declines. As more people get jobs, more money is spent

189

When money is passed from person to person to pay for goods and services, the spending power of the money is multiplied.

on goods and services. As people buy more goods, producers spend more on factories and machines, which, in turn, creates more jobs.

This interaction of the multiplier effect and the acceleration principle affects economic growth. These two factors in combination with changing consumer attitudes make it difficult to predict economic conditions in the future.

REVIEWING THE CONCEPT

Developing Vocabulary

1. Define multiplier effect.

2. Explain how investment spending and the multiplier effect work together.
3. What is the acceleration principle?

Mastering Facts

1. Using an example, explain how the multiplier effect works.
2. The circular flow of money is important to the multiplier effect. Explain why they work together.
3. How does the money people save affect the multiplier?
4. Draw a demand graph that shows the demand for shoes before and after the government lowers taxes.

CASE STUDY

The Multiplier in Action

The interaction of the multiplier effect and the acceleration principle affects the economy of each state and each city as well as the national economy. South Dakota's Governor William Janklow may never use the term multiplier effect, but he knows how it works. Encouraging firms to move to South

Dakota means that investment spending will bring more jobs for his citizens and more money to the state.

South Dakota has several traits that industry finds undesirable. The cold winters, erratic rainfall, and rugged landscape create problems that other areas need not

After Citibank moved into South Dakota, increased investment spending brought more jobs for citizens and more money to the state.

confront. South Dakota is consistently near the bottom of the country's per capita income tables.

Under Governor Janklow some surprising things are happening to the nation's 45th most populous state. South Dakota's two largest cities, Sioux Falls on the eastern edge and Rapid City on the western fringe, are booming. Big banks, led by Citicorp, are moving in, investing millions in construction and payroll. Small manufacturers are relocating to South Dakota. The statewide unemployment rate is less than half the national average.

This growth is not an accident. When Citicorp announced several years ago that it wanted to escape some of New York's consumer loan rate restrictions, South Dakota took advantage of this economic opportunity to attract the banking industry. While other states debated over banking legislation to attract Citicorp, South Dakota's legislature passed a bill welcoming out-of-state banks. One firm, Citibank, built a $25 million Sioux Falls complex that brought jobs and money to South Dakota. With 2,000 workers, Citibank is now the state's third largest private employer.

States like South Dakota that have few large cities have a capital shortage problem. Without large cities to attract industry and business, almost no investment spending occurs. Since the multiplier effect requires spending original dollars, the more money available to spend, the greater the effect of the multiplier. After Citibank opened in Sioux Falls, bank deposits in the city of 81,000 residents increased from $650 million to $6 billion. These bank deposits are a fund from which other firms can borrow in order to invest in South Dakota. This increase in deposits also represents additional money individuals and businesses have been able to save because of an increase in income. Governor Janklow refers to his state's banking and insurance legislation as jobs bills.

In addition to attracting banks, South Dakota has encouraged other businesses to relocate there. The state has no corporate or personal income tax, low workers' compensation and real estate taxes, and a comparatively low cost of living.

"What's wrong with our lot in life?" Governor Janklow asks. "We never really got to prosper. I'm tired of being the farm

191

team for the rest of America." The investment spending of big business coupled with the multiplier effect on the original investment and salaries to workers are bringing prosperity to South Dakota.

ANALYZING THE CASE STUDY

STEP 1 Gather Evidence

1. What steps has South Dakota taken to attract new business? What were the economic tradeoffs of each of its actions?
2. Explain how the addition of new businesses will help South Dakota become more prosperous.

STEP 2 Examine Change

1. What changes are taking place in the type and number of jobs available in South Dakota?

2. Citibank spent $25 million on construction costs alone. If the multiplier was 3, how much additional spending was added to South Dakota's economy?
3. Explain the effects of the additional money available in bank deposits in Sioux Falls.

STEP 3 Predict Further Change

1. What additional changes may occur in the job market in South Dakota?
2. What changes may occur in the population of South Dakota?
3. Explain how the changes may affect South Dakota's two large cities.
4. How might the success of South Dakota in attracting business affect other states? Describe changes other states may take in order to compete with South Dakota.

READING

Frugality in America

by Frank Trippett   (1926-   )

The multiplier and accelerator are two of the factors that determine how a market economy works. However, a market economy also depends on the attitude of consumers toward spending. How much are they spending, and how much are they saving? How have American attitudes toward frugality—careful and efficient management of resources—changed? Changes in these attitudes affect how much Americans spend, and, in turn, the economy. Frank Trippett, a writer for *Time* magazine, looked at how American attitudes toward frugality and spending are changing. In this essay, he examines some economic trends. As you read the excerpt, think about the effects of these trends on the American economy.

66 **D**eep in his recent State of the Union speech, which was mostly devoted to world affairs, the President [Reagan] inserted a two-word sentence of great domestic import: "Eliminate waste." It is likely that a good many Americans reacted to this presidential plea for conservation, as they would to any other, with a silent question: Who—me? Such bewilderment is understandable. The truth is that during the nation's rush to mid-century prosperity the notion of individual frugality practically went out of business. "Prodigality is the spirit of the era," Social Critic Vance Packard declared in *The Waste Makers* 20 years ago. There has been no reason since to change that judgement. "Waste not, want not" has persisted only as a saying, and most people have fallen out of the habit of taking it personally.

The good news is that thanks to the bad news of the energy crisis and skyhigh prices, the prevalent habit of mindless waste may be in the early stages of a reversal. At least some Americans are beginning to pay attention to small savings that were regarded as inconsequential only yesterday. A new scrimpy spirit is most noticeable in direct efforts to conserve gas and other fuels, but it is also emerging in the other routine logistics of daily living.

People are leaning more and more to high-mileage cars. Drivers of all types of autos have begun catching on to the knack of cutting off the engine during long waits. Quite a few Americans have taken to walking or biking on shorter trips, and not just for the exercise. Householders have conspicuously started applying common sense as well as insulation to cut down on heat waste. Why not, it might be asked, with heating oil prices [so high]?

Still, a mix of motives—the atmosphere of crisis as well as financial reasons—underlies the new spirit. More people are scheduling meatless meals. Some are raising vegetables for reasons other than taste. Solid citizens have taken to buying used clothing, and garage sales and tag sales are chic in many neighborhoods. Families are also turning to the secondhand markets for things like bikes and lawnmowers. The oldtime comforter is replacing the electric blanket in some bedrooms. In certain areas people are taking more shoes to shops for repair; in others, the business of mending goods like handbags, belts and golf bags is up.

The do-it-yourself trend in carpentry, plumbing, electrical work and auto repair is winning ever more converts. People seem increasingly willing to channel the refuse of daily existence—cans, bottles, newspapers —into recycling systems. Some restaurants report more calls for doggie bags for taking home leftovers. A few garbage collectors complain about a decrease in good recyclable items in the trash. Observers report an increase in the number of otherwise genteel [polite and refined] people scouting curbside junk heaps for usable stuff such as carpets and furniture. Many people, it is said, are even learning to turn out lights when they are not in use.

Such signs of thrift and prudence have been popping up all over the country, but they have been closely monitored in California. There, in surveys and follow-ups, Stanford University Researchers Dorothy

Leonard-Barton and Everett M. Rogers have been trying to get a fix on how Americans are voluntarily adjusting to the prospect of dwindling resources and limited buying power. Concludes Rogers: "It is possible that while our Federal Government talks about a lot of conservation, we are seeing people voluntarily doing a great deal of frugal living. It's possible that these people represent a prototype for many Americans for tomorrow."

What is certain is that the people turning frugal today are returning to a prototype that was quite typical in the United States not so long ago. Indeed, most Americans once practiced frugality as though it were instinctive, or even religious. It may be well to recall those days for more than nostalgic reasons: they also offer proof that the country has a capability that it could need again if times get truly hard. Moreover, the old ways may even come as an amazement to younger Americans who grew up during the virtually invulnerable affluence [wealth] that followed World War II.

Before that war, although the word recycling was seldom if ever heard, Americans individually recycled food, clothing and other civilized artifacts so assiduously [thoroughly] that what was left could truly be called garbage and trash. Perishables and manufactured stuff alike were subjected to use, reuse and then, by transformation and mending, to yet more use. Food especially got treated as though there would never be quite enough. One day's chicken became next day's hash, and yesterday's leftover vegetable wound up with bones and gristle in soups and stews. Stale bread was crushed into cooking crumbs and egg shells were often used to settle the grounds in boiled coffee.

"Waste not" was more than a motto; it was law. Torn stockings wound up not in the trash but in the sewing basket. Trivial slivers of soap were collected in little wire cages that could be swished through sink water to produce suds for dishwashing. Frayed shirt collars got turned and when the garment became hopeless on the second go-round, the buttons were salvaged and the fabric was channeled into a rag bag, whence it might emerge as a dish cloth, a shoe wiper, a hand towel. Or it might wind up, along with parts of old skirts, dresses, blouses, pajamas and neckties, as part of a patchwork quilt or a rag rug.

Paper of all varieties was hoarded [saved] for reuse as though it were as valuable as fabric. Tissue went into a gift-wrapping kit. Waxy bread packaging became wrappers for school lunches. Brown paper was smoothed and folded for the day on which something had to go out by parcel post. Old newspapers served multiple purposes: they started fires, [and] insulated cots and walls . . . To want not was to salvage even the straight pins that fastened new garments into neat folds. And it was also to maintain bins, boxes and cans as storage vaults for old screws, nails, bolts, rubber bands, paper clips, thumbtacks and—well, name it. In those days every sort of container was coveted, with cigar boxes especially prized by children as chests for personal treasures that did not often fill up entire rooms.

It would be false to suggest that Americans have been unanimously thrifty in all earlier times. The settlement of the continent, as history teaches, was accompanied by a squandering of natural resources and wildlife on a tragic scale. By the ripening end of the 19th century, Thorstein Veblen could chart, in *The Theory of the Leisure Class,* the "conspicuous waste" that had become the crass [tasteless] proof of status among the well off. Still, most Americans were not in that privileged class. In fact, they still had the hang of their frugal daily ways when these became the occasion—with everybody saving everything including tinfoil and kitchen fat for the war effort—of the last great popular conserving binge the nation has known.

Then, suddenly, old-fashioned frugality was out of style. What happened? The answer is that the consumer society got born, the fruit of the nation's determination to extend and expand the economic successes that war production had achieved. Growing production and high employment were the aims, and high and growing consumption was indispensable to the formula. Thrift survived in the moral code, but both commercial and political leaders urged people not to save what they had but to get more of what was available. In a business dip of the late 1950s, somebody asked President Eisenhower what citizens could do to help the situation. Ike's terse reply: "Buy anything." Americans, by and large, became used to doing just that.

The consumer society's success in achieving abundance was stunning, but not all of the costs showed up on the ledger sheets. One of them that did not was the spirit of frugality. It was, as well, violently broken down by the coming of a cornucopia of goods, from plates and cups to razors and lighters, that were made of synthetics and were designed to be used briefly and thrown away. The whole way of doing business soon produced what Futurist Alvin Toffler called a "throw-away mentality".

Now, at last, the success of the consumer economy, as well as its excess, has brought the country right back to the need for individual frugality. It may be that Americans will never again find it necessary, or even feasible, to save slivers of soap and the straight pins out of shirts. Still, the need to curtail waste seems to be homing in again. It is consoling to know that the spirit is there, needing only reawakening by the irresistable force of necessity. **99**

From "The Fall and Rise of U.S. Frugality," by Frank Trippet.

UNDERSTANDING THE READING

1. Explain what the author meant when he said, "'Waste not' was more than a motto; it was law."

2. If the essay is correct in predicting that Americans will be more frugal, saving more and spending less, how will this attitude affect the United States economy?
3. The attitudes of Americans toward the economy and their work are important factors affecting the economy. How do these factors affect economic predictions?

Section 3 Review

Understanding Effects of Spending

1. What effect would an increase in demand for shoes have on total investment spending?
2. Explain how investment spending and the acceleration principle work together.

Effects of Spending Today

1. Americans have become used to the relatively high price of gasoline. What might happen if the price again doubled rapidly? How would it affect the economy of the nation?
2. **Challenge:** As firms and workers move to the Sunbelt, how will the economy of large cities in the Midwest and the Northeast be affected?
3. **Challenge:** What are the costs and benefits for the economy of high levels of spending by consumers and businesses?

Recycling glass is a way to conserve resources.

Americans *at Work*

Meet Mary Farrar
Contractor

Mary Farrar is her husband's boss. However, as she remarked, "Maybe that's not a good way to put it. He'll be working with us." Us refers to Farrar's Hallmark Construction, in Kansas City, Missouri.

After 20 years of being a wife and mother, Mary Farrar took a job as a bookkeeper for a firm that contructed steel-frame buildings. There she learned the economics of building. She soon progressed from keeping payroll and other accounts to proofreading architect's plans for a building. From there, she learned to estimate the costs involved in construction. When the company's owner refused her offer to buy into the firm, her husband urged her to start her own construction company. Mary Farrar took her husband's advice and formed System Erectors Inc.

Farrar's first contract was for erecting two steel frames for warehouses. The contract was for $250,000. It was a shoestring operation. The firm hired workers laid off from other jobs, bought used tools, and had difficulty meeting its payroll. But it had made a start.

System erectors reached $2 million in warehouse construction contracts within two years. Then economic recession struck, and no one wanted warehouses. Beginning over again, Farrar said, is "an entrepreneur's answer to everything." She started a new company, Hallmark Construction.

Like many entrepreneurs, Farrar wanted her new company to be unusual. Hallmark is not an ordinary construction firm. It offers a onestop operation for those who need buildings but are unfamiliar with the processes and economics of construction. Hallmark finds building sites and handles zoning problems. Zoning problems exist because cities and towns divide their communities into zones, or sections. These zones are reserved for residences, businesses, manufacturing industries, and other types of buildings. It is necessary to go to the local government and sometimes to court to change these restrictions. Hallmark Construction also hires architects and takes care of the general contracting. Contractors often negotiate with various companies, called subcontractors to complete particular parts of a project for example, a plumbing firm usually subcontracts to install the plumbing in a building.

Mary Farrar's husband, Jim, a former sheetmetal worker, joined a solid company. Mary, who learned the economics of construction from personal experience, plans to keep it that way.

Obtaining Personal Credit

Suppose a group of your friends decides to take in a movie after school. You do not have enough money in your wallet to pay for a ticket. One of your friends lends you the money. You go to the movie and pay back the loan the following day.

When you borrowed money, you were using credit, or money borrowed for a period of time. Most Americans who use credit pay the lender interest, or a charge for borrowing the money. In the early 1980s, the average consumer in the United States owed $6,300 in credit borrowed. People use credit for several reasons.

First, most people borrow money because they lack cash to buy items they want—especially expensive goods, such as houses, that last a long time. When such goods are bought with credit, the consumer pays for the item gradually or all at once when cash is available later. By buying on credit, the consumer can use the item while paying for it. Second, people use credit for convenience. It is much easier and safer to carry a credit card than cash. Third, credit is used for emergencies. Sometimes unemployment, accidents, or medical expenses occur and cash is not available. Then people may need to borrow funds to help them through a difficult period.

The use of credit can also cause credit problems. Credit buying may cost more than cash purchases because of interest payments. A person who buys too much on credit has to pay a great deal of interest. The usual interest rate on a credit purchase is 1.8 percent per month or 21.6 percent a year on the money owed. Available credit can tempt the consumer to satisfy unlimited wants. Credit can get some people in trouble when it is used irresponsibly.

Obtaining and keeping credit is not difficult for qualified individuals. The following steps outline the basic procedure.

STEP 1   Fill Out an Application

Banks, stores, and lending agencies require you to fill out an application to receive credit. The form usually includes questions about your past credit experience.

STEP 2   Establish Your Character

Institutions granting credit will try to determine whether or not you are an honest and dependable person. You will be asked to list employers, teachers, or others who know you well. These people may be contacted by the institution and asked about your dependability.

STEP 3 Demonstrate Capacity to Pay

Your ability to earn money and use it wisely will be important in obtaining credit. Performing a part-time job well indicates an ability to earn money to repay debts. Maintaining a checking account, building a savings account, and using a bank card all indicate your ability to handle money in a responsible manner.

STEP 4 Repay Your Debts on Time

The best way to obtain credit is to demonstrate that you have successfully used credit before. Consequently, prompt payment is particularly important the first few times you use credit. If you develop the habit of repaying your debts on schedule, you are likely to avoid problems with credit. Then credit can help you run your economic life more smoothly.

ECONOMIC SKILLS TODAY

1. List and explain three reasons for the use of credit.
2. What problems may result from the use of credit?

Enrichment Activities

1. You wish to buy a new car. Investigate the interest charges of at least three sources such as a bank, a credit union, and an automobile dealer's own plan.
2. Collect credit application forms from different department stores. Compare the information asked for on the applications to see similarities and differences.

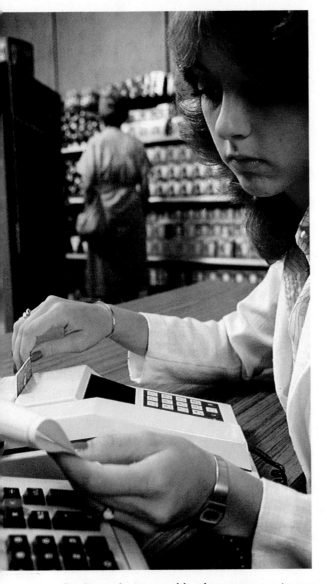

Credit cards are used by the consumer to pay for items. Credit must be paid back with interest, so credit purchases cost more than cash purchases. To obtain a credit card one must demonstrate the capacity to repay debts on time.

CHAPTER SUMMARY

Sources of Income

There are five basic types of income in the United States: (1) employee compensation, (2) proprietor compensation, (3) corporation profit, (4) interest, and (5) rent. Another way to analyze sources of income is by the type of work people perform. There are four basic types: (1) white collar, (2) blue collar, (3) service, and (4) farm. The distribution of income by type of work performed changed as the United States developed from a rural agricultural society into an urban industrial society.

Income Distribution

In the United States market system, incomes are determined by each person's resources—land, labor, and capital. Incomes therefore differ among individuals. The gap between the richest one-fifth of the nation and the poorest one-fifth has remained relatively unchanged since 1947. Median and mean are other terms used to describe how incomes are distributed. The median income is the middle income. The mean is the average income. Income is not the same as wealth. Wealth is any resource that can be used to produce income. In general, wealth is less equally distributed than income.

Effects of Spending

The amount of money people spend multiplies as it ripples through the economy. Each original dollar spent multiplies itself by causing more spending. As the percentage of income spent increases, so does the multiplier. As consumers spend more, firms must invest in capital goods to produce more. This change in investment spending, which results from a change in consumer spending, is called the acceleration principle. The multiplier and acceleraton principle combined with consumer attitudes make economic predictions difficult.

CRITICAL THINKING QUESTIONS

Sources of Income

1. Select from any source, other than this text, five pictures that show people working. Determine from the pictures their major source of income and the type of work they perform.
2. Choose one of the pictures from question 1 and suggest ways the worker could increase his or her income.
3. Give an example of each of the four basic types of work people perform.

Income Distribution

1. Give an example of income an individual may receive from each of the basic resources—land, labor, and capital.
2. In what ways might individuals increase their personal share of the income pie?

Effects of Spending

1. Why is the multiplier effect important for economic growth?
2. If consumers had less money to spend, how would the economy be affected?
3. Give an example of how the multiplier effect, investment spending, and the acceleration principle could work together to affect the economy.

DEVELOPING ECONOMIC SKILLS

1. Name the three major automobile manufacturers in the United States.
2. What percent of the market did each of the three major car manufacturers have in 1946? In 1955? In 1970?
3. Which company or group of companies increased its sales the most between 1965 and 1975?
4. **Challenge:** Based on the relationship between factor and product markets, what assumptions can you make about jobs, income, and purchasing power of workers in the auto industry in 1955? In 1970?

APPLYING ECONOMICS TODAY

1. What evidence might you use to show that we have moved from an industrial society to an information society?
2. Is poverty a relative or an absolute measure? Give your definition of poverty and compare it with the definitions given by your parents and the other students in your class.
3. **Challenge:** An old economic saying is that "power follows property." What property do minority groups possess today, and how do they use it for economic ends?

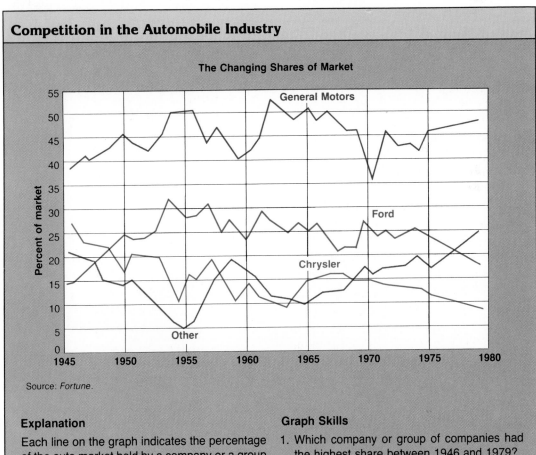

Competition in the Automobile Industry

The Changing Shares of Market

Source: *Fortune.*

Explanation

Each line on the graph indicates the percentage of the auto market held by a company or a group of companies. Imports are included with small domestic companies, in other.

Graph Skills

1. Which company or group of companies had the highest share between 1946 and 1979?
2. Which company or group increased its percentage the most between 1965 and 1979?

CHAPTER 7

Economic Institutions

1 Entrepreneurs

Objective: to understand the factors involved in organizing and operating a small business

2 Corporations

Objective: to understand the organization, advantages, and disadvantages of corporations

3 Unions

Objective: to understand the purpose and structure of unions in the United States market system

202

1 Entrepreneurs

SECTION OVERVIEW

Many children operate their own business, at least on a hot afternoon. They buy a can of frozen lemonade, borrow some cups and a pitcher, and set up a lemonade stand. Many adults wish that they, too, could start their own business. They realize, though, the difficulty and risks involved. As you consider your career, you may dream of being your own boss, of starting your own business. In this section you will learn how small businesses are organized and the challenges they face.

ECONOMIC VOCABULARY

economic institution	sole proprietorship	limited life
entrepreneur	unlimited liability	partnership

Economic Institutions

The capitalist economy of the United States changes rapidly. New products, new technology, and new attitudes develop quickly.

Most businesses in the United States are small enterprises such as this.

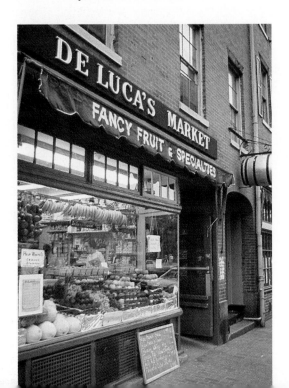

Certain organizations and ideas, though, are quite stable. For example, the family has always been a part of life in the United States. Families are an important part of the economy. Many products, such as houses and laundry detergents, are designed and sold with families in mind. The family is one type of economic institution. An economic institution is an organization or idea that influences economic behavior. Businesses and workers are also types of economic institutions.

Starting a Business

The basic economic institution in the capitalist system of the United States is the business. Businesses determine much of how the economy operates. Starting a business requires more than natural resources, labor, and capital. An entrepreneur must organize these resources. An entrepreneur is an individual who is willing to organize and manage a business in order to make a profit. The entrepreneur answers the basic econom-

203

ic questions about what, how, and how much of a good or service to produce. Many of the nation's business leaders became famous for their ability to organize and manage. Andrew Carnegie in steel, John D. Rockefeller in oil, and Henry Ford in automobiles were entrepreneurs who dominated their industries in the early 1900s.

Sole Proprietorships

Many entrepreneurs start their own businesses as sole proprietorships. A sole proprietorship is a one-owner business. As the graph shows, they are the most common form of business in the United States.

Sole proprietorships are popular for four reasons. First, they are easy to organize. Any individual can start a business. Second, decisions can be made quickly.

Only one person needs to reach a decision before an action can be taken. Third, all profits go to one person. If a sole proprietorship is successful, the owner does not have to share the profits with anyone. Fourth, the owner has pride in the business. Since the success or failure of the business depends primarily on one person, that person feels directly responsible for the company.

The advantages of sole proprietorships explain why so many people start businesses and try to run them alone. However, a sole proprietor sometimes encounters difficult problems in starting a business.

One person alone has limited resources to start and operate a business. The owner has only personal savings and funds that can be borrowed. Because capital is lacking, most sole proprietorships begin small

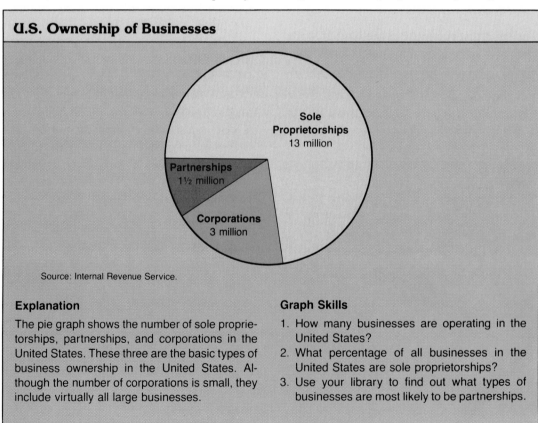

U.S. Ownership of Businesses

Sole Proprietorships
13 million

Partnerships
1½ million

Corporations
3 million

Source: Internal Revenue Service.

Explanation

The pie graph shows the number of sole proprietorships, partnerships, and corporations in the United States. These three are the basic types of business ownership in the United States. Although the number of corporations is small, they include virtually all large businesses.

Graph Skills

1. How many businesses are operating in the United States?
2. What percentage of all businesses in the United States are sole proprietorships?
3. Use your library to find out what types of businesses are most likely to be partnerships.

and fail. Even those that succeed often stay small.

A sole proprietor also must deal with the problem of unlimited liability. Unlimited liability is the concept that a sole proprietor is responsible for all debts of the business. According to the law, the owner and the business are one and the same. If the business fails, the owner must pay the debts. The personal property of the owner, such as a home or car, can be taken to pay the debts of the business. No limit is placed on the amount the owner can lose. High profits can make an owner wealthy, but high losses can ruin an individual.

Still another problem occurs because of the limited life of the business. Limited life is the concept that the business ceases to exist when the proprietor dies. If the owner of a sole proprietorship dies, an entirely new enterprise must be started.

Partnerships

The problems that face a sole proprietorship are serious. Of all new sole proprietorships begun each year, 70 percent fail within five years. To increase their chances of success, entrepreneurs often choose partnership instead of sole proprietorship. A partnership is an association of two or more people in order to run a business. A partnership has many of the characteristics of the sole proprietorship. Partnerships are easy to organize, decisions can be made quickly, profits are shared with only a few people, and the owners are responsible for success or failure of the business.

Like sole proprietorships, however, partnerships are not free of problems. Liability is still unlimited. Like sole proprietors, partners are responsible for the debts of the business. If the business has debts and one of the partners dies, the others are responsible for all debts of the business.

Liability, then, can actually be greater in a partnership than in a sole proprietorship, since each partner is responsible for all the business debts. Partnerships also have limited life. If one partner dies, the business must be dissolved.

The sole proprietorship or partnership needs another condition to survive. Within a free market system, new businesses find easy access to the economy and opportunities to succeed. Nevertheless, the level of competition can be so high that success is very difficult. It is important not only to have the right idea at the right time and the right place, but also to have a great deal of what most consider as luck.

Help for Entrepreneurs

Over the years the government has taken steps to help entrepreneurs. For example, through patents and copyrights the government encourages people to develop new inventions and ideas, and to create new works in the arts. These developments, in turn, benefit others in the economy.

A second form of aid to entrepreneurs comes from the Small Business Administration (SBA). This government agency was created in 1953. It counsels, aids, assists, and protects the interests of small businesses. The SBA makes loans to help individuals expand their businesses. Very few people actually receive government help in starting their business. Most do it with the help of friends, family, and banks.

REVIEWING THE CONCEPT

Developing Vocabulary

1. Define economic institution.
2. Explain why Andrew Carnegie was an entrepreneur.
3. Explain three differences between a sole proprietorship and a partnership.

4. Define unlimited liability.
5. Partnerships and sole proprietorships have a limited life. Explain what limits their life.

Mastering Facts

1. What are the advantages of sole proprietorship of a business?

2. What are the disadvantages of a sole proprietorship?
3. What are the advantages of partnership in a business?
4. What are the disadvantages of a business partnership?
5. What are two ways in which the government helps entrepreneurs?

Starting MICRO D

Most entrepreneurs do not receive government help. They start their businesses because they believe they can earn a profit by providing a product. Lorraine Mecca, for example, always knew she wanted to be her own boss. First, though, she had to find a good opportunity.

After teaching junior high English in Arizona, Mecca moved to Los Angeles, California. She took a job with a Los Angeles distribution firm. Here she worked her way from clerk to production coordinator. However, she did not enjoy her job, and she wanted to learn more about business. She left the job and took business courses at El Camino College.

In 1978, Lorraine married Geza Csige, who had just opened two computer stores. Lorraine and Geza often discussed his computer business. Eventually she began going with him to meetings of the Southern California Computer Dealers Association.

At these meetings, she discovered that many of the dealers had similar problems getting some products. "I came to know all of the dealers in the area. They came to know me. I knew all of their problems, all of the products they were having difficulty getting or selling." Certain accessories for

computers and certain programs were hard to get. This was a distribution problem. Lorraine realized she had the experience to solve the problem. She decided to start her own distribution company.

Like many entrepreneurs, Mecca had to rely on her own resources and those of her family to get started. With $25,000 she had saved from selling a house, and the

Entrepreneurs often depend on family support to start their business.

206

help of a cousin, she began her own company, MICRO D. The firm distributed selected computer parts and programs. Unlike many new businesses, MICRO D was a success from the day it started. During the first full year of operation, MICRO D had sales of $3.5 million.

One reason for Mecca's success was that she realized the problems that entrepreneurs frequently face. Many are good at starting a business but not at running one. Often, entrepreneurs rely too heavily on their own management skills. Mecca overcame this problem by educating herself and hiring the best managers she could find. Speaking of herself and her husband, she said, "We had the benefit of watching an experienced manager work. We were very fortunate that we did not just try to do it all ourselves." The methods followed in managing MICRO D have paid off. Mecca's success in starting MICRO D shows that some entrepreneurs do succeed.

ANALYZING THE CASE STUDY

STEP 1 Clarify the Issue

What is an entrepreneur? Why should Mecca be called an entrepreneur?

STEP 2 Gather Evidence

1. Why did Mecca decide to leave her job in Los Angeles?
2. What need did Mecca see among computer store owners? How did she become aware of this need?
3. What experience did Mecca have that made her think she was qualified to solve the need of computer store owners?

STEP 3 Examine Alternatives

1. How was MICRO D a typical small business started by an entrepreneur?
2. How was MICRO D unusual compared with other small businesses started by entrepreneurs?
3. What trait did Mecca have that would make her successful?

READING

In Praise of Small Business

by Arthur Levitt, Jr.   (1931-   )

In an age of multinational corporations, small businesses are still important. This reading is taken from an article in the *New York Times Magazine* by Arthur Levitt, Jr., chairman of the American Stock Exchange. He discusses some of the hazards small businesses face. As you read, consider how Levitt's comments relate to small businesses in your community.

"**A**s with most people who buy their own businesses, the odds against Robert Johnson were high. He was confronted at the start with a frightening list of problems. After laying out the purchase price, he had no money with which to start building up the business. He had no business experience or training, and he did not know where to go for advice (beyond the help offered by the local Internal Revenue Service office on how to fill out 10 different government reporting forms). There were no tax breaks, no government loans, no expense accounts. Although he

207

purchased the company from his uncle for what he thought was a good price, most everyone else would not have regarded it as a bargain. Since its founding in 1968 the Chicago business—Gamecraft of Illinois, which designed and produced board games—had barely survived. Sales were declining, and stacks of bills were unpaid.

What Johnson did have was a strong conviction that his energy and imagination would make the business succeed. "My sense of my own worth became tied up in the business," he says. "Could I keep it going, make it work?"

With this commitment, Johnson moved the business to his home in suburban Champaign and began living the double life familiar to many American small-business people. After working full time as a university administrator, he would come home at night and "often put in a second eight-hour day, taking care of every little detail of the business, even boxing the games myself and sending them out."

Now, two years later, Gamecraft is making money. No immense profits, to be sure. Johnson, still at the university, has turned the business around. He has put life into its marketing effort, expanded its product line and recruited a business manager. And, he has been sufficiently bitten by the "business bug" to have begun planning how to start a second company.

Johnson has thus become one of a growing number of Americans who have left the routine of wage earning to try to assert their own visions of making it on their own, of trying to succeed in small businesses—from flower shops to print shops, from pizza parlors to Chinese restaurants, from manufacturing plants to service companies.

The popular notion in America is that businesses are growing, with multinationals and huge corporations gobbling up everything in sight. However, during the last few years there has been an astonishing growth in the United States in the birth rate of small businesses. Since 1976, nearly a million Americans have become their own bosses, bringing the total number of self-employed to an all-time high of more than 6.8 million. For 1980, the Dun & Bradstreet Corporation, a business analysis firm, estimated that 533,500 companies were incorporating annually, and that the number of new incorporations in 1980 was 63 percent greater than in 1975.

Entrepreneurs and small businesses offer partial solutions to many current problems.

To grasp the importance of these entrepreneurs, consider that three major economic crises of the 1980s are a lack of jobs, a lack of industrial innovation, and slow growth in output per worker. Then consider that approximately 60 million Americans out of a work force of 97 million find their livelihoods in small businesses. A recent Massachusetts Institute of Technology study found that 66 percent of all new jobs in the private sector were provided by businesses with 20 or fewer employees. In contrast, the National Federation of Independent Businesses has stated that over the last decade *Fortune* magazine's top 1,000 firms, as measured by revenue, created only 10.6 percent of all jobs. Additionally, small companies provide more than 80 percent of the jobs for young blacks and other disadvantaged groups.

Consider, too, a recent National Science Foundation study: It found that small firms produce 4 times as many industrial innovations per research dollar as medium-sized firms and 24 times as many innovations as the largest firms. Finally, consider that small businesses cannot afford to be unproductive. They have no margin for slack. A high output per worker is essential to survival.

Indeed, Johnson and other small-business people are begining to understand their own collective importance. They are realizing that they have interests in common, that they can and should help each other out and that it is to the nation's—and their own—benefit that they do so. They are getting organized in important ways, and developing a sense of unity. These changes may soon make them one of the most potent influences in the economic history of the United States.

It must be said at the start that establishing a business is immensely risky. According to a study by the Small Business Administration, as many as 9 out of 10 new enterprises fail within 10 years.

The roadblocks are formidable. The biggest is, or course, lack of money. To start a business and to keep it going, the vast majority of entrepreneurs must turn, as Johnson did, to personal savings, or to parents, aunts, uncles, friends. The National Federation of Independent Businesses recently asked this question of small-business owners: What was the most important resource for your financing? Forty-five percent answered personal savings, 13 percent said friends, and 4 percent cited private investors. Only 29 percent were financed through banks and other financial institutions, while 1 percent were financed by the government.

Another major problem with entering the small-business world is what Leo Wolk, a Minneapolis insurance agent, terms "a severe lack of sound advice." Dun & Bradstreet estimates that a majority of all business failures are due to poor management. Often business owners recognize their lack of skills or competence in particular areas. However, there just appears to be nowhere for them to turn for reliable advice.

Yet the rebirth of the entrepreneurial spirit is occurring in spite of these obstacles. Why? How does one explain it? One reason is simply population increase. In the years following World War II, the birth rate jumped. The babies of 1946–1960 are now old enough to start their own companies. Another reason is the nation's shift from a manufacturing economy to a service-oriented one. Starting a service-oriented company requires less capital than starting a manufacturing company. But there may be a deeper, more compelling reason, having to do with a change in national attitude.

After the Depression of the 1930s, the word "entrepreneur" often made people think of a scheming promoter or unscrupulous millionaire. Now, however, "entrepreneurial spirit" seems to suggest at once a more down-to-earth figure and a more romantic one. The phrase invokes independence, self-reliance, and courage. **99**

From "In Praise of Small Business," by Arthur Levitt, Jr., in the *New York Times Magazine*.

UNDERSTANDING THE READING

1. Give three statistics that show the growth of small businesses in the American economy.
2. What are the three biggest problems involved in starting a small business? How would you overcome these problems if you started a small business?
3. How does the author explain the rise of small businesses?
4. Would you consider starting or operating a small business? Explain.

Section 1 Review

Understanding Entrepreneurs

1. Give three examples of economic institutions. Explain why each is considered an economic institution.
2. List and explain the steps government has taken to encourage entrepreneurs.

Entrepreneurs Today

1. More than 4,500 businesses in the United States failed in 1981. Using the information you have learned about the American free market system, write a short paragraph explaining why a company may fail.

2. Think about the products you use every day. List those a small business could provide. Explain your choice. Which would need to be made by a large business? Explain your choice.
3. When you choose a full-time employer, would you prefer a small business? Explain why or why not.
4. **Challenge:** The federal government encourages entrepreneurs in several ways. Write a paragraph explaining why you agree or disagree with the federal government's actions.

2 Corporations

SECTION OVERVIEW

There are far more entrepreneurs and partnerships in this country than corporations—approximately six times as many. It is the corporation, however, that provides most of the jobs and the products for people in the United States. Corporations make up only 16 percent of the businesses in the United States, but they produce 87 percent of all income. This section will help you understand how a corporation is organized and the reasons for this dominance.

ECONOMIC VOCABULARY

corporation	board of directors	limited liability	unlimited life
stock	dividend	bond	double taxation

Development of the Corporation

America changed from a farming society to an industrial society between 1860 and 1900. During this time period, many Americans started their own companies. The number of manufacturing companies increased from 252,000 to 335,000. Often, however, one person did not have enough money to start a business. Combining the resources of a number of people and forming a corporation was a way to raise the large amount of money needed.

A corporation is a business that, although owned by one or more investors, legally has the rights and duties of an individual. Corporations have the right to buy, sell, and own property. Corporations may make legal contracts, hire and fire workers, set prices, and be sued, fined, and taxed. A business must obtain a charter of incorporation from a state legislature or Congress to be legally recognized as a corporation.

The corporation was not a new form of business in the mid-1800s. During the early 1600s, English merchants had created trading companies that consisted of stockholders who shared the costs of starting and maintaining colonies. If the colonies were successful, investors shared the profits. American businesspeople 250 years later modified these ideas to finance large industrial projects.

Today, there are about 3 million corporations in the United States. Most are small, but the few large ones control most of the resources corporations own. The graph illustrates this situation.

Corporate Structure

A corporation issues shares of stock which are certificates representing ownership in the corporation. Investors buy and sell these shares of stock. Often hundreds and even thousands of small investors own stock in a single corporation. General Motors, for example, has over 1.5 million individual shareholders, or stockholders.

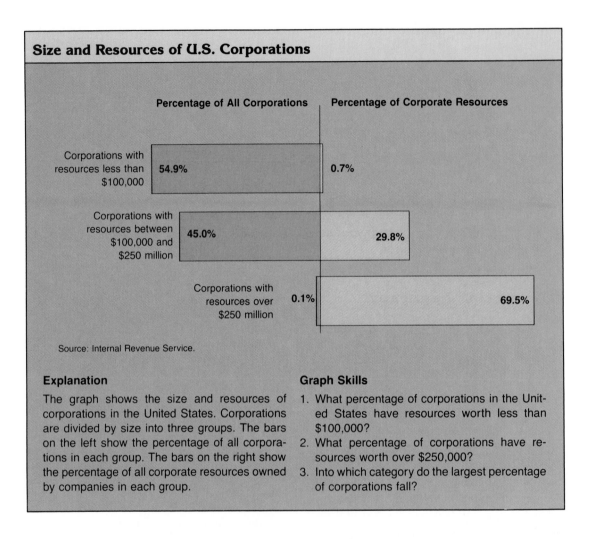

Size and Resources of U.S. Corporations

Percentage of All Corporations

Percentage of Corporate Resources

Corporations with resources less than $100,000
54.9%
0.7%

Corporations with resources between $100,000 and $250 million
45.0%
29.8%

Corporations with resources over $250 million
0.1%
69.5%

Source: Internal Revenue Service.

Explanation

The graph shows the size and resources of corporations in the United States. Corporations are divided by size into three groups. The bars on the left show the percentage of all corporations in each group. The bars on the right show the percentage of all corporate resources owned by companies in each group.

Graph Skills

1. What percentage of corporations in the United States have resources worth less than $100,000?
2. What percentage of corporations have resources worth over $250,000?
3. Into which category do the largest percentage of corporations fall?

Because a corporation may have many owners, the stockholders elect a board of directors. Stockholders have one vote for each share of stock they own.

The board of directors hires individuals to manage the day-to-day operation of the corporation. These individuals include the president and other chief administrators of the company. Most important, the board of directors manages the resources of the corporation in order to produce a profit.

If the corporation makes a profit, shareholders may receive a dividend—a share of the profit paid on the stock. For example, if a corporation's profit allows a $5 dividend per share and an investor owns 200 shares, the total dividend received will be $1,000. The board of directors decides how much of the profit should be divided among stockholders. The board may decide to reinvest some of the profit in the corporation for expansion, modernization, or research and development. The diagram represents the structure of a corporation.

Advantages of Corporations

Corporations have some advantages over sole proprietorships and partnerships. First, a corporation has limited liability. Thus, if the corporation goes bankrupt or is sued, the stockholders lose only the value of their stock. The stockholders, who are the corporation owners, cannot be held

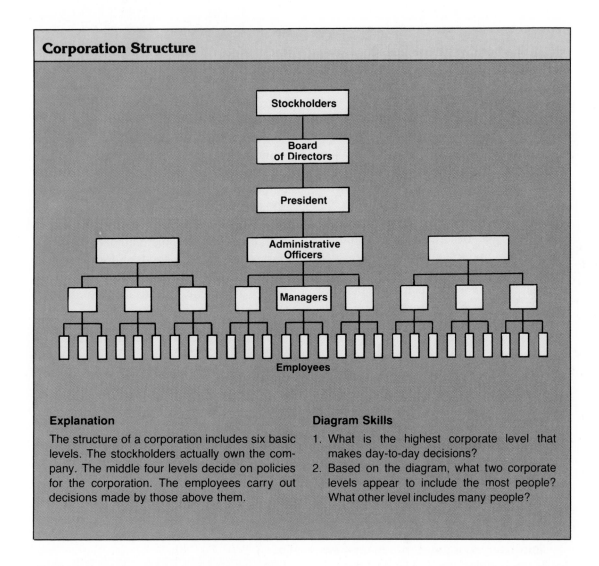

Corporation Structure

Stockholders

Board of Directors

President

Administrative Officers

Managers

Employees

Explanation

The structure of a corporation includes six basic levels. The stockholders actually own the company. The middle four levels decide on policies for the corporation. The employees carry out decisions made by those above them.

Diagram Skills

1. What is the highest corporate level that makes day-to-day decisions?
2. Based on the diagram, what two corporate levels appear to include the most people? What other level includes many people?

personally responsible for any money the corporation owes. Sole proprietors and partners can be held personally responsible for debts of their businesses.

Second, corporations have the ability to raise very large amounts of money. They use this money to change models, replace obsolete equipment, and build new factories. Corporations can raise money by selling bonds, as well as stocks. A **bond** is a certificate that promises to pay the holder of the bond, the investor, a certain amount of money on a certain date. Stocks and bonds differ in two important ways. Bonds, unlike stocks, do not represent ownership

in the corporation. Also, the rate of return on stocks changes; the rate of return on a bond is set when the bond is sold.

Third, a corporation has an **unlimited life.** That is, the corporation continues to function despite death, transfer, or changes in ownership, management, or labor. The work of sole proprietors or partners can end abruptly in such circumstances. This stability attracts small investors.

The fourth advantage of corporations is the ease of ownership transfer. Selling a small business may be difficult; selling shares of stock is relatively easy. The investor also has an advantage. The ability to get

213

out of one business, by selling stock, and into another quickly, by buying stock, is quite useful to small investors.

Disadvantages of Corporations

Corporations have disadvantages as well as advantages. First, individuals forming a corporation must overcome many difficulties. Complex forms must be filed with the state or federal government. A charter must then be issued, investors found, shares sold, and manufacturing or sales begun. The procedure for setting up a corporation is more difficult than that for setting up a sole proprietorship or a partnership. Also, to succeed a corporation must pay stockholders regular dividends and must keep detailed records to satisfy appropriate government agencies.

Second, a corporation's profits are subject to double taxation. A corporation must pay taxes on its profits before the profits are distributed to stockholders as dividends. The stockholders include this dividend money as personal income on their income tax forms. Stockholders pay taxes on this income. The government, then, has taxed the corporation's profits twice.

Third, in corporations with many owners or stockholders the individual share of profits in the form of dividends is comparatively small. In a single proprietorship or parnership, profits are divided among fewer individuals. Therefore, individual incomes are often greater.

Fourth, a corporation's owners do not directly control the business. Most individual stockholders take little interest in management decisions. In contrast, sole proprietors or partners manage their own business. The main concern of the owner-managers is the success of the business. Managers in large corporations, though, may not have invested their own money in the business. Career decisions may be different from, and more important than, decisions to improve the business. For this reason many corporations arrange for management to own shares of stock.

When all the parts of a corporation work well, the corporation will be a successful business venture—and American corporations are successful. The nearly 200,000 manufacturing corporations employ more than 60 percent of all American workers. Corporations dominate every industry and produce goods and services people use every day. The chart lists the 10 largest American industrial corporations.

Largest Industrial Corporations

1. Exxon
2. General Motors
3. Mobil
4. Texaco
5. Ford
6. International Business Machines
7. Standard Oil of California
8. DuPont
9. Gulf
10. Standard Oil of Indiana

Source: *Fortune.*

Explanation

The chart ranks the 10 largest corporations in the United States according to their annual sales. Of the 10 corporations, 7 deal with oil and chemicals. Also on the list are two automobile manufacturers and a producer of office equipment.

Chart Skills

1. Write a one-page history of a corporation in the list. Tell how the company was started, during what years it grew most rapidly, and what product it produces today.
2. Why do you think petroleum and chemicals dominate the list?

REVIEWING THE CONCEPT

Developing Vocabulary

1. Define the following terms:
   a. corporation
   b. board of directors
   c. dividend
   d. limited liability
   e. unlimited life
   f. double taxation

2. Explain what stocks and bonds are and how they differ.

Mastering Facts

1. What rights do corporations have?
2. What does the board of directors do with the corporation profits?
3. List and explain four advantages and four disadvantages of incorporating to operate a business.

CASE STUDY

Theory Z Management

Corporations in American capitalism survive by making profits. Their goal is to constantly increase their profits. However, since World War II ended in 1945, the profits of American corporations have been threatened by increasing competition from companies in other countries. In particular, Japanese corporations have been successful in selling their products in the United States. Much of the Japanese success has resulted from the rapid increase in the output of an average Japanese worker. American corporations are now looking to Japan for ways to increase the output of American workers.

A division of one large American corporation decided to reevaluate its system of management. Though the division was making a solid profit, still, its top executives felt it could improve. Like other executives in American corporations, they had been impressed by the success of their competitors in Japan. They hired a professor from the University of California at Los Angeles, William Ouchi, to help them analyze their management. He had been studying Japanese corporations since 1973. He believed that much of the Japanese success was related to their style of management.

According to Ouchi, Japanese companies are more successful at getting their employees involved with their work. Japanese managers trust their workers more, give them more responsibility, and show them more respect than do traditional American managers. In the United States, individuals are given specific jobs. Workers are closely supervised by their bosses. In Japan, workers have more flexible job assignments. Bosses do not supervise their workers as closely. "In the long run," says Ouchi, "Japanese workers develop more commitment to their job than do American workers." Ouchi believes that American companies can increase their profits by adapting the ideas of the Japanese. He calls the type of management based on Japanese principles, but applied in the United States, Theory Z management.

Ouchi and the top managers of the division held a series of meetings to discuss how the division was run. He explained Theory Z management to them. Then, they designed a five-day seminar for all manag-

Impressed by the productivity of Japanese workers, American managers are studying Japanese management techniques.

ers in the division. He recalls the five-day seminar as a success.

"By the time of the first seminar, there had been a good deal of gossip among the managers. They expected that a new program would be crammed down their throats. The atmosphere in that first seminar was hostile. One of the managers asked point-blank why we thought this new program would work and why we had to force it on them." By the end of the seminar, a change in attitude had taken place. The division's top managers not only had attended but also had participated in teaching the seminar. They had treated the lower-level managers with respect for the first time ever. Repeating this seminar eight times exposed all managers to the same ideas so that they could discuss these new ideas with one another. At this point, no field manager was asked for a commitment to change, but was just expected to consider some new ideas.

Slowly, the ideas of Theory Z spread throughout the division. The attitudes in

the division gradually changed. The traits that Ouchi found in Japanese corporations began to show up in the division. "The emphasis on long-term planning, sharing responsibilities, and group decision-making improved people's attitudes toward work," Ouchi says. The operations of the division began to improve.

Before the change, the division had been turning in operating results of about 88 to 90 percent on such items as quality, reliability, and delivery time. After two years of development work, these same measures ranged from 96 to 98 percent. Before the change, the division contributed approximately $15 million of profit each year to the corporation. During the third year after the change, it contributed $60 million on the same sales volume.

The top group of managers began to work much more cooperatively. Rather than having a guarded approach to one another, they became open and friendly, sharing their disappointments and goals. Finally, they surprised even themselves by sharing the limited time of computer programmers to help one another. They had never shared before. New rules encouraged secretaries to go off and learn something interesting when their bosses were out of town, rather than sitting idly at a desk just to answer the telephones. Turnover of employees dropped sharply, and absenteeism declined. The organization reached a healthier state.

The success of Theory Z, in this division and others, has led many corporations to reconsider their style of management.

ANALYZING THE CASE STUDY

STEP 1 Clarify the Issue

1. Explain what circumstances prompted American managers to study Japanese corporate methods.

2. What important differences between

American and Japanese corporations did Dr. Ouchi find?

3. What evidence suggested to Ouchi that these factors would improve the productivity of American corporations?

STEP 2 Examine Change

1. List and explain three management techniques that a large division of an American corporation used before Theory Z was implemented.

2. List and explain the changes that Theory Z brought about in the techniques listed in question 1.

STEP 3 Consider Costs and Benefits

1. Write a short paragraph explaining what Theory Z cost the corporation. Include social costs as well as money.

2. List and explain the benefits to the corporation from using Theory Z.

STEP 4 Make a Decision

1. Would you have tried Theory Z if you were the head of the division? Why or why not?

2. If you could work under either a traditional or a Theory Z manager, which would you choose? Why?

READING

The Bored Board

by Peter F. Drucker (1909–   )

The board of directors of a corporation is supposed to guide the corporation toward increasing its profits. In this reading taken from his essay, "The Bored Board," Peter Drucker says that boards do very little to guide a corporation. Drucker has published more than 15 books on modern organizations and their management. His books have been translated into more than 20 languages. He is also a frequent contributor to magazines and is an editorial columnist for *The Wall Street Journal.* As you read, determine whether or not Drucker has exaggerated circumstances to make his point.

"All over the Western world boards of directors are under attack and are being changed. . . .

All these pressures assume that the board matters. They assume that the board of directors or of trustees, whether of a business, a university, or a service institution, is truly the "governing body."

But there is little evidence to support this assumption. On the contrary, years of experience indicate that the board has become a work ceremonial and legal fiction. It certainly does not "conduct the affairs of the enterprise"—neither in this country nor in Europe. Life on the board is not juicy and exciting. Rather, it is dull. . . .

I, for instance, served for six years on the board of a fast-growing state university in New Jersey. The board members were genuinely interested in the university. Most of them had considerable experience in teaching, research, and administration. Others had held significant political office. The board met at least once a month, around 5 p.m., and was usually still at work at midnight. Yet we rarely got to the subjects that were uppermost in the minds of the board members: educational policies; the direction of the college; or the relationships between administration, faculty, and students.

Instead, our time was taken up with maternity leaves for Spanish instructors, waiving of fees for foreign students, promotions of people we had never heard about, or the acquisition of real estate for a new parking lot. We often tried to get to the matters we knew to be important, matters in which we also considered ourselves to be competent [knowledgable]. But each time we were sternly reminded by the representative of the State Board of Higher Education (who sat in on every meeting) that state law restricted us to the tedious trivia. She told us at the same time, however, that state law mandated [required] maternity leaves, promotions, and parking lots, so they would go through no matter how we voted.

The same situation exists even in large businesses. Board meetings rarely go beyond similar trivia: approval of a raft [large number] of promotions which have already become accomplished fact; approval of short-term budgets which few of the board members can possibly understand, let alone analyze in depth; approval of last month's operating results, when they have become past history; or spirited debates over a branch manager's right to sign checks. . . .

But where does that leave the board? Does it have any function at all, or is it obsolete? . . . There are six essential functions only an effective board can discharge.

First, institutions need strong, competent management. Only a strong, effective, and independent board can ensure management competence. A strong board is needed to remove a top management that is less than fully competent. . . .

Second, an independent [board] is needed to make sure that crucial questions are being asked: What is our business and what should it be? What is our mission? What are valid "results" in this undertaking? Who are our publics and our constituencies, and what can they legitimately expect from this institution? What are the major directions for the future? What should be abandoned or deemphasized? . . .

Third, an institution needs a "conscience." It needs a keeper of human and moral values and a court of appeal against tyranny and caprice or the equally harmful indifference of bureaucratic routine. It needs someone outside the daily work and the daily relationships who is concerned with what the institution stands for, what its values are, what it considers "right" and "wrong". . . .

Fourth, management itself needs an effective outside board. Top-level managers need people with whom they can talk in confidence, can deliberate, can think aloud. . . .

Fifth, the management of a large institution needs windows that open on the outside world. Inevitably, it sees its own institution as large and important, and the rest of the world as small. . . .

A corporation is governed by a board of directors elected by the shareholders. The board establishes general corporate policies.

Finally, the large institution needs to be understood by its constituencies and by the community. No outsider really understands what goes on "on the fourteenth floor" or "in the president's office." What is so obvious to the decision maker in the executive suite is usually not perceived by the public outside, beginning with people in responsible positions within the organization.

These functions require a very different board than the one we inherited from the nineteenth century. Above all, boards need to accept the idea that they have a responsibility and, with it, specific work of their own. Otherwise, they will not accomplish anything. The first priority in modernization is not to change the board's membership. The first priority is to change the board's role, function, and work. **99**

From "The Bored Board," by Peter Drucker.

UNDERSTANDING THE READING

1. Would most management leaders go along with Drucker's views? Explain why or why not?
2. List and explain the six functions Drucker believes a board of directors should perform.

Section 2 Review

Understanding Corporations

1. Why do individuals form corporations rather than setting up their businesses as sole proprietorships?
2. Why is it sometimes necessary to issue additional shares of stock?

Corporations Today

1. Often large corporations buy or take over other companies. If General Motors took over American Motors, what would be the advantages and disadvantages for each company? For the economy? For consumers?
2. **Challenge:** Recently the United States government used tax money for low-interest loans to Lockheed and Chrysler corporations to keep them from going bankrupt. Use your knowledge of competition and the American market system to criticize or defend the federal government's actions.

3 Unions

SECTION OVERVIEW

In some sports, such as tennis, players win or lose on their own. In other sports, such as baseball or basketball, each player is part of a team. Players on a team work together to achieve a goal. In the economy, only a few people win or lose on their own. Almost everybody is part of a team of workers in a business. In some businesses, workers recognizing their collective strengths and problems have acknowledged their dependence on other workers and formed an organization called a union. Unions are an important institution in American capitalism. In this section you will learn about unions and how they represent the interests of their members.

ECONOMIC VOCABULARY

labor unions	local	collective bargaining
craft unions	federation	strike
industrial unions	independent unions	professional association

Development of Unions

Before 1750, agriculture dominated the economy of the world. Most people lived in rural areas, grew their own food, and made most of the things they needed. New methods to produce power and machines to manufacture products were introduced slowly. During the next 250 years, much of the world became urban and industrial. As the world in which they lived changed, so did the jobs that workers performed. More and more people worked in factories rather than on the land. Increasingly, people worked in groups rather than by themselves. Factory jobs were often unpleasant, dangerous, and low paying. Workers realized that as individuals they could do little to improve their condition. A single employee who complained could be ignored or fired. As a group, however, workers had more strength. The groups workers formed were labor unions. A labor union is an organization of workers to promote the interests of its members.

Labor unions have tried to achieve four basic goals in order to improve the lives of their members: (1) higher wages and benefits, (2) shorter work days, (3) safer working conditions, and (4) better job security. Unions in other countries have tried to reach these goals by gaining some control over company management, including board-level decisions. In the United States, company operations usually have not been a union target.

The first unions were organized in one of two different ways. Craft unions included all workers doing a specific type of work. For example, all carpenters were members of one union. Each group of artisans formed a separate union. These unions developed from earlier associations of skilled craft workers. Industrial unions included all the workers in a given industry. All mine workers, for example, were organized into one union regardless of their particular jobs. Industrial unions often included many factory workers without particular skills. Today, both craft unions and industrial unions exist, but the distinction is less clear than it once was.

The Growth of Unions

The first unions in the United States began in the 1830s. Not until after 1900 did unions grow rapidly. Organizers often faced strong opposition from owners. Violence was not uncommon. Over 700 people have been killed in labor disputes in the United States. Union membership grew most rapidly during the Great Depression of the 1930s. The economic hardships of that era prompted many workers to join unions for the first time. Since 1970, total union membership has grown slowly. The number of nonunion workers has grown more rapidly than has the number of union workers. Consequently, the percentage of all workers who belong to unions has been decreasing.

Structure of Unions

The smallest unit in a union is called the local. A local is the union organization representing the workers in one community or one factory. A local may have only a handful of workers, but some locals have as many as 30,000 members. All locals of a particular craft or industry are united in a national union. If locals from more than one country join together, they form an international union.

Many national and international unions are part of a federation of unions. A federation is a loose organization of national unions that acts as a speaker for all its member unions. In the United States, the largest federation of unions combines two previously independent groups. The American Federation of Labor and Congress of Industrial Organizations, or AFL–CIO, represents over 100 unions, including about 17 million workers. Unions not part of a federation are called independent unions. The United Mine Workers is an example of an independent union.

The basic job of a union is collective bargaining. Collective bargaining is the process of negotiation between workers and owners in which the union is the sole

Union leaders meet with management officials to negotiate wages, working conditions, and employee benefits.

Union Membership, 1900–1980

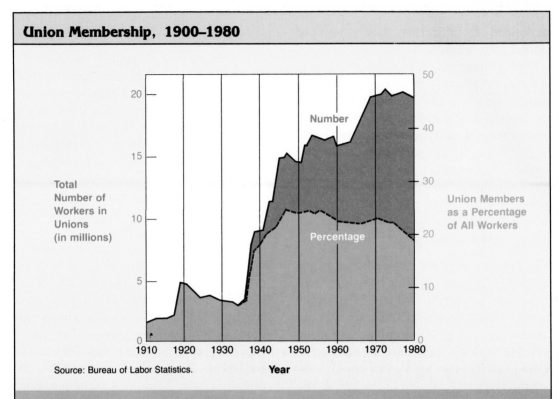

Source: Bureau of Labor Statistics.

Year

Explanation

The graph shows how union membership changed between 1910 and 1980. Membership is measured in two ways. The solid line and the scale at the left indicate how many workers belonged to unions. The dashed line and the scale on the right show the percentage of all workers who belonged to unions. Both lines move upward between 1930 and 1950. Since 1950, the solid line has continued to go up, but the dashed line has begun to go down. The number of union members has increased, but union members are a smaller percentage of all workers in the United States.

Graph Skills

1. How much did the number of union members increase between 1956 and 1980?
2. How much did the percentage of all workers who belonged to unions decline between 1956 and 1980?
3. Explain how this statement could be considered true: "Union membership has increased since 1956." Explain how this statement could be considered false.

representative of all its members. The union and management negotiate over a contract that states the wages, working conditions, and benefits for the employees. Usually a compromise is reached.

If no compromise is reached, the union may use its power to call a strike. A strike is the employees' decision to not work until management agrees to their demands. Generally, the strike is used as the last resort in a dispute. A strike can create strong tensions between workers and management that may last for years. It can disrupt a union as well if not all workers

Largest U.S. Labor Organizations

	Organization	Membership
1.	International Brotherhood of Teamsters	1,891,000
2.	National Education Association	1,684,000
3.	United Automobile Workers	1,357,000
4.	United Food and Commercial Workers	1,300,000
5.	United Steel Workers	1,238,000
6.	American Federation of State, County and Municipal Workers	1,098,000
7.	International Brotherhood of Electrical Workers	1,041,000
8.	United Brotherhood of Carpenters	784,000
9.	International Association of Machinists	754,000
10.	Service Employees International Union	650,000

Source: Bureau of Labor Statistics.

Explanation

The chart shows the 10 largest labor organizations in the United States. The largest is the Teamsters. A teamster is a worker who drives a truck or another vehicle (originally a team of horses) for transporting goods. The National Education Association (NEA) does not consider itself a union. The other eight organizations listed are members of the AFL-CIO, a federation of American unions.

Chart Skills

1. What is the total membership of these 10 organizations? How many people belong to unions in the United States?
2. What is the largest union in the AFL-CIO?

believe a strike is necessary. A strike may hurt company profits by shutting down production. Then it may be harder for the company to afford a wage increase. Finally, workers may not make up the wages they lost during the time they were not working. Strikes are costly to both workers and owners, so both sides prefer to avoid strikes.

Professional Associations

Unions are the most common form of worker organization. In some occupations, people have preferred to form professional associations rather than unions. A professional association is an organization of people in a particular occupation who are interested in improving the methods they use and the conditions in which they work. The American Medical Association (AMA), for example, is a professional association for doctors. It does not bargain collectively on behalf of its members, as would a union. The AMA does try to keep doctors informed of developments in medical research. It also tries to influence the government to pass legislation beneficial to doctors. Other well-known professional associations are the American Bar Association and the Farm Bureau.

Legislation to Help Workers

Over the years, unions have pushed for legislation to protect the rights of workers. The Social Security Act of 1935 established protection for ill and aged workers, as well as some unemployment protection. Also, in 1935 the National Labor Relations Act clarified workers' rights, such as the right to organize. Until this act was passed, these rights were not clearly stated in law.

In 1938, the Fair Labor Standards Act set regulations for working conditions. It limited the labor of children under 14 years old, and established minimum wages for full-time workers at 25 cents an hour. It also set the standard work week at 40 hours. In 1959, the Landrum-Griffin Act gave workers stronger control over their unions in order to prevent corruption.

Unions remain a powerful economic and political force in the United States. They continue to deal with concerns similar to those that prompted their formation. In addition, they must deal with an ever-changing economy based on high technology and its impact on workers. How unions deal with these new technologies will affect the lives of all workers in the years to come.

REVIEWING THE CONCEPT

Developing Vocabulary

1. What is a labor union?
2. Explain the difference between a craft union and an industrial union.
3. Give an example of a union local.
4. What is the purpose of a federation of labor unions?
5. How does an independent union differ from a local union?
6. Explain the process of collective bargaining to settle differences between the union and management.
7. Give an example of when it may be necessary for a group of employees to go out on strike.
8. What is a professional association?

Mastering Facts

1. List the improvements that labor unions have tried to achieve for their members.
2. In the process of collective bargaining, what is the goal of management? Of the labor union?
3. Draw a simple diagram to illustrate how unions are organized.
4. What is the difference between a professional association and a union?

CASE STUDY

Working Together for Success

Changes in the economy have already changed the attitudes of workers in Lordstown, Ohio, say Randy Gasparek. "Everybody in the plant has realized the predicament (trouble) we are in with world competition. We have a close working relationship with management now. We know that if we keep the adversarial (fighting) relationship, we're all going to be out of business." Gasparek, as president of the United Auto Workers local in Lordstown, demonstrates how attitudes between labor and management have changed in the face of foreign competition.

During the 1970s, the Lordstown plant was the scene of a bitter struggle between the workers and the owners of General Motors. General Motors devised the most organized assembly line process in the history of the automobile industry. The plant was to produce 100 Chevrolet Vegas per hour. Each car moved every 36 seconds. Workers had only 5 seconds of recovery time between cars.

The system seemed to be efficient. However, General Motors had pushed the workers hard, and they rebelled. Dan Brooks, a worker at the plant, recalls the problems of the Vega assembly line. "All the jobs were overworked; they [the management] tightened every one up. The only way to get any relief was to let the cars go unfinished." To try to enforce the system, General Motors brought in strict managers. Workers expressed their protest through their union leaders and through vandalism.

Gary Bryner, president of the Lordstown local during the 1970s, said that the managers "would take people one after another and throw them out of the plant. The supervisor would give a direct order to a worker to do a job. One person would refuse, and they would send the worker home. Then, they would turn to the next guy, who would also refuse, and so on down the line. In one stretch 1,400 people were disciplined."

During the 1970s and 1980s, however, relations between the union and management changed. Both sides realized that their economic success depended on meeting the competition from the Japanese. Management softened its approach to the unions. Dave Perrow, a speaker for management, said, "Management style has changed with the times, and we have also mellowed. We have given supervisors additional people training."

Bill Bowers, vice president of the Lordstown local, agrees. "They [management] are not as blunt as they used to be.

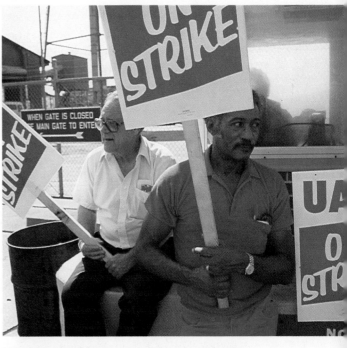

Workers sometimes go on strike when they are unable to agree with management about their contract.

Their goals are the same—they are out to achieve the best they can for the corporation at the expense of the union—but their tactics have changed."

Gasparek, who had once issued tough statements encouraging workers to reject concessions, now agreed that management is more willing than before to listen. "We sit down with management now and talk things out with them."

ANALYZING THE CASE STUDY

STEP 1 Clarify the Issue

1. What caused the Lordstown auto workers to get angry with management during the early 1970s?
2. How did the workers demonstrate their anger over the Vega production system?
3. What response did management make to the angry workers?

1. How did the increase in competition from Japanese automakers change the relationship between the union and management in American auto plants?
2. What evidence suggests that attitudes of company management toward workers were changing?
3. What evidence suggests that attitudes of the auto workers union toward management were changing?

1. From the view of management, what were the costs and benefits of the Vega production system?
2. What were the union's costs and benefits in opposing the production system?

What forces will affect future relations between workers and owners in the auto industry? How will relations change?

READING

The Future of Unions

by Charles B. Craver

Unions' success in ending management's worst treatment of workers has lessened the demand for unions. Consequently, the role of unions is changing. This reading, taken from an article in *The Futurist* magazine, was written by Charles B. Craver, a professor of law at the University of Illinois. It considers the future of unions. As you read, consider whether or not you expect to ever join a union.

66 **A**s the American labor movement begins its second century, it is confronted by challenges that threaten its very existence.

The makeup and geographic distribution of the labor force will significantly affect union strength and organizational potential over the next several decades. Women, who have traditionally been reluctant to unionize, will certainly continue to be a larger part of the labor force.

Another labor force trend is the expanding numbers of minority members. Minority workers are expected to grow from about 12 percent of the work force currently to over 20 percent by the year 2,000. During the next several decades, decreased birthrates and better medical care will combine to produce a substantial increase in another labor-force group—older workers.

One of the most striking changes in the nation over the past decade has involved the explosive growth of the Sunbelt region. The migration of workers and jobs from the Northeast and North Central areas of the country to the South and Southwest is likely to continue—at least for the next several decades. Labor organizations have traditionally found the South and Southwest to be difficult areas to unionize. The labor movement will find such recruitment there to be challenging.

Even traditionally unionized parts of the economy can no longer be taken for granted. Changing worker attitudes and career expectations are challenging the capabilities of union leaders. Earlier workers were satisfied simply to have gainful employment. Today's workers expect more personally rewarding jobs. They reject the authoritarian management policies of the past and strive for greater control over the organization of their work and more opportunities for enjoying their work. They show a similar lack of respect for the role historically played by representatives of the union.

Changes in the composition of the labor force are being matched by significant developments in technology. With the substitution of machines for personal effort, most future factories will need fewer human workers. Future employment opportunities will clearly be found in service and high technology information fields, which have generally not been receptive to unionization efforts.

The internationalization of the world economy will involve the export of American jobs to underdeveloped countries where wages are lower. Labor organizations will need to develop new ways to protect the interests of displaced American workers. They will have to find new methods to effectively confront [challenge] increasingly powerful transnational business enterprises.

As the American economic system changes, it is likely that white-collar personnel will change their perception of labor organizations. The expanding use of technological advancements will cause many white-collar jobs to become more uninteresting. Highly educated but bored employees will increasingly feel frustrated and unhappy. Many white-collar workers may resort to collective action. Teachers, pilots, musicians, and various white-collar service workers have already become strong union members. Within the next several decades, if the American labor movement is able to satisfy the needs of presently unorganized white-collar people, many can be expected to become labor union members.

The continuing migration of workers to Sunbelt states will force unions to direct their organizing efforts to areas that have not been very supportive of trade unions. However, recent trends indicate that the anti-union attitudes historically found in the South and Southwest are being softened. As more northern workers relocate to the Sunbelt and discuss the benefits of union representation with their fellow employees, the work of union organizers should be made easier.

As the labor-force participation rates for minorities and women continue to increase, labor organizations will have to be responsive to the needs of such groups. Labor leaders need to emphasize the fact that unionized black workers earn approximately 30 percent more than

The AFL-CIO is a federation of more than 100 labor unions. Some labor leaders believe that if unions are to meet the challenges of the future, workers will need to form even larger labor federations.

unorganized workers. Labor leaders must demonstrate strong support for equal employment opportunity, since such efforts should bring back the support minorities evidenced for trade unions during the 1930s.

More enthusiastic union support for antidiscrimination principles, particularly for the concept of equal pay for work of comparable worth and the end of sexual harassment in employment environments, should enhance labor support among female workers.

Since workers are most affected by lower level managers, unions should seek programs that would enable workers to influence decisions regarding their immediate work environment and job content. By promoting worker self-esteem, companies could increase productivity while decreasing the number of workers who quit or are fired. Such cooperative ventures could also be used to promote worker job security and advance other employee interest. Future labor organizers will have to go beyond traditional bread-and-butter economic issues through both collective bargaining and the legislative process.

Employees threatened with job losses due to the introduction of new technology or the relocation of their jobs to other states or to different countries are usually most concerned about their employment security. Some labor organizations have sought to lessen the impact of such changes by negotiating agreements that provide employees with pay if they lose their jobs to technology or a change in location. Another method of lessening the impact of reduced employment opportunities is a work-sharing plan under which people would work reduced hours so that more workers would keep their jobs. Unions might induce companies to create large monetary reserves to finance retraining programs. Labor and management leaders should establish retraining opportunities that consider both the skills of workers and the future needs of the corporation and perhaps even the general economy.

The economic condition of unorganized employees has an increasing impact upon unionized workers. The availability of such nonunion people threatens job security of unionized workers. Thus labor officials can best protect their gains by legislation protecting the interests of all workers. Probably the most significant right won by unions is protection from unfair firings. Without such a protection, most employees may be fired at any time for any reason. Since it has been suggested that over one million permanent workers are fired annually without any opportunity for a fair hearing, it is clear that legislation requiring employers to give a reason for firing a worker would significantly protect the employment rights of American workers.

The spread of multinational and even global enterprises during the past several decades has significantly challenged the strength of traditional labor organizations, which generally function within a single nation.

The late labor leader Walter Reuther said that labor organizations must either join together in international union solidarity or separately watch automation, job relocations, and erratic operation of the business cycle bring down the American and Western standard of living. Employee associations must join together to create informal and ultimately formal labor federations in an effort to achieve equality with the employers with whom they deal.

Although labor organizations will have to adapt to entirely different industrial, economic, and managerial environments, there is no reason to believe that they cannot experience continued strength in the coming decades. **99**

From "The Future of the American Labor Movement," by Charles B. Craver, in *The Futurist.*

UNDERSTANDING THE READING

1. List four changes in the economy that will make the job of union organizers more difficult in the future.
2. According to Craver, how can unions adjust to the changes you listed in question 1?
3. According to Craver, how should the relationship between labor unions and management change in the future?

Section 3 Review

Understanding Unions

1. Explain why differences between labor and management sometimes result in physical violence.
2. Explain how a union member may be hurt by a strike. How does a strike affect the company?
3. List and explain two measures the government has taken to protect workers.

Unions Today

1. Check a United States history text for information on why unions began in the late 1800s. What were the working conditions in factories then? Write a paragraph explaining what improvements unions have gained for workers.
2. Talk to your parents, teachers, and other adults. Ask them whether they can think of any incidents in the last 10 years when people were injured as a result of a dispute between labor and management. Discuss your findings in class.
3. **Challenge:** Think about the working conditions and benefits you expect from a full-time employer. Make a list of these expectations and discuss them with other students in your class.

Efficiency in a plant depends on cooperation between management and labor, especially as here, between a supervisor and a worker.

Americans *at Work*

Meet Alexandra Armstrong
Financial Planner

"My test of an investment," said Alexandra Armstrong, "is to ask whether it will make you richer 10 years from now." Armstrong is a financial planner. Financial planners provide their clients with a comprehensive strategy to improve the return on their capital resources without significantly increasing their risk. Her approach to financial planning is cautious rather than aggressive. She prefers to direct her clients to good quality investments that appreciate over the years.

In 1977, after 16 years of experience as a securities analyst and stockbroker, Armstrong became cofounder of her own financial planning company. Working in the nation's capital makes her somewhat unusual among financial planners. "Washington is not a city of entrepreneurs," she explained. Her clientele consists largely of salaried, two-income couples employed by the federal government.

Armstrong finds career government employees generally frugal in their personal spending habits. Many of her clients are in high tax brackets. Nevertheless, the concerns of government employees about layoffs and spending cuts have made them extremely cautious. Armstrong tailors her investment advice to the individual needs of her clients.

In order to increase the spendable income of the people she advises, Armstrong tries to find ways of reducing their taxes. She recommends IRAs, Individual Retirement Accounts, because the interest is not taxed until the owner reaches retirement age. Armstrong also likes other investments providing special allowances that investors can use to reduce their income taxes. Investments in commercial property, such as office buildings and rental apartment complexes, are examples of tax-sheltered investments. Investments in firms involved in energy production—oil exploration, for example—also help to reduce income tax.

Armstrong advises her clients that reducing taxes should never be a goal in itself. The long-term return is what an investor should be considering. She favors quality growth stocks over bonds because bond prices drop when interest rates rise. "It's hard for most people to jump from a savings account to a tax shelter," Armstrong said. "They have to build some tolerance to risk. Buying conservative growth stocks is a first step."

231

Investing in Stocks

Imagine that your favorite uncle just gave you a sum of money, and you want to invest it in the stock market. Your major problem is that you know very little about stocks and how to choose them.

There are a few basic rules of investing. An individual should remember that stock purchases represent rewards and risks. If a company makes money, the stock you purchase probably will appreciate, or grow in value. If the company loses money, the value of your stock will decline as well. Also, a company that loses money may not pay a dividend, a share in the company's profits, to its stockholders.

STEP 1   Pick the Right Kind of Stock

Investors can choose among different kinds of companies and stocks. An investor may buy stock in a company with a history of steady growth. Stock in growth companies tends to appreciate in value over a period of time. For immediate income from stock, the investor may consider well-managed utilities, such as electric companies, that are low risk and have paid consistently good dividends for a long time. An experienced and knowledgeable individual who can afford a riskier venture may choose speculative stocks in companies that are taking greater risks in fields such as new product development.

Some stocks are called blue-chip stocks. They are the shares of large, well-managed firms such as General Motors and General Electric. These companies have always paid good dividends and are not likely to fail. The price of the stock has not fluctuated widely, and their product tends to be in steady demand.

STEP 2   Invest in Several Companies

Successful stock investors buy shares in several companies—they diversify. Investing in several companies spreads the risk. One company in the stock portfolio, or collection of stocks, might not perform well. Nevertheless, the other stocks could do so well that the portfolio would not decline in value.

Investors whose funds are limited may buy shares in a mutual fund. A mutual fund sells shares to customers and then, using the money of all the contributors, buys a large portfolio of stocks. The customer has the advantage of professional management to increase the value of the investment. Another advantage is the ability to spread risk through the large portfolio of the mutual fund.

STEP 3 Take a Long-term Approach

A new investor should take a long-term approach to investing in stocks. Investors rarely make enormous profits in the stock market. However, stock in successful companies will increase substantially in value over a period of several years.

STEP 4 Gather Information

An investor should be informed about the companies being considered for investment. A broker, if requested, will send information on any firm that interests the investor. In addition, business magazines, such as *Forbes* and *BusinessWeek,* the financial pages of large metropolitan newspapers, and the *Wall Street Journal* are excellent sources of information for investors. An investor should read the articles and investment advice that appears in these newspapers and magazines.

Finally, an investor should read and follow the stock market itself. The value of stocks sold on the New York Stock Exchange and other markets are listed daily in most major newspapers. The individual investor may follow a stock by reading the stock market page and studying the dividends paid, the yield of the stock, and its price/earning, or PE ratio. The PE ratio is the relationship between the price of a stock and its earnings. Often, a high PE ratio results when investors bid up the price of a stock because they expect its earnings to increase. Investors interested in steady income from dividends prefer stocks with low PE ratios.

In addition, a buyer of stocks should follow the indications of changing prices Industrial Average. This indicator includes 30 stocks that are representative of the major industries of the country.

STEP 5 Purchase Stock

To purchase stock, an investor must work through a broker. A stockbroker is a person licensed to buy and sell stock on one of the stock exchanges. Brokers charge a fee for their service. Their fee is usually a percentage of the total price of the purchase. Brokers who offer investment advice charge more than do those who simply buy and sell based on the investors' directions.

ECONOMIC SKILLS TODAY

1. Explain the difference between stock dividend and stock appreciation.
2. What is a stock portfolio?
3. Why is investment in a mutual fund advantageous to small investors?

Enrichment Activities

1. Pretend you bought 100 shares of stock in five different companies of your choosing. Using graph paper and stock-market reports, follow the price trends of these stocks over several weeks.
2. Research the major stock market indicators to learn whether any correlation can be found in changes among the indicators. The indicators studied could be:

Dow Jones Industrial Average
S&P 500 Index
NYSE Index
NASDAQ Index
Amex Index

233

CHAPTER 7 Summary and Review

CHAPTER SUMMARY

Entrepreneurs

The basic economic institution in the United States capitalist system is the business. Businesses are started by entrepreneurs who are willing to risk their capital. Entrepreneurs often start as sole proprietors or as partners with one or more other individuals. Sole proprietorships and partnerships are easy to organize, decisions can be made quickly, owners receive all profits, and owners are directly responsible for the company. The disadvantages of sole proprietorships and partnerships include limited resources, unlimited liability, and limited life. In the free market society of the United States, the government has taken steps to encourage entrepreneurs through patents and loans.

Corporations

Corporations became an important part of the American economy in the 1800s. A corporation is a form of business that has the legal rights of a person. Ownership is divided among stockholders. A board of directors, elected by the stockholders, is responsible for directing the corporation's business. The advantages of incorporating a business are limited liability, the ability to raise large amounts of money, unlimited life, specialization of management, and the ease of ownership transfer. The disadvantages of incorporating include the problems involved in setting up a corporation, double taxation, division of profits among many owners, the diversity of managers and owners and their different interests, and the size of some large corporations.

Unions

A labor union is an organization of workers that tries to improve conditions for its members. Unions try to obtain higher wages and benefits, shorter work days, safer working conditions, and better job security. Unions use collective bargaining to obtain these improvements. If no agreement can be reached between the workers and the owners of a business, workers may strike. Most unions are members of the American Federation of Labor and Congress of Industrial Organizations, or AFL–CIO. As a result of government legislation and union actions over the years, the living conditions of workers have improved.

CRITICAL THINKING QUESTIONS

Entrepreneurs

1. Give an example of how you, as an entrepreneur, would obtain and use each of the factors of production.
2. Would you prefer to start your own business or work for someone else? Explain your answer.

Corporations

1. What particular types of businesses receive the most advantages from incorporating? Explain your answer.
2. Explain what factors in the American market system result in the development of large corporations.

Unions

1. Explain why a union might choose to be independent and not join the national federation of unions.

2. Explain why workers in a free market system may decide to form a union.
3. As a worker, explain the advantages and disadvantages of union membership.

DEVELOPING ECONOMIC SKILLS

Use the graph and your economic knowledge to answer the questions that follow.

1. In what years were business acquisitions at their lowest? Their highest?

2. What advantage does a large corporation have in the factor markets? In the product markets?
3. As a business becomes very large, how might its size affect workers? Unions?
4. **Challenge:** If General Foods Corporation, a large food-processing business, owned farms, processing plants, packaging plants, and supermarkets, would such ownership be an advantage to General Foods? The consumers? Explain your answers.

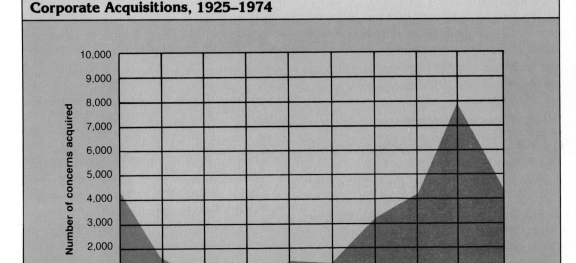

Corporate Acquisitions, 1925–1974

Number of concerns acquired

Source: *Statistical Abstract of the United States.*

Explanation

The graph plots the number of businesses acquired by other companies between 1925 and 1974. The y-axis shows the number of businesses acquired. The x-axis shows the years when they were acquired.

Graph Skills

1. Between which years did the number of business acquisitions rise from about 3,300 to about 4,300?
2. Between which years did the number of business acquisitions fall from 8,000 to 4,500?

UNIT 2 Review

USING ECONOMIC CONCEPTS

Our Market System

1. What is the law of demand? List and explain four factors that may cause the demand curve to shift.
2. What is the law of supply? List and explain the factors that may cause a shift in the supply curve.
3. What is the difference between a change in the supply and a change in the quantity supplied?
4. **Challenge:** Explain the reasons elasticity of demand may vary among products.

Competition in the Market

1. What restrictions limit perfect competition in the real world?
2. In a market economy, how are the four basic economic questions answered?
3. Draw a diagram showing the circular flow of money.

Income and Spending

1. Give an example of each of the five basic types of income in the United States market system.
2. List the four basic categories of workers according to the type of work they do.
3. **Challenge:** Using as an example some money you received and spent recently, explain the multiplier effect.

Economic Institutions

1. What are the advantages and disadvantages of a sole proprietorship? Give an example of each.

2. What advantage do the owners of a corporation have over a sole proprietor?
3. **Challenge:** Explain why workers originally joined together in unions.

APPLYING ECONOMIC SKILLS

Use the chart,"Stock Market Report," to answer these questions.

1. Which stock paid the highest dividend?
2. Which stock rose the most in value over the last two days?
3. Which stock was the least expensive?

Use the chart, "Corporate Profits and Growth," to answer these questions.

1. Compare the growth in sales of the two major food companies listed in the chart. Suggest how competition might help explain the relationship between sales of two companies.
2. Use your library to research one of the companies listed on the chart. Find out what products the company makes. Who are its major competitors?

ECONOMIC REASONING

A popular rock group will be appearing at a local theater. Steve would like to see it and also take his girlfriend. The tickets are $13 each. However, since the group is so popular, Steve knows that he will have to go to the theater the night before and wait in line all night in the cold. He will get to work late the next morning, losing several hours of pay. Even then, he might not be able to get very good seats. On the same night, a less

Stock Market Report, April 17, 1984

A	B	C	D	E	F	G	H	I	J
52-week High	52-week Low	Stock	Div.	PE Ratio	Sales (hds.)	High	Low	Close	Net Change
81	48	Rohm s	1.60	11	48	59¼	58¾	59	– ½
37¾	22¾	Rohrin		6	46	28¾	28⅛	28⅛	– ⅜
18⅞	9⅛	RolinEn		26	1052	11	9¾	10⅞	+1⅛
21⅛	12½	Rollins	.70	165	44	19¾	19⅜	19⅜	+ ¼
30	30¼	RolmCp		21	1368	31	30	30¼	– ¾
7¼	3⅛	Ronson			20	4	3⅞	3⅞	– ⅛
29⅜	15¼	Roper s	.50	7	57	16⅞	16¼	16½	– ¼
34¼	25	Rorer	1.08	15	1125	31⅛	30	30¾	– ⅛
15½	10	Rowan	.08	669	4320	13¾	13⅞	13⅞	– ½
38⅛	23	RC Cos	1.04	21	166	37⅞	37⅞	37⅞.	. . . .
54⅜	40¾	RoylD	2.82	6	1396	53	52⅛	52⅜	+ ⅜
50	32⅝	Rubrmd	.72	15	39	37¼	36	37½	+ ½
14⅛	13¼	RussS n			399	13⅜	13	13⅜	+ ½
25⅛	16⅝	RusTg s	.76	8	139	17½	17⅛	17¼.	. . . .
50	22⅛	RyanH	1.00	8	840	23	22	22⅞	+ ⅛
61⅜	43⅞	Ryders	2.08	10	312	45⅜	45	45¾	+ ⅜
38	16½	Ryind	.60	7	915	17^{6}	16¾	16⅜	–1⅛
29½	12¾	Rymer			1	21	21	21	– ⅜

Source: *Chicago Tribune*, April 17, 1984.

Explanation

The report provides various information about the price, sale and performance of representative stocks on April 17, 1984.

Chart Skills

1. From what source was the stock market report taken?
2. How many kinds of information does the report provide for each stock?

Corporate Profits and Growth

Company	Percent Growth in Sales (5-year average)
Maytag	9.4
General Electric	9.9
Zenith Radio	5.1
Proctor & Gamble	11.3
General Foods	10.0
Campbell Soup	7.7
Hershey Foods	10.0
Coca-Cola	12.8
Pepsi Cola	12.8
Apple Computer	122.3 (3 yr. av.)
IBM	12.8
All-Industry Median	12.4

Source: *Forbes*, January 2, 1984.

Explanation

The chart lists the five-year average growth in sales of all large corporations. The chart also provides the median rate of growth in sales for all industries during the five-year period.

Chart Skills

1. Which corporation showed the greatest growth in sales?
2. Which two corporations showed a 10 percent rate of growth?

popular group is appearing. Tickets are easy to buy and cost only $5 each.

STEP 1 Clarify the Issue

State the basic economic issue that Steve faces in dealing with his problem.

STEP 2 Consider Costs and Benefits

1. List the costs and benefits of buying concert tickets.
2. List the costs and benefits of going to the concert of a less popular group.

STEP 3 Make a Decision

What do you think Steve should do? Explain your opinion.

CURRENT ECONOMIC ISSUES

The United States gains in worker output per hour were the lowest in the industrial world for the years 1977–81. What incentives can companies use to encourage Americans workers to be more productive in the future?

UNIT 3

The Nation's Economy

CHAPTER 8

Measuring Economic Change

1 Gross National Product

Objective: to understand gross national product (GNP) and its application in measuring a nation's economic performance

2 Adjusting GNP

Objective: to understand how GNP is adjusted to make it a more useful economic measurement

3 Economic Indicators

Objective: to understand economic indicators and evaluate their use in predicting economic trends

1 Gross National Product

SECTION OVERVIEW

Everyone wants to be successful. Society often measures success in terms of money. Success also involves personal satisfaction gained from accomplishing a task. However, the satisfaction a person gains from a job is more difficult to measure than the amount of money received. Countries also try to measure the success of their national economies. Analyzing a national economy involves many factors, some of which cannot be measured by data. In this section, you will learn about one measure of an economy's success, gross national product.

ECONOMIC VOCABULARY

microeconomics	gross national product (GNP)	flow-of-product approach
macroeconomics	final goods and services	earnings-and-cost approach

Measuring a Country's Output

The American economy comprises many sectors. Economists study these different parts of the economy in different ways.

Some economists consider specific parts of the economy. These people may study how one product market operates, or the way one group of consumers decides how to spend money. Microeconomics is the branch of economics that analyzes specific factors affecting an economy.

Some economists consider the ways various factors work together in an economy. These people may study changes in the nation's unemployment rate, or the ways the government influences the general economy. Macroeconomics is the branch of economics that analyzes interrelationships among sectors of the economy. Rather than a specific market, macroeconomists study all markets as they work together.

Macroeconomists use various methods to measure the performance of the economy. Statistics measure gross national product, or GNP, which is the value of all goods and services produced for sale during one year. All the goods and services produced must be counted, and their value in dollars and cents determined. For example, every new car and haircut must be included. If a farmer produces 1,000 bushels of apples worth $10 per bushel, that farmer would add $10,000 to the year's GNP. In 1983, the United States GNP was $3.3 trillion.

In the United States the Department of Commerce, an agency of the federal government, computes GNP. Information is collected for every good or service produced in the nation during a year, but not everything is counted. Three factors limit the types of products counted.

First, only goods and services produced during a specific year are counted. Anything produced before or after that year is not added into GNP for that year.

Consumers must make decisions such as whether or not to buy a particular product.

Second, not every good or service produced and sold during the year can be counted. For example, if an individual consumer buys flour, the price paid for the flour is counted as part of GNP. Since it will not be sold again, it is in its final form. However, if a baker uses flour it is counted only as part of the final product the baker produced, such as a loaf of bread. If both the flour the baker used and the bread produced were counted, the flour would be added in twice and so exaggerate the gross national product. To avoid this problem of double counting, economists count a product or service only in its final form. They count the baker's flour in its final product form—that is, as a loaf of bread or a cake. Products in their final form are called final goods and services.

Third, GNP includes only goods sold for the first time. When used goods are resold or transferred, no wealth is created. Since GNP measures the total value of an economy's production, only new goods produced for sale are counted.

Measuring Spending

One way in which economists measure GNP is the flow-of-product approach. Using this method, they count all the money spent on goods and services to determine total value. Each time a new product is sold, GNP increases. For example, when an individual, a business, or a government buys a chair for $50, that purchase causes GNP to increase by $50. The flow of products is shown by the direction of arrows at the top of the diagram.

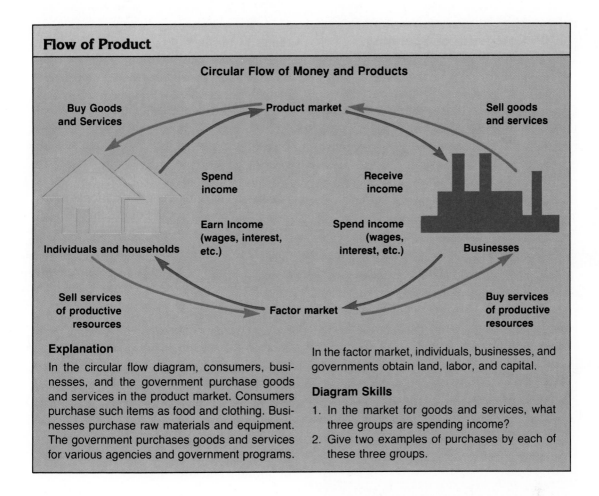

Flow of Product

Circular Flow of Money and Products

Buy Goods and Services

Product market

Sell goods and services

Spend income

Receive income

Earn Income (wages, interest, etc.)

Spend income (wages, interest, etc.)

Individuals and households

Businesses

Sell services of productive resources

Factor market

Buy services of productive resources

Explanation

In the circular flow diagram, consumers, businesses, and the government purchase goods and services in the product market. Consumers purchase such items as food and clothing. Businesses purchase raw materials and equipment. The government purchases goods and services for various agencies and government programs.

In the factor market, individuals, businesses, and governments obtain land, labor, and capital.

Diagram Skills

1. In the market for goods and services, what three groups are spending income?
2. Give two examples of purchases by each of these three groups.

Categories of Spending

Spending for products falls into four categories. The first, and largest, consumer spending, includes all expenditures of individuals for final goods and services. Called personal consumption expenditures, this category accounts for about 65 percent of GNP. The second category includes all spending of businesses for new capital goods. Since these purchases are investments, this category is called gross private domestic investment. It accounts for about 13 percent of GNP.

The third category includes spending of all levels of government. Called government purchases of goods and services, it accounts for about 21 percent of GNP. The

fourth category is net exports of goods and services. Many products made in the United States are sold outside the country, and many products sold in the United States are made abroad. GNP must be adjusted to reflect these conditions. The category for exports accounts for less than 1 percent of GNP. The four categories of spending are shown on the chart.

Measuring Receipts

Another way of determining GNP is the earnings-and-cost approach. This method accounts for all the money received for the production of goods and services.

The flow-of-product approach measures spending; the earnings-and-cost ap-

243

GNP: Categories of Spending

Personal Consumption Expenditures **$2,158.6 Billion**
Gross Private Domestic Investment **$471.3 Billion**
Government Purchases of Goods and Services **$690.2 Billion**
Net Exports of Goods and Services **−$10.6 Billion**

Source: Bureau of Economic Analysis.

Explanation

The chart shows the four categories used in the flow-of-product approach to measuring GNP.

Chart Skills

1. How much money did consumers in the United States spend in 1982?
2. Which category of spending was the smallest part of GNP in 1982? The largest?

proach measures receipts. For example, an economist using this approach to count the value of a chair might include in GNP the $20 for the lumberyard, the $5 for the paint store, the $5 for wear and tear on tools used to make the chair, and the $20 for the labor. The total cost would be $50. By measuring how much money each factor received, the economist can determine that the value of the chair is $50.

Figuring gross national product by counting what people receive requires calculating what the entire country earns for the goods it makes and the services it performs. Included in earnings are such things as business profits, wages and salaries, and taxes the government receives for its services. Also counted are interest on bank deposits, money received as rent, and any other forms of income.

Measuring Economic Success

No way of determining gross national product is entirely accurate. Some data are hard to obtain. Government economists must estimate some information. The two approaches discussed here lead to a rough estimate of the total value of the economy's production in a given year.

Measuring gross national product each year can show whether the economy of a country is growing or shrinking, healthy or sick. GNP is a standard by which the economy as a whole can be judged. The economy is expanding when GNP increases. The economy is contracting when GNP declines. GNP also can be used to compare one country's economy with the economy of another and with itself over time.

What GNP Does Not Measure

Useful as it is, GNP still is less than ideal for determining how well the economy is working. Several economic factors are not measured at all.

First, GNP counts only goods and services that are sold. It does not count those given away free. Since GNP measures only goods and services that command a price, a great deal of productive work is not counted. Housework, volunteer work in hospitals, and gardening are examples of productive work usually not included in GNP. The work of people mowing their own lawns is not included in GNP. The work of garden center employees who mow lawns and get paid for it counts as part of GNP.

Second, GNP does not take into account improvements in efficiency. Americans today produce more goods and services during a 40-hour workweek than their grandparents did during a 60-hour week. Increases in efficiency have allowed people more free time. However, GNP does not reflect this improvement.

Third, GNP does not measure changes in the quality of goods and services produced. It measures only quantity. Television sets, for example, are much better today than they were in 1955. In general, they also cost less. However, GNP shows only that the total value of television sets produced today is greater than their total value in 1955.

The fourth factor not measured creates perhaps the most serious problem in using GNP as an economic standard. GNP cannot show whether the economy is making people's lives better or worse. For example, industry creates air and water pollution. GNP measures the output of industry, but it does not measure the pollution that goes along with that output. GNP does, however, measure the money that must be spent to clean up the air and water.

REVIEWING THE CONCEPT

Developing Vocabulary

Complete each statement with the correct item from the list that follows.

microeconomics
macroeconomics
gross national product
final goods and services
flow-of-product
earnings-and-cost

1. _____ measures the market value of all the final goods and services produced.
2. _____ is the study of the total performance of the economy.
3. The _____ approach to GNP calculates the value of goods and services received.
4. The _____ approach to GNP counts the money received for production.
5. _____ is the study of specific markets.

Mastering Facts

1. What are two different ways of counting the value of goods and services?
2. Why is it useful to have GNP figures available every year?
3. Why does GNP not measure perfectly an economy's productivity?

CASE STUDY

The Value of Your Production

GNP is widely used as a measure of the economy's health, even though it does not measure well all economic activity. GNP summarizes the contributions to the economy from all individuals, companies, and levels of government. Consider your contribution to the nation's overall economy. The money you spend and the goods and services you produce are part of the activity GNP measures.

When GNP is determined by the flow-of-product method, your contribution is measured by your spending. When you spend money, you receive products and services in return. The amounts paid for clothes, movies, concerts, school supplies,

Many economic activities are not counted in GNP.

gifts, and other goods and services are just part of your contribution. They are the easiest to count. In addition, your family buys certain products, such as food, for your consumption. These products also are part of your contribution. You also may cause your family to buy more automobile insurance, a bigger house, or more electricity. The taxes you and your family pay provide the money for police and fire protection, a public library, and national defense. Since no part of these expenses may be attributed directly to you, or to any single individual, all share their cost. Therefore, part of your family's taxes should be considered as your payment for these public services.

When GNP is determined by the earnings-and-cost approach, your contribution is measured by your production. Your major productive resource probably is your labor. The income you receive from working is the measure of the amount of work

you do. If you have a part-time job at a grocery store, for example, your wages are the measure of the value of the goods or services you produced.

Other contributions you make to the nation's economy may not be included in GNP. You may consume or produce products or services without money changing hands. For example, you may do yardwork for your parents but may not be paid. Think of all the services you perform for no pay. You may babysit for younger brothers or sisters, clean the house, repair the car, weed the garden, shovel snow for an elderly neighbor, and do other tasks without pay. Further, some of the activities you do for fun may have an economic value that is not included in GNP. Professional athletics and theater are included in GNP. However, your performance in a school play or basketball game may not be included, even though the activity provides entertainment and perhaps raises money for your school.

Finally, your major form of work is not included at all—your schoolwork. All the efforts you put into producing academic work do not show up in the measurement of the nation's production.

ANALYZING THE CASE STUDY

STEP 1　Clarify the Issue

1. What kind of goods and services does GNP count?
2. Summarize the kinds of goods and services not included in GNP.

STEP 2　Consider Alternatives

1. List five activities that you think contribute most to the nation's production but are not measured in GNP. Estimate the dollar value of each contribution.
2. Estimate the dollar value of your contribution to GNP using the flow-of-product approach and the earnings-and-cost ap-

proach. How close are the estimates you reach by each method?

STEP 3   Predict Change

1. In what different way could GNP be figured so that it would be a more accurate measure?
2. How could your labor be more fairly included?

Enrichment Activity

Some economists have suggested alternatives to GNP that attempt a more accurate measurement of the nation's total production. One is called Net Economic Welfare, or NEW. Use a library to find information on NEW or another alternative to GNP and write a one-page report on it.

READING

Estimating GNP

by Edward Meadows   (1944-   )

When you complete your economics course, you probably will get a single grade evaluating your performance. A full evaluation of your performance would grade how well you did on tests and quizzes, how hard you worked, your contributions in class, and how much you learned. Yet, only a single letter shows on your report card. The growth of the economy is also a complex activity that is often reported by means of one figure. Consequently, an inaccurate GNP, like an inaccurate grade, may shape people's opinions unfairly. In an article in *Fortune* magazine, Edward Meadows points out the difficulties of measuring GNP. As you read, ask yourself how different your perception of the strength of the economy would be if you ignored these difficulties.

❝ Four times a year, the federal government makes a heroic attempt to sum up in a single number all the multifaceted movements of the American economy. What results is gross national product, the statistic relied on as the major index of national prosperity. GNP can't really measure prosperity, of course, for it ignores many of the things that make life worthwhile, such as sunsets and home cooking, and counts all manner of unpleasant things, like the costs of hurricanes and wars. And since the number is jerry-built from incomplete data, it is riddled with error. GNP is eternally being revised. . . .

Revisions are an inescapable fact of life at the Commerce Department's Bureau of Economic Analysis, where the statistics for gross national product are produced. The bewildering truth is that no GNP figure is *ever* final. There are six routine revisions of each original estimate, and major revisions of the whole series every few years.

The main reason for all this tinkering is the immensity of the job.

GNP, which measures the market value of all final goods and services produced in the country over a period of time, is derived from a large number of sources, none of which was designed to make life easy for the BEA's technicians. For example, data on consumer spending comes from the Census Bureau's monthly survey of retail stores and a tally of car sales put out by the Motor Vehicle Manufacturers Association. Information about government purchases is taken from the *Monthly Treasury Statement;* farm income is estimated by the Agriculture Department. These sources do not always meet the standards of accuracy required by economists, and many of the numbers just do not get released in time for quarterly GNP estimates.

So the BEA keeps updating its estimates as new data flow into its Washington offices. The very first quarterly figure is an unpublished "guesstimate," known officially as a projection, which is given only to the President's Council of Economic Advisers and some cabinet members, as well as the Federal Reserve Board. This rough estimate is made fifteen days before the end of every quarter. It becomes raw material for a more refined version that is released to the public about fifteen days after a quarter's close. . . . And since last year the BEA has been putting out yet another estimate seventy-five days after the end of a quarter, when more reliable statistics are in the hands of the bureau's "estimators."

But that's only the beginning. GNP is further revised in each of three successive Julys, when the bureau finally gets hold of comprehensive annual surveys, allowing use of such sources as yearly corporate profit sums reported on tax returns. Then come the occasional, large-scale revisions that the BEA calls "benchmarks" because they set new levels for the series by using data from the Census Bureau's five-year economic census. . . .

Throughout all these estimates and revisions, the BEA's statisticians are juggling two complete sets of numbers that are approximate mirror images of each other. The figure everybody is familiar with is actually the "product side" of the National Income and Product Accounts. . . . The other side of the accounts is the "income side," which totals wages, profits, rents, and interest—all the forms of income people receive for goods and services sold.

The totals from both the product and income sides ought to match each other exactly, since they are merely two different ways of adding up the same transactions. But because the estimation procedure is imprecise, they usually don't match, and the difference is labeled the "statistical discrepancy." . . .

Life gets hectic at the BEA's headquarters when the end of a quarter rolls around. Up on the eighth floor of Washington's dowdy Tower Building, GNP estimators sit at their desks scribbling on ruled work sheets, constantly checking numbers against other numbers to see if they "make sense." There's an estimator for each of the four letters in the

Former Treasury Secretary Donald Regan contemplates statistics collected by the federal government about the nation's economy.

GNP equation, and each of these four chief estimators commands a team of assistants who specialize in separate categories.

For instance, the estimator in charge of consumption expenditures watches over one junior estimator for durable goods, another for nondurable goods, and a third who handles services. As the raw data come in, these statisticians have to process them, adding here, subtracting there, so that the information matches the definitions required for the national accounts. After all, most of the sources used are really designed to serve the administrative needs of the organizations supplying the data. They rarely fit the concepts and timing of the GNP accounts. . . . A few of the estimations involve sheer guesswork, as when, for instance, an estimator "inputes" the income from owner-occupied homes by deciding how much rent such houses would earn if they weren't occupied by their owners. Unlike many government statistical processes, estimating GNP isn't a cut-and-dried mechanical procedure calculated inside the bowels of a computer. . . . The estimators do feed their figures into a computer, but only after considerable exercise of judgment, hunch, and even speculation. . . .

And then there are various attempts to devise a better measure of the national welfare. An oil spill, for example, actually increases GNP because money is spent to clean up the damage. War is an absolute boon to measured economic growth. GNP does not count the value of work done in the household, or recognize the depletion of natural resources . . . Illness and crime are ignored when the data are added up. In short, GNP does not say much about the quality of American life. A few analysts have tried their hand at GNP adjustments—adding household production, for example, and subtracting for all sorts of social ills—to wind up with such notions as "Net Economic Welfare," but these efforts remain curiosities of social science.

Jack Cremeans, at the BEA's Division of Environmental and Nonmarket Economics, explains the problem this way: "There is no consensus on what to add or what to subtract. Economists don't know how to measure 'welfare.'"

He says that when experts do try to correct the GNP's conceptual deficiencies, they find that the Depression years of 1932 and 1937, for instance, turn out to have been "great" years. That's because during those bleak years, there was lots of household production, what with everybody out of work. And recession, contends Cremeans, is the greatest thing in the world for slowing down pollution. With factories idle, the air turns clear and the rivers cleanse themselves of contaminating chemicals. All of which suggests the dimensions of the value judgments required to create any measure of national welfare.

Still, Cremeans has some sympathy for the aims of would-be social accountants. Since 1974 his office has published estimates of expenditures on pollution abatement, which can be substracted from GNP if anyone yearns to do it. Cremeans's office has now started a study to see whether it makes sense to try to sum up the value of household production and account for the depletion of natural resources. If Cremeans decides to go ahead with these or other tabulations, the results will be published as supplementary information alongside pollution-abatement figures. But he insists that the BEA won't get into the business of actually adjusting GNP. "We don't want to louse up a series like the GNP that has been going since 1929," he says.

Perhaps, considering the vast and unruly data that are drawn together and processed to produce the GNP statistics, the wonder is not that the numbers so often need revising, but that they work as well as they do. . . .

As with all the statistics explored in this series, however, the GNP figures must be understood in their proper context. The maddening degree to which these numbers are routinely revised is sufficient evidence of their imprecision. The quarterly estimates can provide some guidance as to whether the economy is picking up speed or slowing down; they are not precise measures of the magnitude of the change.

As George Jaszi, director of the BEA, likes to say, "The GNP statistics are a butter knife, not a scalpel." But even a butter knife, in determined hands, can draw blood. And policymakers who overreact to minute changes in the GNP growth rate are apt to do more damage than if they'd waited out a revision or two. **99**

"Tracking the Ever-Elusive GNP," by Edward Meadows, *Fortune*, May 22, 1978.

UNDERSTANDING THE READING

1. According to Meadows, what are the problems in the Department of Commerce GNP calculation?

2. What importance do the frequent revisions of GNP figures have for economic policy?
3. What are the problems in using GNP as a measure of the national welfare?

Section 1 Review

Understanding Gross National Product

1. Why are final goods and services emphasized in measuring GNP?
2. What must be included if GNP is figured by counting expenditures? By counting income?

Gross National Product Today

1. Why would GNP include electricity for a home but not that for a factory?

2. What groups probably make the most use of GNP figures?
3. **Challenge:** Use the library to research the GNP figures for 1983 or 1984 and analyze the degree of each component's contribution to GNP. Which is highest? Why? Why are imports low?
4. **Challenge:** Use the graphs and your knowledge of economics to answer the graph skills questions.

Gross National Product

Yearly
Percent change from prior year

1973 74 75 76 77 78 79 80 81 82 83

Quarterly
Percent change from prior quarter

1st   2d   3d   4th

Source: Department of Commerce.

Explanation

The graph on the left shows the yearly change in gross national product for each year from 1973 to 1983. The percentage change shows the increase or decrease in GNP from the prior year. The graph on the right shows the quarterly change in gross national product during 1983. The percentage change shows the increase or decrease from the prior quarter.

Graph Skills

1. In what year did GNP decline the most? In what year did it decline the least?
2. In what year did GNP increase the most? In what year did it increase the least?
3. Explain why the quarterly information is less accurate than the yearly information.
4. Compare the 1983 quarterly and yearly percentages. How are they similar? Different?

251

2 Adjusting GNP

SECTION OVERVIEW

Just as grades are an indication of performance in school, GNP is an indication of national economic performance. However, using grades alone as indicators can be misleading. Some classes are harder than others. Your skills probably are greater in one area than in others. You may be happy with a B in one class but disappointed with a B in another. Like grades, GNP figures must be adjusted to take in other factors. In this section, you will learn about two of the adjustments made to GNP.

ECONOMIC VOCABULARY

money GNP	deflation	price index	GNP deflator
current GNP	real GNP	base year	per capita GNP
inflation	constant dollar GNP		

Price Changes and GNP

Gross national product is a measure of production. It is often used to compare the health of the economy in two different years. The unit used to measure GNP is the dollar. The value of each good and service is determined in dollars. Therefore, the GNP figures for a year are called money GNP or current GNP.

In a market economy, the value of a product is its price. Prices change constantly. Each change in price affects GNP. If the prices of all items increase 10 percent, GNP will appear to have increased 10 percent also, even if production remained constant. To remain an accurate measure of production, GNP must be adjusted to account for changes in prices.

A general rise in prices and wages is called inflation. A general decline in prices and wages is called deflation. Numerous factors cause inflation and deflation in a market economy. Among them are changes in the prices of the three basic resources—natural, human, and capital—and the actions of governments.

In 1981 current GNP was $2,954 billion. In 1982, it was $3,073 billion. However, inflation was high in 1982, so the increase in GNP reflected rising prices, not an actual increase in production. Money GNP must be adjusted for inflation or deflation to determine real or constant dollar GNP. Real GNP actually declined slightly from 1981 to 1982.

Price Indexes

In order to determine the rate of inflation or deflation in an economy, economists construct a price index. A price index is a comparison of current prices to the prices of another year. The United States Bureau of Labor Statistics (BLS) computes the Consumer Price Index (CPI) each month to determine price changes in the country. The CPI is made up of about 400 goods and services a typical family purchases. Items include food and beverages, housing, clothes, transportation, medical care, and entertainment. The BLS also computes several other price indexes. Among them is the Producer Price Index (PPI), which is similar to the CPI but includes items producers, rather than consumers, buy. Some of the products included in the PPI are coal, lumber, and grain.

To construct a price index, first, a base year is selected for purposes of comparison. A base year serves as the point of comparison to measure changes in other years. A recent year during which prices generally remained steady is chosen as a base year. It then is the standard for evaluating price changes in all other years. The Consumer Price Index uses 1967 as a base year.

Second, a list of products available in the base year is selected. If the price index is to cover the entire economy, a wide variety of products is chosen. Items might include chewing gum, radios, and movie tickets. If the price index is to measure price changes in only one area, then goods and services are chosen only from that area. For example, a price index for medical care would include only products related to medical care, such as doctors' services and medicine.

Finally, the price of each item in the base year is recorded. All the prices are added together to yield a total amount representing the prices in the base year. This total is given the value of 100. For example, if 1972 is chosen as a base year, 1972 prices are valued at 100. Then prices in all other years being compared are expressed as being higher or lower than those during 1972. If prices in another year add

Sample Price Index			
Product	Price		
	1970 (base year)	1977	1982
One quart of milk	$0.27	$0.37	$0.48
One dozen eggs	0.39	0.56	0.60
One gallon regular gas	0.36	0.62	1.22
Paperback book	0.95	1.95	2.95
Total Cost	$1.97	$3.50	
Index Number	100	178	

Source: Department of Labor.

Explanation

The chart shows a price index. Since 1970 is used as a base year, the total price of goods, $1.97, receives the value of 100. To determine the index number for any other year, divide that year's prices by the result. Then multiply by 100 to change the answer from a decimal to a whole number. To calculate the index number for 1977, divide the current price, $3.50, by base price, $1.97. Then multiply the quotient, 1.78, by 100 to get the index number, 178.

Chart Skills

1. Calculate the total 1982 cost of the four items in the sample price index.
2. What is the index number for 1982 using 1970 as the base year?
3. What is the percentage of price increase for these items between 1970 and 1982?

up to half of the 1972 total, then the price index for the year compared is 50. If the sum is twice the 1972 amount, then the price index is 200. The chart shows an example of a price index.

Adjusting GNP for Inflation

Economists also compute the GNP deflator, another type of price index. The GNP

Comparing Money and Real GNP

Year	Money GNP ($ billion)	GNP Deflator	Real (1972) GNP ($ billion)
1960	507	68.7	738
1965	691	74.4	929
1970	993	91.5	1,085
1975	1,549	125.8	1,231
1980	2,633	178.6	1,474
1981	2,954	195.1	1,514
1982	3,073	206.9	1,485
1983	3,309	215.6	1,535

Source: Bureau of Economic Analysis.

Explanation

The chart shows gross national product for various years from 1960 to 1983. Money GNP for 1975 was $1,549 trillion, and the GNP deflator was 125.8. Dividing the money GNP, $1,549 trillion, by the GNP deflator, 125.8, and multiplying by 100 gives real GNP, $1,231 trillion. Real GNP provides a more realistic basis for comparing two or more years in which prices differed. The base year used in the chart is 1972. Therefore, the GNP deflator is computed on the basis of 1972 equaling 100.

Chart Skills

1. What was the trend in real gross national product through 1983?
2. What is the base year?
3. Does dividing money GNP by the GNP deflator always result in a lower real GNP? Explain your answer.
4. Explain what happened to the productivity of the United States between the years 1981 and 1982.
5. What two components used in calculating real GNP are calculated from a base year?

Gross National Product (GNP)

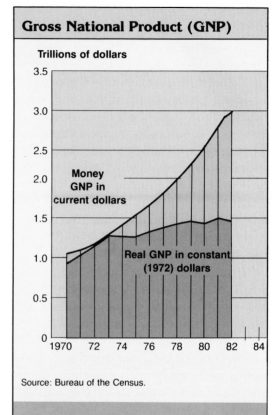

Source: Bureau of the Census.

Explanation

The graph illustrates the difference between money GNP and real GNP. The rate of growth appears to be much greater before adjustment for price changes than after application of the GNP deflator.

Graph Skills

1. In 1982, what was the money GNP? What was real GNP?
2. What does the area between the two lines on the graph represent?
3. Explain why money GNP and real GNP were the same in 1972.

deflator measures the price changes of all goods and services using 1972 as the base year. The purpose of this index is to remove from gross national product the effects of inflationary price changes that do not re-flect changes in productivity. Therefore, the money GNP is divided by the GNP deflator and the quotient then is multiplied by 100. Real GNP enables economists and government planners to compare GNP in different years to determine the economy's growth rate.

Growth of per Capita GNP

Year	Real (1972) GNP (billions)	Population (millions)	Real (1972) GNP per Capita
1960	$ 737	180.7	$4,079
1965	929	194.3	4,781
1970	1,086	205.1	5,295
1975	1,232	216.0	5,704
1980	1,474	227.7	6,473
1981	1,514	229.8	6,588
1982	1,485	232.1	6,398
1983	1,535	234.2	6,554

Source: Bureau of Economic Analysis.

Explanation

The chart shows gross national product before and after adjustments for population growth. To find per capita GNP, economists divide the constant dollar GNP by the number of people in the country. Per capita GNP in 1960 was $4,079. In other words, the value of all the goods and services that were produced in the United States in 1960 amounted to $4,079 per capita, or person.

Chart Skills

1. What is the trend in population growth in the United States?
2. In what years did real GNP increase in the United States? Decrease?
3. In what years did per capita GNP increase in the United States? Decrease?
4. Real GNP almost doubled from 1960 through 1982. During the same period, per capita GNP increased from $4,079 to $6,398. Explain why per capita GNP did not double along with real GNP.

Per Capita GNP in 12 Countries

Country	Per Capita GNP 1980 (in constant 1979 dollars)
Switzerland	16,210
United States	10,408
Canada	9,189
Japan	8,946
Czechoslovakia	7,437
Soviet Union	4,861
Peru	819
Philippines	631
Ethiopia	134
Bangladesh	112

Source: Arms Control and Disarmament Agency.

Explanation

This chart shows the wide range of per capita GNP among the countries of the world. The leading countries are highly industrialized.

Graph Skills

1. Which country had the highest per capita GNP in 1980? The lowest?
2. Compare the locations of the countries. What pattern exists?

Adjusting GNP for Population

Unadjusted, gross national product also shows the effect of population changes. Remember that gross national product measures production. If the population increases, production probably will increase, too. To determine the significance of production changes, economists need to know per capita GNP. Per capita GNP is the total production of a nation's economy divided by its population.

Per capita GNP also is useful in comparing the economies of countries. For example, the United States population is much larger than that of France. So comparing real GNPs of the United States and France would not show truly the difference in the two countries' production.

REVIEWING THE CONCEPT

Developing Vocabulary

1. Define inflation and deflation.
2. What is the difference between money GNP and real GNP?
3. Explain the use of a base year in constructing a price index.

255

4. What is the purpose of constructing a price index?
5. Define GNP deflator.
6. What is the meaning of per capita?

Mastering Facts

1. What steps are followed in constructing a price index?

2. Explain why real GNP is better than money GNP as an indicator of the United States economic health.
3. How is per capita GNP determined?
4. What are the two principal price indexes that economists use to determine the rate of inflation or deflation? What does each include?

Comparing Costs of Education

Adjustments to GNP make it a more accurate measure of production. These adjustments also influence each of the items that make up GNP. Government spending for public education is just one small part of GNP. Analyzing how such spending has changed over time can show how the cost of your education compares with the cost of your parents' education. Depending on the figures used, the comparisons can lead to very different conclusions. Compare the three following statements.

Statement A. Between 1960 and 1980, government spending on public education skyrocketed. In 1960, the nation spent $15.6 billion on education. By 1980, this amount had risen dramatically, to $96 billion. In the short span of 20 years, government spending for public education had increased 514 percent.

Statement B. Between 1960 and 1980, government spending on public education increased moderately. In current dollars, spending increased 514 percent. In constant dollars, spending increased 133 percent. Part of this increase resulted from an increase in the number of students.

Statement C. Between 1960 and 1980, government spending on public education

stayed fairly stable. In 1960, expenditures for education accounted for 3.1 percent of GNP. By 1980, that percentage had risen to 3.6 percent. An increase of only 0.5 percent barely affects the economy.

ANALYZING THE CASE STUDY

STEP 1   Read Charts

1. What was the net change in total expenditures for public education in current dollars? In constant dollars?
2. What was the percent change in per capita expenditures in current dollars? In constant dollars?
3. What was the net change in the percentage of total GNP that the government spent for education?

STEP 2   Consider Alternatives

1. Match each sentence below with the statement (A, B, or C) in the Case Study that would best support it.
   a. Since the United States has barely increased government spending for public education since 1960, it should spend more now.
   b. The United States cannot afford to

Government Spending on Public Education 1960–1980

	1960	1980	Net Change	Percentage Change
Total expenditures (billions)				
in current dollars	$ 15.6	$ 96.0	$ 80.4	514.0
in constant (1980) dollars	$ 41.3	$ 96.0	$ 54.7	133.0
Per pupil expenditures				
in current dollars	$ 472	$2,491	$2,019	427.8
in constant (1980) dollars	$1,247	$2,491	$1,244	99.7
Per capita expenditures				
in current dollars	$ 87	$ 424	$ 337	387.0
in constant (1980) dollars	$ 230	$ 424	$ 194	84.0
Percentage of total GNP spent for education	3.1	3.6	0.5	16.0

Source: National Center for Education Statistics.

Explanation

The chart shows how total expenditures, per pupil, and per capita expenditures for education changed between 1960 and 1980. Amounts are given in both current and constant (1980) dollars. The chart also shows the percentage of the GNP spent for education in 1960 and 1980. The final column in the chart, percentage change, compares the net change with the 1960 level of spending.

Chart Skills

1. Explain why the changes in current dollars apear to be much larger than those in constant dollars.
2. Explain why the amounts for 1980 in current dollars and in constant dollars are the same.
3. Why are the per pupil expenditures much higher than the per capita expenditures? Which figures would opponents of increased education spending probably cite?

continually increase federal government spending for public education as it did between 1960 and 1980.

c. As long as the economy continues to grow, the United States can afford to maintain its moderate rate of growth in federal government spending for public education.

2. What statistics do people use to support their belief that education spending should increase rapidly?

3. What statistics do people use to support their belief that education spending should not increase?

STEP 3 **Make a Decision**

With which of the three statements do you agree most? Explain your position in a one-paragraph statement.

Enrichment Activity

Find out how much your school district or state spent for public education in 1960. Your library may have copies of the local newspaper, school budgets, or tax records that will help you. Describe in a one-page report how spending for education has changed in your community since 1960.

257

GNP Comparisons

by Alex Rubner   (1920-   )

Colleges often use high school grades to compare the abilities of applicants for admission. Most admissions directors recognize that two students with identical grades from two different schools may possess very different abilities. Similarly, GNP is often used to compare the abilities of two different economies to produce wealth. According to British economist Alex Rubner, people should recognize that two countries with identical GNPs may actually have very different abilities to produce wealth. This reading is taken from Rubner's book, *Three Sacred Cows of Economics*. As you read, consider how comparing GNPs of different countries can be misleading.

"Sometimes the pleasure of cultivating roses comes from beating one's own past efforts or from surpassing the excellence of roses planted by an envious neighbor. Such comparisons can indeed often determine the intensity of enjoyment experienced by botanical enthusiasts. Yet it is also not uncommon for some dedicated gardeners to glow with joy when—without any thought for the size and fragrance of other roses—they lovingly behold the blooms of roses which they have grown from a cutting, nurtured, watered, and manured with dedication.

Unlike roses, GNP figures by themselves can never generate joy. To say that the national cake has a value of $X or creates Y amount of usefulness means nothing in isolation. Such numbers only become significant once they are contrasted with the quantities of other GNPs. The primary reason for calculating GNPs is to make possible comparisons over time and with other countries.

It is, of course, common ground that the path of GNP comparisons is strewn with imponderable nails. The majority of economists claim that despite these nails, such comparisons do deliver a powerful message on relative standards of wealth. A minority claim that the resultant knowledge is flimsy. Some critics even argue that these GNP comparisons may actually do harm by producing distorted pictures which take up effort that could be used to study national welfare by other, better indicators.

No one, to my knowledge, has ever been guilty of claiming that the measurement of national output is, in itself, a worthy job. Clearly there is no meaningfulness in simply producing a series of GNP figures. What, then, is the reason for all this effort? The per capita GNPs are said to provide a measuring stick for national standards of economic health. In addition, they reflect countries' ability to support international organizations and countries' need to receive aid.

Once one accepts that the collection of comparative GNPs is motivated by the purpose of comparing the health of other economies, one has moved away from the field of objectivity which characterizes other national measurements, such as how many dogs live in a country, or the average birthrate. I believe that measuring health depends on subjective criteria and national peculiarities. The GNP enthusiasts are caught between the devil and the deep sea. So far as their output tables are concerned, they may represent correct and objective data but, on their own admission, these are by themselves meaningless. Once statisticians use these figures to compare the strength of different economies, they are no longer measuring objective matters, because GNP values do not accurately mirror relative national standards of poverty or wealth. GNP comparisons cannot be both objective and meaningful.

There are several reasons why GNP does not satisfactorily compare the standards of living in different eras and countries. A nation's welfare is not necessarily linked to its output.

If the Dutch and Kenyan GNPs both record $100 million of road building, this could mean that the inhabitants of the Netherlands have benefited from 10 miles of new roads and the Kenyans only of 5 miles; this difference would be due to the flat countryside of the Netherlands and the mountainous terrain of Kenya. The costs of supplying 1 gallon of water and the price charged for it may be 5 times higher in Kuwait than in Ireland. It is wrong to suggest that a mile of road and a pint of water create different amounts of value according to the varying national costs of producing them. Yet this is the way GNP is usually determined.

Further, all values are treated alike as equally useful. Thus, when a dictator recruits 1 million persons to dig a canal and then employs another million to fill it in again, the output values of these 2 million people are seen as helping GNP in that country. When the Burmese built pagodas, Burmese GNP increased. Some economists believe that just as individuals with the same income must be assumed to have the same standard of living, so nations with the same GNP output must be deemed to have the same standard of living.

Assume my friend Joe and I both have the same income but I *must* wear spectacles to earn my living, while he need not. Since I must pay an average of $20 to care for and occasionally replace these glasses, my standard of living is lower than his.

When countries A and B both have a $500 per capita GNP, level of living in each cannot always be determined from this figure. If, for example, country A feels it has to spend $200 per capita on military preparations while country B does not, then country B will have a higher standard of living.

Comparisons over time are also difficult. The British 1970 GNP is in every way bigger than that of 1870. Part of today's national cake, however, includes output that does not bring about a superior standard of living. It satisfies needs that have been created by the urbanization of the economy. This urbanization has raised living costs.

Town life results in higher expenditure on lighting, roads, and sewage disposal. Distribution costs go up because of the packaging and transportation costs added to base prices of food. If high buildings are more expensive to construct per square foot of dwelling, then part of the resultant increased housing costs are due to urbanization. If one assumes that people like spending some of their leisure time in rural surroundings, the additional expenses of traveling to the countryside must be counted as another cost element caused by the rural-urban transformation.

The farm worker may regard with envy the steel worker who drives to work in his car. The farm worker walks for 5 minutes to his workplace while the latter must drive bumper-to-bumper to the steel plant which is 20 miles from his home. Of course, we are better off today than we were 100 years ago, but the 1970 GNP of the urbanized United Kingdom overstates this superiority when compared with the 1870 GNP of a less urbanized Britain.

Climatic conditions represent another reason GNP comparisons are often misleading. Assume that Kuwait spends 6 percent of its national output to remove salt from sea water and manufacture air-conditioners, while Holland expends only 1 percent of its GNP on these two items. Let us further assume that Kuwait's per capita income is 5 percent larger than that of Holland. Would it not be rash to conclude from these figures that Kuwait enjoys a standard of living which is 5 percent higher than that of the Dutch?

Countries which do not have a consistently warm climate must expend a large part of their national product on efforts to combat cold. A few years ago an estate agent tried to convince me to move to the Bahamas and, for that purpose, to buy a plot of land from him. I was given a brochure which explained that though the costs of many articles in the Bahamas were higher than in Britain, this should not frighten one from living in this sunny paradise. Clothing is more expensive than in the United Kingdom. However, since the climate is tropical, shorts and beachwear can be worn the whole year round; thus total expenditure on clothing tends to be less than in the United Kingdom. He did not succeed in selling many plots to the residents of foggy London—but the logic of his argument remains true.

A definite conclusion can be drawn from our survey of GNP comparisons: the problems raised do not allow for a final solution. There are no objective, scientific GNP data. Comparisons of national income yield haphazard answers. The subjective nature of all such exercises is clear to both producers and consumers of the resultant figures; the game is harmless. There is nothing sacred about the GNP cow. **"**

From *Three Sacred Cows of Economics*, by Alex Rubner.

UNDERSTANDING THE READING

1. According to Rubner, what is the basic problem in using GNP to compare the wealth of two countries?
2. How can differences in climate cause GNP comparisons between countries to be misleading?
3. What does Rubner mean when he says, "Comparisons of national income yield haphazard answers"?

Section 2 Review

Understanding Adjusting GNP

1. Explain why economists adjust gross national product for inflation.
2. What is the purpose of a price index?
3. Why is the GNP deflator used?
4. For what reason do economists adjust gross national product to obtain a per capita GNP?

Adjusting GNP Today

1. List two ways the United States might increase its real GNP over the next 10 years.
2. What are the consequences of a nation's not increasing its GNP?
3. **Challenge:** Explain how the BLS Statistics calculates a GNP deflator.

GNP of Industrial Nations

Country	Total GNP (billions, constant 1979 dollars)			Per Capita GNP (constant 1979 dollars)		
	1971	1975	1980	1971	1975	1980
United States	1,826.3	1,991.7	2,370.0	8,882	9,307	10,408
France	426.5	490.6	575.1	8,313	9,309	10,709
Great Britain	346.0	371.1	403.8	6,211	6,624	7,210
West Germany	603.3	646.9	769.1	9,842	10,467	12,485
Japan	656.0	796.9	1,044.9	6,205	7,140	8,946
Soviet Union	966.9	1,153.4	1,290.8	3,987	4,541	4,861
Mexico	77.1	98.3	129.1	1,491	1,675	˙1,901
Canada	161.4	192.5	220.5	7,473	8,479	9,189

Source: Arms Control and Disarmament Agency.

Explanation

The chart shows both the total GNP and per capita GNP of eight industrial countries for the years 1971, 1975, and 1980.

Chart Skills

1. Explain why per capita GNP is more useful than total GNP in comparing the growth of several countries.

2. Which of the countries listed had the highest per capita GNP in 1971? 1975? 1980?
3. Which of the countries listed had the highest real GNP in 1971? 1975? 1980?
4. Which of the countries listed had the lowest per capita GNP in 1971? 1975? 1980?
5. State and explain two conclusions you can draw from the information on the chart.

3 Economic Indicators

SECTION OVERVIEW

A crystal ball that predicted the future would be in great demand. Then, if you knew that the stereo you wanted would be half-price in a month, you would wait to buy it. In reality, however, you must make guesses or predictions about the future, and make plans based on those guesses. Business planners, investors, and government policy-makers also must make predictions about the future. Sometimes indicators help individuals to make predictions. In this section, you will learn about economic indicators that help planners to make predictions about the future of the economy.

ECONOMIC VOCABULARY

economic indicators   coincident indicators   composite indexes
leading indicators   lagging indicators

Predicting Economic Activity

Many people want to know as much as they can about the economy. They believe that such knowledge is a powerful tool for successful participation in the economy. Business managers must make investment and production decisions. If the economy is growing, businesses need to buy capital equipment and build new factories. Consumers need to plan their savings and expenditures. Government planners need to know how much they will collect in taxes and how much they will need to spend for different programs.

The gross national product is a measure of current economic performance and growth, but GNP gives no indication of future growth. Economists, working for the United States Department of Commerce, have therefore developed three groups of economic indicators, or statistics, to help them measure economic performance. By studying these statistics, economists try to predict how the economy of the United States will change in the future.

This businessman is explaining a chart that illustrates predictions about his company's earnings. Both governments and businesses attempt to identify economic trends.

In the first group are leading indicators. They measure a wide variety of business activities that tend to rise or fall just before a major change in economic activity. The leading economic indicators include information on the number of workers employed, construction activity, and the formation of new businesses. All three of these business activities will increase as demand increases and the economy begins to expand. Industry will begin hiring new workers to increase production, and new factories will be built. Entrepreneurs, seeing the opportunity for profit in a growing economy, will form new businesses, such as consulting firms, restaurants, and stores.

The second group comprises coincident indicators. They measure business activities that change at about the same time that shifts occur in general economic activity. Economists look at four coincident indicators: total industrial production, total industrial sales, personal income, and the number of employees on industrial payrolls. An increase or decrease in any or all of these four areas indicates the present state of the economy.

A change in demand, increase or decrease, throughout an economy happens slowly. In addition, when demand changes, a lag, or interval, occurs before suppliers recognize the change and can begin to increase or decrease their production. Therefore, when industrial production and sales rise, the economy is already expanding. The same is true of personal income and the level of industrial employment. For this reason, these indicators are termed coincident indicators.

In the third group are the lagging indicators. They decline or rise after a change in general economic activity has occurred. Two of the lagging indicators, interest rates charged by banks on loans and the amount of money owed, increase or decrease after a general rise or decline in the economy. For example, assume that demand for shoes increases. Before borrowing money to buy more capital equipment and build new factories, shoe manufacturers will wait to be sure the economy is still growing. Other business planners and entrepreneurs also are waiting. As more firms borrow to expand, the amount of money owed slowly increases. This demand for the limited supply of capital causes interest rates to rise. By this time, economic expansion is well under way and may even have leveled off. Money owed and interest rates have lagged behind the change in economic activity.

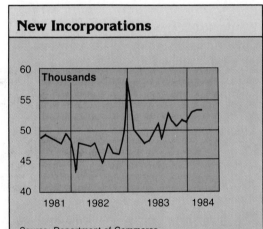

New Incorporations

Source: Department of Commerce.

Explanation

The graph shows the numbers of new corporations formed from January 1981 to March 1984. Not all new businesses are corporations. However, the trend shown here reflects the general pattern of new business formation.

Graph Skills

1. In what period were the most corporations formed? The fewest?
2. During what time of the year does the formation of new corporations usually increase? Decrease?
3. What does the large increase in late 1982 indicate about the economy?

The length of time workers remain unemployed and the amount of goods manufacturers have produced but have not yet sold also are lagging indicators. The amount of change in each lagging indicator provides information for determining the extent and effects of expansions and contractions, or declines, in the economy.

Composite Indexes

Following and interpreting all economic indicators is time-consuming. The Commerce Department, therefore, lists a composite index, or single number, for each of the three sets of indicators. These composite indexes are an average of all the indicators in each category. Like the Consumer Price Index, each composite index uses 1967 as a base year. Thus, a value of 100 is assigned to the figures for that year.

Of these indexes, the composite index of leading economic indicators is the most closely watched. This index comprises three major categories.

The first category of statistics that make up the composite index of leading economic indicators is employment. This category includes the average workweek of factory workers and the layoff rate. Employees may be laid off temporarily until business increases and they are recalled. When the economy is growing, the average number of hours worked per week increases. Employers prefer to increase the hours of existing employees before hiring new employees. As the number of employees needed increases, then, fewer employees are laid off and possibly some laid-off employees are recalled or rehired.

The second category in the leading indicators index is production. Orders for capital equipment, building permits for new houses, and new orders for consumer goods point to an increase in economic growth. Orders for capital equipment and consumer goods indicate a willingness to spend and confidence in the future. Housing construction means future spending for appliances, carpeting, and furniture.

The third category of leading indicators includes measures of business activity. Among them are the number of new businesses formed, the price of stocks, and waiting time for delivery of factory orders. The more orders a factory receives, the longer the wait until new factories can be built. Long waits indicate a growing economy. These three figures also change shortly before a major change in economic activity.

Predicting the Economic Future

Economists cannot make absolutely accurate forecasts. Since 1945, however, the composite index of leading economic indicators has proven reasonably accurate. This index has turned upward approximately three months prior to each of the last seven economic recoveries.

Use of the economic indexes presents some problems for the business planner or investor. For instance, the length of time between a change in the composite index and an upturn or downturn in the economy varies from three to nine months. Another problem is that indicators can become self-fulfilling prophecies. That is, by predicting an event they cause it to occur. When a possible downturn in economic activity is publicized, consumers and investors begin saving. Fear of being unemployed or losing money on an investment decreases spending, thereby further contributing to the downturn. Similarly, when an upturn is predicted businesses begin to expand to take advantage of the predicted change.

Even with their problems, the various economic indicators are better than nothing. Without them, business planners would have little information on which to act. Estimating the economy then would be only a matter of luck.

REVIEWING THE CONCEPT

Developing Vocabulary

1. Explain the purpose of analyzing an economic indicator.
2. List and define the three categories of economic indicators.
3. What is a composite index?

Mastering Facts

1. Explain why information on the average workweek and the construction of new houses would be considered leading economic indicators.
2. Choose one of the lagging indicators and explain why it fits that description.
3. How is a composite index calculated?
4. What group of economic indicators is related to the present? For what reason do they have that name?

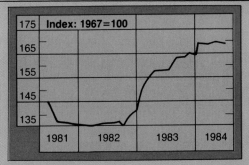

Leading Economic Indicators

Index: 1967=100

| | 1981 | 1982 | 1983 | 1984 |

Source: Department of Commerce.

Explanation

The graph represents the average of the 10 leading economic indicators. The base year, 1967, has a value of 100.

Graph Skills

1. What time period is covered?
2. The January 1984 leading indicators index is 165. Explain what this number means.
3. Compare this graph to the new corporations graph. How are they similar? Different? Make a prediction for the rest of 1984. Based on occurrences in 1984, was your prediction accurate?

Computer Predictions

The use of economic indicators to forecast economic changes received a boost with the development of computers. In 1951, the Census Bureau began using UNIVAC I to help sort and measure all types of information about the United States, including economic indicators. UNIVAC I was the first commercial computer. Economists now use computers regularly to develop complex models of the way the economy operates. Some models include over 1,000 equations to describe economic activity. However, during the late 1970s, as in the early 1950s, many economists failed to anticipate the extended period of inflation. Their failure shook the public's confidence in economists.

Economist Henry C. Wallich tried to explain why so many members of his profession did not forecast the prolonged trend of recent inflation. Wallich is a member of the Federal Reserve Board of Governors, which oversees much of the nation's policy on money and banking. According to Wallich, the problem was not that the statistics were poor. The difficulty was in the assumptions of the economists.

Wallich believes that the first problem was a change in people's attitudes in the early 1980s. "We economists have done a poor job of forecasting because people have changed their response to inflation. The last time people were hit by a great upsurge in prices—in 1974—they stopped spending and increased their savings. That's been the traditional response."

During the upsurge in prices in 1979 and 1980, forecasters predicted that the traditional response would occur again. However, said Wallich, consumers did the opposite. They began "spending more to beat inflation." Rather than increase their savings so that they could afford to buy items at higher prices, consumers decided to purchase what they wanted as soon as possible before prices increased even more.

According to Wallich, this shift was "a very fundamental change. It has thrown off computer-forecasting models. You need a certain number of years before such a trend can be cranked into the models. Forecasts are based in large part on past experience, but now we have very little hard data. Improvement can come only after you get a backlog of history."

A second problem, Wallich said, was that economists tend to follow the forecasts of other economists. "You see a herd instinct among economists. First a few people predict a recession, and then there is a movement in that direction by others. If something happens, we may all flip in the opposite direction."

Finally, economists missed predicting the inflation of 1979–1981 because they kept looking for a recession to develop. Wallich believes that economists are more likely to miss on inflation than on recession. "It's not unfair to say that economists are quick to forecast recession because they are afraid they will miss it when it comes. We have our professional pride. A recession is a well-defined phenomenon statistically. You can catch it with a model and a forecast, so everybody makes a great point of not overlooking it."

Despite the problems in recent years, Wallich still believes that forecasts will improve. "Eventually, the changes we have seen recently will get into the computer, and the forecasting system will work again, after a fashion."

Wallich admits, though, that computer projections may never be completely reliable. "It could very well be that we should rely less on computers and go more with our common sense."

ANALYZING THE CASE STUDY

STEP 1 Define Key Terms

1. What did Wallich mean when he said economists have a herd instinct?
2. How is a recession defined?

STEP 2 Consider Alternatives

1. Explain why American economists expected consumer spending to decline as inflation increased.
2. How did consumer spending patterns change in the late 1970s?
3. What alternative to computer projections did Wallich suggest? What are the costs and benefits of this alternative?

STEP 3 Predict Further Change

1. According to Wallich, why will computer forecasts about the economy become more accurate? Do you agree? Explain.

Clues to the Future

by Art Buchwald   (1925-   )

The composite index of leading economic indicators is one attempt to predict how the economy will change. Still, forecasts are not reliable. In the following reading, the author humorously attacks the ways economists make their predic-ictions. The author, Art Buchwald, is one of the nation's best-known political humorists. This reading is taken from one of his columns. As you read, consider the difficulties economists face in making predictions.

"Washington—You're going to hear a lot about "economic indicators" this year. An economic indicator is a clue to what is really happening to the economy. From these hints, economists can make fantastic predictions of which way the country will tilt in the next 12 months.

A man who works with nothing but economic indicators is Dr. Fredrich Strasser, who is in charge of the Input-Output Institute of Physical Economics. A visit to Dr. Strasser's Institute produced some very interesting but frightening information.

Dr. Strasser said that at the moment all his economic indicators were pointing up. "More people are starting to travel on the airlines, which is a very good thing," he told me. "At the moment, though, it's still possible to book a flight without difficulty and have a comfortable ride without people sitting on your lap. But if things keep getting better, the airports won't be able to handle the traffic. The planes will be overbooked, baggage will be lost and the airlines will have a very good economic year."

"Wait a minute," I said. "Are you trying to say that if the economy gets better in this country, things will get worse?"

"Of course I am. Everyone knows the price of a good economy is a breakdown in services that the economy provides. The more refrigerators people buy, the less chance they have of getting them repaired. The more cars that are sold, the bigger pollution and traffic problems you have. The more the country consumes, the less opportunity there is of getting rid of the garbage."

Dr. Strasser said one of his best economic indicators is the behavior of shop clerks, hotel reservation people and headwaiters. "The nicer they are," he said, "the more trouble the country is in. During the recent recession we found shop clerks, hotel people and headwaiters the most courteous they had been since the economic downturn of the early sixties.

"This indicated to us that things were very bad. Lately we've been spot-checking, and we've discovered that the hotel people are getting snippety again, the clerks in stores are starting to ignore customers, and in

Economic forecasting is much more reliable than fortune-telling or palm-reading. Since all three make predictions about the future, however, all are capable of some error.

some good restaurants the headwaiters, for the first time in two years, are becoming their old obnoxious, patronizing selves. This shows that things are picking up, and the country could be in for a good year."

"It's fantastic how you people arrive at your conclusions," I said.**"**

From "Clues to the Future," by Art Buchwald.

UNDERSTANDING THE READING

1. List the economic indicators Dr. Strasser used.
2. What is Buchwald's main point in this column?
3. Explain why you agree or disagree with the statement, "if the economy gets better in this country, things will get worse."

Section 3 Review

Understanding Economic Indicators

1. Who uses economic indicators?
2. Explain why personal income is a coincident indicator rather than a leading or lagging one.
3. Which is the most widely used composite index? Why?

Economic Indicators Today

1. Listen to a business report on television or read the financial page of the newspaper. What is predicted for the economy in the next six months? What information was used to make the predictions?
2. In many major cities the United States Department of Commerce, Bureau of Labor Statistics, has a telephone number to provide a recorded message on current economic information. If such a listing appears in your telephone book, call the number, record some of the information, and discuss it in class.
3. **Challenge:** How might economic forecasts become self-fulfilling prophecies?

Americans *at Work*

Meet Fred Roman
Auditor

Fred Roman works for one of the largest public accounting firms in the world. Roman's work as an auditor involves examining and checking financial records. He was one of the subjects Studs Terkel interviewed for his book, *Working*. In the following excerpt from that book, Fred Roman talks about what his job entails.

"The company I work for doesn't make a product. We provide a service. Our service is auditing. We are usually hired by stockholders or the board of directors [of a company]. We will certify whether the company's financial statement is correct. They'll say, 'This is what we did last year. We made X amount of dollars.' We will come in to examine the books and say, 'Yes, they did.' . . . We do [our investigating] on a spot check basis. Some companies have five thousand individual accounts receivable [money owed to the company]. We'll maybe test a hundred . . .

We work with figures, but we have to keep in mind what's behind those figures. What bugs me about people in my work is that they get too wrapped up in numbers. To them a financial statement is the end. To me it's a tool used by management or stockholders . . .

We have a computer . . . It has taken the detail drudgery out of accounting . . . The term [auditor] scares people. They believe you're there to see if they're stealing nickels and dimes out of petty cash. We're not concerned with that. . . . What we're really doing is making sure things are reported correctly . . .

Is my job important? . . . It's important to people who use financial statements, who buy stocks. It's important to banks . . . It's necessary in this economy, based on big business."

Auditors check businesses' financial records.

Reading an Annual Report

Just as teachers send out report cards each term, corporations issue annual reports summarizing the progress made in the past year. Stockholders and potential investors use the annual report to evaluate the performance of the corporation. The ability to read an annual report is a basic skill for understanding how a business operates.

STEP 1 Understand Annual Reports

The annual report is a message to the stockholders—the owners—of a corporation from the corporate management. The report tells the stockholders the company's financial status at the end of the year and what management sees for the future. Also, the annual report fulfills a legal requirement. The Securities and Exchange Commission (SEC), a federal agency, requires publicly held corporations to publish financial information about their firm. With such information, investors can make educated decisions. Libraries stock annual reports of major corporations.

STEP 2 Read the Financial Information

Annual reports generally are divided into two sections. The first section contains a letter to the stockholders from the chief executive officer (CEO) of the corporation. Accompanying this letter summarizing the corporation's performance is a chart of financial highlights. Also frequently included in the first section is an overview of the corporation's organization.

The second section includes statistics on the company's performance. Most of the information appears in charts and graphs.

The balance sheet is a chart that includes the assets (items of value the company owns) and its liabilities (debts or claims against the assets of the company). The balance sheet represents the financial picture of the firm at one instant in time.

The income statement shows the profit or loss of the company for the year. This chart reports the income the company received from sales, interest, and other sources. The operating costs—salaries, advertising, maintenance—subtracted from the income yields the profit or loss.

The statement of stockholders' investment, or equity, includes information on the company's stock, such as number of shares outstanding and issued.

The statement of changes in financial position shows the sources of money the company spent and how it was used. This chart includes some information from both the balance sheet and the income statement.

STEP 3 Analyze Corporate Success

Various parts of the annual report can be used to determine whether a corporation is profitable. In addition to reporting on this current year, most corporations include in their annual reports comparisons of the current year's and the prior year's financial information.

The income statement shows whether income increased or decreased over the last year, as well as earnings per share of stock. The balance sheet shows any spending to expand by purchasing property, plants, or equipment. This chart also indicates whether the firm's long-term debt is increasing or decreasing. The financial highlights part states the dividends paid per share. Investors usually want such information in deciding whether the stock fits their investment goals.

Also important to stockholders and investors is the company's return on sales. This percentage is calculated by dividing profit by total sales or revenue. If a firm sold $1 million worth of its products and its profit was $100,000, return on sales would be 10 percent.

Investors can also determine the rate of return on their investment adding up the dividends received for the year and dividing the total by the stock price.

STEP 4 Evaluate Performance

Whether a particular company's stock is a good investment depends on the investor's goals. If the goal is income, the investor would consider a company that has consistently paid high dividends over the years. If the goal is a long-term gain, the investor would consider a company that has growth potential. The company may not pay dividends since it will be using profits to expand. However, if the company grows and stays profitable, the price of its stock will increase. The investor willing to wait may see the stock price rise and so produce a long-term gain. Since each industry's needs differ, investors compare the reports of several companies in the industry.

ECONOMIC SKILLS TODAY

1. Determine the rate of return on investment for the following stock:
   Quarterly dividend per share, $1.35
   Price of stock, $25.00
   Is this stock a better investment than a money market account? Than a savings account? Explain.
2. How does a firm determine whether it has earned a profit or suffered a loss?
3. Why is an investor interested in a balance sheet? Statement of stockholder's equity? Income statement?

Enrichment Activities

1. Obtain a copy of an annual report and read the financial highlights section. Explain whether or not this firm's stock is a good investment and why.
2. Find out when and why the Securities and Exchange Commission was established. Explain the economic conditions that prompted creation of the SEC. How are the members of the SEC chosen?

CHAPTER SUMMARY

Gross National Product

Microeconomics is the study of individual markets; macroeconomics concerns the systems and changes in the total economy. One measure of the condition of a country's economy is gross national product (GNP). GNP is a measure of the final value of all goods and services produced during one year. Two methods are used to compute GNP. One is the flow-of-product approach, which counts all the money spent on goods and services. The other is the earnings-and-cost approach, which counts all the money received for producing goods and services. GNP provides a way of judging whether the economy is expanding or contracting. Gross national product also provides a method of comparing the economies of different countries.

Adjusting GNP

To use GNP as a standard of measurement, money value must be adjusted to remove the effects of price changes and population growth. To remove the effects of price changes, a price index is constructed to determine the amount of price change from year to year. A base year serves as the standard of comparison. The total price of goods and services chosen for the base year is assigned the index value of 100. Then, prices for other years are expressed as being more or less than those of the base year. The GNP deflator is a price index used to remove the effects of price changes from money GNP and convert it to real GNP. Dividing real GNP by the country's total population determines the per person, or per capita, real GNP.

Economic Indicators

Business and government planners, investors, and consumers make decisions based on their expectations of future economic performance. To help predict expansion or contraction of the economy, government economists identified a number of indicators. They fall into three categories: leading, coincident, and lagging. Leading economic indicators rise or fall just before a major change in economic activity. Coincident economic indicators change at about the same time that shifts occur in general economic activity. Lagging economic indicators rise or fall after a change in economic activity.

CRITICAL THINKING QUESTIONS

Gross National Product

1. Explain the two methods used to determine gross national product.
2. List and explain the four categories of spending included in the flow-of-product approach to measuring GNP.
3. List and explain the reasons why GNP is not completely accurate.
4. Estimate the effect on people's lives of a 10 percent population increase over the next 20 years and a doubling of real per capita GNP.

Adjusting GNP

1. How is GNP is adjusted for inflation?
2. Why, for comparisons, is per capita GNP often more useful than total GNP?
3. Using a United States history textbook, research the expansion and contraction periods in the United States economy.

Expansion and contraction are parts of the business cycle and will be listed in the index. Explain whether a pattern emerges from these expansions and contractions.

Economic Indicators

1. How do leading, coincident, and lagging economic indicators differ?
2. How is a composite index of economic indicators compiled?
3. Would an increase in help-wanted advertising be a leading, coincident, or lagging indicator? Explain your answer.

DEVELOPING ECONOMIC SKILLS

1. Copy the form below. Construct a bar graph to show the rise in prices from 1970 to 1982 for one of the categories shown on the chart.
2. Using the same format, make a bar graph comparing the 1983 prices of the six major consumer categories.

APPLYING ECONOMICS TODAY

1. During the winter of 1983 and the spring of 1984, economic growth was increasing. Decide how this condition might affect the job possibilities of a graduating high school senior.
2. **Challenge:** How will expansion and contraction of economic activity affect your life in the next five years? Write a paragraph detailing changes that might occur in your life as a result of each situation.

CPI for Selected Product Groups

Product Group	1974	1975	1976	1977	1978	1979	1980	1981	1982	1983
Food and beverages	158.7	172.1	177.4	188.0	206.3	228.5	248.0	267.3	278.2	284.4
Housing	148.8	164.5	174.6	186.5	202.8	227.6	263.3	293.5	314.7	323.1
Apparel and upkeep	136.2	142.3	147.6	154.2	159.6	166.6	178.4	186.9	191.8	196.5
Transportation	137.7	150.6	165.5	177.2	185.5	212.0	249.7	280.0	291.5	298.4
Medical care	150.5	168.6	184.7	202.4	219.4	239.7	265.9	294.5	328.7	357.3
Entertainment	139.8	152.2	159.8	167.7	176.6	188.5	205.3	221.4	235.8	246.0

Source: Bureau of Labor Statistics.

Explanation

The chart shows the increase in prices of items in six product groups for each year from 1974 to 1983. These six items include the major expenses of most families in the United States. To construct the Consumer Price Index, the Bureau of Labor Statistics collects information from 85 areas across the country. The Bureau collects statistics each month.

Chart Skills

1. Which three product groups showed more than a 100% increase in prices between 1974 and 1983?
2. Which product group showed the smallest increase in prices during the period?
3. List two expenditures that are not included in any of the categories shown here that might be major expenditures for some families.

CHAPTER 9

National Economic Goals

1 Economic Growth

Objective: *to understand economic growth and the rises and declines that make up the business cycle in a market economy*

2 Full Employment

Objective: *to understand the nation's goal of full employment and the barriers to its accomplishment*

3 Stable Prices

Objective: *to understand the nation's goal of stable prices and recognize the causes and effects of changes in price*

1 Economic Growth

SECTION OVERVIEW

If you ever have ridden on a roller coaster, you probably remember feeling the sudden changes of direction, the sharp rises and declines, the variations in speed. The economy of a market system seems to resemble a roller coaster. A market economy rises and falls, sometimes with startling speed. The changes in the economy, though, have far greater impact on you than do the changes on a roller coaster. The direction and speed of the economy directly affect the number and type of jobs available and the amount of profit a company earns. For this reason, economic growth is a national goal. In this section, you will learn about economic growth and the rises and declines that make up the business cycle in a market economy.

ECONOMIC VOCABULARY

business cycle	contraction	depression	productivity
expansion	trough	autonomous investment	full potential
peak	recession	induced investment	

The Business Cycle

The growth of the United States economy is measured by changes in real gross national product. During periods of increasing real GNP, the national economy is expanding. When real GNP declines, the economy is contracting. These changes determine the business cycle, a pattern set by growth or decline in real GNP. The business cycle includes four phases: expansion, peak, contraction, and trough.

A business cycle begins with expansion, a period of growth in real GNP. During expansion, economic recovery occurs. In general, jobs are available, employment is high, and wages increase. Expansion continues until it reaches a peak, the highest point in a business cycle. The peak is a period of prosperity and boom. After a

peak, production slows down and unemployment increases. This period of decline in real GNP is called a contraction. The lowest level the economy reaches during a business cycle is called a trough. Following the trough is another period of expansion that marks the beginning of the next business cycle.

Any slowdown in economic activity may be called a contraction. Sometimes, during the contraction phase of the cycle real GNP declines for two consecutive quarters, or six months. Then the economy is in a recession. If a recession is severe and persistent, many people out of work and many businesses closed, the period may eventually be called a depression.

Business cycles have always characterized capitalist economies. During the expansion phase, businesses see their sales

Four Phases of the Business Cycle

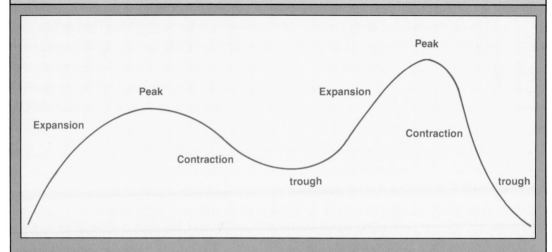

Explanation

The line graph shows two business cycles. Each cycle is divided into four phases—expansion, peak, contraction, and trough. Each phase within each business cycle can reflect a different quantity and duration, from boom to severe depression. The line on this graph shows how business cycles can differ.

Graph Skills

1. In what direction is the curve moving during expansion? What does the direction represent in terms of growth or decline?
2. Explain the difference between a peak and a trough in a cycle.
3. What differences between the two cycles do the curves in the line suggest?

increasing, so they increase production. Firms continue to increase the supply of products until demand declines and sales begin to fall. If businesses have not correctly forecast the peak in the cycle, an excess of products will exist after the peak has been reached.

The supply of unsold goods contributes to the contraction phase because new workers are not needed until the excess products are sold. During the contraction phase, sales will be slow. After the trough is reached, demand will begin to increase again. Then, businesses must increase production in order to meet the growing demand of the expansion phase. The length of each business cycle, and each phase within it, varies.

The economy's growth varies from week to week and month to month. How-ever, over several decades the relative strength of expansion and contraction in each cycle determines the general trend of the economy. For example, the period between 1945 and 1975 saw several complete business cycles. The expansion phases of the business cycles were stronger than the contraction phases. So, overall, the economy grew between 1945 and 1975.

Influencing Economic Growth

In a business cycle, the economy goes through periods of growth and decline. These changes, though, are part of a longer economic trend. Several factors influence the general trend of the economy.

The rate of population growth is an important influence on the economic trend. If population increases while production of

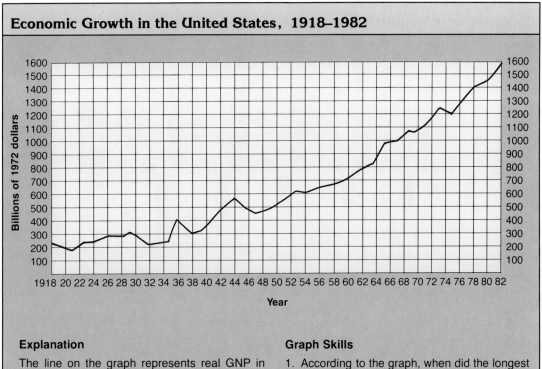

Economic Growth in the United States, 1918–1982

Billions of 1972 dollars

Year

Explanation

The line on the graph represents real GNP in billions of 1972 dollars. The United States economy went through 12 major business cycles between 1918 and 1982. These cycles are measured by increases and decreases in real GNP. Within each major cycle, smaller fluctuations in real GNP occurred.

Graph Skills

1. According to the graph, when did the longest business cycle occur? The shortest?
2. How much did real GNP grow between 1918 and 1980?
3. During which decade did real GNP increase most steadily? During which decade did the rate of growth vary the most?

goods and services remains the same, everyone's share of goods and services will be smaller. The total production must be divided among more people. At times, though, population growth can cause economic growth. An increase in the number of workers, for instance, means that production can increase. More people also signal greater demand. A combination of increasing supply and increasing demand can cause an economy to enter a long expansionary phase of the business cycle.

The kind of population growth also is important. If the population grows because of a higher birthrate, demand for certain kinds of goods and services—diapers and day care, for example—will increase soon. Later, demand for classrooms and teachers will increase. If population growth results from immigration, the effects will be different. Immigrants will need training in new jobs and, often, a new language. Families will require immediate housing. If the population grows because people are living longer, entirely different demands will increase. The country will need more medical care for the aged and more retirement centers. Community recreation programs will need to consider activities the elderly enjoy. Each kind of population growth produces its own set of demands for goods and services.

277

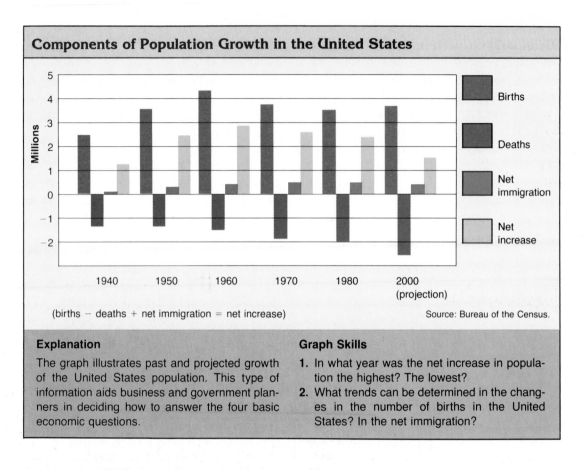

Components of Population Growth in the United States

Millions

1940 1950 1960 1970 1980 2000 (projection)

- Births
- Deaths
- Net immigration
- Net increase

(births − deaths + net immigration = net increase)

Source: Bureau of the Census.

Explanation

The graph illustrates past and projected growth of the United States population. This type of information aids business and government planners in deciding how to answer the four basic economic questions.

Graph Skills

1. In what year was the net increase in population the highest? The lowest?
2. What trends can be determined in the changes in the number of births in the United States? In the net immigration?

Another important factor that influences the general trend of the economy is the investment spending of businesses on capital resources, such as machines, tools, and factories. Investment spending works with the multiplier effect and acceleration principle to stimulate the economy. Through investments, businesses can start or maintain economic growth, an expansion phase of the business cycle. Investments may be either of two kinds, autonomous or induced.

Autonomous investment results from influences outside the economy. New inventions are a good example. When farmers first used machine-driven harvesters, the amount of land they could farm increased greatly. Other examples of outside forces that affect investments are wars and discoveries of new deposits of such resources as oil and gold.

Induced investment is encouraged by factors in the economy. Such investment results from the countless decisions of consumers, bankers, business leaders, and governments. Examples of such decisions include increased government spending, tax cuts, and wage increases. All permit consumers to buy more goods and services than producers can make. Then producers will invest in new plants and equipment so that they can meet the higher demand.

Investment often results in greater productivity—the efficiency with which goods can be produced. As workers increase their output per hour, the economy can produce more as a whole. If each worker is producing more this year than last year, economic growth will occur even if population and investment stay the same. Increased productivity has been an important source of economic growth in the

278

United States. Two factors that have improved productivity are expanded education and capital investment. Education increases workers' skills, helping them to produce more because of special training. Capital investment raises productivity by providing new equipment for faster, more skillful completion of tasks. These improvements stimulate an upswing in the business cycle.

Finally, consumer attitudes and expectations influence the general trend of the economy. Changes in people's attitudes affect the whole economy. Loss of confidence in government policies might cause consumers to worry about the future. As a result, they may begin to spend less.

A change in attitude about inflation also may cause a change in consumer spending patterns. Such a change took place in the late 1970s. In previous infla-tionary periods when consumers were faced with a rapid rise in prices, they reduced spending and increased savings. Rather than pay a higher, or inflated, price, consumers saved their money, waiting for lower prices. This action brought on a recession. In the most recent period of inflation from 1976 to 1980, though, people increased their spending to beat inflation. Consumers wanted to buy before prices went up even higher.

The Circle of Economic Activity

The many factors that affect the economy are interrelated. No change can occur in any factor without causing an almost immediate change in the others. For example, if people start spending more money, output will increase. People buying more goods and services encourage businesses to produce more to keep up with demand. In-

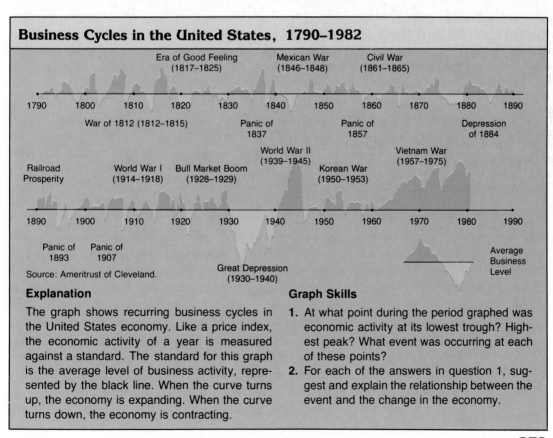

Business Cycles in the United States, 1790–1982

Era of Good Feeling (1817–1825)
Mexican War (1846–1848)
Civil War (1861–1865)

1790 1800 1810 1820 1830 1840 1850 1860 1870 1880 1890

War of 1812 (1812–1815)
Panic of 1837
Panic of 1857
Depression of 1884

Railroad Prosperity
World War I (1914–1918)
Bull Market Boom (1928–1929)
World War II (1939–1945)
Korean War (1950–1953)
Vietnam War (1957–1975)

1890 1900 1910 1920 1930 1940 1950 1960 1970 1980 1990

Panic of 1893
Panic of 1907
Source: Ameritrust of Cleveland.
Great Depression (1930–1940)
Average Business Level

Explanation

The graph shows recurring business cycles in the United States economy. Like a price index, the economic activity of a year is measured against a standard. The standard for this graph is the average level of business activity, represented by the black line. When the curve turns up, the economy is expanding. When the curve turns down, the economy is contracting.

Graph Skills

1. At what point during the period graphed was economic activity at its lowest trough? Highest peak? What event was occurring at each of these points?

2. For each of the answers in question 1, suggest and explain the relationship between the event and the change in the economy.

creased output, in turn, means that more people are working. More people earning income will lead to even more spending. The relationship works the other way, too. If a factory slows down production, people working there will be earning less money. They will then be spending less, so other firms will decrease production.

The interaction of the different parts of the economy is complex. Ideally, all parts would work together so that the economy could operate at its full potential. Full potential is the output that would result if all the economy's human, capital, and natural resources were used as much as possible. This economic state never happens. A gap always separates the potential output of the economy from the actual output. Some unemployment always exists. Some idle factories always can be found. The economy comes nearest to reaching its full potential at the peak of a business cycle. However, immediately after a peak, the economy begins to contract. In a free—private—enterprise market system, the ups and downs of the business cycle will never be completely smoothed out.

REVIEWING THE CONCEPT

Developing Vocabulary

1. Write a brief definition of each of the following:

   business cycle
   expansion
   peak
   contraction
   trough
   full potential
   productivity

2. What is the difference between a recession and a depression?

3. Explain how induced investment and autonomous investment differ.

Mastering Facts

1. Explain the cause-and-effect relationship that exists among the four phases of the business cycle.

2. How does population growth affect economic growth? Give examples to illustrate your answer.

3. Explain autonomous and induced investment using an example for each that was not included in the text.

CASE STUDY

Purchasing a Car

Economic growth is affected by each person's individual economic decisions. In a multitrillion-dollar economy such as that of the United States, the influence of any single individual is small. Still, each purchase influences the direction of the business cycle. For example, consider your impact on the economy when you buy a car.

The decision to buy a car will affect demand in various ways. The purchase itself represents a part of demand. In addition, the money paid for the car will, in turn, be used to pay the people who work for and sell services to the car dealers. Each of these people then will be able to buy more products. After you own the car, you will need to pay for gasoline, tires, insurance, and repairs. Each of these expenditures will increase demand as the money flows through the economy.

During economic expansions, consumers buy more large, durable goods such as cars.

The car purchase also influences the total supply of goods in the economy. Each individual or business that profits from your expenditures is encouraged to supply more of the items it produces. If you buy a car that gets higher gas mileage, auto producers will be encouraged to manufacture more high-mileage cars. In addition, you many need to work extra hours to pay for and maintain the car. The decision to work extra hours means giving up some free time and so contributes to the supply of labor.

The decision to buy a car also will affect and be affected by the point where the economy stands in the business cycle. Consumers are most likely to purchase a car during an expansion. The ability to pay for a car depends on your income. You are more likely to have a job and thus an income during a period of expansion. Further, you are more likely to be optimistic that you will keep your job and receive a

pay raise. Your purchase will promote further expansion of the economy.

You are less likely to buy a car during a contraction. Consumers feel less secure about jobs, and wages are less likely to increase. However, if you can afford to buy a car during a contraction you may be able to find a good car at a low price. Since sales decrease during a contraction, dealers are willing to sell cars at a lower profit. Your purchase of a car during the period of economic decline will help to shorten the contraction phase. When you and others increase spending, the economy will begin to expand again.

ANALYZING THE CASE STUDY

STEP 1   Clarify the Issue

1. List three ways in which your decision to purchase a car affects the demand for products in the economy.
2. Explain how a car purchase stimulates an increase in production.

STEP 2   Examine Costs and Benefits

1. List five benefits that you and others gain from your purchase of a car.
2. List three costs that you and others pay in your purchase of a car.
3. What are the costs and benefits to the entire economy when you decide to purchase a car?

STEP 3   Consider Alternatives

1. Would your purchase help the economy more during expansion or contraction?
2. During what part of the business cycle would suppliers probably have more cars for sale than consumers want to buy? When would suppliers be more likely to lower prices?
3. In terms of effect on the economy, how would buying a foreign-made car differ from buying an American-made car?

1. Using library sources, find out what happened to the nation's economy when American car manufacturers' sales declined in the 1970s. Find out which groups suffered the most and which groups benefited from the decline.

2. Find a newspaper article that indicates the current stage of the nation's business cycle. Try to find out when economists think the next peak or trough will occur.

READING

Creative Destruction

by Joseph Schumpeter   (1883-1950)

Joseph Schumpeter was an unusual economist. Most economists have tried to reduce business cycles, but Schumpeter believed they were good because they resulted from invention and innovation. Schumpeter believed that constant change was the strength of capitalism. In constantly developing new products and new ideas, entrepreneurs cause the destruction of old products and ideas. Schumpeter thought that this process, which he called creative destruction, caused the business cycles that are part of a capitalist system. In this reading taken from *Capitalism, Socialism and Democracy,* Schumpeter describes the role of entrepreneurs and the process of creative destruction. As you read, decide whether or not you think business cycles are helpful to the economy in the long run.

    "The key point is that capitalism is an evolutionary process. It may seem strange that anyone can fail to see so obvious a fact . . . . Yet the bulk of our ideas about modern capitalism persistently neglect it.

    Capitalism is a form or method of economic change; it can never be stationary. And this evolutionary character of capitalism is not merely due to wars, revolutions, growth in population, and uncertainties of the monetary system. The fundamental impulse that keeps the capitalist engine in motion comes from the new consumers' goods, the new methods of production or transportation, the new markets, and the new forms of industrial organization that capitalist enterprise creates.

    The history of capitalism is a history of revolutions. Consider the development of the iron and steel industry, from the charcoal furnace to our own type of furnace. Other examples are the history of power production from the water wheel to the modern power plant and the history of transportation from the mailcoach to the airplane. The opening up of new markets, foreign or domestic, and the development from small

Thomas Edison's inventions created new industries, and caused others to decline.

shop and factory to such giant concerns as United States Steel illustrate the same process of industrial growth. This growth constantly revolutionizes the economic structure from within—constantly destroying the old one, constantly creating a new one. This process of creative destruction is the essential fact about capitalism. This is the environment of capitalism in which every capitalist enterprise must live.

However, many economists accept the situation of the moment as if there were no past or future to it. They almost never try to see behavior as a result of past history. Economists do not see the present situation as an attempt to deal with a situation that is sure to change. Action should be seen as an attempt by firms to keep on their feet when the ground is slipping away from under them. In other words, the problem that is usually studied is how capitalism deals with existing structures; whereas the real problem is how it creates and destroys existing structures. As long as this is not recognized, the investigator does a meaningless job. As soon as it is recognized, the economist's outlook on capitalism and its social results changes considerably.

The person responsible for the creative destruction of capitalism is the entrepreneur. The function of entrepreneurs is to reform or revolutionize the pattern of production. This is accomplished by exploiting an invention or, more generally, by exploiting an untried way of producing a new commodity or producing an old one in a new way. Entrepreneurs open up new sources of supplies, develop new outlets for products, and reorganize industries. Examples of entrepreneurs revolutionizing production can be found in everything from automobiles to toothbrushes. This kind of activity is primarily responsible for the recurrent periods of prosperity and recession. New products and methods destroy the equilibrium of an economy. To undertake such new things is difficult. It constitutes a distinct economic function.

People resist new ideas in many ways, from simple refusal either to finance or to buy a new thing, to physical attack on the person who tries to produce it. To act with confidence beyond the range of the familiar to overcome that resistance requires aptitudes that are present in only a few people. These people carry out the entrepreneurial function. This function consists in getting things done. **99**

From *Capitalism, Socialism and Democracy*, by Joseph Schumpeter.

UNDERSTANDING THE READING

1. What did Schumpeter mean when he referred to capitalism as an evolutionary process?
2. Why did Schumpeter criticize economists who treat capitalism only in terms of existing structures?
3. According to Schumpeter, how is an entrepreneur responsible for the creative destruction of capitalism?

Section 1 Review

Understanding Economic Growth

1. How does investment spending affect economic growth? Mention the multiplier effect and acceleration principle in your answer.
2. Why are consumers' attitudes an important factor in the performance of a market economy?
3. List and explain three reasons why an economy in reality never operates at its full potential.

Economic Growth Today

1. Productivity can be increased through education and capital investment. Write a short paragraph explaining how you think the United States is encouraging productivity in either of these two ways.

2. The economy expands or contracts as a result of the workings of complex, interrelated factors. Explain, step by step, the changes that occurred when consumers increased spending rather than saving their money during the inflationary period 1976–1980.
3. **Challenge:** Firms often try to increase productivity by giving workers rewards. For instance, besides the salary they receive some workers are paid an additional amount of money for each item they sell or produce. Explain why each of the following workers might resist having a pay raise tied to an increase in productivity: teacher, assembly line worker, writer, truck driver, salesclerk, airline pilot, miner.

2 Full Employment

SECTION OVERVIEW

The goals individuals set reflect their beliefs and priorities. Studying for an exam rather than going to a party with friends implies that to you education is more important than parties. Choosing an expensive stereo over a cheap one may reflect a knowledge and appreciation of music or a desire for status. The goals stressed for the United States economy reflect Americans' beliefs about what is important. The idea that jobs should be available for as many people as possible reflects a desire to use national resources fully. Americans also believe that work is good for people. In this section, you will learn about the economic goal of full employment.

ECONOMIC VOCABULARY

full employment

unemployment

unemployment rate

frictional unemployment

cyclical unemployment

seasonal unemployment

structural unemployment

The National Labor Force

Over 115 million people, some 64 percent of all Americans, are in the national labor force, either working or looking for work. Those who are working produce the nation's goods and services. The wages they receive become the money they spend as consumers. Full employment, a condition in which as many people as possible can find a job, is a national economic goal. Not everyone who wants a job can find one, though. Unemployment is the condition of wanting, but not having, a job.

Measuring Unemployment

The Bureau of Labor Statistics (BLS) of the Department of Commerce measures the level of employment in the United States. It reports the unemployment rate each month. The unemployment rate is the percentage of the labor force that is unemployed and actively looking for a job. The labor force contains all the people between 16 years of age and retirement who are employed or looking for a job. The BLS obtains information on unemployment from government employment offices and through extensive surveys of a sample of households in the United States. The unemployment rate is calculated by dividing the number of unemployed persons by the total number of persons in the labor force.

The unemployment rate is only an estimate. The figure does not include people who once wanted a job but have stopped looking for work. These people have searched unsuccessfully for employment and are no longer trying. Further, the government considers people employed if they did any work for pay during a certain

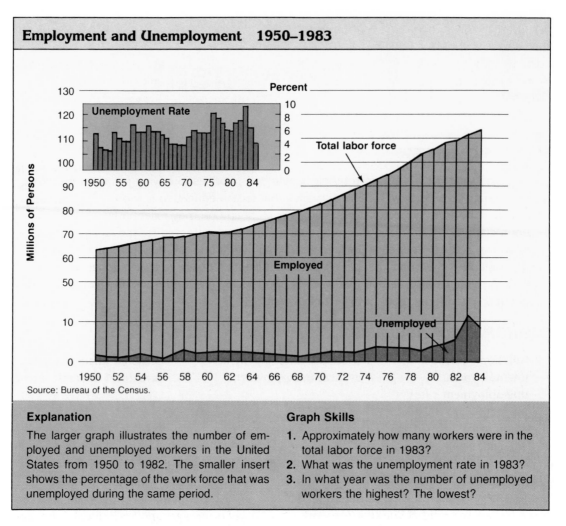

Employment and Unemployment 1950–1983

Unemployment Rate

Source: Bureau of the Census.

Explanation

The larger graph illustrates the number of employed and unemployed workers in the United States from 1950 to 1982. The smaller insert shows the percentage of the work force that was unemployed during the same period.

Graph Skills

1. Approximately how many workers were in the total labor force in 1983?
2. What was the unemployment rate in 1983?
3. In what year was the number of unemployed workers the highest? The lowest?

week. Therefore, a person who wants a full-time job but can find only part-time work is not counted in the unemployment rate. The government also considers workers employed if they worked in a family business 15 or more hours in the week, even if they received no pay.

Because of these limitations, the unemployment rate usually understates the actual level of unemployment. According to economist Lester Thurow, the difference between the official rate and the actual rate of unemployment can be large. Thurow estimates that in 1983, when the official rate was 11 percent, the actual level of unemployment was 17 percent.

Types of Unemployment

Various factors cause unemployment. These factors, alone or combined with others, cause different types of unemployment. Four basic types of unemployment can be identified.

First, frictional unemployment occurs when people are out of work because they are temporarily between jobs. Workers who are changing jobs or entering the job market for the first time face frictional unemployment. Some frictional unemployment will always be present because the labor force always will include some workers who have left one job and are looking for another. In a healthy economy, manufacturing techniques and the demand for various products are always changing. Some workers must transfer from declining industries to expanding industries.

Frictional unemployment has risen in recent years. People change jobs more often now than they once did. In particular, the rates of leaving and reentering the work force have been higher for workers under 21 and adult married women. Each time a person reenters the work force, looking for a job, that person is counted as unemployed until employment begins.

Second, cyclical unemployment occurs when workers lose their jobs because of changes in the business cycle. During the contraction phase, people usually save more because of uncertainty about the future. Consumers postpone spending for expensive, durable goods, such as cars, houses, and large appliances. When consumer demand declines, unemployment in these industries increases. When business picks up and an expansion phase begins, these workers often are rehired. Therefore, many people who are unemployed for cyclical reasons live on their savings. Many, however, take temporary jobs while waiting for the economy to improve.

Third, seasonal unemployment results from annual changes in the weather or weather-related changes in demand for certain products. Seasonal unemployment occurs in such industries as farming. When crops are harvested, the demand for workers is high. After the harvest, the demand for labor drops drastically. The construction industry in the North also is subject to high seasonal unemployment because of the cold winter weather.

Fourth, structural unemployment results from a basic change in the economy that makes the skills of certain workers obsolete or useless. Structural unemployment may occur when owners decide to move their business to another location. For example, if a company decides to move a factory from the United States to another country, it no longer needs the skills of its American workers. Often, structural unemployment occurs because of a change in technology. Computers now do work that typesetters once did. So the skills of some typesetters are no longer needed. In industrial economies, structural unemployment occurs frequently.

Structural unemployment is more serious than the other three types of unemployment. The others are often temporary. When structural unemployment occurs, though, jobs often are permanently lost. Consequently, employers, unions, and the government have funded training programs to help workers learn new skills.

Effects of Unemployment

Unemployment affects the economy's workers in several ways. Those not working are often without a source of income. Many workers are covered by unemployment insurance. This government program provides some income to a worker for a specific period of time after a job loss. However, these payments do not necessarily continue until the worker finds a new job. Economist Lester Thurow estimated that in 1983 only 40 percent of unemployed workers received unemployment compensation.

Besides the loss of income, unemployment brings other hardships. People without work often blame themselves for their problems. They think they have failed in some way because they cannot find work. In fact, though, unemployment may not be their fault at all. They may simply be victims of economic forces beyond their control. For example, they may have been laid off because of a slowdown in their industry.

Or the entire country may be suffering from a recession. No matter what its cause, however, unemployment brings suffering to those out of work.

Unemployment also hurts the entire economy. When an individual is not working, the economy loses the benefits of that person's productivity.

Full Employment

The problems of unemployment are a serious economic concern. Consequently, full employment has become a national goal. Full employment does not mean that 100 percent of the people who want to work have jobs. Full employment means achieving the lowest rate of unemployment possible in the economy, allowing for frictional and seasonal unemployment. Some frictional unemployment will always exist.

REVIEWING THE CONCEPT

Developing Vocabulary

Complete each statement with the correct term from the list that follows.

full employment
unemployment
unemployment rate
frictional unemployment
cyclical unemployment

seasonal unemployment
structural unemployment

1. The number of unemployed persons divided by all people 16 years of age or older who are employed or looking for a job yields the _____.
2. _____ is unemployment resulting from a change in demand related to weather conditions.
3. The type of unemployment that includes people who are out of work because they are changing jobs or entering the job market is _____.
4. _____ occurs when as many people as possible can find a job.
5. _____ is a condition of wanting a job but being unable to find one.
6. _____ results when the economy is contracting.
7. Unemployment that results when a basic change in the economy ends the need for certain skills is _____.

Mastering Facts

1. How and by whom is the unemployment rate determined?
2. Is the unemployment rate accurate? Explain why or why not.
3. Explain why structural unemployment is the most serious type of unemployment.

The Pain of a Recession

The high cost of unemployment often affects entire communities during a recession or depression. During the recession of the early 1980s, cities with large automobile factories and other heavy industry were hard hit. Fond du Lac, Wisconsin, felt the recession earlier than many communities. By the fall of 1980, when the nation's unemployment rate was 7.8 percent, unemployment in Fond du Lac was climbing to over 10.5 percent. By the end of 1982, the nation's unemployment rate would approach 11 percent.

Fond du Lac, a town of 34,400, had three large industries—outboard motors, auto parts, and homebuilding materials. All three industries laid off or fired large numbers of workers during the 1970s. Some, like Ray Wittkop, were forced to retire early. According to Wittkop, age 59, "They called me in at 11 o'clock one day and said they were retiring me. There hadn't been any inkling. I felt like a whipped dog."

The effects of the widespread joblessness were far reaching. Workers who lost their jobs, or were concerned that they would soon be laid off, cut back on expenses. Downtown merchants soon saw their sales fall. Over 600 retail workers were laid off because of the decline in sales. The decline did not hurt all parts of the city's economy equally. According to Sue Emmanuel, manager of the Fox Jewelry Store, jewelry sales declined but repair work was brisk.

Some of the unemployed workers in Fond du Lac wanted to leave to find work in other communities. However, because of the depressed economy the market for houses declined sharply. Many people wanted to sell their homes, but few people were looking to buy. As a result, housing prices declined. Unemployed workers hoping to sell their house and move to an area where jobs were more plentiful were faced with a difficult choice. They had to either sell their home at a low price or keep it and hope to find work in the area before falling behind on mortgage payments.

The community's economic problems led to other problems related to the stress of unemployment. People who lost their jobs faced an uncertain future. They did not know when they would be able to find work again. The tension of constantly looking for work took its toll on many. The incidence of family abuse and violence, drug addiction, and depression increased. Social workers and psychiatrists advised people on how to deal with the tension of joblessness. They encouraged people to keep up their friendships and think of ways to develop new skills. The resources of Fond du Lac to deal with the problems of unemployment were limited. In normal conditions, the city needed only a few mental health workers. The city welfare budget was only $60,000.

Unemployment in Fond du Lac resulted from a combination of structural and cyclical changes. Structural changes in the national economy, such as the decline of the automobile and steel industries, caused the loss of thousands of jobs. In addition, the unusually sharp contraction in the business cycle in the 1970s created greater than normal cyclical unemployment. The result was that in the early 1980s Fond du Lac faced the highest unemployment it had faced in almost 50 years.

ANALYZING THE CASE STUDY

STEP 1 Clarify the Issue

1. What was the nation's unemployment rate in 1980? What was the unemployment rate in Fond du Lac?
2. What industries in Fond du Lac were hit hard by the recession?

STEP 2 Examine the Results

1. List three economic effects of the recession on Fond du Lac. How did each effect contribute to the others?
2. List four noneconomic effects of the recession on Fond du Lac. Which of

these effects hurt people other than those unemployed?

STEP 3   Make a Decision

Which of the following would you consider unemployed? Which would the government consider unemployed?

1. Ed, a high school senior, would like to work part time, but he cannot find a job.

2. Bob, age 54, was laid off after working in a steel mill for 30 years. Because of his age, he no longer looks for work.

3. Susan practiced law for 15 years. At age 45, she stopped working so that she could travel. She lives comfortably off the income from her investments.

READING

Why We Still Can't Wait

by Coretta Scott King   (1927-   )

When you finish your education, you probably will want to work full time. Yet, if unemployment is high, the chances are 1 in 8 that you will not find a job. According to Coretta Scott King, a civil rights leader, everyone who wants to work should be able to find a job. As you read, consider the effects of full employment on individuals and the economy, and the moral issue involved in full employment.

66 In 1963, when my husband, Martin Luther King, Jr., sat in the Birmingham jail during the civil rights campaign in that city, he received a letter from a group of concerned white clergymen. While they recognized the clear justice of his cause, they wondered whether it would not be better to ask for less and accept that one must wait for progress.

My husband's answer, written on scraps of paper and smuggled out of his cell, was one of the great documents of the civil rights movement. The "letter from a Birmingham jail" laid out for all Americans the moral and social reasons why we can't "wait."

I was reminded of Martin and the letter recently when I went to Washington to testify in favor of a bill that would commit the government to take all practical steps to lower unemployment to 3 percent for adults within four years. Although the issue was different—full employment rather than civil rights—and involved both black and white Americans, once again the less fortunate were being told that practical men had decided for them that it would be better to "wait."

My husband can no longer raise his voice in reply, but there is no question what his answer would be. There are three burning reasons why America's jobless cannot wait for some far-off day before we have full employment.

Coretta Scott King, civil rights activist and social critic, argues in favor of a full employment policy.

The first reason is that our current high unemployment is nothing less than a guarantee that America's future will hold deterioration rather than progress. The men and women breadwinners of America are not isolated individuals but a pivot on which the whole health of our community depends. A man with a decent job is a provider for his children and a model for their behavior. He is the support of his aging parents and a force for stability in his neighborhood and city. Clean and safe streets, decent housing, adequate medical care, and even racial peace are all goals that can come only from a base of stable jobs. Without decent jobs, neither the "special programs" of the cautious nor the pious lectures of the uncaring can do anything but add the insult of indifference to the injury of unemployment.

Nothing less than the future of America is at stake. Right now a new generation is growing up, all too many in homes where the parents are without work. Tolerating high unemployment in 1980 will be nothing less than a guarantee that we shall walk down dirty streets, past bitter youths and sad-eyed old men, on into the 21st century. High unemployment is nothing less than a vile investment in continuing decay.

The second reason why America's unemployed cannot wait is that the last 30 years have offered compelling proof that waiting is no solution at all. Do we really need to be reminded that the many postwar cycles of prosperity and recession have always left millions of Americans behind? Millions of people involuntarily work part time or shuffle from one poverty-level job to another, all of them excluded from the unemployment rate we watch so closely.

Genuine full employment requires a major improvement of our educational system and expanded job training to prepare the unemployed for good jobs. It requires tax and regulatory policies to ensure that jobs are located where people can reach them, and not policies that encourage the export of jobs to foreign countries. It requires major investment in mass transit, in energy, and a host of projects that will benefit all America. And not a single one of these things will be achieved by waiting. Full employment will be achieved by forceful government action or it will not be achieved. The proposal that we wait is in reality the proposal that we do nothing.

The final and most compelling reason why America's unemployed cannot be told to wait is that full employment is at base a moral issue, and questions of justice cannot be solved by waiting. We who support full employment know full well that there are realistic limits to our economic capacity, and we do not ask for miracles. All we seek is an America where every person is given the chance to productively contribute to our country and where everyone can receive a fair and equitable share of the wealth that production creates. There is no economic mystery in this, only a simple demand for justice. The current government policy, on the other hand, is deeply unfair. Accepting unemployment to control inflation amounts to choosing the people at the very bottom of the economic pyramid to bear the entire economic burden. In the so-called war against inflation, America's 10 million unemployed have been made the administration's unwilling army.

Yet, there are those who try to avoid this moral issue. Full employment is indeed a just and decent goal, they say, but it is just too complex to be solved with a clear and direct government commitment to its elimination.

To be frank, I cannot but consider this the most reprehensible evasion of all. Since when have we begun to decide our ethics on the basis of how difficult they are to fulfill? In 1963 we did not decide our view of the Civil Rights Act on the basis of whether it would create complex problems. What we asked was whether God created all people equal. In 1965 we did not ask how much the Voting Rights Act would cost in terms of federal inspections. We asked if America was indeed to be a land of justice and a country of free people.

And so today what we must ask is not whether full employment will be simple or convenient or cheap, but whether tolerating unemployment is morally right or wrong.

For myself, if the alternative to full employment is simply to wait, to tolerate in silence the shattered dreams of jobless youth and the broken hearts of laid-off old men, then my choice is clear.

America's jobless cannot "wait," not only because waiting is no solution and not only because waiting has social consequences that are frightening to contemplate, but because to do nothing when we have the capacity to act is morally and socially wrong. **"**

"Why We Still Can't Wait," by Coretta Scott King, in *Newsweek*.

UNDERSTANDING THE READING

1. According to Coretta Scott King, how would full employment benefit the economy of the nation?
2. What moral issue is involved in full employment?
3. Do you believe the nation should commit itself to full employment regardless of the cost? Explain.

Section 2 Review

Understanding Full Employment

1. Explain why frictional unemployment has risen in the last 15 years.
2. How are supply and demand and cyclical unemployment related?
3. List and explain two social and two economic effects of unemployment.

Full Employment Today

1. Are the unemployment rates for the nation and your state the same or different? Why might they be different?
2. **Challenge:** Explain why unemployment would affect different socioeconomic groups in different ways.

3 | Stable Prices

SECTION OVERVIEW

Ask your parents or grandparents how much they earned on the first job they remember. Their wages were probably far less than any amount you have ever been paid. Also ask how much they paid to see a movie. Once again, the low price may surprise you. Since your parents and grandparents were your age, prices and wages have increased almost continuously. In this section, you will learn about the causes and effects of changes in price.

ECONOMIC VOCABULARY

demand-pull inflation   cost-push inflation   stagflation

Inflation and Deflation

All modern countries attempt to maintain stable prices. In a market system, however, prices rise and fall according to supply and demand. When the supply of goods and services increases more rapidly than spending, sellers compete for consumers' money by lowering prices. When spending increases more rapidly than the supply of available goods and services, prices rise until a new equilibrium price is reached. The new equilibrium price rarely lasts a long time.

Economists in the 1800s believed that imbalances between demand and supply would be only temporary. They believed that the invisible hand of the market system would automatically stabilize prices. However, modern industrial societies have experienced periods of both rising prices—inflation—and falling prices—deflation. Price stability has been the exception rather than the rule. In modern industrial societies, inflation occurs more often than deflation. Economic expansion usually pushes up wages and prices. However, economic contraction often does not cause wages and prices to decrease. Since 1900, only two major deflationary periods have occurred: one during the early 1920s and the other during the 1930s—the Great Depression.

Inflation, though, has been very common since 1900. Inflation in Germany after World War I was so high that many people wanted to be paid each day so that they could spend their money before prices rose. During the early 1980s, the rate of inflation in some countries rose to over 100 percent a year. In the United States, inflation did not exceed 5 percent until the late 1970s. During the early 1980s, however, it increased to more than 15 percent and became an important political issue.

Supply and demand govern the market system. The causes of inflation can begin in either one.

Demand-Pull Inflation

Demand-pull inflation is an increase in the general level of prices caused by an increase in demand. Since not enough goods and services are produced for everyone

293

who wants to buy, sellers can charge higher prices. During a period of demand-pull inflation, producers try to increase production to meet demand. If the nation is operating close to full potential, however, expanding production is difficult.

One cause of demand-pull inflation is government spending to finance a war. The sudden increase in demand for guns and soldiers causes inflation. Because of the multiplier effect and acceleration principle, demand soon affects the entire economy. Often during wars, jobs are plentiful and wages are high because of war production. Demand-pull inflation can also occur during boom periods. For example, the United States was not at war during the mid-1950s, when prices and demand rose together. Demand-pull inflation can occur whenever demand increases. The demand resulting from higher wages and higher profits also may cause inflation.

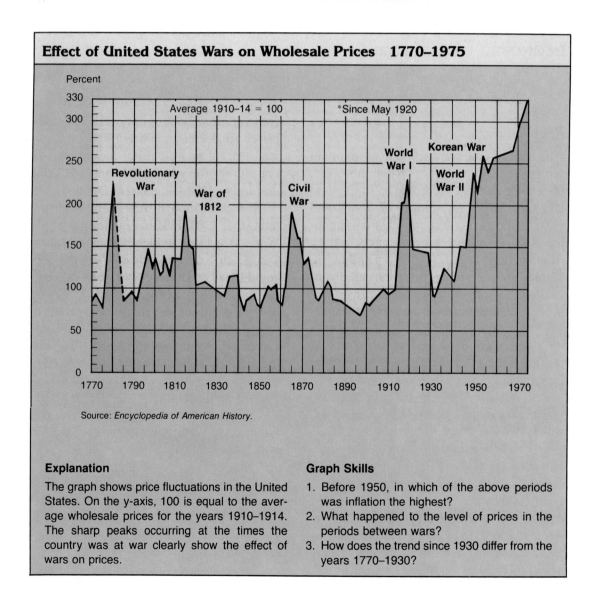

Effect of United States Wars on Wholesale Prices   1770–1975

Source: *Encyclopedia of American History.*

Explanation

The graph shows price fluctuations in the United States. On the y-axis, 100 is equal to the average wholesale prices for the years 1910–1914. The sharp peaks occurring at the times the country was at war clearly show the effect of wars on prices.

Graph Skills

1. Before 1950, in which of the above periods was inflation the highest?
2. What happened to the level of prices in the periods between wars?
3. How does the trend since 1930 differ from the years 1770–1930?

Cost-Push Inflation

A change in the supply side of markets also can cause inflation. Cost-push inflation is an increase in the general level of prices caused by an increase in production costs.

Increases in the cost of any good used in production can cause inflation. For example, in 1980 lack of rain damaged the corn crop, so corn production decreased. In 1979, corn production amounted to 7.9 billion bushels. In 1980, the supply was 6.6 billion bushels. The drop in supply caused the average per-bushel price of corn to increase from $2.50 to $3.11. Since every corn-containing product then increased in price, inflation increased in 1980.

The largest expense in producing many goods and services is labor. For example, wages constitute 70 percent of the cost of factory production. For this reason, cost-push inflation is sometimes called wage-push inflation. When producers pay higher wages, they increase the prices of the products they make to pay for the increased wages. Wage increases do not necessarily cause inflation, however.

If a corresponding increase in productivity accompanies the rate of wage increases, inflation does not occur. For example, if the workers' output rises 4 percent, their wages can rise 4 percent without causing cost-push inflation. Since the workers' production has increased, the owner can either increase output or cut back the work force by 4 percent. Either way, a price increase is not needed.

Inflation and Unemployment

Both demand-pull and cost-push inflation usually occur when the economy is near full employment. When most people are working, demand is strong and wages are high. Often, too, the economy is growing. However, in the 1970s inflation was high but employment was not. The economy seemed to stagnate. It was not growing fast enough to provide jobs. The combination of rising prices and high unemployment is called stagflation. Between 1975 and 1979, inflation and unemployment each averaged about 7 percent.

Effects of Inflation

Inflation makes planning for the future difficult. If inflation is high, then prices measured in current dollars will increase much more rapidly than prices measured in constant dollars. For example, because of inflation $100 worth of goods in 1967 would cost $297 in 1983. More dollars are required to buy goods. Hence, the value of each individual dollar is less. In 1967, a dollar would buy a can of three tennis balls. In 1984, after 17 years of inflation, a dollar would buy only one tennis ball. In terms of tennis balls, or most goods, a 1967 dollar was worth about 3 times a 1984 dollar.

For individuals whose income rose as fast as inflation, such price increases did not cause a problem. However, consider the effect of inflation on a person who retired in 1967 with a pension of $100 a week. In 1967, that amount would have been a comfortable income. However, in 1984 that $100 would buy only about one-third as much as it did in 1967. The pensioner's money income had remained constant, but his costs had increased. In other words, the income in current dollars had not changed, but the income in constant—real—dollars had declined.

Banks suffer from high inflation also. Loans for homes are often repaid over a 30-year period. Banks predict a certain level of inflation when they set interest rates. If inflation is higher than expected, the banks will earn less profit.

One of the effects of high inflation, then, is to drive up the interest rates charged for borrowing money. The higher a bank believes inflation will be, the more it charges for loaning money. These high interest rates, in turn, hurt businesses that depend on consumer loans, such as the auto and housing industries.

Inflation rates also influence the ways people invest their money. If inflation is low, more people leave their money in banks, where it will earn interest. However, if inflation is high, more people invest in gold, art, or other items that will increase in price with inflation.

The rate of inflation varies for different products. Consequently, it affects some groups more than others. Between 1967 and 1984, prices for basic necessities, such as food, housing, and medical care, increased more rapidly than did prices for clothes, furniture, and appliances. The percentage of income poor people spend on food, housing, and medical care is higher than that which wealthy people spend. Inflation, then, hurts the poor more than the rich. Further, workers in unions often have enough bargaining power to receive wage increases that match inflation. Workers without the protection of a union, however, often cannot keep pace. Inflation generally hurts nonunion more than union workers.

Inflation increases taxes, even though the government does not raise them in fact. Income taxes are based on amount of income. As income increases, the percentage paid for income tax also increases. Say that a salary of $20,000 in 1983 is taxed at 16 percent, or $3,200. The following year, inflation is 10 percent. If the salary increased enough to cover inflation, it now will be $22,000. However, that extra $2,000 pushes the salary into the next higher tax bracket—say, 17 percent. Now the tax bill is 17 percent of $22,000, or $3,740. Though

The Effects of Inflation

Product	Increase in Prices 1967-1983 (percent)
Women's clothing	71.4
Men's clothing	88.3
Refrigerator	91.4
Shoes	109.7
Furniture	117.2
Ground beef	156.5
Food for home	182.5
Food away from home	221.0
Electricity	240.7
Train fare	264.5
Gasoline	289.5
Airline fare	320.7
Hospital room	527.6
Fuel oil	576.5

Explanation

Inflation affects some goods and services more than others. The average price of all goods and services tripled between 1967 and 1980. The chart shows how much the prices of various products increased between 1967 and 1983.

Chart Skills

1. On the chart, what three items increased in price the most? The least?
2. Draw a bar graph to illustrate the increase in prices of the products listed.
3. Put each item in the chart into one of the following groups: (1) food, (2) clothing, (3) energy and transportation, (4) furniture and appliances, and (5) medical expenses. Which group increased the most? Which group increased the least?

real income remained the same, the tax burden increased by $540.

As do most other economic issues, inflation has benefits as well as costs. Inflation helps people in debt because it makes dollars less valuable. Then borrowed money can be repaid with less valuable dollars. For example, consider a person who in 1967 took out a loan to buy a house. Payments are $300 a month for 30 years. In 1967, those payments were high. In 1984, though, $300 was much more affordable. Since dollars declined in value, the loan was repaid with cheaper dollars.

Full Employment, Stable Prices

Price stability, like full employment, is a national goal that has been difficult to achieve. Achieving both at once has been even more difficult. During the expansion phase of a business cycle, unemployment often decreases. As demand increases, so do jobs, but greater demand drives up prices, causing inflation. During the contraction phase of the cycle inflation often decreases. Since the amount supplied is greater than that demanded, some producers lower prices. However, decreased demand increases unemployment.

Though the nation wants both full employment and stable prices, it sometimes must choose between higher unemployment and higher inflation. Unemployment is particularly hard on the workers who lose their jobs, and hard on their families as well. Inflation hurts all consumers, particularly those with fixed income or nonunion jobs. Each problem prevents the economy from reaching its full potential. Consequently, promoting stable prices and full employment is everyone's concern.

REVIEWING THE CONCEPT

Developing Vocabulary

1. What is inflation? Deflation?
2. Explain how demand-pull and cost-pull inflation are similar. How do they differ?
3. Define stagflation.

Mastering Facts

1. In the market system, what circumstances result in deflation? Inflation?
2. List and explain three changes in spending, saving, or living habits that may result from inflation.
3. How does the nation's business cycle affect prices?

The Pain of Inflation

Between 1967 and 1980, the United States suffered from high inflation. Yet, not everyone complains about that period. For example, James Roscoe believes that the high inflation of the 1960s and 1970s did not hurt him. According to Roscoe, "I was in a lot worse shape back in 1967 than I am now. In fact, I am now much better off."

Roscoe is a long-time veteran of the police force of Cambridge, Massachusetts. Though his salary increases did not keep pace with the overall rate of inflation, he did not need some of the most inflated items. For example, housing prices in his area went up sharply, but the Roscoes had bought their home in 1957 for $15,000. By the end of the 1970s, they had paid off the mortgage. The increase in housing costs pushed up the inflation rate, but it did not hurt the Roscoes. Instead, they benefited from the inflation in housing. Now, when James retires the Roscoes can move into a smaller home and sell their current house at a substantial profit.

Other people do not think they survived inflation as well as the Roscoes. Carl and Dorothy Danielson are retired. They live in Largo, Florida. Carl was a Lutheran minister and now receives a pension from the church. This pension, even when combined with social security payments, does not quite meet the couple's needs. Dorothy cleans house for a neighbor, and Carl does repair and yard work around Largo. "Without the extra money it would be awful slim pickings," said Carl.

The threat of inflation is real to people on a fixed income. They cannot easily raise their income to keep up with inflation. People receiving government aid were among those hurt most. The average recipient's after-tax income declined 16.5 percent between 1967 and 1978.

The threat the Danielsons feel represents one of the most serious problems of inflation. Rising prices threaten to undercut their financial preparations. The fear of continuing inflation is hard to overcome.

Frustration sometimes causes families to change their plans. Steve and Karen Pavich manage two farms near Richgrove, California. They want to have children, but they are unsure they will be able to afford them. Karen said, "You want to hear about inflation? I'll tell you about inflation. There's petrochemical inflation, energy inflation, machinery and steel inflation, wage inflation, and all of it comes down on the farmer. It just corks me off. It seems like we're always having to work harder and harder just to stay where we are."

The threat and frustration of inflation often combine to create a sense of hopelessness. Arthur Garcia, a Chicago steel worker, sees no solution. "You really want to revolt, but what can you do?"

ANALYZING THE CASE STUDY

STEP 1 Define Key Terms

1. What is inflation?
2. In what way do the Danielsons feel they are threatened?

STEP 2 Gather Evidence

1. What suggests that inflation hurt the Roscoes less than the Danielsons?
2. How much did income for the average government aid recipient decline between 1967 and 1978?

STEP 3 Examine Costs and Benefits

1. What were the costs and benefits of inflation for the Roscoes? The Danielsons? The Paviches?
2. What is the psychological cost of inflation for Albert Garcia?

READING

The Other Side of the Coin

by Bruce Catton   (1899-1978)

If inflation continues, teenagers 25 years from how may be impressed that you earned only $4 an hour in high school, whereas they earn $16. You will understand, though, that $4 was as valuable to you then as $16 is to them. Historian Bruce Catton thinks that too many adults draw the wrong lesson from seeing the effects of inflation. This reading is taken from an article Catton wrote for *American Heritage* when he was 79 years old. As you read it, consider how inflation affected Catton.

"Set any group of adults talking about the good old days and it will not be long before someone brings up the subject of inflation. The good old days, apparently, were the days when a dollar was worth a dollar, and the general decline in everything from moral standards to how people dress can be measured by the decline in the dollar's power to purchase. If the adults engaged in the discussion date back any distance at all, each one will have his own little story to show inflation's tragic effects. As a matter of fact, I have my own inflation story, and propose to tell it now.

Away back in the early years of the present century, when I was a good five years old, my older brother and I were walking down the village street one summer afternoon when we found a nice, shiny 25-cent piece lying on the sidewalk. This represented unimaginable wealth. Pocket money we never had. We legged it down the road to the resort town of Beulah, three-quarters of a mile away, where moneyed gentlemen like ourselves could find things worth buying.

Our first port of call, of course, was the soda fountain, where each one of us had a tall chocolate ice-cream soda. This was a once-a-year delicacy, at best, always enjoyed through the bounty of some grownup. Here we were, on our own, spending 5 cents apiece with great abandon. When the last drops went noisily up the straws and down our throats, we still had 15 cents.

We strolled about, enjoying the sensation of being wealthy. To help ourselves enjoy it, we bought a 5-cent box of Cracker Jack, which I recall as a sort of popcorn-and-molasses confection, and ate it to the final fragment as we walked. Then it occurred to us to go to the candy store, where after long discussion we invested 5 cents in chocolate drops. (I suppose that is what they were called. Or maybe, by stretching the words' meaning a bit, they were called chocolate creams. They were big, with firm white centers and a slick chocolate coating, and they came three for a penny.) For a nickel one got quite a sackful, and we took ours and went and sat on a dock and ate them all.

Down to the last nickel, now. By unanimous consent, we bought a package of chewing gum. This meant that we were stocked up for a long time to come. You never threw away a used stick of chewing gum in those days; you fastened it in some safe place—the underside of a chair or table was best—and next day you brought it out and started all over again. That final nickel was wisely spent.

If I were inventing this, I would make a moral tale of it by reciting that we both got stomachaches and could not eat any supper, but it did not happen that way. We had no pains, and our appetites were at the normal level when evening came. The day had simply been a gift from the gods, and there was no price to pay.

So that is my little story about inflation, and I probably ought to go on and point out how much farther a 25-cent piece went in those days than it could possibly go today. But somehow I can't. For the simple fact is that if it went farther in those days, it had a great deal farther to go and a lot more to carry. It was harder to get; and the inescapable fact is that in the brave preinflation era there was a great deal of plain, unadulterated poverty.

In that era of 5-cent ice cream sodas, the going wage for a grown man (aside from the highly skilled trades) was 15 cents an hour. Working a 10-hour day and a 6-day week, which was about standard, a man could take home $9 on Saturday evening. With that he had to support a family. Prices were low, to be sure—they had to be low—but hardly anybody had anything to spare. The average boy never finished high school, because he had to go to work.

I know, horrible tales can be told about the bad effects of inflation; it can destroy the reliability of fixed assets, give pampered youth a false set of values, undermine pension and retirement plans, and raise a great number of very serious problems. But I don't want to hear any more about those things. I had a good long look at the other side of the coin, and it destroyed more than it conserved. There was something radically wrong about a system under which the discovery of one 25-cent piece would shed a radiance that is still bright 60-odd years later. **99**

"The Other Side of the Coin," by Bruce Catton, in *American Heritage.*

UNDERSTANDING THE READING

1. What economic problems did Catton remember from his youth?
2. What did Catton and his brother buy with the quarter they found?
3. Explain what Catton meant when he said, "I had a good long look at the other side of the coin, and it destroyed more than it conserved."

Section 3 Review

Understanding Stable Prices

1. In a market system, what circumstances result in deflation? Inflation?
2. Explain how a general lowering of the income tax might cause inflation. Would this circumstance result in demand-pull or cost-push inflation?
3. Explain how a rapid rise in the price of oil might cause inflation. Would it be considered demand-pull or cost-push inflation? Why?

Stable Prices Today

1. Explain how inflation might affect an individual saving for a car or a family saving to purchase its first home.
2. What is the difference between money income and real income? Explain why it is important for wage earners and consumers to understand this difference.
3. **Challenge:** Some economists consider inflation a tax on savings. To what extent is this idea true?

Americans at Work

Meet Sandra Hunt
Biologist

Sandra Hunt remembers her father saying to her, "You have to make something of yourself." She started saving for college when she was 15. Hunt worked at two jobs to pay for her bachelor's degree in biology from the University of Texas. "Whenever I got tired, I kept reminding myself that J. C. Penny, founder of the department store chain that bears his name, made and lost three fortunes before he made one he kept. I hadn't even lost one yet."

At age 27, Hunt set up her own biological testing laboratory to provide sanitation tests for restaurants and special tests for cosmetics manufacturers. She began by buying the equipment of her employer, whose business was failing. The first year Hunt took in $54,000. In 1982 she hit $1 million. Her secret was giving her clients better service than they had received from anyone else. For example, she helped one local restaurant start an employee bonus system for cleanliness. Another time a client told her, "It sure is hard breaking someone away to take you that sample." When she heard that, she started a courier service to carry clients' samples, saving them the trouble. "It was common sense," she said.

In 1978, sales for BioSearch reached $400,000. In that year, Hunt returned to school. She enrolled in the business school of Southern Methodist University. She began to work on her master's degree in business administration.

On her way to success in the testing business, Hunt made some mistakes. She lost $50,000 investing in electric cars and silver mines. Then she realized, as she said, "I was relying on someone else to do it right, not on myself. I will never again get into something I cannot control."

In 1983 Hunt merged BioSearch into Professional Service Industries, Inc., which provides a wide range of laboratory testing sevices for clients. Before the merger, Hunt had 500 clients and 3 laboratories. Now, as a major PSI shareholder, she has taken over three more labs and two archaeological surveying offices.

Hunt works 14 hours a day learning about her clients. She is constantly learning about the economic problems her clients face. Better service through a better understanding of these problems continues to be Hunt's way to success. Successful management requires long working days. Nevertheless, Hunt likes her work in Professional Service Industries. She is happy to report that her father gave her good advice.

Recognizing Trends

If industries could predict consumers' preferences, they could increase profits. Firms use various methods to analyze trends and make predictions—economic indicators, surveys, viewer ratings, sample markets. The following steps show how firms obtain information to aid in identifying trends.

STEP 1   Gather Data

A manufacturer who was considering introduction of a new type of cereal would not be able to question every American who eats cereal. Researchers select a sample, or small group, out of the total population. To be useful in determining what age group eats the most cereal, a sample could not include a disproportionately large number of very old or very young people. A sample that did would be biased; it would not represent the population. Two conditions are required to avoid a biased sample.

First, the sample must be randomly chosen. For example, from a list of all residents in a town, every 50th name may be included in the survey group.

Second, individuals chosen must represent all the subgroups in the population being studied. A sample to determine whether a new cereal appealed to students would include students of both sexes, all grade levels, all social classes, and all neighborhoods. This method is called a stratified sampling.

The size of the sample is another important factor. If the sample is too small, the information will have no value. If the researcher questions only 10 students regarding a cereal, the results will not reflect the opinions of all students. In surveys aimed at large populations, a researcher questions about 1,000 people.

STEP 2   Graph Information

Putting the information gathered on a graph enables the researcher to better determine whether a trend exists. For instance, a film producer wants to produce a movie, but is not sure whether a comedy will be profitable. A researcher obtains the box office information on attendance at comedies for the last 12 months. A graph is drawn showing the months on the x-axis and the number of customers on the y-axis. Points are marked on the graph, and a line is drawn to connect the points.

STEP 3   Interpret Results

The line on a graph of study results is not always easy to intrepret as an upward or

downward sloping curve. For instance, Congress might want to determine the effect of a tax increase on total government revenue. Higher taxes could mean higher revenues. However, raising taxes might discourage people from working hard because they had to pay so much of their income in taxes. If tax rates were lowered, people would have more money to spend. More money in the economy would increase employment and business activity in general, thereby increasing tax revenue.

One person who interpreted the relationship between tax rates and tax revenue was Arthur Laffer, a government economist. Laffer thought that taxes in 1981 were already too high. He believed that a tax cut would stimulate economic activity and thus increase tax revenue. A graph showing the relationship Laffer predicted is called a Laffer Curve.

ECONOMIC SKILLS TODAY

1. What economic trends would provide useful information for a stock investor? A homebuilder? An entrepreneur considering opening a restaurant?
2. If a movie producer wanted to determine whether a movie appealed to the general public, would all the students in your school provide a random sample on which to judge the movie's appeal? Why or why not?

Enrichment Activity

Survey at least 15 students on the number of times they went to a movie theater in each of the past three months. Graph the results and determine the trend in movie attendance during this period.

Movie Attendance at Comedies

Total attendance (1,000s) vs. Date of movie (January, July, December)

Explanation

The graph represents the attendance at comedies shown at a theater during one year.

Graph Skills

1. Copy the graph. Sketch a straight line on your graph that comes close to as many points as possible.
2. What is the general trend in attendance at comedies during the year?

The Laffer Curve

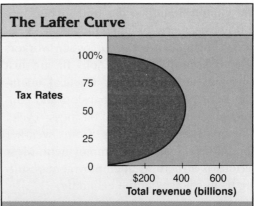

Explanation

This curve suggests the total amount of government revenue from different tax rates.

Graph Skills

1. As tax rates increase from 25 percent to 50 percent, what happens to total revenue?
2. What happens to total revenue as tax rates increase from 50 to 75 percent?

CHAPTER SUMMARY

Economic Growth

Economic growth is reflected in the business cycle—a pattern of growth and decline in real gross national product. The business cycle comprises four phases: expansion—increase in employment, wages, and production; peak—the high point in real GNP; contraction—decline in real GNP and increase in unemployment; and trough—the low point in economic activity and real GNP. Following the trough is another period of expansion, which begins the next business cycle.

Full Employment

Unemployment is the condition of wanting but not having a job. The Bureau of Labor Statistics reports the unemployment rate in the United States each month. There are four basic types of unemployment. Frictional unemployment occurs when workers are temporarily between jobs or are just entering the job market. Cyclical unemployment results from expansion and contraction phases of the business cycle. Unemployment resulting from weather conditions is seasonal unemployment. Most serious is structural unemployment resulting from changes in the economy.

Stable Prices

In a market economy, prices rise and fall according to supply and demand. A general rise in prices is called inflation. A general decline in prices is called deflation. Economists have determined two major causes of inflation. Demand-pull inflation results from an increase in demand. Cost-push inflation results from an increase in production costs. Both ripple through the economy, causing a general rise in the level of prices. Between 1975 and 1979, the United States suffered from rising prices and high unemployment—stagflation.

CRITICAL THINKING QUESTIONS

Economic Growth

1. Using the graph on page 254, column 2, determine how much the real GNP increased in 1970–1980. Form a hypothesis on how this change affected consumers. Talk to adults to learn whether your hypothesis is correct. Write a paragraph reporting your results.
2. Identify and list the effects that approaching zero population growth in the United States might have on the country's economic growth.
3. **Challenge:** Research information regarding the educational systems in another industrialized country, such as the Soviet Union, Japan, or England. Determine whether a relationship exists between productivity and education. Write a paragraph about your results.

Full Employment

1. Indicate the type of unemployment that results from each of the following:
   a. a textile mill moves from Massachusetts to South Carolina
   b. oil-exporting countries collectively raise oil prices
   c. schools are open nine months a year
2. What are the potential social and eco-

nomic consequences of continued high levels of unemployment?

3. In general, how would government spending affect unemployment levels?

Stable Prices

1. How would inflation affect a retired couple living on a fixed pension?
2. List and explain three reasons for the government's lack of success in achieving full employment and stable prices.
3. Which directly affects the most people, inflation or unemployment? Which is more harmful to the economy? Why?
4. Explain three reasons why the economy never operates at full potential.

DEVELOPING ECONOMIC SKILLS

Use the chart and your economic knowledge to answer the questions.

1. Is there a cause-and-effect relationship between energy use and economic growth? Explain your answer.
2. You may use natural gas to heat your home, cook, or dry clothes. You use gasoline, a petroleum product, as fuel for a car. Explain how you use coal.

APPLYING ECONOMICS TODAY

1. Develop a list of factors that make up a successful economy. Explain the reasons for your choices.
2. **Challenge:** Is it possible to have an economy functioning at its full potential and not have inflation? Explain your answer.
3. **Challenge:** Inflation affects individuals and businesses in many different ways. The effects of inflation depend on the economic circumstances of the individual or firm, such as source of income, amount of savings, ownership of real

Energy Use in a Lifetime

Year of Birth	Tons Coal	Barrels Petroleum	Cubic Feet Natural Gas
1920	303	233	408,000
1930	253	449	922,000
1940	228	631	1.3 million
1950	223	1,070	2.7 million
1960	155	1,394	4.7 million
1970	182	1,871	7.4 million
1980	228	2,028	6.5 million
1982	226	1,782	5.7 million

Source: Energy Information Administration.

Explanation

The chart shows the amount of coal, petroleum, and natural gas that people born in different years are expected to use during their lifetime. A person who was born in 1920, for example, is expected to use 303 tons of coal, 223 barrels of petroleum, and 408,000 cubic feet of natural gas.

Chart Skills

1. What three different units of measure are used in the chart?
2. According to the chart, people born in what year will use the least amount of coal during their lifetime?

estate, and amount of debt. Explain the effects of inflation on:

a. a senior citizen who has $85,000 in savings, whose only income is from social security and interest on her savings, and who rents an apartment.
b. an automobile dealer who owns both his house and the land and building for his business, but has no savings and no other sources of income.
c. a factory worker who owns her house, has $30,000 in savings, and also owns a small apartment building.
d. a car mechanic who rents a house and has $10,000 in savings.
e. the president of a family-owned bank who owns his home but has no other assets or sources of income.

CHAPTER 10

The Role of Government

1 Aiding the Economy

Objective: *to understand how the actions of the federal government promote economic activity*

2 Economic Rights

Objective: *to understand the role of government regulations in promoting national economic rights*

3 Public Goods

Objective: *to understand how and why governments at all levels supply public goods and services*

1 Aiding the Economy

SECTION OVERVIEW

You make many economic decisions for yourself. You decide whether or not to take a job, buy a product, or start a savings account. In a market system, individuals or businesses make most economic decisions. The government, however, has an important role. For example, the federal government regulates interstate and foreign commercial activity. The government does not make many decisions for people, but it does make some basic decisions that determine how the economy operates. In this section, you will learn about government's role in promoting economic activity.

ECONOMIC VOCABULARY

English system   metric system

Government's Economic Role

In a market system, the federal government promotes the general welfare through policies that encourage economic growth and stability. Economic growth and stability depend on the ability of businesses to settle disputes between themselves and with workers and investors. The rights of all—employers, workers, investors, consumers—must be protected.

Economic decisions require timely information. Investors, employers, and government agencies must be able to communicate with others. Sales statistics and marketing information must be up to date.

Finally, a single, acceptable currency and system of weights and measures provide the basis for economic growth and stability. Government also encourages economic activity by providing basic services, such as a court system, mail delivery, copyright and patent laws, a system of weights and measures, and a national currency.

Settling Disputes

Competition in a market system sometimes leads to conflict. For example, two businesses may disagree over the terms of a contract. These disagreements may lead to lawsuits. Federal and state governments fund court systems to provide for the settlement of disputes.

In industry, conflicts occur between employers and workers. In 1935, Congress passed the landmark National Labor Relations (Wagner) Act, which gave workers the right to organize labor unions and bargain collectively. By recognizing the right of workers to form unions, Congress eliminated one of the major sources of conflict between labor and management.

Collective bargaining requires employers and union representatives to get together and discuss pay, benefits, and working conditions. The result of collective bargaining is a contract between management and workers. The contract covers a limited period, one or more years, and guarantees the level of wages, benefits, and working conditions. More than 95 percent of contract negotiations are settled peacefully without work stoppages.

The NLRB

The National Labor Relations Act set up the National Labor Relations Board (NLRB). The NLRB may go into plants to oversee elections, look for unfair labor practices, and issue court orders. Workers in a plant sometimes disagree over which national union to join. In these cases, the NLRB conducts a secret-ballot election to determine who will represent the workers in collective bargaining. In disputes between employers and employees, either side may ask the NLRB to investigate the controversy.

Encouraging Creators

The government sets up rules to promote certain activities that are beneficial to society. For example, society wants to encourage people to be creative. New products and new works of art can benefit everyone. Therefore, the government grants patents to inventors and copyrights to writers and other artists. Patents and copyrights give people who develop new ideas exclusive right to profit from these ideas for a certain period of time.

Strikes for Right to Organize

Year	Strikes for the Right to Organize (percent)	Strikes for Wages, Hours, and Other Issues (percent)
1935	47	53
1940	50	50
1945	20	80
1950	19	81
1955	20	80
1960	16	84

Source: *Historical Statistics of the United States.*

Explanation

The chart shows the percentage of strikes related to various issues that occurred between 1935 and 1960.

Chart Skills

1. Compare the first two years shown with the last four years shown. What generalization can you make about the causes of strikes?
2. Explain how the labor law passed in 1935 may have influenced the reasons for strikes.

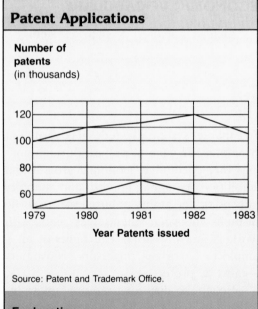

Patent Applications

Number of patents (in thousands)

Year Patents issued

Source: Patent and Trademark Office.

Explanation

The graph shows the number of patent applications the government received and the number of patents it issued for the years 1979 to 1983.

Graph Skills

1. How many patent applications did the government receive in 1982? How many patents were issued in 1982?
2. In 1983, patent application fees increased. According to the law of demand, what should have happened to the number of applications? Does the graph supply evidence of such an occurrence? Explain.

308

Providing Information

Economic activity depends on up-to-date information. For example, the decision to market a new product requires a variety of information—surveys of consumer tastes; census figures on family size, income, and spending habits. The government collects and distributes large amounts of information. The federal government gathers statistics on the prices, sales, and production of many products. The U.S. Government Printing Office makes information available to the public. Government statistics provide business managers with information that is useful for analyzing economic trends and making successful economic decisions. The government also finances scientific research projects in many areas, including defense, health, energy, space, transportation, education, and agriculture. Private industries, as well as individuals, often benefit from government-funded research. For example, integrated circuits, lasers, and nuclear energy are among government-sponsored developments.

The government's role in distributing information is perhaps one of its best-known functions. The United States Postal Service provides inexpensive, reliable transportation of letters and packages. The government also regulates all telephone companies to aid communication. Efficient communication makes the entire economy operate more efficiently.

Setting Money and Measures

Another function of government is to provide a national currency. If an economy is to operate smoothly, everyone in a country must use the same system of money. People

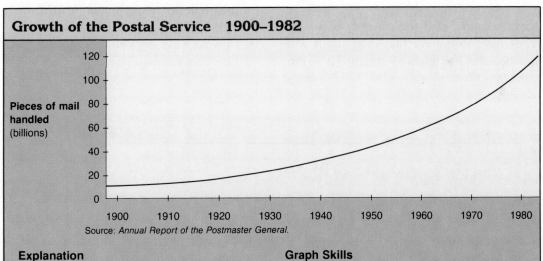

Growth of the Postal Service   1900–1982

Pieces of mail handled (billions)

Source: *Annual Report of the Postmaster General.*

Explanation

The graph shows the increasing volume of mail handled by the United States Postal Service. Although the United States Postal Service is responsible for by far the largest number of pieces of mail handled in the country, private companies compete with the postal service for some of the mail-handling business. These private services compete especially in the rapid delivery of letters and parcels.

Graph Skills

1. How many pieces of mail were handled in 1900? In 1980?
2. The population of the United States was 76 million in 1900. It was 232 million in 1980. Compare the number of pieces of mail handled per capita in 1900 and in 1980. Which is greater?
3. What do you think will be the trend in volume of mail handled by the United States Postal Service to the year 2000?

The government establishes a system of weights and measures and a system of currency.

federal government's duty to establish a single system of currency for the United States. For this reason, the government charters and regulates national banks.

Similarly, the government establishes the system of weights and measures that the country uses. It then guarantees that a 1-pound can of coffee in New York contains the same amount of coffee as a 1-pound can in California.

REVIEWING THE CONCEPT

Developing Vocabulary

1. What is a patent?
2. What is a copyright?

Mastering Facts

1. Give two reasons why a government needs to promote economic activity.
2. What basic rule benefiting workers did the federal government establish in 1935? What agency?
3. In what ways does government information help business?

have to know what their money is worth. They have to believe that their funds will not become worthless overnight. It is the

---

CASE STUDY

English or Metric?

On average, Americans use weights and measures in total about 20 billion times a day. How items are weighed or measured affects everyone. Currently, the United States uses the English system, a system of weights and measures in which the basic units are the foot for length, the pound for weight, and the quart for liquid volume. Most other countries in the world use the metric system, a system of weights and measures in which the units are the meter for length, the gram for weight, and the liter for liquid volume.

The federal government has considered proposals to change from the English to the metric system. Since weighing and measuring are so important to everyday life in America, these proposals have generated heated controversy.

Ernest L. Boyer, a former United States Commissioner of Education, said that eventually the United States would switch to the metric system. "Metric will not happen overnight but it will happen. No country can survive in a world of measurement isolation."

Boyer and other proponents of the metric system argue that metric is easier to learn and use than is the English system. The effect on the economy would be tremendous, they say. Industries that compete in worldwide trade would benefit the most. Now, the companies have to produce items in two versions, one measured in English units for the United States, and one measured in metric units for the rest of the world. Consequently, says Boyer, metric makes good economic sense.

66 The simple fact is that the world continues to get smaller, and the business of the nations of the world has become inextricably interlocked. The nation's largest industries, which once so vigorously opposed a uniform system of measurement, are now leading the way since their marketplace has now become worldwide. A uniform measurement of equipment, tools, products, and replacement parts is absolutely crucial. Scientists around the world use metric measurement in their work because accuracy and universality are essential. Most of us use 35 millimeter cameras. The engine sizes of cars are stated in liters. We watch the Olympic Games with all measurements in metric. Coca Cola, 7-Up, Pepsi Cola, Dr. Pepper, and Shasta now market their products in liter containers. Of the nation's top 1,000 industries, more than 60 percent use metric—or they are in transition. 99

Boyer believes a switch to metric makes good sense economically. The government could aid the entire economy, especially the part active in world trade, by ordering a switch to metric.

J. W. Batchelder, author of the book, *Metric Madness,* opposes the switch to met-

The 35 millimeter camera is an example of the metric system in use today in the United States. Many of the Nation's industries use the metric system in part.

ric. He also bases his views on how the change would affect the economy. He believes the cost of changing would be very high. With or without the metric system in the United States, he points out, American companies are able to market abroad. Batchelder opposes government intervention to support the metric system. "If the metric system really possessed overall advantages compared with our system, then obviously competition would long ago have forced widespread metric usage in the United States."

Competition has prompted many industries to switch to metric. The food, computer, chemical, paper, and business machine industries use metric extensively. The auto industry in the United States is steadily converting to metric.

General Motors began its conversion to metric in the 1970s. At first, the company used metric measurements on all its new designs intended for the General Motors world market. This design change was the first step in the production of a car the firm would market everywhere in the world. By 1979, 27 out of 34 car models were built mostly according to metric measurements. By the mid-1980s, General Motors was almost completely metric.

The cost of converting to the metric system at General Motors proved to be much lower than originally expected. By 1980, the cost had come to about $9 million, less than 1 percent of the estimate made in the 1960s. At the same time, the change brought unexpected savings. One General Motors division cut costs by $1.5 million because standard metric measures permitted reduction in the number of required wire sizes from 57 to 7.

In some auto-related industries, however, the movement to metric has been slow. For example, by the mid-1980s only about 10 percent of all the nation's gasoline pumps showed sales in liters. Still, some big oil companies stuck with their pledge to shift gradually in the 1980s to complete metric measurement. The federal Department of Transportation announced plans to change highway distance signs to kilometers. Public complaints, though, halted the change before long. People not adjusted to metric did not want to change.

Despite Americans' reluctance to change systems, the debate over metric continues. The American National Metric Council, funded by contributions from major corporations, labor unions, and business associations, expects complete changeover by the end of the century. David Gorin, president of the council, said in 1982 that "the entire metric planning effort could be completed within five to seven years and implementation completed generally by the year 2000." In achieving such a changeover, the exporting industries will be leading the way.

ANALYZING THE CASE STUDY

STEP 1 Define the Problem

1. What problems arise when nations use different weights and measures systems?
2. What are the problems in America's use of two standards of weights and measures—the metric and the English?
3. If the use of a single system of weights and measures is advantageous, should the United States require metric, or retain its current system?
4. Why has the United States been slow to adopt the metric system?

STEP 2 Gather Evidence

1. What industries in the United States use the metric system?
2. What advantages does the metric system have over the English system?
3. What advantages does the English system have over the metric system?

STEP 3 Consider Alternatives

1. List the costs and benefits involved in the decision of the United States on adoption of the metric system.
2. List the consequences of retaining the English system in the United States.

STEP 4 Make a Decision

Should the United States retain the English system, change to the metric system, or allow both systems to be used? Give at least two reasons to support your decision.

Enrichment Activities

1. Find out which nations use the metric system. List five of these nations that are important trade partners of the United States.
2. Spend one day using the metric system in all of your activities. Make a list of metric weights and measures that you use during the day.

A Crop of Myths

by George F. Will   (1941-   )

The rules that government sets affect all industries. Often, though, the rules are designed to protect or help a particular industry. George F. Will, a political columnist, has written for the *National Review,* the *Washington Post,* and *Newsweek.* This reading is taken from one of his newspaper columns. He is known for his conservative views on the economy and politics. According to Will, agriculture is one industry that has benefited from government support. As you read, consider how Congress has aided agriculture.

It was, we now know, an astonishing week. On February 12, 1809, Charles Darwin and Abraham Lincoln were born. Three days later came Cyrus McCormick. He, too, transformed the 19th century. He was part of the revolution in American agriculture.

Modern agriculture is a capital-intensive form of manufacturing that proves wrong some American political and economic myths. Agriculture is, arguably, the most successful American industry, and the one most continuously shaped by government policy. The idea that there is today, or once was, a clear distinction between public and private sectors is disproved by the history of American agriculture.

McCormick's career foreshadowed the evolution of agriculture. He began as a farmer and ended as an industrialist. In six weeks, in his 23rd year, he invented a reaper, a machine used to harvest wheat. Before he died in 1884, he had pioneered many of the mass-production techniques that would be developed by another mechanic, Henry Ford.

A broader paradox of American agriculture is suggested by Thomas Jefferson's life. Jefferson shared the American suspicion that those who work in cities are apt to be less virtuous citizens than farmers. Jefferson, however, was an early student of new agricultural technologies. These new technologies eventually would make it possible for a small farm population to feed a thoroughly urbanized nation. Although Jefferson distrusted energetic government as much as he celebrated agriculture, American agriculture is one of American government's success stories, the product of energetic development policies.

Two hundred years ago, labor was cheap and land was so plentiful that farmers regarded it as something to be used up, and they used it wastefully. Machinery was a plow; energy came from human and animal muscle; fertilizer was animal waste. But federal undertakings, from land distribution through rural electrification and price supports, have made agriculture, in part, a government enterprise.

First, government aimed at broad distribution of farmland. But by 1890, just 64 years after Jefferson's death, the census indicated that the

Modern farmers depend on technology to improve production.

frontier was closed. Then government policy aimed at increasing the productivity of land. The system of colleges begun in 1862 by the Morrill Act sponsored agricultural research. The government also sponsored a system to distribute this information to farmers. The National Reclamation Act of 1902 set up government funds to help irrigate dry land in the West. The Federal Farm Loan Act of 1916 deepened government involvement.

In 1908, the Country Life Commission expressed Theodore Roosevelt's desire to promote the institutionalization of agriculture. "Farmers must learn," he said, "the vital need of cooperation with one another. Next to his comes cooperation with the government. . . ."

Professor Earl O. Heady notes that "by the 1920s the per capita income had risen high enough for the domestic demand for food to have become highly inelastic. That is, incomes had risen to the level where consumers were able to buy all the food they needed and further increases could have little effect on food consumption."

Increased food production was apt to mean decreased prices. Not surprisingly, in 1929 the Hoover Administration committed itself to the task of "preventing and controling surpluses in any agricultural commodity."

Farmers are thought of as the last examples of individualism and pure private enterprise. Increasingly, however, farmers are industrialists whose production processes depend on research and large amounts of capital. Farmers have become deeply involved with public policy. Most farmers do not eat what they produce. They eat what they find at the supermarket—that showcase of abundance made possible by two centuries of government promotion of agriculture.

Those were fortunate pioneers whose wagons sank into the heavy soil of the Midwest, and who did not push beyond that ancient seabed—the world's finest stretch of farmland. McCormick's machine was especially suited to farming that prairie. But perhaps the most important agriculture machinery has been the machinery of government. **99**

From *The Pursuit of Virtue and Other Tory Notions,* by George Will.

UNDERSTANDING THE READING

1. List four examples of government actions that promoted agriculture.
2. According to Will, how does a supermarket demonstrate the effect of government support for agriculture?
3. What would happen to the agriculture industry if government programs ended? Formulate some hypotheses.

Section 1 Review

Understanding Aiding the Economy

1. In what ways did the National Labor Relations Act affect employers' rights?
2. Explain how patents and copyrights may benefit everyone.
3. Which of the following statements are true and which are false? Reword those that are false to make them true.
   Having a national currency enables people to know what their money is worth from day to day.
   Having a national currency means that money cannot lose its value.
   Granting patents discourages people from coming up with new products.
4. Explain the consequences of complete adoption of the metric system in the United States.

Aiding the Economy Today

1. What might be the economic effect of a policy requiring the federal government to guarantee loans from financial institutions to help save the nation's businesses from bankruptcy?
2. **Challenge:** Many homes and businesses have video recorders. When programs are taped using these recorders, producers and others involved with the original program do not receive any payment. Should a law be passed requiring payment of a certain amount to the producers of movies and TV shows when a video recording is made? Should movie and television writers and actors also be paid on the same basis? What economic effects might result?

2 Economic Rights

SECTION OVERVIEW

As an individual, you feel you have certain rights. Among the rights important to you may be the right to drive a car and the right to own goods. It is sometimes necessary for parents or another adult to protect the rights of children. Similarly, it is sometimes necessary for the government to protect an individual's rights. In this section, you will learn about the role of government in protecting economic rights.

ECONOMIC VOCABULARY

right	destructive competition	merger
regulatory agencies	price fixing	property rights

Regulations to Protect Rights

A right is an action or benefit that is just, good, or proper. The Declaration of Independence includes life, liberty, and the pursuit of happiness as inalienable rights. Among the rights the French fought for in 1789 were liberty, equality, and fraternity. In both these instances, individuals felt that it was the government's responsibility to protect their rights.

Among the economic rights protected in the United States are the right to compete in an open market, consumer and property rights, and the right to personal safety. In the United States, government regulatory agencies often enforce economic rights. Regulatory agencies are the bureaus, commissions, offices, and agencies that interpret and enforce regulations on economic activity. Usually they are attached to the executive branch of government.

Regulatory agencies face a large job in dealing with complex activities that require specialized knowledge. Agencies often hire people from the businesses or professions being regulated in order to obtain the specialized knowledge needed. Since knowledge and conditions change rapidly, agencies must constantly update their standards and procedures. When regulatory agencies are slow to change, they may enforce obsolete or unnecessary regulations. Complementing the federal government's regulatory powers are state and local laws to regulate education, the licensing of professionals, and zoning.

The cost of regulation is sometimes very high. Taxes pay the salaries of thousands of scientists, lawyers, and inspectors who work for regulatory agencies.

Preserving Competition

An important right in a market economy is the right to free competition. The government tries to prevent unfair or destructive competition. Destructive competition occurs when competing businesses threaten the economy or safety of a community.

316

Pricing goods so low as to force all other companies in the same line out of business is one example of destructive competition. For this reason, pricing has come under government regulation.

The Robinson-Patman Act of 1936, for example, prohibits manufacturers from charging some customers less than others, unless the lower price is based on costs that are actually lower. Thus, a manufacturer cannot arbitrarily set a wholesale price for a chain store and then ask a higher one from an independent merchant. This ban helps the independent merchant to stay in business. Nevertheless, such restrictions on competition often can result in higher prices for the consumer.

The opposite of destructive competition is competition that is too weak. For example, when firms get together and agree on the prices they will charge for similar products, competition declines. Setting prices by mutual agreement among competitors is called price fixing. Such agreements are illegal in the United States. Company executives sometimes have been fined or even jailed for price fixing. Laws against price fixing are designed to strengthen competition. The government also may use the antitrust laws to break up combinations of business firms in order to increase competition in an industry.

Several antitrust laws regulate mergers among companies. A merger is a joining of two companies, one of which remains in control of the organization. Mergers of competitors reduce competition.

In some situations, such as natural monopolies, no competition exists. Natural monopolies are businesses in which competition would be inefficient or impossible. Utilites are examples of natural monopolies. Allowing two or more electric companies to string power lines, for instance, would be inefficient. Thus, one firm usually serves a large area.

The government closely regulates the monopolies it permits. Electric companies, for example, are subject to government regulation of their rates and business practices. A former monopoly no longer permitted involves the telecommunications industry. The breakup of American Telephone and Telegraph Company in 1984 provides a recent example of the government's role in curbing monopolies.

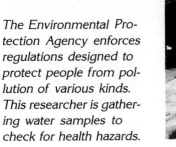

The Environmental Protection Agency enforces regulations designed to protect people from pollution of various kinds. This researcher is gathering water samples to check for health hazards.

317

Federal Legislation to Promote Competition

Year Enacted	Law	Provisions
1887	Interstate Commerce Act	Established the Interstate Commerce Commission and gave it the power to forbid price fixing and rate discrimination by railroads.
1890	Sherman Act	Outlawed "combinations in restraint of trade"; prohibited individuals or companies from monopolizing or trying to monopolize any market.
1914	Clayton Act	Outlawed price discrimination that favors certain customers; prohibited agreements under which manufacturers sell only to dealers who refuse to handle competitors' products; prohibited certain mergers if they reduce competition.
1914	Federal Trade Commission Act	Established the Federal Trade Commission; prohibited "unfair methods of competition" and practices that reduce competition.
1950	Celler-Kefauver Act	Tightened controls over mergers that might reduce competition.
1974	Antitrust Procedures and Penalties Act	Increased penalties for violating antitrust laws and placed restrictions on the President's authority to grant antitrust immunity.
1975	Parens Patrial Act	Gave states' attorneys general the right to sue antitrust violators for damage on behalf of citizens of the state harmed by violations; required large companies to notify the government of planned mergers; strengthened federal antitrust investigating powers.

Explanation

The chart lists the major acts of Congress that promote competition.

Chart Skills

1. What industry was the subject of the first antitrust legislation mentioned on the chart?
2. Which acts regulate mergers or combinations of businesses?

Protecting Property Rights

Property rights are the rights of an owner to use goods, services, or opportunities. Laws against theft and trespassing are examples of regulations that protect property rights.

Regulation of radio airwaves is another example. At the start of the radio era, several stations sometimes tried to broadcast over the airwaves on the same frequency. Then, none of their programs could be heard very clearly. Since nobody can claim to own the air, the government decided to regulate the use of airwaves. It assigned a frequency to each station and forbade any other station from broadcasting on that frequency. The right to broadcast on a particular frequency became a property right. Each television channel also is regulated in the same way. Because radio and television stations now earn huge profits, the government also requires them to show that they are serving the public interest. Usually the stations must ask people within their broadcasting area what issues interest and concern them. The station then is expected to devote a certain amount of time to locally produced programs dealing with those issues.

Protecting People's Rights

Consumers and workers have rights that the government protects. The government tries to ensure that products sold in the market are fresh, safe, and accurately labeled. Truth-in-lending laws require lenders to provide information about the actual costs of a loan. Safety devices in cars, the testing of new drugs, and the inspection of restaurant kitchens are other examples of government efforts to protect consumers.

318

Federal Regulatory Agencies

Year Established	Agency	Functions
1887	Interstate Commerce Commission	Regulates freight rates, passenger fares, and business practices (such as mergers and safety standards) of interstate railroads, trucks, buses, pipelines, bridges, ferries, barges, and terminals; encourages fair wages and good working conditions in the transportation industry.
1914	Federal Trade Commission	Tries to prevent or stop unfair business practices, such as false advertising and price-fixing agreements; enforces labeling laws; may challenge proposed business mergers in court.
1934	Federal Communications Commission	Regulates interstate telegraph and telephone rates and service; issues frequency bands and broadcasting licenses to radio and television stations; regulates the Communications Satellite Corporation, which owns and operates the American part of the global satellite system.
1934	Securities and Exchange Commission	Regulates stock markets; requires companies that sell stocks and bonds to provide the public with information on finances and other matters; licenses brokerage firms and investment advisers.
1961	Federal Maritime Commission	Regulates rates, services, and agreements of shipping firms and port operators; makes sure that owners and charterers of large passenger vessels have enough money to pay claims for accidental injuries and deaths or to refund fares if voyages are canceled.
1970	Environmental Protection Agency	Establishes and enforces standards limiting pollution; sponsors research and provides assistance to local and state governments to combat pollution; administers funds to clean up hazardous waste sites.
1974	Nuclear Regulatory Commission	Licenses and supervises the operation of civilian nuclear power plants; may fine or close down any nuclear power plant that it judges to be a danger to public health.
1977	Federal Energy Regulatory Commission	Administers interstate sales of electricity and natural gas; grants licenses for hydroelectric power projects; approves changes in service of utility companies; approves proposed oil and gas pipeline routes; sets wholesale electric rates, natural gas prices, and charges for oil pipeline shipments.

Explanation

The chart lists the major commissions that regulate business practices. These regulations are designed to protect individuals and businesses from unfair or dangerous practices.

Chart Skills

1. Which agencies described in the chart regulate transportation?
2. What is regulated by the two agencies established in the mid-1970s?

Another goal of the nation is to ensure workers' rights to safe workplaces. In 1970, Congress established the Occupational Safety and Health Administration (OSHA) to promote safe working conditions. OSHA sets standards for fire safety and exposure to dangerous chemicals, and determines what safety equipment is required in factories. The actions of state and local governments, together with federal laws, have reduced the number of people injured or killed at work.

The federal government helps to guarantee a clean environment by regulating the amount and type of waste products a company can produce. Also regulated is the construction of new dams, roads, and other large structures that may greatly affect the environment. The primary government agency responsible for enforcing environmental regulations is the Environmental Protection Agency (EPA). The EPA tries to reduce air, water, and noise pollution, and the dangers from waste disposal.

Air Pollution Index, 1975–1981

Type of Pollution	Pollution Level (1975=100)		
	1975	1978	1981
Carbon monoxide	100	85	75
Ozone	100	101	86
Sulfur dioxide	100	80	73
Lead	100	92	43
Nitrogen dioxide	100	113	104
Particles	100	98	97

Source: Environmental Protection Agency.

Explanation

The chart shows the level of air pollution for six major types of pollution. The first five listed are chemicals. The sixth type, particles, measures the level of dust in the air.

Chart Skills

1. How did the level of most types of pollution change between 1975 and 1981?
2. Would air pollution get worse or better during a recession? Explain.

REVIEWING THE CONCEPT

Developing Vocabulary

1. Why did the federal government establish regulatory agencies?
2. What is the relationship between price fixing and destructive competition in a market economy?
3. Define merger.
4. List and explain the rights of a property owner, consumer, and worker.

Mastering Facts

1. Explain why the government tries to control the effects of natural monopolies.
2. How does federal antitrust legislation relate to the market system?
3. Describe the functions of three federal regulatory agencies.
4. Describe five examples of federal, state, and local government efforts to protect consumer rights.

CASE STUDY

Lemon Cars and Consumer Rights

Government regulations have increased throughout the history of the United States. Consumer protection laws, for example, have become increasingly important. The products most people purchased 200 years ago were food and tools. Most consumers could tell before purchase whether a product was defective. As the nation industrialized, consumers began to purchase more items that were complex. Television sets, for example, have hundreds of parts. Few consumers now have enough knowledge to evaluate a television set be-

fore buying it. Cars, with over 15,000 parts, are even more complex. Consumers now must rely more on the reputation of a business and the regulations of government than they did before industrialization.

Bob Mitchell, a newspaper reporter in Valparaiso, Indiana, purchased a new car that had the types of problems consumers fear today. Mitchell bought the car in the spring of 1981. For about three months, the car ran well. Then, suddenly, the heat light went on, indicating that the engine was overheating. Bob's problems began.

Some states have passed lemon laws to protect auto owners such as this one from defective products.

During the next 12 months, the car was in and out of the repair shop. Repeated efforts of the mechanics could not solve the problem of overheating. The warranty covered some of the repair work, but not over $2,000 of it. By July 1982, the need for repairs seemed as great as ever.

Bob finally decided he had purchased a lemon—a poorly constructed car with several defective parts. He traded in his car and bought one from another company. Even then, his troubles did not end. His payments for buying and repairing his lemon lasted until 1985.

During the early 1980s, several states passed laws designed to protect consumers like Bob. These laws, called lemon laws, give consumers certain rights if they buy a new car that has recurring problems. The lemon laws provide that if repairs take the car out of use for a specified period during the first year, the owner may present the

case to a mediation panel. The panel can decide to award the owner a new car or return the purchase price. If dissatisfied with the mediation panel's decision, the consumer may sue or take the car manufacturer to court.

People disagree over the need for lemon laws. Some, such as car manufacturers, argue that very few cars are lemons. Consumer groups insist that many owners must return for the same repair over and over. In some cases, consumers face the frustration of having some repairs lead to the need for others as well.

Another disagreement between supporters and opponents of lemon laws concerns the role of the government. Automakers and dealers insist that risk is involved in buying any complex machine. They claim that consumers should assume that risk instead of trying to avoid it through government regulation. Besides, they point out, remedies for dissatisfaction already exist, and are voluntarily offered. Consumers can take their complaints directly to the company without using lemon laws. The auto industry points to procedures outlined in every car owner's manual. First, the owner can return the car to the dealer for repair or replacement. Second, when not satisfied with the results of direct dealer contact, the consumer can appeal to a mediation panel. Manufacturers and some dealer associations have established such panels. Failing there, the owner can take the matter to court.

Lemon law supporters point out that the average new car now costs $10,000 to $12,000, a sizable investment. The ordinary buyer cannot check every part. A manufacturer, in effect, signs a contract that the product will operate properly. Lemon laws provide a relatively inexpensive means of enforcing that contract. Mediation panels seem biased in favor of sellers. They do little to protect the consumer. Besides, critics claim, if voluntary procedures were satisfactory, the public would not favor lemon laws.

Finally, supporters and opponents of lemon laws disagree over the economic costs of lemon laws. According to opponents, lemon laws will increase the cost of automobile ownership. They might encourage a mechanic to replace a defective part instead of repairing it. Replacements usually cost the consumer more than repairs. Lemon laws also tend to discourage manufacturers from strengthening the guarantees they give when they sell a car.

In addition, lemon laws could force manufacturers to pass on the costs of repair or replacement to all consumers by increasing the costs of buying a new car. Lemon law supporters argue that manufacturers should not be allowed to make consumers pay for carelessness that leads to lack of uniform quality in their products. The producer should pay the economic costs of poor production, they say.

ANALYZING THE CASE STUDY

STEP 1 Define the Issue

1. Define the terms lemon, lemon law, and mediation panel.
2. In a sentence or paragraph, explain how lemon laws relate to the nation's pursuit of economic goals.

STEP 2 Consider Alternatives

1. What action can consumers take now if they get a lemon? Find out how many consumers have used mediation panels to get satisfaction regarding their car purchases. Are mediation panels used enough to justify their costs?
2. List and explain the ways lemon laws may involve both benefits and costs to the consumers.
3. List and explain the ways lemon laws may involve both benefits and costs to the manufacturers.
4. If lemon laws are successful in the car industry, would similar laws be useful for other items requiring major investments—houses, for instance?

STEP 3 Make a Decision

Do you support passage of a lemon law? Give at least three reasons.

Enrichment Activity

Find out whether your state has a lemon law. Summarize its contents. List the steps involved in replacing a defective car. Propose five questions you would like to ask a car dealer regarding lemon laws.

The Jungle

by Upton Sinclair   (1878-1968)

American attitudes toward government regulation changed as the nation industrialized. In general, the change in attitudes occurred slowly. The Federal food inspection laws existed that before 1906 were weak and not enforced. In 1906, however, Upton Sinclair's novel, *The Jungle,* shocked the public into demanding stronger government regulations for the meat-packing industry to promote public health. Sinclair's experience working in a Chicago meat-packing plant gave him firsthand knowledge of the unsanitary conditions in that industry. In 1906, Congress passed the Pure Food and Drug Act and the Meat Inspection Act. Because of the public outcry, these laws were tougher and more vigorously applied than earlier laws. As you read the following excerpts from *The Jungle,* consider whether the costs of government regulation are worth the benefits.

66 **W**hen visitors came to the Chicago stockyards they did not see any more than the packers wanted them to. They went into a room from where there is no returning for hogs. It was a long narrow room, with a gallery along it for visitors. At the head there was a great iron wheel, with rings here and there along its edge. As the wheel turned, a hog was suddenly jerked off his feet and borne aloft. There were high squeals and low squeals, grunts, and wails of agony; there would come a momentary lull, and then a fresh outburst, louder than ever, surging up to a deafening climax. It was too much for some of the visitors.

Meantime, heedless of all these things, the men upon the floor were going about their work. There was a long line of hogs; each vanished with a splash into a huge vat of boiling water.

The carcass hog was scooped out of the vat by machinery. It was then passed between two lines of men. There were men to scrape the back; there were men to clean the carcass inside, to trim it and wash it. At the end of this, every inch of the carcass had been gone over several times; and then it was rolled into the chilling room.

Before the carcass was admitted here, however, it had to pass a government inspector, who sat in the doorway and felt of the glands in the neck for tuberculosis. He was quite willing to explain to you the deadly nature of the poisons which are found in tubercular pork. While he was talking with you, you could hardly be so ungrateful as to notice that a dozen carcasses were passing him untouched.

Then the visitors might go across the street to where they did the killing of beef—where every hour they turned four or five hundred cattle into meat.

The Pure Food and Drug Act and the Meat Inspection Act, passed in 1906, made the laws tougher in the meat packing industry.

There were men to cut the carcasses, and men to split it, and men to cut it and scrape it clean inside. There were some with hoses which threw jets of boiling water upon it. Others who removed the feet added the final touches. In the end, as with the hogs, the finished beef was run into the chilling room, to hang until its appointed time.

And then the visitors were taken to the pickling rooms, and the salting rooms, the canning rooms, and the packing rooms, where choice meat was prepared for shipping in refrigerator cars, destined to be eaten in all the four corners of civilization.

But the visitors did not see the diseased meat or the injuries of the workers. There were the men in the picklerooms, for instance, that had all the joints in their fingers eaten by the acid, one by one. Of the butchers and all those who used knives, you could scarcely find a person who had the use of his thumb; time and time again the base of it had been slashed. The hands of these men would be crisscrossed with cuts, until you could no longer pretend to count them or to trace them.

There were those who worked in the chilling rooms, and whose special disease was rheumatism; the time limit that a man could work in the chilling rooms was said to be five years.

Worst of any, however, were the fertilizer men, and those who served in the cooking rooms. These people could not be shown to the visitors, for the odor of a fertilizer man would scare any ordinary visitor at a hundred yards.

Neither did the visitors learn how the meat that was taken out of pickle would often be found sour. The packers would rub it with soda to take away the smell and sell it to be eaten on free-lunch counters. Also the miracles of chemistry gave any sort of meat, fresh or salted, whole or chopped, any color and any flavor and any odor they chose.

There was never the least attention paid to what was cut up for sausage; meat that was moldly and white would be dosed with borax and glycerine, and dumped into the hoppers. There would be meat that had tumbled out on the floor, in the dirt and sawdust, where the workers had tramped and spit uncounted billions of disease germs. There would be meat stored in great piles in rooms; and the water from leaky roofs would drip over it, and thousands of rats would race about on it.

These rats were nuisances, and the packers would put poisoned bread out for them. The rats would die, and then rats, bread, and meat would go into the hoppers together. This is no fairy story and no joke. **99**

From *The Jungle,* by Upton Sinclair.

UNDERSTANDING THE READING

1. List the dangers to workers and consumers that Sinclair described.
2. What might have been the economic consequences to meat packers of tougher and better enforced inspection laws?
3. At the time Sinclair wrote *The Jungle,* a few large companies controled meat packing in America. Would the operation of free market forces have brought about changes in meat-packing methods? Explain why or why not.
4. How can you be sure that the meat you buy is safe to eat?

Section 2 Review

Understanding Economic Rights

1. Why is destructive competition considered undesirable?
2. What tradeoffs are involved in the Robinson-Patman Act of 1936?
3. In what ways do consumers pay for protection? Do you think they should pay at all? Why or why not?
4. Why is the broadcast industry regulated in regard to frequencies?
5. What do truth-in-lending laws have to do with consumer rights?
6. Would a mediation panel set up by the automobile industry be biased against consumers? Explain your answer.

Economic Rights Today

1. Do you think radio and television stations within a broadcasting area should be required to devote time to locally produced programs that deal with public-interest issues? Give reasons for your opinion.

2. **Challenge:** Gasoline service stations have often engaged in price wars, undercutting competitors to try to attract customers. Do you think this practice should be banned by law? Explain why or why not?

3. **Challenge:** Attempts have been made to pass laws requiring used car dealers to list for customers the defects of each product they sell. Do you think such laws would be economically sound? Why or why not?

4. Why might a car driven by "Ralph Nader's mother" be desirable? Would this type of advertising influence you?

"I happen to know Ralph Nader's mother drives this model."

326

3 Public Goods

SECTION OVERVIEW

You use some products without paying the full price for them. If you swim in a city swimming pool or play tennis on a public tennis court, you benefit from the taxes that paid for the facilities. Everyone shares in paying for these facilities through taxes. Since not everyone is a tennis player or a swimmer, many people get no use from such expenditures. The government provides a wide variety of goods. Many of them benefit a large group of people, though few, if any, benefit everyone equally. In this section, you will learn how and why the government supplies goods and services to the public.

ECONOMIC VOCABULARY   public goods   third-party benefits

Defining Public Goods

Those who use them pay for most goods and services. The price of an apple, for instance, covers the cost of growing, picking, packaging, and transporting it. Whether the apple is bought or not depends on whether its benefits seem equal to or greater than the money the potential buyer must pay for it. However, people enjoy some kinds of goods and services without paying the full price. Economists call them public goods. Public goods are goods and services used collectively and often paid for through the government. Public schools, highways, and police protection are examples of public goods.

A public good benefits many people at once, even those who do not pay for it. In other words, it has third-party benefits. A third-party benefit is a purchase benefit that goes to a person who is neither the buyer nor the seller in the purchase. If your neighbor installs a light in a dark place near your home to discourage vandalism, that light will benefit you also. The light has third-party benefits. Only the person who buys an apple, though, can use it. Once it is consumed, no one else can eat it. Many goods provided through government have third-party benefits. A person can use the local park without preventing others from using it. All can swim at a public beach. Everyone benefits from the country's system of national defense.

The Need for Public Goods

The market system usually produces only goods and services whose full cost is paid by the user. Many public goods would be too expensive for most people to enjoy if private businesses provided them. Therefore, the market system produces only a few public goods.

Since the market system does not supply many public goods, the government provides most of them. National defense and space programs, parks, roads, public health programs, and police and fire service are examples of goods and services that yield large third-party benefits. Usually, they are provided through the government rather than through the market system.

These citizens are in line to receive unemployment compensation, one of the public goods supplied by the government.

The federal government also manages social security, a system to provide for various groups who are in need of assistance. Workers pay a portion of the funds for social security through payroll deductions. These payments appear as amounts labeled FICA, for Federal Insurance Contributions Act, the law that established the system. Because the money is deducted from the paycheck, as in income tax, most people think of social security payments as a tax. Other contributions to the system come from employers and the federal government. This money is then used to pay social security benefits, such as payments to retired, disabled, and unemployed workers.

Fire protection is a good example of the reason the government has become the major producer of public goods. In the early 19th century, fire protection was the responsibility of private companies that competed with one another. A homeowner would sign a contract with one fire company. If a fire broke out, that company would come to fight it. If a neighbor had a contract with another firm, that company would not come unless the fire spread to the neighbor's house. In this system, fires tended to spread rather quickly. People without enough money to pay for a fire protection contract simply watched their homes burn. Dissatisfaction with this system led to the creation of public fire departments, each serving a large area.

Choosing Public or Private Goods

Private companies could provide most public goods. Schools, hospitals, and parks are examples of products that both government and private companies provide. Some people believe, in fact, that private companies should supply more of these items.

A recently proposed alternative would make education subject to market competition. The government would give students coupons, called vouchers, to be used like money to pay for education. Individuals could decide to spend their vouchers at private schools or public schools. Many different voucher plans have been suggested. All of their supporters claim that students would get a better education if they could simply go out and buy whatever kind of education they wanted.

Some people think that the government could better provide some private goods that the market system now supplies. One example is health care. Those who support a national health care plan claim that more people would have access to better care if the government offered and largely paid for it. Funds could be raised through some system of taxation. Proponents of this sort of care say that health care is so important that all people should have it, regardless of their income. If health care were a public good, poor people would have a chance to achieve a standard of care similar to that of wealthy people. Equality is one reason why education is a public good. The same logic could also be applied to other goods, such as housing.

These examples show that the line between public goods and private goods is not always easy to draw. Economists' attempts to clarify the issue raise several questions. Are third-party benefits involved? Is the good or service one that benefits many people at once, even those who do not use it directly? Can the free market provide it? Can the government do a better job of providing the good or service?

Two issues are involved in any debate over whether or not to make a good a public good—choice and responsibility. Should people who do not want a specific good or service still have to pay for it with their taxes? Does the government have the right to make this choice for people? Should a good or service be limited to only those who can afford it? Would society as a whole be better off if it were available to everyone? Does the government have the responsibility to provide it?

REVIEWING THE CONCEPT

Developing Vocabulary

1. Give six examples of public goods.
2. Explain the meaning of third-party benefits, and give three examples not included in the text.

Mastering Facts

1. How is the United States social security system funded? What types of benefits does social security provide?
2. What caused police and fire protection to become public goods?
3. What are examples of goods that are offered both publicly and privately?

CASE STUDY

Paying for Public Goods: Education

One of the most important and most expensive public goods is education. Funding for public education, though, varies throughout the United States. Jane Middleton and George Chosen are two high school students who attend two very different public high schools.

Jane goes to a high school in a suburb along the shore of Lake Michigan, north of Chicago. In addition to the standard courses, her school offers a great variety of electives. They include six different classes in history, two classes in creative writing, journalism, Chinese, advanced trigonometry, calculus, and several science courses. The school also offers a host of athletic activities for both males and females, and extensive programs in music and other arts. Most teachers in the school have at least a master's degree. Their salaries average $25,000 a year.

George attends high school in a medium-sized city in Alabama. His school offers American and world history; Spanish and French; four years of English; mathematics, including trigonometry and ad-

The amount of money spent on education varies widely from state to state and from city to city.

vanced algebra; and general science, biology, and botany. Football, basketball, and baseball for boys make up the athletic program. Mixed glee club and band are the only two music activities the school offers. All the teachers in George's school have bachelor's and some have master's degrees. Their average salary is about $15,000.

The Chicago suburban school can offer much more than the Alabama school, largely because it has more money. In 1982–1983, the average expenditure per pupil in Illinois was $3,209. In Alabama it was $1,545, about half as much.

While George Chosen's school district spent about the Alabama average per pupil, Jane Middleton's was spending more than $4,000, well above the Illinois average. Much of the money for schools comes from a property tax. Each property owner pays a tax to the school district based on the value of the property owned. Jane lives in a wealthy area where the average home is worth over $100,000. Thus, in her district the property tax produces relatively high revenue for education.

The property tax as a means of supporting public education has been chal-

lenged. Some people believe that such a system leads to inequality among districts, even within states. In 1973, the United States Supreme Court entered the debate in the case of *San Antonio Independent School District* v. *Rodriquez*. The Court ruled then that the property tax for education was constitutional. Nevertheless, the Court acknowledged that reliance on the property tax did create inequality of educational opportunity. In 1976, the California Supreme Court held that the use of the property tax for schools violated the state constitution because such use discriminated against children in poor school districts. This ruling did not eliminate the property tax as a source of school revenue in California. However, the amount of state funding for education there did increase.

Just as local property tax funding of schools varies from district to district, so does state support for public education. New Hampshire has neither an income nor a sales tax. There, local sources pay 89 percent of school expenses. The state pays 7 percent and the federal government pays the remaining 4 percent. In Illinois, state funding comes to 36 percent; in Alabama,

330

62 percent. In Hawaii the state funds nearly 90 percent of school expenditures.

Federal aid to education also varies widely. In Mississippi, federal funds account for almost 20 percent of all education expenses. In Wyoming, federal funds provide only 3 percent. Overall, the federal government pays about 7 percent of the cost of operating public schools.

Some observers believe that the federal government should increase its aid to public education. Increasing federal aid, they say, would reduce financial inequalities among districts. These people argue that all American children, regardless of where they live, are entitled to equal educational opportunity. Some states and communities will always be less well off than others. Therefore, the federal government should supply sufficient money to bring all schools up to a certain minimum expenditure per pupil. What that minimum should be is open to debate. In 1982–1983, expenditures per pupil ranged from Alaska's high of $6,301 to Alabama's low of $1,545.

Those who oppose increasing federal aid usually oppose the control over schools that goes with it. Federal control, they say, damages the traditional concept of local responsibility for schools. The strength of public schools in the United States has always been their close association with the needs and values of their local communities. Greater reliance on the federal government could damage this association.

Frequently, increases in federal spending would lead to more equitable distribution of a public good. However, greater equality often has its costs. Consequently, the conflict over spending for education or other public goods is likely to continue. In the future, you will be a provider rather than a consumer of education. Consider how you think funds for public education should be obtained and distributed.

ANALYZING THE CASE STUDY

STEP 1 Clarify the Issue

1. Explain how public education is an example of a public good.
2. How does federal policy on public education affect national economic goals?
3. How do economic differences among communities and states affect funding of public education?

STEP 2 Understand the Evidence

Which of the following statements are true and which are false? Reword the false ones to make them true.

1. Federal funds account for 10 percent of the school expenditures in the nation.
2. Federal funds provide 10 percent of the education funds in each state.
3. All states spend the same amount of money per student.
4. Local taxes are the largest source of education funds in each state.
5. Federal education aid rose in the 1960s.

STEP 3 Evaluate Costs and Benefits

1. Explain why poor communities are more likely than wealthy areas to support increased federal funding of education.
2. Explain why individuals who own several pieces of property are more likely than those who own none to support increased federal funding for education.
3. What could be the consequences, good and bad, when local communities accept more funding from state and federal sources for public education?
4. What are the third-party benefits of public education?

STEP 4 Make a Decision

Should the increased costs of public education come from local communities or state or federal government? Write a paragraph explaining your position.

Free to Choose Education

by Milton and Rose Friedman

One public good that affects almost everyone is public education. Critics of the current educational system argue that increased competition among schools would bring improvements. One of these people is Milton Friedman, a prominent economist. For over 30 years, Friedman taught at the University of Chicago. In 1976 he won the Nobel Prize in Economics. Friedman advocates less government regulation of much of the economy. In this reading, adapted from Milton and Rose Friedman's book, *Free to Choose: A Personal Statement,* they explain why they support a voucher system. As you read about the Friedmans' proposal, consider how you would use an education voucher.

"One way to achieve a major improvement, to bring learning back into the classroom, especially for the currently most disadvantaged, is to give all parents greater control over their children's schooling. . . . One simple and effective way to assure parents greater freedom to choose, while at the same time retaining present sources of finance, is a voucher plan. . . .

Suppose . . . the government said to you: "If you relieve us of the expense of schooling your child, you will be given a voucher, a piece of paper redeemable for a designated sum of money, if, and only if, it is used to pay the cost of schooling your child at an approved school." The sum of money might be $2,000, or it might be a lesser sum. . . . But whether the full amount or the lesser amount, it would remove at least a part of the financial penalty that now limits the freedom of parents to choose. . . . That would both give every parent a greater opportunity to choose and at the same time require public schools to finance themselves by charging tuition. . . . The public schools would then have to compete both with one another and with private schools.

This plan would relieve no one of the burden of taxation to pay for schooling. It would simply give parents a wider choice as to the form in which their children get the schooling that the community has obligated itself to provide. . . . [Consider five of the possible criticisms of the voucher plan.]

[One] objection to the voucher plan is that it would raise the total cost to taxpayers of schooling—because of the cost of vouchers given for the roughly 10 percent of children who now attend parochial and other private schools. That is a "problem" only to those who disregard the present discrimination against parents who send their children to nonpublic schools. Universal vouchers would end the inequity of using tax funds to school some children but not others.

Under the current system, public school students such as these attend whatever school serves the district in which they live. Milton and Rose Friedman believe the voucher system would force schools to compete with one another for students.

[A second concern about vouchers is the fear that they would promote racial segregation.] Discrimination under a voucher plan can be prevented . . . by redeeming vouchers only from schools that do not discriminate. A more difficult problem has troubled some students of vouchers. That is the possibility that voluntary choice with vouchers might increase racial and class separation in schools and thus exacerbate [increase] racial conflict and foster an increasingly segregated and hierarchical society.

We believe that the voucher plan would have precisely the opposite effect; it would moderate racial conflict and promote a society in which blacks and whites cooperate in joint objectives, while respecting each other's separate rights and interests. . . . Integration has been most successful when it has resulted from choice, not coercion. Nonpublic schools, parochial and other, have often been in the forefront of the move toward integration.

[A third possible problem with vouchers is] their likely effect on the social and economic structure. . . . [This] question has . . . perhaps divided students of vouchers more than any other. . . . Some have argued that the great value of the public school has been as a melting pot, in which rich and poor, native and foreign-born, black and white have learned to live together. That image was and is largely true for small communities, but almost entirely false for large cities. There, the public school has fostered residential stratification, by tying the kind and cost of schooling to residential location. It is no accident that most of the country's outstanding public schools are in high-income enclaves [communities].

[A fourth concern is over the creation of new schools.] Private schools now are almost all either parochial schools or elite academies. Will the effect of the voucher plan simply be to subsidize these, while leaving the bulk of [the students from poor families] in inferior public schools? What reason is there to suppose that alternatives will really arise?

The reason is that a market would develop where it does not exist today. Cities, states, and the federal government today [spend substantially more] on elementary and secondary schools . . . than the total amount spent annually in restaurants for food. The smaller sum surely provides an ample variety of restaurants for people in every class and place. The larger sum, or even a fraction of it, would provide an ample variety of schools.

[Finally, opponents] claim that vouchers would destroy the public school system, which, according to them, has been the foundation and cornerstone of our democracy. Their claims are never accompanied by any evidence that the public school system today achieves the results claimed for it—whatever may have been true in earlier times. . . .

The threat to public schools arises from their defects, not their accomplishments. In small, closely knit communities where public schools, particularly elementary schools, are now reasonably satisfactory, not even the most comprehensive voucher plan would have much effect. The public schools would remain dominant, perhaps somewhat improved by the threat of potential competition. But elsewhere, and particularly in [poverty-stricken urban areas] where the public schools are doing such a poor job, most parents would undoubtedly try to send their children to nonpublic schools. **99**

Adapted from *Free to Choose: A Personal Statement*, by Milton and Rose Friedman.

UNDERSTANDING THE READING

1. Explain how a voucher plan would work. To what extent, if any, would a voucher plan change education from a public to a private good?
2. What are the Friedmans' responses to the objections to vouchers?
3. Do you support or oppose a voucher system? For what reasons?

Section 3 Review

Understanding Public Goods

1. What questions differentiate a public from a private good?
2. Which of the following statements are true and which are false? Reword the false ones to make them true.
   Public goods have third-party benefits.
   A clear line exists between public goods and private goods.
   Producing public goods involves government in making choices.

The federal government pays for social security benefits.

Public Goods Today

1. List the economic consequences of having private firms deliver all mail.
2. Do renters pay property taxes? Explain.
3. **Challenge:** What would be the economic consequences of total federal funding of health care?

334

Americans at Work

Meet Henry Cisneros
Mayor of San Antonio

Back in 1843, when Texas was still an independent nation, the city of San Antonio had a Mexican-American mayor. Not until 1981, when Henry B. Cisneros won mayoral election, did San Antonio have its second Mexican-American mayor. After he served his first two-year term, the citizens of San Antonio reelected Cisneros by 94 percent of the vote.

Cisneros's interest in city government grew out of a conference on public issues in which he participated at West Point, New York, when he was a junior at Texas A&M University. Of the discussions there, he said, "I was badly outclassed by people from universities such as Williams, Harvard, and Stanford. On the flight back, I felt like I had just woken up. I came back my senior year and decided the city was what I wanted to do."

Cisneros was not quite 34 when first elected mayor of San Antonio. By then he had compiled an impressive list of academic and civic awards to his credit. He had earned a PhD in public administration, been an administrative assistant in city government, served with the National League of Cities, won a Ford Foundation grant, and been elected to the San Antonio city council. In addition, he had taught public administration at Massachusetts Institute of Technology and at the University of Texas at San Antonio.

As mayor, Cisneros has several opportunities to influence the San Antonio economy. Each year he proposes changes in the city government's taxing and spending policies. Decisions to increase or decrease taxes, to hire or fire city workers, and to fund or not fund programs all affect the city's economy.

Cisneros works with business leaders to promote economic growth. He tries to coordinate the efforts of the city government, banks, factories, neighborhood groups, and schools to ensure that the San Antonio economy grows steadily.

In 1983, Cisneros received increased national attention when President Reagan appointed him to a special commission to study the problems in Central America. Cisneros is a young leader with great potential. How does Cisneros respond to questions about his ambitions for higher office? "I think the job of mayor of San Antonio is tough as can be," he said. "The mayor's office is not a position you can take time off from. I have no plans beyond doing what I have been trained for, being a good urban leader, a city leader."

Consumer Protection

A recent survey reported that 1 out of every 4 consumers complained about a product or service during the past year. Accidents, mistakes, poor communications, and, at times, dishonesty all cause problems for consumers. Many people feel they have no way to communicate with or obtain justice from a big, impersonal business. Educated consumers can deal effectively with their buying complaints. Consider the following steps to take when dissatisfied with a product or service.

STEP 1   Shop Carefully

The first step in consumer protection is to know the product you are buying and the reliability of the seller. Talk with friends to find out where they shopped, and what brand they chose and why. Carefully read advertisements, labels, and guarantees.

If unsure about the features of an item, ask questions of the salesperson. For example, does the car insurance policy cover theft of a tape deck installed in the car? Also be sure the products are not damaged when purchased.

STEP 2   Take Problems to the Store

When problems develop in a product or service, contact the store as soon as possi-

ble. Try to talk with the person who sold you the product. Explain the problem simply and with courtesy. Most consumer problems can be straightened out quickly. Stores usually will immediately replace faulty merchandise.

STEP 3   Talk to Supervisors

If the salesperson who helped you is unable to resolve the problem, ask to see that person's supervisor. Supervisors frequently have more flexibility in handling problems. Continue to talk to people at higher and higher levels in the company until you reach a supervisor who can help. Keep a written record of people talked to and what they said. The chances for success increase if you can demonstrate your intention of following the problem until someone in the company can resolve it.

STEP 4   Contact Outside Agencies

After talking to everyone in a company who can help, contact consumer protection agencies. Besides government agencies, many private business groups provide help for consumers. Some of them, such as the Better Business Bureau, handle complaints about almost any type of good or service. Others, such as the Major Appliance Con-

Consumer Assistance Agencies

Type	Name	Description
Private	Better Business Bureau	This nonprofit organization of businesses encourages businesses to adopt fair practices.
	Major Appliance Consumer Action Panel (MACAP)	This group helps resolve disputes between consumers and producers of major home appliances, such as television sets and washing machines.
Local government	Varies in different cities	City offices usually handle complaints about health, safety hazards, and other activities regulated by city ordinances.
State government	Varies in different states	State agencies usually handle complaints about insurance, real estate, utilities, and other activities regulated by state laws.
Federal government	Consumer Products Safety Commission (CPSC)	This agency tests and sets safety standards for such products as toys, appliances, tools, and sports equipment.
	Food and Drug Administration (FDA)	This agency tests and approves drugs, cosmetics, and food additives, and methods of preparing, handling, and selling food.
	Federal Trade Commission (FTC)	This agency sets and enforces standards for advertising, selling, and other business practices.
	Federal Communications Commission (FCC)	This agency licenses and sets standards for radio and television stations.

Explanation

The chart shows some of the major agencies that help settle problems between consumers and businesses.

Chart Skills

1. Which agency regulates advertising?
2. If you had a problem with a stereo, which of these agencies might be able to help you?

sumer Action Panel, consider consumers' problems with certain types of goods.

STEP 5 File a Lawsuit

As a last resort, you may decide to file a lawsuit—an expensive and time-consuming process. If the claim is not large, a suit can be filed in the Small Claims Court. Claims here do not require a lawyer. Court personnel provide the forms and explain how to complete them. If the claim is large or complex, it may be necessary to hire a lawyer who specializes in handling consumer complaints.

ECONOMIC SKILLS TODAY

1. List the steps a consumer may take if a sweater purchased from the local department store shrank even though the washing directions were followed.
2. In what sort of situation do you think a lawsuit would be needed to deal with a consumer problem?

Enrichment Activity

Obtain from the local office of the Better Business Bureau information on a store in your area. Write a paragraph summarizing the information.

337

CHAPTER SUMMARY

Aiding the Economy

Supply and demand in a free market form the basis of the United States economy. However, the government passes the rules or laws that provide the framework for the market system. Contract laws, rules for collective bargaining, and a national currency system contribute to a smoothly running economy.

Economic Rights

One of the many roles of government in the United States is to protect the economic rights of producers, consumers, property owners, and workers. Consumers are entitled to the highest quality at the lowest price as determined by competition. Government rules work to ensure competition and eliminate price fixing. Laws and the court system protect property owners against theft and other violations of property rights. Laws regulating working conditions protect workers' rights.

Public Goods

Public goods and services benefit people collectively. Government often pays for these goods and services through tax revenue. Public goods improve the welfare of citizens. A public good often has third-party benefits; it may benefit even those who do not pay for it. People disagree on the question of who should provide public goods. Some people believe private companies could supply public goods. Other people believe that the government could better supply some private goods that the market system now provides.

CRITICAL THINKING QUESTIONS

Aiding the Economy

1. Explain the benefits of collective bargaining for both the workers and the employer in settling disputes.
2. Write a short paragraph stating whether you think public employees, such as police officers, firefighters, and teachers, should be allowed to strike. If collective bargaining fails, what other alternatives are available?
3. Do you believe it would be advantageous for the United States to use only the metric system? Why or why not?
4. How did government policy concerning agriculture shift in emphasis over time, and why might agriculture be called a government enterprise?

Economic Rights

1. Is a clean environment—air and water free of pollution—an economic right of all citizens? If so, who should pay the cost of maintaining the environment: Producers, who pass the cost on to consumers through higher prices? The government, which raises various taxes to pay the costs?
2. At what stage of economic development can a country consider spending on such products as clean air and water?
3. Using an American history textbook, find out what conditions led to passage of the Interstate Commerce Act and the Sherman Act. How did these acts contribute to an efficiently operating market economy? Do they still perform an important function?
4. Government regulation is a controversial issue in the United States. Some

groups believe government regulations reduce competition and limit economic efficiency. Others think that government regulations are important in maintaining the rights of consumers, workers, and property owners. Write a paragraph explaining your support for or opposition to government regulations in the area of workers' rights, property owners' rights, or consumers' rights.

Public Goods

1. Would it be economically advantageous for a family with children to move from a state that spends little per pupil on education to one that spends a higher amount? Explain your answer.
2. What kind of tax to raise revenue for education would you consider the most fair to the most people? Why?
3. In many countries, the government owns all railroads and airlines. Would that arrangement work in the United States? Why or why not?
4. The federal government has spent billions of dollars developing the space shuttle system. Is that because the system is a public good, or might there be other reasons?
5. Can subsidies be justified economically? Explain your answer.

DEVELOPING ECONOMIC SKILLS

Use the chart and your economic knowledge to answer the questions.

1. What competition exists among businesses in the fast-food industry?
2. What advantage does the consumer gain from this competition?
3. What government regulations affect the fast-food industry? Use the chart, Consumer Assistance Agencies, on page 337.

Leading Franchises

Company	Number of Franchises in 1983	Minimum Capital Needed	Franchise Fee in 1983
McDonald's	5,247	$227,000	$12,500
Hardee's	1,135	600,000	10,000
Taco Bell	780	142,000	45,000
Popeye's	385	500,000	15,000
Wendy's	1,598	500,000	15,000
Pizza Inn	445	150,000	15,000

Source: *Entrepreneur.*

Explanation

The chart lists six fast-food restaurants that *Entrepreneur* magazine rates among the 10 best franchises (the legal right to market a company's goods or services) in the United States. The franchise ranking is based on growth rate, years in business, and several other financial factors.

Chart Skills

1. For which of these restaurants is the franchise fee the smallest? The largest?
2. Which of these restaurants had the largest number of franchises? The smallest number of franchises?

APPLYING ECONOMICS TODAY

1. Every day the government affects individuals in numerous ways. Write a short list of government rules, policies, or regulations that affected you today.
2. Identify three government regulations that conflict with economic efficiency. How can this problem of conflict be resolved?
3. **Challenge:** Members of a church dating to Revolutionary War times must decide whether to sell the property to a company that is planning to erect an office building on the site. The sale will bring a great deal more than enough money to build a new church. On what basis do you think the members should decide? Explain your reasoning.

CHAPTER 11

Monetary Policy

1 Forms of Money

Objective: to understand the various forms and economic functions of money

2 The Money Supply

Objective: to understand the methods of measuring and controlling the nation's money supply

3 The Federal Reserve

Objective: to understand the operations of the Federal Reserve System and how it influences the money supply

1 Forms of Money

SECTION OVERVIEW

Most people use money almost every day. It is so common that many people rarely think about why money is important and what gives it value. For example, a $1 bill and a $100 bill are almost identical in appearance. The paper and ink used to make each are the same. The value of each, however, is quite different. In this section, you will learn about the forms of money and the important role of money in the economy of the United States.

ECONOMIC VOCABULARY

money	checking account	time deposit
barter	check	legal tender
currency	demand deposits	near money

Defining Money

Money is a fundamental part of a capitalist system. In general, money is any object that is used as a means of exchange, a store of value, and a standard of value. It is something people see and use almost every day. No market economy could get along without it. Though money is commonplace, its forms and functions are complex.

The familiar green paper bills and metal coins used in the United States are only two of the forms money can take. In the past, many things served as money— beads, shells, dogs' teeth, cattle, stones, tobacco, fishhooks, and even slaves. Precious metals, especially gold and silver, have been a favorite form of money. Some of the things used as money—fishhooks or cattle, for example—also have had value as consumer goods. Most of the items used as money, however, have had value only because people agreed that they could be exchanged for goods and services. In other words, what is used as money often has little value of its own. Its value comes from the products for which it can be exchanged.

The Functions of Money

In most modern economies, money serves several functions. First, as a means of exchange money is used to trade for goods and services. When a person takes $5 to a grocery store and buys food with it, the money is being used as a means of exchange. Less complex societies often do not use money at all. They simply barter, or trade, one product for another. Two farmers may trade a bushel of wheat for a jar of milk, for example. The more complex a country's economy, the harder it is to use a system of trading one good for another. Money is the answer to that problem.

Second, as a store of value people use money to save their wealth for the future. Storing goods is not so easy as storing money. Many goods, such as food, spoil quickly. Others, such as cars, take up a lot of space. But money can be kept in a bank or a safe or a pocketbook until it is needed.

Third, as a standard of value money is used to compare the worth of one product with that of another. Everyone knows about how much a dollar will buy. People can therefore compare the worth of one $100 item with other items worth the same amount of money. The value of all the goods and services the economy produces can be determined by adding up their prices. In this way, of course, economists determine GNP.

Forms of Money

In the United States, money comes in several forms. Money in the form of paper bills and metal coins is called currency. The supply of currency is only about $700 per capita. Most money is in the form of checking accounts.

A checking account is a bank account in which money has been deposited. A withdrawal can be made at any time using a check. A check is a written order to a bank to pay a certain amount of money to the person or business to whom the check is made. Depositing $100 in a bank checking account increases the sum the depositor can draw on by that amount. From then on, the depositor need not have $100 in paper bills or coin in order to buy something worth $100. Simply writing a check will cover the cost. Checking accounts are also known as demand deposits, because their owners have the right to demand them from the bank whenever they wish.

Sometimes, time deposits also are considered a form of money. A time deposit is a bank deposit that can be withdrawn at a certain time in the future, or on advance notice. Time deposits cannot be withdrawn using a check. A savings account is an example of a time deposit.

Almost all firms use checks to pay their bills, and most people also are paid by check. Checks are more convenient and safer to use than currency. They are flexible in that they can be written for any amount. They provide a legal record of financial transactions. However, although most people and institutions accept them, checks are not legal tender. Legal tender is money that, by law, must be accepted in payment of a debt. The only legal tender in the United States is currency.

Several other things are used like money. Economists call things used for some, but not all, of the functions of money near money. Credit cards, for example, allow a purchaser to borrow money from the seller of the purchased goods. Credit cards are a common way to purchase goods and services. If the card is used to buy gasoline, the gas station will record the name and number and send it, along with the bill for the gasoline, to the credit card company. The credit card company will then pay the gas station and send the buyer a bill for the amount of the gasoline. Credit cards are not money, though, since they can be traded only for certain products from certain companies. Money can be exchanged for anything.

When savings accounts are used as a store of value, savers deposit their money for use in the future instead of in the present. The bank book is a record of a person's deposits and the interest the bank paid for use of the money. Insurance policies, stocks, and bonds are stores of value and can be exchanged for money. They are other examples of near money.

The Role of Money

Money is very important in our society. As a store and a standard of value and as a means of exchange, money helps the economy run smoothly. We can judge the worth of such diverse things as pets, paintings, medical care, and car washes. Then we can compare their value using the amount they cost. The market system determines how much money everything is worth. People whose jobs are thought to be more important get higher salaries than those whose jobs are considered less important. Thus, people often are judged by how much money they earn.

You have your own beliefs about the value of goods, services, jobs, and people. Often the value you place on an item will differ from its monetary value. You may feel that some things are priceless and others are not worth as much as they cost. Your own values dictate what you are willing to do for pay.

REVIEWING THE CONCEPT

Developing Vocabulary

Write a brief definition for each of the following terms:

money	demand deposits
barter	time deposit
currency	legal tender
checking account	near money
check	

Mastering Facts

1. What is money really worth?
2. List three advantages that checks have over currency.
3. Why are savings accounts considered near money rather than money?
4. List 10 items that have been or could be used as money.

CASE STUDY

Scrip Money

Money is so important to a capitalist system that people will invent it if they do not have it. Can you imagine paying for groceries or other items with money made of cardboard, wood, or rubber? Many Americans did during the early 1930s, when regular money was often difficult to obtain. The unusual printed money was called scrip. **Scrip** is paper money or tokens issued for temporary use in an emergency. Local governments and businesses issued scrip during the Depression to temporarily replace regular money. Though not legal, scrip did help people to survive in difficult times.

In 1929, the nation entered the worst economic depression of its history. At that time, Betty Meier was 19. Betty remembers the long lines outside banks. Many people demanded their money from banks, but the banks closed because they did not have enough cash. "My parents were lucky," said Betty. "They got their small savings out before the bank closed." However, her parents were afraid to invest their savings. Even after the banks reopened, they kept their money in a box in the attic of their home. "My parents spent very little during the depression years. No one could tell when times would get better." Most people refused to spend or invest money, and the demand for goods greatly decreased. The decline in demand caused more workers to lose their jobs. Those losses, in turn, lowered the money supply even more.

What were people supposed to do as money became more and more scarce?

Betty remembers trading bread her mother made to get a used winter coat for her sister. Betty heard stories that Madison Square Garden in New York accepted everything from potatoes to spark plugs to cover the price of admission to boxing events. Bartering, however, was often time-consuming and difficult to work out.

Money was still needed—so people began to make their own. Betty's aunt was paid in scrip issued by the school district where she taught. "I went to the grocery store to get potatoes. The clerk took my aunt's school scrip and gave me paper money printed by his store." City governments and individuals began to use scrip.

Scrip was backed by a person's reputation, funds in a closed bank, corn, buildings, equipment, or so on. Local citizens realized that if scrip were not accepted, such services as fire protection, police protection, and hospitals could not operate.

Most scrip money was illegal, but the government knew that it was necessary. By 1932 over 400 American communities were issuing scrip. According to *Collier's* magazine, scrip was "a magnificent testimonial to the courage, imagination, and resourcefulness of the American people."

This piece of "oyster money" was one of the many types of scrip that were used in some communities during the Great Depression.

ANALYZING THE CASE STUDY

STEP 1   Clarify the Issue

1. List three differences between scrip money and legal currency.
2. Why did people in the 1930s feel they needed to use scrip?

STEP 2   Evaluate Costs and Benefits

1. What problems did scrip solve?
2. What are the costs and benefits in bartering for goods today?

STEP 3   Make a Decision

1. Why do you think the federal government allowed scrip money to be used?
2. What does this case study suggest about the forms of money?

READING

Mammon and the Archer

by O. Henry   (1862-1910)

Money can be exchanged for any product. However, money cannot buy everything. This reading considers what money can and cannot buy. The reading, like that in Section 1 of Chapter 1, was written by William S. Porter (O. Henry). As you read, consider how your use of money reflects your values.

"Old Anthony Rockwall, retired manufacturer and proprietor of Rockwall's Eureka Soap, looked out the library window of his Fifth Avenue mansion. And then Anthony Rockwall, who never cared for bells, went to the door of his library and shouted "Mike!"

"Tell my son," said Anthony to the answering menial, "to come in here before he leaves the house."

When young Rockwall entered the library, the old man laid aside his newspaper, looked at him with a kindly grimness on his big, smooth, ruddy countenance, rumpled his mop of white hair with one hand and rattled the keys in his pocket with the other.

"You're a gentleman," said Anthony, decidedly. "They say it takes three generations to make one. They're off. Money'll do it as slick as soap grease. It's made you one. By hokey! it's almost made one of me."

"There are some things that money can't accomplish," remarked young Rockwall, rather gloomily.

"That's why I asked you to come in. There's something going wrong with you, boy. I've been noticing it for two weeks. Out with it. If it's your liver, there's the Rambler down in the bay, coaled, and ready to steam down to the Bahamas in two days."

"Not a bad guess, dad; you haven't missed it far."

"Ah," said Anthony, keenly, "what's her name?"

Richard began to walk up and down the library floor. There was enough comradeship and sympathy in this crude old father of his to draw his confidence.

"Why don't you ask her?" demanded old Anthony. "She'll jump at you. You've got the money and the looks, and you're a decent boy. Your hands are clean. You've got no Eureka soap on 'em. You've been to college, but she'll overlook that."

"I haven't had a chance," said Richard. "Every hour and minute of her time is arranged for days in advance. I must have that girl, dad, or this town is a blackjack swamp forevermore. And I can't write it—I can't do that.

"I'm allowed to meet her with a cab at the Grand Central Station tomorrow evening at the 8:30 train. We drive down Broadway to Wallack's at a gallop, where her mother and a box party will be waiting for us in the lobby. Do you think she would listen to a declaration from me during that six or eight minutes under those circumstances? No, dad, this is one tangle that your money can't unravel. We can't buy one minute of time with cash; if we could, rich people would live longer."

"You say money won't buy time? Well, of course, you can't order eternity wrapped up and delivered at your residence for a price, but I've seen Father Time get pretty bad stone bruises on his heels when he walked through the gold diggings."

That night came Aunt Ellen to brother Anthony at his evening paper, and began discourse on the subject of lovers' woes.

"He told me all about it," said brother Anthony, yawning. "I told him my bank account was at his service."

"Oh, Anthony," sighed Aunt Ellen, "I wish you would not think so much of money. Wealth is nothing where a true affection is concerned. Love is all-powerful."

At eight o'clock the next evening Aunt Ellen took a quaint old gold ring from a motheaten case and gave it to Richard.

"Wear it to-night, nephew," she begged. "Your mother gave it to me. Good luck in love she said it brought. She asked me to give it to you when you had found the one you loved."

Young Rockwall took the ring reverently and tried it on his smallest finger. It slipped as far as the second joint and stopped. He took if off and stuffed it into his vest pocket.

At the station he captured Miss Lantry out of the mob at eight thirty-two.

"To Wallack's Theatre as fast as you can drive!" said Richard loyally.

At Thirty-Fourth Street young Richard quickly thrust up the trap and ordered the cabman to stop.

"I've dropped a ring," he apologized, as he climbed out. "It was my mother's, and I'd hate to lose it. I won't detain you a minute—I saw where it fell."

In less than a minute he was back in the cab with the ring.

But within that minute a crosstown car had stopped directly in front of the cab. The cabman tried to pass to the left, but a heavy express wagon cut him off. He tried the right, and had to back away from a furniture van that had no business to be there. He tried to back out, but dropped his reins and swore dutifully. He was blockaded in a tangled mess of vehicles and horses. The entire traffic of Manhattan seemed to have jammed itself around them.

"I'm very sorry," said Richard, as he resumed his seat, "but it looks as if we are stuck. They won't get this jumble loosened up in an hour. It was my fault. If I hadn't dropped the ring we—"

At 11 o'clock that night somebody tapped lightly on Anthony Rockwall's door.

"Come in," shouted Anthony, who was in a red dressing-gown, reading a book of the adventures of pirates.

Somebody was Aunt Ellen.

"They're engaged, Anthony," she said, softy. "She has promised to marry our Richard. On their way to the theatre there was a street blockade, and it was two hours before their cab could get out of it.

"And, oh, brother Anthony, don't ever boast of the power of money again. A little emblem of true love—a little ring that symbolized unending affection—was the cause of our Richard finding his happiness. He dropped it in the street, and got out to recover it. And before they could continue the blockade occurred. He spoke to his love and won her there while the cab was hemmed in. Money is worthless compared with true love, Anthony."

The story should end here. I wish it would as heartily as you who read it wish it did. But we must go to the bottom of the well for the truth.

The next day a person with red hands and a blue polka-dot necktie, who

346

called himself Kelly, called at Anthony Rockwall's house, and was at once received in the library.

"Well," said Anthony, reaching for his checkbook, "it was a good amount of soap. Let's see—you had $5,000 in cash."

"I paid out $300 more of my own," said Kelly. "I had to go a little above the estimate. I got the express wagons and cabs mostly for $5; but the trucks and two-horse teams mostly raised me to $10. The motormen wanted $10, and some of the loaded teams $20. The cops struck me hardest—$50 I paid two, and the rest $20 and $25. But didn't it work beautiful, Mr. Rockwall? And never a rehearsal, either! The boys was on time to the fraction of a second. It was two hours before a snake could get below Greeley's statue.

"You didn't notice," said he, "anywhere in the tieup, a kind of a fat boy without any clothes shooting arrows around with a bow, did you? **""**

"Mammon and the Archer," by O. Henry.

UNDERSTANDING THE READING

1. What exchanges did money permit in this story? Did Anthony Rockwall's money really buy time?
2. Which function of money does the gold ring illustrate? What besides monetary value is stored in the ring?
3. What was the cost of Richard Rockwall's two hours alone with Miss Lantry? What function of money does this cost illustrate?

Section 1 Review

Understanding Forms of Money

1. Identify the function that money serves in each of the following situations:
   Jane Dunn collects $50 for her part-time job in the supermarket.
   On her way home, Jane puts $15 in her savings account.
   Jane visits a store where she compares the prices of personal computers.
2. Why are checks not legal tender?
3. List five examples of near money other than savings accounts.
4. Explain the difference between a savings account and a checking account.
5. Which of the following statements are true and which are false? Reword the false ones to make them true.

   a. Money comes in a variety of forms.
   b. Currency can be goods or services.
   c. Near money can perform the same functions as money.
   d. Credit cards are a type of money.
   e. Money has absolute value in itself.

Forms of Money Today

1. Explain why the high price of an item might make it attractive to some people.
2. What problems might occur if barter were the only means of exchange today?
3. Are a cashless society and a society without money the same or different? Explain your answer.
4. **Challenge:** What are the possible dangers in a cashless society?

2 The Money Supply

SECTION OVERVIEW

Your personal supply of money changes often. Increases and decreases in your supply of money probably affect how much you spend. Similarly, the amount of money in the total economy changes often. Changes in the economy's money supply are more complex than changes in a personal money supply. Still, these fluctuations in the money supply influence not only how much spending occurs and but also the general level of business activity. In this section, you will learn how the money supply expands and contracts.

ECONOMIC VOCABULARY

reserve   M-1A   M-1B   M-2

Expanding the Money Supply

The money supply of the United States is constantly changing. Sometimes it expands and sometimes it contracts. The government prints new bills and mints new coins every year to replace those that are worn. It also changes the money supply to meet people's needs.

The supply of checking account money, or demand deposits, also changes. Suppose that bank customer John Winslow deposits $10,000 of his earnings in a checking account. What does the bank do with the $10,000? It puts the money to use by lending it to people and charging interest.

Banking laws in the United States require a bank to put a certain percentage of its deposits in reserve. A bank's reserve is the money the bank must set aside and not loan to anyone. Assume that the bank's reserve must be 10 percent of total deposits. Of John Winslow's $10,000, the bank keeps $1,000 in reserve. The other $9,000 it lends to anyone able to pay it back with enough interest.

Next, Jane Diaz asks to borrow $9,000 from the bank to pay her tuition at Bailey Medical School. She signs an agreement to pay back the money with interest. The bank then gives her a check for $9,000, which she pays to the medical school. The school puts the money into its bank account. That bank holds 10 percent ($900) in reserve and lends the rest, $8,100, to George Graham, who wants to buy a computer from the ABC Computer Company. When ABC deposits Graham's $8,100 in its bank, the bank keeps 10 percent ($810) in reserve and lends the rest, $7,290, to Justine Craig so that she can buy a new car. The Adams Auto Agency deposits Craig's $7,290—and so the process continues, with a succession of borrowers and depositors.

None of these transactions involved currency. All were completed through checking accounts. This series of deposits caused the total supply of checking account money to expand. John Winslow still has $10,000 in his checking account. The Bailey Medical School has $9,000 in its account. The ABC Computer Company has $8,100 in its account. The Adams Auto Agency has $7,290 in its account. So how much is in all the checking accounts? The sum of $10,000, $9,000, $8,100, and $7,290 is $34,390. In other words, the original $10,000 in checking account money grew, because of loans, to a subtotal of $34,390.

Limits to Money Supply Growth

This expansion of the money supply does not continue forever. A deposit in a checking account can increase the money supply by about 5 times the original amount. Several factors stop the process of expansion or even reverse it.

First, federal law requires the bank to keep a percentage of its demand deposits in reserve, usually 10 to 20 percent. Banks cannot loan out all of the money people deposit. After John Winslow's original deposit, each successive deposit was less.

Second, expansion will stop if the bank stops making loans. Lending may cease if the bank cannot find any more people it believes will be able to repay a loan. Also, if people stop putting their money into checking accounts, the bank will not be able to make loans.

Finally, if many people suddenly withdraw their money all at once, the bank must do more than stop making loans. It will have to start calling for payment of its loans so that it can increase its reserves.

Measuring the Money Supply

Determining the supply of money in the economy is difficult. Economists disagree on what to include when measuring the money supply. Consequently, several different measures are used. The most common are M-1A, M-1B, and M-2. M-1A includes all currency and all deposits in standard checking accounts. Of the three, it is the most limited measure. M-1B is M-1A plus money in accounts that are similar to checking accounts but pay interest. M-2

Expansion of the Money Supply

Stage	Deposits		Reserves	Loans
1. John Winslow	$ 10,000		$ 1,000	$ 9,000 to Diaz
2. Bailey Medical School	9,000		900	8,100 to Graham
3. ABC Computer Company	8,100		810	7,290 to Craig
4. Adams Auto Agency	7,290		729	6,561
Subtotal	$ 34,390		$ 3,439	$30,951
Additional deposits	65,610		6,561	59,049
Total	$100,000		$10,000	$90,000

Explanation

At each stage, an individual or company makes a deposit to a bank, which keeps 10 percent for reserves. The other 90 percent is used for loans. The process begins with a $10,000 deposit. The following three deposits are also shown. Eventually, with the addition of other deposits, the sum of all the deposits in the banks would be $100,000.

Chart Skills

1. After four stages, how much money had been deposited? How much then was added?
2. What was the total of all loans that resulted from the series of deposits?
3. Explain what would happen to the amount of money available for loans if banks used 60 percent of their deposits for loans.

includes M-1B plus savings deposits. Of the three, M-2 is the most comprehensive measure of the economy's money supply. Money in savings accounts cannot be used immediately to purchase products, but it is often easily available to depositors.

Growth of the Money Supply

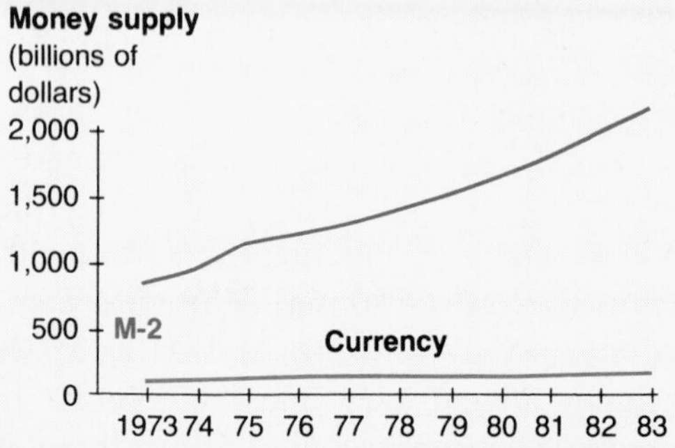

Money supply
(billions of dollars)

Source: Federal Reserve System.

Explanation

The graph shows two different measures of the supply of money. Between 1973 and 1983, currency increased from $12 billion to $139 billion. M-2, which includes currency, increased from $861 billion to $2,098 billion.

Graph Skills

1. What types of money besides currency are included in M-2?
2. How much was M-2 in 1983? How much was the supply of currency in 1983?

Credit and the Money Supply

In a way, the money supply seems to be based on magic. You put some money in a bank, and suddenly there is more money. The magic, of course, is people's credit—trust in the ability of borrowers to repay loans. The money you put in the bank is yours because you can count on the bank to pay it back. The bank, in turn, can count on being able to pay you back because it can count on its borrowers to pay it back.

Borrowing from a bank is not the same as borrowing from a friend. If you do not repay your friends, they may be hurt or angry. But if you cannot pay them back, they probably will understand. If you do not pay back the bank, you will lose more than your good name or credit. If a large number of people, acted as you did, the whole banking system would collapse.

REVIEWING THE CONCEPT

Developing Vocabulary

Write a definition of each of the following: M-1A, M-1B, M-2.

Mastering Facts

1. Give four reasons why the banking system's ability to create money is limited.
2. How does failing to repay a bank loan differ from failing to repay a loan from a friend or relative?

CASE STUDY

What Type of Account?

The problems of the Federal Reserve System (Fed), the nation's central banking system, in measuring the money supply have increased in recent years. Changes in banking regulations have allowed many new types of accounts. The deposits in some of these accounts are almost like money. In order to accurately count the money supply, the Fed must decide how to count these deposits.

Assume that you received $1,000 in paper money. Because it is paper money, or currency, it is counted as part of M-1A. Since M-1A is included as part of M-1B and M-2, the $1,000 also is considered part of those measures.

If you decide to open a checking account with the cash, you will not affect the money supply directly. Regular checking accounts are included in M-1A, M-1B, and M-2. However, if you put the $1,000 into a NOW (negotiated order of withdrawal) account rather than a regular checking account, your influence will be different. NOW accounts were permitted nationwide in 1981. A NOW account is similar to a checking account but earns interest. Money in these accounts is not considered part of M-1A but is part of M-1B. Therefore, by starting a NOW account you will decrease M-1A. M-1B and M-2 remain the same.

If you establish a savings account rather than a checking account, your influence on the money supply will again be different. M-2 is the only one of the three measures that counts savings deposits. Therefore, your deposit will not be considered part of M-1A or M-1B. It will still be part of M-2.

Your deposit will have not only a direct effect but also an indirect effect on the money supply. If you keep your money in a shoebox at home, it will not circulate and create more money. However, if you deposit it in a bank, the bank can then lend it to people who want to borrow. This process increases the money supply.

The type of account you choose will determine the amount of money the bank will be able to lend. The Federal Reserve has established different reserve requirements for different types of accounts.

For checking accounts, the reserve requirement is between 7.00 and 16.25 percent. The percentage varies depending on the size and location of the bank. For savings accounts, the reserve requirement is only 3 percent. Consequently, banks can lend more money from $1,000 deposited in savings than from the same amount deposited in checking.

Many people constantly shift money from one account to another. Accurately measuring the money supply is virtually impossible. Like many other economic statistics, estimates provide the best information available.

ANALYZING THE CASE STUDY

STEP 1   Define Key Terms

1. How does a NOW account differ from a checking account?
2. What is the difference between M-1A and M-1B?
3. What is M-2?

STEP 2   Consider Alternatives

1. How would the money supply of the nation change if 50 percent of the money in checking accounts were withdrawn and placed in safe deposit boxes?
2. What bank policies would encourage you to put your money in the bank?

STEP 3   Predict Further Change

1. If you decided to use all your savings to buy a house, what would be the effect on the money supply?
2. If you transferred your money from a savings account to a NOW account, what would be the effect on M-1B? M-2?

Enrichment Activity

Use a library to find out how the development of NOW accounts influenced the money supply. Find out how the Fed changed its methods of measuring the money supply to reflect these changes.

The Grapes of Wrath

by John Steinbeck   (1902-1968)

During economic growth, the money supply expands through a series of loans and deposits. However, during the contraction phase of the business cycle people may have trouble in repaying their debts. During the 1930s, low crop prices and poor harvests hurt farmers. Many had borrowed money to buy their land. When they could not repay the loans, the banks took ownership of the land. The banks could then try to sell the land and get their money back. This reading taken from John Steinbeck's novel, *The Grapes of Wrath,* describes some problems the farmers faced. As you read, consider how you would have responded if you had been a farmer.

66 The owners of the land came onto the land, or more often a spokesman for the owners came. They came in closed cars, and they felt the dry earth with their fingers, and sometimes they drove big earth drills into the ground for soil tests. The tenants, from their sun-beaten dooryards, watched uneasily when the closed cars drove along the fields. And at last the owner men drove into the dooryards and sat in their cars to talk out of the windows. The tenant men stood beside the cars for a while, and then squatted on their hams and found sticks with which to mark the dust.

In the open doors the women stood looking out, and behind them the children—corn-headed children, with wide eyes, one bare foot on top of the other bare foot, and the toes working. The women and the children watched their men talking to the owner men. They were silent.

Some of the owner men were kind because they hated what they had to do, and some of them were angry because they hated to be cruel, and some of them were cold because they had long ago found that one could not be an owner unless one were cold. And all of them were caught in something larger than themselves. Some of them hated the mathematics that drove them, and some were afraid, and some worshiped the mathematics because it provided a refuge from thought and from feeling. If a bank or a finance company owned the land, the owner man said the Bank—or the Company—needs—wants—insists—must have—as though the Bank or the Company were a monster, with thought and feeling, which had trapped them. These last would take no responsibility for the banks or the companies because they were men and slaves, while the banks were machines and masters all at the same time. Some of the owner men were a little proud to be slaves to such cold and powerful masters. The owner men sat in the cars and explained. You know the land is poor. You've scrabbled at it long enough, God knows.

The squatting tenant men nodded and wondered and drew figures in the dust, and yes, they knew, God knows. If the dust only wouldn't fly. If the top would only stay on the soil, it might not be so bad.

The owner men went on leading to their point: You know the land's getting poorer. You know what cotton does to the land; robs it, sucks all the blood out of it.

The squatters nodded—they knew, God knew. If they could only rotate the crops they might pump blood back into the land.

Well, it's too late. And the owner men explained the workings and the thinkings of the monster that was stronger than they were. A man can hold land if he can just eat and pay taxes; he can do that.

Yes, he can do that until his crops fail one day and he has to borrow money from the bank.

But—you see, a bank or a company can't do that, because those creatures don't breathe air, don't eat side meat. They breathe profits; they eat the interest on money. If they don't get it, they die the way you die without air, without bacon. It is a sad thing, but it is so. It is just so.

The squatting men raised their eyes to understand. Can't we just hang on? Maybe the next year will be a good year. God knows how much cotton next year. And with all the wars—God knows what price cotton will bring. Don't they make explosives out of cotton? And uniforms? Get enough wars and cotton'll hit the ceiling. Next year, maybe. They looked up questioningly.

We can't depend on it. The bank—the monster—has to have profits all the time. It can't wait. It'll die. No, taxes go on. When the monster stops growing, it dies. It can't stay one size.

Soft fingers began to tap the sill of the car window, and hard fingers tightened on the restless drawing sticks. In the doorways of the sunbeaten tenant houses, women sighed and then shifted feet so that the one that had been down was now on top, and the toes working. Dogs came sniffing near the owner cars and wetted on all four tires one after another.

Sure, cried the tenant men, but it's our land. We measured it and broke it up. We were born on it, and we got killed on it, died on it. Even if it's no good, it's still ours. That's what makes it ours—being born on it, working it, dying on it. That makes ownership, not a paper with numbers on it.

We're sorry. It's not us. It's the monster. The bank isn't like a man.

Yes, but the bank is only made of men.

No, you're wrong there—quite wrong there. The bank is something else than men. It happens that every man in a bank hates what the bank does, and yet the bank does it. The bank is something more than men, I tell you. It's the monster. Men made it, but they can't control it.

The tenants cried, Grandpa killed Indians, Pa killed snakes for the land. Maybe we can kill banks—they're worse than Indians and snakes. Maybe we got to fight to keep our land, like Pa and Grampa did.

And now the owner men grew angry. You'll have to go.

But it's ours, the tenant men cried. We—

No. The bank, the monster owns it. You'll have to go.

We'll get our guns, like Grampa when the Indians came. What then?

Well—first the sheriff, and then the troops. You'll be stealing if you try to stay, you'll be murderers if you kill to stay. The monster isn't men, but it can make men do what it wants.

But if we go, where'll we go? How'll we go? We got no money.

We're sorry, said the owner men. The bank, the fifty-thousand-acre owner can't be responsible. You're on land that isn't yours. Once over the line maybe you can pick cotton in the fall. Maybe you can go on relief. Why don't you go on west to California? There's work there, and it never gets cold. Why, you can reach out anywhere and pick an orange. Why, there's always some kind of crop to work in. Why don't you go there? And the owner men started their cars and rolled away.

The tenant men squatted down on their hams again to mark the dust with a stick, to figure, to wonder. Their sunburned faces were dark, and their sunwhipped eyes were light. The women moved cautiously out of the doorways toward their men, and the children crept behind the women, cautiously, ready to run. The bigger boys squatted beside their fathers, because that made them men. After a time the women asked, What did he want?

And the men looked up for a second, and the smolder of pain was in their eyes. We got to get off. A tractor and a superintendent. Like factories.

Where'll we go? the women asked.

We don't know. We don't know.

And the women went quickly, quietly back into the houses and herded the children ahead of them. They knew that a man so hurt and so perplexed may turn in anger, even on people he loves. They left the men alone to figure and to wonder in the dust.

After a time perhaps the tenant man looked about—at the pump put in 10 years ago, with a gooseneck handle and iron flowers on the spout, at the chopping block where a thousand chickens had been killed, at the hand plow lying in the shed, and the crib hanging in the rafters over it.

The children crowded about the women in the houses. What we going to do, Ma? Where we going to go?

The women said, we don't know, yet. Go out and play. But don't go near your father. He might whale you if you go near him. And the women went on with the work, but all the time they watched the men squatting in the dust—perplexed and figuring. 🙰

From *The Grapes of Wrath,* by John Steinbeck.

UNDERSTANDING THE READING

1. Explain how the bank loans to the farmers increased the money supply. What would happen to the money supply if the farmers were unable to repay their debts?

2. If the banks did not take the land, what would happen to the financial condition of the banks?

3. What would you have done if you had been the banker? The farmer?

Section 2 Review

Understanding the Money Supply

1. Copy the forms below. Complete the forms to show how the banking system can increase the money supply. Suppose that $50,000 is deposited in the First National Bank. The reserve requirement is 10 percent. Assume that a borrower is loaned the 90 percent, and that the money is deposited in a second bank; and then repeat the process for the third and fourth banks.

Increasing the Money Supply

First National Bank
Amount deposited _____
Amount required for reserves _____
Total available for loans _____

Second National Bank
Amount deposited _____
Amount required for reserves _____
Total available for loans _____

Third National Bank
Amount deposited _____
Amount required for reserves _____
Total available for loans _____

Fourth National Bank
Amount deposited _____
Amount required for reserves _____
Total available for loans _____

Explanation

The chart when completed will show how the banking system can increase the money supply. Directions for completing the chart appear in question 1.

Chart Skills

1. How much money was available for loans in each bank?
2. What was the total amount of money available for loans from all the banks? How does this amount compare with the amount of money deposited?

2. Explain how each of the following actions affects the money supply.
a. The public decides to hold more cash and keep less of its money in demand deposits in banks.
b. The Federal Reserve lowers the required reserve for checking accounts from 12 to 8 percent.
3. Explain why the owner men in *The Grapes of Wrath* said that the bank was something more than men?

The Money Supply Today

1. Suppose the reserve requirement for banks was increased from 10 percent to 20 percent. How would this change affect the bank's ability to lend? What effect might the change have on the economy of the nation?
2. If the United States were suffering from high inflation, could a change in the reserve requirement help reduce inflation? Explain your answer.
3. **Challenge:** What, if anything, can people like the tenants in *The Grapes of Wrath* do about the economic situation in which they find themselves?

During the depression migrant workers took to the roads to find work.

3 The Federal Reserve

SECTION OVERVIEW

Most people keep some money in savings accounts. This money provides a reserve for future use. In addition, banks pay interest on deposits and provide loans to those who want to borrow. If you have not done so already, you probably will use a bank someday for savings, checking, and loans. Banks, in turn, also need to keep reserves, not only to earn interest on their money but also to borrow when their funds are low. The Federal Reserve System provides these services. In providing them, the Federal Reserve greatly influences the nation's money supply. In this section, you will learn how the Federal Reserve operates and how it influences the money supply.

ECONOMIC VOCABULARY

monetary policy

reserve requirement

discount rate

open-market operations

easy money

tight money

The Federal Reserve Structure

The money supply of the United States changes constantly. The Federal Reserve System (Fed), the nation's central banking system, influences the rate of growth or decrease in the money supply.

The Federal Reserve System was established in 1913. About 5,000 of the 15,000 banks in the nation are members. All banks chartered by the federal government are required to join the system. These banks have the word *national* in their name. Banks chartered by states may choose to join or not join the Fed. For a small fee, nonmember banks may obtain most of the Fed's services.

Prior to March 1980, nonmember banks were not required to comply with the Fed's reserve requirement. Then, Congress passed the Depository Institutions Deregulation and Control Act of 1980. One provision of this law requires all financial institutions that receive deposits from the public to maintain reserves in the Federal Reserve System. Even though less than half of all banks are members, the 5,000 member banks control about 75 percent of all assets held by banks.

The country is divided into 12 Federal Reserve regions. In each one is a Federal Reserve Bank to serve the member banks in that region. Also, 24 branch banks are in the system.

The Federal Reserve Board of Governors oversees the 12 regional banks and the operation of the system. The President appoints the 7 board members to 14-year terms. The Senate must confirm these appointments. The President also appoints the chairman, who is the most visible public figure on the board. The Federal Reserve Board reports to the President and Congress. However, the operations of the Fed are not subject to the approval of either the President or Congress.

Twelve Regions of the Federal Reserve System

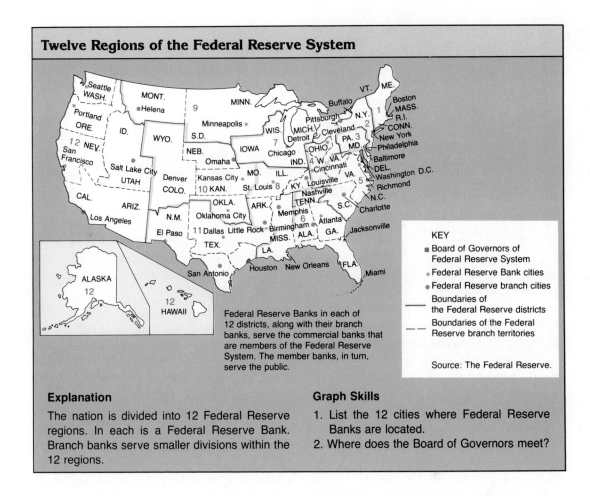

Federal Reserve Banks in each of 12 districts, along with their branch banks, serve the commercial banks that are members of the Federal Reserve System. The member banks, in turn, serve the public.

KEY
■ Board of Governors of Federal Reserve System
● Federal Reserve Bank cities
● Federal Reserve branch cities
— Boundaries of the Federal Reserve districts
-- Boundaries of the Federal Reserve branch territories

Source: The Federal Reserve.

Explanation

The nation is divided into 12 Federal Reserve regions. In each is a Federal Reserve Bank. Branch banks serve smaller divisions within the 12 regions.

Graph Skills

1. List the 12 cities where Federal Reserve Banks are located.
2. Where does the Board of Governors meet?

The Federal Advisory Committee of 12 commercial bankers confers with the Board of Governors. Each of the 12 Federal Reserve Banks selects a member of the Federal Advisory Committee. These committee members advise the board on banking conditions in their district.

Monetary Policy

The most important function of the Fed is to carry out the government's monetary policy. Monetary policy is the government's effort to influence the money supply and interest rates. Bank loans to businesses during economic growth expand the money supply. When banks reduce the amount of lending, the money supply contracts.

If banks do not lend money, people cannot buy houses or cars or any of the other expensive products for which they need borrowed money. Thus, the demand for these products goes down. Production declines and workers are laid off. The result is rising unemployment.

The money supply can expand too rapidly, however. Then production goes up quickly in response to increased spending. As the spending for goods and services increases, prices tend to rise as well. If prices rise too rapidly, inflation results.

Tools of the Federal Reserve

Two laws set up and later altered the Federal Reserve System, increasing its power. Now it has three important tools to influence the money supply.

357

The San Francisco Federal Reserve Bank serves nine western states.

First, the Fed can determine what percentage of its deposits a bank must keep in reserve. This proportion is called the reserve requirement. If the reserve requirement is 10 percent, a bank must keep in reserve $1 of every $10 it receives in deposits. It can lend $9 of every $10. If the requirement is raised to 20 percent, $2 must be kept in reserve and $8 can be lent. By raising the reserve requirement, therefore, the Fed is contracting the money supply. By lowering the reserve requirement, it is expanding the money supply.

Second, the Federal Reserve System lends money to banks and, like any other bank, charges interest on its loans. The discount rate is the interest rate banks must pay to borrow money from the Fed. By raising the discount rate, the Fed discourages banks from borrowing. Then the banks have less money to lend to customers. By lowering the discount rate, the Fed encourages banks to borrow from it. Then the banks have more money to lend to customers. Raising the discount rate contracts the money supply. Lowering the discount rate expands the money supply.

Third, the Fed is permitted by law to buy and sell government bonds. The Federal Open Market Committee directs the sale of United States government bonds. A government bond promises that the gov-

ernment will pay the owner the purchase price of the bond, plus interest, at the end of a certain period of time. When the Fed sells a bond and receives a check, money is transferred to the Fed out of the bank that issued the check. This action reduces the amount of money the bank has on hand for loans. When the Fed buys bonds from banks, money flows in the opposite direction. The Fed's bond sales contract the banks' money supplies. The bond purchases expand the banks' money supplies. Fed sales and purchases of government bonds are known as open-market operations.

Easy and Tight Money

Easy money results when the Fed expands the money supply. In other words, money is easy to borrow because banks have more available to lend. Tight money results when the Fed contracts the money supply. Money is scarce and hard to borrow. Easy money leads to increased demand and production, lower unemployment, and higher prices. However, it can also increase inflation. Tight money leads to lower demand and production, increased unemployment, and lower prices. At the same time, it can lead to a recession.

Money as a Product

Another way to consider the influence of the Federal Reserve System is to think of money as a product. The Fed controls the supply of the product. If the quantity of a product increases, the product's value, as measured by price, decreases. The price of money is the interest rate. When the quantity of money increases, the interest rate will decrease. Because money is less valuable, prices of goods and services will increase. An easy money policy promotes expansion and often inflation.

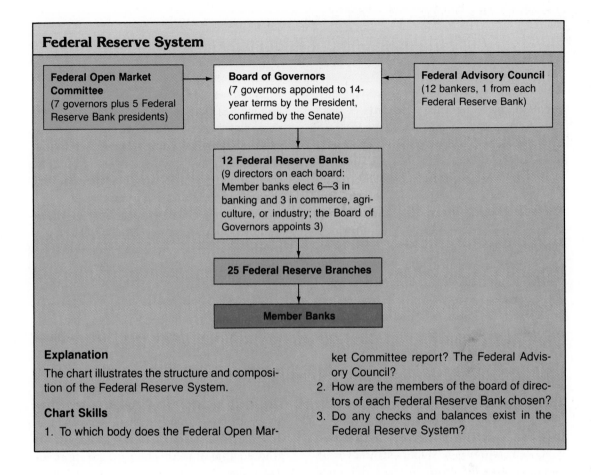

Federal Reserve System

Federal Open Market Committee
(7 governors plus 5 Federal Reserve Bank presidents)

Board of Governors
(7 governors appointed to 14-year terms by the President, confirmed by the Senate)

Federal Advisory Council
(12 bankers, 1 from each Federal Reserve Bank)

12 Federal Reserve Banks
(9 directors on each board: Member banks elect 6—3 in banking and 3 in commerce, agriculture, or industry; the Board of Governors appoints 3)

25 Federal Reserve Branches

Member Banks

Explanation

The chart illustrates the structure and composition of the Federal Reserve System.

Chart Skills

1. To which body does the Federal Open Market Committee report? The Federal Advisory Council?
2. How are the members of the board of directors of each Federal Reserve Bank chosen?
3. Do any checks and balances exist in the Federal Reserve System?

In the opposite direction, a tight Federal Reserve money policy promotes recession and usually deflation. When the money supply contracts, money is scarcer. Scarcity makes the value of money greater. Dollars are worth more; hence, they will purchase more goods and services.

Both easy money and tight money policies have proponents and opponents. What the Fed does is usually controversial. When unemployment is high, the Fed may pursue an easy money policy. When prices are too high, the Fed may promote tight money. Striking a balance between these two extremes is not an easy task. Making it even harder is the difficulty in getting accurate information about the economy quickly enough to make the right decision.

REVIEWING THE CONCEPT

Developing Vocabulary

Write a brief description of each term:

monetary policy
reserve requirements
open-market operations

easy money
tight money
discount rate

Mastering Facts

1. What effect does lowering the reserve requirement often have on unemployment? Explain your answer.
2. Would a rise in the discount rate increase or decrease the money supply? Explain your answer.
3. If the money supply is too high, should the Fed sell or buy government securities? Explain your answer.

The Impact of the Fed

The Fed's controversial decisions have great impact on the economy. Consequently, the person who chairs the Board of Governors that oversees the Fed is a powerful, controversial individual. A survey of American leaders in the early 1980s picked Chairman of the Board of Governors Paul Volcker as the second most powerful person in the nation. Only the President ranked higher. Volcker's policies have shaped the economy of the 1980s.

Paul Volcker became chairperson of the Board of Governors in the summer of 1979. When he was appointed, inflation was very high—at over 12 percent. The first goal was to bring down inflation. "We had a sense, in the summer of '79, that psychologically and otherwise inflation was getting ahead of us. I suppose we're interested in inflation in the end because the economy, over a long period of time, cannot operate very well without a stable currency." In order to slow inflation, Volcker tightened the money supply.

How might a tight money policy affect you? If you were going to borrow money to buy a car, a tight money policy would cost you money. Higher interest rates would mean that your car would be more expensive. The same problem would face you if you were planning to take out a loan to attend college.

Tight money policies could help you, though, if you already had money saved. An increase in interest rates means money is getting more valuable. So, the money you had in a savings account would be worth more. You could receive a higher interest rate for allowing a bank to use your money.

By the summer of 1981, inflation was slowing down. Volcker and the Fed began to ease the tight policy. Borrowing money became easier. Loans for cars, houses, and college tuition became less expensive. Further, businesses could now borrow money more cheaply for expansion. For individuals, cheaper money could mean that finding a job might be easier since businesses were expanding and hiring workers.

Volcker's decision to follow an easier money policy, though, may have hurt you as well as helped you. Many feared that an easy policy would increase inflation. Then, the money saved to pay the costs of college or trade school would be less valuable. Prices would go up faster.

Volcker believes that the battle against inflation must continue. "What we're aiming for," said Volcker, "is a situation in which people can proceed about their business without worrying about what prices are going to do over the next year, 2 years, 3 years, 10 years, and can take it for granted that they're going to be more or less stable."

Volcker realizes, however, the difficulty of managing the money supply to keep growth steady without inflation. He realizes that the Fed's policies are important

The Fed's actions influence interest rates.

technically—how they affect the actual money supply—and psychologically—how they affect the way people think.

"You do get in that dilemma," Volcker acknowledges. "Sometimes, the technical analysis runs in the same direction as the psychology, so making policy is easy. But sometimes they run in opposite directions. Then policies do create a dilemma. And the psychology often runs to extremes. You go back to early '80—I mean, people were really scared! 'The Federal Reserve isn't restrictive at all; this thing is never going to stop, credit expansion is going to go on forever.' Of course, within three weeks the view was all changed, but that was the psychology that existed. And you're tempted to respond to the psychology. Sometimes I think you have to. But on purely technical grounds it can be a mistake.

"You know, what seems technically right isn't right if the psychology is running in the other direction and it makes no impact. It can be very hard to deal with in the short run. Sometimes it means there is no right policy."

ANALYZING THE CASE STUDY

STEP 1   Define the Issue

What is the difference between a tight money policy and an easy money policy?

STEP 2   Evaluate Costs and Benefits

1. List the economic costs and benefits to you from a tight money policy.
2. List the economic costs and benefits to you from an easy money policy.

STEP 3   Consider Alternatives

When would you benefit most from an easy money policy? A tight money policy?

Enrichment Activities

1. Talk to three car dealers or bankers. Find out how much interest rates for car loans have changed since 1980. Compare these changes with changes in the policies of the Federal Reserve.
2. Research Paul Volcker's training in economics and attitudes on politics. Write a one-page report on his background for his job.

READING

Who Controls the Money?

by Arthur Burns   (1908-   )

From 1970 to 1978, Arthur Burns was chairperson of the Federal Reserve System. In March 1975, Burns appeared before the Senate Banking Committee to answer questions about the Fed's goals for the coming year. This reading is taken from the record of the committee meeting.

BURNS: Of late, there has been some concern in the Congress and elsewhere that supplies of money and credit were not growing fast enough. We in the Federal Reserve know that the growth rates of money and credit that are fitting at any point in time depend on basic economic conditions. At present, our nation has very high rates of unemployment and idle factories. Thus, even though an upturn in business activity may be near at hand, the restoration of full employment of our labor and capital resources will remain a central aim of public policy for many months to come.

The Federal Reserve System is now seeking a moderate rate of expansion in the total supplies of money and credit. We believe that the course we are following will promote an increase of from 5 to 7.5 percent in currency and checking account supplies over the next year. This is a rather high rate of expansion by past standards. But it is not too high when the numbers of idle resources are great and prices are rising.

SENATOR PROXMIRE (Wisconsin, committee chairperson): By telling us the Federal Reserve Board's present views as to the right ranges of growth in the total supply of money and credit for the next year, you have aided the cause of informed, intelligent government.

As to your specific plans, the Joint Economic Committee heard other testimony last week. This was that we need an 8 to 10 percent growth in money supply over the next year if economic recovery is not to be nipped in the bud and if unemployment is to be reduced to 6 percent by the end of 1977. Why are these others wrong?

BURNS: I am not going to say they are wrong. Their views differ from mine. I have found, Senator, that most economists move from platform to platform these days and from one hearing room to another. They pay very little heed to the business cycle. They have never even studied it thoroughly. Or, if they have, they have forgotten what they once knew. In particular, they give very little attention to the turnover of money.

Members of the economics profession put a great deal of emphasis on the stock of money. In my judgment, they are stressing the wrong thing. Far more important than the stock of money is the willingness to use the existing stocks.

The important factor in the business cycle is not the stock of money but the rate of turnover of money. This depends on the state of confidence. If you look at the record, you will find that in the first year of recovery, it is the rate of turnover of money that shoots up dramatically in contrast to the change in the existing stock. This is the main source of our difference with other economists.

SENATOR PROXMIRE: Can you tell us what your proposal will do for unemployment and prices in the next year?

BURNS: The monetary path we are on is quite enough in our judgment to assure a strong economic recovery. With recovery, unemployment will, of course, come down.

SENATOR PROXMIRE: How much will it go down by the end of the year? Will it go down 1 percent—half of 1 percent?

BURNS: I don't know, Senator, any more than you do or anybody else.

Arthur F. Burns was chairman of the Federal Reserve from 1970 to 1978.

SENATOR PROXMIRE: Will it be below 9 percent?

BURNS: I would hope so.

SENATOR PROXMIRE: What do you assume as to the inflation rate at the end of the year?

BURNS: I remain an optimist. If we act responsibly in the budget and monetary areas, the rate of inflation may come down to 5 percent.

SENATOR PACKWOOD (Oregon): If we go ahead with a $70-billion deficit next year and the tax cut we passed, will we have a good enough recovery without increased inflation? Or is $70 billion too much?

BURNS: It may well be too much. If so, you ought to undo some of the actions you have taken before. If you find that it is too much, then you ought to welcome a bill from the President lowering it. And if he is slow in doing that, you ought to get the jump on him.

SENATOR BIDEN (Delaware): Congress is faced with the questions as to what effect our actions will have on interest rates. If the Fed can't or shouldn't concentrate on that, who should? How should we handle interest rates?

BURNS: You know, you could leave interest rates alone. After all, we have highly competitive money and capital markets. If you are going to engage in price-control exercises, you ought to turn to those sectors of the economy where you have pockets of monopoly. Wages is one of them. We don't talk about wages. And yet we have pockets of monopoly in the field of labor.

SENATOR PROXMIRE: Are you telling us that if you had an 8 or 9 percent growth in the money supply, and with unemployment at an 8 percent level, even with that kind of stimulus you wouldn't be able to slow down in time to stop?

BURNS: Senator, economists have a very poor record in forecasting recoveries. If they can't see where the recovery will come from, they conclude it won't come at all or will be a mild one. It's not given to us to see. We have millions of decision-making units in this country. Let's give them a chance to do their part.

You know, we seem to forget we have a dynamic, private-enterprise system. So many economists and so many others in private or political life talk as if the government pushes the economy, as if the economy is a purely passive thing. The economy contains recovery forces of its own. And now, I think, in the private economy the recovery forces are under way. **"**

From *U.S. News & World Report.*

UNDERSTANDING THE READING

1. In what situation was the economy when Burns spoke to Congress?
2. What did Burns say that suggests agreement with Volcker's idea that attitudes toward using money are as important to the economy as is the total money supply?
3. Explain what Burns meant when he said, "We seem to forget we have a dynamic private-enterprise system."

Section 3 Review

Understanding the Federal Reserve

1. Which of the following statements are true and which are false? Reword the false ones to make them true.
a. Bank reserves cannot limit the expansion of a bank.
b. Banks cannot expand the money supply from deposits in checking accounts.
c. Banks regulate their reserve deposits.
d. The Federal Reserve System can lend money to banks.
e. The Federal Reserve System can buy and sell corporate bonds to regulate the money supply.
f. The Federal Reserve System's monetary policy greatly influences the nation's supply of money.

The Federal Reserve Today

1. Can the government just print money to pay its debts? Why or why not?
2. Explain why the government is concerned about the size of the money supply. How does the money supply affect the economy as a whole?
3. **Challenge:** Who should control money and credit?

Americans *at Work*

Meet Robert Hsi
Developer

Robert Hsi wants people to think of more than oil when they think of Houston. If Hsi has his way, Houston's 10-block Chinatown will soon be supplemented by Tang City, a multimillion-dollar, 140-shop mall 20 miles from the downtown area.

Hsi is president of UCO Development Company, based in Hong Kong, the developer of Tang City. "We think there is a need for a planned Chinatown." Hsi stated. Houston's Asian population, mostly Chinese, has grown to nearly 35,000, more than 2 percent of the city total. The 300 Chinese restaurants represent an increase of 200 over 5 years.

Many architects and others engaged in Houston's Tang City project are Chinese-Americans. The big store in the mall will be Everybody's, a Hong Kong store described as the Chinese version of Sears, Roebuck.

Hsi looks forward to seeing various Chinese interests develop the areas adjacent to Tang City. The possibilities include an office park, a townhouse complex, and an Oriental-style hotel, as well as one or more restaurants.

Developers such as Hsi try to forecast economic trends. The demand for various types of businesses changes constantly. Developers try to attract new businesses to meet changes in demand in area. Some developers work primarily on organizing residential rather than business areas. Developers succeed or fail based on how well they analyze changes in the economy.

Hsi believes that this development can be profitable. First, land values are lower than they are in more settled areas, so the cost of development will be less. Second, Tang City will be near the area where many Chinese people live. Third, highway access is good. Hsi believes that if the economy in general holds up, attracting renters for the nearly 140 shop units available will not be hard. The $7.5 million that Robert Hsi's company is investing in Tang City could well pay off handsomely.

UCO Incorporated, parent company of UCO Development, has interests in Singapore, Malaysia, and Taiwan, as well as in Hong Kong. UCO's chairman, Jefferson Chen, who adopted the name of Thomas Jefferson, says the mall will be the centerpiece of Tang City Plaza. He wants its Chinese archway to have a bust of Confucius. Undoubtedly, UCO's real estate and other interests in the United States will increase. In the future, China's influence will be felt in parts of the country other than Houston.

Financing a Car Loan

Borrowing money to buy an expensive item has become more and more common. You may be financing a loan during the next several years. Borrowing intelligently requires an understanding of the two basic ways to determine repayment. Assume that you want to purchase a car but do not have the entire amount of money needed. The following steps will help determine the best way to finance a loan.

STEP 1   Compare Loan Sources

Numerous loan sources are available to borrowers. Loans for major purchases can be obtained from credit unions, banks, finance companies, or, for cars, the car dealers. If all other factors are equal, your choice will depend on which source will charge the lowest rate of interest.

Before 1969, individuals borrowing money had difficulty in determining the best deal. In that year, however, Congress passed the truth in lending law requiring the lender to tell the actual cost of a loan. Call banks, finance companies, and other lenders. Ask them what annual interest rate they charge on auto loans and the method used to calculate repayment. Compare answers to find the best finance source.

STEP 2   Compute Interest

Even though the truth in lending law exists, it is important to understand the two basic methods of figuring interest—simple and compound. Using the simple interest method, the borrower repays the principal—the amount borrowed—and interest in one single payment to the lender.

For example, to purchase a car you would like to borrow $2,000 at 8 percent interest. You will repay the loan in 12 months. Interest can be calculated using the formula $I = P \times R \times T$. In the formula, I is interest, P is principal, R is rate of interest (percent), and T is time, in years, before the money is repaid. Hence, $2,000 $\times 0.08 \times 1 = \$160$—the amount of interest charged. The total to be repaid at the end of the year is $2,160—that is, $2,000 principal plus $160 interest.

The repayment schedule for most loans actually is calculated by using compound interest—the add-on method. Payments are broken into even parts—12 months, for example—and that portion—one-twelfth—of interest and principal is paid back each month. Using the add-on method, the borrower must know the annual percentage rate (APR) or total finance charge on the loan rather than just the loan interest rate, as in simple interest.

If a monthly payment plan were used, repayment of a $2,000 loan at 8 percent would cost you approximately $180 per month—$2,160 divided by 12 months. Using a monthly repayment plan, you have possession of the entire $2,000 you borrowed for only one month. Then you are paying the loan back in equal portions. Monthly repayment of the principal and interest increases the annual percentage rate (APR) from 8 percent to 14.8 percent. It is not necessary to know how to calculate this APR. Remember, though, that by law the lender must tell you the rate. Using the APR as a guideline, borrowers can more easily decide which loan is best suited to their purposes.

STEP 3 Determine Repayment Time

Interest rate is one important factor that affects the cost of a loan. The other factor is the length of time before the loan is completely repaid. As car prices have increased, so have the amount borrowed and the time required to repay the loan. Borrowers tend to see the lower monthly payments on longer-term loans as an advantage. Often, borrowers fail to realize that a longer repayment time increases the total cost of the loan.

ECONOMIC SKILLS TODAY

Use the chart and your economic knowledge to answer the questions.

Enrichment Activity

Study the interest chart and complete the activity accompanying it.

Repaying a $2,000 Loan

Years	Monthly Payment	Total Repayment
1	$175.65	$2,107.80
2	92.11	2,210.64
3	64.35	2,316.60
4	50.54	2,425.92

Explanation

The chart shows the cost of repaying a $2,000 loan at 10 percent interest over different lengths of time. The cost is shown as a monthly payment and the total cost of repayment.

Chart Skills

1. How much are monthly payments on a three-year loan?
2. How much interest must be paid on a four-year loan?

Monthly Loan Payments

Term Amt.	1 Yr.	2 Yrs.	3 Yrs.	4 Yrs.
at 9.75%				
$1,500	131.70	69.05	48.23	37.87
$2,000	175.60	92.06	64.30	50.49
$2,500	219.50	115.08	80.38	63.11
at 10%				
$1,500	131.88	69.22	48.41	38.05
$2,000	175.84	92.29	64.54	50.73
$2,500	219.79	115.37	80.67	63.41
at 11%				
$1,500	132.58	69.92	49.11	38.77
$2,000	176.77	93.22	65.48	51.70
$2,500	220.96	116.52	81.85	64.62

Explanation

The chart shows the cost of repaying loans.

Chart Skills

1. What is the monthly repayment on a 4-year loan of $1,500?
2. How much is the total repayment on a 1-year loan of $2,500?

CHAPTER SUMMARY

Forms of Money

Money is necessary in most economies. It serves as a means of exchange and a store and standard of value. Currency, used in modern societies, fulfills these functions. In addition to currency, people may use checks and credit cards to purchase goods and services. Savings accounts, stocks, and bonds are stores of value that can easily be exchanged for money. All of these forms of money and near money help the economy run smoothly.

The Money Supply

The money supply in the United States fluctuates constantly. These fluctuations result from a number of factors, including consumers' willingness to borrow money and the percentage of their deposits the bank is required to keep in reserve. The money supply increases when the demand for loans is high and the reserve requirement is low. The combination of these two factors tends to drive up interest rates, and so may lower demand. Economists use M-1A, M-1B, and M-2 to measure the supply of money and level of economic activity in the United States.

The Federal Reserve

The federal government, through the Federal Reserve System, works to control the money supply and interest rates in the United States. The Federal Reserve has three important tools to carry out monetary policy. First, the Fed sets the percentage of deposits a bank must keep in reserve. Raising or lowering the reserve requirement decreases or increases the amount of money being created. Second, the Fed determines the discount rate. Lowering or raising the discount rate charged to member banks makes money more or less easily available. Third, the Fed, using its open market operation, buys and sells government bonds. When the Fed sells bonds, the money it receives is no longer available for other business transactions. Hence, the money supply decreases. When the Fed buys bonds, the money banks receive increases the supply of money available for business transactions. In this way, the Fed pursues a policy of easy or tight money.

CRITICAL THINKING QUESTIONS

Forms of Money

1. Think about the purchases you made last week. How would they have been more difficult in a barter system? Use three examples in your answer.
2. The government determines the type of currency in use in a country, but the market system determines its value. Using your three examples from question 1, explain how the value of your money was established.
3. Ask three adults how often they use credit cards. In a paragraph based on their replies, explain how the use of credit cards makes the Fed's job of controlling the money supply more difficult.

The Money Supply

1. Explain why it is important to be able to increase or decrease the money supply.

2. Collect two articles from major newspapers or news magazines about the recent expansion or contraction of the money supply. Analyze the reasons for this expansion or contraction.
3. Find the current reserve requirement for banks. Beginning with a deposit of $50,000 and using the current reserve requirement, calculate the amount of money that could be created. Assume that all money not required for reserves will be lent.

The Federal Reserve

1. Of the three methods the Fed uses to expand and contract the money supply, which would obtain the fastest results? The slowest? The longest lasting? Explain your answers.
2. The Federal Reserve System provides many pamphlets to educate consumers. Call your local Fed office and find out what information is available and how you can obtain it.

3. Consider the present state of the economy. If you were in charge, would you pursue an easy or tight money policy? Explain the reasons for your choice.

DEVELOPING ECONOMIC SKILLS

Use the graph and your economic knowledge to answer the questions that follow it.

APPLYING ECONOMICS TODAY

1. Check through newspapers to determine whether the Fed is currently pursuing an easy or tight money policy. Explain how this policy affects consumers. Use three examples in your answer.
2. Ask at four banks about their policy on low-interest loans to pay college tuition. How do their interest rates and payback terms compare?
3. **Challenge:** What, if any, is the relationship between the money supply and the business cycle?

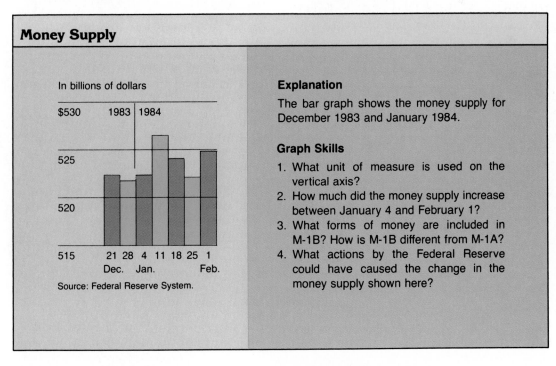

Money Supply

In billions of dollars

$530   1983 | 1984

525

520

515   21 28 4 11 18 25 1
       Dec.   Jan.   Feb.

Source: Federal Reserve System.

Explanation
The bar graph shows the money supply for December 1983 and January 1984.

Graph Skills
1. What unit of measure is used on the vertical axis?
2. How much did the money supply increase between January 4 and February 1?
3. What forms of money are included in M-1B? How is M-1B different from M-1A?
4. What actions by the Federal Reserve could have caused the change in the money supply shown here?

CHAPTER 12

The Federal Budget

1 Taxes

Objective: *to understand and evaluate the different types of taxes government collects*

2 Expenditures

Objective: *to understand government expenditure and debt*

3 Fiscal Policy

Objective: *to understand government policies on taxes and spending*

1 Taxes

SECTION OVERVIEW

Consider all the government goods and services you use. For example, you use schools, roads, and parks. These things are paid for through taxes. You pay taxes on the income you earn and often on the goods and services you buy. In addition, you may sometimes pay indirect or hidden taxes. The price of a gallon of gasoline usually includes both state and federal taxes. In this section, you will learn about different types of taxes and how to evaluate them.

ECONOMIC VOCABULARY

tax	regressive tax	tax incentive
progressive tax	proportional tax	

Types of Taxes

Businesses and individuals receive most of their income by selling goods or services to people who want to buy them. Governments do not have voluntary buyers of their services. Therefore, people are required to fund governments by paying taxes. A tax is a compulsory payment of money to support a government. In return for paying taxes, the citizens receive government services. Schools, roads, national defense, and aid to the poor are some of the services government provides.

The federal, state, and local governments in the United States all collect taxes. The federal government receives over half of all taxes paid. Sources of its revenue include personal income, corporate, and excise, or sales, taxes.

The largest share of federal tax revenue comes from the personal income tax. This tax is based on an individual's income. It accounts for over one-third of the federal government's tax revenue. Corporate in-

Virtually every working person in the United States must file yearly income tax returns. These returns are used to calculate the differences between the amount of tax the person owes and the amount that he or she has already paid during the year.

come taxes supply about 8 percent of the government's total income. A small percentage of government revenue comes from excise, or sales, taxes and customs duties. An excise tax is either paid by the producer or added to the price of an item or service when it is sold. Important sources of federal excise tax revenue are tobacco, liquor, gasoline, and airplane fares. Additional federal revenue comes from the estate and gift taxes. The first is imposed on a person's estate after death. The second is imposed on gifts of cash, stocks, land, and other items.

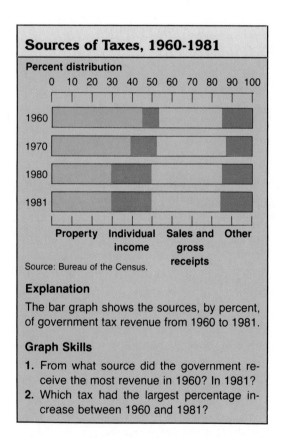

Sources of Taxes, 1960-1981

Percent distribution

Property | Individual income | Sales and gross receipts | Other

Source: Bureau of the Census.

Explanation

The bar graph shows the sources, by percent, of government tax revenue from 1960 to 1981.

Graph Skills

1. From what source did the government receive the most revenue in 1960? In 1981?
2. Which tax had the largest percentage increase between 1960 and 1981?

To supplement their tax income, state and local governments receive revenue from the federal government. Federal grants account for about one-fifth of the income of state and local governments.

Effects of Taxes

The people affected by taxes vary according to the tax. Some, such as the income tax, affect nearly everyone. The excise tax on airline fares, however, affects only those who fly. Some taxes are structured so that wealthy people pay more than poor people. A progressive tax takes a larger percentage of a rich person's income than of a poor person's income, since the wealthy are better able to pay taxes.

The graduated income tax is structured as a progressive tax. For example, a family whose income is $75,000 a year may be taxed at 30 percent of that income. At the same time, a family whose income is $15,000 a year may be required to pay only 15 percent. The richer family will pay $22,500; the poorer family, only $2,250. Suppose that both families had to pay the same percentage of their income in taxes (say, 20 percent). Then, the family with the larger income would pay $15,000 and the family with the smaller income, $3,000. In the first situation, the richer family would be left with $52,500; in the second, $60,000. The poorer family would be left with $12,750 in the first situation and $12,000 in the second.

Some taxes take a larger share of a low income than of a high one. They are called regressive taxes. Sales taxes on food, for example, tend to be regressive. The percentage of income poor people must spend on food is higher than the proportion others spend. Therefore, the percentage of income the poor pay in sales tax is higher.

Another type of tax is neither progressive nor regressive. A proportional tax takes the same percentage of everyone's income. A tax that took 15 percent of each family's income would be a proportional tax. In practice, no tax takes precisely the same amount from both rich and poor.

Evaluating Taxes

Almost any change in taxes causes controversy. Usually, arguments concern one of five issues.

The first issue is legality. Is the tax proposal legal? For example, in 1895 the Supreme Court declared the personal income tax unconstitutional. Ratification of the Sixteenth Amendment in 1913 changed the Constitution. Then, Congress was allowed to collect an income tax.

The second issue is clarity. What does the tax proposal mean? Tax laws are often hard to understand. Thousands of lawyers and accountants work full time helping people and businesses decide what they are legally required to pay in taxes.

The third issue is efficiency. Can the tax be collected easily? Some taxes, such as the sales tax, are easy to figure and collect. Others, such as property taxes, are less efficient. Property taxes are not only hard to calculate but also expensive to collect.

The fourth issue involves consequences. How will the tax affect people and the economy? Increasing taxes makes goods and services more expensive. During the oil shortage of the 1970s, some people wanted to increase the tax on gasoline. Increasing the cost of gasoline, they said, would discourage consumption and help conserve the supply of oil. Tax increases affect both consumers, by raising prices, and producers, by decreasing the quantity demanded. Tax increases also affect economic growth and government revenue.

The fifth controversial tax issue is fairness. Is the tax proposal fair? People define fairness in different ways. They disagree over which tax is fairest—progressive, regressive, or proportional. Changes in tax laws always affect different groups of people in different ways. Increasing taxes on gasoline, for example, would take money from all people who drive a car to work. However, mass transit agencies and bicycle manufacturers probably would benefit because their products would be relatively less expensive.

Tax Incentives

Much of the debate over taxes concerns tax incentives. A tax incentive—sometimes called a tax break—is a law that decreases taxes for a certain group of people or economic activity. The largest tax incentive is available to employers who contribute to health insurance and retirement funds for their workers. By reducing employers' taxable income, this tax incentive encourages employers to contribute to such services.

The second largest tax incentive is useful to individuals who pay interest on their debts. The yearly interest paid can be deducted from taxable income. This incentive especially benefits people who want to buy a home. Much of the cost of buying a home is the interest paid on the loan. By allowing a tax deduction for these interest payments, the government lowers the actual cost and encourages people to purchase homes. The federal government also allows tax deductions to the blind, the elderly, and the poor.

Many tax incentives are available to businesses. The government allows businesses to deduct some of the cost of replacing old equipment. The percentage of taxes corporations pay on income varies widely as a result of tax incentives.

When tax law changes are debated, taxpayers can offer good arguments for keeping the incentives that help them. Ending the deduction for interest paid on home loans, for example, would increase the cost of buying housing. Fewer people would be able to afford homes. In effect, both buyers and sellers of housing would suffer economically.

Corporate Income Tax by Industry

Industry	Actual Tax Rate (percent)
Automobiles	48
Trucking	40
Electronics, appliances	29
Farm equipment	24
Retailing	23
Oil and refining	19
Airlines	16
Metal manufacturing	10
Aerospace	7
Crude oil	3
Commercial banks	2

Source: Congressional Joint Committee on Taxation.

Explanation

The chart shows the variation among industries in the percentage of income tax that corporations in the industry pay.

Chart Skills

1. Which industry in the chart benefits the most from tax incentives?
2. Which four industries in the chart are related to transportation?

REVIEWING THE CONCEPT

Developing Vocabulary

1. What is a tax?
2. Explain the difference between a progressive and a regressive tax. Give examples of each.
3. What is a proportional tax?
4. Define tax incentive.

Mastering Facts

1. List some of the goods and services governments provide. Could these goods and services be provided without government. Why or why not?
2. What are the major sources of tax revenue for the federal government?
3. List and explain five areas of controversy surrounding taxes.
4. Describe two of the largest tax incentives. What type of activity do they encourage? Who benefits from them?

CASE STUDY

Taxing Experiences

Taxes are never popular. Politicians try to reduce taxes if possible. In 1981, President Reagan proposed a 25 percent cut in the federal personal income tax over a three-year period. When Congress passed the tax cut, Tom Dugan, a Chicagoan, expected his tax to decrease. Other changes, however, he had not expected.

During 1981, 1982, and 1983, Dugan's entire income, as a salesperson, averaged $20,000 per year. Because of the tax cut, Dugan's federal income tax decreased from $3,787 in 1981 to $3,450 in 1982, and $3,096 in 1983.

At the same time the federal government cut income taxes, it also reduced the funds distributed to the states for various programs. Besides, 1981 and 1982 were years of economic recession, when sales and incomes decline. Consequently, tax revenues decreased. The combination of lower federal payments and recession caused state and local governments to increase their income, sales, and property taxes in order to maintain revenue.

The Illinois state income tax increased from 2.5 percent to 3.0 percent. Dugan's state income tax bill went from $475 in 1981 and 1982 to $570 in 1983, a difference of $95. The federal tax on gasoline went from 5 cents to 8 cents a gallon. The Illinois gasoline tax rose from 5 cents to 10 cents. Dugan bought about 800 gallons of gasoline a year. Thus, the additional 8 cents in taxes cost him an additional $64 a year. Then, increased property taxes caused the rent on Dugan's apartment to increase from $450 to $475 a month. His housing cost for 1983 was $300 more than it had been for 1981. Finally, the Cook County sales tax on all goods except food and medicine increased from 6 percent to 7 percent. Since Chicago is part of Cook County, this increase affected Dugan. Since Dugan made most of his purchases in Cook County, the sales tax increase cost him an additional $120.

Tom Dugan's experience was not unique. People in other states experienced much the same situation. Michigan raised its income tax from 4.6 percent to 5.6 percent. Detroit's resident income tax rose from 1.5 percent to 2.0 percent. New York City placed a 10 percent surcharge (additional tax or fee) on the local income tax for individuals whose income was greater than $20,000. Vermont raised its sales tax from 3 percent to 4 percent and its tax on diesel fuel by 14 cents a gallon. Florida's sales tax rose from 4 percent to 5 percent. New Jersey's gasoline tax jumped from 5 cents to 13 cents a gallon.

States that did not increase taxes cut budgets. Citizens then had to pay for services previously supplied by government—garbage pickup, snow removal, recreational activities. Spending cuts also resulted in the loss of thousands of state jobs.

During the 1980s, Tom Dugan and millions of other Americans awoke to an important fact of economic life: what government gives with the one hand, it can take away with the other.

Tax cuts affect social welfare spending.

ANALYZING THE CASE STUDY

STEP 1 Gather Evidence

1. How much did Dugan's federal income tax decrease between 1981 and 1983?
2. List the tax increases that affected Dugan between 1981 and 1984.

STEP 2 Interpret Information

1. How did Dugan's total taxes change between 1981 and 1984?
2. Explain why the decrease in federal income tax may have caused increases in other taxes.

STEP 3 Make a Decision

1. In 1981, would you have supported the federal tax cut proposal? Explain.
2. In 1984, would you have changed your decision about the tax cut? Explain.

Enrichment Activity

Research the structure and purpose of one of these proposed tax reforms and report your findings to the class: flat rate income tax, guaranteed income program, negative income tax.

Principles of Taxation

by John Stuart Mill   (1806-1873)

Controversy over taxation is as old as taxation itself. In the middle of the last century, British philosopher and economist John Stuart Mill published his views on the basic principles of taxation. As you read, think about the major taxes paid in the United States—personal income, property, and sales taxes. Do these taxes follow Mill's principles of taxation?

66 The four qualities most wanted in any system of taxation have been set down by Adam Smith. These are as follows:

1. The citizens of every country ought to help support their government as best they can in proportion to their abilities. That is, they should give in proportion to the income they enjoy under the protection of the state.

2. The tax each person is bound to pay ought to be certain, not arbitrary. The time, method, and amount of payment must be clear and plain. If not, all will be more or less at the mercy of the tax collector, who may then be willing to raise the tax or to threaten the same. An uncertain taxation can only promote corruption. Certainty, by contrast, is so important that even some degree of inequality is to be preferred to a very small amount of uncertainty.

3. Each tax ought to fall due at the time, or in the way, it is most fit for the subject to pay it. A tax on the rent of land or of houses can be paid at a regular term or when money is most apt to be at hand. Taxes on luxury goods can, of course, be paid at the time of sale.

4. Every tax ought to be so managed that it will take out—and keep out—of the pockets of the people as little as possible beyond what it brings in to the public treasury. Waste is less to be feared when the number of officers in the tax service is kept down; it is less likely when the tax does not offer a temptation to smuggling; and it is less when the people are not subject to the frequent visits of tax gatherers, or to the restrictive trade practices that create them.

Of the four maxims, equality of taxation is least understood. Why should equality be the rule in tax matters? For the reason that it should be the rule in all state affairs. A government ought not to distinguish between persons or classes in the claims they have on it. What sacrifices the government requires from one of them should bear as heavily or as lightly on all. In this way, the least sacrifice will be felt by the whole.

If any one bears less than his or her fair share of the burden, another must suffer more. The lightening of the one's share is not so great a good as the increased burden on the other is an evil. Equality of taxation, therefore, means equality of sacrifice. It means sharing what each person gives towards the costs of government so that no one will feel any more or less trouble than anyone else. This standard of perfection cannot, of course, be fully reached; but our first need is to know what perfection is.

Some people, it seems, are not content with mere justice as a basis on which to ground their rules of finance. They must have something more suited to the subject. What pleases them best is to look on the tax of each person as a sum paid for value, or services, received. In this view, those who have twice as much property to be protected receive twice as much protection. Therefore, they ought, on the principles of bargain and sale, to pay twice as much for it.

We find here a strange kind of reason. It cannot be agreed that to have the protection of 10 times as much property is to be 10 times as much protected. Nor can it be said that to protect £1,000 a year costs the state 10 times as much as to protect £100 a year. The same judges, soldiers, and sailors who protect the one protect the other; and the larger income does not even always call for more policemen.

Do we want to guess the degree of benefit that different persons derive from the protection of the state? Then we must think who would suffer most if that protection were withdrawn. And the answer to this question must be that those who are the weakest in mind or body, whether by birth or condition, would suffer the most. Indeed, it is slaves and children who best fit this description. If there were any value, therefore, in this notion, then those who are least able to help or defend themselves would be those who most need the protection of the government. Therefore, these persons should pay the greatest share of its cost. Yet here we have the reverse of the true idea of justice. The true idea consists not in imitating the inequalities and wrongs of nature but in correcting them.

Government is so clearly a concern of all that to try to calculate those who are most interested in it is a worthless chore. If a person or class receives so little as to make the question necessary, then there is more than taxation that is wrong. The thing to do is to repair the defect, not recognize it.

When money is donated for a cause everyone supports, all are thought to have done their part when each has given according to his or her means. In the same way, this should be the principle of taxation. One can find no better ground for justice. **99**

From *Principles of Political Economy*, by John Stuart Mill.

UNDERSTANDING THE READING

1. Summarize the four qualities Smith thought desirable in taxation.
2. According to Mill, should people pay taxes according to how much they depend on the government for protection? Explain your answer.
3. Would Mill support a progressive or regressive income tax? Why?

Section 1 Review

Understanding Taxes

1. What is an excise tax? Give three examples of excise taxes.
2. From what sources do state governments obtain funds?
3. What is the purpose of a progressive tax?
4. Why does the federal government provide tax incentives?

Taxes Today

1. Are federal and local government taxes on gasoline progressive or regressive? Explain your answer.
2. The tax incentive that allows individuals to deduct interest payments from their taxable income benefits many Americans. List and explain three benefits to the economy from this tax incentive.
3. Itemize the pay you received and the purchases you made over the last two weeks. How much did you pay in taxes?
4. **Challenge:** Reducing government spending would eventually result in lower taxes. Since everyone wants to pay less in taxes, why is a spending reduction so difficult to achieve?
5. Who does the man with the briefcase represent in the cartoon below?

THE WALL STREET JOURNAL

"We believe that in a previous life you were J. Winthrop Harris, who died owing us $4,500."

2 Expenditures

SECTION OVERVIEW

All spending decisions reflect values. Choosing a baseball game over a movie, or a Cadillac over a Chevrolet, indicates an individual's values. In the same way, government spending should reflect a society's values. Individuals aim to spend within the limits of personal income. However, the government over the past 50 years often has spent more than it received in income. In this section, you will learn about government expenditures and debt.

ECONOMIC VOCABULARY

deficit	national debt	government securities	crowding out

Government Expenditures

Each year, Congress establishes the federal budget. Congress generally modifies a budget that the President proposes. Then it passes a revised budget. Since 1974, income security has been the largest category of federal spending—34 percent for 1985. Income security includes retirement and disability payments for federal employees, unemployment insurance, and social security payments to retired and handicapped workers. Defense spending makes up the second largest category at 29 percent. Interest payments on the national debt constitute the third largest expenditure—13 percent in 1985.

The amount spent on each federal program varies from year to year. In general, defense spending increases when the nation is at war. Spending on income security programs increased from $25.7 billion in 1965 to $282.5 billion in 1983. Interest on the national debt, at $144.8 billion in 1984, was larger than the total federal budget 19 years ago. In 1965, total federal spending was $118.4 billion.

State and local government spending varies from state to state and place to place. Overall, state and local governments spend the largest percentage of their income on education. Other large expenditures are for highways, aid to the poor, health care, and police and fire protection.

Every year, federal, state, and local governments spend over $20 billion to build and repair streets and highways.

Federal Government Expenditures

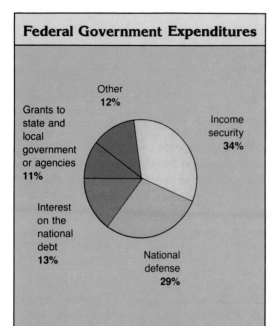

Grants to state and local government or agencies **11%**

Other **12%**

Income security **34%**

Interest on the national debt **13%**

National defense **29%**

Explanation

The pie graph shows the distribution of federal government expenditures for 1985. The total budget for the year was $925.5 billion.

Graph Skills

1. How much money was spent for interest on the national debt?
2. In a library, find the federal budget for 1960. Compare it with the budget for 1985. List three ways in which the two budgets differ.

The National Debt

Government spending often exceeds government revenue. A deficit occurs when the income for a year is less than the expenditures for the year. When the government adopts a deficit budget, it must borrow money to pay its bills for the year. The national debt is the money that the federal government has borrowed because expenses exceeded tax revenue. Interest payments on the national debt are a major item in the budget. The national debt usually increases rapidly during wars.

The national debt is owed to a variety of groups. A portion of the debt is owed to workers as they become eligible to collect social security payments. The rest is held by American banks, foreign lenders, corporations, state and local governments, individual citizens, and the Federal Reserve. This portion is held mainly in the form of government securities. These bonds promise to pay the owner the purchase price of the bond plus interest. Government securities are sold in the market much like any other product or service. Some government securities, such as government savings bonds, are payable only after several years. Others, such as Treasury bills, are payable in only three to six months.

Ownership of National Debt

Owner	Amount (billions)	Percent
U.S. government accounts	$ 239.0	17.4
Federal Reserve Bank	155.4	11.3
Commercial banks	176.3	12.8
Individuals	128.5	9.3
Corporations	35.5	3.0
Foreign and international creditors	160.8	11.7
Mutual savings banks and insurance companies	70.4	5.0
State and local governments	131.4	9.5
Others	279.9	20.0
Total	$1,377.2	100.0

Source: Treasury Department.

Explanation

The chart shows how much of the national debt different types of creditors hold.

Chart Skills

1. How much money does the United States government owe to foreign and international creditors? To individuals?
2. How much money does the United States government owe to banks, corporations, and insurance companies all together?

Effects of the National Debt

The national debt has long been a subject of controversy. When it was much smaller than it is today, many people thought that the nation would collapse if the debt got much bigger. The debt did get a lot bigger, but the nation did not collapse. The debt grows because people are willing to lend money to the government. They are willing to lend money because they are fairly sure that the United States government will be able to pay off its loans as promised.

Many people worry about the size of the national debt. They argue that no household or business can afford to remain in debt forever, and neither can the government. Yet, many economists believe that the size of the debt is not very important. They argue that as long as the economy is healthy and strong, the government will continue to receive income. That is, it will collect taxes. So it will always be able to make its annual payments on the debt.

The debt does have several effects on the economy. The national debt increases the demand for money. When the government borrows money, it may cause interest rates to increase. Then, crowding out may result. Crowding out occurs when heavy government borrowing causes interest rates to increase, thereby preventing other potential borrowers from taking out loans. Government borrowing may, in effect, use money that could be lent to businesses or individuals. Crowding out reduces business expansion and home purchases.

The national debt also influences the total demand for goods and services in the economy. Government spending, like consumer and business spending, increases total demand. A growing national debt means that the federal government is spending more than it receives in taxes. This situation promotes higher employment and higher prices, and it may have an inflationary effect on the economy.

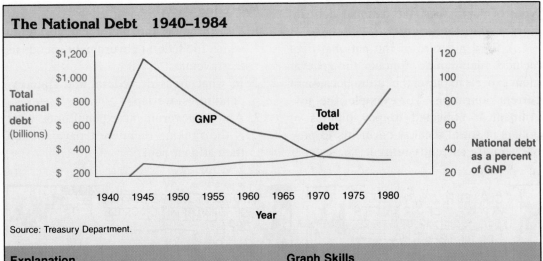

The National Debt   1940–1984

Total national debt (billions) — left axis: $1,200, $1,000, $800, $600, $400, $200

GNP   Total debt

National debt as a percent of GNP — right axis: 120, 100, 80, 60, 40, 20

Year: 1940 1945 1950 1955 1960 1965 1970 1975 1980

Source: Treasury Department.

Explanation

The graph shows two ways to measure the national debt. The red line shows the debt in current dollars. The scale for this line is on the left vertical axis. The blue line shows the debt as a percent of the gross national product. The scale for this line is on the right vertical axis.

Graph Skills

1. Between 1945 and 1984, what was the general trend in the total debt of the United States? In the national debt as a percentage of the GNP?
2. Explain why the graph shows that the national debt is both increasing and decreasing.

Measuring the National Debt

Like measuring other economic information, measuring the national debt is not easy. Depending on what is included, the national debt can be measured in four different ways.

The first measure includes only the money borrowed to pay current government bills. Usually when people refer to the national debt, this measure is used.

Some people believe that the federal debt should include loans guaranteed by the federal government, known future government expenditures, and potential obligations. A second measure of the national debt, then, would include the amount of money borrowed by agencies, corporations, or individuals but guaranteed by the federal government. For example, the government guarantees repayment of certain loans to college students. Though the government is not actually in debt, it could be forced to pay out money if the student cannot repay the loan. By including these types of guarantees, the national debt increases 10 to 15 percent.

A third measure of the national debt includes the amount of money the government expects to pay in the future because of current obligations. For example, the government is obligated to pay billions of dollars in social security payments to people who are currently retired. These types of obligations almost quadruple the national debt.

Finally, the debt of the nation can be measured by the potential obligations of the government. For example, the government operates an insurance program for banks and farmers. If all insured banks failed, all insured crops were destroyed, and all other possible claims on the government were made, the total obligation of the government in 1983 would have been $6.8 trillion, about 5 times the national debt.

REVIEWING THE CONCEPT

Developing Vocabulary

1. What is a deficit?
2. Explain what the national debt is and to whom it is owed.
3. What is a government security? Give two examples of government securities.
4. What do most people worry about in the deficit according to the cartoon?

Mastering Facts

1. List three of the major categories on which the federal government spends its tax revenue.
2. In what areas do federal and state expenditures overlap?
3. Among government expenditures, what is the ranking of interest payments on the national debt?

Chicago Tribune, April 18, 1984.

The Balanced-Budget Amendment

During their campaigns for the Presidency, both Jimmy Carter and Ronald Reagan promised to balance the federal budget. However, federal expenditures have continued to exceed income. Between 1969 and 1979, personal income in the United States rose 158 percent; total federal government expenditures rose 263 percent. Federal tax receipts rose significantly less than expenditures. As a result, deficits have occurred during every year since 1969.

An amendment to the Constitution proposed in Congress in 1982 would require Congress to balance the budget every year. The provisions of the amendment would allow for two exceptions. Congress could waive the balanced budget requirement by a simple majority in any year during which the nation was fighting a declared war. In years of peace, Congress could pass a deficit budget only if a three-fifths majority of both houses agreed. In addition, Congress could not raise taxes as a proportion of national income unless the members specifically voted to allow such an increase. A deficit could occur legally, however, if tax collections fell below the amount predicted by Congress.

The proposed balanced-budget amendment aroused a great deal of controversy in the nation. Robert List, former governor of Nevada, supported the amendment. William O'Neill, who became governor of Connecticut in 1981, disagreed with List. Compare the following statements of List and O'Neill. Decide whether or not you would support an amendment to the Constitution requiring a balanced budget.

Robert List believes the economy of the United States has gotten out of control. He sees the doubling of the national debt between 1972 and 1982 and the endless tide of deficits as the reasons for the unwieldy economy. List does not think that Congress can balance the budget on its own, since Congress lacks the will to stand up to special interest groups. These groups pressure the Congress for appropriations to the concerns they promote.

List supports the requirement that three-fifths of the Congress must vote to authorize deficit spending in peacetime instead of the simple majority vote now needed. The proposed amendment would make Congress and individual lawmakers accountable for any deficit spending. By placing a heavier burden on lawmakers who approve deficits, the amendment would slow government spending.

List believes that people are demanding fiscal responsibility. He cites one opinion poll showing that an overwhelming 90 percent of the public believe the deficit poses a serious problem for the nation. Another opinion poll indicates that 79 percent of the American people favor a balanced-budget amendment. The amendment making it harder to go into debt has much popular support. List is wary that Congress might still find ways to continue deficit spending. He stresses the need to watch Congress very closely.

To balance the budget, Congress must either raise taxes or cut spending. List feels that what Congress would do is open to speculation. He is confident, however, that

Congress would not start slashing in areas where people supported government spending. List believes that if Congress passes the amendment, the states will quickly ratify it.

Nevertheless, he is also aware that, in some states, bureaucrats and public officials fear a loss of federal money. Therefore, they oppose the amendment for selfish reasons. List criticizes the congressional opponents of the proposed amendment who take credit for all the federal expenditures in their district or state while blaming the federal deficits on all the other members of Congress. List claims, "that just is not going to work anymore."

William O'Neill opposes the amendment for a balanced budget. Locking the amendment into the Constitution would restrict the flexibility in spending necessary to hold the country together, especially in difficult economic times.

According to O'Neill, the problems state and federal government face are com-

What is a simple definition of deficit financing?

pletely different. Many of the expenditures that contribute to the deficit involve federal, not local, problems. Highway and rail systems, health and welfare programs, and employment policy can be solved only at the federal level. Holding the line on federal expenditures would amount to Congress walking away from its responsibilities. Such a stance would weaken, rather than strengthen, the country.

O'Neill also believes that the amendment would hurt relations between the federal government and the states. To balance the budget, Congress would have to cut the dollars going to the states even more drastically then has already been done. The states would then have to assume the burden of funding programs for which the federal government had paid.

O'Neill thinks that social programs should remain among the obligations of government at all levels. The states might better handle some items in the federal budget, but many responsibilities must be shared between the two levels of government.

Finally, O'Neill opposes the amendment because he thinks it would result in a basic change in the democratic process. The amendment would require three-fifths of the members of both houses to approve any deficit spending. Two-fifths of the members—a minority—could, therefore, block some proposed spending.

O'Neill foresees the election of fiscally responsible people to Congress as a way of solving the problem. He also looks at the possible results of immediate action to balance the budget. If Congress attempted to balance the budget now, the cuts in spending would result in additonal millions of unemployed people. O'Neill would rather see people working and paying taxes, even if they are holding public-service jobs, than standing in breadlines or living on welfare.

O'Neill realizes that most people would support balancing the federal budget. However, if they were asked about what they thought of cuts in their social security or in the grants for their children's education, they would respond very differently.

ANALYZING THE CASE STUDY

STEP 1 Gather Evidence

1. Explain why the proposed amendment would allow Congress to deficit spend during wartime.
2. In your opinion, would the balanced-budget amendment decrease government spending? Why or why not?
3. According to O'Neill, what does current law say about the federal expenditures and the budget?

STEP 2 Evaluate Costs and Benefits

1. How does the balanced-budget amendment affect government expenditures? Are there any costs or benefits to the government? Explain your answer.
2. How does government spending affect taxpayers? Will taxpayers benefit from the proposed amendment? If so, how?
3. How does the balanced-budget amendment affect various groups of citizens? Are there any costs or benefits for the elderly? College students? The wealthy?

STEP 3 Make a Decision

1. Write a paragraph explaining why you support or oppose the amendment to balance the budget.

Enrichment Activity

Divide the class into two groups. Ask one group to prepare a defense of the balanced-budget amendment. Ask the other group to prepare arguments against the proposed amendment. Allow class time for debate.

Wasteful Expenditures

by Robert Heilbroner   (1919-   )
and Lester Thurow   (1938-   )

Everyone who pays taxes wants the government to provide the most services for the least money. Yet, according to economists Robert Heilbroner and Lester Thurow, measuring waste in government spending for public goods is difficult. This excerpt is taken from their book, *Five Economic Challenges.* As you read, consider how you evaluate the way government spends your taxes.

66 **I**s government spending wasteful? First, we must understand that waste in government means something different from waste in private business.

The only standard for waste in the private sector, so far as the kind or quantity of output is concerned, is the bottom line, whether or not the business makes a profit. The output of cigarettes, pornography, shoddy merchandise, or fake medicines is not considered a waste if the producing company makes money. Unsold merchandise is worthless, but the same merchandise, if tastes change, can be very valuable.

The public sector is basically different from the private sector. With minor exceptions, it does not sell its output. Therefore it cannot justify what it produces by pointing to market demand. Moreover, much public output consists of publicly shared things, such as defense or justice. For such public goods or services, there is no conceivable market test to determine whether the level of output is right. Instead we use a political test—voting—in place of the market.

We vote for or against the general economic programs of candidates or parties. Within Congress or the state legislatures, our representatives vote again. The process is the subject of intense efforts to influence the voters. Most citizens will vote for government programs that increase their income. They will vote to lower those expenditures that increase the income of others. Thus if each of us were to scrutinize the government's budget, we could easily find areas to cut. The problem is, of course, that another citizen may gain from the very activity that we would eliminate. The objective, then, is to find cuts in expenditures that will win voting majorities.

How does a legislator assess the worthwhileness of a proposed expenditure? A public expenditure is rarely planned to make money. Therefore, a legislator must try to estimate the public benefits from the expenditure and compare these against its cost. These benefits may be fairly easy to calculate. When a government agency plans to build a hospital, legislators can estimate what a comparable private hospital might earn. Even if the public hospital provides its services free, these services are surely worth that much to the public simply because it has saved expenses it would otherwise have made at a private facility.

But often the benefits of a project are exceedingly difficult to calculate. How can we estimate the benefits of a new road? By the tolls that might be collected? But what about the indirect benefits gained by townspeople who are now served more rapidly and efficiently? What about the businesses that spring up alongside the new road? What about improvements in the landscape if billboards are banned?

In short, there is no accurate way of determining the value in money of a public project. We can make more or less sophisticated guesses and estimates, but these estimates always contain a large element of uncertainty. We can easily overestimate—or underestimate—the benefit of a project.

Once a project is decided on for better or worse—a road, a school, a training program—considerations of cost effectiveness are exactly the same as they are in a factory, a private house, or any other private venture. The principle is the use of the most economic combination of inputs to achieve a given output.

A second consideration that economists can offer to legislators is the concept of opportunity cost. The true cost of any public project (like that of any private one) is not the dollars it takes, but the alternative projects that cannot be undertaken because resources are committed to the first. The opportunity cost of weapons is not measured in dollars, but in the alternative goods those dollars might have brought forth.

Opportunity costs are difficult to apply to public projects because the returns from these projects, as we have emphasized, include so many nonmonetary gains. Hence, in practice, most legislators consider each year's appropriations in terms of increases or decreases to existing commitments.

Suppose, for example, that you are considering the federal budgetary appropriation for community development, a $7-billion commitment in the previous year. In all likelihood, most of your discussion would be concentrated on whether the appropriation should be increased or diminished by, say, half a billion dollars. Your review of the opportunity costs of the project would focus on whether or not that half-billion dollars would be a useful addition to the nation, compared with other uses to which those funds might be put (including their use by taxpayers if you decided to lower taxes by half a billion dollars). Legislators rarely consider the opportunity costs of entire programs.

Economists talk a lot about the regulating forces of supply and demand in the private sector. In the public sector the corresponding regulating force is inertia. Inertia is the tendency for conditions to remain the same. Whatever exists tends to persist. This is, of course, one of the

People determine through voting whether the level of spending for public goods and services such as defense and justice is correct.

reasons why it is difficult to cut government back. That is not saying, however, that government functions are therefore useless or wasteful. It is also difficult to eliminate private goods that are generally regarded as useless or wasteful or counterproductive, such as our ghastly TV commercials, when supply and demand keeps them there. The sword cuts two ways. There is waste in the market, defined by nonmarket standards, and there is waste in the public sector, defined by market standards.

This seems a good place to make a final assessment of the whole problem of how our resources are distributed by votes and by private spending. . . .

We should remember that the voting process tends to be used, in a capitalist system, only when the market mechanism does not work well, or even work at all. The market is the principal method by which capitalism distributes goods. It does so in a very simple manner. Each person who goes into a store, or who places an order by phone, or who enters the market in any other way, is entitled to buy as much as his or her income and wealth permit. This is also a voting system of a kind, only it is one dollar, one vote; not one person, one vote.

Just the same, all market systems have two failings. Markets cannot allocate some kinds of public goods. For example, there is no way of selling national defense just to those with the dollars to buy it. A defense system such as a navy will protect all citizens, whether they have paid for the navy or not.

Because there is no way of selling public goods, we decide how much defense or air traffic control to provide by voting for them. If enough individuals want these things, we provide them. If not, not. The result may be wasteful. However, it is a waste that results because there is no way to allocate votes by dollars.

Second, markets distribute certain kinds of goods in ways that outrage the public. When a new vaccine comes onto the market, we do not want it to be bought up only by rich people. Or when a family falls into poverty, for whatever reason, we do not want it to starve on the streets. Therefore every market system includes certain goods or services from the dollar voting system and entrusts them to the political voting system. We ration new vaccines by need, and we provide free or very inexpensive basic food or shelter to the poor.

In conclusion, we believe all market economies must have public sectors. **"**

From *Five Economic Challenges*, by Robert Heilborner and Lester Thurow.

UNDERSTANDING THE READING

1. How is waste measured in the private sector? Why does this standard not apply to the public sector?
2. According to Heilbroner and Thurow, what are two failings of all market systems? Why is a public sector needed?
3. Do you believe government expenditures and private business expenditures should be evaluated on different standards? Explain.

Section 2 Review

Understanding Expenditures

1. How does the government obtain the money to pay its bills when they exceed tax income?
2. Why do people buy and hold government securities?
3. Explain how the national debt results in a redistribution of income.
4. Explain how the national debt results in higher interest rates for everyone.
5. Why do higher interest rates affect the whole economy?
6. Explain the four ways of measuring the national debt. What is the result of each?

Expenditures Today

1. List two ways that citizens can be involved in government budget decisions.
2. Explain one advantage and one disadvantage of a constitutional amendment requiring a balanced budget.
3. **Challenge:** Look at the graph of government expenditures on page 380. Decide which area, in your opinion, should be cut in order to balance the budget. Write a paragraph defending your choice.

3 Fiscal Policy

SECTION OVERVIEW

Government taxes influence your spending habits. If taxes were lower, you would have more money to spend. Higher taxes decrease the amount you can purchase. Similarly, government expenditures may influence personal income. If the government decides to open more day care centers, more jobs are created. Government spending affects millions of people. A change in tax laws, for example, may affect every taxpayer. As a result, government has a significant influence on economic activity. In this section, you will learn how government policies on taxes and spending influence the economy.

ECONOMIC VOCABULARY

fiscal policy
demand-side economics

supply-side economics
automatic stabilizers

Basic Economic Aims

The revenues and expenditures of the national government form the budget. The government's fiscal policy is carried out through budgeted income and spending. Fiscal policy consists of government decisions on spending and taxation designed to achieve national economic goals. The government tries to combine fiscal policy and monetary policy to promote stable prices, full employment, and economic growth. The government's fiscal policy influences the economy in two ways.

First, fiscal policy can lead to an increase or decrease in the total amount of income consumers and businesses are able to spend. The more money consumers and businesses spend, the more likely it is that output, spending, and income will go up. Then, unemployment will fall and prices will rise. The less money consumers and businesses spend, the more likely it is that output, spending, and income will go down. Then, unemployment will rise and prices will fall.

How can the government affect the amount of money businesses and consumers spend? One obvious and important way is through its power to collect taxes. By raising taxes, the government decreases total spending. This action tends to stop price increases by slowing down economic activity. Tax increases, therefore, are used to fight inflation. By lowering taxes, the government increases the amount of money that can be spent. Then, output tends to go up. When output rises, more people are working and earning income. Tax cuts, therefore, are used to stimulate the economy and fight unemployment.

Second, the government's fiscal policy influences the economy through government expenditures. Government can increase or decrease the amount of goods and services it buys. Increases in government spending increase the demand for products. This demand, in turn, helps businesses to prosper and employment to increase. Like other increases in demand, however, government spending can push prices higher.

One way in which the government can discourage price increases is by reducing its spending. Decreases in government spending lower the total demand for goods and services. Though lower demand can help to hold down prices, it may lead to more unemployment.

Supply-side Economics

Traditionally, fiscal policy has centered on the use of government taxes and expenditures to increase the demand for goods and services. Such policies are called demand-side, or Keynesian, economics. Some econ-omists believe that fiscal policy should emphasize supply rather than demand. Supply-side economics is a set of government economic policies designed to promote economic growth by encouraging businesses to increase the supply of goods and services. These policies include lowering taxes on investments and reducing government regulations on trade, workers' safety, and the environment.

Stabilizing the Economy

Many government policies are designed to promote steady economic growth and reduce inflation. These policies tend to reduce demand during economic expansion and increase demand during contractions.

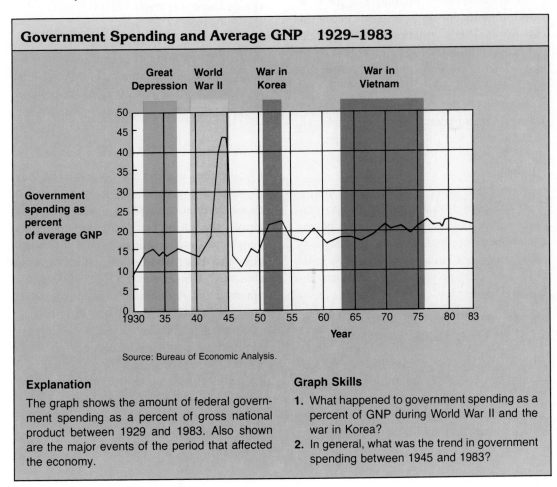

Government Spending and Average GNP   1929–1983

Government spending as percent of average GNP

Source: Bureau of Economic Analysis.

Explanation

The graph shows the amount of federal government spending as a percent of gross national product between 1929 and 1983. Also shown are the major events of the period that affected the economy.

Graph Skills

1. What happened to government spending as a percent of GNP during World War II and the war in Korea?
2. In general, what was the trend in government spending between 1945 and 1983?

Congressional representatives analyze and debate the nation's fiscal policy. They determine the level of taxes and expenditures of the federal government.

The progressive income tax helps to slow inflation during periods of economic expansion. When inflation increases, people move into higher tax brackets. Higher taxes, in turn, tend to reduce consumption and increase federal revenue. When the economy contracts, unemployment increases. Unemployment compensation provides income for the unemployed and assures that demand will not decrease too rapidly.

The federal income tax and unemployment compensation are part of the government's fiscal policy. The graduated income tax and unemployment compensation are called automatic stabilizers because they are built into the economy to stabilize the business cycle.

Debate Over Fiscal Policy

Fiscal policy is controversial for a number of reasons. The government does not spend money and collect taxes simply to regulate unemployment and inflation. The main reason for taxes and spending is the need to provide the programs and services that citizens demand. Sometimes, these programs cost so much that the government has to raise taxes even when such action will have a negative effect on the economy. For example, a large tax increase to pay for a war will mean that consumers have less money to spend. The result may be unemployment in industries that are very sensitive to reduced consumer spending—the automobile industry, for instance.

What is more, when the government decides to cut spending, programs that are very important to some people may be cut back or even stopped. Since members of Congress must face reelection every two or six years, they are reluctant to vote for cuts in federal government spending. Thus, politics makes it harder for the government to use its level of spending as a way to regulate the economy.

For all these reasons, fiscal policy as a way of controlling the economy is more complicated than monetary policy. Even though complex, however, fiscal policy is very important.

Fiscal Policy and Social Values

Fiscal policy is also social policy. The ways in which a government collects and spends money reflect the nation's values. For example, the nation has decided to encourage people to donate money to schools, hospitals, and other nonprofit organizations and charities. Consequently, the government allows a tax deduction to people who donate money. Both direct spending and tax deductions result in subsidies for certain groups. Each subsidy reflects certain social values. Some subsidies are controversial. They reflect the values and interests of only special groups within the society. Others are accepted by nearly everyone. They reflect values that most Americans share, or at least never question.

REVIEWING THE CONCEPT

Developing Vocabulary

1. Give three examples of how government applies fiscal policy.
2. Define supply-side economics.
3. Identify some automatic stabilizers and explain how they work.

Mastering Facts

1. Explain how the government's taxing policy affects the economy.
2. How does government spending affect the economy?
3. Why is government fiscal policy controversial? Use examples in your answer.

CASE STUDY

Guns or Butter?

Government spending reflects the nation's values. The government must choose its purchases from a variety of goods and services. Its decisions greatly affect national and personal prosperity. Such decisions usually are made on the basis of national needs. The mix of products the federal government purchases reflects the varied needs of the nation.

The phrase "guns or butter" is often used to refer to the mix of military and civilian goods a country can produce. The expression originated during World War II, when countries did not have enough re-

These workers depend directly on defense spending for their jobs.

sources to produce both military and civilian goods. If a nation needed tanks and guns, it reduced or stopped making cars and refrigerators. In time of war, the choice was obvious. Nations spent more for guns and less for butter. In times of peace, the choices are most difficult.

The Council on Economic Priorities, a private organization that studies the social and environmental responsibilities of corporations, has researched the impact of the guns or butter questions on our economy. The council concluded that:

1. Defense spending creates fewer jobs than other kinds of government spending. For example, $1 billion spent on defense creates only 28,000 new jobs, but $1 billion spent on education creates 71,00 new jobs.
2. Skilled professionals, engineers, and scientists fill jobs created by defense spending. The nation's unemployed do not benefit directly from defense jobs.
3. Industrial nations that spend the most on guns and the least for butter do not enjoy great economic growth. The United States and Great Britain, for example, rank as top spenders for defense among such nations, but rank at the bottom for productivity growth.

393

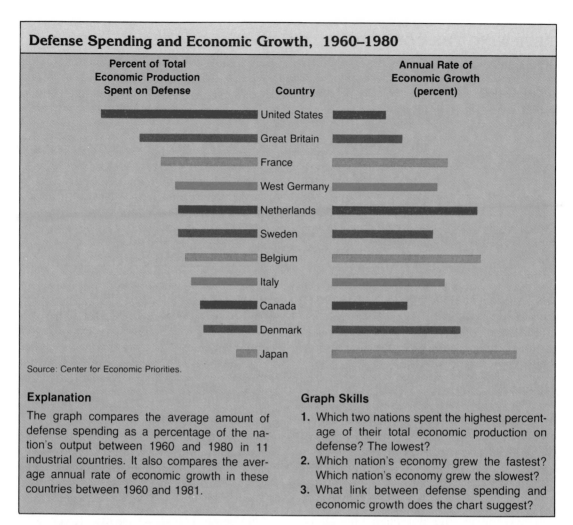

Defense Spending and Economic Growth, 1960–1980

Percent of Total Economic Production Spent on Defense	Country	Annual Rate of Economic Growth (percent)
	United States	
	Great Britain	
	France	
	West Germany	
	Netherlands	
	Sweden	
	Belgium	
	Italy	
	Canada	
	Denmark	
	Japan	

Source: Center for Economic Priorities.

Explanation

The graph compares the average amount of defense spending as a percentage of the nation's output between 1960 and 1980 in 11 industrial countries. It also compares the average annual rate of economic growth in these countries between 1960 and 1981.

Graph Skills

1. Which two nations spent the highest percentage of their total economic production on defense? The lowest?
2. Which nation's economy grew the fastest? Which nation's economy grew the slowest?
3. What link between defense spending and economic growth does the chart suggest?

In short, the council concluded, defense spending is not so beneficial to the economy as other types of spending. The people of the nation may decide that high defense spending is needed, despite its effect on the economy. Government expenditures must reflect all the needs of a nation, not just those of its economy.

ANALYZING THE CASE STUDY

STEP 1   Clarify the Issue

1. State at least two quesitons a government must answer regarding the mix of spending for military and civilian goods and services.

STEP 2   Evaluate Possible Outcomes

1. Identify the consequences of each of the following alternatives in time of peace.
   Increase spending for guns.
   Increase spending for butter.
   Spend equal amounts for both guns and butter.
2. Which of the three alternatives best promotes peacetime economic prosperity?
3. Which of the three alternatives best promotes the noneconomic needs of society during a time of peace?

STEP 3   Make a Decision

Decide which peacetime alternative you support. Explain your decision.

394

Does Money Matter?

by John Maynard Keynes   (1883-1946)

John Maynard Keynes is widely considered the most influential economist of this century. Like Adam Smith in the 1700s and Karl Marx in the 1800s, Keynes has shaped the way today's economists view economic problems. Keynes book, *The General Theory of Employment, Interest, and Money,* shifted the focus of the study of economics. Keynes believed that the government could promote economic prosperity through the use of fiscal policy to influence the total demand for goods and services in the economy. Through carefully planned taxing and spending policies, government could prevent the economy from experiencing severe depressions. The reading reflects Keynes's belief that the government should put idle resources to work. It is taken from a speech Keynes gave near the end of World War II. Great Britain had been severely damaged by bombing raids during the war. Near the end of the war, people began to consider how to rebuild the country. As you read, consider how a large public works project would help Great Britain.

"For some weeks you have enjoyed the dreams of planning. But what about the nightmare of finance? I am sure there have been many listeners who have been muttering: "That's all very well, but how is it to be paid for?"

Let me begin by telling you how I tried to answer a famous architect who doubted all the grand plans to rebuild London with the phrase, "Where's the money to come from?"

"The money?" I said. "But surely, Sir John, you don't build houses with money? Do you mean that there won't be enough bricks and mortar and steel and cement?"

"Oh no," he replied, "of course there will be plenty of all that."

"Do you mean," I went on, "that there won't be enough labor? For what will the builders be doing if they are not building houses?"

"Oh no, that's all right," he agreed.

"Then there is only one conclusion. You must be meaning, Sir John, that there won't be enough *architects.*" But there I risked offending him, I was trespassing on the boundaries of politeness. I hurried to add: "Well, if there are bricks and mortar and steel and concrete and labor and architects, why not assemble all this good material into houses?" But he was, I fear, quite unconvinced.

"What I want to know," he repeated, "is where the money is coming from."

395

To answer that would have got him and me into deeper water than I cared for, so I replied rather shabbily, "The same place it is coming from now."

He might have countered (but he didn't): "Of course I know that money is not the slightest use whatever. But, all the same, my dear sir, you will find it hard not to have any."

Had I given him a good and convincing answer by saying that we build houses with bricks and mortar, not with money? Or was I only teasing him? It all depends what he really had in mind. He might have meant that the burden of the national debt, the heavy taxation, the fact that the banks have lent so much money to the government and all that, would make it impossible to borrow money to pay the wages of the makers of the raw material, the building labor, and even the architects. Or he might have meant something quite different. He could have pointed out that those who were making houses would have to be supported while working. Will the rest of us, after supporting ourselves, have enough to support the builders as well as ourselves while they are at work?

In fact was he really talking about money? Or was he talking about resources in general—resources in a wide sense, not merely bricks and cement and architects?

If the first, if it was some problem of finance that was troubling him, then my answer was good and sufficient. No doubt there is a technical problem, but it is one which today we understand. It would be out of place to try to explain it in a few minutes, just as it would be to explain the technical details of bridge-building or the internal combustion engine or the surgery of the thyroid gland. As a technician in these matters I can only say that the technical problem of where the money for reconstruction is to come from can be solved, and, therefore, should be solved.

Now, let me turn back to the other interpretation of what my friend may have had at the back of his head—the adequacy of our resources in general, even assuming good employment, to allow us to devote a large body of labor to capital works which would bring in no immediate return. Here is a real problem, fundamental yet essentially simple, which it is important for all of us to try to understand.

The first task is to make sure that there is enough demand to provide employment for everyone. The second task is to prevent a demand greater than the possibilities of supply. This causes inflation. For the physical possibilities of supply are very far from unlimited. Our building programs must be related to the resources which are left after we have met our daily needs and have produced enough exports to pay for what we require to import from overseas.

It is extremely difficult to predict accurately in advance the scale and pace on which plans can be carried out. In the long run almost anything is possible. Therefore do not be afraid of large and bold schemes. Let our plans be big, significant, but not hasty. Rome was not built in a day. The

During World War II, parts of Great Britain, such as this section of London, were destroyed by bombing raids. The economist John Maynard Keynes suggested establishing government work programs to repair the damage.

building of the great architectural monuments of the past was carried out slowly, gradually, over many years.

You cannot improvise a building industry suddenly or put part of it into storage when it is excessive. Tell those concerned that we shall need a building industry of a million workers—well and good, it can be arranged. Tell them that we shall need a million and a half or two million—again well and good. But we must let them have in good time some reasonably accurate idea of the target. For if the building industry is to expand in an orderly fashion, it must have some reason to expect continuing employment for the larger labor force.

Not all planning is expensive. Even the planning of London to give space and air and perspective costs nothing to the nation's resources and need not involve a charge on the budget. There is heaps of room, enough and more than enough, in a replanned London. We could get all the housing we need if a third of the present built-up area was cleared altogether and left cleared. To build may be costly. Let us offset that expense by a generous policy, here and there, of not building.

Where we are using up resources, do not let us submit to the harmful idea of the last century that every enterprise must justify itself in cash income, with no other measure of value but this. I should like to see the memorials to those who fought in World War II take the shape of an enrichment of the civic life of every great center of population.

Why should we not set aside, let us say, £50 million a year for the next 20 years to add, in every major city of the country, the dignity of an ancient University or a European capital to our local schools and their surroundings, to our local government and its offices. Above all, let us provide a local center of refreshment and entertainment with an ample theatre, a concert hall, a dance hall, a gallery, a British restaurant, canteens, cafes, and so forth.

Assuredly we can afford this and much more. Anything we can actually do we can afford. Once done, it is there. Nothing can take it from us. We are immeasurably richer than our predecessors. Is it not evident that some mistaken reasoning governs our action as a country if we are forced to be so much poorer than they in the riches of life?

Yet these must be only the trimmings on the more solid, urgent, and necessary outgoings on housing the people, on reconstructing industry and transport, and on replanning the environment of our daily life. Not only shall we come to possess these excellent things. With a big program carried out at a proper pace we can hope to keep employment good for many years to come. We shall, in very fact, have built our new cities out of the labor which we were mistakenly keeping unused and unhappy in enforced idleness. **"**

From *How Much Does Finance Matter?*, by John Maynard Keynes.

UNDERSTANDING THE READING

1. Explain what Keynes meant in his question: "But surely, Sir John, you don't build houses with money?"
2. According to Keynes, what are the costs of not building?
3. How did Keynes think that a large construction program in Great Britain would help society?

Section 3 Review

Understanding Fiscal Policy

1. How are fiscal policy and the federal budget related?
2. What is the relationship between fiscal policy and monetary policy?
3. Explain the expected results of applying supply-side economics.
4. How do presidential and congressional elections affect the federal government's fiscal policy?
5. What kind of fiscal policies are called Keynesian economics? For whom and why were they so named?

Fiscal Policy Today

1. What is the main reason for government taxation and spending?
2. What fiscal policy should be followed to reduce inflation? What other effects would this policy produce?
3. **Challenge:** When is direct government spending preferable to a tax cut as a method stimulating the economy?
4. **Challenge:** Compare the supply-side philosophy of economics to the deficit spending concept. In what situations should each be used? What are the effects of each?

Americans *at Work*

Meet Diana Guetzkow
Entrepreneur

"There are not many countries where someone can do what I did here," Diana Guetzkow said about her adopted country, the United States. Born in West Germany of Polish refugee parents, Guetzkow came to America as a child. She earned a degree in physics, then a PhD in foreign policy. Now she is president and chief executive officer of Netword Inc., of Riverdale, Maryland. Netword Inc. is certified by the Postal Service to be part of its electronic mail system. Electronic mail uses a computer to transmit people's messages over telephone lines for a fee. Guetzkow's husband, Daniel, is executive vice president.

The Guetzkows' company illustrates the relationship between technology and economics. Electronics makes it possible to transmit messages over long distances instantaneously—a need of many businesses. The Postal Service supplies this service through private companies. By the end of 1983, Netword Inc. transmitted approximately 270,000 letters.

Before starting Netword, Guetzkow was working for the Energy Department. Then she decided she wanted to go to work for herself. To organize Netword Inc., Guetzkow had to attract investors. She found 40, who contributed $100,000. With this money, Guetzkow got her business started.

Later, when the company offered 3 million shares of stock for public sale at $1 each, investors quickly purchased them. The sale gave the company additional operating funds until income increased.

Guetzkow attributes her success in part to her personality. "I have the character of an entrepreneur. . . . I'm the classic story of someone who had to fight adversity at a young age and find an inner strength." Studies show that entrepreneurs are often very independent, hard working individuals. In addition, entrepreneurs must be willing to take risks.

The economics of organizing a business are important. However, the entrepreneur must believe deeply in the enterprise and be willing to sacrifice to get under way. To Diana Guetzkow, it matters not whether the entrepreneur is male or female. "It's equally tough," she said. "I don't know that we're going to succeed. But we work hard, we're honest, and we have a good product." Those are the beginnings of any firm's success.

Understanding the National Budget

A budget is a plan for coordinating income and spending. A budget contains a list of sources and amounts of income, as well as kinds and amounts of expenses. Because expenses and income vary, most budgets contain some estimated figures.

The federal government's budget, as well as that of many business firms, is based on a fiscal year that differs from the calendar year. A fiscal year is an accounting period of 12 months. Those months may or may not be the same as the months of the calendar year. The 1984 federal budget year began on October 1, 1983, and ended on September 30, 1984.

Fiscal policy is accomplished through the use of the federal budget. The following steps will help you understand the process and limitations of the United States budget.

STEP 1 Understand the Process

Budget preparation begins about a year and a half before the budget goes into effect. The President asks the head of each department (defense, state, transportation, etc.) to prepare a budget. These budgets are sent to the President's Office of Management and Budget (OMB). At the hearings that follow, the department heads must defend their proposed expenditures. The OMB also receives estimates of government tax revenues from the Department of the Treasury.

The spending and income figures are revised several times. Finally, they are assembled into a budget, which the President sends to Congress for approval. The Congressional Budget Office along with the proper committees of both the House and Senate analyze the budget. After much debate and perhaps amendments, Congress passes appropriations bills specifying how much money each government department may spend. If proposed spending exceeds the spending target, Congress may have to revise the budget later by cutting spending or raising taxes. Congress may authorize a budget that has a deficit or a surplus.

The revised budget is then sent to the President in appropriations bills for his signature or veto. The OMB receives the authorized funds from the Treasury Department and distributes them to the government departments. The General Accounting Office, another federal agency, checks to make sure each department properly follows its budget.

STEP 2 Analyze Expense Categories

The categories in the federal budget—energy, defense, education—represent national goals. However, it is sometimes difficult to determine what a particular budget classification includes. For instance, the main function of the Department of Energy is to develop, promote, and conserve energy. Still, some defense spending on nuclear weapons appears in the energy budget.

STEP 3 Examine Areas of Controversy

The amounts the federal government budgets for different purposes will always be controversial. The goals of individuals and communities vary. One group of citizens will favor defense spending while others want to give priority to social services. The government must make tradeoffs in deciding how to spend limited funds.

Another area of controversy is deficit spending. Most citizens agree that the country should spend no more than its income, and that government spending should be reduced rather than taxes increased. However, no general agreement exists on the programs that should be eliminated in order to reduce spending.

STEP 4 Balance the Budget

Many candidates for federal offices have promised to balance the budget. That task has proved more difficult than most suspected because Congress has less control over the federal budget than individuals have over personal budgets.

Nearly half of the 1982 federal budget was spent on entitlements—payments required by law. Social security, military, and other federal pensions, and medicare and medicaid are entitlement programs.

The defense budget is a target of spending cuts. Almost 75 percent of the defense budget is used to pay salaries, maintenance, and training costs—all difficult to cut. Agreements with allies also add to defense costs.

Finally, reducing or discontinuing the interest paid on the national debt would be an admission of bankruptcy. The result would be a loss of faith in the United States government, an inability to borrow, and economic disruption.

All these expenses leave only about 12.4 percent of a typical budget for Congress to appropriate as it chooses. The 12.4 percent represents a potential political problem, since every program has protective beneficiaries and constituents.

ECONOMIC SKILLS TODAY

1. List the steps required to draw up the federal budget. How does this process differ from setting up a personal budget?
2. What problems with past and future data would develop from attempts to simplify the budget categories?

Enrichment Activities

1. Write a letter to the President explaining how the budget could be balanced.
2. Choose an entitlement program to investigate. Present a case for keeping it, modifying it, or dropping it.

CHAPTER SUMMARY

Taxes

Governments collect taxes to pay for the goods and services they provide. Federal government taxes fall into four major categories: income, excise or sale, estate and gift, and customs (duties). Many state and local governments also impose taxes on income, sales, and property. There are three types of taxes. Progressive taxes take a larger percentage of higher incomes and a smaller percentage of lower incomes. Regressive taxes have the opposite effect. Proportional taxes take the same proportion of everyone's income. Controversy often surrounds the legality, clarity, efficiency, effect, and fairness of taxes. Governments give tax incentives to individuals and businesses to promote certain social or economic behavior. Tax incentives are a major source of controversy.

Expenditures

Tax revenues finance government expenditures. The major expenditures of the federal government include social welfare, defense, interest on the federal debt, and grants to state and local governments. The major expenditures of state and local governments are education, public aid, highways, health care, and police protection. Government spending often exceeds revenue, causing a deficit. Governments then borrow to pay their bills. The effects of federal government borrowing and the size of the national debt have long been controversial subjects. The effects of the national debt include redistribution of income, higher interest rates, and increased demand for goods and services.

Fiscal Policy

Government fiscal policy represents government's attempt to achieve certain goals through taxing and spending. Increasing or decreasing taxes changes the amount of spendable income and influences the economy. The amount and kind of government spending also affect the economy. Government spends to meet the demands of citizens for certain programs and services. Controversy arises when pursuing taxing and spending policies to achieve social goals conflicts with fiscal policy necessary to achieve economic goals.

CRITICAL THINKING QUESTIONS

Taxes

1. Income tax credits for tuition payments is a recurring issue in the United States. What are the advantages or disadvantages that would result from income tax credits for tuition? Explain whether you are or are not in favor of such credits, and why or why not.
2. In general, what impact does the graduated income tax have on individuals and businesses? How do taxes affect the allocation of resources?

Expenditures

1. How does the concept of opportunity costs apply to government spending?
2. List four major effects of deficit spending. Explain their costs and benefits.
3. Explain the relationship between the national debt and the Federal Reserve System. What would happen to monetary policy if the national debt were paid off?

4. How does the national debt affect the relationship between the public sector and the private sector?

Fiscal Policy

1. If you were a member of Congress, what fiscal policy would you support to combat inflation? How would you defend your choice to any constituents who would be hurt by it?
2. How do the multiplier effect and the accelerator principle affect fiscal policy?
3. In what ways are supply-side and demand-side economics similar? How do they differ?
4. Fiscal policy and monetary policy do not always work toward the same goals. Explain why.

DEVELOPING ECONOMIC SKILLS

Use the cartoon and your economic knowledge to answer the following questions.

1. What is a Keynesian?
2. What is a supply-sider?
3. In view of the answers to the questions 1 and 2, what do you think a monetarist is?
4. What is the cartoonist's view of the government's attempts to regulate the economy? Explain how the cartoonist illustrated this view.

APPLYING ECONOMICS TODAY

1. Using news magazines or a recent United States history textbook, research the views of each of the candidates for President in the last election. What measures to strengthen the economy did each emphasize? What did each see as the cause of the country's economic condition?
2. **Challenge:** When government fiscal policy causes interest rates to rise, what action can the Federal Reserve Board take to stop the increase? What are the short-term effects of this policy? The long-term effects?

"....FIRST I WAS A KEYNESIAN .... NEXT I WAS A MONETARIST...THEN A SUPPLY-SIDER ... NOW I'M A BUM...."

UNIT 3 Review

USING ECONOMIC CONCEPTS

National Economic Measurements

1. How do macroeconomics and microeconomics differ?
2. What does GNP measure?
3. Explain the purpose and construction of a price index.
4. List and explain the three types of economic indicators.
5. **Challenge:** How do inflation and deflation affect GNP measurements?

National Economic Goals

1. List and explain the four phases of the business cycle.
2. Draw a diagram illustrating the circle of economic activity.
3. How does unemployment affect the nation's economy?
4. How does inflation affect those who owe money? Those who have loaned money? The economy? Taxpayers?
5. **Challenge:** Why are full employment and stable prices difficult to achieve?

The Role of Government

1. How does the government provide for settlement of disputes?
2. How does the government encourage inventors and artists?
3. Explain the function of a national currency and system of measurement.
4. How does the government provide for free competition in the United States?
5. **Challenge:** What controversy exists over who supplies public and private goods? Include an example in your answer.

Monetary Policy

1. In modern economies, what functions does money serve? Explain your answer.
2. How does a bank's reserve requirement affect the money supply?
3. How do various types of bank accounts affect M-1A, M-1B, and M-2?
4. How is the economy affected by easy money? By tight money?
5. **Challenge:** Explain how monetary policy is carried out in the United States.

The Federal Budget

1. From what sources does the federal government receive its revenue?
2. How do progressive, regressive, and proportional taxes differ?
3. Explain the purpose of the national debt and how it is financed.
4. In what two ways does fiscal policy influence the economy?
5. What are automatic stabilizers and how do they influence the economy?
6. Explain the difference between supply-side and demand-side economics.
7. **Challenge:** Explain why, as a way to control the economy, fiscal policy is more complicated than monetary policy.

APPLYING ECONOMIC SKILLS

The ratio of self-employed men to self-employed women 10 years ago was almost 3 to 1. That is, for every business a woman owned in the United States, men owned almost three. Today that gap has narrowed. Use the graph and your economic knowledge to answer the questions.

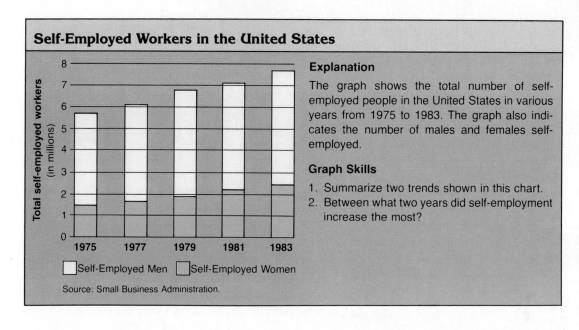

Self-Employed Workers in the United States

Total self-employed workers (in millions)

1975 1977 1979 1981 1983

☐ Self-Employed Men   ☐ Self-Employed Women

Source: Small Business Administration.

Explanation

The graph shows the total number of self-employed people in the United States in various years from 1975 to 1983. The graph also indicates the number of males and females self-employed.

Graph Skills

1. Summarize two trends shown in this chart.
2. Between what two years did self-employment increase the most?

CURRENT ECONOMIC ISSUES

According to a March 1984 Department of Labor survey, more than 6 of every 10 mothers of children under 18 are in the labor force. This statistic indicates a 44 percent increase in working mothers since 1970. Use this information to help you answer the following questions.

1. As more mothers enter the labor force, what types of products will be in greater demand? Will this affect the GNP?
2. How will the increase in working mother's affect the size of the labor force?

ECONOMIC REASONING

Karen Kuen was finishing her senior year in high school. She had been looking forward to attending a nearby college until her father lost his job. For 25 years, Mr. Kuen had worked on an assembly line where he made parts for American car engines. Mr. Kuen spent four months looking for another job, but he was unable to find anything at comparable pay. Now he is working at a gas station but hopes he will be called back to his former job.

Karen's family expects her to get a full-time job so that she can contribute something toward paying the family's bills rather than adding to them with college tuition. Karen is depressed and feels that all of her hard work in high school was a waste of time and effort.

STEP 1   Define the Problem

1. What is Karen's problem?
2. What is Mr. Kuen's problem?
3. What is the family's problem?

STEP 2   Clarify the Issue

1. Is Karen's future the central issue?
2. Is the family's need for additional income the main issue?

STEP 3   Consider Alternatives

1. List the alternatives available to Karen.
2. What are the costs and benefits of each alternative available to Karen?

STEP 4   Make a Decision

If you were in Karen's situation, what would you do?

Using Economics Today

CHAPTER 13

Challenges to the Market Economy

1 Industrialization

Objective: to understand the economic characteristics and problems of industrialized countries

2 Equal Opportunity

Objective: to understand the non-economic influences that sometimes disrupt competition in the market system

3 Equity and Efficiency

Objective: to understand that the goals of equity and efficiency cannot always be attained

1 Industrialization

SECTION OVERVIEW

Individuals develop from infants to children, to adolescents, and finally to mature adults. Each of these stages has its own developmental characteristics. Economies also develop in stages, each with distinctive characteristics. In this section, you will learn about the characteristics and problems of industrialized economies.

ECONOMIC VOCABULARY

technology   industrial economy   bureaucracy

Beginnings of Industrialization

Technology is the study and application of scientific principles and skills to solve problems, build machines, and make work easier and more productive. After about 1750, machines were used to increase the production of goods, and new sources of power to run the machines were developed. The industrial economy emerged as factories replaced home workshops.

Industrial economies depend on business, especially large-scale manufacturing and profit-making businesses. Several characteristics are common to all industrial economies. First, huge amounts of energy must be supplied to run the machinery for mass-producing goods. Second, large amounts of money are necessary to purchase land and machinery. Third, workers are needed to operate equipment. Last, the great output of goods requires an extensive transportation and communication network. Industrialized economies must provide energy, capital, workers, and communication and transportation facilites.

Both costs and benefits resulted from industrialization. A benefit of industrialization was the improvement in the overall quality of life because more products were available at lower prices. Another benefit is increased leisure time for recreational activities. Today, countries continue to promote industrial growth as a way to better the living conditions of their citizens and increase the influence of their government.

The costs of industrialization have changed as industrial economies have matured. During the initial period of industrialization, the costs included long working hours, low wages, dangerous jobs, and crowded and unsanitary living conditions. Workers demanded, and over a long period of time gradually obtained, an eight-hour workday and higher wages. Working and living conditions improved.

Industrialization still carries both benefits and costs. Increased productivity has been beneficial in raising the standard of living of people in industrialized countries. Also, more goods are available at lower prices. The present costs of industrializa-

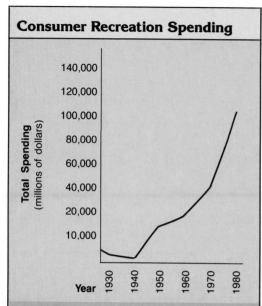

Consumer Recreation Spending

Total Spending (millions of dollars)

140,000
120,000
100,000
80,000
60,000
40,000
20,000
10,000

Year: 1930, 1940, 1950, 1960, 1970, 1980

Explanation

The graph shows the increase in individual spending for recreation. This spending includes purchases of sporting goods, toys, books, magazines, radios, television sets, stereo equipment, and admissions to movies, concerts, and athletic events.

Graph Skills

1. How much did consumers spend on recreation in 1930? 1980?
2. Suggest two reasons that might explain why recreation expenditures increased between 1930 and 1980.

job of making a product. With specialization, productivity increases and costs decrease. However, specialization can prevent a worker from contributing to the job in a creative or thoughtful way. The work may become monotonous and tedious. Workers sometimes complain of a lack of job fulfillment. Since workers are responsible for only a small part of the product, they lose the pride that results from doing a job well or making a quality product.

Assembly line workers in large factories sometimes have a sense of lost individual identity. Workers may feel overwhelmed by the impersonality of their work and the corporate bureaucracy. A bureaucracy is a system for operating an organization based on formal policies or rules, rigid organization, and written records. Employees sometimes feel they have little control over their working lives since they have little power to make job-related decisions or contributions in a large corporation.

Need for Mobility

Before industrialization, workers seldom changed jobs or moved to a new location. Today, the average worker will change jobs three times and move four times during the working years. Specialization contributes to this mobility. Workers usually live in the area where demand exists for their particular skill. Job advancement sometimes requires a change of residence. When an employer does not fully use a worker's skills, the worker may decide that changing jobs is necessary to obtain a higher level job and an increase in salary.

Job mobility often disrupts traditional living patterns. Lasting friendships and family ties are difficult to maintain after relocation. Few, if any, adult residents of many modern suburbs were born there. Dislocation from families and friends often has led to feelings of loss and loneliness.

tion include unsatisfying jobs, a mobile work force, increased demand for highly educated workers, interdependence of countries, and the continual need to increase demand for new goods and services.

Unsatisfying Jobs

Increased productivity is based on division of labor and specialization. Workers trained to perform each specialized task in a total job can complete the job faster than could untrained workers. An assembly line worker performs one particular part of the

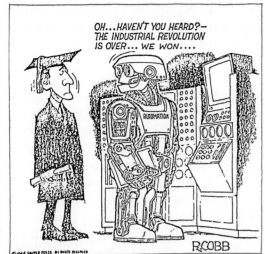

Reprinted courtesy Sawyer Press. © 1968, Sawyer Press. All rights reserved.

Who does the person on the left represent? In what way has the Industrial Revolution been lost? Who is the loser?

Importance of Education

Advances in technology have changed industrial production methods. These new methods often result in new or improved products. In addition, new methods often change how people work. As the automobile was developed in the early 1900s, fewer people relied on horses for transportation. As a result, society needed fewer horseshoe makers but more mechanics.

Technology changes more quickly today than ever before. Consequently, people preparing to enter the job market now need to be flexible, expecting to change the way they work during their lives. One way to prepare for changes in the job market is to acquire a sound education. Individuals who can think clearly and communicate well will have the flexibility to benefit from technological advances.

Interdependence

The effects of industrialization influence nations as well as individuals. Before indus-trialization, countries and societies tried to be economically self-sufficient. Citizens could satisfy their needs without importing goods. In England, for example, people raised sheep for wool. The wool was card-ed, spun, and woven into cloth. The cloth was sewn into clothes. All the labor and resources needed to produce clothes were provided by English men and women. England had no need to depend on others for that economic need. Before industrialization, people lacked the variety of products available today but did not go without the necessities of life.

With the introduction of factories and the growth of trade and transportation, countries began to specialize based on their climate, resources, and available labor supply. Productivity increased, providing more products at lower cost. As specialization increased, so did interdependence. Countries traded resources and products. Countries now depend more on one another than ever before. In 1982, the United States needed to import 15 percent of its oil. Oil-exporting countries can limit their exports or increase prices.

The interdependence of importing and exporting countries has increased with industrialization. When an import such as oil is restricted, production in factories slows down. Wars, revolutions, and weather conditions also can affect the availability of imports. Individuals, companies, and nations depend on the resources and economic policies of others. Modern industrialized societies depend on the resources and products of others. Disruption of trade in one country often causes global problems.

Limits to Growth

In his book, *Stages of Economic Growth,* economist Walt Whitman Rostow described how societies develop the necessary preconditions for growth, take off into in-

411

"SO that's where it goes! Well, I'd like to thank you fellows for bringing this to my attention."

dustrial development, and finally reach full development—economic maturity. Many nations, including the United States, have mature economies. Unfortunately, complex problems exist for mature economies. Among the problems are the need to constantly increase demand for new goods and services and the need for a continuing supply of natural resources.

In a mature economy, most people have the food, clothing, and shelter they need or can afford. Economic growth requires increased demand. Unless a demand exists for new goods and services, no new jobs will be created for the labor force. Rostow suggested three alternative courses for growth in the mature economy: (1) encourage population growth; (2) engage in wars that require military supplies; or (3) use labor to produce social goods, such as parks, hospitals, and cultural centers. Some businesses in the United States attempt to create demand by means of advertising and planned obsolescence. Some goods become obsolete, which means they go out of style and consequently require replacement. Mature industrial economies are a recent economic development. Such problems as maintaining full employment have not yet been solved.

Industrial economies also require a continuing supply of natural resources to maintain production. These resources are used as energy or raw materials in the manufacture of capital and consumer goods. One result of the manufacturing process is pollution. Another is the reduced supply of resources. Some resources, such as wood, are renewable; others, such as oil, are not. Many people are concerned about the depletion of natural resources and the environmental damage caused by pollution. Both pollution of the environment and the limited supply of natural resources restrict the growth of industrial economies.

REVIEWING THE CONCEPT

Developing Vocabulary

1. Define technology.
2. What are the characteristics of an industrial economy?
3. What is a bureauracy?

Mastering Facts

1. What production methods does industry use to increase productivity?
2. Why is the United States often called a mobile society?
3. In the cartoon on this page, why is the person speaking pretending to be surprised at what is is shown?

Corporate Power

As industrial societies developed, government power increased. As the bureaucracies of government and industry expanded, the influence of the individual declined. Ralph Nader has devoted his life to returning some power to citizens. Since the mid-1960s, Nader has worked to make available to average citizens information and legal power to enhance their influence in corporate and government decisions. Nader is the country's best-known consumer activist and founder of most of the modern consumer rights movements.

Historically, the consumer movement began in women's magazines at the turn of the century. Women protested the high rate of inflation and contaminated foods. Consumer issues then were often regarded as women's issues. Nader, a Harvard lawyer, changed this focus.

Ralph Nader was born in Winstead, Connecticut, to Lebanese immigrant parents who owned a bakery and delicatessen. "It was kind of a community center. People came there and talked about how they felt about issues," said Nader. His parents and his New England origins endowed him with a sense of hard work and a belief in the idea of citizen participation.

Nader did his undergraduate work at Princeton and obtained his law degree from Harvard in 1958. Nader said he chose to study law "because it was a way of working for justice. Also, legal work was an approved way of learning about power."

While studying at Harvard, Nader wrote a paper, "Automotive Design Safety and Legal Liability." He explained, "the subject appealed to me because I was interested in seeing if you could apply the law to humanize a technology." In 1965, Nader wrote the bestseller, *Unsafe at Any Speed.* This book blamed the country's automobile manufacturers for the safety problems and the resulting deaths of millions of Americans. "I was representing people injured in car accidents, and I kept thinking, 'What is this? You can spend the next 50 years doing this and you'll never do much about the problem.' What I wanted to do was prevent injuries."

The publication of his book identified Nader as someone who was interested in defending the rights of individuals. Consumers found in Ralph Nader a spokesperson who would help them fight the government and corporate bureaucracies.

Before Nader, consumers were not well organized. They did not have the powerful, well-financed lobbies that corporations and unions could afford. No one represented consumer views to Congress. In 1969, Nader started Public Citizen, a national research and lobbying organization for citizen issues. Dozens of local public-interest research groups followed, as well as the Health Research Group, the Center for Science in the Public Interest, the Critical Mass Energy Project, and the Center for the Study of Responsive Law. Nader thinks of these organizations as projects. "I always wanted to create Johnny Appleseed kinds of projects that would eventually run on their own. What a real leader does is prod, prove, inspire, initiate. That way the multiplier effect gets going."

Nader is most proud of giving people the opportunity to participate. Nader backed the Freedom of Information Act, which expands the individual's rights. Indi-

Ralph Nader travels throughout the country to encourage people to form organizations to protect their rights as consumers.

viduals may examine any files that such organizations as schools, credit bureaus, and governments keep on them. 'It implemented the old point that information is the currency of democracy," said Nader. "All kinds of articles have been written because researchers had access to material and information through this act."

Not all of Nader's efforts have been successful. He supported a corporate accountability bill and a bill to make airbags mandatory in cars. Both of these bills failed. However, several laws related to auto safety, pollution, and worker health and safety have resulted from Nader's work. These laws are lasting accomplishments. Enforcement of these consumer protection laws may vary with changing administrations, but the laws exist.

Some of Nader's critics complain that his work has limited influence. Nader, of course, does not agree.

"The way I see the consumer movement is that it is a force to put the citizen in charge of the economy. The corporation is now in charge of the economy. The movement goes to the core of the value systems of the society. The more corporate power there is, the less freedom you have in this country and the more invasion of privacy. You're up against adversaries that know no shut-down time. General Motors operates worldwide 24 hours a day. There's a fundamental unfairness—corporations have all the rights that human beings have, but they have privileges and immunities that human beings don't have under our Constitution. Yet, we're all equal under the law, GM and you.**"**

ANALYZING THE CASE STUDY

STEP 1   Examine the Issue

1. Explain Ralph Nader's view of the rights of individuals in our society.
2. What conditions shaped Nader's view?

STEP 2   Gather Evidence

1. What are the specific problems that Ralph Nader addresses?
2. What problems do consumers have when dealing with large organizations?

STEP 3   Consider Alternatives

What actions can individuals take when, for instance, a manufacturer refuses to correct a defect in a product?

STEP 4   Make a Decision

Write a paragraph listing specific actions you can take when a manufacturer refuses to replace a defective product. How could you organize support from others?

The Age of Bureaucracy

by John Lukacs   (1924–   )

Businesses, government agencies, and other organizations establish bureaucracies to handle their work fairly and efficiently. At times, however, the rigid policies, rules, and patterns of organization in bureaucracies result in less efficiency. John Lukacs, a professor of history at Chestnut Hill College in Philadelphia, believes that bureaucracies are found in several aspects of life in the modern world. As you read this selection by Lukacs, consider the effects, both positive and negative, that the bureaucracies of government, business, and educational institutions have on your daily life.

"The United States may have led the world into the democratic age. Yet it is possible that the entire democratic period of history may have been an episode and that the age of aristocracies is followed not by the age of democracy but by the age of bureaucracy. Two hundred years after its birth, the United States has been unable to avoid the degeneration [decline in efficiency] of some of its institutions.

The main source of this decay is the rise of bureaucracy and of the bureaucratic mind . . . .The inclination to administer, to standardize, to regulate, to reorganize, to define—and therefore constrict [limit]—personal activity and private choice is endemic [widespread] in so-called private institutions, corporations, businesses as much as in public ones.

Bureaucratization is constricting not only our channels of production but those of our intellectual commerce. It has affected the American language, which, as late as 50 years ago, was simpler and more direct than English as spoken in England. Americans—sometimes but not always—used to laugh at intellectuals who expressed themselves in complicated terms. Now the relatively uneducated and half-educated often express themselves in long words and surrealistic [unreal] abstractions.

Bureaucratic language, by its very nature, is abstract, lengthy, and vague, wherefore an awful lot of things in this country are now couched in abstractions. This is not merely a matter of esthetics [beauty] or of linguistic purity; it reflects a now widespread sluggishness of mind. The pace at which ideas move—the process whereby even the most reasonable ideas are translated into practice—is disturbingly slow and complex and often impossible.

Large numbers of people adapt their entire personalities to the bureaucratic system—or lack of system. This [situation] is true in almost every field of life, from politics to publishing, from art criticism to corporate business.

Consider the Vietnam War: Whatever its meaning in retrospect, it was the first war in the history of this country—and perhaps of any country—where a great nation slowly slid into a little war through reams of memoranda prepared by the often anonymous governmental and military bureaucracy in Washington.

Or consider when the New Deal began in 1933—and it did contribute to the burgeoning of the governmental bureaucracy—the entire White House staff numbered less than 50. Fifty years later it consisted of 600 or more and this includes only full-time White House employees.

Bureaucratization does not only clog up the movements of life and of mind; it tends to falsify their essence. Here is an example that concerns me deeply:

There is now an appetite for history—for all kinds of history—among the American people that never existed before. We have at least three times as many local historical societies as 40 years ago. Books dealing with history—on all kinds of levels, to be sure—outsell fiction by a very large margin. Novelists such as Mailer and Vidal are obsessed with history. The "documentary"—a new and hybrid [mixed] genre [form]—is more and more widespread on television, in the movies, even in the theater.

Yet this has developed at the very time when the educational bureaucracy—including professional historians—thoughtlessly allowed

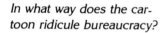
In what way does the cartoon ridicule bureaucracy?

416

the elimination of history courses from our schools and colleges. They did not only go along with what seemed to be "relevant"; they failed to see what was really going on. They contributed to a cultural development that was not only harmful and false but which in the future will give an impression to historians of the American people that is wrong.

In sum, the bureaucratization of life restricts the choice before most Americans by making those choices . . . more and more predictable. Yet Americans are not a predictable people. They can reverse some of these bureaucratic tendencies more rapidly than almost any other people in the world.

As Edmund Burke, the first great supporter of American independence, said, "The people should never be regarded as incurable [unchangeable]." For their sake, the repetition of a few antibureaucratic slogans is not enough; what we must have is a healthy skepticism [doubt] about the shibboleths [myths] of "progress."

We must rethink the entire meaning of that word. **99**

From *U.S. News & World Report.*

UNDERSTANDING THE READING

1. Explain how Lukacs uses each of these words to express his opinion about bureaucracies: degeneration, decay, constrict.
2. According to Lukacs, how does the elimination of college history courses show the problems of bureaucracies?
3. Why does Lukacs have hope that bureaucracies will not continue to grow in the future?

Section 1 Review

Understanding Industrialization

1. List and explain three advantages to a society of industrialization.
2. List and explain three disadvantages to a society of industrialization.
3. Why is it difficult for mature economies to continue growing?
4. What are three courses for growth that Rostow suggested? Which would you choose? Why?

Industrialization Today

1. Do you think you are economically better off than your parents? Than your grandparents? Explain your answer, using specific examples.
2. Do you think you are better educated than your parents? Than your grandparents? Explain your answer.
3. List and discuss three problems arising from a job-related move.
4. **Challenge:** What costs were involved in improving your living standard? In providing for your education?
5. **Challenge:** List three resources the United States must import. List three products the United States exports that are necessary to the importing country.

2 Equal Opportunity

SECTION OVERVIEW

Waiting in line at a movie theater or store is frustrating. Generally, however, individuals in the back respect the rights of those ahead of them. Everyone had an equal opportunity to arrive early and be first in line. In the same way, everyone wants a fair chance at economic success. The goal of equal opportunity in all areas—education, employment, housing—has not yet been reached. However, equal opportunity represents an important economic objective. In this section, you will learn why equal opportunity remains an important economic goal.

ECONOMIC VOCABULARY   discrimination

Competition and Discrimination

In the market system, competition answers the basic questions of what, how, for whom, and how much. Competition among producers is for the highest profits. Competition among consumers is for the best goods and services at the lowest prices. Obtaining the highest profits and the best goods at the lowest price are the only motives the market system considers. They are the only motives that are, strictly speaking, economic.

The real world, however, is more complex. Other motives besides profit and value demand consideration. One of the most important motives is prejudice. It often results in discrimination. Discrimination is the act of treating people in different ways on a basis other than individual merit. Discrimination often results in unfair treatment of individuals.

Perhaps the most familiar kind of discrimination is racial. For example, an employer may refuse to hire someone because of that person's race, regardless of skills. The opposite also happens. In order to make up for previous discrimination against the race, an employer can hire a worker because of that worker's race. Employers also may refuse to hire people because of their sex, age, or religion. Finally, employers discriminate when they pay certain kinds of workers less money than others who do the same work.

Discrimination also exists in the product market. People are sometimes denied apartments or credit because of their race, religion, sex, or age. Consumers discriminate when they refuse to buy from people of a different race, religion, or political viewpoint, or when they deliberately buy from those whose beliefs they do share.

Legal Discrimination

Most forms of race and sex discrimination are now illegal in the United States. Laws also prohibit some kinds of discrimination because of age. Not all forms of discrimina-

418

tion are bad, however. By economic reasoning alone, anyone with enough money to buy a car should be allowed to own and drive one. Few of us, though, would want 10-years-olds to drive. Perhaps your uncle owns a shoe store, and you would rather buy shoes from him than from someone else. That preference, too, is a form of discrimination against which no one would want to pass a law.

Another form of discrimination that has wide support in the United States allows people to work at certain jobs only when they have earned a license. All physicians and lawyers, for example, must pass examinations in order to practice their trade. Also licensed are real estate and insurance sellers, teachers, and plumbers. Such discrimination is legal and necessary in order to maintain standards of skill, competency, and safety.

Costs of Discrimination

How does discrimination affect the workings of the market economy? The market system predicts that competition will produce the most efficient mix of resources and the greatest consumer satisfaction. Discrimination of any kind, then, reduces that efficiency and satisfaction. Resources are used and goods and services distributed in different ways. Race and sex discrimination, for example, keep qualified people from contributing to the country's resources. The results are waste and inefficiency. Hiring one's relatives to do work for which they are not qualified results in poor work. Refusing to buy in stores owned by members of a certain race or religion prevents the free movement of goods and services. The result may be higher prices or poorer quality products.

The effects of discrimination are hard to measure precisely. For example, wage rates vary widely among different groups. As a group, men often are better paid than women. In September 1983, the average pretax monthly income was $1,294 for single men and $706 for single women. On average, a woman with a bachelor's degree will earn $523,000 during her lifetime. A man with a bachelor's degree will earn $1,190,000 during his lifetime.

Some wage differences may result from higher levels of training and experience. However, not all of the inequality in wages and salaries results from such differences. Discrimination appears to account for part of the difference. Similarly, discrimination probably is responsible for part of the difference in unemployment rates among different groups.

Unemployment by Sex, Race, Age

Group	Unemployment Rate 1983 (percent)
All workers	10.0
Male	10.0
Female	9.9
White	8.6
Black	20.6
Hispanic	14.0
16–19 years	23.1
20–24 years	14.8
25–34 years	9.7
35–44 years	6.9
45–54 years	5.7
55–64 years	5.4

Explanation

The chart shows the unemployment rate for different groups in the economy.

Chart Skills

1. Which racial or ethnic group had the highest rate of unemployment in 1983?
2. What pattern exists in the unemployment rate of different age groups?

Many people now enjoy equal opportunity in the work place regardless of race or sex.

The economic costs of discrimination were a factor when Congress passed the Civil Rights Law of 1964. This far-reaching law makes several forms of discrimination illegal. One part of the law specifically forbids discrimination on the basis of race, color, religion, sex, or national origin in hiring, promoting, training, and other conditions of employment. In 1967, the law was amended to include a ban on discrimi-

nation on the basis of age against workers between 40 and 70 years old. In addition to outlawing discrimination by employers, the law also forbids discrimination by unions and the government. Ending discrimination promotes equality for all.

The federal agency responsible for enforcing the ban on hiring discrimination is the Equal Employment Opportunity Commission (EEOC). The EEOC also enforces the laws on equal pay for equal work.

REVIEWING THE CONCEPT

Developing Vocabulary

1. Define discrimination.

Mastering Facts

1. How does the market system deal with noneconomic motives?
2. How does discrimination affect people who want to enter any of the professional occupations?
3. How does discrimination affect the working of the market model?
4. Explain how discrimination against people in a society may cause higher prices and a less productive economy.

CASE STUDY

The Gender Gap

Jennifer Szemler, airline pilot, and Grace Clements, riveter—these women work in occupations once closed to women. Today, federal law prohibits discrimination in hiring and pay on the basis of sex. However, an income gender gap, a difference between the wages of men and those of

women, still exists. On the average, women earn 60 cents for every dollar men earn. Does this gap indicate that discrimination against women still exists?

Polly Madenwald, an officer of the International Federation of Business and Professional Women's Clubs, thinks that

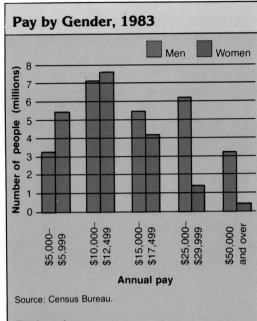

Pay by Gender, 1983

Men ▮ Women ▮

Number of people (millions) — Annual pay

Source: Census Bureau.

Explanation

The bar graph shows the number of men and the number of women at various levels of pay from $5,000 to over $50,000.

Graph Skills

1. Which three categories of pay included the largest number of men?
2. Which category of pay appears to include the highest percentage of men?

women in the United States do not yet have equal opportunity. "Occupations have opened up, but we're not financially better off. We're making less money than we were 20 years ago. We're still at the low end of the wage scale, and a lot of women are not getting as many fringe benefits as men because those are tied to income."

The information in the two charts supports Madenwald's views. More and more women are in jobs once commonly held by men. However, men still dominate high-paying jobs.

Some believe that the gender difference in pay results from the market forces of supply and demand. Women sometimes have less education and experience than men. Also, women may be more likely than men to choose low-paying careers.

Mary Corcoran disagrees with those who blame the income gender gap on the free market. Corcoran, a researcher at the University of Michigan, said: "Women are consistently paid less than men with similar qualifications, even if the women work in occupations where most workers are men." According to Corcoran, differences in education and experience account for less than 35 percent of the income gender gap.

One effort to narrow the income gender gap is the drive to develop a scale comparing different jobs. The scale would give points for, among other things, knowledge and skills, mental demands, accounta-

Jobs by Gender, 1983

Occupation	Percentage of Women, 1970	Percentage of Women, 1980
Nurse	97.4	95.9
Grade school teacher	83.9	75.4
Editor and reporter	40.2	49.3
Real estate agent	32.5	45.2
Lawyer	4.8	13.8
Police officer	3.8	6.0
Carpenter	1.3	1.6

Source: Department of Commerce.

Explanation

The chart shows the percentage of women in seven different occupations in 1970 and 1980.

Chart Skills

1. In which occupations did women hold more than 50 percent of the jobs in 1970? What had happened to the percentage of women in these occupations by 1980? What had happened to the percentage of women in the other occupations?
2. Write a sentence summarizing the changes shown in the chart.

Women are increasingly entering fields traditionally dominated by men.

bility, and working conditions. When the points were added up, jobs with equal totals would be determined to be of comparable worth. Comparable-worth jobs, according to supporters, should have similar pay scales. Low-paying jobs, such as nursing, that employ largely women are worth as much to employers or society as comparable jobs dominated by men, such as plumbing. Therefore, by right and by law they should be paid the same amount. The legal basis for comparable worth is the 1964 Civil Rights Act. This act contains a provision on equal pay for equal work.

A 1982 study in Minnesota found that the mostly female registered nurses, with a rating of 275 points, earned $1,732 per month. The mostly male vocational education teachers also rated 275 points, but they earned $2,260. A female health-program representative with 238 points earned less than a male steam boiler attendant with 156 points. The average entry-level salary for male employees was about the same as the average salary for women who had worked for the state for 20 years.

Many states are taking steps to avoid court battles over comparable worth. The Iowa legislature appropriated $10 million to study and adjust state wage scales. Nearly every state in New England has begun preliminary job-rating studies.

To date, comparable-worth debates have been limited largely to workers in state and local governments. Economists say that supply and demand may force private corporations to match government wages in order to compete for qualified employees. Such competition could force the closing of some businesses earning small profits.

Supporters of comparable worth believe that in view of the skills and responsibility required, teaching, secretarial work, and other traditionally female-occupied jobs are underpaid. Opponents of comparable worth say that fairly comparing different types of work is difficult.

ANALYZING THE CASE STUDY

STEP 1 Define Key Terms

1. Define equal opportunity employment.
2. What is the income gender gap?
3. What is comparable worth?

STEP 2 Gather Evidence

1. In 1982, how many women in the United States earned between $5,000 and $5,999? How many men?
2. Which income category included approximately the same numbers of men and women?
3. How many more men than women earned over $50,000 in 1982?
4. List two occupations in which the per-

centage of women increased almost 10 percent between 1970 and 1980.

STEP 3 Consider the Issues

1. Explain how market forces may cause the income gender gap.
2. Explain how Mary Corcoran views the income gender gap.

STEP 4 Propose a Solution

1. What are the problems of the comparable worth solution?

2. Suggest a way the income gender gap could be closed. List two costs and two benefits of your solution.

STEP 5 Draw a Conclusion

1. Do you believe women have equal opportunity in the United States? Write a paragraph supporting your opinion.
2. Would comparable worth as a solution to the income gender gap in the United States affect traditional ideas about male and female roles? Why or why not?

READING

Racial Discrimination

by Alan Pifer   (1921–   )

Discrimination limits competition in the market. Efforts to ensure equal opportunity have been only partially successful. In this reading, Alan Pifer, president of the Carnegie Corporation of New York, analyzes the continuing economic problems blacks faced in the 1980s. As you read the excerpt, consider how racial discrimination harms the economy.

66 In 1977, I noted in my annual report that opportunities for blacks had increased in the last 15 years. However, I also noted that there had been extensive failure measured against the nation's highest ideals. I tried to discover the reasons for this and what could be done about it. I ended my report by asking the nation to revive the moral vision of the 1960s and to recognize that it is in the self-interest of all Americans to make this vision become reality. Some say that racial discrimination is not an important issue any longer. They believe that the way is now fully open for individual blacks, solely through motivation and merit, to earn their place in the sun.

In short, it appears that the very successes that blacks can point to with pride are working against them. These successes provide a convenient excuse to pull back on efforts to ensure equal opportunity for blacks and for weakening strict laws protecting their rights.

Now, my assessment of black economic progress, sad to say, is somewhat gloomier; progress continues, but there are clear indications of a worsening situation for the black poor.

Many blacks are now in offices and holding managerial positions.

On the brighter side, blacks as a group, by almost all measures of economic change, have continued until very recently to make steady gains. They have improved their educational attainment and employment status at a faster rate than have whites. In addition, the occupational distribution of blacks continues to become more diversified. Greater numbers of blacks are competing successfully for prestige jobs in the managerial and professional occupations. As a result, college-educated blacks have achieved virtual income equality with their white counterparts. The average income of all black males [in the United States] has reached about 77 percent that of white males, and black women now earn incomes equal to white women.

The most dangerous signs for the future, however, concern the condition of lower-income black families. The income gap between black and white families, after narrowing to less than 39 percent in 1969, has widened to 43 percent. Black family income has been affected more seriously than white by the heavy loss of jobs in the cities. It has also been affected by the increase of white women into the labor force. Whether white women are in direct competition with blacks is debatable, but there is no doubt that their wages have raised the income levels of white families compared with black, where two or more workers have traditionally existed. Furthermore, the percentage of black males without work continues to be very high. Of the black children living in poverty, most are in families without a working father.

These figures are frightening. They reveal a widening gap in income between upper- and lower-income blacks. In a recent issue of *Ebony* magazine, the editors made clear their belief that unless significant change occurs, a growing [division] between the black ghetto resident and the black college graduate is likely to result. Whether this is so, I am in no position to judge. I only know that, however one analyzes the problem and its causes or cures, there is a group of blacks at the core of urban life who have been untouched by the civil rights movement, who have not benefited from affirmative action or antidiscrimination laws, who will be bypassed in the next economic boom, who are isolated and largely alienated and forgotten except when incidents of [racial] violence command our attention.

The next decade will be a critical time for black progress. It will require continued vigilance and organized pressure by blacks and their white allies just to sustain the gains of the recent past. At the same time, attention must now also be paid to that segment of the black population which remains totally excluded from the good life and which presents, as I suggested, both a moral and practical danger to the well-being of the society of which we are all a part. It is vital that we develop the analyses, the language, and the leadership that can arouse once more a sense of collective and individual responsibility to help those less fortunate than ourselves. That was the hallmark of the 1960s. It is in our national self-interest to do so.**"**

From *Vital Speeches of the Day.*

UNDERSTANDING THE READING

1. What evidence does Alan Pifer use to suggest that discrimination in the United States has lessened?
2. According to Pifer, what division between socioeconomic groups of blacks is developing?
3. What problems do poor blacks continue to face?
4. Why does Pifer conclude that equal opportunity is a matter of self-interest for all Americans?

Section 2 Review

Understanding Equal Opportunity

1. Explain how hiring a worker can be a discriminatory act.
2. Explain why the economy of the United States would be more efficient if discrimination were ended.
3. Give three examples of discrimination that are acceptable to most people.

Equal Opportunity Today

1. Do you think society discriminates economically against children? Adolescents? Explain your answer.
2. Does the United States government support some forms of economic discrimination? Explain your answer.
3. List three jobs that you think should require a license for a worker. Give reasons for your opinion.
4. **Challenge:** Give evidence of age discrimination in the economy. Summarize the arguments for and against age discrimination. Which opinion do you support? Why do you support it?
5. **Challenge:** Explain three steps you could take if you thought you were a victim of a form of discrimination.

3 Equity and Efficiency

SECTION OVERVIEW

Imagine that the economic system could be made either more fair or more efficient. The system could not be both fair and efficient. Which would you choose? First, you would have to decide exactly what was meant by fairness and efficiency. Then, you would have to consider how increasing one would influence the other. For example, making the economy more efficient might make it less fair. Or, making it more fair might make it less efficient. In reality, fairness and efficiency are two important economic goals. Like other economic goals, they are sometimes in conflict. In this section, you will learn how the economy tries to achieve both equity and efficiency.

ECONOMIC VOCABULARY

equity   technical efficiency   economic efficiency   cost–benefit ratio

Economic Goals

A nation pursues many goals. Some of the economic goals pursued in the United States, have been freedom, efficiency, equity, full employment, stability, and economic growth. How countries use their resources to pursue such goals is a question economists study. One of the things they have learned is that conflicts are inevitable.

Take, for example, two of the goals, equity and efficiency. Equity means equal, or just. An action is equitable when it conforms to a group's ideas about what is just or fair. If two boys spend their summer mowing lawns, and each does as much work as the other, they will think it fair to evenly divide their earnings. If one of the partners provides the power mower and pays for the gas, the two probably will agree that in fairness the first boy will get more money than the second.

What Is Efficiency?

Efficiency means at least two things. First, technical efficiency is using the least amount of resources to produce the best product. Put another way, efficiency means getting the most production possible from a given amount of resources. For example, the boys in the mowing business may decide that their power mower burns too much gas. By trading it in for a mower with a more efficient engine, they will use fewer resources—gasoline—to produce the same amount of work.

Second, economic efficiency means that, over the long run, the benefits of an economic activity are greater than its costs. Put another way, the cost–benefit ratio is favorable. A cost–benefit ratio is a comparison between the costs and the benefits of an action. For example, a lawn-mowing business is economically efficient if, at the end of the summer, the total amount of money earned is greater than the costs of buying the mower, paying for gas, cleaning and repairing tools, and so on. The cost–benefit ratio is favorable.

Sometimes, the two goals of equity and efficiency conflict with each other. Suppose that one of the boys in the lawn-mowing business was hurt in an accident and could not work. How should the profits be divided at the end of the summer? Should the boy who was injured get any of the money? He helped set up the business. He was ready to work, and would have worked hard if he had not been injured. Nevertheless, he did none of the mowing. If he received some of the profits, the boy who did the actual work would have less money. He could not, therefore, buy shovels to set up a winter snow-shoveling business. The money the lawn-mowing business produced would thus not be used efficiently. To deny the injured boy any of the money earned during the summer would go against many people's ideas of fairness, however.

This problem could be multiplied many times over throughout the whole country. For example, the old and the seriously disabled may not be able to contribute much to the nation's economy. If the real economy were exactly like the market model, those who could not contribute would not receive anything. In other words, in the market model the people who could not support themselves might not survive. In the real economy, considerations of equity have led the government to provide support for such people. These might take the form of food stamps or welfare payments. Most Americans have solved the conflict between equity and efficiency by deciding that they would rather not live in a totally competitive economic system. They do not think the competitive market system is fair or humane.

Not everyone agrees on what equity and efficiency mean. For example, some people do not think that it is fair for those who do not contribute to be supported by those who do. Furthermore, not everyone agrees on what is the most efficient way to use resources.

Making Tradeoffs

Countries must always make tradeoffs. Governments must decide how much of one goal they are willing to give up to achieve some part of another goal. For example, fairness might mean raising taxes to provide money for those who are out of work. Yet, higher taxes could stop firms from expanding their operations. Then jobs might be scarcer. At some point, therefore, the country would be forced to reach a compromise between total fairness and total efficiency. Such decisions are never

To avoid the high cost of hospitalization, tradeoffs must be made. Fewer hospital staff, as well as more treatment in clinics and doctors' offices are some tradeoffs that can be made.

easy. They always mean that some people will be better off and some people worse off than they were before the decision.

REVIEWING THE CONCEPT

Developing Vocabulary

1. Is equity the same as equality? Give examples to demonstrate how they are alike or different.
2. What is the difference between technical efficiency and economic efficiency?

3. Give an example of a favorable cost–benefit ratio.
4. Give an example of an unfavorable cost–benefit ratio.

Mastering Facts

1. How do national goals affect the country's economy?
2. What is the relationship between technical efficiency and a cost–benefit ratio?
3. How does the market system provide for society's nonproducers?

Equal Pay for Teenagers

One question of equity that directly affects high school students is the minimum wage law. The minimum wage is part of the Fair Labor Standards Act, which Congress passed in 1938. According to this law, workers must be paid a minimum amount of money per hour. Since 1981, the minimum wage has been $3.35. A full-time worker being paid the minimum hourly wage would earn $6,700 per year.

Some people argue in favor of a subminimum wage for people under 18 years of age. Supporters of the subminimum wage say that it is inefficient to make businesses pay $3.35 for workers who lack experience, may not produce $3.35 per hour in value, and are learning on the job.

Two individuals who disagree on this issue are Walter E. Williams, professor of economics at Temple University, and Sol C. Chaikin, president of the International Ladies' Garment Workers Union.

Walter E. Williams argues for a subminimum wage for teenagers that is 30 to 40 percent less than the adult minimum wage. Williams claims that employers have little incentive to pay a teenager $3.35 per hour when that worker can produce only $2 per hour in goods or services. Many youths lack experience and skills, and cannot work as productively as adults. Williams claims that teenage unemployment increases each time the minimum wage is raised and the number of jobs the minimum wage covers is expanded.

According to Williams, a subminimum wage for teenagers would benefit the public. Ineffective youth employment programs, paid by tax dollars, could be discontinued. Williams believes that the costly programs have done little to alleviate the high youth unemployment rate. In addition, more young people would get early work experience. They would learn how to

428

Some teenagers find employment as laborers, as these two who are doing yardwork.

get jobs, how to maintain a work routine, and how to perform as part of a work force.

Sol C. Chaikin opposes a subminimum wage for teenagers. Chaikin claims that no basis exists for the argument that an increase in the minimum wage increases teenage unemployment. Nor does he think that a subminimum wage would create additional jobs for young people. Chaikin believes that teenage unemployment is related to the health of the general economy. When the economy is growing and the market for the products of business is expanding, employment of both older workers and teenagers rises.

Chaikin supports a single minimum wage, although he thinks that the present minimum wage is low. He claims that the minimum wage makes up a smaller proportion of the average industrial wage today than in the 1950s. Industrial workers' wages have increased because of inflationary pressures, but the minimum hourly wage has not kept pace.

Chaikin believes that a subminimum wage for teenagers would create another problem. An employer might hire people 17 to 18 years of age, and then fire them when they qualified for the minimum wage. The employer could then hire other 17-year-olds at the subminimum wage.

ANALYZING THE CASE STUDY

STEP 1   Define the Issue

1. Explain what is meant by a subminimum wage for workers.
2. How does a subminimum wage relate to the issue of equity? Discrimination?

STEP 2   Consider the Arguments

1. List three points Williams uses to argue for a subminimum wage. Identify each as fact or opinion.
2. List three points Chaikin uses to oppose a subminimum wage. Identify each as fact or opinion.

STEP 3   Weigh the Consequences

Make a chart listing the advantages and disadvantages of a subminimum wage.

STEP 4   Make a Decision

Do you support or oppose a subminimum wage? Give at least two reasons to support your answer.

Justice and Growth

by Robert Reich

The balance between equity and efficiency affects everyone in an economy. If the wages of workers in grocery stores were cut in half, the grocery industry would be more efficient but less equitable. Robert Reich thinks that equity and efficiency are not always in conflict. Reich, an economist for the Federal Trade Commission, believes that some nations are better than the United States in providing both. As you read this excerpt, ask yourself how achieving both goals will benefit you.

"By any measure, the economies of Sweden, Germany, and Japan outperformed ours between 1971 and 1981. Even though they are more dependent on imported oil than we are, their productivity increased at a faster rate. Their levels of unemployment also remained lower. Citizens in these countries are likely to enjoy a higher standard of living than our own citizens during the 1980s.

This growth has been accomplished along with, not in opposition to, social justice. The distribution of income in these countries is more equitable than it is in the United States. The poorest people in these countries receive a larger share of their nation's output than do the poor in the United States. The gap between the highest-paid and the lowest-paid workers is smaller in these three countries than in the United States. Swedish, Japanese, and West German executives earn only about 40 to 60 percent more money than the lowest-paid workers in their companies. In the United States it is not unusual for executives to take home three times the pay of the lowest-paid workers. Some five-year pacts for corporate officials run to $8 million or more.

Social security and unemployment insurance are more generous in Sweden, Japan, and West Germany than they are in the United States.

In addition, employees have more job security and better working conditions abroad. In Sweden, Japan, and West Germany workers cannot be fired arbitrarily; yet the vast majority of United States employees can be dismissed without notice or reason. Employees in these countries are less likely to miss work because of a strike or other type of dispute with management. Workers in all three other countries participate in management decision-making through various types of committees. In the United States there is little opportunity for labor participation in management.

Nor have these countries sacrificed health, safety, and the environment in pursuit of growth and productivity. Unlike the United States, each has a substantial national health insurance program, financed by government and industry. Infant mortality (a measure of public health) is substantially lower in Sweden, Japan, and West Germany than it is in the United States. Industrial accidents per 100,000 people are fewer in

Equity and Growth in Four Countries 1982

Category	Sweden	West Germany	Japan	United States
Income received by poorest 10% of population (percent)	2.4	2.9	3.2	1.5
National income spent on social security (percent)	20.1	19.9	9.7	9.3
Unemployed workers receiving compensation (percent)	90.0	75.0	59.0	58.0
Workers in unions (percent)	83.0	40.0	40.0	21.0
Days of labor lost because of strikes and industrial disputes per 1,000 workers	39	56	244	1,349
Average number of vacation weeks per year	5	4	4	2.5
Infant mortality rate per 1,000 live births	8	9	8.9	14.1
Industrial accidents per 100,000 workers	2.4	2.5	3.7	3.1
Total population in 1983 (millions)	8.331	61.543	119.205	234.193
Life expectancy at birth (years)	NA	73	76	74
Adult illiteracy (percent)	0.5	0.5	0.5	0.5
GNP per capita in 1980 (1979 dollars)	13,032	12,485	8,946	10,408
Taxes in 1981 (percent of GNP)	51.3	37.3	26.9	31.2
Tax revenues per capita in 1981 (1981 dollars)	6,933	4,133	2,634	3,832

Source: *Statistical Abstract of the United States* and *The New Republic*.   NA, not available.

Explanation

The chart compares the performance of four industrial nations in eight categories. The categories reflect the distribution of wealth, the degree of cooperation between labor and management, and the general health of the society.

Chart Skills

1. What percentage of unemployed workers receive compensation in Sweden?
2. Does the chart suggest that high union membership increases the problem of strikes? Explain.

Sweden and West Germany than in the United States, although Japan's record is worse than ours in this regard. And environmental regulation in each of these countries is at least as strict as it is now in the United States. The environments of these countries are less contaminated by carbon monoxide, hydrocarbons, and nitrogen oxides than ours.

How have our international competitors managed to achieve unparalleled growth and social justice? In advanced industrial countries productivity and economic growth depend not so much on overall level of investment as upon how investment is used. Within complex industrial systems there are so many potential critical transactions that the amount of resources available for investment may be less important than how the investment is directed and absorbed. Put simply, the organization of an advanced economy can encourage productivity in two ways. One way is to channel investment into industries or processes capable of yielding high output. The other is to generate high morale and motivation in the work force. Productivity can be discouraged by doing the opposite.

Is social justice necessary to productivity in an advanced industrial economy? That is the central question that we must begin to address in earnest. **"**

From *The New Republic*.

Japan's industrial success is due to the harmony in the workplace.

UNDERSTANDING THE READING

1. What evidence does Robert Reich offer to show that Japan, Germany, and Sweden are more equitable than the United States?
2. How does equity promote efficiency?
3. Suggest two ways in which the United States can increase both its equity and its efficiency.

Section 3 Review

Understanding Equity and Efficiency

1. Do equity and efficiency conflict? Explain your answer.
2. Does the minimum wage affect teenage employment? Explain.
3. **Challenge:** Many people argue that increasing environmental regulation decreases economic growth and productivity. What evidence in the reading contradicts this argument?

Equity and Efficiency Today

1. Do you think a minimum wage has an inflationary effect on the economy? Why or why not?
2. Suggest two ways to improve the economy of the United States. Explain how each change that you suggested would affect the equity and efficiency of the American economy. How would each change affect you?

Americans
at Work

Meet Nino Guidici
Pharmacist

Nino Guidici worked 40 years as a pharmacist in a drugstore in Chicago. Studs Terkel interviewed Nino Guidici for his book, *Working*. In this excerpt from that book, Nino Guidici talks about the changes he has observed in the pharmacy business over his long career.

"The corner drugstore, that's kinda fadin' now. The small store is on its way out. Can't do the volume. In the old days they took druggists as doctors . . . All we do [now] is count pills . . . Today was a little out of the ordinary. I made an ointment. Most of the ointments come already made up. Doctors used to write their own formulas and we made most of these things. Most of the work is now done in the laboratory. The real druggist is found in the manufacturing firms . . . We just get the name of the drugs and the number and the directions. It's a lot easier. You used to fill maybe twenty, twenty-five prescriptions a day by hand. Nowadays you can fill about 150. . . .

In the old days we just used simple drugs . . . but it's got so highly developed . . . I like it better this way. If you had to make up everything and the physician had to write down a prescription with all the ingredients, you could hardly exist in this economy. Everything is faster, it's better. People wouldn't get relief out of medicine in them days like they get today.

In the days I went to pharmacy school, you only went two years. Now it's six. . . . The young ones [now] know a lot more chemistry . . . they're prepared to go to the manufacturing end of it. . . . When I first started out, you dispensed very little medicine for children after they were seven or eight . . . [now] we fill a lot of ointments for 'em. We sell a lot more cosmetics than we did.**"**

Pharmacies have long been a part of the business scene in America.

ECONOMIC

Protecting Your Employment Rights

Discrimination has always been a part of the economy of the United States. Virtually every minority group—German, Irish, Polish, Chinese, black, Hispanic—has been the victim of unfair treatment. Until the 1950s, laws often upheld unequal treatment of ethnic and racial groups and women.

Now, discrimination is clearly illegal, although it has not ended. Equal employment opportunity is a national goal. According to the law, everyone has an equal opportunity to get a job. However, in practice some problems still exist. People need to protect their employment rights.

Minority and Female Employment, 1982

Occupation	Percentage of Minorities	Percentage of Women	Occupation	Percentage of Minorites	Percentage of Women
All occupations	11.6	42.8	File clerk	22.9	83.8
Accountant	9.9	38.5	Secretary	7.2	99.1
Computer programmer	10.4	29.4	Carpenter	5.8	1.9
Engineer	7.3	4.4	Auto mechanic	8.9	0.6
Lawyer	4.6	14.1	Baker	13.3	41.5
Dentist	6.2	4.6	Textile worker	26.7	61.0
Physician	14.5	13.7	Taxicab driver	28.7	9.8
Nurse	12.3	96.8	Private household worker	32.4	96.5
Economist	6.9	25.0	Cook	19.7	51.9
Teacher	10.1	70.6	Police officer	10.7	5.7
Bank official	5.5	37.5	Farm laborer	15.1	15.9
Insurance agent	6.2	23.9	Fire fighter	8.9	0.9

Source: Bureau of Labor Statistics.

Explanation

The chart shows the percentage of jobs in various occupations held by members of minority groups and women. Women make up approximately 45 percent of the labor force; minorities constitute about 20 percent of the labor force. Minority groups include blacks, Hispanics, Asian-Americans, and others.

Chart Skills

1. Which three occupations include the highest percentage of minorities? The lowest?
2. Which three occupations include the highest percentage of women? The lowest?
3. Do you believe that minorities and women are discriminated against in the area of employment? Explain your answer.

STEP 1   Know Your Rights

The major law that protects your right to equal opportunity is the Civil Rights Act of 1964. Your right to equal opportunity is the right to be judged solely on your ability to perform a job. In addition to the right to equal opportunity in hiring, your rights include equal opportunities for training, promotion, and pay. Employers must give all employees equal chances to improve their situation after they are hired. According to a 1963 law, people who do equal work and have equal backgrounds must receive equal pay.

STEP 2   Look for Equal Opportunity

According to the law, all employers must provide equal opportunity in hiring and promoting workers. Many employers advertise their support for the law by stating in their help-wanted notices that they are an "equal opportunity employer." Such employers are likely to be aware of their duties under the law.

Many employers today have established affirmative action plans. These employers attempt to find qualified minorities and women to fill openings in job categories dominated by whites and males. Businesses accepting large contracts with the federal government are required to have affirmative action plans. In order to check on their success in attracting a wide variety of applicants, companies often request information on the sex, race, and age of applicants for jobs.

STEP 3   Report Suspected Violations

If you suspect that you have not received fair treatment, you should contact your local EEOC office or the national office, at 2401 E Street NW, Washington, D.C. 20506. In most cases, charges must be filed within 180 days of the incident. The EEOC will investigate the complaint to determine whether reasonable cause exists to believe that discrimination has occurred. When possible, the EEOC settles the dispute through negotiation between the worker and the employer. If the EEOC investigation indicates that a law was broken, the agency may file a lawsuit in federal court. However, cases involving discrimination are often hard to settle. People disagree on what traits actually are required for a job. Further, proving discrimination is difficult.

ECONOMIC SKILLS TODAY

1. When were laws to protect the right to equal employment opportunity passed in the United States?
2. What events or changes motivated Congress to pass these laws?
3. What are affirmative action plans? Who benefits from such plans? What are the costs involved in such plans?
4. What would you do if you thought your employment rights were violated?

Enrichment Activity

One limit to equal opportunity for all is attitude: certain jobs are considered "men's work" and other jobs "women's work." To learn whether attitudes have changed, compare 10 magazine ads from 1960 with 10 current advertisements that show people at work. Do you see evidence in the ads that attitudes toward equal opportunity have changed since 1960?

CHAPTER SUMMARY

Industrialization

As societies become industrialized, the overall quality of life improves and leisure time increases. However, new problems also develop. Work on assembly lines is monotonous, and workers lose some of their sense of identity. Transfers to new locations disrupt lives. Important job skills today may be unnecessary in the future. Industrialization increases specialization, and countries depend on one another for some necessary goods. Industrialization also uses up supplies of natural resources and pollutes the atmosphere.

Equal Opportunity

Equal employment opportunity for all is a national goal. Discrimination inteferes with this goal. Enforcing laws against discrimination is difficult. The results of discrimination are waste and inefficiency.

Equity and efficiency

The national goals of equity and efficiency sometimes conflict. Countries must make tradeoffs between these goals. In the United States, considerations of equity have led the government to provide support for many people who cannot contribute much to the nation's economy.

CRITICAL THINKING QUESTIONS

Industrialization

1. Bring to class at least three pictures that illustrate different problems of industrialization. Explain how each picture illustrates the problem. What could you change in these pictures to indicate improvements.
2. **Challenge:** Some countries have tried to improve working conditions for assembly line workers. Write a paragraph suggesting several ways to improve assembly line work.

Equal Opportunity

1. How do noneconomic motives distort the market system? Give examples.
2. In a market system, what factors would determine the employment of a woman? An individual in a wheelchair? A minority worker?
3. **Challenge:** The United States has made some tradeoffs to make up for or eliminate discrimination. Give some specific examples of these tradeoffs.

Equity and Efficiency

1. Describe two situations in which equity and efficiency conflict. How would you resolve the conflict?
2. **Challenge:** Would you prefer to live in a totally competitive economic system? Why or why not?

DEVELOPING ECONOMIC SKILLS

1. How did the percentage of blacks, Indians, and Orientals in the total work force change between 1970 and 1980?
2. In 1980, which groups of workers formed a higher percentage of the total work force than of the manager group?
3. During which year did the number of managers in each category more closely reflect the entire work force? What

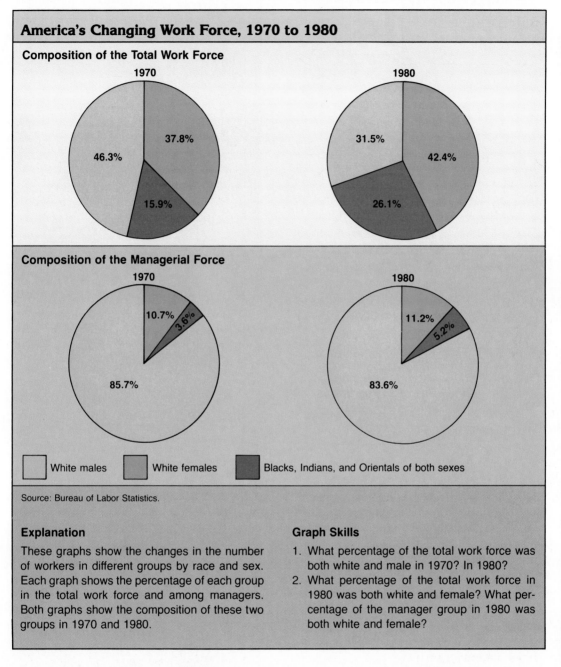

America's Changing Work Force, 1970 to 1980

Composition of the Total Work Force

1970

37.8%
46.3%
15.9%

1980

31.5%
42.4%
26.1%

Composition of the Managerial Force

1970

10.7%
3.6%
85.7%

1980

11.2%
5.2%
83.6%

☐ White males   ☐ White females   ■ Blacks, Indians, and Orientals of both sexes

Source: Bureau of Labor Statistics.

Explanation

These graphs show the changes in the number of workers in different groups by race and sex. Each graph shows the percentage of each group in the total work force and among managers. Both graphs show the composition of these two groups in 1970 and 1980.

Graph Skills

1. What percentage of the total work force was both white and male in 1970? In 1980?
2. What percentage of the total work force in 1980 was both white and female? What percentage of the manager group in 1980 was both white and female?

change in the economy between 1970 and 1980 does this situation suggest?

APPLYING ECONOMICS TODAY

1. Affirmative action refers to the deliberate policy of recruiting, training, and promoting members of groups that have been discriminated against in the past. Attack or defend the following statement: "Affirmative action is nothing more than a new form of discrimination. The minorities should not get any favorable treatment and should pull themselves up by their own bootstraps like everybody else."

1 Energy

Objective: *to understand the importance of oil and other forms of energy in the industrialized economy*

2 Cities

Objective: *to understand how economic reasoning can help identify urban problems and evaluate solutions to improve city life*

3 The Environment

Objective: *to understand and evaluate the economic issues involved in protecting the environment*

1 Energy

SECTION OVERVIEW

People use energy every day—for electricity, heat, and transportation. Production of the items you take for granted—food, clothes, and appliances—requires energy. Fuel supplies the energy to operate factories, light offices, heat buildings, and run vehicles. The United States and other highly industrialized countries import large quantities of fuel. Any change in the price or supply of fuel affects the entire economy. In this section, you will learn how important oil and other sources of energy are to the economy.

ECONOMIC VOCABULARY

fossil fuels   solar energy   embargo   cartel   gasohol

Sources of Energy

Throughout history, people have developed various sources of energy to help them do their work and improve their living conditions. One of the first forms of energy that people used was fire. Later, wind and water supplied energy for transportation and simple machinery. Domestic animals provided energy to pull plows and wagons. The inventions of the steam engine, electricity, and the gasoline engine introduced new stages in energy development and increased productivity. Recently, nuclear energy has begun to contribute to the productivity of the economy.

Since the invention of the steam engine, societies have depended on fossil fuels to supply energy. Fossil fuels, such as coal, oil, and natural gas, developed from the remains of prehistoric plants and animals. Today, fossil fuels supply 97 percent of the world's energy needs. The amount of fossil fuel people burn has nearly doubled every 20 years since 1900. Such rapid consumption of this type of energy may exhaust the world's supply of fossil fuels. Engineers predict that oil will become scarce in the early 2000s and the earth's natural gas reserves will be exhausted within about 30 years. Coal, the most plentiful fossil fuel, is expected to last another 300 to 400 years.

Sources other than fossil fuels fill some of the world's energy needs. For example, water power provides about 2 percent of the world's energy and 4 percent of the energy used in the United States. Solar energy, given off by the sun, is used in some places to heat homes and generate electricity. Winds, tides, and the heat of the earth's interior are among other sources of energy people use today.

The Importance of Oil

The United States uses one-third of the world's total energy output. Almost half of this energy comes from oil. Oil is easier to obtain, transport, and burn than coal. For

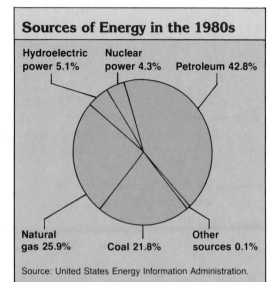

Sources of Energy in the 1980s

Hydroelectric power 5.1%
Nuclear power 4.3%
Petroleum 42.8%
Natural gas 25.9%
Coal 21.8%
Other sources 0.1%

Source: United States Energy Information Administration.

Explanation

The pie graph illustrates the six major sources of energy in the United States in 1980s.

Graph Skills

1. What is the chief source of energy in the United States?
2. How might this graph have looked in 1940? In 1900?

many years the United States was able to supply its own growing petroleum needs. However, by World War II American energy demands had expanded so much that the nation had begun to rely on foreign sources of oil. Today, the United States ranks as the second largest producer of petroleum in the world. Only the Soviet Union produces more. Nevertheless, the United States still must import a large amount of oil because of its huge demand.

The outbreak of war between Israel and the Arab states in 1973 and revolutionary upheaval in Iran during 1979 disrupted the flow of oil from the Middle East. The two developments made clear the economic importance of oil. These two developments in the Middle East also illustrate the economic problems that can result from a nation's dependence on imports.

The Rise of OPEC

Since 1970, major problems for the United States have developed in obtaining imported oil. The largest oil-exporting area is the Middle East. Nations there that export oil include Saudi Arabia, Iran, Iraq, Kuwait, the United Arab Emirates, and Libya. Saudi Arabia is the leading supplier.

In 1950, the oil-producing countries began to raise prices. Then, in 1960, middle eastern oil-producing countries formed the Organization of Petroleum Exporting Countries, or OPEC, a cartel. A cartel is a group of industrial businesses, often operating in different countries, that combine to control the price, production, and sale of a commodity. A cartel acts in the same manner as a monopoly. The membership of OPEC, a cartel formed to control oil, has

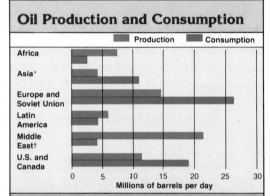

Oil Production and Consumption

Production Consumption

Africa
Asia*
Europe and Soviet Union
Latin America
Middle East†
U.S. and Canada

0 5 10 15 20 25 30
Millions of barrels per day

Source: *The Americans.* *Excludes Soviet Union and Middle East.
†Excludes Egypt and the Sudan.

Explanation

The graph shows the difference between the production and consumption of oil in areas around the world.

Graph Skills

1. Which geographic area imports the most oil? The least?
2. Which geographic area exports the most oil? The least?
3. Which areas produce more oil than they consume?

grown to include several nations outside the Middle East.

For many years, OPEC members quarreled among themselves and did little to control oil prices. After the Arab–Israeli war began in 1973, however, the Arab producers united to impose an embargo on sales to many of the countries that had supported Israel. An embargo is a government order prohibiting or restricting a country's exports or imports. The price per barrel of oil almost doubled between 1973 and 1974. Oil-exporting nations increased their earnings from $40 million in 1973 to $120 million in 1974.

In late 1979, the price jumped again as a result of an Iranian revolution. Iran, which produces 10 percent of the world's oil supply, became hostile to some Western nations. The new government in Iran reduced production and raised the price of its oil. The outbreak of a war between Iran and Iraq and the destruction of refineries and terminals jeopardized oil exports from the Persian Gulf region. Anticipated shortages helped keep prices high. Industrial nations that rely on oil could only buy OPEC oil at the new, higher prices.

The Effects of OPEC

The rapid rise in oil prices concerned Western nations for two reasons. First, economists were afraid that the money oil exporting countries earned would not be invested in the West. A break in the circular flow of money between consumers and producers in the world economy could cause a breakdown in the world trading system. Second, the higher cost of energy would burden the economies of not only the industrialized world but also the developing countries.

During this period, however, the world trading system did not break down. OPEC nations spent their oil money on development projects and imports. The income that OPEC nations received for their oil was rapidly spent or invested in the industrialized world. Yet, the increased price of oil has significantly affected the economies of industrialized nations. Increases in the price of oil led to three economic consequences.

First, since oil is an important factor in the production of goods and services, the high oil price led to increases in many of their prices, thereby causing inflation. Inflation decreased demand because consumers were not always willing to pay the higher prices.

Second, individuals, businesses, and the government initiated measures for conserving fuel. Consumers purchased smaller cars and drove less. The United States

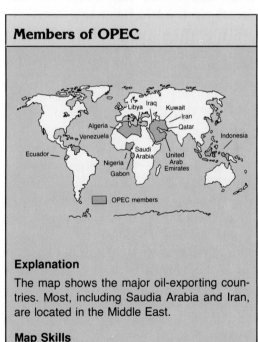

Members of OPEC

Explanation

The map shows the major oil-exporting countries. Most, including Saudia Arabia and Iran, are located in the Middle East.

Map Skills

1. Name the 13 OPEC members.
2. Oil imports to the United States are shipped over a vast distance. What is the approximate distance between the Middle East and the United States?

441

government set a 55-mile-per-hour speed limit on national highways. Cars use less gasoline per mile at this speed than at higher speeds. Many thermostats were set lower. Conservation practices also decreased demand. The nation experienced a recession in 1975. Unlike previous recessions, this one did not end inflation. Economists were at a loss to develop strategies to improve the unusual situation.

A third effect of the huge rise in oil prices was the intensified search for alternative sources of energy. Industrial nations increased their efforts to develop new fuel sources and use substitutes for oil, such as coal. Nuclear power was emphasized. Industries also spent money to develop alternative such sources of energy, as solar power, hydropower, wind-generated power, and gasohol—a fuel made from 10 percent alcohol and 90 percent gasoline. The recession, along with the use of alternative fuels, reduced the flow of dollars and European currencies to OPEC.

Solving the Energy Problem

Three questions must be kept in mind in thinking about meeting energy requirements. First, how should the nation share existing energy supplies? Second, how should the United States seek more fuel supplies and develop new forms of energy? Third, how can the United States answer both of these questions in ways that do not conflict with other economic goals, such as high levels of production and growth?

Sharing energy supplies involves decisions about the price of oil and other fuels, such as coal and natural gas. The price of fuel determines who will get it and how much will be available. The federal government can influence fuel prices by changing its fuel taxes. By increasing or decreasing those taxes, the government can affect the quantity of fuel demanded. As demand changes, so will supply. In addition, through tax credits and other incentives the government can encourage exploration to discover new supplies of fuel and the use of alternative fuels.

The government could ration fuel in order to ensure that everyone would be able to get at least the amount needed to do business, run a car, or heat a home. However, during rationing profits remain low, and companies have little incentive to explore for new sources. In the long run, rationing might bring back the long lines at gas pumps, the closed businesses, and the cold houses of the mid-1970s.

A final problem remains to be solved. How can enough energy be developed to run an industrial economy without ruining the natural environment at the same time?

These coal miners are going to work in a West Virginia coal mine. Like oil, coal is an example of non-renewable energy source.

REVIEWING THE CONCEPT

Developing Vocabulary

1. Name three kinds of fossil fuels.
2. What is a cartel?
3. To an exporting country, what are the economic consequences of an embargo?
4. How does gasohol help to conserve oil?

Mastering Facts

1. What share of the world's total energy output is produced from oil? What sources of energy produce the remaining energy output?
2. What geographic area is the major source of oil today? List four countries in this area.
3. What is OPEC, and why was it formed? What effect does OPEC have on the world's oil supply? What countries are OPEC members?
4. Explain how governments can control the supply and the users of their limited energy sources.

Trash Power

Disposing of society's trash is a big problem in an urban society. Americans throw away hundreds of thousands of tons of garbage each day. As the United States developed from a largely agricultural to an industrial economy, the amount of goods produced greatly increased. In recent years, too, manufacturers have emphasized the production of disposable goods—items used only once or twice and then thrown away.

To most of us, the main problem is carrying the garbage out of the house for the pickup. Beyond that, we think little about it. However, business and government must deal with larger disposal issues.

Traditionally, cities have used a number of methods for disposing of garbage. Many cities use waste as landfill. Others burn it in huge incinerators. For years, New York City hauled garbage out to sea and dumped it. However, these methods often create or add to other problems. Sea dumping creates environmental hazards, and the traditional ways of burning garbage contribute to air pollution. Communities often do not want garbage landfill sites within their vicinity.

Another problem many communities face is the rising cost of energy. Garbage disposal and high energy costs are two separate problems. However, researchers have developed technologies based on using one problem, garbage disposal, to help solve the other, the high cost of energy production.

John M. Kehoe, Jr., senior vice-president of Signal Resco Company, is involved in building plants to produce energy from garbage. "Yes, there is a refuse to energy business," he explained. "Resco has six plants built or planned, representing a total investment of $960 million." The purpose of these plants is to convert garbage into steam. The steam then is used to generate electricity.

The conversion of waste to energy received a boost from the environmental movement of the 1960s, along with a new wave of national interest in conservation. Burning trash to produce energy conserves

Garbage processing centers such as this can convert waste to energy. The energy can generate electricity and help run manufacturing plants.

the nonrenewable fuels, such as gas and oil, normally used to generate electricity.

The number of cities turning garbage into energy has been increasing. In Saugus, Massachusetts, the Signal Resco plant supplies steam to a jet-engine factory, which uses it to generate electricity. Garbage trucks from Boston and 16 other towns haul 1,500 tons of trash to the Saugus plant each day. Signal Resco has another processing center in Pittsfield, Massachusetts, which produces energy for a company manufacturing paper for United States currency. The streetlights and some of the homes and businesses in Columbus, Ohio, use electricity generated by a garbage processing plant. A factory in Miami also burns garbage to produce energy.

In the 1980s, New York and Los Angeles announced plans to build several plants. Some experts predict that by the year 2000, half of the nation's garbage will be used to produce energy. The trash that you and others set out for collection will be converted to electric power for operating all types of lights and appliances.

John Kehoe is optimistic about the economics of garbage as a fuel. "Resco could build plants wherever large volumes of waste must be trucked more than 20 miles." One area he is studying for a possible plant is New Jersey, which has an abundance of industrial waste. Each industrial waste site is a "Kuwait of garbage," he said gleefully.

ANALYZING THE CASE STUDY

STEP 1 Clarify the Issue

1. What is meant by trash?
2. Is trash an appropriate name for waste materials used to produce energy?
3. What did John Kehoe mean when he referred to each industrial waste site as a "Kuwait of garbage"?

STEP 2 Propose Alternatives

1. List five items that you or your family regularly discard as trash. Suggest how each of these items could be recycled.
2. Could any of the items listed in question 1 be used to produce energy?

STEP 3 Evaluate Costs and Benefits

List the economic costs and benefits of using trash to produce energy.

STEP 4 Predict Changes

1. What economic changes would encourage more cities to turn trash to energy?
2. Suggest some actions that the federal government could take to encourage cities to recycle trash.

Enrichment Activity

Find out how other nations use waste products to produce energy. Denmark and India are two nations already extensively involved. What can the United States learn from other nations?

Thinking Soft

from Newsweek

Wherever you go—home, school, or community—energy-consuming machines surround you. The appliances in your home, the heating and lighting in your school, the traffic lights and cars on city streets all require fuel. The demand for energy is constantly rising. Societies must decide how to meet this demand. Physicist Amory Lovins, an American consultant, is one of the world's most influential energy thinkers. He is a member of the Energy Research Advisory Board of the United States Department of Energy. With his wife and colleague, L. Hunter Lovins, he has co-authored many books and technical papers. Both are active in energy policy in about 15 countries, lecturing and consulting for a wide range of groups. A London resident, Lovins has served as the British representative of the Friends of the Earth Inc. since 1971. This excerpt from *Newsweek* explains Lovins's controversial views on energy.

66 **L** ovins's basic thesis is that the hard energy path—a growing reliance on huge centralized electric-power systems that depend on fossil fuels and nuclear energy—is inefficient and dangerous. Lovins also believes hard energy is inappropriate to United States energy needs. Instead, he argues, the nation should embark on a soft energy path. Countries should reduce their massive energy appetite through "technical fixes" that can cut energy waste in half. What energy requirements after reductions in use remain should be filled with flexible and harmless power sources such as solar and wind energy, *biomass* conversion (producing liquid fuels from farm and forestry wastes) and *cogeneration* (using industrial waste heat to generate electricity).

"I start by asking what are we trying to do with all this energy and what is the best way to do each job," Lovins explains. What he finds, he says, is an economy that burns 29 percent of its fossil fuels to produce its highest-grade form of energy, electricity. However, all but 8 percent of power requirements could be filled by lower-grade fuels. This is "superfluous, wasteful and expensive," he wrote in an essay in *Foreign Affairs,* "like cutting butter with a chain saw."

Electricity is increasingly expensive to generate—demanding a capital investment so huge it could cripple the economy. Growing dependence on highly centralized, complex power systems, Lovins says, makes the society ever more open to damage and disruption. "A small fault or a few discontented people become able to turn off a country," he notes. At the same time, individuals will find themselves increasingly at the mercy of "an alien, remote and perhaps . . . uncontrollable technological elite." The result could be a loss of civil liberties and the rise of "friendly fascism."

445

A solar home is an example of soft energy. Soft energy could replace today's highly centralized power systems.

The soft path, on the other hand, poses none of these dangers, Lovins insists. "It can be understood and controlled by the people who depend on it." Soft energy relies on a number of simple (though sophisticated), labor-intensive technologies. Neighborhood rooftop solar collectors would replace huge, remote power stations. "Fluidized-bed" boilers that can burn everything from coal to garbage cleanly would replace giant coal-conversion plants. Since the soft path would not use nuclear power, he argues, "it is the only way to come up with an intellectually consistent nonproliferation policy."

Lovins maintains that technologies on which the soft path depends are already available. He believes that the transition could be made within the next 50 years without forcing major social changes. What's crucial, he says, is that the transition begin soon—before the hard path's momentum ends all other options.

Lovins came to energy policy by way of climatology, the science dealing with climates, after an education that included studies in music, classics, law and experimental physics at Harvard and Oxford. His only formal degree is a Master of Arts from Oxford, which has led some to question his qualifications as a scientist. "He's impressed a lot of people who don't know anything about energy and depressed a lot of people who do," says one oil executive. Specifically, critics insist that Lovins has overestimated the costs of hard technology, while underestimating the costs of soft. They also claim that many of the soft technologies Lovins touts are actually years away from availability.

Still, Lovins's basic thesis has yet to be disproved, and his influence is widening daily. His essay in *Foreign Affairs* broke the record for reprint requests within a year of publication. And many of its readers are influential enough to act on its recommendations. Indeed, the day after he talked with Lovins, President Carter told an international energy conference that the world should consider alternatives to nuclear power. While it would take a capital investment of $200,000 to $300,000 to produce a nuclear-energy capacity equivalent to one barrel of oil, Carter noted,

446

"recent studies I have read show that we can gain the equivalent of a barrel of oil per day by conservation at very little or no cost." The author of those studies: Amory Lovins. **99**

From Newsweek.

UNDERSTANDING THE READING

1. On what kinds of energy sources does a hard energy policy rely? A soft energy policy?
2. Switching to the soft path to energy might involve what economic costs? Economic benefits?
3. What social considerations are involved in choosing between hard and soft energy policies?
4. What political considerations are involved in a hard energy policy?
5. To what was Lovins referring when he argued that taking the soft path "is the only way to come up with an intellectually consistent nonproliferation policy?"

Section 1 Review

Understanding Energy

1. What share of the world's total energy output does the United States consume?
2. What two factors contributed to United States reliance on imported oil?
3. Why did the price of oil rise in the 1970s?
4. What two major concerns did the rapid rise in oil prices cause in the Western world? Why?
5. What is a nonrenewable source of energy? List three different nonrenewable sources of energy.
6. What are three alternative, renewable, sources of energy?
7. List and explain three possible effects of rationing fuel.
8. List six methods of generating power, and one advantage and disadvantage of each method.
9. What is the difference between hard and soft energy?

Energy Today

1. In the 1970s, oil was in short supply; by the early 1980s, the world was experiencing an oil glut. How might this turnaround have happened?
2. List and explain five ways that you, as a consumer of energy, can conserve fuel.
3. Consider the community in which you live. How could the community conserve energy? What source of energy exist that are not being used?
4. How does the market system answer the question of energy allocation?
5. **Challenge:** How might rising energy costs affect each of the following?

a. inflation   **e.** standards of living

b. GNP growth   **f.** transportation costs

c. employment   **g.** government spending

d. education   **h.** taxes

2 Cities

SECTION OVERVIEW

If you want to enjoy a major league baseball game, you must live in or travel to a city. Cities provide support for museums. Opera companies, symphony orchestras, and theaters find audiences in the cities. Nevertheless, American cities are suffering from numerous problems resulting from population shifts that occurred after World War II. The problems of cities affect almost everyone. They are issues that involve value judgments and are debated worldwide. Although these problems go beyond economics to social reform, economic analysis can clarify the costs and benefits of the various proposed solutions. In this section, you will learn how economic reasoning can help to identify urban problems and evaluate solutions to improve city life.

ECONOMIC VOCABULARY

| urbanologist | inner city | central city | metropolis | capital flight |

Changing Cities

During the Depression and World War II, the lack of money and military priorities limited housing construction in the cities. When the war ended, a great construction boom began in the suburbs. Highway construction and the increase in mass transit systems encouraged suburban growth. Many of the white middle class families that could afford the move went to the suburbs.

Cities became crowded as new groups moved in. People came from rural areas, blacks from the South, and Puerto Ricans, Mexicans, and Cubans from their native lands to replace the white middle class in cities. These groups often had little education, few skills, and no money.

As the population shifted, a circular pattern of city development became evident. Urbanologists, who study the problems of cities, described this pattern.

A downtown shopping district, luxury hotels, banks, and office buildings consti-

tute the center of the city. A beltline of factories, warehouses, and shipping yards often encircles this core. The residential areas, where most of the people live, begin beyond the industrial belt. The oldest and most run-down buildings are in the residential area closest to the center of the city. This area, called the inner city, often suffers from a high crime rate.

The next circle outward is made up of the homes and apartments of unskilled or blue collar workers. At the outer edge of the city are the homes of the middle class. The area within the city boundaries is referred to as the central city, or the core city. The suburbs form a ring around the central city. The city and its suburbs together is a metropolis, or metropolitan region.

Problems of Cities

Large cities require police, health, traffic, sanitation, and educational facilities far more complex than those needed in a rural

448

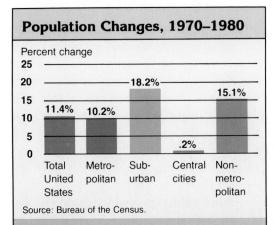

Population Changes, 1970–1980

Percent change

Area	Percent change
Total United States	11.4%
Metropolitan	10.2%
Suburban	18.2%
Central cities	.2%
Non-metropolitan	15.1%

Source: Bureau of the Census.

Explanation

The graph shows changes in population between rural and urban areas. Metropolitan includes the city and its suburbs. During the period from 1970 to 1980, the United States population increased 11.4 percent.

Graph Skills

1. Which area grew the most? The least?
2. What explanation can you give for the difference in growth between areas?
3. What was the trend in population growth in the 1970s?

---

addition, cities lose the taxes these businesses once paid.

Not all city problems are economic. Some are political and social. Among the problems cities face are slum housing, poverty, inadequate education, decreasing job opportunities, high public aid costs, inadequate transportation and recreational facilities, and air and water pollution. Economics can help analyze solutions to the problems cities face. Using the concept of opportunity cost, economists can show that each time resources are used in one way, all other uses of those resources are sacrificed. Each solution has its own price. Economists can suggest better ways to pay the third-party costs and distribute the third-party benefits.

Transportation Problems

For the past 30 years a major question in transportation policy has been how to divide city spending between highways and such mass transit systems as buses, subways, and trains.

Many of the people who moved to the suburbs continue to work in the city and drive their cars there each day. Cars account for 90 percent of the travel in cities. The results are traffic jams, air pollution, and the sprawl of highways and parking lots. In addition, the use of public transportation has fallen significantly. During rush hours, however, city owned and operated public transportation frequently handles up to 50 percent of the commuters.

Two problems exist. One is dealing with the rush-hour traffic jam, and the other is maintaining both highways and public transportation. Economists have suggested ways of solving both problems at once. For example, users of mass transit during rush hours could pay more and off-hours users less. This solution encour-

setting. Money from taxes provides the revenue to pay for these added services. As people with low or no income increasingly inhabit large cities, government revenues must be spread thin to cover the rising costs of providing more services to more people. The poor need more police and fire protection, more specialized education, and more emergency medical care than do higher income groups. The result is a drain on the city's revenues.

Cities try to bolster their revenues by increasing taxes. As a result, cities often have higher taxes than do suburban areas.

Cities are also hurt by capital flight, the movement of businesses and jobs to suburbs and other outlying areas. The urban poor find it difficult or impossible to commute to these new jobs outside the city. In

449

Mass Transportation, 1940–1982

Year	Total Passengers
1940	13,098,000
1945	23,254,000
1950	17,246,000
1955	11,529,000
1960	9,395,000
1965	8,253,000
1970	7,332,000
1975	6,972,000
1980	8,671,000
1982	8,085,000

Source: American Public Transit Association.

Explanation

The chart lists the number of passengers carried on mass transportation vehicles, such as commuter trains, subway cars, and buses, between 1940 and 1982.

Chart Skills

1. In which year was public transportation used most? Least?
2. What might explain the sharp drop in use of mass transportation vehicles between the years 1945 and 1950?
3. Summarize the trends shown in this chart.

ages a tradeoff—fewer passengers during rush hours and more passengers at other times during the day. A cost of this solution could be a dramatic decrease in mass transit use during rush hours, along with a decrease in revenue, unless the increased transit fare is less than the cost of driving alone or car pooling.

Another possible solution could require highway users to pay more in gasoline taxes. The increased cost of using highways might encourage many automobile users to switch to mass transit. Revenue for the maintenance and improvement of mass transit systems then would rise. Increased use of mass transit also would spread the costs over many more riders, thereby possibly reducing fares. In addition, traffic jams would be reduced, as would air pollution and the need for parking lots.

In this solution to the problems of urban transportation, tradeoffs involve decreases in traffic jams and air pollution for inconvenience to former drivers and larger crowds on public transportation during rush hours. Among the costs of this solution are dissatisfied gas station owners and a possible decline in the number of people willing to work in the city. A change in city administration also could result as voters showed their displeasure.

Other solutions could be studied. The cost of parking could be increased to encourage more people to leave their cars at home. Local tax incentives could be given to people who use mass transit. Large subsidies could be granted to public transportation systems. New trains, traveling at high speeds, might make cars a less attractive way of getting to and from work.

The study of economics can point out the costs and benefits of various solutions. The job of economists is to consider all the connections among problems. Then they can explain what each solution will cost in terms of resources, time, money, labor, and so on.

Education Problems

A national crisis in the United States concerns the quality and cost of city education systems. The costs of maintaining school systems have rapidly increased while the number of students has decreased. However, city schools show little progress in educating the new urban population, many of whom do not complete high school. For every 1,000 children who entered 5th grade in 1973, 944 entered high school in 1977, and only 745 graduated in 1981.

Economists can study the problem, comparing gains in achievement with the costs of new programs. Costly programs could be maintained in response to parental or teachers' union demands. However, communities should be able to assess intelligently the educational program's value. Tradeoffs and opportunity costs have to be analyzed to enable parents and administrators to make educated choices.

Livable Cities

Making cities livable means more than just making them clean, safe, and healthy. They must be turned into the kinds of places where people want to live. Individuals want to live in safe communities that reflect their values and give them a sense of pride. Economists can aid city planners and administrators in making cities more livable.

"Henderson's made a remarkable adjustment to city living."

How has the new apartment-dweller adjusted to urban life?

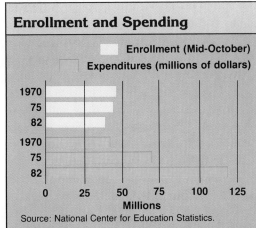

Enrollment and Spending

□ Enrollment (Mid-October)
□ Expenditures (millions of dollars)

Millions

Source: National Center for Education Statistics.

Explanation

The graph illustrates the decline in students accompanied by increased costs for public schools in the United States.

Graph Skills

1. By how many students did enrollment drop between 1970 and 1982?
2. How much more money was spent in 1982 than 1970?
3. What was the percent of increase in expenditures between 1970 and 1982?
4. How would each of the following help to explain the increased spending: rate of inflation, per-pupil expenditures, spending as a percentage of GNP?

REVIEWING THE CONCEPT

Developing Vocabulary

1. Explain why the field of urbanology developed only recently.
2. What forms the boundary of the central, or core, city?
3. In what ways does a metropolis differ from a city?
4. What does capital flight mean?

Mastering Facts

1. What groups make up the majority of the population in most large cities? Why have these groups moved to the cities?
2. What group makes up the largest part of the population of the suburbs? Why did this group leave the cities in the 1940s and 1950s?
3. Why do the poor living in a city require more city services?
4. List five problems that cities face today. For one of them, propose a solution, and list its costs and benefits.
5. List the costs and benefits of public transportation to society.

Bicycles versus Automobiles

John Dawkins sold his car five years ago and bought a bicycle. Since then, his bicycle has been his principal means of transportation in the city.

Dawkins is well satisfied with his choice of transportation. "I have more money for other things," he said. "The average price of a car today is around $10,000. Gas is expensive and I don't have to pay for insurance, license plates, or city license fees. My bike requires much less maintenance than a car; and when it rains or is really cold, I ride the bus."

About a century ago, the bicycle was an important means of personal transportation. With the introduction of the automobile, Americans abandoned the two-wheeler. The bicycle remained a means of transportation only for those too young to drive legally. For others, the bicycle became a form of recreation.

In some developing countries, though, fun is not the principal purpose in owning a bicycle. China is an example of a nation on two wheels. Millions of Chinese go to and from work and school on bicycles. People in many highly developed industrial nations, such as Denmark and Sweden, also use bicycles for transportation.

The expense of automobiles goes beyond their purchase price and maintenance costs. The popularity of the automobile has contributed to urban sprawl. Roads, parking lots, and service stations occupy up to 60 percent of the land in some American cities, as well as in Cairo, São Paulo, Mexico City, Paris, and Tokyo.

Automobiles contribute to air pollution and are responsible for the death or injury of thousands of people each year. Since the first recorded automobile fatality, in New York City in 1893, automobiles have accounted for the deaths of more American citizens than all the wars in which the nation has fought.

Bicycles are more energy-efficient than cars. Dawkins explained, "Riding my bicycle, I use only one-fifth the energy to get to work that I would use if I walked. I get there faster and stay healthier at the same time." Cars transfer only 20 percent of their fuel's potential energy, but a bicycle transfers 80 to 98 percent.

John Dawkins is not a typical American in his use of the bicycle. Dawkins started no trend, and no one expects Americans to turn back the clock to days when bicycles were prominent on city streets. Even if the car were not tied closely to the national economy, Americans would be unlikely to give up the freedom and convenience of owning and driving a car. However, environmentalists have suggested that citizens of developing nations should think twice before becoming dependent on cars.

Some cities, such as Madison, Wisconsin, have constructed special lanes for bicycles.

ANALYZING THE CASE STUDY

STEP 1 State the Problem

1. Describe how the car contributes to three urban problems.
2. What tradeoffs have individuals and communities made in relying on cars?
3. What are the opportunity costs of producing cars?

STEP 2 Consider Possible Solutions

1. Analyze the effect of using bicycles on each of the three problems in Step 1. State how bicycles might make the problem worse, and how bicycles might help to solve the problem.

2. List two other advantages and disadvantages of riding bicycles when compared to driving cars.
3. What benefits does the auto industry provide to the economy? What other industries would be affected if auto sales declined sharply?

STEP 3 Make a Decision

1. Decide whether or not the government should subsidize energy-efficient forms of transportation, such as bicycles. Write a paragraph explaining and defending your position.

Future Communities

A Photo Essay

The photo essay illustrates some future cities that architects have proposed as possible answers to current urban problems. As you study the photographs, consider how each suggests a solution to an urban problem.

Instant City by Stanley Tigerman

It is planned that these structures could be erected above existing expressways that run between cities. The bottom section of each building contains four stories, which could be used for service and parking needs. The next section of three stories could provide space for industry and commerce, as well as education. There would be five stories of office space. There are then three other sections—each with seven stories—for residential use.

A city of the future as imagined by an architect. Note the many highways and lack of traffic jams.

453

Tetrahedronal City by Buckminister Fuller

Tetrahedronal City would be built to house 300,000 families, each with a balcony and outside view. All the machinery necessary to run the city would be located inside the tetrahedron. The structure would be built so that it could float on water. Each city would measure 2 miles to an edge. The whole city could be floated out into the ocean and anchored at any point. The city can start with a thousand residents and expand slowly to house a million people without ever changing its shape.

Tomorrow's city: a modern Pyramid.

Habitat by Moshe Safdie

This version of Habitat was built for the Montreal Expo in 1967. One of the advantages of this type of dwelling is that it can be built on the construction site itself. The structure is made up of many separately built boxes. After each box is built, it is attached to the other boxes in a zigzag pattern. People get to their apartments by elevators and stairs and by covered bridges that connect them. A special advantage of Habitat is that it is built over and around existing structures, without tearing them all down first.

Habitat—one answer to overcrowding.

Manhattan Dome by Buckminster Fuller

Buckminster Fuller has created many domes, although they are smaller than this proposed dome over Manhattan. One of the dome's advantages is that it is extremely strong. Another is that the larger domes seem to disappear into the sky. They become transparent when it is bright outside, and opaque when it is overcast. There are problems, too. The floor area is small compared to the height, and the skin of the dome is hard to clean. Perhaps the real question the dome raises is this: can you change a city without changing the city?

The dome is another idea for the future.

454

UNDERSTANDING THE READING

1. If you were planning a new city, which of these innovations, if any, would you favor? Why?
2. How might each of these solutions make cities more livable?
3. What problem is each of the designs supposed to solve?
4. Are there any disadvantages to each of the designs? Explain your answer.
5. Choose one of the new cities and answer the questions based on your choice.
   a. What kinds of relationships between people might this city foster?
   b. What tradeoffs must be made to produce this city?
   c. Would you like to live here? Explain.
   d. Is the city economically feasible?

According to this cartoon, what is one danger of living in a city?

Section 2 Review

Understanding Cities

1. Draw a diagram showing the circular pattern of city development.
2. What effects has the automobile had on cities? List at least three.
3. What are the third-party costs and benefits of automobile use?
4. Develop a solution, not based on those suggested in the text, for the transportation problem of cities.
5. What educational problems exist in schools in large cities?
6. Develop a solution for the education problems large cities face. What tradeoffs are involved? What are the opportunity costs of your solution?
7. List three ways cities reflect the problems of the mature economy.
8. Which solution to urban problems mentioned in this section would be worth trying? How could it be implemented?

9. Is Habitat a good name for Safdie's city design? Why or why not?

Cities Today

1. Using the largest city near your home or the one where you live as an example, explain whether it fits the circular development pattern of cities.
2. List and explain what characteristics, in your opinion, make a city livable. Explain why you chose these characteristics. Are they common to most cities?
3. List three advantages and three disadvantages of living in a large city.
4. Are cities worth saving? Explain why or why not.
5. **Challenge:** If you were a city manager, how would you divide your city's money between roads and public transit? Explain your choices.

3 The Environment

SECTION OVERVIEW

The environment includes all the forces and features of a particular place. Climate, air, water, plants and animals, food chain, and people are all parts of the environment. It has been changing rapidly since the Industrial Revolution, and waste and contamination endanger it. In this section, you will learn about the economic issues involved in protecting the environment.

ECONOMIC VOCABULARY

environmental pollution   externalities   government subsidy   acid rain

A Changing Environment

People have been changing the environment throughout history. Campfires have sent smoke into the air. Wood has been taken from forests. Animals have been raised for food and their bones left to litter the area. Recently, however, changes have been more drastic.

Since the Industrial Revolution, people and factories have put huge amounts of pollutants into the earth's air and water systems. Pollution has increased to the point where some plant and animal species are endangered. Poisonous, or toxic, wastes have entered our food chain. Even the atmosphere is affected. Recently, concern about pollution has grown. The government, businesses, and individuals now are taking steps to control pollution.

Another consequence of industrialization and population growth is the depletion of the water supply. Industrial plants have dramatically increased the demand for water. Manufacturing processes and a growing population require ever-increasing amounts of water. Some areas of the country suffer from a shortage of usable water.

The Problem of Pollution

Today, pollution affects many areas of the environment. People pollute the air and water by adding unclean substances to them. Environmental pollution refers to the ways people pollute their surroundings. For example, factories and motor vehicles add harmful gases to the air. Industries pour the waste products of the manufacturing process into lakes and rivers. Noises from construction and traffic are sometimes deafening. People ruin natural surroundings by littering. Hazardous waste products, such as poisonous chemicals and radioactive materials, are not always disposed of properly. Nearly everyone causes environmental pollution in some way.

Measuring the Cost of Pollution

Firms measure production expenses by adding the costs of all resources used to make the product—land, labor, and capital. Expenses do not include the price of resources that have no market value, such as water and air; therefore, pollution costs usually are not part of production costs.

Such accounting is an economically sound business practice. Profit depends on producing the best product for the lowest price.

Economists call the costs of pollution external costs, or externalities. They are costs of production that neither the producer nor the consumer of a product pays directly. Pollution is a social, or third-party, cost paid by society and external to the market system. A negative externality results when costs are shifted to people not directly involved in producing or consuming the product. A positive externality results when benefits are shifted to people not directly involved in a transaction. Pollution is a negative externality. Education is a positive externality. As the level of education rises, crime and public aid payments tend to decrease. The market system does not work well in dealing with externalities.

Controlling Pollution

Government can pass laws to regulate the processes that create pollution. Public policy results when concerned groups initiate a movement to protect the environment and to make others aware of the dangers in pollution. Such groups undertake efforts to educate the public. For example, many groups have tried to distribute information about acid rain—rain that has a high acid content. Some research shows that pollution from automobiles, factories, and burning coal causes the acid level in rain to increase. Highly acidic water can kill vegetation in forests and lakes. Pictures of graceful egrets and sandpipers covered with oil, or forests turned brown by acid rain provoke a public appeal for government regulation. People want laws passed to control pollution. The purpose of such legislation would be to stop individuals or firms from polluting.

Economists understand that government regulations do not transfer the cost of pollution to just the business causing the pollution. Changing production to include antipollution methods increases the cost of producing an item. The firm's costs rise; therefore, each item costs more to produce. Firms increase the price of the product to cover the cost of antipollution equipment or to pay the fines for polluting. The supply curve shifts to the left. According to the law of demand, as the price of an item increases, smaller quantities are bought. The amount of decrease will depend on the elasticity of demand. Employees also pay the costs of pollution because as less is sold, fewer employees are needed. Three groups pay the costs of regulation—buyers, sellers, and employees.

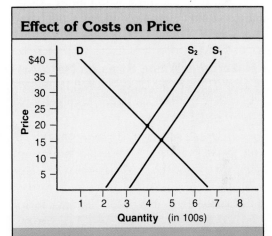

Effect of Costs on Price

Explanation

The graph shows the effect of higher costs on equilibrium price. The line S_1 is the supply curve before government regulations increase costs. The line S_2 represents the supply curve after antipollution costs have been included.

Graph Skills

1. What is the equilibrium price before antipollution regulations?
2. What is the equilibrium price after antipollution regulations?
3. How did the increased equilibrium price affect demand(D)?

457

In order to protect the nation's environment from pollution, the United States government set up an independent agency, the Environmental Protection Agency (EPA). The EPA establishes and enforces environmental protection standards and conducts research on the effects of pollution. The EPA provides grants and technical assistance to help local governments cope with pollution problems. The EPA also administers the Comprehensive Environmental Response, Compensation and Liability Act of 1980. This law set up a large fund of money, $1.6 billion, to clean up hazardous toxic waste sites and prosecute individuals and firms who do not obey government regulations.

Another way to attack the pollution problem is to tax those who pollute. Companies could be required to pay a tax based on the amount of pollutants they release into the environment. If companies could clean up their pollution for less than the tax, they would do so. If the tax cost less than installing a smoke scrubber or constructing and maintaining a cooling tower, the company would pay the tax. The government would use the tax money to clean up the environment.

From an economic point of view, the tax is similar to government regulations. The tax raises the cost of production and again shifts the supply curve. Buyers, sellers, and workers share the cost of controlling pollution. Regulation affects all polluters alike, but taxes allow firms some freedom of choice. This freedom of choice may help small firms to remain in business.

Finally, pollution can be controlled through government subsidies. A govern-

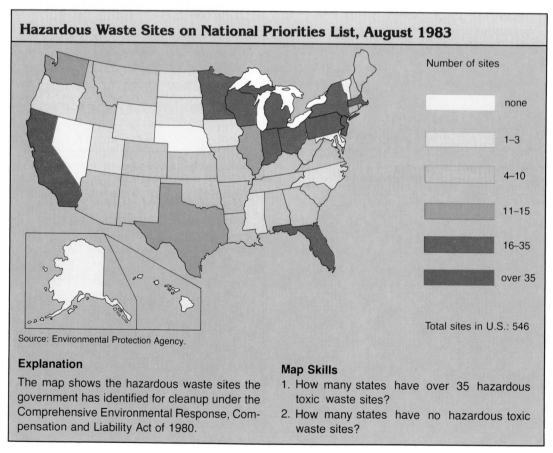

Hazardous Waste Sites on National Priorities List, August 1983

Number of sites

	none
	1–3
	4–10
	11–15
	16–35
	over 35

Total sites in U.S.: 546

Source: Environmental Protection Agency.

Explanation
The map shows the hazardous waste sites the government has identified for cleanup under the Comprehensive Environmental Response, Compensation and Liability Act of 1980.

Map Skills
1. How many states have over 35 hazardous toxic waste sites?
2. How many states have no hazardous toxic waste sites?

ment subsidy is a grant of money to a firm or individual for a project that aids the public well-being. All taxpayers share the cost of government subsidies. The government, in this example, would be paying firms to clean up the environment. Subsidies can take the form of an agreement to lower taxes after a promise to install antipollution devices.

Economists often object to subsidies because they hide the real economic costs of clean production of goods and services. When subsidies are given, antipollution costs are divided among all taxpayers rather than just the producer and consumer of the product. Subsidies remove pollution costs from the market system. Producers and consumers do not know the pollution cost of a particular good or service. In contrast, the use of government regulations and taxes allows the market system to handle the otherwise hidden costs of pollution.

Other Environmental Problems

Pollution is not the only environmental problem industrialized nations face. A shortage of usable water creates another problem. Even though more rain falls in the United States than is used each year, 92 percent evaporates immediately or runs off to the oceans. In addition, the nation's water resources are unevenly distributed. The agricultural states of the Southwest get less than 30 inches of rainfall a year, whereas the Pacific Northwest receives more than 50 inches. Most southwestern states use water that was deposited underground over thousands of years. Of all the water the United States use for irrigation, power, or personal consumption, 25 percent comes from underground sources. The use of underground water has been increasing rapidly. In 1950, the nation took 12 trillion gallons of water out of the ground. By 1980, the amount had increased to 24 trillion gallons. Each day 21 billion more gallons are used than are replaced by natural seepage. Some engineers predict that by 2000 the water supply in parts of Nebraska will be so depleted that farming in those areas will be impossible.

Depletion of underground water reserves causes the earth's surface to crack or sink. Arizona farmers have used so much ground water that cracks up to 25 feet wide have appeared on the desert floor between Tucson and Phoenix. California's San Joaquin Valley has dropped by nearly 30 feet in some places. Houston is slowly sinking as water is pumped from beneath it.

Another environmental concern is the loss of many species of plants and animals. Among the animals that have become extinct in the United States since 1750 are the Wisconsin cougar, eastern elk, plains wolf, passenger pigeon, and great auk. The nation's endangered species list contains over 200 vanishing plants and animals, and 50 other species are listed as threatened. Some scientists predict that the worldwide loss will increase to one species a day by the year 2000.

Air pollution from industries can affect areas far from factories.

The loss of plants and animals not only decreases the richness and variety of the earth's environment but also could seriously affect the world's economies. Removing one plant or animal affects 20 to 25 others in the interdependent plant and animal world. Scientists do not know how much strain this interdependent system can manage before it collapses. A cure for a disease or a crop to feed people in less developed countries may be contained in the genes of an endangered plant or animal species.

Economics and the Environment

Economics teaches people to analyze problems. Economists try to find the costs of each kind of environmental damage. The costs of environmental damage are sometimes hard to measure. How does one measure the value of a species of tiny fish that will be destroyed by the construction of one dam? Economists also want to know the costs of preventing damage. For example, what would be the costs, in terms of goods, services, and jobs, of not building a dam? Tradeoffs and opportunity costs must be considered. Saving the environment while destroying the economy would solve nothing. Allowing the economy to grow bigger and bigger while ruining the earth would be suicidal.

REVIEWING THE CONCEPT

Developing Vocabulary

1. What is environmental pollution? Give three examples.
2. Explain the economic meaning of externality. Give two examples.
3. What is a government subsidy?
4. Why is acid rain dangerous?

Mastering Facts

1. Explain why pollution recently has become an important concern.
2. For what reason is the cost of pollution not considered a business expense in a market economy?
3. Explain who pays the cost of controlling pollution when the government passes laws or levies taxes to reduce pollution. Draw a graph to illustrate your answer.
4. Why does the United States suffer from a water shortage even though more rain falls than is used?

CASE STUDY

Acid Rain

"We live off the land, with the land, and respect the land," said Hilary Waukau, vice-chairman of the Menominee Indian Tribal Legislature for the reservation in Wisconsin. "It is Mother Earth, and it is sacred to us. The white man in his technological society forgets that. Our reservation should not be made a garbage dump for the white man's industrial waste."

One form of industrial waste that affects the Menominee reservation is acid rain. The acid can cause fish egg cases to dissolve and can destroy lake food chains. All lake life slowly dies. Eventually, the

Acid rain is steadily destroying this statue. Polluted rainwater can destroy the food chain in a lake.

used to see 1,000 swallows perched on wires. Not long ago he counted only 18.

"We know we have acid rain," said Steve Dodge, a mining and planning specialist for the Menominee. "The question is, what is the solution to acid rain?" The Menominee solution is to oppose any kind of industrial development that threatens the environment. Many people agree that strong action must be taken to reduce or end acid rain. The National Academy of Sciences estimates the damage from acid rain at $5 billion. In all, acid rain has caused environmental damage in 31 states.

Not everyone agrees with the Menominee. Industries that burn coal believe that not enough is known about acid rain to warrant a costly program of regulation.

The cost of stopping acid rain is an important concern. The Edison Electric Institute predicts that controlling utility company pollution could raise electric bills by $938 a year for some families. National Coal Association president Carl Bagge said, "It would be irresponsible national policy to impose these costs on the American public while significant and legitimate scientific questions remain."

Another possible solution exists. Government could require industries to burn coal with a low sulfur content. Coal miners, however, are divided on this issue. Miners in Wyoming and West Virginia, where low sulfur coal exists, favor the idea. Miners in Illinois, where coal has a high sulfur content, oppose it.

Members of Congress have introduced at least a dozen bills on acid rain. The bills range from upholding the idea of more research to the installation of more scrubbers to reduce pollution. None of these bills has passed. Meanwhile, environmental damage to the nation that could prove irreversible continues.

lakes become crystal clear but contain no living plants or animals.

Bill Marleau, a retired New York forest ranger, no longer sees the brook trout and water lilies that led him to build a cabin in Woods Lake 21 years ago. He said, "The way I look at it, everything in nature depends on food. Acid rain destroys the food supply of the birds and animals that feed on fish. This affects the food supply of animals that don't depend on the insects and fish in the lake." On August evenings Marleau

STEP 1 State the Problem

1. What is acid rain? Why is it a problem?
2. List three factors that make a solution to the problem of acid rain hard to find and put into practice.

STEP 2 Propose Solutions

1. Suggest three possible solutions to the acid rain problem.

STEP 3 Evaluate Costs and Benefits

1. List the economic costs and benefits of each solution you proposed in Step 2.
2. List the tradeoffs involved in each solution you proposed.

STEP 4 Make a Decision

1. What particular solution would you favor? Write one paragraph defending your position.

Enrichment Activity

Find out whether any of your electricity comes from coal-fired power plants. If so, how would your proposed solution affect your electricity rates?

READING

Silent Spring

by Rachel Carson   (1907–1964)

If any one event caused Americans to become aware of environmental pollution, it was the publication of *Silent Spring* in 1962. The author, Rachel Carson, was a marine biologist. The following excerpt set the theme of the book. As you read, consider the accuracy of the predictions Rachel Carson made.

There was once a town in the heart of America where all life seemed to live in harmony with its surroundings. The town lay in the midst of a checkerboard of prosperous farms, with fields of grain and hillsides of orchards where, in spring, white clouds of bloom drifted above the green fields. In autumn, oak and maple and birch set up a blaze of color that flamed and flickered across a backdrop of pines. Then foxes barked in the hills and deer silently crossed the fields, half hidden in the mists of the fall mornings.

Along the roads, laurel, viburnum and alder, great ferns and wild flowers delighted the traveler's eye through much of the year. Even in winter the roadsides were places of beauty, where countless birds came to feed on the berries and on the seedheads of the dried weeds rising above the snow. The countryside was, in fact, famous for the abundance and variety of its bird life, and when the flood of migrants was pouring through in spring and fall, people traveled from great distances to observe them. Others came to fish the streams, which flowed clear and cold out of the hills and contained

Brook trout from a stream in upper New York State die from pollution.

shady pools where trout lay. So it had been from the days many years ago when the first settlers raised [built] their houses, sank their wells, and built their barns.

Then a strange blight crept over the area and everything began to change. Some evil spell had settled on the community: mysterious maladies swept the flocks of chickens; the cattle and sheep sickened and died. Everywhere was a shadow of death. The farmers spoke of much illness among their families. In the town the doctors had become more and more puzzled by new kinds of sickness appearing among their patients. There had been several sudden and unexplained deaths, not only among adults but even among children, who would be stricken suddenly while at play and die within a few hours.

There was a strange stillness. The birds, for example—where had they gone? Many people spoke of them, puzzled and disturbed. The feeding stations in the backyards were deserted. The few birds seen anywhere were moribund; they trembled violently and could not fly. It was a spring without voices. On the mornings that had once throbbed with the dawn chorus of robins, catbirds, doves, jays, wrens, and scores of other bird voices there was now no sound; only silence lay over the fields and woods and marsh.

On the farms the hens brooded, but no chicks hatched. The farmers complained that they were unable to raise any pigs—the litters were small and the young survived only a few days. The apple trees were coming into bloom but no bees droned among the blossoms, so there was no pollination and there would be no fruit.

The roadsides, once so attractive, were now lined with browned and withered vegetation as though swept by fire. These, too, were silent, deserted by all living things. Even the streams were now lifeless. Anglers no longer visited them, for all the fish had died.

In the gutters under the eaves and between the shingles of the roofs, a white granular powder still showed a few patches; some weeks before it had fallen like snow upon the roofs and the lawns, the fields and streams.

No witchcraft, no enemy action had silenced the rebirth of new life in this stricken world. The people had done it themselves.

This town does not actually exist, but it might easily have a thousand counterparts in America or elsewhere in the world. I know of no community that has experienced all the misfortunes I describe. Yet every one of these disasters has actually happened somewhere, and many real communities have already suffered a substantial number of them. A grim specter has crept upon us almost unnoticed, and this imagined tragedy may easily become a stark reality we all shall know.

What has already silenced the voices of spring in countless towns in America? **99**

From *Silent Spring,* by Rachel Carson.

UNDERSTANDING THE READING

1. Economically, what problems would result if no birds flew or sang?
2. Except to those who like to eat fish, why would the loss of fish cause environmental problems?
3. Carson stated, "The people had done it themselves." What did the people gain in return for their actions?

Section 3 Review

Understanding The Environment

1. List four types of environmental pollution and the causes of each type.
2. Give examples of positive and negative externalities. Explain your choices.
3. List and explain three ways to attack the problem of pollution.
4. Why was the Environmental Protection Agency (EPA) created?
5. Who pays the costs of government subsidies to control pollution?
6. What are economists' objections to the use of government subsidies as a way to control pollution?
7. Why is the disappearance of some plant and animal species a cause of concern to many people?
8. How can economists help to solve environmental problems?

The Environment Today

1. What would be the costs of banning cars and factories from highly polluted areas of the country?
2. What third-party economic benefits flow from pollution control?
3. What actions do you think should be taken to control pollution in the United States? Explain your choices.
4. What actions can you, as an individual, take to decrease pollution?
5. **Challenge:** Some Eastern cultures believe that deriving the greatest amount of utility from the least amount of consumption is a desirable goal. List two examples of American consumption patterns indicating that many people do the opposite—that is, derive minimal utility from maximum consumption.

Americans
at Work

Meet Elizabeth Bailey
University Dean

"Never lean back and assume people recognize that you are doing a good job. Be receptive to outside job offers and try to have visibility outside your own organization," said Elizabeth Bailey. This attitude on professional advancement has led Bailey to a varied and interesting career.

Elizabeth Bailey was the first woman appointed to head one of the country's top-rated business schools. She is dean of the Graduate School of Industrial Administration at Carnegie-Mellon University, a leading engineering school and research center in Pittsburgh.

Bailey has not always been involved in education. Before going to Carnegie-Mellon, she held a much different position. She was appointed by President Carter to serve on the five-member Civil Aeronautics Board (CAB). President Reagan later promoted Bailey to CAB vice-chairman. The CAB, an independent agency of the federal government, regulated United States airlines. Before deregulation, the CAB set air fares and air service mail rates, issued permits to United States airlines for domestic and international routes, and was the first regulatory agency to set up a consumer affairs office. As a member of the Civil Aeronautics Board, Bailey put her econom-

ic knowledge and her enthusiasm for the free-enterprise system to use. Her work on the CAB aided deregulation and led to intense price competition among airlines.

Bailey found her work in Washington challenging and exciting. "I know lots of people who went to work for the government and found they were bored. I never had that experience. In fact, I never had as much fun professionally as I did in deregulating the airlines. Every time I step onto a plane I get to reap some of the benefits of my work in Washington."

Bailey's new job as dean will again use her economic skills. Her first task at Carnegie-Mellon will be to raise $15 million. The school needs money, she said, to create new courses, especially on "how to manage the introduction of automation into the workplace."

Deans are sometimes overwhelmed by administrative detail and lose sight of students. Bailey recognizes students' needs, and she wants Carnegie's business students to gain real-world experience. "I want our students to find out how an organization really works—not how the employees' handbook says it works. Once you understand how the real world works, you can then make it work for you."

Preserving the Environment

Waste and pollution threaten the world environment. Every American consumes 13 tons of goods a year. More than 142 tons of pollutants—three-fourths of a ton for every American—are released into the atmosphere every year. Our highways yearly gather 20 million cubic yards of trash.

Recycling and consuming carefully will conserve natural resources, contribute to your health, and save you money. In addition, you can join environmental protection groups and act to increase public awareness of environmental problems.

STEP 1 Recycle and Conserve

Recycling saves energy and raw materials, protects the environment, and cuts waste disposal costs. Save newspapers, magazines, and other paper products and recycle them. Recycling just half of the world's used paper would meet almost 75 percent of new paper demand and would free 20 million acres of forestland from paper production. Recycling paper also conserves energy. Less energy is required to produce recycled paper than to manufacture paper from wood.

Save your aluminum cans for recycling. Throwing away an aluminum beverage container wastes as much energy as discarding such a can half-filled with gasoline. Extracting aluminum from ore requires 20 times as much electricity as recycling the metal. In addition to recycling centers, several types of reverse vending machines have been developed to accept used aluminum cans and dispense coins or redeemable coupons in return. If your local supermarkets do not have reverse vending machines, encourage them to install some.

Use water carefully. Turn off faucets when not in use and repair leaks. Use clothes washers and dishwashers only when full. A brick in the toilet tank of every home in Chicago would conserve 100,000 to 300,000 gallons of water per day and save money on water bills. Instead of filling a bathtub, use a shower if one is available. Showering requires much less water than does tub bathing.

Conserve electricity. Avoid electrical gadgets. Turn off lights, and use less heating and cooling. Be sure your home is properly insulated to reduce heating and cooling needs.

When in need of auto parts, visit a junkyard. About 25 percent of the nation's 11,000 junkyards now are clean, well-lighted recycling centers where car parts are removed from junk cars, cleaned, wrapped, cataloged, and shelved.

The Car Recycling Industry

Total annual sales (United States and Canada)	$4 billion
Total employment (United States and Canada)	80,000
Total number of vehicles handled annually (United States)	8 million

Source: Automotive Dismantlers and Recyclers Association.

Explanation

The chart shows sales, employment, and the number of vehicles handled annually in the automotive recycling industry.

Chart Skills

1. How might the repair of old cars affect the new car industry?
2. List two economic changes that would encourage people to repair their cars rather than buy new ones.

STEP 2   Consume Carefully

As consumers, you and your family can shop and use products carefully. Buy returnable bottles and return them. Avoid the use of paper products. Avoid using plastic, which decomposes very slowly. Scientists estimate that a million years will be required for the evolution of microorganisms capable of breaking down plastics. Plastic production uses chemicals derived from natural resources, such as coal, petroleum, and water. Avoid buying individually wrapped packages. They are often more expensive and they waste natural resources.

When washing clothes, use only the amount of detergent required, and try to avoid phosphate detergents. Algae eat phosphates, multiply rapidly, and destroy lakes. Avoid aerosol spray cans. Many scientists believe the fluorocarbons used in aerosol cans reduce the ozone layer protecting the earth. Depletion of the ozone layer may cause skin cancers, damage to plant life, and even global climate changes.

Do not buy clothes and commercial products made from the skins of endangered animals. Between 1950 and 1970, 95 percent of the alligators in the everglades were killed for their hides.

STEP 3   Support Conservation Efforts

Many environmental protection groups exist on both national and local levels. The following national organizations are dedicated to environmental causes: Friends of the Earth, National Auduborn Society, National Wildlife Federation, Sierra Club, Wilderness Society. Write for information to learn more about their work.

Libraries contain many books on environmental problems and the actions that individuals and groups can take to preserve the environment.

ECONOMIC SKILLS TODAY

1. List five steps that you can take to save energy and protect the environment.
2. From newspapers and magazines, cut out at least two pictures that show litter, waste, or other environmental problems. What actions could be taken to reduce the problems?

Enrichment Activity

Write to at least one environmental protection group and obtain pamphlets explaining their goals and the actions citizens can take to protect the environment.

CHAPTER SUMMARY

Energy

Fossil fuels provide 97 percent of the world's energy. Of the fossil fuels, oil is the easiest to obtain, transport, and burn. Many countries rely on imported oil for energy. The price of oil has increased significantly since 1973, when the Arab oil-producing nations imposed an embargo on sales to the United States and many of its allies. In industrialized nations, the rapid rise in oil prices contributed to a recession accompanied by inflation. Rising prices encouraged nations to find and develop alternative sources of energy.

Cities

Since 1945, white middle class residents of American cities have been moving to suburbs. Cities have been increasingly occupied by groups with lower incomes and less education and skills. The need for public services—police and fire protection, specialized education, medical care—also has increased. However, city revenue has decreased. Economists can aid in offering solutions to some of the cities' problems. For example, in the areas of transportation and education, economists can study various solutions and try to determine the costs in goods, services, and jobs.

The Environment

Environmental pollution is a major problem in industrialized countries. The costs of pollution are external to the market system. Often, therefore, the government must take action to control pollution. The government may regulate polluting industries or levy taxes against polluters. Regulations and taxes pass the costs of pollution on to the buyers and sellers of the product and the employees who produce the product. The government also may subsidize industries to clean up pollution. Government subsidies pass on the cost of controlling pollution to all taxpayers.

CRITICAL THINKING QUESTIONS

Energy

1. How does an oil price increase spread through a nation's economy? Explain your answer.
2. If the use of fossil fuels declined and the use of alternative forms of energy—nuclear, geothermal, solar—rose, what would be the effect on jobs? On costs?
3. When the price of such a commonly used product as gasoline increases dramatically, how does a market economy adjust? How does a command economy adjust? Compare the reactions of the two economic systems.

Cities

1. Propose a solution to the problem of declining revenue coupled with increasing costs of maintaining city government. Explain the third-party costs and benefits, if any, of your solution.
2. Choose any other problem that cities face and propose a solution. Explain the tradeoffs and opportunity costs involved in your solution.
3. List all the benefits that cities provide to society. List the costs to society of maintaining cities. Compare your lists. If you determine that the costs outweigh the

benefits, what alternative lifestyle should replace cities.

The Environment

1. The Environmental Protection Agency checks pollution levels in factories. When pollution levels are too high, the EPA levies fines for each day that pollution levels exceed standards. Who pays for these fines?
2. If a clean environment can be maintained only at the cost of limiting economic growth, decide what tradeoffs between environment and growth are acceptable. How do these tradeoffs affect other groups in the population?
3. Using a polluting industry, determine the effects of each of the three methods of attacking the pollution problem: regulation, taxes, and subsidies. Which of the three methods is more favorable to the producer? The employees? The consumer? The uninvolved taxpayers? Explain your answers.

DEVELOPING ECONOMIC SKILLS

1. Explain why the real dollar and current dollar price of oil differs.
2. The spread between the price of oil in real dollars and the price in current dollars increased significantly between 1979 and 1982. Explain the cause of this wider spread.
3. What two periods saw the greatest increases in the price of oil? What caused these increases?

APPLYING ECONOMICS TODAY

1. Many smaller communities share the problems that plague cities. List the economic and social problems of your community. How many are similar to those of cities described in this chapter? Are any different?
2. Do Americans waste energy? List the instances of energy waste that you observe during one day. List ways in which each could have been avoided.

Oil Prices, 1960–1983

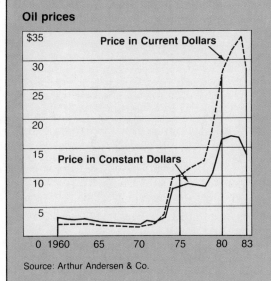

Oil prices

Source: Arthur Andersen & Co.

Explanation

The graph shows the price of oil per barrel in both constant dollars and current dollars for the period 1960 to 1983. The Organization of Petroleum Exporting Countries (OPEC) was formed in 1960. In the 1970s, OPEC influence over world oil prices increased.

Graph Skills

1. What was the highest price for oil in current dollars between 1960 and 1983?
2. In what year were the current and constant dollar prices for oil the same? What does this tell you about base year for the constant dollar measurements?
3. Describe three effects of an increase in oil prices on the economy of the United States.

CHAPTER 15

International Trade

1 Trade Restrictions

Objective: to understand and evaluate the various restrictions placed on international trade

2 Balance of Payments

Objective: to understand how currency exchange rates affect the nation's balance of payments and the economy

3 Worldwide Business

Objective: to understand how multinational corporations affect the national and world economies

1 Trade Restrictions

SECTION OVERVIEW

When people make purchases, money is traded for the item purchased. Someone who buys a loaf of bread wants the bread. The baker who sells the bread wants the money. People performing specialized work earn money. Countries also specialize in what they produce. Two countries trade with each other because each will be better off as a result. In this section, you will learn why countries trade with other countries, and why and how this trade can be restricted.

ECONOMIC VOCABULARY

comparative advantage   tariff   revenue tariff   protective tariff   quota   dumping

Reasons for Trade

The most successful way to deal with scarcity is to use existing resources more efficiently. A common way is to specialize. A country that can produce an item more efficiently than can another has a compara-

tive advantage in producing that item. For example, the soil and climate of the United States give it a comparative advantage over Japan in producing corn.

Nations sometimes base their trading policies on political, rather than economic, grounds. For example, after the Soviet

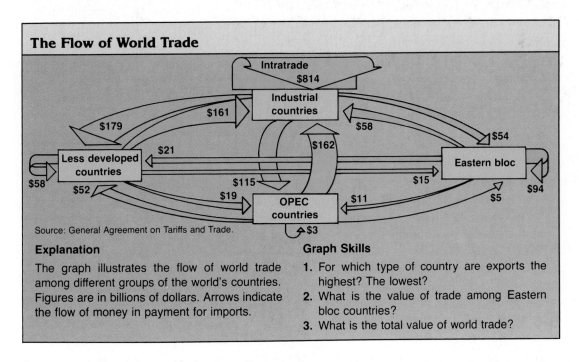

The Flow of World Trade

Intratrade $814

Industrial countries

$161 $179 $58 $54

$162

Less developed countries $21   Eastern bloc

$58 $52 $115 $15 $94

$19   OPEC countries $11 $5

$3

Source: General Agreement on Tariffs and Trade.

Explanation

The graph illustrates the flow of world trade among different groups of the world's countries. Figures are in billions of dollars. Arrows indicate the flow of money in payment for imports.

Graph Skills

1. For which type of country are exports the highest? The lowest?
2. What is the value of trade among Eastern bloc countries?
3. What is the total value of world trade?

Union invaded Afghanistan in December 1979, President Carter banned the sale of high-technology equipment to the Soviet Union. These high technology items included computers and oil-drilling equipment. Grain sales to the Soviet Union also were severely restricted. An example of how politics can foster trade is the support that the Soviet Union has provided for Cuba through trade with that nation over the last 20 years. Economic reasons have little to do with this Soviet–Cuban trade.

Limits on Trade

Despite the advantages of free trade, many nations impose limits on trade. The four main types of trade restrictions are tariffs, subsidies, quotas, and cartels.

A tariff is a tax placed on imported goods. Tariffs are of two kinds—revenue and protective. A revenue tariff raises money for the government. For this reason, revenue tariffs are generally low so that consumers will continue to purchase the taxed goods. A protective tariff taxes an imported good so that the price becomes as high as, or higher than, the similar domestic manufactured product. Protective tariffs make imported products more expensive and encourage people to buy goods produced in their own country. For example, if the cost of producing a pair of shoes is $20 in the United States and $10 in Italy, Italian shoes could be cheaper. Americans then would buy Italian shoes to save money. To encourage domestic shoe purchases, the federal government could levy a tariff of $15 per pair on imported Italian shoes.

A subsidy can be thought of as a tariff in reverse. Instead of taxing the foreign product, the government gives a subsidy—grant of money—to the industry that is suffering from foreign competition. In the shoe example, the government would grant

Similar restaurants exist around the world.

a subsidy to the nation's shoe industry. Shoe manufacturers could then meet some of their production costs through the subsidy and charge less than foreign producers for their products.

A quota is a limit on the amount of goods that can be imported into the country. A quota on shoes, for example, might limit shoe imports to 100 million pairs a year. If Americans buy 500 million pairs of shoes each year, most of the market will go to American producers. Usually, quotas are imposed when tariffs and subsidies have failed to protect domestic industries from foreign competition.

A cartel is a group of companies or countries that band together to restrict competition. The members of the cartel agree to limit the supply and control the price of a particular good. Members meet regularly to decide how much to sell and how much to charge for their product.

Sometimes, tariffs and subsidies are applied on a regional rather than a national basis. For example, in the late 1950s six Western European nations—Belgium,

France, Italy, Luxembourg, the Netherlands, and West Germany—formed the European Economic Community (EEC), usually called the Common Market. Later, Denmark, Great Britain, Greece, and Ireland also joined. The EEC established common tariffs against products from non-EEC nations. At the same time, the countries eliminated tariffs among themselves. Mexico and most South American nations have imitated these policies in the formation of the Latin American Free Trade Association (LAFTA) and the Central American Common Market (CACM).

Reasons for Trade Restrictions

Supporters of tariffs argue that these taxes provide domestic job protection and aid industrial development. Proponents also believe that tariffs are important to the national defense.

In industrialized countries, full employment is a national goal, and unemployment causes real and continuous concern. Labor unions often support trade restrictions to limit imports of goods produced by inexpensive foreign labor. Steel workers have tried to keep foreign-made cars out of company parking lots to protest the foreign-made steel used in the cars. Labor leaders prefer trade restrictions so that domestic workers need not compete with cheap foreign labor.

Inefficient industries often require protection. Many economists believe that inefficient industries should be phased out so that resources can be used elsewhere. In the short run, protection can help workers in inefficient industries to maintain their jobs. However, because prices are high as a result of protection, people buy less of the product. Substitutes for high-priced products may be found, and the industry eventually will die.

Trade restrictions also are supported to protect infant industries. By limiting competition, tariffs can help a new manufacturing industry to develop. A protective tariff may help a new or infant industry to gain strength and experience before having to face foreign competition. The problem is to determine when protection should be removed so that the industry can compete on its own.

Tariffs also can stop foreign competitors from putting established domestic industries out of business. Some foreign suppliers use dumping to gain an unfair share of a nation's markets. Dumping involves selling a product in a foreign market at a price lower than the cost in the home market. Once the domestic manufacturer has been forced out of business, the foreign supplier is free to raise prices.

Another argument in favor of tariff restrictions is based on national defense. Specialization and trade result in interdependence. Many nations do not want to depend on other countries for products necessary to national defense, such as oil and steel. Many economists believe that a nation should use tariffs to develop industries needed for national defense. This argument raises the problems of determining which industries are critical to national defense and recognizing that the protected industries may be inefficient. Protection removes the necessity to produce the best product at the lowest price. Trade restrictions also may protect an industry for which the country does not have an advantage based on climate, natural resources, or labor supply.

Effects of Trade Restrictions

All trade restrictions limit world trade, reducing the total number of goods and services produced. Without specialization, resources are not used as efficiently as possible. Fewer goods and services are available to consumers, and fewer jobs exist. The world economy produces at less than maximum efficiency.

Trade restrictions also raise prices. For example, if 300 million pairs of shoes can be manufactured in the United States and 200 million in Italy, the supply of shoes available on the American market is 500 million pairs. Say that the government sets a protective tariff of $15 a pair and an import quota of 100 million pairs on Italian shoes. As a result, American manufacturers produce and sell more shoes. Employment in the United States may increase, but competition decreases. Domestic producers can charge higher prices for their shoes.

American consumers, however, must pay more for a pair of shoes and choose from a smaller supply. Also, foreign workers have less money to buy American goods. Thus, unemployment in the businesses involved in the United States export industry increases.

Trade limits in one country usually lead to the imposition of limits in other countries. If the United States places a high tariff on shoes made in Italy, then Italy may impose tariffs on American goods that are sold in Italy.

Improving World Trade

In general, nations recognize that specialization and trade benefit everyone. The advantages of global trade include the production of more goods, the improvement of living standards in the trading countries, and the increased operating efficiency of the world economy.

To encourage world trade, the United States passed the Reciprocal Trade Agreements Act of 1934. The law authorized the President, rather than Congress, to make agreements setting the exact tariff rate for individual products. The law provided for the reduction of tariffs on items specified in trade agreements between the United States and other countries. According to this law, the United States could grant the most favorable tariff rates on products from another country in return for similar trade benefits with that country. A country that receives this reduction in tariffs is known as a most favored nation.

For example, suppose that the United States and Italy had a trade agreement in which the United States recognized Italy as a most favored nation. Italy would enjoy any tariff reduction that the United States

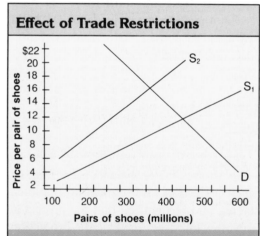

Effect of Trade Restrictions

Explanation

Lines D and S_1 represent the supply and demand of shoes before trade restrictions. Line S_2 represents the supply of shoes after trade restrictions.

Graph Skills

1. What is the equilibrium price before restrictions? After restrictions?
2. From how many pairs of shoes can consumers choose before trade restrictions? After trade restrictions?

Trade Balance of Selected Countries

Country	Imports $ (millions)	Exports $ (millions)
China	21,566	21,560
France	115,743	92,756
Ghana	1,106	1,063
Japan	131,930	138,930
Panama	1,540	315
Saudi Arabia	35,244	120,240
Soviet Union	72,960	79,003
United States	254,884	212,275
Zaire	672	662

Source: United Nations.

Explanation

The chart shows the total imports and exports of selected countries in 1982. Countries with industrial economies generally have higher volumes of trade than do countries with little industry.

Chart Skills

1. Which countries on the chart imported more than they exported?
2. Which countries on the chart exported more than they imported?
3. Which country on the chart has the greatest difference between its imports and its exports? Use your library to find out this country's major imports and exports.
4. Use your library to find out the five leading imports and exports of the United States.

granted to any other country on a specified product. Italy would extend to the United States a similar tariff reduction granted to any other country on a specified product. American and Italian producers then would find it easier to sell those particular items in each other's country.

The international General Agreement on Tariffs and Trade (GATT) encompassed 22 countries in 1947. By the 1980s, the group had expanded to 89 countries. Signers of the GATT meet periodically in an effort to lower tariffs and settle trade disputes. The GATT also restricts member countries from banning or limiting imports from the other participants.

The Export-Import Bank is a United States government lending agency that makes loans available to importers and exporters. The bank also can lend money to foreign governments to help them develop international trade.

REVIEWING THE CONCEPT

Developing Vocabulary

1. What is a comparative advantage?
2. How do a revenue tariff and a protective tariff differ?
3. How does a quota differ from a tariff?
4. Explain dumping and give an example.

Mastering Facts

1. What is the relationship between specialization and trade?
2. On what principles do nations base their trade policies?
3. How do subsidies restrict trade?
4. What are the long-range effects of trade restrictions?
5. Give two examples of common market arrangements. How do they work? What are their costs and benefits?
6. How does the Reciprocal Trade Agreements Act encourage world trade?

Limit Car Imports

Imported Japanese cars account for almost one-fourth of all cars sold in the United States. During the recession from 1979 through 1982, sales of American cars declined. In 1982, sales of domestically produced cars reached a 24-year low of 5.7 million; unemployment in the American auto industry exceeded 20 percent. As a result of declining sales, the United States asked Japanese car manufacturers to limit their exports to the United States. In April 1981, the Japanese agreed to a voluntary quota of 1.7 million cars per year for three years. In April 1984, the agreement was extended a fourth year and the quota increased to 1.85 million cars. In 1985, the agreement ended. Japanese automakers immediately announced their intention to increase car exports to the United States.

Trade restrictions on Japanese cars have been debated in the United States for over 10 years. Douglas Fraser, president emeritus of the United Auto Workers, and Reubin O'D. Askew, United States special representative for trade negotiations between 1971 and 1981, disagree on limiting imports of Japanese cars. Study the arguments Fraser and Askew used to support their positions, and decide whether you agree or disagree with each.

Douglas Fraser thinks the United States government should pressure the Japanese to build cars here in order to save jobs for United States workers. Although Fraser supports free trade in principle, he thinks that free trade no longer operates fairly. The Japanese impose many subtle restrictions on trade. The United States open market policy has worked against the job security of the United States auto worker.

Fraser acknowledges that United States car makers share part of the blame for the flood of Japanese imports. United States companies continued to manufacture more profitable large cars too long, neglecting the small car market. As United States consumers began to buy smaller cars, Japanese manufacturers met their needs. The Japanese got an exclusive hold on the small-car market.

Fraser fears that if some restraint is not put on the Japanese, the flood of imports will increase until the Japanese have exhausted their capacity to export cars. Since consumers tend to stay with a car if they are satisfied with its performance, the United States automobile industry could suffer permanent damage.

Fraser claims that he does not approve of trade restrictions that limit consumer choices. He asserts that the United States automobile industry needs the competition and discipline that the European and Japanese manufacturers provide. Fraser would in certain cases, however, recommend either a marketing agreement to limit imports or legislation requiring that Japanese car manufacturers whose sales volume in the United States is high use numerous parts made in the United States. If such measures were not successful, Fraser would support tariffs or quotas.

As layoffs in the three big United States automobile companies continue, Fraser thinks the time has come for the administration to get tough. Other industrialized countries have asked the Japanese to behave in a responsible manner, and the Japanese have responded. If the United States administration would pressure the

Limiting the importation of Japanese cars: will it help or hurt the U.S. economy?

Japanese companies, it would be a step in the right direction.

Like Fraser, Reubin O'D. Askew expresses concern over the high levels of unemployment in the United States automobile industry. Unlike Fraser, he is not in favor of imposing any form of import restrictions. Askew believes that such restrictions would have an adverse effect on the United States economy. Limiting the number of imported subcompact cars would force consumers to either buy larger, less efficient cars or postpone buying until smaller cars become available. The high cost to the consumer would increase inflation. The use of larger cars also would raise gasoline consumption.

Askew believes that the number of jobs created by import restrictions would be very small, whereas the costs of even temporary limits on imported cars would be very high. Askew cites the Council of Economic Advisers' estimate that every job gained by import restraint would add about $100,000 in costs to the consumer.

Askew foresees a gradual recovery of the United States automobile industry as manufacturers become responsive to public demands for smaller, more fuel-efficient cars. He points to one study estimating that the imported share of the car market could be cut from 26 percent to 10 percent within a decade. As United States car companies become more competitive, foreign companies will find it harder to sell their cars in this country.

Askew thinks that the Japanese are afraid the United States automobile industry will regain its previous market share. Therefore, the Japanese are reluctant to invest in car production in this country. He believes, however, that foreign automobile manufacturers have a responsibility to invest here. The government will continue to press the Japanese to make investments in this country. Askew cites examples of Japanese automobile industry investment. By the mid-1980s, Japanese firms had invested in plants in California and Tennessee.

In addition to governmental pressure on the Japanese to invest in this country, Askew points to government efforts to get the Japanese to open up their market. Although the Japanese have no tariff on cars, they do impose a 6 to 8 percent tariff on car parts. The Japanese also require that imported cars be individually tested. The United States government is making some progress in persuading the Japanese to remove these trade restraints.

Askew is aware of the trade restrictions Europeans have set up to limit imports to a certain percentage of their domestic markets. These European markets have not been so competitive as the United States market. Askew does not think that copying other nations' trade restrictions is in the best economic interest of the United States.

"As a nation that's trying to furnish the leadership to open up free trade," he explained, "we must recognize that if the United States starts to be seen as protectionist, this can influence other nations. If the world trading system turns inward, we could suffer substantially; every time there's been a contraction of world trade, countries like the United States, with tremendous potential for export expansion, have been hurt."

ANALYZING THE CASE STUDY

STEP 1   Clarify the Issue

1. What policies do Askew and Fraser favor on the issues of protectionism and free trade?
2. Do Askew and Fraser agree that other countries restrict foreign trade? Explain your answer.

3. Summarize the position of Askew regarding free trade and the position of Fraser regarding protectionism.

STEP 2   Gather Evidence

1. What evidence does Fraser use to support imposing trade restrictions on Japanese cars?
2. What evidence does Askew use to support free trade?
3. Who will benefit from car import restrictions? Who will pay for those benefits?

STEP 3   Make a Decision

Decide whether you support trade restrictions or free trade in foreign cars. Write a paragraph explaining your choice.

READING

International Trade

by J. A. Hobson   (1858–1940)

English economist and journalist J. A. Hobson achieved wide popularity as a lecturer and writer around the turn of the century. Hobson criticized classical economics, which centered on people's automatic response to inflexible economic laws. Hobson held the unpopular view that economic theory was linked to the problems of social welfare and should be used as a guide to reform. His works include several books on economics. As you read Hobson's views on international trade, think about the costs and benefits of trade restrictions.

❝A century and a half ago a band of British immigrants landing in North America made their way into an extreme southern part of the province of Ontario, Canada. They settled down in a fertile valley crossed by a river. Along the banks they built clusters of log huts that grew into a large and prosperous village. The north side of the river had most of the better grazing land, and a creek running down from the neighboring hills made it easier to develop a lumber mill on that side. But the south side had land more fertile for wheat and better protection for fruit and vegetables. There were specially favorable plots of soil on either side under the shelter of the hills. Advantages of climate, soil, or position led to special sorts of cultivation and industries connected with the two settlements. A few blacksmiths, carpenters, weavers, tailors, and shoe-makers settled, according to personal convenience or family connections, on the north or south side of the stream. Far from other settlements, this village, with its neighborhood of farmers, lumbermen, etc., formed a self-supporting industrial community. There was a bridge across the river so that people and goods passed freely back and forth. Market arrangements enabled every special advantage of soil or position, or any special skill which some artisan or manufacturer might possess, to be most fully used. Producers gained because the whole body of customers were free to buy what they had to sell.

Here was a simple example of the economy of division of labor on a basis of free exchange. It was evidently an advantage for the villagers living on either side of the stream to have close contact and free trade. Anyone suggesting that the bridge should be broken down, or that a toll should be set up for people and goods passing across, so that each side could supply its own needs, would have been called a lunatic.

Now it came to pass, after the American revolution, that a line dividing the frontiers between Canada and the new United States was drawn. The river passing through the village was the boundary line. Politically the village was cut in two. The inhabitants of the northern part remained Canadian citizens, obeying the laws and paying the taxes of Ontario. The inhabitants of the southern part became citizens of the United States. In time the political division might affect the feelings of the two sets of villagers toward one another and lead to a lessening of social exchange. However, could political disagreements make that division of labor and that freedom of exchange, which were an advantage formerly, less advantageous? Would it be any less damaging than before to break down the bridge, or put a toll on the goods which sought a market across the stream? It would be possible, as it was before, to break the economic community into two, following the line of the river. But it would be just as evident that every person who had anything to sell would have only half the market he had before. Everything he wanted to buy was similarly restricted in the supply available to him. It might be possible for all the villagers to supply themselves with all they needed by dealing with neighbors on their own side of the stream. This would mean losing their share of the natural advantages or special skill belonging to some villagers on the other side. The new restrictions on the market for the things which they are in a superior position to make, rob them of part of the fruits of their own industry. Each village loses, both as buyer and as seller, by any limits put on that free trade which existed before.

The political division does not affect the true economy of industry. It was previously an advantage for the young men and women who grew up on the north side to take up land or a trade upon the south side if a better opportunity presented itself. Such freedom of movement led to a better development of the whole district, an advantage in which all would share. Similarly, if any thrifty farmer on the south had money and saw a better use for his savings by putting up a sawmill on the north side, it would hurt the interests of all the villagers on either side to stop him from this profitable use of his capital. All villagers would gain more by the cheaper timber his sawmill would supply than by any other use to which he could put his savings on his own side of the stream. Under such circumstances any interference with the free flow of labor or capital is as injurious as any interference with freedom of markets. For the inhabitants of either or both sides to adopt a law which kept the growing population to its own side of the frontiers [borders], or put restrictions on imports which could be produced better or more cheaply on the other side, would be a suicidal policy.

If the villagers on the north, out of some mistaken patriotism, adopted such a policy, they could damage the villagers of the south. However, they would damage themselves to a somewhat greater extent. The cost of collecting the tolls, keeping out smugglers, and administering the whole protective policy, would fall on them. Supposing, however, that they were so foolish as to try this economic separation, would the villagers of the south gain by copying the restrictions? Why should they stop northern capital from coming in and developing their resources or stop skilled labor from crossing the stream to help northern capital in their work? Why should they prevent their villagers from getting the better or cheaper produce which the northerners still wanted to supply? To follow the bad example of the north would be to double the injury for their citizens as well as for the others, and to saddle themselves with the same costs of administering the policy.

So long as the village was all inside Ontario, cooperation among all its members, by division of labor, freedom of markets and full liberty of movement for capital and labor, aided the common welfare of the village. The soil and other natural conditions might be much more favorable on the south than the north, so that young workers and new savings went chiefly to the development and settlement of that section. But it would be evident that the villagers who stayed on the northern side were better off, because of the fuller development of the better resources on the southern side. If any foolish sentiment had operated to keep their workers and capital from seeking more profitable employment across the river, they would have been heavy losers. Now this economy could not be reversed or even modified by the political event which split the little industrial community into two political communities. What was good business before would remain good now. Any political interference with the freedom of movement for men and goods would injure business. If either of the sections of the village would be improved by restrictions, further barriers between the two parts of the north divided by the creek which ran into the river would also be advantageous. This policy of subdivision might be carried so far as to make each street and finally each family a self-contained individual community.

This illustration sets forth the simple and sound doctrine of industrial and commercial relations between nations. What these two sections of the frontier village are to one another, are also the two nations to which they relatively belong, Canada and the United States. If free flow of capital and labor and products is advantageous for both sides of the divided village, so is it for the two nations. What is true for Canada and the United States is true for any other nations, whether possessing a common frontier or not. The inhabitants of every country benefit by the freest possible intercourse with all other countries. In that way they can get most wealth, utilizing most completely and effectively any special qualities of natural resources or acquired skill they may possess. Nations profit by sharing the advantages which the inhabitants of other countries possess. **"**

From *The Science of Wealth*, by J. A. Hobson.

UNDERSTANDING THE READING

1. Is J. A. Hobson in favor of protectionism or free trade? Explain your answer.
2. In Hobson's example, if the villagers in the north adopted trade restrictions, who would benefit? Who would be hurt? Why?

Section 1 Review

Understanding Trade Restrictions

1. What are the advantages of specialization and trade? The disadvantages?
2. Why are revenue tariffs generally lower than protective tariffs?
3. How do protective tariffs aid domestic industry? Give an example.
4. What is the difference between a cartel and a quota?
5. How might trade restrictions contribute to national defense? How might they hinder national defense?
6. Do trade restrictions protect American jobs? Explain your answer.
7. In the long run, do trade restrictions help or hurt inefficient industries? Explain your answer.
8. In what ways do trade restrictions affect a nation's consumers?
9. How does the multinational General Agreement on Tariffs and Trade (GATT) affect world trade?
10. What is the function of the Export-Import Bank?

Trade Restrictions Today

1. Do you think that American businesses should be allowed to engage in trade with nations that the United States government regards as enemies of the country? Why or why not?
2. **Challenge:** Why are the prices of some foreign goods lower than the prices of similar American goods?

2 Balance of Payments

SECTION OVERVIEW

Americans who plan vacations outside the United States can obtain foreign money—French francs, German marks, Japanese yen—from their local banks. Firms that import goods from other countries also can obtain foreign currency. Countries maintain records of the movement of money and all other international transactions. The money tourists and businesses spend outside the United States affects currency rates and the balance of payments among countries. In this section, you will learn how currency exchange rates affect the nation's balance of payments and the economy.

ECONOMIC VOCABULARY

balance of payments	exchange rate
current account	floating exchange rates
capital account	depreciate
foreign exchange markets	special drawing rights (SDRs)

Trade Among Countries

Countries import and export goods. Trade makes up an important part of the economy of industrialized nations. The total value of world trade, as measured by the exports of all countries in 1980, was $1,988 billion. Exports represent between 7 percent and 9 percent of United States GNP.

Countries record all of their international transactions. All money flowing into the country to pay for exports and to be invested is recorded. All money flowing out of the country to pay for imports and military expenses overseas and to be invested abroad also is recorded.

The balance of payments is the difference between the money flowing into and out of a country. If the amount of money leaving the country is larger than the amount coming in, the country has a nega-tive balance of payments. A positive balance of payments represents more money coming into than leaving a country. The balance of payments account is the result of two main categories of transactions among nations—the current account and the capital account.

The current account represents the value of exports and imports of goods and services, tourist spending, investment income, military transactions, and pensions and other transfers of money. The capital account includes money that Americans invest abroad and foreigners invest in the United States. These investments consist of long-term deposits in financial institutions, purchases of stocks and bonds, and ownership of factories and buildings. Also included in the capital account are short-term loans. Foreigners can lend money to American individuals, banks, businesses, or, by

United States Balance of Payments Account

	1980	1981	1982
Current Account ($ millions)			
Exports of goods and services	269,628	288,378	264,178
Imports of goods and services	−291,721	−310,338	−294,660
Income to foreigners from investments in the U.S.	− 42,875	− 52,760	− 56,842
Income from U.S. investments abroad	72,445	86,243	84,146
Capital Account ($ millions)			
U.S. assets abroad	− 86,052	−110,601	−118,045
Foreign assets in the U.S.	54,922	80,678	87,866

Source: Bureau of Economic Analysis.

Explanation

The chart represents a brief summary of flow of money in and out of the United States from 1980 to 1982.

Chart Skills

1. In what year was the balance of payments in the current account negative?

2. Was the balance of payments in the capital account negative or positive during 1980, 1981, and 1982?

3. According to the chart, what was the total United States balance of payments for 1980, 1981, and 1982?

---

buying government securities, the United States Treasury. Americans also lend money for short terms all over the world.

Obtaining Foreign Currency

Importing increases the amount and variety of goods available. More goods exist than could be produced domestically. However, importing also requires buyers to obtain foreign currency. When an American car dealer buys German cars, the dealer must pay in German marks rather than dollars. Similarly, a German must obtain dollars to purchase American products. Individuals and small businesses obtain foreign currency from banks. American banks arrange the delivery of German marks to the German car manufacturer. In the same way, banks in Germany provide dollars for delivery in the United States.

Banks and large firms buy foreign currency on the foreign exchange market. On foreign exchange markets, people buy and sell currencies in the same way that stocks are bought and sold on stock exchanges. The price of a currency is called its exchange rate because it represents the amount of one currency that must be given in trade or exchange for another.

The rate of exchange for major currencies—the American dollar, French franc, German mark, Japanese yen—is determined by floating exchange rates. In the system of floating exchange rates, supply and demand determine the value of one nation's currency in relation to those of other nations. As a result, currency rates fluctuate from day to day. Therefore, as Americans purchase more British goods, the demand for British pounds rises, as does the equilibrium price.

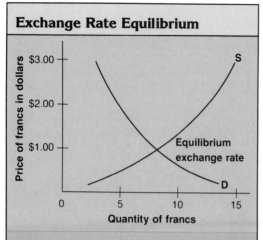

Exchange Rate Equilibrium

Explanation

The demand for francs is represented by D and the supply by S. As demand increases—foreigners demand more French products, invest in French securities, travel to France—the equilibrium price rises.

Graph Skills

1. At the equilibrium price on the graph, how many francs can be exchanged for $1.00?
2. How is a new equilibrium price determined?

Currency Exchange Rates

	New York Tues.	Home Mkt. Tues.	New York Mon.
	(In U.S. dollars)		
British pound........	1.2628	1.2620	1.2680
Canadian dollar......	0.7631	0.7628	0.7637
	(In foreign units to U.S. dollar)		
French franc	9.0080	9.0600	9.0150
Japanese yen	241.68	241.85	242.12
Swiss franc.........	2.4245	2.4235	2.4095
West German mark ...	2.9455	2.9435	2.9370

Based on average of late buying and selling rates. Home markets: London, Toronto, Paris, Tokyo, Zurich and Frankfurt.

Source: *Wall Street Journal*, November 6, 1984.

Explanation

The financial listing states the value of foreign currencies in relation to the dollar. For example, at the time of reporting, a Canadian dollar was worth only 76 cents in American money. A British pound could be exchanged for $1.26. The remaining currencies are shown in foreign units. A dollar could be exchanged for 9 French francs or 241.68 Japanese yen.

Chart Skills

1. At the time of reporting, how much would a $400 American television set cost in Canadian dollars? In French francs?
2. For how many yen would a suit made in Germany and costing 600 German marks sell in Japan?

The value of a currency on the foreign exchange market changes in relation to other currencies. For example, University of Chicago economist George Stigler was awarded the Nobel prize in 1982. The Nobel Prize carries a monetary award of 1.15 million Swedish kronor. In mid-1982, the cash value of 1.15 million kronor was $182,000. Because the demand for the dollar was strong in relation to the demand for the kronor, by December 1982, when Stigler received the award, the amount in dollars had shrunk to about $155,000.

When the demand for the dollar is strong, the dollar is said to be strong. When demand for it decreases rapidly, it is said to be weak. During 1982 the demand for the dollar increased, increasing the dollar's worth in relation to other currencies and vice versa. The rate of exchange for currencies is reported daily in the financial section of newspapers.

Effects of Exchange Rates

Fluctuations in currency exchange rates affect a nation's economy in numerous ways. Currency rates affect prices, interest rates, and employment.

By affecting prices, floating exchange rates affect the sale of American goods abroad, as well as the sale of all goods traded among countries. If the exchange rate for Japanese yen were 245 yen for $1.00, the price of a Japanese television set at 73,500 yen would be $300. If the demand for yen increased so that $1.00 would buy only 200 yen, the same television set would cost $367.50. At the new rate, Americans would buy fewer Japanese goods.

If a large amount of Japanese yen, or any other currency, accumulates in the hands of foreign banks, business firms, and individuals, the price of the money in relation to other currencies tends to fall. Supply has increased faster than demand. Currency is said to depreciate in a floating system when the value of a currency falls in relation to other currencies.

Price changes resulting from currency fluctuations affect many people. When the dollar is strong in relation to the yen, Japanese goods become cheaper. A strong dollar makes imports cheaper. Then consumers gain because competition from foreign goods keeps down prices and, therefore, inflation. However, a strong dollar makes exports more expensive, and so hurts farmers who export their crops and industries that export products. American tourists abroad gain when the dollar is strong because their dollars buy more goods and services there. Users of imported raw materials gain as production costs decrease.

When the value of the dollar falls in relation to other currencies, the number of American tourists abroad decreases and the price of imports rises. Exports increase because American goods cost less.

Currency exchange rates affect interest rates. As the demand for and value of the dollar increases, interest rates rise because fewer dollars are available for lending. As interest rates rise, foreign investment increases to take advantage of high interest rates. Again, the demand for the dollar increases. Large deficits in the United States budget also add to rising interest rates, crowding out smaller borrowers.

Fluctuations in currency values affect employment. As exports decrease, some sectors of the economy suffer. Since one-sixth of the United States economy depends on exports, each $20 billion in the trade deficit equals 500,000 more jobless. Foreign exports may drive inefficient American firms out of business, thus increasing unemployment. Some economists see this situation as an advantage, since only the most competitive industries survive. In the future, the United States economy will gain from industries strong enough to compete internationally. However, in the short run many Americans may lose their jobs.

Overall, a strong currency and less expensive imports increase the desire for protection against imports. In the United States, the steel and automobile industries, among others, have asked the President and Congress for trade restrictions against cheap imports.

Surpluses and Deficits

Exchange rates affect a nation's balance of payments. As the value of a currency increases, imports become cheaper and exports correspondingly more expensive. Imports increase and exports decrease. A growing current account deficit results as money to pay for exports flows out of the country. However, a strong currency generally results in a capital account surplus as investment increases and interest rates rise, causing money to flow into the country. The capital account surplus helps to offset the current account deficit.

The United States, like other countries, prefers a surplus in the current account showing foreign purchases of American-made goods. Purchases of American-made goods stimulate production, provide jobs, and raise incomes in the United States.

Capital inflows carry two dangers, depending on whether the capital represents short-term or long-term investment. Short-term money seeks the highest possible interest return. If interest rates fall, however,

Americans must exchange their dollars for other currency to use in other countries.

funds quickly flow out of the United States, seeking a higher return elsewhere. When dollars flow abroad, they are not available for spending here and cannot stimulate domestic investment.

Long-term capital investment implies a degree of foreign control of American enterprises. When accompanied by a strong dollar, the stable political climate encourages long-term foreign capital investment in the United States.

An International Currency

To consumers, the real value of the dollar is based on what it will buy in the United States. However, many other nations use the dollar as an international currency and are concerned about the dollar's stability. In 1970, the International Monetary Fund (IMF) invented a new form of money. The IMF is a part of the World Bank set up under the direction of the United Nations. The new money, called Special Drawing Rights (SDRs), or sometimes paper gold, is

an internationally recognized currency available to nations in need of funds. According to a set of complicated rules, a country can borrow SDRs from the IMF and use them to buy back its own currency from other countries.

All major countries hold SDRs in addition to gold and supplies of one another's currencies. SDRs also can be used in place of dollars to settle international payments.

REVIEWING THE CONCEPT

Developing Vocabulary

1. What is the difference between a negative and a positive balance of payments?
2. What does the current account of a nation represent?
3. What is included in the capital account?
4. What is the purpose of foreign exchange markets in international trade?
5. How do floating exchange rates affect the balance of payments?
6. Why do currencies depreciate in value?

Mastering Facts

1. Explain why the process of trading between nations is more complex than trading within a country.
2. How do floating exchange rates affect the prices of exports? Of imports? Of domestically manufactured products?
3. List three groups that either benefit from or are hurt by a strong United States dollar. Explain the reasons for your answers. How would these groups be affected by a weak dollar?
4. Why do countries prefer to have a surplus in their balance of payments current account rather than capital account?
5. What are the current exchange rates for the Japanese yen, the German mark, and the British pound? The *Wall Street Journal* and other major newspapers carry this information.

A Trip to England

Constance Trickett anticipated an exciting summer vacation. Connie had thoroughly enjoyed her first visit to England in the 1970s. Last year she decided to take another trip there. A travel agency arranged flights, hotel accommodations, car rental, and theater tickets. Friends in London had sent magazines and catalogs so that Connie could plan some shopping trips.

The confirmation of travel arrangements and the London magazines arrived on the same morning. The prices surprised Connie. She knew that air fares had increased with rising fuel costs, and she had heard that inflation had been more severe in England than in the United States. However, travel articles had stressed the growing purchasing power of the dollar compared with other currencies. During Connie's trip to England in 1972, the exchange rate for the British pound was $2.50. When Connie planned her present trip, a British pound was worth only $1.35.

Increased costs worried Connie, and she decided to prepare a budget. Fortunately, she had saved her records from the earlier trip. Connie listed each item and the price paid in pounds and dollars in both 1972 and 1984.

Connie could see how much the strong dollar had lowered costs for her trip. The 1984 vacation would cost four times as many pounds but only twice as many dollars as the earlier trip. Still, $2,600 seemed like a lot of money.

Then Connie remembered how she had learned to compare prices in her high school economics class. The Consumer Price Index could be used to convert prices in a current year to comparable prices in a base year (current price / CPI × 100 = price in base year). If Connie could check the CPIs for 1972 and 1984, she could convert the cost of the trip to a base year and compare prices. The local librarian told Connie that with 1967 as the base year the CPI in 1972 was 125.3; in 1984, 303.5. Using the formula, Connie determined, first, that the 1972 trip cost $969.07 in 1967 dollars. Second, she found that the 1984 trip to England would cost only $851.31 in 1967 dollars.

Knowing that her trip in 1984 would really be cheaper than the earlier trip made

Comparison of Two Trips				
	1972 Pounds	1972 Dollars	1984 Pounds	1984 Dollars
Air fare	128.00	320.00	481.37	649.85
Hotel	65.00	162.50	395.00	533.25
Meals	85.30	213.25	267.50	361.13
Car rental	37.50	93.75	98.50	132.98
Gasoline	52.00	130.00	73.60	99.36
Train fare	5.00	12.50	35.00	47.25
Theatre	15.00	37.50	32.50	43.88
Hairdresser	1.25	3.13	7.00	9.45
Gifts	25.04	62.60	124.40	167.94
Clothing	71.60	179.01	399.00	538.35
Total	485.69	1,214.24	1,913.87	2,583.74

Explanation

The chart shows the cost of various goods and services purchased by Connie on her trips in 1972 and in 1984. The chart gives costs in both pounds and dollars.

Chart Skills

1. How much did air fare increase, in dollars, between 1972 and 1984? In pounds?
2. If the value of the dollar had been less, how would the cost of Connie's trip in pounds have changed? Explain.

Connie feel better. However, she was still worried. She put the problem aside for a few days, but when the travel agency requested a deposit to hold the hotel room she had to decide. As she looked over the figures once more, Connie wondered how she had managed in 1972 when her salary was half her present salary. She used the CPI again and found her answer. In 1972 Connie's salary had been $15,225—$12,151.84 in 1967 dollars. Her current salary, $31,962, was only $10,531.14 in 1967 dollars.

Connie's income had not kept pace with inflation. The 1984 trip to England would take a larger percentage of her salary than had the earlier trip. She would shop less during this trip.

ANALYZING THE CASE STUDY

STEP 1   Clarify the Issue

1. What economic reasons made a trip to England in 1984 a good idea?
2. If other Americans use the same reasoning, how will the increase in tourists abroad affect the balance of payments?

STEP 2   Identify Change

1. How has the fluctuation in currency exchange rates affected tourism?
2. How had inflation between 1972 and 1984 affected Connie's salary?

STEP 3   Predict Further Change

1. What steps has the United States taken to control inflation?
2. What factors have contributed to the strong United States dollar?

READING

American World Trade

by the Council of Economic Advisers to the President

International trade and the place of the United States in the world economy has become an important concern of the federal government. The 1983 Annual Report of the Council of Economic Advisers, chaired by Martin Feldstein, addressed the issues of trade restrictions, the effects of floating exchange rates, and the international debt problem. As you read this excerpt from the *Annual Report*, consider how various aspects of international trade affect the United States balance of payments.

❝ D uring the 1970s, the world's market economies became more closely linked than ever before. Exports and imports, as a share of gross national product (GNP), reached record levels for most industrial countries. International lending and direct foreign investment grew even faster than world trade. This closer linkage of economies was mutually beneficial. It allowed producers in each country to take greater advantage of their country's special resources and knowledge. At the same time, it allowed each country to consume a wider variety of products, at lower costs, than it could produce itself.

Underlying the growth in world trade and investment was a reduction of barriers to trade. The postwar period was marked by a series of agreements to liberalize trade.

In spite of its huge benefits, however, this trading system is now in serious danger. Within the United States, demands for protection against imports and for export subsidies have grown. A combination of factors have led to the view that we are becoming uncompetitive in world markets. In Europe, a growing structural unemployment problem, aggravated by recession, has increased protectionist pressures. In the developing countries, financial problems are pushing many countries back toward exchange controls and import restrictions.

These problems must not be allowed to disrupt world trade. If the system comes apart—if the world's nations allow themselves to be caught up in a spiral of retaliatory trade restrictions—a long time may pass before the pieces are put back together. . . .

Concern over the international competitiveness of the United States is high. It is argued that United States business has steadily lost ground in the international marketplace. This supposed poor performance is often attributed to two causes—failures of management in the United States and the support given to foreign businesses by their governments. Contributing to the view of declining competitiveness is the United States deficit in merchandise trade, especially the imbalance in trade with Japan.

Changes in the United States trade performance must, however, be put into the context of changes in the United States role in the world economy. This wider approach reveals that much of the concern about long-run competitiveness is based on misperceptions. The recent strength of the dollar has created a temporary loss of competitiveness. However, the United States has not experienced a continuing loss of ability to sell its products on international markets. Changes in the relationship of the United States to the world economy have made the United States look less competitive by some traditional measures.

The United States share of world trade and world GNP did decline throughout the 1950s and 1960s, reflecting the recovery of the rest of the world from World War II, together with the narrowing of the huge United States technological lead. In the 1970s . . . this long decline leveled off.

The changing structure of the United States balance of payments contributed to the view that we were not competitive.

In the 1950s and early 1960s, the United States normally had a trade surplus and invested heavily in other countries. In the years after 1973, the United States normally had a trade deficit, and annual investment by foreigners in the United States began to approach United States investment abroad. The shift in the trade balance was closely connected with the shift in investment flows.

There is no question, however, that increased foreign competition has forced some sectors of the United States economy to contract. This is partly a result of the fact that trade has become more important to the United States economy. Specialization by nations is the reason for international trade. If the United States is to expand its trade, our economy must become more specialized. Some sectors will grow and others will shrink.

The "problem" of diminshed market power in some sectors actually results from a desirable aspect of trade—the fact that trade increases competition. One of the major benefits of an increasingly open economy is the reduction of monopoly and market power, increasing efficiency and helping consumers. . . .

During 1982, the dollar rose against other major currencies to its highest level since the beginning of floating exchange rates in 1973. The strength of the dollar provided some benefits to the economy by reducing import prices and controlling inflation. On the other hand, the strong dollar caused severe problems by decreasing the cost competitiveness of United States exports.

What the rise of the dollar seems to reflect is a rise in the demand for United States assets. In order to buy United States assets, foreigners must first obtain dollars. The increased demand for dollars drives up the exchange rate.

Many observers believe that other factors besides interest rates help explain the dollar's strength. The United States is still regarded as the most politically and economically stable of the market economies and has become a financial shelter in troubled times. The worldwide search for financial security may partially explain this country's rising capital account surplus and its growing current account deficit.

The rise of the dollar was associated with a large rise in the production costs of United States firms relative to foreign competitors. This rise in relative costs has at least temporarily reduced the international competitiveness of United States industry dramatically. Other United States exporting and import-competing sectors, especially agriculture, have also been hurt.

Despite this decline in competitive position, not until the third quarter of 1982 did the United States trade deficit begin to show a significant increase. This delay was in line with previous experience of the effect of exchange rates on trade. The full effect of changes in exchange rates on the volume of exports and imports is felt only after some time has passed. Some trade takes place under contracts signed in advance and customers do not always change suppliers immediately . . . Some estimates suggest that the full negative effect is not felt for more than two years.

If large budget deficits continue, real interest rates may rise again, sustaining or even increasing the high exchange rate of the dollar. In this case, the trade deficit could remain high for several years. A large and sustained trade deficit would result in an economic recovery which would be "lopsided" in the sense that exporting and import-competing sectors would not share in the gains.

The temporary adverse effects of a strong dollar create pressure to do something for the exporting and import-competing sectors. Three kinds of policies might be used: (1) intervention by the federal government in the form of protection or export subsidies, (2) direct intervention in the foreign exchange market, and (3) changes in monetary and fiscal policy.

First, the negative effect of the strong dollar on the competitiveness of many United States firms has fueled pressures for protective trade policy. These pressures must be resisted. Protecting import-competing industries or subsidizing exports is not just a harmful long-run policy. With a floating exchange rate, such policies would fail to improve the trade balance or create employment even in the short run.

An increase in exports or a reduction in imports would lead to an increased demand for or reduced supply of dollars on the world market, raising the exchange rate. This would lead to a further loss of competitiveness. Governments cannot simultaneously protect every industry.

Market-distorting policies reduce the efficiency of the economy. The effects would prove still worse if, as is likely, United States actions were to provoke foreign retaliation.

The second policy available to the federal government to counteract the strong dollar is intervention in the foreign exchange market. Since March 1981, the United States has refrained as much as possible from direct intervention in the foreign exchange market. This unwillingness to intervene is based on doubts about whether exchange-market intervention is effective or desirable. Action by the government would probably have little effect on the exchange rate because of the sheer size of world financial markets.

Although the government cannot significantly affect exchange rates through direct intervention, monetary and fiscal policies do indirectly affect the exchange rate. A third strategy for bringing the dollar down would involve looser monetary policies—increasing the supply of dollars. Tighter fiscal policies—higher taxes and less government spending— would also lower the exchange rate of the dollar. Both of these changes would tend to lower real interest rates (at least in the short run), making the flow of money into the United States less attractive and thus driving down the value of the dollar.

Despite its unfortunate effects on the United States balance of trade, however, tight money is the prime weapon in the fight against inflation. Under fixed exchange rates, the heaviest costs of monetary contraction and controlling inflation fell on the interest-sensitive areas of the economy, such as construction and durable consumer goods. With floating exchange rates, however, much of the burden also falls on exporting and import-competing sectors . . .

A tighter fiscal policy would also lower real interest rates and lead to a lower dollar. Under fixed exchange rates, budget deficits crowded out domestic investment. With a floating exchange rate, budget deficits crowd out exporting and import-competing products as well. A reduction in deficits would lead—with some lag—to an improvement in the trade balance as well as higher investment.

The strength of the dollar has put considerable strain on the resolve of the United States to remain committed to free trade. The most effective strategy the United States can pursue for its exporting and import-competing sectors is to get its overall economic house in order—above all, by bringing budget deficits and real interest rates under control. **"**

From *The Annual Report of the Council of Economic Advisers,* February 1983.

UNDERSTANDING THE READING

1. How has the structure of the United States balance of payments changed in the years since 1973? What was responsible for the changes?
2. What three kinds of policies might the federal government use to counteract the negative effects of the strong dollar on the United States balance of payments? Explain how each would work.
3. How does a strong United States dollar affect you and your family?

Section 2 Review

Understanding Balance of Payments

1. List and explain three examples of long-term investments.
2. Why is the price of a currency on the foreign exchange market called the currency's exchange rate?
3. Why do currency exchange rates fluctuate from day to day?
4. What caused economist George Stigler's Nobel Prize award to decrease from $182,000 to $155,000?
5. What effect do floating exchange rates have on interest rates?
6. How is employment in the United States affected by floating exchange rates?
7. List and explain two reasons for the increase in the amount of foreign invest-

ment in the United States.
8. What motivates industries to demand trade restrictions?

Balance of Payments Today

1. Explain why you agree or disagree with the following comment: "Most trade between people, regions, or nations benefits one trading partner at the expense of the other."
2. **Challenge:** Suppose that Texas became an independent nation. In view of the major products and services of Texas— oil, cattle, aerospace technology—what would be the principal positive and negative items in the Texas balance of payments accounts with the United States?

3 Worldwide Business

SECTION OVERVIEW

Businesses grow and change. A company may be successful in producing a product or service for the United States market. Then, based on its success, the company may begin to export a small amount of its product. As the company builds its exports, it may think of itself as an international company. Finally, the company may realize that the potential of the world market could mean additional revenue. Plants are built overseas, and the company's philosophy changes to that of a multinational. In this section, you will learn what a multinational is and how multinational corporations affect the national and world economies.

ECONOMIC VOCABULARY   multinational corporation

Worldwide Corporations

In the past few decades a new factor has entered international trade—the multinational corporation. Multinational corporations produce products in more than one country, thus helping to distribute their goods and services on a global scale. What makes multinationals so special is their enormous size.

About 7,300 multinationals exist today. Approximately 300 of them operate in more than six countries and have annual sales of more than $100 million. Two-thirds of these 300 large multinationals are based in the United States.

Multinational corporations, have business interests that crisscross the globe. For example, PepsiCo produces Pepsi Cola in more than 500 plants in over 100 countries. Ford Motor Company comprises a network of over 55 subsidiary corporations, 40 of them foreign based. Nestlé Chocolate, a Swiss firm, receives over 90 percent of its revenue from outside Switzerland. Phillips Lamp Works, a huge Dutch multinational, has business operations in 68 countries. By the year 2000, experts predict, multinals will account for half of all production in the non-Communist world. The gross sales of large multinationals exceed the GNP of some countries.

Effects of Multinationals

Companies derive some benefits from operating in several countries. First, goods manufactured in a foreign country where they are sold save transportation costs and are not subject to import tariffs or quotas. Second, earnings from foreign operations are not subject to United States income taxes unless the profits are brought back to the United States. Third, multinational firms can use resources efficiently. Raw

National GNP and Corporate Gross Sales

Nations and Corporations	$ Billions	Nations and Corporations	$ Billions	Nations and Corporations	$ Billions
United States	2,614.1	Sweden	119.3	Greece	44.6
Soviet Union	1,423.8	Switzerland	114.4	Iraq	39.1
Japan	1,152.6	ROYAL DUTCH PETROLEUM	100.0	STANDARD OIL OF INDIANA	35.0
West Germany	848.3	MOBIL	74.0	Philippines	34.2
China	552.0	Austria	77.7	Colombia	32.0
United Kingdom	445.4	BRITISH PETROLEUM	65.0	GULF OIL	32.0
Italy	368.1	Yugoslavia	73.2	Taiwan	32.0
Canada	243.3	FORD MOTOR COMPANY	70.0	IBM	29.1
Brazil	248.4	TEXACO	70.0	GENERAL ELECTRIC	27.2
Netherlands	173.6	Hungary	57.9	SHELL OIL	27.0
India	159.4	South Africa	64.5	Portugal	23.3
East Germany	146.0	STANDARD OIL OF CALIFORNIA	50.0	Pakistan	25.1
Mexico	142.4			Malaysia	23.3
GENERAL MOTORS	126.0				

Sources: Dun and Bradstreet; *Statistical Abstract of the United States.*

Explanation

The chart compares the GNP of selected countries with the gross sales of selected corporations. Corporations appear in capital letters.

Graph Skills

1. What is the largest corporation listed?
2. What is the business of most of the corporations listed here?

materials can be purchased in areas where they are plentiful. Labor-intensive production can take place in countries where the wages of workers are low. Capital can be borrowed in countries where banks charge borrowers a low rate of interest.

Critics of multinationals claim that American jobs are lost because money is invested in foreign production facilities rather than in United States plants. Critics also claim that multinationals drain tax revenues from the United States. Under the current United States tax law, a multinational company can deduct from its United States tax obligations all taxes paid to foreign governments.

Multinational corporations have made government control of the economy more difficult. During periods of inflation, governments follow a tight money policy, raising taxes and cutting spending to slow the economy. Normally, tight money policies would reduce companies' plant and equipment spending. However, the ability of multinational companies to borrow money abroad to finance investment at home makes government policy less effective. During economic recessions, governments increase the money supply to stimulate the economy. Multinational corporations then may use money borrowed at low interest rates to increase production in another nation's economy.

Control of Multinationals

Political questions arise as a result of the size and influence of multinational companies. Supporters of multinationals argue that by operating in several countries at once, these giant corporations act as a force for peace. For example, more than 1,000 agreements are in force between Western corporations and Communist countries.

Such ties encourage cooperation between different economic systems.

The United Nations has compiled a code of conduct for multinationals. Its principles include respect for the national ruling authority, obedience to the law, and noninterference in the internal politics of the countries where the multinational operates. Whether governments can enforce this code against companies that are sometimes as large as or larger than the government is uncertain.

Nevertheless, once a multinational company has entered a foreign nation it is bound by the laws and traditions of that country. By tradition, for example, individuals working for giant corporations in Japan are never fired. Any foreign firm operating in Japan would be obliged to follow this unwritten law. Government expectations also may influence multinationals. Company business decisions often involve closing unprofitable plants or building new plants. However, if business decisions cause serious problems for the host country's economy, the government will try to influence business policies.

Important changes are occurring and will continue to occur in the world. New kinds of jobs will open, new kinds of homes will be built, and new problems and shortages will have to be faced. New discoveries and ideas will change the ways in which we think about ourselves and our world. Advances in communications will continue to change business practices and the way people relate to one another. Nations will have to face the growing power of multinational corporations and the demands of poor nations for a fair share of the world's resources. New opportunities and new challenges will result.

REVIEWING THE CONCEPT

Developing Vocabulary

What is a multinational corporation?

Mastering Facts

1. List and explain three benefits that multinational corporations gain from operating in several countries.
2. What criticisms have been leveled at multinational corporations?
3. How may multinational corporations affect their host countries?
4. How may host countries affect the operations of multinationals?

Sony's Innovation

For over 20 years, Sony has been one of Japan's great multinational corporations. It was founded just after World War II, and has earned an international reputation for quality and new product development. Its global approach to marketing has placed Sony stocks in trade on 23 stock exchanges in 12 countries. Sony's main line of business is consumer electronics—transistor radios, transistorized television sets, and home video recorders.

Much of the credit for Sony's success goes to Sony's chairperson, Akio Morita. Because Sony's goal is to be first with the best, the company spends more than 8 percent of its sales revenue to finance research and development. Said Morita, "If we stop, we will be beaten just as American industry was beaten by the Japanese."

Morita built plants in the United States and Europe that have helped Sony to win shares of the markets in those countries. In 1983, Europe accounted for about 24 percent of Sony's sales compared with 13 percent in 1974, when Morita opened Sony's first European plant in Wales. However, by building plants near his markets Morita also increased wage costs. Other Japanese multinationals, such as Matsushita and Sanyo, moved into cheaper labor areas, building plants in Mexico, Taiwan, and Malaysia.

Sony's rapid switches from one product to another are attributed to Morita's sixth sense in innovation. Sony's management worried when Morita became obsessed with the Walkman. "He brought in this little radio," an executive recalled, "and I thought, 'Sony will build that?' " By 1983, Sony had built over 7 million Walkmans.

Akio Morita made his first trip to the United States in 1953 to license Western Electric transistor technology. Since that time, Morita has become more an industrial statesman and less an operating executive. He frequently flies the Paris, New York, Tokyo circuit. He plays tennis with Virginia Wade, gives interviews, and seems absorbed by his career as wise man, serving on such boards as the United States–Japan Advisory Commission. "I am quite involved with trade matters," he said, "because I am one of the few businessmen who can deal with them."

Being an international statesman has not dampened Morita's enthusiasm for new products. He recently spent time in an equipment-packed movie director's van parked outside New York's Plaza Hotel. There he met with movie producer Francis Ford Coppola. Since 1980, Morita has provided Coppola with experimental television equipment and specially priced goods, such as Sony's professional video camera and its state-of-the-art videotape recorder. In return, Sony receives favorable publicity and a Hollywood test area for devices that Morita believes will reshape the movie business. Coppola plans to shoot his next picture directly on Sony's advanced video recording machines. He will then transfer the end result to 35mm film. Coppola expects this technique to drastically cut production time. With Sony's help, Coppola may be the first to produce a major feature film directly on video recorders.

Morita, however, dreams of selling Sony's advanced equipment not just to filmmakers but also to owners of small, 150-seat video theaters. Of Sony's future, Morita says, "The whole technology is changing. I already feel the turning point. We are going up."

ANALYZING THE CASE STUDY

STEP 1   Gather Evidence

1. What evidence exists that Sony is a multinational corporation?
2. How has Morita contributed to Sony's development as a multinational?

STEP 2   Identify Change

1. According to Morita, why must Sony's research continue? How much of its revenue does Sony spend on research?
2. How has Sony contributed to changes in the electronics industry?
3. What effect has the development of such multinationals as Sony and Masushita had on Japan? On the United States? On world markets?

STEP 3   Predict Further Change

Write a paragraph explaining your view of future changes resulting from the continued growth of multinational companies in either the world economy or the United States economy.

A World Economy

by Peter F. Drucker   (1909–   )

Multinational corporations make large targets for critics. Some criticisms are valid; others are more myth than reality. Peter Drucker, consultant, speaker, and writer tries to separate the myths from the realities. In this reading, Drucker discusses the multinational as a response to the emergence of a genuine world economy. As you read, consider why national governments sometimes view the multinationals as a threat.

"The multinational represents the most important and most visible innovation of the postwar period in the economic field. The multinational corporation is also a symptom of a much greater change. It is a response to the emergence of a genuine world economy. . . . The developing world economy is fundamentally independent, has its own demand patterns, its own institutions—and in the Special Drawing Rights (SDR) even its own money and credit system in early form. . . .

This, understandably, appears as a threat to national governments. The threat is aggravated by the fact that no one so far has a workable theory of the world economy. As a result, there is today no proven, effective, predictable economic policy: witness the helplessness of governments in the face of worldwide inflation.

The multinationals are but a symptom. Reducing their influence can only aggravate the disease. But to fight the symptoms instead of finding a cure has always been tempting. It is, therefore, entirely possible that the multinationals will be severely damaged, and perhaps even destroyed, within the next decades. If so, this will be done by the governments of the multinationals' home countries, the United States, Great Britain, Germany, France, Japan, Sweden, Holland, and Switzerland . . . [which] account for at least three-quarters of the multinationals' business and profits. The developing nations can contribute little to saving or destroying multinationals. They are not important enough to the multinationals (or to the world economy) to have a major impact.

But at the same time the emergence of a genuine world economy is the one real hope for most of the developing countries. This is especially true for the great majority which by themselves are too small to survive as "national economies" under present technologies, present research requirements, present capital requirements, and present transportation and communications facilities. The next twenty years are the years in which developing countries will both most need the multinationals and have the greatest opportunity of benefiting from them. These will be the years when the developing countries will have to find jobs and incomes for the largest number of new workers into the labor force. At the same time, the developed countries will experience a sharp contraction of the number of new entrants into their labor force—a contraction that is already quite far advanced in Japan and in parts of western Europe. The jobs that the developing countries will need so desperately for the next ten years will, to a very large extent, require the presence of the multinationals—their investment, their technology, their managerial competence, and above all their marketing and export capabilities.

The best hope for developing countries, both to reach political and cultural nationhood and to obtain the employment opportunities and export earnings they need, is through the power of the world economy. Their tool, if only they are willing to use it, is the multinational company—precisely because it represents a global economy and cuts across national boundaries.

The multinational, if it survives, will surely look different tomorrow, will have a different structure, and will be "transnational" rather than "multinational." But even the multinational of today is—or at least should be—a most effective means to constructive nationhood for the developing world. **99**

From *Toward the Next Economics*, by Peter F. Drucker.

UNDERSTANDING THE READING

1. What, according to Drucker, are the long-run consequences of the development of a world economy?
2. As head of state of a less developed country, what guarantees would you require of a multinational corporation that wanted to open a production facility in your country?
3. In general, what is the objective of multinational corporations?

Section 3 Review

Understanding Worldwide Business

1. In what ways have multinationals affected government's economic control?
2. What principles are contained in the United Nations code of conduct for multinational corporations?
3. Why do some host countries feel threatened by multinational corporations?
4. List three benefits a multinational corporation offers to the people and economy of a host country.

5. List three costs a multinational corporation exacts from the people and economy of a host country.

Worldwide Business Today

1. List three multinationals that produce goods and services that you use on a regular basis.
2. **Challenge:** If you were a chief of state of a small, poor country, would you seek to attract multinationals? Why or why not?

Americans *at Work*

Meet Seeley Lodwick
Farmer

Fifty years ago, the income of a farmer depended largely on weather conditions and the size of the farm crop. Today more than ever before, farmers depend on the world economy as well as foreign agricultural prices. Prices for such major crops as corn, soybeans, wheat, and cotton often are influenced by world political conditions, foreign exchange rates, and prices of foreign agricultural products, as well as the weather and domestic production.

Seeley Lodwick owns a farm in Wever, Iowa. Lodwick currently serves as a member of the United States International Trade Commission (ITC). The ITC is the federal government's research agency for international trade.

Two out of every five acres of United States farmland grow crops for export. Lodwick believes farmers need to understand international economics in order to run their farms profitably. "Years ago many of us would try to decipher whether farm prices were going to rise or fall by judging the likely size of the crop here in the Midwest. Today, the size of our midwestern neighbors' crops has less to do with the level of our prices than the size of crops in Brazil, Argentina, Canada, or South Africa, or the volatile swings in world currencies on the Zurich exchange. Now the agricultural supply and demand outlook cannot be accurately assessed without an eye to the international situation."

In recent years, farmers have suffered from a widening gap between income and expenses. The prices of fertilizers and farm machinery have increased faster than crop prices. Many farmers have been driven out of business. Others keep their farms while working at other jobs. Seeley Lodwick hopes his present position will enable him to help farmers.

Today's farmer faces many uncertainties.

Personal Banking

If you had held a job 50 years ago, you might have been paid in cash rather than by check. Consumers paid for purchases in cash and often had little money left over for a savings account in a financial institution.

Today, cash is used in fewer transactions. Substitutes for currency, such as credit cards and checks, are widely accepted. A wise consumer of personal banking services must know the types of financial institutions, kinds of savings and checking accounts, and interest rates being paid.

STEP 1   Choose a Financial Institution

One type of financial institution in which savers may deposit funds is the commercial bank. Commercial banks are similar to corporations in that stockholders own them. Commercial banks are established to make profits, which are distributed as dividends to stockholders.

Mutual savings banks are owned by, and operated for the benefit of, their depositors. In addition to interest earned on deposits, depositors are paid any profits in the form of dividends.

Savings and loan associations were organized primarily to make long-term loans for buying or building houses. Savings and loans do not offer customers safe deposit boxes or regular checking accounts; however, they do offer special checking accounts called NOW accounts.

Credit unions are nonprofit financial associations operated for the benefit of their members. Generally, credit unions can charge members lower rates for loans and pay higher interest on deposits than can other financial institutions. Depositors buy shares with their deposits and receive dividends from profits earned.

The choice of a financial institution will be based on a number of factors. Tradeoffs involve convenience of use, interest rates, and services offered.

STEP 2   Decide on Savings Goals

Numerous savings accounts are available, as are different methods for calculating interest. Interest compounded most frequently earns the most for depositors.

Money may be deposited into a passbook savings account, a certificate of deposit (CD), or a money market mutual fund. A passbook savings account pays the least interest. However, any amount may be deposited or withdrawn from a passbook account at any time.

Certificates of deposit (CDs), require that funds stay on deposit for a specified

period of time. CDs earn a higher rate of interest than passbook savings accounts.

Insured money market mutual funds pool the money of depositors in order to invest in securities that pay high interest rates. The interest rates on money market mutual funds change monthly. These funds generally offer free limited checking services. Money market mutual funds require a minimum balance of $2,500 and certain minimum withdrawals.

STEP 3   Manage a Checking Account

To use a checking account wisely, the checkbook record must include each deposit, each check written, and the existing balance. Checkbook registers are designed specifically for keeping the account records.

Each month the bank sends a statement showing the checks paid from your account —cleared—and your deposits. Included in the statement are canceled checks and copies of deposit slips for the month. The statement must be verified by checking your balance on the day the statement was issued against the bank's balance.

To verify the checking account statement, put a checkmark in your check register in the appropriate column to show that the check has cleared and been returned to you. Next, circle the deposits shown on the returned slips in your check register. Enter any service charges in the register and subtract them from the balance. Find the balance after the last cleared check. Add any circled deposits included in the statement that appear below this balance. Subtract any deposits not circled and not included in the statement that appeared above the balance. Go through your check

register for checks written before the last cleared check. Add the amount of these checks to your balance. The resulting figure should agree with the bank's statement.

ECONOMIC SKILLS TODAY

Using the checks and deposits listed below, determine the balance in your checking account on December 20, January 1, and January 15.

Enrichment Activities

1. Visit a local bank and find out how to open a checking account. Is there a minimum deposit? What types of checking accounts are available? How much do checks cost? Are there any other costs? What other services are available?
2. Visit a local savings and loan. How do the services available differ from those available at the bank?

Balancing a Checkbook

Deposits:

12/15	$1,258.03
12/30	$ 845.58

Checks:

#306, 12/28	Car insurance	232.00
#307, 12/28	gas company	49.00
#308, 12/28	charge card	152.08
#309, 12/28	Cash	250.00
—, 1/02	Service charge	5.00
#310, 1/05	Cash	165.00
#311, 1/10	Rent	250.00

Explanation

This is a sample of entries in a checkbook.

Chart Skills

1. How much were deposits in total?
2. How much were checks in total?

CHAPTER SUMMARY

Trade Restrictions

Specialization of nations and the resulting international trade benefits all countries. Trade restrictions—tariffs, quotas, cartels, subsidies—limit world trade and result in fewer jobs, fewer goods and services, and higher prices. Limits on trade often are imposed to protect infant and strategic industries and the wages and jobs of domestic workers. Retaliation against another country's restrictions is another goal. Several agreements and laws encourage trade among nations.

Balance of Payments

A country's balance of payments, made up of the current and capital accounts, shows money flowing into and out of a country. The foreign exchange rate affects a nation's balance of payments. To import products, businesses must buy foreign currency on the foreign exchange market. The prices of currencies on the foreign exchange market fluctuate according to supply and demand. All people are affected by currency fluctuations. To aid countries that need to borrow, the World Bank established special drawing rights (SDRs).

Worldwide Business

Multinational corporations produce goods and services in more than one country. Producing goods and services in more than one country results in greater efficiency. Critics, however, charge that multinationals take jobs and tax revenues from the United States. Multinationals raise political questions because of their size and power.

CRITICAL THINKING QUESTIONS

Trade Restrictions

1. Define the four main types of trade restrictions and explain the effect of each on trade.
2. If free trade is advantageous to all, why did the United States place restrictions on cars imported from Japan?
3. In and around your house look for any major items not made in the United States. Explain why these items, rather than their American-made counterparts, were purchased.
4. Explain how the European Economic Community influences trade around the world.

Balance of Payments

1. Explain what determines the value of a currency and how the international exchange rate is set.
2. What factors have changed the positive balance of trade of the United States to a negative balance?
3. The slogan, "Buy American," has been a popular one. Using your knowledge of trade and the world economy, defend or oppose this slogan.
4. What are SDRs? How do they serve as a form of international currency?

Worldwide Business

1. List and explain the problems and benefits for a host country that result from multinational corporations.
2. How have multinational corporations changed economists' ideas about how the world economy works?
3. Explain how multinational corporations

have made government control of the economy more difficult.

4. How do the traditions of a country influence the behavior of a multinational corporation working within that country?

5. Explain what problems multinationals might face that companies operating in only one country do not face.

DEVELOPING ECONOMIC SKILLS

1. Construct a line graph to illustrate the figures shown in the chart. Draw one line showing total car sales in the United States. Draw another line showing Japanese imports. During which year were non-Japanese auto sales the highest?

2. What groups or individuals would benefit from trade restrictions placed on Japanese imports?

3. In 1981, the Japanese government agreed to limit automobile exports to 1.68 million cars a year for 1982 and 1983. Describe the effect of this policy on the economies of the United States and Japan. How might this agreement influence world trade policies?

APPLYING ECONOMICS TODAY

1. Since 1982 the value of the dollar has been the highest since floating exchange rates began. How does this level affect the United States consumer? The U.S. tourist abroad? U.S. investment abroad? Developing nations?

2. What is the relationship between the strength of the dollar and high United States interest rates? Do you benefit or suffer from high interest rates?

3. What is the relationship between a strong dollar and the United States balance of payments deficit?

4. How do trade restrictions affect multinational corporations?

5. **Challenge:** In what areas does the United States have an advantage in regard to trade? Is this advantage the same as it was 25 years ago? Why?

Car Sales in the United States

Year	Total Car Sales (millions)	Japanese Car Sales in the United States
1973	0.5	0.75
1974	9.0	1.00
1975	9.0	0.75
1976	10.5	1.00
1977	11.5	1.50
1978	11.5	1.75
1979	10.5	1.75
1980	8.5	2.00

Explanation

The chart shows total car sales and the number of Japanese cars sold in the United States from 1973 to 1980.

Chart Skills

1. What percentage of the total car sales were Japanese imports in 1973? 1975? 1978? 1980?

2. Summarize the trend in sales of Japanese cars in the United States from 1973 to 1980.

Less Developed Countries

1 Development Problems

Objective: *to understand the problems developing countries face*

2 Patterns of Change

Objective: *to understand the patterns of development in less developed countries*

3 Global Economics

Objective: *to understand the close interdependence among the countries of the world today*

1 Development Problems

SECTION OVERVIEW

Psychologist Abraham Maslow believed that human needs form a pyramid. Fundamental physical needs—hunger, thirst, safety—make up the bottom of the pyramid. These basic physcial needs must be satisfied before individuals can begin to consider the higher psychological needs to feel competent, achieve, and gain recognition. Many of the people in less developed countries go to sleep hungry every night. Education, health care, and the future remain unimportant as long as every day is spent in trying to obtain enough to eat. In this section, you will learn about the problems less developed countries face.

ECONOMIC VOCABULARY   less developed country (LDC)   subsistence agriculture

Characteristics of LDCs

Half of the almost 5 billion people in the world live on a diet of less than 1,500 calories per day. Most of these malnourished people live in what the United Nations terms less developed countries (LDCs). LDCs have five general characteristics: (1) low per capita GNP, (2) a traditional economic system, (3) limited technology, (4) few imports, and (5) a growing population.

First, a less developed or developing country is one in which per capita GNP is low relative to the per capita GNP in such industrialized nations as Canada, Great Britain, and the United States. Low per capita GNP means that the total amount of goods and services the nation produces is small compared to its population. Generally, resources are used to produce only the necessities of life.

Second, the LDC's economy usually follows a traditional system, based on subsistence agriculture, which supplies only enough food to feed the population. Most people live on small farms that produce just enough food to feed the immediate family. Farming offers the only hope for getting the food they need to survive. Some developing countries may grow small surpluses for export, but many do not produce enough food to feed their people and must try to import grain.

Third, people in LDCs have limited skills, tools, and machines to increase production. Educational opportunities are limited, since all children must work. The proportion of people in LDCs who learn to read is low—generally less than 25 percent.

Fourth, developing countries can afford to import only small amounts of goods and services. LDCs usually do not produce enough food or goods to trade. Therefore, to buy food, capital equipment, and the services of technicians, these countries must borrow money. In periods of worldwide economic contraction, borrowing funds and, therefore, receiving needed goods is very difficult.

Fifth, the populations of LDCs are increasing rapidly. People produce many children, hoping that enough will survive to care for their parents in the future. Living conditions are often unsanitary, and medical care is poor, however. Thus the life expectancy is only two-thirds as long as that of developed countries.

A Subsistence Economy

To exist, people must be able to feed themselves. To progress economically, a country must produce a surplus of food. A surplus allows some workers to leave farms and obtain jobs building roads, dams, power lines, and factories needed for future economic growth.

A surplus also provides capital that can be invested to further expand production. When farmers sell their crops, they can use the money to buy tools and fertilizer to produce a larger surplus. Eventually, a cycle of progress may begin to lift the LDC from the cycle of subsistence agriculture. Eventually, enough food may be produced to begin trading crops overseas. Then the country can earn the needed currency to purchase capital equipment and the personnel to train workers in the use of new equipment. Developing countries, recognizing the value of foreign trade, sometimes have exported food the inhabitants need. The tradeoff between exporting food and consuming it domestically can be difficult for developing countries.

Infant Death, Life Expectancy, and Adult Literacy

Country	Infant Death Rate (percent)	Life Expectancy (years)	Adult Literacy Rate (percent)
India	12	51	36
Malawi	14	46	25
Indonesia	9	47	62
Bolivia	16	52	63
Malaysia	3	67	60
Mexico	6	65	76
Brazil	9	62	76
Soviet Union	4	70	99
Japan	1	76	99
Saudi Arabia	12	53	15
United States	1	73	99

Source: UNESCO.

Explanation

The chart contains the most recent estimates of the infant death rate, life expectancy, and adult literary rate for selected countries.

Chart Skills

1. Are the infant death rate, life expectancy, and adult literacy rate related?
2. How do the statistics in the chart reflect economic development?

Percentage of Workers in Agriculture, 1978

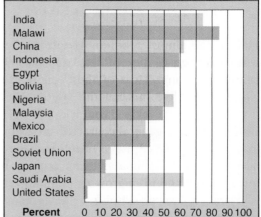

Source: *The World Book.*

Explanation

The graph shows percentage of working population in farming in selected countries.

Graph Skills

1. Which country had the largest percentage of the working population in farming?
2. How are economic development and the percentage of farm workers related?

Communications Resources

Country	Telephones (number per 1,000 people)	Daily Newspapers (copies per 1,000 people)	Televisions (number per 1,000 people)	Radios (number per 1,000 people)
Bangledesh	1	5	1	8
Bolivia	9	39	54	89
Ghana	7	31	5	163
Soviet Union	89	396	303	490
United States	788	282	624	2,099
Venezuela	58	176	123	385

Source: Statistical Office of the United Nations.

Explanation

The chart shows the number per 1,000 people of telephones, televisions, radios, and copies of daily newspapers in selected countries around the world.

Chart Skills

1. Which two countries appear to have the best communication systems? Explain.
2. Explain how a poor communications system would slow economic development.

Natural Resources

Some poor countries have few natural resources. For example, the African countries of Ethiopia and Somalia have poor soil. Consequently, agricultural production in these countries is low. Many LDCs are rapidly using up their minerals, topsoil, and other nonrenewable natural resources. In some cases, synthetic substitutes have lowered the demand for the resources of tropical countries. For example, the development of synthetic rubber filled some of the demand for natural rubber. LDCs that produced natural rubber, such as Malaysia and Indonesia, faced new competition.

The lack of mineral fuels, such as oil and coal, has forced dependence on imported oil. The recent rapid increase in the price of that fuel harmed many developing nations. People began to use wood as the principal fuel for heating and cooking, and trees and bushes were destroyed. The resulting loss of topsoil from erosion further reduced farm output.

Political Problems

Worldwide communications have made people in developing countries well aware of the contrast between their poverty and the prosperity of developed countries. In their desire for economic growth, people of LDCs often turn to their government for leadership.

Fulfilling the demands of the citizens requires extraordinary skills of government leaders. As a result, developing countries often suffer from unstable political conditions. When the demands of the people are not met, the government may be replaced. Constant changes of government slow down economic decisions.

REVIEWING THE CONCEPT

Developing Vocabulary

1. Give your definition of a less developed country (LDC).
2. What is subsistence agriculture?

Mastering Facts

1. List the five characteristics that developing nations have in common.
2. Why is a production surplus important to economic growth? Why do LDCs have few surpluses?
3. What factors contribute to poverty in less developed countries?
4. Why do LDCs often suffer from unstable political conditions?

Life in Zaire

For many years, Sister Mary Rose had wanted to be a missionary. Her doctorates in English and theology and fluency in French, however, had led to a teaching career at the college level. In 1984, at the age of 55, Sister Mary Rose was finally granted the opportunity to work in a developing country. She spent some time in Zaire Air, a village outside the city of Lambdka, Zaire, learning Lingala, the language generally spoken. These months were a preparation for her eventual destination of Brazzaville, the Congo. While in Zaire Air, Sister Mary Rose sent the following letter to friends in the United States.

66Greetings to each of you from Zaire. I have been assigned a mission in Brazzaville, Congo, at a special school for the handicapped—mentally, physically, or educationally—poor. I am happy over my assignment.

While you were freezing in winter temperatures, I have been sweltering in the hot, humid climate of Mbandaka, the former Equatorville, in Zaire. The equator runs through the city. Mbandaka has the worst climate in Zaire because the city is in a valley, below sea level. This makes the weather very humid and oppressive. However, the nights are usually cool. Here I feel I am in an entirely different world, time, even civilization. No amount of mission preparation can prepare one for the actual extremes of poverty, primitive lifestyle, and almost total lack of basic hygiene. To see starving babies on television is one thing, but to experience the actuality is another.

Here in the village where we live, dusty roads exist instead of paved streets. One- and two-room houses built of mud bricks and thatched with palm branches for roofs house the people. Inside the houses—I have entered the ones of the destitute elderly in our village—I was shocked to see only a bamboo bed covered with rags, a stool or two, and a few dilapidated pots on the dirt floor. The fire for cooking is sometimes in the middle of the room, but in the dry season most people build their fires outdoors. The fires are all built in the same fashion with three stones on which the pot rests. As the fire burns, wood is pushed in toward the center.

Families eat from a common pot. Their staple food is manioc—the starchy root of a tropical plant. If the family can afford it, fish is added, rarely meat, for meat is too expensive. The people eat only one meal a day.

At 4:30 A.M. I am awakened by the women talking very loudly as they begin their long trek to the fields 10 or 15 miles away. One seldom sees a car. Only a few officials own them, and the general poverty is such that most of the people here have no hope of even owning a bicycle in their lifetime. In the evening I see the long trek home from the fields and am appalled [shocked] to see old women with huge baskets of wood on their backs. They are bent almost in two by the weight. Younger women carry large baskets of heavy manioc or other produce.

Most of the people in our village . . . have a well. Even in the 'city' of Mbandaka the faucets are located at intervals with several families, sometimes many, sharing one water spigot. Last week I went with Sister Jo Ann to visit some of the homes in her parish and could not believe I was in a so-called city. The shacks of the poor in the United States seem like rich townhouses in comparison.

One of the things I have learned to reverence [respect] here is water. We have electricity only three hours a day—6 P.M. to 9 P.M. During this time a motor pumps water from the cistern [tank for storing rainwater] to the water tank for our daily water supply. However, we are now in the dry season, and about two weeks ago our cistern went dry. Now the novices [new members of a religious order] take a 20-minute walk each day to a spring to obtain our drinking water. The water is boiled and filtered before we use it for drinking. All the water for bathing, laundry, and cleaning must be hauled in our truck in large tanks from the priests' house, which has city water. Our two wells on the property are almost dry. Yesterday, when I drew up a bucket, the water was very cloudy with a reddish-brown dust. However, the dust will settle after a couple of hours. We are praying for rain, but we still have two months of the dry season.

Because the electricity is on for only three hours in the evening, I dress by candlelight at 5 A.M. The candle for our morning Mass is not a symbol but a necessity to see the words. Our cooking is done on a woodstove.

As I cross the garden in the morning after breakfast, I feel like I am living in another age. The novices are busy pounding out manioc in wooden bowls as they have done for decades.

Since malnutrition is a very urgent problem here, our sisters work with mothers of babies. The mothers are asked to bring their babies to be weighed and examined. The sisters keep a chart on each baby. Every day we furnish a hot porridge for all the toddlers, four years old or under. At 10 A.M., when the church bell rings, the children come streaming into the churchyard with bowls and pots of all descriptions, sit on little benches under the trees, and patiently wait for their bowl to be filled. One bowl had a hole which was plugged with a piece of bamboo. While the children are eating, the mothers are being given a demonstration on how to prepare this food and how to increase the protein in their diet by adding crushed peanuts, beans, etc. Manioc is filling, but has no nutritional value—thus the severe malnutrition. Other sisters teach the women how to sew, care for the babies, etc. One sister teaches teenagers who have never had an opportunity to attend school. Other sisters work in the clinic and hospital with the elderly who have tuberculosis. TB is prevalent here. I would love to tell you about my exciting trip into the equatorial forests to visit our three mission posts, but that will have to wait. . . .

Know that I am counting on your prayers as I begin my work in the Congo, and that you are gratefully and affectionately remembered.**"**

Sister Mary Rose's letter describes life in Zaire. The problems are common to most developing countries today.

ANALYZING THE CASE STUDY

STEP 1   Gather Evidence

1. Describe the houses in Zaire Air.
2. What do the people eat? Is the food nourishing?

3. What evidence is there of the comforts of city life?

STEP 2 **Clarify the Issue**

1. Are most of the people poor? Explain your answer.
2. How do most families make their living?
3. Is there evidence of the use of tools and machines to increase productivity?
4. Do educational facilities exist for the people?

STEP 3 **Draw Conclusions**

How does Zaire exemplify the five characteristics of less developed countries? Write a paragraph supporting your answer.

READING

Population and Poverty

by T. R. Malthus   (1766-1834)

The Reverend Thomas Malthus was an English economist. Best known among his many contributions to the growing science of economics is his book, *An Essay on the Principle of Population*, published in 1798. Malthus believed that because of the limited food supply the number of people born always exceeded the number that could survive. War, famine, and disease were necessary to kill off the extra population. Human misery and poverty were inevitable unless population could be controlled. Improved methods of agriculture have increased the supply of food and proved Malthus wrong. However, the rapid population growth of this century has led to renewed interest in Malthus's theories. As you read, consider whether the ideas he expressed are true.

❝In an inquiry concerning the improvement of society, the mode of conducting [the way of examining] the subject which naturally presents itself, is,

1. To investigate the causes that have hitherto [until now] impeded [slowed] the progress of mankind towards happiness; and,

2. To examine the probability of the total or partial removal of these causes in [the] future.

The principal object of the present essay is to examine the effects of one great cause [closely] united with the very nature of man. . . .

The cause to which I allude, is the constant tendency in all animated life to increase beyond the nourishment prepared for it. . . .

Through the animal and vegetable kingdoms Nature has scattered the seeds of life abroad . . . but has been comparatively sparing in the room and the nourishment necessary to rear them. The [people] contained in this earth, if they could freely develop themselves, would fill millions of worlds in the course of a few thousand years. Necessity . . . restrains them. . .

Population has this constant tendency to increase *beyond* the means of subsistence . . . [Let us examine] what would be the natural increase of population, if left to exert itself [grow] with perfect freedom; and what might be expected to be the rate of increase in the production [of food] under the most favorable circumstances of human industry. . . .

In the northern states of America, where the means of subsistence have been more ample . . . than in any of the modern states of Europe, the population has been found to double itself . . . in less than twenty-five years. In the back settlements, where the sole [only] employment is agriculture, and vicious customs and unwholesome occupations are little known, the population has been found to double itself in fifteen years. Even this extraordinary rate of increase is probably short of the utmost power of population. [Some people] suppose a doubling possible in so short a time as ten years. . . .

It may safely be pronounced, therefore, that *population, when unchecked,* goes on doubling itself every twenty-five years, or *increases in a geometrical ratio* [1, 2, 4, 8, 16, 32, etc.]. . . .

The rate according to which the productions of the earth may be supposed to increase, it will not be so easy to determine. Of this, however, we may be perfectly certain, that the ratio [rate] of their increase in a limited territory must be of a totally different nature from the ratio of the increase of population. A thousand millions are just as easily doubled every twenty-five years by the power of population as a thousand. But the food to support the increase from the greater number will by no means be obtained with the same facility [as easily]. Man is necessarily confined in room. When acre has been added to acre till all the fertile land is occupied, the yearly increase of food must depend upon [improvement] of the land already in possession. . . .

The science of agriculture has been much studied in England and Scotland; and there is still a great portion of uncultivated land in these countries. Let us consider at what rate the produce [food production] of this island might be supposed to increase under circumstances the most favorable to improvement.

If it be allowed that by the best possible policy and great encouragements to agriculture, the average produce of the island could be doubled in the first twenty-five years, it will be allowing, probably, a greater increase than could with reason be expected.

In the next twenty-five years, it is impossible to suppose that the produce could be quadrupled. It would be contrary to all our knowledge of the properties of land. It must be evident to those who have the slightest acquaintance with agriculture . . . that the additions that could yearly be made to [the production of food] must be gradually and regularly diminishing.

Let us suppose that the yearly [increases in food production], instead of decreasing, . . . were to remain the same. . . . In a few centuries it would make every acre of land in the island like a garden.

It may be fairly pronounced, therefore, that, considering the present average state of the earth, *the means of subsistence,* under circumstances the most favorable to human industry, *could not possibly be made to increase faster than in an arithmetical ratio* [1, 2, 3, 4, 5, etc]. . . .

The necessary effects of these two different rates of increase, when brought together, will be very striking. Let us call the population of this island eleven millions; and suppose the present produce equal to the easy support of such a number. In the first twenty-five years the population would be twenty-two millions, and the food being also doubled, the means of subsistence would be equal to this increase. In the next twenty-five years, the population would be forty-four millions, and the means of subsistence only equal to the support of thirty-three millions. . . . At the conclusion of the first century, the population would be a hundred and seventy-six millions, and the means of subsistence only equal to the support of fifty-five millions, leaving a population of a hundred and twenty-one million totally unprovided for.

Taking the whole earth, . . . and, supposing the present population equal to a thousand millions, the human species would increase as the numbers 1, 2, 4, 8, 16, 32, 64, 128, 256, and subsistence as 1, 2, 3, 4, 5, 6, 7, 8, 9. In two centuries the population would be to the means of subsistence as 256 to 9. . . .

In this supposition [example] no limits whatever are placed to the produce of the earth. It may increase for ever . . . yet . . . the increase of the human species can only be kept down to the level of the means of subsistence by the constant operation of the strong law of necessity. . .

The ultimate check to population appears then to be a want of food, arising necessarily from the different ratios according to which population and food increase. But his ultimate check is never the immediate check, except in cases of actual famine.

The immediate check may be stated to consist in all those customs [such as war] and all those diseases, which seem to [result from scarce food supply]; and all those causes, [such as hard labor] which tend prematurely to weaken and destroy the human frame [body]. . . .

The sum of all these . . . checks, taken together, forms the immediate check to population. . . . [Yet, in most countries] there is a constant effort in the population to increase beyond the means of subsistence. This . . . subjects the lower classes of society to distress, and prevents any great permanent [improvement] of their condition.

These effects seem to be produced in the following manner. The constant effort towards population [increase] which is found to act even in the most vicious societies, increases the number of people before the means of subsistence are increased. The food, therefore, which before supported eleven millions, must now be divided among eleven millions and a half. The poor consequently must live much worse, and many of them be reduced to severe distress. The number of laborers also being above the [amount] of work [available, salaries and wages] must tend to fall, while the price of provisions [food and shelter] would at the same time tend to rise. The laborer therefore must do more work, to earn the same as he did before.

During this season of distress the discouragements to marriage and the difficulty of rearing a family are so great, that the progress [growth] of population [slows]. In the mean time, the cheapness of labor, the [large number] of laborers, and the necessity [of finding work encourage farmers] to employ more labor upon their land, to turn up fresh soil, and to [improve production until the food supply may match the population's needs]. The situation of the laborer being then again tolerably comfortable, the restraints to population are in some degree loosened; and, after a short period, the same [cycle is repeated]. . . . **99**

From *An Essay on the Principle of Population*, by Thomas R. Malthus.

UNDERSTANDING THE READING

1. What does Malthus believe is the main reason why people have not progressed toward happiness?
2. How does the maximum rate at which food production can be increased compare to the increase of population?
3. What are the checks on population growth?
4. What are the checks on increases in food production?
5. Explain the cycle that develops as a result of increases in population and food production.

Section 1 Review

Understanding Development Problems

1. How does low per capita GNP affect per capita income?
2. Why are educational opportunities limited in LDCs?
3. Why is it difficult for LDCs to import needed goods and services?
4. Why is life expectancy lower in LDCs than in such developed countries as the United States?
5. Explain why most of the people in LDCs are farmers.

Development Problems Today

1. Choose a developed and a developing country and compare their characteristics. How do they differ?
2. **Challenge:** How would the climate of Central America affect progress and economic development?
3. **Challenge:** What type of soil makes up parts of central Africa? How does such soil affect progress and economic development there?

2 Patterns of Change

SECTION OVERVIEW

The process of economic development is normally slow and requires cooperation among many groups. First, the developing country must recognize its need to improve the living standard and then must try to bring about such change. The developing country may establish a national plan for growth. Sources of funding must be found to finance projects. Finally, the groundwork must be established to allow market forces to work in the country as development occurs.

ECONOMIC VOCABULARY

infrastructure   foreign aid   development assistance

Problems of Development

Improvement in the standard of living may be a goal of every country, but because of differences in each country, improvement in the living standard may be difficult to attain. Such traits as positive work attitudes, an emphasis on education, and slow population growth may lead to an improved standard of living. A large supply of capital and a stable government also promote economic growth.

Every country has physical and human resources. Physical resources are the tools and materials of production, such as machinery, equipment, and land. Human resources include the labor force of a country and the skills that individuals in the labor force possess. Such resources are part of a country's capital.

Several factors determine the productivity of both types of resources. Physical capital, such as machinery, may become more productive with technological advances. A country itself may become more productive as the amount of available physical capital increases.

Human capital also may differ among countries. As a country develops, the quality of the human capital usually improves. Human capital must develop beyond agricultural skills. Besides growing food, the people must learn how to build roads and operate machinery. Naturally, as a country develops further even more skills are required, especially in such service areas as health care and education.

In the past, developing countries have improved their educational systems in order to improve the quality of their human capital. The construction of vocational and agricultural schools and research facilities in developing countries has improved the training of students for jobs in various areas of business and government.

Resistance to Change

In some developing countries, people's deep-rooted attitudes toward economic ac-

514

Educational Levels in Developing and Developed Countries

	Primary School Enrollment (Percent)	Higher Education Enrollment (Percent)
United States	98	55
Japan	101	30
France	112	25
Sweden	97	37
Spain	109	22
Saudi Arabia	64	7
Israel	96	26
Kenya	108	1
Russia	106	21
Mexico	120	15
Bahamas	135	3
Singapore	107	8
India	76	9
China	117	1

Source: World Bank.

Explanation

The chart shows the percentage of two age groups enrolled in school in several countries.

Graph Skills
1. Which two countries had low enrollments in primary schools?
2. What is the relationship between the level of development and the percent of its population enrolled in higher education programs?

tivity make progress slow and difficult. People's skepticism toward new ways of producing goods has prevented some countries from introducing modern technology.

For example, during the late 1970s the Indonesian government tried an experiment to increase the catch of fish in one community. They supplied people with motorized fishing boats equipped with nylon nets and other special equipment. Each boat carried a 12-person crew. Because of the new boats and equipment, each person on a boat had an opportunity to become far richer than the other people in the community. The community reacted angrily to the experiment, which would have made some people wealthier than others. Within a month, all the new boats had been destroyed. Observers of the incident concluded that the residents preferred that everyone remain equal rather than allow a select few to rise above the rest.

A similar reaction to change in the developing countries has occurred because of the population growth issue. In the early 1980s, rapid population growth was canceling out most economic progress.

Population Growth

The standard measure of a country's wealth or poverty is its per capita gross national product. Even though a country's GNP is rising, its population may be increasing at a faster rate. Then, per capita GNP declines as total production is divided by an ever more numerous population. At a growth rate of 1 percent per year, a country's population will double in 70 years. A 3 percent rate means that the population will double in 23 years.

The Role of Government

One of the key factors in economic development is government. For economic development to occur, the government in a country must be stable. The government also must be willing to promote economic development and to undertake directly the development of major construction projects for public works.

Governments in less developed countries tend to be unstable and to change often. Instability discourages individuals from risking their savings in order to begin a business. When government is stable, individuals are more confident about the future. Consequently, people are more willing to risk investments.

Once a government is stable, it can begin the proper planning and develop-

Population Growth in Selected Countries

Country	Average Annual Rate of Population Growth 1980–1983 (percent)	Estimated Population 1983 (millions)	Estimated Population 2025 (millions)
Less Developed Countries	NA*	NA*	6,818.300
Algeria	3.2	20.695	62.900
Bangladesh	3.1	96.539	221.800
Brazil	2.3	131.305	291.300
China	1.5	1,059.802	1,469.300
Ecuador	3.1	8.811	25.700
Kenya	4.1	18.580	82.300
Malaysia	2.3	14.995	28.800
Nigeria	3.3	85.219	285.500
Saudi Arabia	3.4	10.443	31.000
Developed Countries	NA*	NA*	1,376.800
France	0.5	56.604	57.100
Soviet Union	0.8	272.308	355.000
United States	0.9	234.193	305.800
World Total	1.8	4,722.000	8,195.100

*Not available.

Sources: U.S. Bureau of the Census; Population Division of the United Nations.

Explanation

The chart shows average annual rates of population growth and population estimates for 1983 and 2025 various less developed and developed countries and for the world.

Graph Skills

1. Is population growth in the developed countries slow or rapid?
2. Are population growth rates of less developed countries rapid or slow?

ment of the country's infrastructure. The infrastructure of a nation includes its highways, bridges, dams, schools, communications system, and other facilities on which other parts of the economy depend. All of these projects are costly, and in virtually all circumstances are undertaken by government. The infrastructure provides the foundation for future private development.

Government may take several steps to promote private economic activity. For example, government can attempt to raise interest rates to encourage savings. Some governments reduce the taxes of businesses that provide new jobs or goods for export. Others subsidize the sale of certain items to encourage production of selected goods.

Efforts to overcome development problems must involve the entire country in planning for proper growth, educating the population, developing the appropriate in-frastructure, and slowing population growth. Government's role is to lead the way in such efforts. Development problems are interrelated and must be dealt with in that way.

Funding Economic Development

Economic development in a country requires vast sums of money. Sources of funding for economic development may come from within the country itself or from other governments, international organizations, and private banks and other businesses. Most developing countries pay for over 80 percent of their economic development with their own taxes, savings, and export earnings.

One source of money to develop a country may be a foreign government. Funds provided by one nation to another in

Foreign Aid Distributed and Received, 1982

Country	Total Aid ($ Millions)	Aid as Percent of GNP	Aid per Capita ($)
Selected Distributing Countries			
Australia	882	0.57	59
France	4,028	0.75	74
Italy	814	0.24	14
Japan	3,023	0.29	29
Kuwait	1,295	4.86	NA*
Norway	559	0.99	136
Soviet Union	1,850	0.14	NA*
Sweden	987	1.02	119
Saudi Arabia	4,428	2.82	NA*
United States	8,202	0.27	35
United Arab Emirates	563	2.06	NA*
Selected Recipients			
Bangladesh	1,414	11.46	—
Egypt	1,472	4.63	—
India	2,570	1.59	—
Jordan	1,088	29.73	—
Pakistan	1,126	3.75	—
Sudan	736	10.95	—
Syria	1,450	9.31	—
Tanzania	749	12.83	—
Turkey	1,035	1.75	—
Vietnam	1,140	11.23	—

*Not Available.

Source: Organization for Economic Cooperation and Development.

Explanation

The chart shows amounts of government aid that several countries distributed and received. The first column shows the total volume of aid. The second and third columns show aid compared to the GNP and population of the country.

Chart Skills

1. Explain why the United States, Kuwait, and Norway each could claim to give more foreign aid than any other country on the chart.
2. Which country on the chart receives the highest percentage of its total GNP from foreign aid?

order to promote development are called foreign aid or development assistance. Aid may be in the form of either an outright grant, which need not be repaid, or a loan, which the nation must pay back to the lender. Often, countries give aid for a specific project or purpose. A foreign aid loan carries a low rate of interest and may be repaid over a long period of time.

Developing countries also receive financial assistance from various international organizations. Two of the largest of these organizations are the United Nations and the World Bank.

United Nations organizations provide assistance in such areas as agricultural production, forestry and fisheries development, worker and teacher training, adult education, health care, and population control. The World Bank is the largest international organization providing funds for economic development. In close cooperation with the United Nations, the World Bank lends money to over 100 developing countries for specific development projects. The money borrowed must be repaid over a 15- to 50-year period.

Funds for developing countries also come from private banks. As the economies of developing countries become stronger, the countries may qualify for loans from private banks. Such loans may go either directly to the government or to a private business in the developing country. In many instances, banks work together to provide loans for development projects.

Private businesses in developed nations assist developing countries by supplying equipment or machinery on special terms or investing directly in the less developed country. Through this type of industrial assistance, workers are trained and acquire job skills. Companies often can make their product at a lower cost than they could in the developed country.

Finally, developing countries gain development funds from foreign trade earnings. As a country develops, it usually increases the amount of goods it exports to other countries. By exporting goods, the developing country receives money that it then can spend on additional development projects, such as roads, schools, and factories. Often, a country's first exports are mining or agricultural products.

Development Gains

Economic development still poses many unsolved problems. Nearly a billion people still live in extreme poverty and have little hope of improving their situations during their lifetime.

Despite some gains in living standards in developing countries, in the poorest countries improvements come slowly. GNP per capita in the poorest countries has increased in recent years, but at only half the rate of the other developing countries.

Gains in education in less developed countries are very uneven. Most of the training programs are offered to men but not to women. Since fewer girls than boys attend school in developing countries, the literacy rate for men is higher than that for women. In addition, jobs tend to be open primarily to men. Such conditions increase the inequality of opportunity between men and women. By neglecting to provide opportunities for women, the developing countries are wasting half of their potential human capital. Thus, they are foregoing potentially significant production gains.

Three Developing Countries

Developing as well as developed countries may have either a market or a command economic system. For example, Cuba, Venezuela, and Thailand are developing countries. Cuba has a command economy; Venezeula and Thailand, market economies. These three countries are similar but also quite different.

Since 1959, Cuba has had a centrally planned, or command, economy. All industry in Cuba has been nationalized, or state owned, since 1968. Cuba's major exports, like those of almost all developing countries, are agricultural goods. The major imports are manufactured and processed goods. Since 1961, Cuba has received over $8 billion in foreign aid, mostly from the Soviet Union. Primary education is especially emphasized. All children ages 6 through 14 must attend school. The schools are free, the costs paid by the state. In the early 1980s, the literacy rate was 96 percent. Like most developing countries, Cuba has taken steps to reduce population growth. The rate of growth in the early 1980s was 1.2 percent, down nearly 40 percent from the growth rates between 1960 and 1978.

The private sector dominates Thailand's free market economy. The basis of the Thai economy is agriculture. Over 60 percent of Thailand's export earnings come from the sale of fruits, corn, rubber, and rice. Major imports to Thailand are machinery, equipment, and manufactured products. Since 1946, Thailand has received nearly $ 3 billion in financial assistance from the United States and the World Bank. Such aid assisted the government's road building, irrigation, education, and agricultural projects. The literacy rate in the early 1980s was 70 percent. Schooling is free and compulsory for seven years. The annual population growth rate in the early 1980s was 2.3 percent, which the government viewed as excessive. Steps are being taken to reduce it.

Venezuela, also a free market country, has been able to accelerate its standard of living in the past decade because of its large oil resources. Over 80 percent of Venezuela's export earnings come from petroleum. Most of Venezuela's imports are machinery, equipment, and other manufactured products. The country often has a large trade surplus because of its oil exports. The major sources of foreign aid to Venezuela —$874 billion since 1946—have been the United States and the World Bank. Venezuelan industry is changing from small-scale to large-scale enterprises as the nation uses its oil earnings to promote growth. This strategy of industrial development and diversification aims at replacing oil as a source of revenue when the oil reserves are exhausted. Education in Venezuela is free and compulsory for six years. The current literacy rate is 74 percent.

REVIEWING THE CONCEPT

Developing Vocabulary

1. What is the difference between physical resources and human resources?
2. Give four examples of the infrastructure of your community.

Mastering Facts

1. Explain how improvements in education help a country to develop its economy.
2. Summarize the difference in the population growth in developed and less developed countries.
3. Describe three ways that governments in less developed countries can aid economic development.

CASE STUDY

Growing Up in the Philippines

Young people around the world face decisions about their education, career, and family. The options of a 17-year-old living in a less developed country, though, are somewhat different from yours.

Juan Mendez is the pseudonym of a real person in the Philippines. He is 17 years old and lives in a small community 30 miles west of Manila. For him, as for young people in less developed countries around the world, life centers on agriculture. Everyone farms. The economy of Juan's area is based on rice. Work changes as the time of year shifts. Each season brings a different kind of work in the rice paddies—first planting, then weeding, and then harvesting the crop.

In addition to growing rice, many people have other jobs. Juan's father, for example, sells insecticides and fertilizer. Juan's parents also sell fish that they catch and vegetables that they raise. Their cash income is very low. Juan and his family raise the food they need. Since they have little cash, however, Juan's parents accumulate savings very slowly. They cannot accumulate rice to store for their old age. Rather, they expect Juan to care for them when they are too old to farm.

For several generations, Juan's ancestors had grown a crop of rice each year. They used the same type of rice and the same method of growing it each year. Several years ago, though, Juan's parents were among the first people in his community to experiment with new farming methods.

Initially, the farmers tried a new type of seed that required fertilizer. When the harvest was in that year, they realized that the new seeds and fertilizer produced a larger crop than had the old seeds. The extra harvest each year gave them an opportunity to sell more of their rice.

Juan's parents next tried another innovation, irrigation. His parents borrowed money from a bank to buy a water pump. The family now could raise a second crop of rice during the dry season. By raising two crops of rice each year, the family had a larger food supply. Again, they produced a surplus of rice to sell.

The money they were able to save allowed Juan's parents to slowly improve the family's standard of living. For example, they moved the family out of their bamboo house and into a small house they had built of cement blocks.

The increase in his family's wealth also allowed Juan more opportunities. When he was younger, Juan had expected to grow up and become a farmer, as was his father. With its increased income, Juan's family was able to send him to school through eighth grade. Usually, young people are needed to help in the fields, but Juan's parents could spare him from the farm. Further, they could afford to pay his tuition.

Juan's education and experience in farming made him eligible for a training program operated by his country's department of agriculture. Students in the program would spend two years at a high school in a nearby city. Then they would be employed to travel from village to village, working with farmers. They would try to teach farmers more efficient methods.

Juan's parents had moved a step beyond subsistence agriculture. Juan now had an opportunity to go one more step. By taking that step, he could help others to increase their productivity. With the money he earned, he could help his brothers and sisters stay in school.

Farmers in the Philippines often use traditional methods for growing rice.

To join or not join the training program was an economic decision with significant consequences for Juan and his family. Like other economic decisions, Juan's decision involved tradeoffs for both him and his family. Though the program was a wonderful opportunity, the costs were high. Juan had never really considered leaving his home community. Moving away from his family would be difficult. Economic development often requires individuals and families to make difficult choices.

ANALYZING THE CASE STUDY

STEP 1   Clarify the Issue

1. Summarize the basic problem facing less developed countries. How is this problem evident in the Philippines?
2. What decision did Juan face because of his education and experience?

STEP 2   Examine Change

1. Why could Juan go to school?
2. How would entering the training program benefit Juan? How would the program help the Philippines to develop?

STEP 3   Make a Decision

If you were Juan, would you enter the training program? Explain your decision.

Enrichment Activities

1. Agricultural production increased sharply in several less developed countries during the 1970s. This change was called the green revolution. Find out what led to the green revolution and how it changed agricultural production.
2. Find five pictures showing technological advancement in less developed countries. Write a brief explanation describing the use of technology in each picture.

READING

A Strategy for Development

by Barbara Ward   (1914-1981)

If they want to grow, the less developed countries of the world must carefully determine how to use their sources. In this reading, Barbara Ward suggests a strategy for developing countries. Ward, a British economist, studied the problems of economic development for much of her life. She was on the staff of *The Economist*, a British news magazine. As you read, consider what role Ward assigns to developed countries in encouraging economic development.

What sort of policies can help the developing nations in the crucial years that lie ahead? . . . Let us be clear first of all over the general aim. During the next twenty to thirty years we hope to see a majority of the developing nations pass through the sound-barrier of sustained growth. Moreover, we want these societies to have political elbow-room

Foreign aid is one source of funds for education in developing countries.

with a measure of autonomy [self-government] for different groups and political power organized on a plural basis. We do not specify institutions or ideologies; but we hope for open societies in an open world. How shall we set about it?

The first point to make is that some general strategy is needed. And strategy is inseparable from a sustained effort through time. The rhythm of growth is not the rhythm of annual budgeting appropriations. Unless the Western nations bring themselves to accept the need for five- and ten-year programs, they will even waste what they do spend, for it will not be geared into a genuine strategy of growth.

The next point is that the scale of aid must be adequate. Patchy development, a little here, a little there, does not lead to sustained growth. In every developing economy, there comes a time when, for perhaps two decades, a 'big push' is needed to get the economy off the launching-pad and into orbit.

Not all nations come to that point at the same time. There seems to be a certain pattern of progress and expansion, and different economies are ranged at different points along the line. First there is a phase that one might call the 'pre-investment' phase. Nearly everything needed for a 'big push' in investment is still lacking. Educated people are not available, training is minimal, capital overheads or infrastructure—power, transport, harbors, housing—have still to be built. At this stage, the country must be prepared for a later plunge into investment and help with education and training, investment in infrastructure, surveys of resources, and some preliminary planning, are the great needs.

But at the next stage . . . the big investments begin to pay off. The ground is laid, rapid growth can be secured. It is at this point that large-scale capital aid from abroad can offset local poverty and lack of capital, thereby sparing governments the cruel choice of using totalitarian methods to compel people to save. . . .

Given that we accept the philosophy of a 'big push' in aid and investment, once the pre-conditions of growth have been realized, where should the capital be directed? It is quite impossible to define a general strategy since each country varies so much in its capacities, in its endowment [supply] of resources, in the scale of its internal market, and

522

its export prospects. But perhaps one or two general points are worth making here. The first is that investment in education must continue to receive strong emphasis. Recent studies suggest that between sixty and fifty per cent of the gains in productivity made in the West in the last half-century spring from better trained minds, from more research, and more systematic use of the economy's brain-power. At present, most of the developing economies are only in the very first stages of the needed advance in education. Africa is strewn [filled] with societies where not more than ten per cent of the people are literate, where perhaps only one per cent ever reach secondary levels of schooling. . . . No modern economy can be built on this basis.

A second critical area is that of farming. Modernized agriculture is, as we have seen, indispensable to the creation of general momentum in the economy. There are two separate needs: to encourage the structural changes which modern agriculture demands—the land reforms, the consolidation of holdings, the building of an influential co-operative movement; and to ensure a sufficient flow of capital into farming. The great variety of modern techniques, new fertilizers, new seed, new methods in planting and tilling, are nearly all costly. So is the scale of credit needed to launch a successful co-operative system. So last of all are the agricultural extension systems without which the farmer cannot learn what new opportunities are open to him. In the past, agriculture has been all too often the last on the government's priority list. Modern experience suggests it should be moved to the top.

The third area of expansion—industry—shows such universal variety that most generalizations have little value. However, one or two comments have some validity. Programs will lead to a better use of resources if capital is recognized for what it is in all developing economies: extremely scarce. Its price should be high, even if this idea upsets the more usual concept that basic [goods and] services should be kept cheap in order to stimulate growth.

Another aspect of the same problem is that since foreign exchange is the scarcest of all forms of capital, it may be necessary, by high import duties or by auctioning [selling] import licences, or by other measures, to ensure that the entrepreneur who gets his hands on foreign exchange pays for its full value. This approach may contradict another tendency—to overvalue a developing nation's currency so that its exports will buy a maximum amount of foreign supplies. . . .

A developing government should aim its policies at ensuring the quickest rate of capital accumulation. Profits should be strongly encouraged, in public as in private enterprise, and tax-systems arranged so that all the incentives are towards their reinvestment. This again does not always arouse much enthusiasm among planners brought up to believe in the inherent immorality of profits and ready to run essential public services on a 'no profit, no loss' basis. But profits are one of the chief means by which resources can be put at the disposal [use] of the investors in society. . .

When it comes to the actual content of industrial policy, it must fit local conditions. Most countries can begin to produce locally some of the goods they import, provided protection is given. The [first] stage of consumer industry only awaits a determined government and some local entrepreneurial talent. But large-scale industry depends upon the availability of crucial raw materials. And it depends, too, upon the scale of the internal market. Five large steelplants in India, where over four hundred million people make up the market and where iron ore and cokingcoal are available, make perfect sense. East Europe's proliferation of steel-mills after 1948 did not. Clearly, developing governments would be well advised to look round and see whether by customs unions or common markets with their neighbours they may not increase the size and efficiency of their industrial units without risk of over-production.

To all these changes—in education, in farming, in industry—there are more than economic consequences. Investment in people, investment in new techniques, investment in new forms of activity, all widen and strengthen the managerial and professional class and increase the training and scope of the manual worker. That gradual extension of the middle class to cover more and more of the nation's citizens is set in motion. With it goes a brighter hope of rational politics and civil rights. **99**

From *The Rich Nations and the Poor Nations,* by Barbara Ward.

UNDERSTANDING THE READING

1. Describe the conditions in a country during the pre-investment phase.
2. Discuss the importance of farming in the development of a country.
3. Explain the role of profit, risk, and incentive in economic development.
4. What action did Ward recommend that developed nations take?

Section 2 Review

Understanding Patterns of Change

1. Explain the effect of improved technology on the level of productivity.
2. Why is improving human capital important in a developing country?
3. How can government affect the level of economic development in a country?
4. What funds for economic development are available to a country?
5. What role can foreign businesses play in the development of a country?

Patterns of Change Today

1. Describe the unresolved economic development problems in LDCs.
2. What common problems face Cuba, Venezeula, and Thailand today?
3. **Challenge:** Compare and contrast the role of education in developed and less developed countries.

3 Global Economics

SECTION OVERVIEW

Today, the world's economies have merged into an interdependent global economy. The expanding volume of trade conducted among nations reflects their economic interdependence. Other signs of a growing global economy are the amount of foreign investment and the expansion of multinational companies. The oil crisis during the early 1970s made clear the degree of global economic interdependence. However, changes in trade patterns recently have caused hardship in some countries and prosperity in others.

ECONOMIC VOCABULARY   global economy

Trade and Development

The trade patterns of a less developed country often change as the country's economy grows. Less developed countries generally export minerals and agricultural products and import manufactured goods. As the country develops, its total trade usually increases. Exports of minerals and agricultural products make up a smaller percentage of its total trade. For example, the United States was a less developed country in the 1700s and 1800s. The country's major exports were cotton, tobacco, wood, and grain. As the economy of the United States developed, it both imported and exported more manufactured goods. Today, the United States still exports a high volume of agricultural goods. However, the nation also exports machinery, chemicals, and other processed goods, and imports such items as cars and cameras.

Other countries have followed a similar pattern. For example, India now exports woven textiles and clothing in addition to raw cotton. Colombia exports paper, greeting cards, furniture, and flooring materials in addition to logs and raw lumber. As countries develop, they depend more on other countries, and others depend more on them. Together, the nations of the world form a global economy, into which most of the national economies have merged as world trade has grown.

The Problem of Debt

As developing countries mature, their citizens demand better services and greater economic growth. To meet these demands, the developing countries often borrow funds from private banks throughout the world. The borrowers must be able to pay interest on the loans and also gradually repay the loan principal. Getting deeply into debt thus can become a problem. Recently some developing countries' significant debt repayment problems have caused major banks to hesitate over lending additional funds for development.

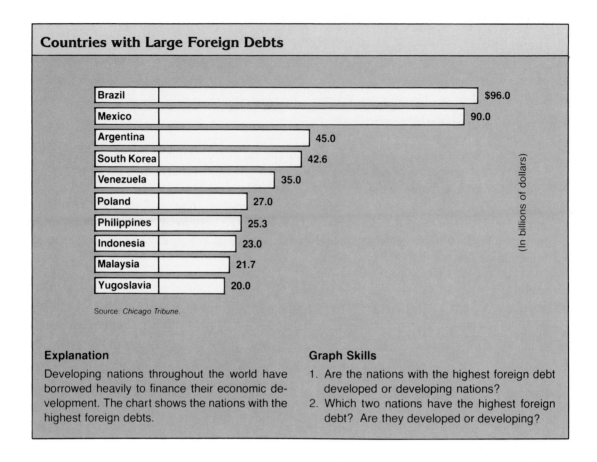

Countries with Large Foreign Debts

(In billions of dollars)

Brazil	$96.0
Mexico	90.0
Argentina	45.0
South Korea	42.6
Venezuela	35.0
Poland	27.0
Philippines	25.3
Indonesia	23.0
Malaysia	21.7
Yugoslavia	20.0

Source: *Chicago Tribune*.

Explanation

Developing nations throughout the world have borrowed heavily to finance their economic development. The chart shows the nations with the highest foreign debts.

Graph Skills

1. Are the nations with the highest foreign debt developed or developing nations?
2. Which two nations have the highest foreign debt? Are they developed or developing?

Cartels

Many developing countries control significant amounts of raw materials and natural resources on which the developed countries depend. Acting alone, many of the developing nations that have an abundance of a natural resource had very little power to bargain with the more developed countries of the world. However, some of these less developed countries joined together in cartels to set production limits on the resources they sold to the developed countries. By working together, they found they had great control over prices. By jointly limiting production of raw materials for export, the less developed countries were able to raise prices in the world market. Another advantage to limiting production is, of course, conservation of the countries' nonrenewable natural resources.

The Organization of Petroleum Exporting Countries (OPEC), for example, is an oil cartel. By banding together, some developing countries are able to earn significant amounts of money. These funds they then used to promote further development.

A New Economic Order

The differences between developed and developing countries are immense. According to the World Bank, in the early 1980s the developed countries contained roughly 18 percent of the world population but produced over 62 percent of world output. The United States, with approximately 6 percent of the world population, produced over 22 percent of world output. At the same time, developing nations with about half of the world population generated only about 15 percent of world output.

Significant changes must occur in many of the developing nations before their inhabitants rise above the base subsistence level. Long-term progress in economic development is rarely possible without a government able to maintain stability. In some countries, the government maintains order by maintaining broad popular support. In others, the government keeps order by dictatorial means.

REVIEWING THE CONCEPT

Developing Vocabulary

1. Define global economy.
2. Explain how and why a global economy developed in the world.

Mastering Facts

1. How do a country's exports change as its economy develops?
2. What countries in South America have large foreign debts?
3. How do cartels help to promote development in some LDCs?
4. Compare the per capita production of LDCs to that of developed nations.

CASE STUDY

Trade and Countertrade

It is clear, according to Roderick M. Hills, that countertrade is actually a form of currency exchange. Hills, chairman of Sears World Trade, a unit of the giant retailing and financial services company, depicts countertrade as an important form of international trading for many countries —especially developing countries. Countertrade may be considered a form of bartering between a developed country and developing countries. Sears, Hills noted, "sold several thousand head of breeding swine to a Latin American company that paid us in pesos because it couldn't get dollars. We quickly used the pesos to buy sugar there, which we sold to a Chicago food manufacturer."

Such trading involves a high level of risk and a thorough understanding of markets in all countries involved. In short, it is not a method of trading that businesses in developed countries favor. Nevertheless, "such countertrading," Hills emphasized, "is hard to admire—rather, it is an unpleasant fact of economic or political life or perhaps of business naiveté."

Importing countries normally must pay for American goods in dollars they have earned from previous exports to the United States. However, if the United States wants few of a developing country's goods for export, that country's dollar exchange opportunities are very limited. Countertrade provides a way for the United States to trade with countries that have few dollars. In 1982, countertrade accounted for 30 percent of global trade—up from about 2 percent a decade earlier.

Mr. Hills had a warning for individual businesses, though. "Anyone who uses countertrade or barter as a means of building a business, instead of overcoming trading or currency problems, is asking for trouble. Too much can go wrong. In our case with the [sale of hogs], we viewed the operation as basically a currency trading deal. The goods involved didn't matter; the value we received did. After all, the value of any currency is measured against other currencies or some goods that embody a store of value."

Mr. Hills considers his hog-peso-sugar deal as a series of independent barter operations carried on in free trade conditions. He declared, however, that countertrade is essentially a set of rules imposed on trading partners. They have little or no choice other than to comply with those rules if they want to do business.

ANALYZING THE CASE STUDY

STEP 1 Clarify the Issue

1. Describe a countertrade exchange between two countries.
2. Describe the conditions in a country that wants to countertrade.

STEP 2 Gather Evidence

1. Give an example of countertrade.
2. How has the volume of countertrade changed over the past decade?

STEP 3 Draw Conclusions

1. Why do countries engage in countertrade exchange?
2. How does countertrade differ from the traditional method of trading products between countries?
3. What are the benefits of countertrade to a developing nation?
4. Explain the possible problems associated with countertrade.

READING

The Global Challenge

by Aurelio Peccei   (1908–   )

The world faces tremendous economic challenges in the future. Economists disagree sharply about how to meet these challenges. The Club of Rome is a worldwide group of over 100 scientists, business leaders, and scholars who study global trends. Their reports are widely debated and sometimes controversial. Aurelio Peccei, co-founder of the Club of Rome, wrote the following article for a book of essays about the future, *Through the '80s.* As you read, consider whether or not Peccei's suggestions are practical.

"It is my perception that the world is in worse shape now than it was 10 years ago—and is getting worse. . . .

We are now heading into an even more complex and difficult decade. I have pretty well given up predicting what will happen unless we act. The

Club of Rome now concentrates instead on what may happen if present circumstances prevail.

In the following key areas, it is relatively easy to see what will happen.

1. Population. This is the worst problem we face and it affects all of us. Today there are 4.5 billion people in the world. Projections show that between now and the end of the century there will be two billion more people. There are not enough resources on this planet to care for them. So if population is not controlled, we will not be able to control anything else. . . . When people's basic needs are not being met, there will be increased social tension, more civil and military violence, more unemployment, less food and less shelter. Because of this, practically everything will be unmanageable.

2. Economic Affairs. The economy will take slight up and down curves, but the overall projection is a downward trend in the next decade. The world economy will be under greater stress as prices continue to increase in the area of foodstuffs, transportation, energy supplies, and raw materials. Because of this, economic enterprise will become harder.

3. Military Activities. There will be larger arsenals in the world; they will be more powerful; and there will be more occasions to use them. Because of this, the picture is becoming more worrisome. Right now, it is estimated that each person in the world is sitting on the nuclear equivalent of 10 tons of explosives. . . .

4. Science and Technology. The problem here is that 40 percent of the world's scientists are working on military preparations rather than producing technology for the betterment of the world. And the scientific gains that we've made—in areas such as genetics and microelectronics—aren't being handled well by people. We still retain values our forefathers gave us, which are no longer valid in our civilization.

5. Ecosystems. Four ecological areas necessary to sustain life—ocean fisheries, forests, pastures, croplands—are under great stress today. This does not mean much in countries like Canada where there are vast spaces and policies of reforestation, but in other parts of the world, tropical rain forests are being destroyed and deserts are advancing. If we continue to burn tropical forests down to make way for highways and settlements, and to cut them down to produce lumber, we will be destroying the very basis of life and food. . . .

What is to be done? The new project of the Club of Rome is to work to make the world more governable. By this, we mean a more regional approach to the new international order.

Today the world is a fragmentation of more than 150 nations. Each is fiercely nationalistic, but we must realize how much interdependence there is. . . .

I think it is impossible for 150 [countries of the world] to continue to be selfish.

What the Club of Rome is proposing is a plan to try to make the south of the globe as governable as the north.

In the north there are five giant communities: Western Europe, the Soviet bloc, North America, China, and Japan. In the south, however, there are 120 nation-states without any community.

We are therefore suggesting that in areas such as East Africa, West Africa, Latin America, and Southeast Asia, they should get together and try to speak with one voice.

Such a process will no doubt be long, tortuous, and painful. But it is certainly within the realm of possibility if we all accept the basic principles involved. Indeed, I consider it essential if a true sense of global community is to evolve. **99**

From "The Challenge of the '80s," by Aurelio Peccei, in *Through the '80s.*

UNDERSTANDING THE READING

1. What are the results of uncontrolled population growth?
2. What are the potential dangers to mankind when the ecosystems are endangered?
3. What does Peccei recommend to make the southern hemisphere more governable? Why might this suggestion be controversial?

Section 3 Review

Understanding Global Economics

1. What is the usual pattern of trade between a developed country and one that is developing?
2. What problems arise as developing nations mature?
3. What would be the benefits and costs to countries joining in a cartel?
4. Describe the imbalance between production and population in LDCs.

Global Economics Today

1. Explain how changes in the global economy have made the countries of the world more interdependent.
2. **Challenge:** Should the United States encourage the development of a new economic order? What would be the role of the United States in its development?

These tourists are visiting England. Money moves from one country to another when tourists spend.

Americans
at Work

Meet Naomi Friedman
Plumber

Naomi Friedman decided to become a plumber after she called one to fix a problem in her home in 1975. She was impressed at how easily the plumber did the job and at how much money he made. Friedman, who lives in Oakland, California, realized that, despite improvements in technology, skilled craft workers were still in great demand.

Friedman's first challenge was to learn the trade. Finding a plumber to take her on as an apprentice proved almost impossible. The local union and private companies were not interested in helping her get started. They wanted male plumbers. "Most of the time I'd go into plumbing companies and the receptionist would laugh at me, which was very frustrating."

Finally, Friedman found an independent plumber who was willing to teach her the trade. In return, she had to agree to work nine months without pay. After the nine months, Friedman started her own business. Four years later, Friedman became a licensed plumber.

Customers who called Friedman were often surprised when she appeared at their home. People expected to see the customary male plumber. Friedman says she has received few complaints from people about being charged $35 an hour for her services, the union wage scale. Though she felt that initially the union treated her unfairly, she realized that it was helpful in her business. She said, "I know I couldn't charge $35 an hour if it weren't for the unions."

Friedman remembers her own hard start and uses her experience to help others. In particular, she has tried to encourage other women and minorities to enter plumbing. In 1972, less than 5 percent of all plumbers were black. Less than 0.1 percent were female. By 1982, over 6 percent were black and 0.8 percent were female. Friedman gave up four months of work to help coordinate the first national conference for women in the trades. In addition, she has spent time teaching plumbing to interested young people.

Friedman believes that plumbing has a sound future. The United States has approximately 500,000 plumbers. Changes in technology are not likely to decrease the demand for their skills. "Sewers are the basis of our civilization. There's a lot of money in them. Most people don't argue over a bill when you're fixing their sewer." Friedman benefits from a well-known economic fact—one person's need can become another person's gain.

Buying Insurance

People buy insurance to protect themselves against financial loss from floods, fires, accidents, sicknesses, crime, and other misfortunes. To obtain insurance, a person must sign a contract with an insurance company. This contract is known as a policy. The policy states that the person, or policyholder, agrees to pay small, regular sums of money to the insurance company. These payments are known as premiums. In exchange for premiums, the insurance company agrees to pay the policyholder certain sums of money in the event that particular losses listed in the policy occur. Such payments made by the insurance companies are known as benefits.

In your lifetime, you will probably buy many different kinds of insurance. Buying insurance can be complicated because so many types of policies are available. However, there are a few simple steps that you can follow to ensure that you obtain the policies that are best suited to your needs.

STEP 1 Identify Your Insurance Needs

In general, you need insurance whenever you run a risk of significant financial loss. For example, if you own a car, you will need auto insurance to protect yourself from accident losses. If you buy a house, you will need homeowner's insurance to protect yourself from fire, flood, or theft losses. Most people also need health insurance to protect themselves against losses caused by disease or disability.

As your life changes, your insurance needs will also change. For example, if you marry and have children, and if you contribute a large portion of your family's income, you will probably want to buy life insurance. This insurance will protect your family from the financial hardship that could follow your death. Since individual insurance needs change over time, be sure to reevaluate your needs whenever major events in your life occur.

STEP 2 Research Policies and Firms

Once you have decided that you need a particular kind of insurance, do some research to find out what kinds of policies are available and which of these policies is best suited to your needs. Read books, magazines, encyclopedia articles, and other sources of information about types of insurance policies. Ask your friends, relatives, and acquaintances about the companies with which they do business and about the policies they hold.

STEP 3 Talk to Insurance Agents

Insurance policies are sold by representatives of insurance companies known as agents. Before choosing a particular company or policy, do some comparison shopping. When talking to an agent about a particular policy, make sure that you find out exactly how much the policy will cost, what losses are covered by the policy, what losses are *not* covered by the policy, and how much the company will pay in benefits for each loss that the policy covers.

STEP 4 Inform Your Agent

Once you choose a particular agent and a particular policy, make sure that you pay your premiums on time. Failing to do so may result in cancellation of your policy. If you find that you no longer need a particular policy, ask your agent to cancel it. Do not simply allow your policy to lapse. Some companies will not reinsure someone who has allowed a policy to lapse without canceling it. Whenever your address changes and whenever new insurance needs arise, inform your agent. Developing a courteous, professional relationship with your agent will help to ensure that you will receive proper service.

Insurance Premiums and Benefits

Premiums ($ billions)	Benefits ($ billions)
78.49	70.52
health	insurance
48.11	34.31
life	insurance
40.51	32.40
auto	insurance
10.13	7.62
homeowner's	insurance
75.96	45.75
other types of	insurance
Total: 253.2 billion	Total: 190.6 billion

Source: *World Book Encyclopedia*

Explanation

This graph shows the the amount of insurance premiums and benefits paid in 1982.

Graph Skills

1. Compare the total payments of consumers and insurers.
2. What percentage of all insurance premiums were paid for health insurance?

ECONOMIC SKILLS TODAY

1. List four major types of insurance and explain the reasons for buying each.
2. Give two reasons why a person should talk to more than one agent before buying insurance.

Enrichment Activities

1. Imagine that you are a wage earner, that you have dependents, and that you want to buy life insurance. Find out what types of life insurance are available. Describe the advantages and disadvantages of each major type.
2. Renters, as well as homeowners, often buy insurance to protect their personal property. Contact an insurance agent and find out what types of renters' insurance are available. Compare and contrast the policies described to you and then choose the policy that you think is best for you. Explain the reasons for your choice.

CHAPTER 16 | Summary and Review

CHAPTER SUMMARY

Development Problems

The less developed countries (LDCs) face five major economic problems: (1) low per capita GNP; (2) inefficient farming methods; (3) lack of the skills, tools, and machines; (4) dependence on borrowing; and (5) rapidly increasing populations. In addition, many LDCs suffer from unstable political conditions that make economic planning difficult. Some LDCs have few natural resources.

Patterns of Change

To improve the standard of living of their people, LDCs usually try to (1) create positive work attitudes, (2) educate their citizens, (3) encourage slow population growth, (4) build capital resources, (5) create a stable government, and (6) develop a sound economic infrastructure. These steps toward economic growth may be financed by the government of the LDC or by aid from foreign governments, international organizations, and private banks.

Global Economics

Advances in transportation and communications have merged countries into one interdependent global economy. In this global economy, trade and borrowing to finance growth play important roles. LDCs often export raw materials. As their economies develop, they begin to export manufactured and processed goods. Some LDCs take advantage of global interdependence by forming cartels. Vast differences still exist between the less developed and the more developed countries.

CRITICAL THINKING QUESTIONS

Development Problems

1. Before the coming of modern technology, cloth and clothes were made by hand. Compare and contrast this traditional method with the modern method of factory production. What are the advantages and disadvantages of each? Why have so many Americans become interested in recent years in traditional crafts and do-it-yourself projects?
2. To understand why populations increase so rapidly, think about this problem: Suppose that you were offered a choice between receiving $1 million today or 2 cents today, 4 cents the next day, 8 cents the next day, and so on, for 30 days. Which would you choose? To find out, start by writing 2 cents at the top of a sheet of paper. Double this amount 30 times to see how much you would have at the end of a month.

Patterns of Change

1. Based on what you learned in this chapter, explain why a good education system is essential to a healthy economy.
2. The technological devices that are used for communication between people are an important part of the infrastructure of any economy. The telephone is one such technical device. Name four more devices used for communication and explain why such devices are important to an economic system.
3. One South American country has had over 50 political revolutions in the past 100 years. Would you expect it to have a sound economy? Why or why not?

Global Economics

1. Imagine a country with the following chief exports: spices, coffee beans, rice, and silk. Is this a developed country or a less developed country? How did you choose your answer?
2. Name six products that you own or use that were produced in other countries.
3. Review the information on monopolies given in Chapter 5. Is a cartel a monopoly? Defend your answer.
4. Imagine that you have been elected mayor of a city in which there are economically depressed neighborhoods. To improve conditions in these neighborhoods, you decide to use the same methods used by the planners in less developed countries. What methods could you use?

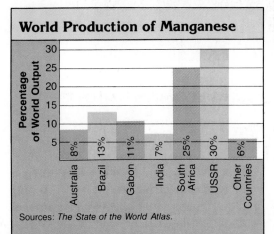

World Production of Manganese

Sources: *The State of the World Atlas.*

Explanation

This graph shows the production of manganese, a metal used for strengthening steel.

Graph Skills

1. Which country produces the most manganese?
2. Predict how a cartel of manganese producers would affect the United States.

DEVELOPING ECONOMIC SKILLS

Use the graph and your knowledge to answer the questions that follow.

1. Which two countries control most of the world's production of manganese?
2. What percentage of the world's manganese is produced by Australia, Brazil, Gabon, India, South Africa, and the USSR combined?
3. If all of the countries listed on the graph wanted to establish a cartel, could they do so? If such a cartel were established, which countries in the cartel would have the most power to influence the price set by the cartel?

APPLYING ECONOMICS TODAY

1. During the 1970s and 1980s, many of the less developed countries have been at war. These countries include El Salvador, Honduras, Nicaragua, Morocco, Algeria, Iran, Iraq, North and South Yemen, Ethiopia, Somalia, Rhodesia, Mozambique, Vietnam, Laos, and Kampuchea. What effect might these wars have had on the possibilities for economic development in the countries involved?
2. **Challenge:** Is it possible for countries to import and export information? Explain your answer. Is transferring information from country to country any different from transferring other types of information?
3. **Challenge:** As developed countries continue to grow, they use up many nonrenewable resources. However, many less developed countries have these same resources in abundance. For example, the continent of Africa is rich in untapped iron ore. Explain how the leaders of less developed countries might be able to use these facts to their advantage in the future.

535

UNIT 4 Review

USING ECONOMIC CONCEPTS

Challenges to the Market Economy

1. List and describe the benefits and costs of industrialization.
2. Describe the kinds of problems that face a mature industrial economy.
3. How does discrimination hurt a market system economy?
4. Why are equity and efficiency sometimes in conflict?
5. **Challenge:** How can the goals of equal opportunity and equity be achieved in a market economy?

Current Economic Issues

1. Describe the impact that the rapid rise of oil prices in the 1970s had on the economies of the United States and Europe.
2. List four energy sources that could replace fossil fuels.
3. Explain the reasons for the increase in the problems cities have faced during the past 40 years.
4. What measures can the government take to decrease pollution? How are the costs paid? Who pays them?
5. **Challenge:** Explain the impact that the use of soft energy—for example, solar power to heat homes—would have on the environment.

International Trade

1. What kinds of restrictions can be imposed on international trade? Explain the reasons why countries resort to these measures.
2. How does the strength or weakness of a country's currency affect the prices of its exports, the country's employment rate, and the restrictions the country imposes on imports?
3. Explain how exchange rates affect a country's balance of payments.
4. How have multinationals contributed to the development of a world economy?
5. **Challenge:** Explain the effect of the United States budgetary deficit on the value of the dollar.

Less Developed Countries

1. Describe five basic problems that less developed countries face in trying to improve their economies.
2. How can less developed countries promote economic development?
3. Summarize how a country's trade pattern changes as its economy develops.
4. **Challenge:** What are the costs and benefits to a country of accepting foreign aid?

APPLING ECONOMIC SKILLS

Use the graph and your economic knowledge to answer the following questions.

1. What evidence suggests that Canada is more developed than Mexico?
2. Which country has a positive balance of trade? How did you find the answer?
3. Cite two statistics suggesting that the economy of Mexico was facing severe problems. List two statistics suggesting that Mexico had a large supply of resources to help in solving its problems.
4. List three other statistics that would indicate the level of development of the countries shown in the graph.

Comparing Three Economies			
Category	United States	Canada	Mexico
Population (millions)	232	24	71
GNP ($ billions)	2,614	243	142
Inflation (percent)	7.1	11.3	32.8
Oil Reserves (billion barrels)	29.8	7.3	57.0
Exports ($ billion)	233.7	70.3	19.4
Imports ($ billion)	273.4	66.5	23.1

Source: *U.S. News and World Report.*

Explanation

This graph compares the economies of the United States, Canada, and Mexico.

Graph Skills

1. Which nation had the largest GNP per capita?
2. Predict which statistics would increase if the price of oil increased sharply.

ECONOMIC REASONING

Risa and Heather are going to Mexico for two weeks this summer. They plan to stay at hotels and eat in restaurants. After studying Spanish four years in school, they want to see whether their investment of time and effort was worthwhile.

The two girls know that currencies fluctuate. They wonder when they should change their dollars into Mexican pesos. They could change their currency immediately, wait until just before they leave, or change it as they travel in Mexico. Another alternative would be to charge their expenses and pay the bills after they return.

They expect to spend about $850 each. On the business page of the newspaper, they find that the current exchange rate is 189 pesos per dollar. A month ago, the rate was 205 pesos per dollar. During the past year, the exchange rate fluctuated between 185 and 384 pesos per dollar.

STEP 1   Gather Information

1. List five questions Risa and Heather might try to answer before they decide when to change their currency.
2. What sources of information could Risa and Heather use to find out more about the exchange rates between American dollars and Mexican pesos?

STEP 2   Analyze Costs and Benefits

1. Describe the monetary risks Risa and Heather are taking by converting their currency now, just before they leave, and as they travel.
2. What nonmonetary issues would the two girls consider as they decided when to change their currency?

STEP 3   Make a Decision

1. In what conditions should Risa and Heather immediately change their currency? In what conditions should they wait?

CURRENT ECONOMIC ISSUES

1. Compare the reading by John Lukacs in Chapter 13 with the reading by John Naisbitt in Chapter 6. As society moves into the information age, will it have more or less bureaucracy than it has today? Explain the consequences of your prediction for the economy.
2. In the 1970s, the price of oil increased sharply. If that situation occurs again, what changes will occur in the economy of the United States? How will demand for other forms of energy change? How will the environment be influenced? How would a sharp oil price increase affect world trade?

Glossary

This glossary explains many of the important words and ideas needed to understand economics. Each entry consists of a short explanation and the number of the page where the term is used.

acceleration principle, the principle that a change in consumer spending creates a need for a change in investment spending (189).

acid rain, rain that has a high acid content. Acid rain can kill vegetation (457).

annual report, a yearly report made to stockholders by the management of a corporation. The report tells about the corporation's activities during the preceding year, describes the corporation's financial status at the end of the year, and explains the corporation's plans for the future (270).

asset, an item of value. An individual's assets might include money; property such as stocks, land, copyrights, or patents; and intangibles such as job skills, education, and work experience (270).

automatic stabilizers, built-in elements of the economic system that act to counter the business cycle. Automatic stabilizers include the graduated income tax and unemployment compensation (392).

autonomous investment, investment that results from noneconomic changes. A new invention may increase autonomous investment (278).

axis, either of the two perpendicular lines used to construct a graph. The horizontal axis is the x-axis; the vertical axis is the y-axis (8).

balance of payments, the difference between the money flowing into and that flowing out of a country (482).

balance sheet, a chart that shows the assets and liabilities of a corporation. A balance sheet summarizes a corporation's financial condition at one instant in time (270).

barter, a method of exchange in which one good or service is traded for another without the use of money or any other medium of exchange. Barter is common in traditional economies (341).

base year, a year chosen as a standard against which to measure economic activity during other years. For example, the Bureau of Labor Statistics uses 1967 as a base year for determining the consumer price index (253).

blue collar workers, people who work outdoors or in factories. Carpenters, plumbers, bricklayers, truck drivers, and laborers on assembly lines are all blue collar workers (173).

board of directors, a group of people elected by shareholders to manage the resources of a corporation. The administrators who oversee the day-to-day operations of a corporation are usually hired by the board of directors (212).

bond, a certificate that promises to pay the holder a certain amount of money on a certain date. Corporations sell bonds to investors in order to raise money for expansion (213).

budget, a plan for coordinating income and spending. The federal budget is a document showing, among other things, how much money the federal government expects to receive and spend during one year (400).

bureaucracy, a system for operating an organization based on rules, policies, organization, and written records (410).

business cycle, the pattern of growth or decline in real GNP. The business cycle includes four phases: expansion, peak, contraction, and trough (275).

capital, wealth, either in money or property, owned by a person or firm and used to produce goods or more wealth (6).

capital account, money that Americans invest abroad and foreigners invest in the United States, including short-term loans (482).

capital flight, the movement of businesses and jobs to suburban or outlaying areas from cities. Cities are hurt by capital flight (449).

capital goods, goods used to produce other items. Tools, machines, and buildings are examples of capital goods (7).

capital resources, the money or property, such as tools or buildings, used to produce consumer goods or services. To keep its operations up-to-date, a business must continually renew or replace its capital resources (6).

capitalism, a type of market system in which private individuals and businesses own most of the resources. The economy of the United States is an example of capitalism (55).

cartel, a group of businesses or countries that act together to control the price, production, and sale of a product (440).

central city, the area within the city boundaries of a large urban area (448).

check, a written order to a bank to pay a certain

amount of money to an individual or organization (342).

checking account, a bank account from which money can be drawn by writing a check (342).

chief executive officer (CEO), the highest management official in a corporation. The chief executive officer is usually chosen by the board of directors (270).

circular flow of money, the path in which money travels through the economy. Producers pay workers. These workers, who are also consumers, purchase goods from producers (158).

coincident indicators, statistics that measure business activities that change at about the same time as shifts in general economic activity. Coincident indicators include total industrial production, total industrial sales, personal income, and the number of employees on industrial payrolls (263).

collective bargaining, negotiations between management and union officials in which the union acts as the sole representative of a group of workers. In collective bargaining, management and labor try to agree on a contract that is acceptable to both groups (221).

command system, an economic system in which central planners make most of the basic economic decisions. The government-controlled economies of China and the Soviet Union are command systems (37).

communism, an extreme form of socialism, in which workers control the means of producing goods and services (79).

comparative advantage, the ability of one country to produce a good or service more efficiently than another country. The United States has a comparative advantage over most countries in growing corn because of its soil and climate (471).

complementary products, products that are used in combination with one another. Lettuce, tomatoes, and salad dressing are complementary products. A shift in demand for one will be accompanied by a shift in demand for the others (109).

composite indexes, an economic measurement that averages several other economic indicators. Indexes for employment, production, and signs of business activity are often combined into one composite index (264).

constant dollar GNP. See **real GNP** (252).

consumer, a person who buys goods and services for personal use (5).

consumer cooperative, a form of business in which the consumers who purchase from the business share ownership. Cooperatives in the United States include credit unions, mutual insurance companies, and health plans (81).

consumer goods, products that satisfy people's economic needs and wants. Food, clothing, and cars are examples of consumer goods (5).

Consumer Price Index (CPI), a statistic showing changes over time in the prices of selected goods and services purchased by consumers. See also **price index** (253).

contraction, the phase of the business cycle in which real GNP declines. During a contraction, production slows down and unemployment increases (275).

copyright, the exclusive right to publish or perform a literary, artistic, or musical work for a certain number of years (142).

corporation profit, the income that a corporation has after paying all of its expenses. Corporate profits can be reinvested in the corporation or paid to stockholders as dividends (171).

corporation, a form of business organization in which one or more shareholders own the business, and which has the legal rights and duties of an individual. A corporation may be owned by many people (211).

cost-benefit ratio, the comparison between costs and benefits of an action (426).

cost-push inflation, an increase in the general level of prices caused by an increase in production costs (295).

craft union, an organization that represents a group of laborers, all of whom do the same kind of work (220).

credit, money borrowed for a period of time. Many Americans buy houses and cars on credit (198).

crowding out, the decrease in borrowing by businesses related to high government borrowing. Government borrowing may drive up interest rates, thereby crowding out businesses that cannot afford to pay the high rates (381).

culture, the entire way of life of a society. A society's culture includes its language, housing, food, clothing, religion, family life, and political system (37).

currency, money in the form of paper bills and metal coins. In the United States, currency is manufactured by the Bureau of the Mint, a division of the Treasury Department (342).

current account, the value of exports and imports of goods and services, tourist spending, investment income, military transactions, pensions, and other transfers of money in and out of a country (482).

current GNP. See **money GNP** (252).

cyclical unemployment, unemployment that occurs because of changes in the business cycle. Some unemployment inevitably accompanies any slowdown, or contraction, of general economic activity (287).

deficit, the difference between income and expenditures for a given year when the expenditures exceed the income. A government deficit results whenever a government spends more than it collects in revenue (380).

deflation, a general decline in prices and wages. During periods of deflation, the supply of goods and services exceeds the demand for them. As a result, prices may fall, and businesses may lower their output, thus increasing unemployment (252).

demand, the quantity of a good or a service that consumers want at each of its possible prices. Prices usually increase when the demand for a product is greater than the supply (55).

demand curve, a line, plotted on a graph, that shows how much of a product consumers will demand at various possible prices (106).

demand deposit, a checking account, so called because the person who deposited money in the account has the right to demand the return of the money at any time (342).

demand schedule, a chart that shows how much of a product consumers will demand at various possible prices. Producers use demand schedules to determine the best possible prices for their products (106).

demand-pull inflation, an increase in the general level of prices caused by an increase in demand (293).

demand-side economics, the theory that government can promote economic stability by increasing or decreasing spending and taxes at different parts of the business cycle. According to the theory, the government can influence total demand for goods and services enough to even out the business cycle. Also known as **Keynesian economics** (391).

depreciate, to decrease in value. A currency depreciates when its exchange rate falls in relationship to other currencies (485).

depression, a severe and persistent recession that results in business closings and massive unemployment. The United States experienced a period of depression following the stock market collapse of 1929 (275).

deregulation, the process of lessening governmental control of an industry or industries. After deregulation of the airlines, these companies became more competitive (50).

destructive competition, competition among businesses that threatens the economy or safety of a community. Setting artificially low prices that force other companies out of business is destructive competition (316).

development assistance, funding from one country to another in order to promote development. Also known as **foreign aid** (517).

differentiated competition, a form of imperfect competition in which producers are numerous and prices vary greatly. Also known as **monopolistic competition** (141).

discount rate, the interest rate that banks pay to borrow money from Federal Reserve Banks. The Federal Reserve can decrease the money supply by raising the discount rate (358).

discrimination, the act of treating people differently, based on something other than individual merit. Discrimination often results in unfair treatment of individuals (418).

distribution of income, the division of money received for work or property. Progressive income taxes help to even the distribution of income (179).

dividend, a payment to a stockholder from a corporation. A dividend is paid for each share of stock that the stockholder owns (212).

division of labor, the separation of a job into several tasks, each of which is the responsibility of a different worker. Factories use division of labor to increase productivity (69).

double taxation, the practice of taxing corporate profits twice. Corporations pay taxes on their profits before distributing these profits as dividends. Shareholders then pay taxes on these profits again in the form of income taxes on the dividends that they have received (214).

dumping, selling a product in a foreign market at a lower price to force domestic manufacturers out of business, which then leaves the foreign supplier free to raise prices (473).

earnings-and-cost approach, a method of computing the gross national product, or GNP. This method determines the total value of goods and services produced by counting all the money received for them (243).

easy money, the result of an expansion of the money supply by the Federal Reserve Bank, giving banks more money to loan. Easy money leads to increased demand and production (358).

economic efficiency, a state in which the benefits of economic activity outweigh the costs (426).

economic indicators, statistics that help economists to measure economic performance. See **leading indicators, coincident indicators,** and **lagging indicators** (262).

economic institution, an organization that influences economic behavior. Families, businesses, and labor unions are all economic institutions (203).

economic model, a plan of an economy. A model helps an economist to analyze problems, seek solutions, and make comparisions among events (23).

economics, the study of how people and countries use their resources to produce, distribute, and consume goods and services (5).

elasticity of demand, the degree to which changes in the price of a product cause changes in the quantity of the product demanded. The demand for automobiles is highly elastic, but the demand for salt is not (107).

elasticity of supply, the degree to which changes in the price of a product cause changes in the quantity of the product supplied. The supply of record albums is highly elastic, but the supply of automobiles is not (116).

embargo, a governmental order prohibiting or restricting a country's imports or exports (441).

employee compensation, income earned by working for others. Employee compensation includes wages, salaries, and fringe benefits such as health insurance and retirement plans (171).

English system, a system of weights and measurements in which the basic units are the foot for length, the pound for weight, and the quart for liquid volume. The English system is still widely used in the United States (310).

entrepreneur, an individual who organizes and manages a business to make a profit (203).

environmental pollution, the addition of unclean substances to natural resources. Industries pouring their waste matter into rivers are environmental polluters (456).

equilibrium price, the price at which the amount of a product that producers will supply and that consumers will demand is the same. If a demand curve and a supply curve are plotted on the same graph, the equilibrium price will be at the intersection of the two curves (124).

equity, equality or fairness. An action is equitable when it is perceived as fair (426).

expansion, the phase of the business cycle in which real GNP increases. During an expansion, economic recovery occurs, and both employment and wages increase (275).

exchange rate, the amount of one currency given in trade or exchange for another (483).

externalities, costs of production which neither the producer nor the consumer pays directly. An industry's cost of repairing the effects of pollution is an externality, because society pays (457).

factor markets, markets or exchanges for land, labor, and capital. The job market is the factor market in which people look for work and employers seek workers (148).

factors of production, the resources needed to produce goods and services. Factors of production include land, labor, and capital (148).

farmworkers, people who work on their own or others' farms (173).

Federal Reserve System (the Fed), the central banking system of the United States. The Federal Reserve influences the increase or decrease in interest rates and the money supply (356).

federation, a loose organization of national unions that acts as a speaker for all its member unions. The AFL-CIO is the largest such federation in the world (221).

final goods and services, products in their final form as used by consumers. A shirt is a final good, but the cotton used to make it is not (242).

fiscal policy, government decisions on spending and taxation designed to achieve national economic goals. Stable prices, full employment, and economic growth are three goals of national fiscal policy (390).

fixed expenses, regularly occurring expenses that are set in advance. Most Americans have several fixed expenses, including mortgage or rent payments, auto payments, and insurance premiums (32).

floating exchange rates, a system of exchange rates in which supply and demand determine the value of nations' currencies in relation to one another (483).

flow-of-product approach, a method of computing the gross national product, or GNP. This method determines the total value of goods and services produced by counting all the money spent on them (242).

foreign aid. See development assistance (517).

foreign exchange markets, the market in which people, banks, and other businesses buy and sell currencies. The foreign exchange markets work in much the same way as the stock exchange (483).

fossil fuels, fuels developed from the remains of prehistoric plants and animals. Fossil fuels include oil, coal, and natural gas (439).

freedom of exchange, the right of buyers and sellers to purchase, trade, or sell goods on whatever terms they can agree. Government-enforced price controls limit freedom of exchange (57).

frictional unemployment, unemployment that occurs when people are temporarily between jobs. Some frictional unemployment will always be present in a market economy (286).

full employment, the condition in which everyone who wants to work can find a job (285).

full potential, the output that would result if all the resources of an economy were used as much as possible. In practice, full potential is never completely realized (280).

gasahol, an alternative fuel made from a mixture of alcohol and gasoline. The development of gasahol was a response to a huge increase in oil prices in the 1970s (442).

geographic specialization, the tendency of persons and businesses within a region to produce goods and services that make use of the resources of that region. The paper industry in Wisconsin, which makes use of the state's abundant timber resources, is an example of geographic specialization (69).

global economy, the overall economy into which most of the national economies have merged as world trade has grown (525).

GNP deflator, a statistic for measuring the price changes of all goods and services using 1972 as the base year (253).

government securities, bonds issued by the federal government that promise to pay the owners the purchase price of the bonds plus interest after a specific period of time. Government securities include savings bonds and treasury bills (380).

government subsidy, a grant of money from a government to a firm or individual to aid the public well-being (459).

graph, a diagram that shows the changing values of one or more variables. Graphs can show changes or trends in the economy (8). See also **variable** (8).

grid, the framework of a graph, made with two perpendicular lines called axes.(8).

gross national product (GNP), the value, in dollars, of all final goods and services produced for sale during one year. The United States GNP increased from about $7.4 billion in 1878 to over $3.3 trillion in 1983 (241).

hidden costs, costs that are not reflected in the market prices of goods and services. For example, building an airport may involve such hidden costs as increased traffic and noise pollution (87).

human resources, the skills, talents, expertise, and experience that people can use to produce goods and services. The large and well-educated American labor force provides a wealth of human resources. See also **labor** (514).

imperfect competition, the situation that exists when a market is only partially competitive.

See **differentiated competition, monopoly,** and **natural monopoly** (140).

income, the money that a person receives in exchange for work or sale of property (179).

income statement, a statement that shows a firm's profit or loss during a single year. The statement lists revenues and expenditures for one year (270).

independent union, a union that is not part of a federation. The United Mine Workers is an independent union (221).

induced investment, investment encouraged by factors in the economy. Any economic decision that results in increased consumer demand, such as tax cuts or wage increases, will lead to induced investment (278).

industrial economy, an economy characterized by large-scale manufacturing and profit-making businesses. After about 1750 an industrial economy emerged in Europe as factories replaced home workshops (409).

industrial union, an organization that represents all the workers in an industry, regardless of the type of work each performs (221).

inflation, a general rise in prices and wages. During a period of inflation, the demand for goods and services generally exceeds the supply (252).

infrastructure, a country's system of highways, bridges, dams, schools, communication networks, and other facilities on which its economy depends (516).

inner city, the residential area closest to the center of a city. Often, the inner city is an old and poor section (448).

interest, money paid or received for lending money. Individuals receive interest for money they deposit in banks. People pay interest on loans they receive from banks (171).

investment spending, spending on capital goods. An increase in investment spending usually leads to economic expansion (188).

invisible hand, a term eighteenth-century economist Adam Smith used to describe the tendency of competing self-interests to promote the common good. According to Smith, an individual who "intends only his own gain" is "led by an invisible hand to promote . . . that of society (56)."

Keynesian economics. See **demand-side economics** (391).

labor union, an organization of workers formed to promote the interests of its members. Labor unions enable workers to bargain collectively for better wages, benefits, and working conditions (220).

Laffer Curve, a graph suggesting that, in certain conditions, a tax cut will stimulate economic activity and therefore actually increase tax revenue (303).

lagging indicators, statistics that tend to rise or fall after a change in general economic activity has occurred. Two lagging indicators are interest rates banks charge on loans and the amount of money owed (263).

law of demand, the principle that as the price of an item increases, a smaller quantity will be bought, and as the price decreases, a larger quantity will be bought (106).

law of supply, the principle that as the price of an item increases, so will the amount of the item producers are willing to supply, and as the price of the item decreases, so will the amount supplied (115).

leading indicators, statistics that tend to rise or fall just before a major change in economic activity. Some leading indicators include statistics on the number of workers employed, construction activity, and the formation of new businesses (263).

legal tender, money that, by law, must be accepted in payment of a debt. In the United States, currency is the only legal tender (342).

less developed country (LDC), a country with low per capita income and GNP. LDCs are poor countries with such problems as inadequate food supplies and few educational opportunities (505).

liability, a debt or claim against the assets of an individual or corporation. The assets and liabilities of a corporation are listed on the balance sheet that accompanies the corporation's annual report (270).

limited liability, a condition in which owners of businesses can lose only the amount of their investment. Stockholders in corporations have limited liability (212).

limited life, a condition in which a business ceases to exist when the owner, or one of the owners, dies or leaves the business. Businesses that are partnerships and sole proprietorships have limited life (205).

local, a union organization representing the workers in one community or factory (221).

M-1A, a measurement of the nation's money supply that includes all currency and all deposits in standard checking accounts (349).

M-1B, a measurement of the nation's money supply that includes all currency, and all de-

posits in standard and interest-bearing checking accounts (349).

M-2, a measurement of the nation's money supply that includes all currency, all deposits in standard and interest-bearing checking accounts, and all savings deposits (350).

macroeconomics, the branch of economics that analyzes the relationships among sectors of the economy. Macroeconomists study the money supply, interest rates, the trade deficit, inflation, and other issues (241).

market systems, economic systems in which most basic economic decisions are made by merchants, consumers, and businesspeople. The economy of the United States is a market system (37).

mean, the average value of a group of numbers. The mean is determined by dividing the total quantity by the number of units. Thus, the mean of the numbers 2, 7, and 9 is 18 divided by 3, or 6 (181).

mechanization, the use of machines to increase production. Mechanization is one reason for the efficiency of modern factories (70).

median, the middle number in a list of numbers arranged in order. In the series 1, 2, 3, 4, 5, the median is 3 (180).

merger, a joining of two companies. Usually, one company gains control of the other in a merger (317).

metric system, a system of weights and measures in which the basic units are the meter for length, the gram for weight, and the liter for liquid volume. The metric system is the most widely used system of weights and measures in the world (310).

metropolis, a metropolitan region, or the area of the city and its suburbs together (448).

microeconomics, the branch of economics that analyzes specific factors affecting an economy. For example, the study of how best to market a particular product would be a microeconomic study (241).

monetary policy, the government's effort to influence interest rates and the money supply in order to cause changes in the economy as a whole. Monetary policy is carried out and, to a large extent, determined by the Federal Reserve (357).

money, any object used as a medium of exchange or a store or standard of value (341).

money GNP, the gross national product of any year stated in the dollars of that year. Also known as **current GNP** (252).

monopolistic competition. See **differentiated competition** (141).

monopoly, the situation in which one seller supplies all the demand for a particular product or service. For example, electrical companies often have a monopoly in a limited geographical area (141).

multinational corporations, large corporations that produce products in more than one country (493).

multiplier effect, the tendency of an initial amount of spending to stimulate further spending. For example, if three people in turn receive and then spend a dollar, the total amount of spending associated with this dollar bill is three dollars (187).

mutual fund, a trust or corporation that pools the resources of several small investors in order to buy a large and usually diverse group of stocks. By buying shares in a mutual fund, even a small investor can have the advantage of professional investment management (232).

national debt, the money that the federal government has borrowed because its expenditures have exceeded its revenues. In 1984, the national debt of the United States exceeded the $1.5 trillion mark (380).

natural monopoly, a monopoly that results when a product or service can be supplied most cheaply by a single producer. Public utilities, such as electric and water companies, are natural monopolies (141).

natural resources, raw materials, such as land, water, oil, timber, iron ore, and coal, from which goods are made. The United States is rich in some natural resources, such as timber and coal, but poor in others, such as tin (6).

near money, items used for some but not all of the functions of money. Credit cards are examples of near money (342).

nonrenewable resources, resources that cannot be replaced quickly. Oil and natural gas are nonrenewable resources (87).

NOW account, a bank account that is similar to a checking account but pays interest to the depositor. The letters NOW stand for negotiable order of withdrawal (351).

occupational specialization, the tendency of workers to concentrate on developing one skill or set of skills rather than several that are unrelated. For example, doctors often specialize in one type of medicine (69).

oligopoly, a type of imperfect competition in which there are few producers and little price variation. The gasoline industry is an example of an oligopoly (141).

OPEC, the Organization of Petroleum Exporting Countries, an oil cartel including several leading petroleum producing countries (440).

open-market operations, sales and purchases of government bonds by the Federal Reserve. The Fed can decrease the money supply by selling bonds to banks and increase the money supply by buying back these bonds (358).

opportunity cost, the value of the time, money, goods, and services given up in making a choice. The opportunity costs of going to college include the loss of income and work experience (22).

partnership, an association of two or more people in order to run a business (205).

patent, an official document granting an inventor the exclusive right to make, use, or sell an invention for a specified number of years. Thomas Edison held patents on many important inventions (142).

peak, the highest point in a business cycle. The peak is a period of prosperity, generally followed by a contraction, or slowdown, in economic activity (275).

per capita, per person (255).

per capita GNP, the total production of a nation divided by its population (255).

perfect competition, the situation that exists when a market is completely competitive. In such a situation, all economic decisions are made solely on price (139).

physical resources, the tools and materials of production (514).

planned economy. See **command systems** (46).

poverty level, the minimum amount of money, determined by the federal government, that an individual or a family requires to meet basic needs (18).

price fixing, agreements among companies on the prices they will charge for similar products. Price fixing weakens competition and is illegal in the United States (317).

price index, a comparison of current prices with the prices of another year or period of time. Two important price indexes compiled by the Bureau of Labor Statistics are the Consumer Price Index, or CPI, and the Producer Price Index, or PPI (252).

private property, resources owned by individuals and businesses. In the United States, almost all businesses are private property (57).

producer, a person or group of persons that makes the goods or provides the services that consumers use. Producers usually sell their goods and services to consumers (5).

Producer Price Index (PPI), a statistic showing changes over time in the prices of selected goods and services purchased by producers. See also **price index** (253).

production possibilities model, a graph that shows the production choices open to a country. A graph of this kind illustrates the tradeoffs a country must make to increase production of an item (23).

product market, a market in which consumers buy the goods and services that they want or need. Food, clothing, housing, and medical care are some of the items purchased on the product market (149).

productivity, the efficiency with which goods and services are produced, as measured by output per worker per hour. Increasing productivity is one important means of achieving economic growth (278).

professional association, an organization of people in an occupation who are interested in improving the methods they use and the conditions in which they work. The American Medical Association and the Farm Bureau are examples of professional associations (223).

profit, the difference between the cost to make something and the price at which it sells. Companies use profits to invest in new capital goods and to pay dividends to stockholders (56).

profit motive, the desire to make money. The profit motive encourages producers to respond quickly to changing demands (56).

progressive tax, a tax by which government takes a larger percentage of a rich person's income than of a poor person's income. The graduated income tax is a progressive tax (372).

property rights, the rights of an owner to use goods, services, or opportunities. Laws against theft protect property rights (318).

proportional tax, a tax by which government takes the same percentage of everyone's income, whether poor or rich (372).

proprietor compensation, income earned by people who work for themselves. Proprietor compensation is the money left over after a sole proprietor pays all expenses (171).

protective tariff, a tax on an imported good that forces up the price of the good (472).

public goods, goods and services used collectively and often paid for through the government. Public schools, highways, and police protection are all public goods (327).

quota, a limit on the amount of a good that can be imported (472).

real costs, the various resources used in producing a good or a service. The real costs of building a house include such materials as timber and brick, the labor of the builders, and the wear and tear on tools (22).

real GNP, the gross national product of a country adjusted for inflation or deflation. Real GNP is measured in dollars of a certain year. Also known as **constant dollar GNP** (252).

recession, a decline in real GNP that lasts for two consecutive quarters, or six months. A recession is part of the contraction phase of a business cycle (275).

recycling, the process of using materials over again. Aluminum cans can be recycled to make new cans (16).

regressive tax, a tax by which government takes a larger percentage of a poor person's income than of a rich person's income. A sales tax on food is a regressive tax because poor people spend a higher percentage of their income on food than do rich people (372).

regulatory agencies, governmental bodies that issue, interpret, and enforce regulations on economic activities. The Securities and Exchange Commission, Federal Communications Commission, and Food and Drug Administration are regulatory agencies (316).

rent, income from fees charged to people for the privilege of using property temporarily. A payment for occupying a hotel room is a kind of rent (171).

reserve, the money that a bank must set aside and not lend to anyone (348).

reserve requirement, the percentage of its deposits that a bank must keep in reserve, as determined by the Federal Reserve. The Fed can increase the money supply by lowering the reserve requirement or decrease the money supply by raising this requirement (358).

resource, a person or thing used in making goods or providing services. People, time, coal, oil, money, tools, buildings, and machines are examples of resources (5).

resource specialization, the tendency of a person, business, or region to produce goods or services using easily available resources (69).

revenue tariff, a tax on imported goods designed to raise money for a government. Since revenue tariffs tend to be low, they do not decrease imports significantly (472).

right, an action or benefit that is just, good, or proper. Economic rights protected by law in the United States include the right to compete in an open market, consumer and property rights, and the right to personal safety (316).

sample, a small, representative group chosen from an entire population for purposes of study or research. Gathering economic statistics usually involves studying the characteristics of a representative sample (302).

savings bonds, government securities that are payable after a period of years (380).

scarcity, the situation that exists when demand for a good, service, or resource is greater than supply. Underdeveloped countries suffer from a scarcity of trained scientists, engineers, technicians, and professionals (6).

scrip, paper money or tokens issued for temporary use in an emergency. During the Depression, local governments and businesses issued scrip to substitute for currency (343).

seasonal unemployment, unemployment that results from weather-related changes. Farming and construction are two industries in which seasonal unemployment occurs (287).

Securities and Exchange Commission (SEC), a federal agency that oversees the buying and selling of stocks and bonds. The SEC requires corporations to issue annual reports (270).

service, an action performed for the benefit of one or more other people. Haircutting, housecleaning, and teaching are all services (5).

service workers, people who provide services to other individuals or businesses. Janitors, barbers, and nurses are service workers (173).

social interdependence, the reliance of people on one another. Specialization and division of labor have led to increased social interdependence (70).

socialism, an economic system in which the public owns and controls most of the capital goods. In socialist countries, most basic economic decisions are made by government planners (78). See also **command economy.**

solar energy, energy given off by the sun and harnessed to generate heat and electricity (439).

sole proprietorship, a one-owner business. Sole proprietorships are the most common form of business institution in the United States (204).

special drawing rights, (SDRs), a new form of money, invented by the International Monetary Fund, available to nations in need of funds. SDRs are an internationally recognized currency (486).

stagflation, the combination of high unemployment (stagnation) and rising prices (inflation). The United States experienced stagflation between 1975 and 1979, when inflation and unemployment in the nation each averaged about 7 percent (295).

stock, a certificate representing partial ownership of a corporation. A large corporation issues millions of shares of stock (211).

strike, a decision by a group of employees not to work until management agrees to meet certain demands (222).

structural unemployment, unemployment that results from basic changes in the economy making the skills of certain workers unnecessary. Retraining programs are often used to combat structural unemployment (287).

subsistence agriculture, agriculture that provides only enough food for the population (505).

substitution effect, changes in demand for a product or service caused by changes in the prices of substitute products or services. As the price of home heating oil increased in the 1970s, the demand for wood and other substitute fuels increased (108).

supply, the quantity of a good or a service that producers will provide at each of its possible prices. Prices usually decrease when the supply of a product is greater than the demand for it (55).

supply curve, a line on a graph showing the quantity of a good or a service that producers are willing to supply at different possible prices (115).

supply schedule, a graph that shows how much of a product sellers will supply at different possible prices. In general, supplies will increase as prices increase and decrease as prices decrease (114).

supply-side economics, the theory that government can promote economic growth by encouraging businesses to increase the supply of goods and services. Government can encourage such increases by lowering taxes on investments and deregulating (391).

tariff, a tax placed on imported goods (472).

tax, a compulsory payment of money to support a government. In return for paying taxes, citizens receive government services, such as schools, roads, national defense, and aid to the poor (371).

tax break. See **tax incentive.**

tax incentive, a law that decreases taxes for a certain group of people or taxes associated with a particular economic activity. Also known as a **tax break** (373).

technical efficiency, use of the least amount of resources to produce the best product (426).

technology, the study and application of scientific principles to solve problems, build machines, and make work easier (409).

Theory Z management, a management technique aimed at increasing the productivity of workers by giving them more responsibility for and control over their own jobs. According to this theory, workers produce at higher levels if their managers treat them with respect (215).

third-party benefit, a benefit that goes to a person who is neither the buyer nor the seller in a transaction. For example, neighbors may benefit from increased property values when one family on their block remodels its home (327).

tight money, the scarcity of money that results when the Federal Reserve contracts the money supply. As the supply of money tightens, interest rates and unemployment often increase (358).

time deposit, a bank deposit that can be withdrawn only at a specified time in the future or on advance notice (342).

tradeoff, a loss of one benefit or advantage in order to gain another. When people choose between two possible uses of their resources, they are trading off one for the other (22).

traditional systems, economic systems in which decisions are made based on custom, habit, religion, or law. In many of the developing countries of Africa, traditional economic systems exist along with command and market systems (37).

transfer payment, money that one person or group gives to another even though the receiver has not provided a specific good or service. Gifts, inheritances, and aid to the poor are examples of transfer payments (172).

treasury bills, government securities that are payable after three to six months (380).

trend, a tendency in a certain direction. Economists try to find trends in economic activities by compiling statistical information (302).

trough, the lowest point in a business cycle. The trough is followed by a period of expansion that marks the beginning of another business cycle (275).

unemployment, the condition of wanting but not having a job. See also **unemployment rate** (285).

unemployment rate, the percentage of the work force that includes people actively looking for jobs but unable to find them (285).

unlimited liability, a sole proprietor's responsibility for all the debts of the business (205).

unlimited life, the ability of a corporation to continue to exist and function despite death, transference, or other changes in its ownership, management, or labor. Since they have unlimited life, corporations tend to be more stable than sole proprietorships or partnerships (213).

urbanologist, a person who studies the special problems of cities (448).

variable, anything that can have a number of different values. A graph usually shows the relationship between two variables, one measured on the y-axis and the other represented by the x-axis (8). See also **axis.**

voucher plan, a method of financing schools in which the government issues coupons, or vouchers, to parents who use them to pay for their child's education (332).

wealth, resources that can be used to produce income. Wealth includes savings, stocks, land, and other forms of property (181).

white collar workers, people who work in offices. Secretaries, accountants, insurance agents, and computer programmers are all white collar workers (173).

zero point, the point at which the vertical and horizontal axes of a graph meet (8).

zero-sum game, a game in which someone wins when someone else loses. Economist Lester Thurow views income distribution as a zero-sum game (184).

Index

When a word is defined in the text, the page number on which it is defined is underlined. The letter *c*, *g*, *m*, or *p* following a page reference indicates a chart, graph, map, or photograph. Additional text information usually is included. References to other entries in the index are italicized.

Text Acknowledgments

Chapter 1

20–21, Excerpted from *Economics: An Introductory Analysis* by Paul Samuelson; copyright © 1973 by McGraw-Hill, Inc., reprinted by permission of McGraw-Hill, Inc.; **28–30**, Excerpted from *Building a Sustainable Society* by Lester R. Brown; copyright © 1981 by World-watch Institute, by permission of W. W. Norton & Company, Inc.

Chapter 2

41–45, Excerpted from *Life in a Turkish Village* by Joe E. Pierce; copyright © Holt, Rinehart and Winston; **50–54**, "The Art of Queuing," from *The Russians* by Hedrick Smith; copyright © 1976 by Hedrick Smith, reprinted by permission of Times Books, a Division of Random House, Inc.; **60–62**, pp. 18–19 from *The Making of Economic Society*, 5th Ed., by Robert L. Heilbroner; copyright © 1975, reprinted by permission of Prentice-Hall, Inc., Englewood Cliffs, N. J.

Chapter 3

73, Reprinted from *USA Today;* copyright © 1983 USA Today, with permission; **80–82**, Excerpted from *Dollars and Sense*, February 1981 issue; **82–86**, Reprinted from *U.S. News & World Report* issue of May 9, 1983; copyright © 1983, U.S. News & World Report, Inc.; **89–90**, Excerpted from "Disappearing Jobs" by Bruce Gilchrist and Ariaana Shenkin, from *The Futurist*, February 1981, reprinted by permission of The Futurist, published by the World Future Society, Washington, D.C.; **91–93**, "Technology for the Poor" by Paul R. Ehrlich and John P. Holdren, from *Saturday Review;* copyright © 1971, reprinted by permission; **95**, Excerpts from "Margaret Richards," from *Working: People Talk About What They Do All Day and How They Feel About What They Do*, by Studs Terkel; copyright © 1972, 1974 by Studs Terkel, reprinted by permission of Pantheon Books, a division of Random House, Inc.

Chapter 4

121–123, Excerpted from "Popcorn Industry," from *Everybody's Business: An Almanac;* **129–132**, Excerpted from *The Making of Economic Society*, 5th Ed., by Robert L. Heilbroner; Copyright © 1975, reprinted by permission of Prentice-Hall, Inc., Englewood Cliffs, N.J.

Chapter 5

145–147, Excerpted from "The Parable of the Parking Lots" by Henry G. Manne, reprinted with permission of the author, from *The Public Interest*, No. 23 (Spring 1971) pp. 10–15; copyright © 1971 by National Affairs, Inc.; **154–156**, Excerpted from *Global Reach* by Richard J. Barnet and Ronald E. Muller; copyright © 1974 by Richard J. Barnet and Ronald E. Muller, reprinted by permission of Simon & Schuster, Inc.

Chapter 6

176–178, Excerpted from *Megatrends;* copyright © 1982 by John Naisbitt, published by Warner Books, Inc.; **184–186**, Excerpted from *The Zero-Sum Society: Distribution and the Possibilities for Economic Change* by Lester C. Thurow; copyright © 1980 by Basic Books, Inc., Publishers, reprinted by permission of the publisher; **192–196**, Excerpted from "The Fall and Rise of U.S. Frugality," from *Time*, March 3, 1980; copyright © 1980 Time Inc., all rights reserved, by permission from *Time;* **197**, Excerpted from "Iron Lady" by Barry Stavro, from *Forbes Magazine*, November 21, 1983; copyright © Forbes Inc., 1983, reprinted by permission of Forbes Magazine.

Chapter 7

206–207, Excerpted from *Nation's Business*, June 1984; **207–210**, Excerpted from "In Praise of Small Business" by Arthur Levitt, Jr., from December 6, 1981, *New York Times Magazine;* copyright © 1981 by The New York Times Company, reprinted by permission; **215–216**, Excerpted from *Theory Z* by William Ouchi; copyright © 1981, Addison-Wesley, Reading, MA, Pgs. 58, 59 & 161–167, reprinted by permission; **217–219**, Excerpted from "The Bored Board" by Peter Drucker, appeared in *The Wharton Magazine*, Fall 1976; **226–229**, Excerpted from "The Future of Unions" by Charles Craver, from *The Futurist*, October 1983; by permission of The Futurist, published by the World Future Society, Washington, D.C.

Chapter 8

247–250, Excerpted from "Tracking the Ever-Elusive GNP" by Edward Meadows, from *Fortune;* copyright © 1978 Time Inc.; **258–260**, Excerpted from "The Crux: GNP Comparisons," from *Three Sacred Cows of Eco-*

nomics by Alex Rubner, published by Granada Publishing Limited. **267–268**, "Clues Reveal a Better Economy" by Art Buchwald, from *The Failure of Success*, reprinted with permission of the author; **269**, Excerpts from "Fred Roman," from *Working: People Talk About What They Do All Day and How They Feel About What They Do*, by Studs Terkel; copyright © 1972, 1974 by Studs Terkel, reprinted by permission of Pantheon Books, a division of Random House, Inc.

Chapter 9

282–284, Adapted and abridged from Chapters VII & XII (3rd Edition) of *Capitalism, Socialism and Democracy* by Joseph A. Schumpeter; copyright © 1942, 1947, by the Trustees under the will of Elizabeth Boody Schumpeter; copyright © 1950 Harper and Row, Publishers, Inc., reprinted by permission of Harper & Row, Publishers, Inc.; **288–289**, Excerpted from *Time*, August 11, 1980; **290–292**, "Why We Still Can't Wait" by Coretta King; copyright © 1976 by Newsweek, Inc., all rights reserved, reprinted by permission; **297–298**, Excerpted from "Who Does Inflation Hurt?" from *Time*, January 15, 1979; **298–300**, "The Other Side of the Coin" by Bruce Catton, from *American Heritage;* copyright © 1978 American Heritage Publishing Co., Inc., reprinted by permission from American Heritage (April/May 1978); **301**, "Don't Just Get Married" by Toni Mack from *Forbes Magazine, November 21, 1983;* copyright © Forbes Inc., 1983, reprinted by permission of Forbes Magazine.

Chapter 10

313–315, Excerpted from "A Crop of Myths," from *The Pursuit of Virtue and Other Tory Notions* by George Will; copyright © 1982 by The Washington Post Company, reprinted by permission of Simon & Schuster, Inc.; **332–334**, Adapted and excerpted from *Free to Choose* by Milton and Rose Friedman; copyright © 1980 by Milton and Rose D. Friedman, reprinted by permission of Harcourt Brace Jovanovich, Inc.

Chapter 11

352–354, Excerpted from *The Grapes of Wrath* by John Steinbeck; copyright © 1939, renewed © 1967 by John Steinbeck, reprinted by permission of Viking Penguin, Inc.; **365**, Excerpted from "The Great Mall of China" by Jessica Greenbaum, *Forbes Magazine*, December 6, 1982; copyright © Forbes Inc., 1982, reprinted by permission of Forbes Magazine.

Chapter 12

386–389, Excerpted from *Five Economic Challenges* by Robert L. Heilbroner & Lester C. Thurow; copyright © 1981 by Heilbroner & Thurow, published by Prentice-Hall, Inc., Englewood Cliffs, N.J. 07632. **399**, Excerpted from "Inner Strength" by Jeff Bloch, *Forbes Magazine,* November 21, 1983; copyright © Forbes Inc., 1983 reprinted by permission of Forbes Magazine.

Chapter 13

415–417, "The Age of Bureaucracy Has Replaced the Era of Democracy" reprinted from *U.S. News & World Report*, August 13, 1984; copyright © 1984, U.S. News & World Report, Inc.; **420–422**, Excerpted from *USA Today*, November 28, 1983; **423–425**, Excerpted from "Prospects for Black Progress in the 1980's" by Alan Pifer, Dec. 1, 1980 issue *Vital Speeches of the Day*, by permission of City News Publishing Company; **430–431**, Excerpted from "The Liberal Promise of Prosperity" by Robert B. Reich, from *The New Republic*, Feb. 21, 1981; copyright © 1981 The New Republic, Inc., by permission of The New Republic; **433**, Excerpted from "Nino Guidici," from *Working: People Talk About What They Do All Day and How They Feel About What They Do* by Studs Terkel; copyright © 1972, 1974 by Studs Terkel, reprinted by permission of Pantheon Books, a division of Random House, Inc.

Chapter 14

462–464, "A Fable for Tomorrow," from *Silent Spring* by Rachel Carson; copyright © 1962 by Rachel L. Carson, reprinted by permission of Houghton Mifflin Company; **465**, Excerpted from "Visibility 101" by Stanley W. Angrist, from *Forbes Magazine*, September 26, 1983; copyright © Forbes Inc., 1983, reprinted by permission of Forbes Magazine.

Chapter 15

497–498, pp., 75–77 from *Toward the Next Economics* by Peter F. Drucker; copyright © 1974, by Peter F. Drucker; reprinted by permission of Harper & Row, Publishers, Inc.; **499**, Excerpted from Grinnell, IA, *Herald-Register*, July 16, 1984, and October 18, 1984.

Chapter 16

521–524, Excerpted from *The Rich Nations and the Poor Nations* by Barbara Ward; copyright © 1962 by Barbara Ward, by permission of W. W. Norton & Company, Inc.; **528–530**, Excerpted from *Through the '80's*, "Postscript" by Aurelio Peccei; copyright © 1980 World Future Society, by permission of the World Future Society, Washington, D.C.; **531**, Excerpted from "Pipe Dream" by Roger Neal, from *Forbes Magazine*, November 21, 1983; copyright © Forbes Inc., 1983, by permission of Forbes Magazine.

The authors and editors have made every effort to trace the ownership of all copyrighted selections found in this book and to make full acknowledgment for their use.

Picture and Cartoon Credits

Cover

Copyright © Vasarely Sin—Hat—3, 1968
Vasarely Museum, Chateau Museum
Gordes, France. All Rights Reserved.

Table of Contents

V, Chuck O'Rear/West Light; vi, CAMERIQUE/H. Armstrong Roberts

Chapter 1

2, 3, Cameron Davidson/Bruce Coleman, Inc.; 4, Jamie Tanaka/Bruce Coleman, Inc.; 6, H. Armstrong Roberts; 13, The Quarasan Group, Inc.; 17, CAMERIQUE/H. Armstrong Roberts; 18, J. P. Laffont/Sygma; 20, The Bettmann Archive; 23, John Lei/Stock Boston, Inc.; 26, CAMERIQUE/H. Armstrong Roberts; 29, J. Meyers/H. Armstrong Roberts; 30, Drawing by Henry Martin; © 1980 The New Yorker Magazine, Inc.; 31, McDougal, Littell and Company

Chapter 2

36, J. L. Atlan/Sygma; 38, Jerry L. Hunt/Bruce Coleman. Inc.; 40, W. Bayer/Bruce Coleman, Inc.; 43, Richard Kalvar/Magnum Photos; 47, Gary Stallings/Tom Stack & Associates; 49, M. Koene/H. Armstrong Roberts; 51, Bruno Barbey/Magnum Photos; 54, Drawing by Stayskal; The Tampa Tribune, all rights reserved; 57, Bruce Davidson/Magnum Photos; 59, Richard Howard/Black Star; 61, Charles Harbutt/Archive Pictures; 63, D. P. Herskowitz/Bruce Coleman, Inc.; 65, Harley L. Schwadron

Chapter 3

68, Stewart M. Green/Tom Stack & Associates; 70, 72, CAMERIQUE/H. Armstrong Roberts; 73, The Wall Street Journal-permission, Cartoon Features Syndicate; 75, Brown Brothers; 76, Bruno Barbey/Magnum Photos; 79, William J. Warren/West Light; 81, Courtesy McCollum Photos; 88, C. Foussat/H. Armstrong Roberts; 90, Peter Arnold; 92, Owen Franken/Stock Boston, Inc.; 94, Sebastiao Salgado/Magnum Photos; 95; J. P. Laffont/Sygma

Chapter 4

102, 103, CAMERIQUE/H. Armstrong Roberts; 104, Steve Leonard/Black Star; 107, Richard Pasley/Stock Boston, Inc.; 120, R. C. Paulson, Jr./H. Armstrong Roberts; 122, Gerard Murrell/Bruce Coleman, Inc.; 128, Lee Foster/Bruce Coleman, Inc.; 130, Charles Harbutt/Archive Pictures; 133, Courtesy Don Lusk; 135, Mark Sherman/Bruce Coleman, Inc.

Chapter 5

138, Jeff Foott/Bruce Coleman, Inc.; 148, Harry Wilks/Stock Boston, Inc.; 153, Donald Dietz/Stock Boston; 155, Charles Harbutt/Archive Pictures; 158, Eugene Richards/Magnum Photos; 160, Chip Henderson/West Light; 163, The Bettmann Archive; 164, Drawing by Henry Martin; © 1980 by The New Yorker Magazine, Inc.; 165, Jim Mendenhall, Photo courtesy of Proctor & Gardner Inc.; 167, Stock Boston, Inc.

Chapter 6

170, Andrew Sacks/Black Star; 171, Frank Siteman/Stock Boston, Inc.; 175, Eugene Richards/Magnum Photos; 177, Ellis Herwig/Stock Boston, Inc.; 178, Harley L. Schwadron; 181, Ivan Massar/Black Star; 183, Charles Gupton/Stock Boston, Inc.; 186, James Sugar/Black Star; 190, Bruce Coleman, Inc.; 191, Courtesy photo; 196, Bruce M. Wellman/Tom Stack & Associates; 197, Greg Anderson/Gamma Liaison Agency; 199, Charles Harbutt/Archive Pictures

Chapter 7

202, J. P. Laffont/Sygma; 203, Edith G. Haun/Stock Boston, Inc.; 206, Chuck O'Rear/West Light; 208, Richard Kalvar/Magnum Photos; 216, Ethan Hoffman/Archive Pictures; 219, Tom Campbell/West Light; 221, Susan McElhinney/Archive Pictures; 225, Eli Reed/Magnum Photos; 228, Daniel Brody/Stock Boston, Inc.; 230, Raoul Hackel/Stock Boston, Inc.; 231, Courtesy Alexandra Armstrong Advisors

Chapter 8

238, 239, Annie Griffiths/Bruce Coleman, Inc.; 240, Craig Aurness/West Light; 242, Sybil Shelton/Peter Arnold; 246, John Lei/Stock Boston, Inc.; 249, Dennis Brack/Black Star; 262, Pierre Kopp/West Light; 268, John Running/Stock Boston, Inc.

Chapter 9

274, J. Urwiller/H. Armstrong Roberts; 281, Bruce Coleman, Inc.; 283, Brown Brothers; 291, Gilles Peress/Magnum Photos; 301, Peter Calvin/Camera 5

Chapter 10

306, J. P. Laffont/Sygma; 310, Cary Wolinsky/Stock Boston, Inc.; 311, Rick Smolan/Stock Boston, Inc.; 314, Wayne Miller/Magnum Photos; 317, Michael Yamasita/West Light; 321, Mary A. Root, APSA/Hillstrom Photos; 324, Jim Pozark/Gamma Liaison Agency; 326, Drawing by F. B. Modell; © 1966 The New Yorker

Magazine, Inc.; **328**, John Lei/Stock Boston, Inc.; **330**, Dave Darnell/Black Star; **333**, James Sugar/Black Star; **335**, Harry Benson/Gamma Liaison Agency

Chapter 11

340, CAMERIQUE/H. Armstrong Roberts; **344**, Smithsonian Institution Negative No. 84-3962; **355**, United Press International Photo; **358**, Mike Mazzaschi/Stock Boston, Inc.; **360**, Shelly Katz/Black Star; **363**, United Press International photo; **365**, John Grossman

Chapter 12

370, Dennis Brack/Black Star; **371**, CAMERIQUE/H. Armstrong Roberts; **375**, J. L. Atlan/Sygma; **378**, The Wall Street Journal-permission, Cartoon Features Syndicate; **379**, Wendell Metzen/Bruce Coleman, Inc.; **382**, Jeff Macnelly; Tribune Media Services, Inc.; **384**, Harley L. Schwadron; **388**, Greenwood/Gamma Liaison Agency; **392**, Owen Franken/Stock Boston, Inc.; **393**, United Press International photo; **397**, Brown Brothers; **399**, David Burnett/Contact; **403**, William Schorr, Tribune Media Services, Inc.

Chapter 13

406, **407**, R. Krubner/H. Armstrong Roberts; **408**, Jim Anderson/Black Star; **411**, R. Cobb; Sawyer Press; **412**, Drawing by Stevenson; © 1970, The New Yorker Magazine, Inc.; **414**, Rick Friedman/Black Star; **416**, Drawing by Eldon Dedini; © 1975, The New Yorker Magazine,

Inc.; **420**, Alex Webb/Magnum Photos; **422**, Cary Wolinsky/Stock Boston, Inc.; **424**, Stacy Pick/Stock Boston, Inc.; **427**, Charles Gupton/Stock Boston, Inc.; **429**, Alex Webb/Magnum Photos; **432**, Craig Davis/Sygma; **433**, Sybil Shelton/Peter Arnold

Chapter 14

438, Randall Taylor States/Bruce Coleman, Inc.; **442**, Dennis Brack/Black Star; **444**, Peter Menzel/Stock Boston, Inc.; **446**, Richard Choy/Peter Arnold; **451**, Drawing by Lawrence Butler; **452**, Daniel Brody/Stock Boston, Inc.; **453**, **454**, Courtesy Intentional Educations; **455**, The Wall Street Journal-permission, Cartoon Features Syndicate; **459**, Earl Dotter/Archive Pictures; **461**, Don & Pat Valenti/Hillstrom Photos; **463**, Ted Speigel/Black Star; **465**, Courtesy Carnegie-Mellon University

Chapter 15

470, Owen Franken/Stock Boston, Inc.; **472**, Chuck O'Rear/West Light; **477**, Dennis Brack/Black Star; **486**, Eric Carley/Stock Boston, Inc.; **499**, Peter Marlow/Magnum Photos

Chapter 16

504, Jim Tuten/Black Star; **520**, CAMERIQUE/H. Armstrong Roberts; **522**, Owen Franken/Sygma; **530**, Cary Wolinsky/Stock Boston, Inc.; **531**, Ed Kashi/Gamma Liaison Agency

Staff Credits

Director of Social Studies: *Mercedes B. Bailey*

Editor: *Jim Strickler*

Associate Editor: *Joanne Stack*

Production Coordinator, Social Studies: *Maury B. Cain*

Design and Production: *The Quarasan Group, Inc.*

Publisher and Editor-in-Chief: *Joseph F. Littell*

Administrative Editor: *Kathleen Laya*

Managing Editor: *Geraldine Macsai*